FISKE GUIDE TO COLLEGES 2007

Also by Edward B. Fiske

Fiske Guide to Getting into the Right College with Bruce G. Hammond

Nailing the New SAT with Bruce G. Hammond

Fiske What to Do When for College with Bruce G. Hammond

Smart Schools, Smart Kids: Why Do Some Schools Work?

Using Both Hands: Women and Education in Cambodia

Decentralization of Education: Politics and Consensus

When Schools Compete: A Cautionary Tale with Helen F. Ladd

Elusive Equity: Education Reform in Post-Apartheid South Africa with Helen F. Ladd

FISKE 2007
GUIDE TO
COLLEGES

EDWARD B. FISKE

former Education Editor of
the *New York Times*

with Robert Logue
and
the *Fiske Guide to Colleges* staff

SOURCEBOOKS, INC.®
NAPERVILLE, ILLINOIS

Published by Sourcebooks, Inc.
P.O. Box 4410
Naperville, Illinois 60567-4410
(800) 432-7444
Fax: (630) 961-2168
www.sourcebooks.com

ISBN-13: 978-1-4022-0660-3
ISBN-10: 1-4022-0660-7
Twenty-Third Edition

Your comments and corrections are welcome.
Please send them to:

Fiske Guide to Colleges
P.O. Box 287
Alstead, NH 03602
Fax: (603) 835-7859
Email: editor@fiskeguide.com

Printed and bound in the United States of America
DR 10 9 8 7 6 5 4 3 2 1

To Sunny

Contents

Index by State and Country

The colleges in this guide are listed alphabetically and crossreferenced for your convenience. Below is a list of the selected colleges grouped by state. Following this listing, you will find a second listing in which the colleges are categorized by the yearly cost of attending each school.

Index by Price

	PUBLIC	PRIVATE
$$$$	More than $7,000	More than $30,000
$$$	$6,000–$7,000	$27,000–$30,000
$$	$5,000–$6,000	$22,000–$27,000
$	Less than $5,000	Less than $22,000

Price categories are based on current tuition and fees and do not include room, board, transportation, and other expenses.

PUBLIC COLLEGES AND UNIVERSITIES

PRIVATE COLLEGES AND UNIVERSITIES

Inexpensive—$

Adelphi University, 1
Albertson College, 7
Alfred University, 12
Alma College, 16
Austin College, 41
Baylor University, 53
Birmingham-Southern College, 60
Brigham Young University, 72
Calvin College, 105
Centre College, 118
Cooper Union, 168
Dallas, University of 176
Dayton, University of, 185
Deep Springs, 187
DePaul University, 197
Elon University, 217
Gordon College, 263
Guilford College, 270
Hendrix College, 294
Hollins University, 303
Hood College, 307
Hope College, 310
Houghton College, 312
Howard University, 314
Illinois Institute of Technology, 319
Marquette University, 397
Millsaps College, 426
Morehouse College, 33
Oglethorpe University, 484
Presbyterian College, 513
Prescott College, 515
Principia College, 521
Randolph-Macon Woman's College, 528
Rice University, 546
Ripon College, 550
Rochester Institute of Technology, 555
Southwestern University, 600
Spelman College, 35
Sweet Briar College, 631
Texas Christian University, 643
Trinity University, 650
Tulsa, University of, 660
Warren Wilson College, 688
Wells College, 703
Wheaton College (IL), 711
Xavier University of Louisiana, 741

Moderate—$$

Agnes Scott College, 3
Albion College, 9
Allegheny College, 14
American University, 19
Antioch College, 23
Atlantic, College of the, 37
Beloit College, 55
California Institute of Technology, 102
Case Western Reserve University, 113
Catholic University of America, The, 115
Clarkson University, 144
Cornell College, 171
Denver, University of, 195
DePauw University, 199
Drexel University, 207
Earlham College, 213
Eckerd College, 215
Emerson College, 220
Eugene Lang College, The New School for Liberal Arts, 225
Florida Institute of Technology, 235
Furman University, 246
Goucher College, 265
Grinnell College, 267
Gustavus Adolphus, 273
Hampden-Sydney College, 278
Hiram College, 296
Illinois Wesleyan University, 322
Ithaca College, 349
Kalamazoo College, 357
Knox College, 367
Lake Forest College, 372
Lawrence University, 375
Lewis & Clark College, 380
Loyola University New Orleans, 387
Macalester College, 389
Manhattanville College, 393
Marlboro College, 395
Mills College, 424
Muhlenberg College, 440
Northeastern University, 471
Ohio Wesleyan University, 491
Pacific, University of the, 500
Puget Sound, University of, 523
Redlands, University of, 531
Rhodes College, 543
Richmond, University of, 548
Rose-Hulman Institute of Technology, 560

St. Benedict, College of, and St. John's University, 564
St. Olaf College, 574
Saint Louis University, 576
San Francisco, University of, 579
South, University of the (Sewanee), 591
Southern Methodist, 598
Stetson University, 621
Susquehanna University, 626
Syracuse University, 633
Wabash College, 683
Washington and Jefferson College, 693
Washington and Lee University, 695
Whittier College, 718
Willamette University, 720
Wittenberg University, 732
Wofford College, 734
Wooster, The College of, 736

Expensive—$$$

Babson College, 43
Barnard College, 48
Boston College, 62
Bryn Mawr College, 78
Claremont McKenna, 130
Clark University, 141
Colorado College, 153
Davidson College, 182
Denison University, 192
Drew University, 204
Emory University, 222
Fairfield University, 230
Fordham University, 239
Hartwick College, 282
Holy Cross, College of the, 305
Lafayette College, 370
Lehigh University, 377
Notre Dame, University of, 476
Occidental College, 481
Pepperdine University, 508
Pomona College, 136
Rensselaer Polytechnic Institute, 536
Rhode Island School of Design, 541
Rochester, University of, 553
Rollins College, 558
Santa Clara University, 581
Scripps College, 139
Smith College, 588
Ursinus College, 664

PRIVATE COLLEGES AND UNIVERSITIES

The Best Buys of 2007

Following is a list of 45 colleges and universities
that qualify as Best Buys based on the academic offerings
in relation to the cost of attendance.
(See page xviii for an explanation of how Best Buys were chosen.)

Public

University of Aberdeen (Great Britain)
University of Arizona
University of British Columbia (Canada)
University of California at Berkeley
University of Colorado
University of Florida
Georgia Institute of Technology
University of Iowa
University of Kansas
University of Mary Washington
McGill University (Canada)
New College of Florida
University of North Carolina at Asheville
University of North Carolina at Chapel Hill
University of St. Andrews (Great Britain)
University of Texas at Austin
University of Toronto (Canada)
University of Washington
University of Wisconsin

Private

Adelphi University
Baylor University
Brigham Young University
California Institute of Technology
Case Western Reserve University
Centre College
Cooper Union
Deep Springs College
Earlham College
Elon University
Grinnell College
Hendrix College
Howard University
Illinois Institute of Technology
Macalester College
Morehouse College
Olin College of Engineering
Randolph-Macon Woman's College
Rice University
University of the South (Sewanee)
Spelman College
Trinity University (TX)
Wabash College
Warren Wilson College
Washington and Lee University
Wheaton College (IL)

Introduction

FISKE GUIDE TO COLLEGES—AND HOW TO USE IT

The 2007 edition of *Fiske Guide to Colleges* is a revised and updated version of a book that has been a bestseller since it first appeared two decades ago and is universally regarded as the definitive college guide of its type. Features of the new edition include:

- Updated write-ups on more than 300 of the country's best and most interesting colleges and universities
- A section titled "Sizing Yourself Up," with a questionnaire that will help you figure out the kind of school is best for you
- A Guide for Preprofessionals that lists colleges and universities strong in nine preprofessional areas
- A list of schools with strong programs for students with learning disabilities
- Designation of the 43 schools that constitute this year's Best Buys
- Statistical summaries that give you the numbers you need, but spare you those that you do not
- Authoritative rankings of each institution by academics, social life, and quality of life
- The unique "If You Apply…" feature, which summarizes the vital information you need about each college's admission policies—including deadlines and essay topics
- A section on the top Canadian and British universities in response to the fact that a growing number of students and families in the United States have become aware of the educational bargains lurking just across the border to the north. These universities offer first-rate academics—easily the equivalent of the flagship public institutions in the U.S.—but at a fraction of the cost.

Picking the right college—one that will coincide with your particular needs, goals, interests, talents, and personality—is one of the most important decisions any young person will ever make. It is also a major investment. Tuition and fees alone now run at least $5,000 at a typical public university and $25,000 at a typical private college, and the overall tab at the most selective and expensive schools tops $40,000. Obviously, a major investment like that should be approached with as much information as possible.

That's where *Fiske Guide to Colleges* fits in. It is a tool to help you make the most intelligent educational investment you can.

WHAT IS THE *FISKE GUIDE TO COLLEGES*?

Fiske Guide to Colleges mirrors a process familiar to any college-bound student and his or her family. If you are wondering whether to consider a particular college, it is logical to seek out friends or acquaintances who go there and ask them to tell you about their experiences. We have done exactly that—but on a far broader and more systematic basis than any individual or family could do alone.

In using the *Fiske Guide*, some special features should be kept in mind:

- The guide is **selective**. We have not tried to cover all four-year colleges and universities. Rather, we have taken more than 300 of the best and most interesting institutions in the nation—the ones that students most want to know about—and written descriptive essays of 1,000 to 2,500 words about each of them.
- Since choosing a college is a matter of making a calculated and informed judgment, this guide is also **subjective**. It makes judgments about the strengths and weaknesses of each institution, and it contains a unique set of ratings of each college or university on the basis of academic strength, social life, and overall quality of life. No institution is right for every student. The underlying assumption of the *Fiske Guide* is that each of the colleges chosen for inclusion is the right place for some students but not a good bet for others. Like finding the right husband or wife, college admissions is a matching process. You know your own interests and needs; the *Fiske Guide* will tell you something about those needs that each college seems to serve best.

- Finally, the *Fiske Guide* is **systematic**. Each write-up is carefully constructed to cover specific topics—from the academic climate and the makeup of the student body to the social scene—in a systematic order. This means that you can easily take a specific topic, such as the level of academic pressure or the role of fraternities and sororities on campus, and trace it through all of the colleges that interest you.

HOW THE COLLEGES WERE SELECTED

How do you single out "the best and most interesting" of the more than 2,200 four-year colleges in the United States? Obviously, many fine institutions are not included. Space limitations simply require that some hard decisions be made.

The selection was done with several broad principles in mind, beginning with academic quality. Depending on how you define the term, there are about 175 "selective" colleges and universities in the nation, and by and large these constitute the best institutions academically. All of these are included in the *Fiske Guide*. In addition, an effort was made to achieve geographic diversity and a balance of public and private schools. Special efforts were made to include a good selection of three types of institutions that seem to be enjoying special popularity at present: engineering and technical schools, those with a religious emphasis, and those located along the Sunbelt, where the cost of education is considerably less than at its Northern counterparts. This current edition also includes several colleges that in recent years have significantly increased their academic quality and appeal to students.

Finally, in a few cases we exercised the journalist's prerogative of writing about schools that are simply interesting. The tiny College of the Atlantic, for example, would hardly qualify on the basis of superior academic program or national significance, but it offers an unusual and fascinating brand of liberal arts within the context of environmental studies. Likewise, Deep Springs College, the only two-year school in the *Fiske Guide*, is a unique institution of intrinsic interest.

HOW THE *FISKE GUIDE* WAS COMPILED

Each college or university selected for inclusion in the *Fiske Guide to Colleges* was sent a packet of questionnaires. The first was directed to the administration and covered topics ranging from their perception of the institution's mission to the demographics of the student body. Administrators were also asked to distribute a set of questionnaires to a cross section of students.

The questions for students, all open-ended and requiring short essays as responses, covered a series of topics ranging from the accessibility of professors and the quality of housing and dining facilities to the type of nightlife and weekend entertainment available in the area. By and large, students responded enthusiastically to the challenge we offered them. The quality of the information in the write-ups is a tribute to their diligence and openness. American college students, we learned, are a candid lot. They are proud of their institutions, but also critical—in the positive sense of the word.

Other sources of information were also employed. Administrators were invited to attach to their questionnaires any catalogs, in-house research, or other documents that would contribute to an understanding of the institution and to comment on their write-up in the last edition. Also, staff members have visited many of the colleges, and in some cases, additional information was solicited through published materials, telephone interviews, and other contacts with students and administrators.

The information from these various questionnaires was then collated by a staff of journalists and freelance writers and edited by Edward B. Fiske, former education editor of the *New York Times*.

THE FORMAT

Each essay covers certain broad subjects in roughly the same order. They are as follows:

Academics	**Housing**
Campus setting	**Food**
Student body	**Social life**
Financial aid	**Extracurricular activities**

Certain subtopics are covered in all of the essays. The sections on academics, for example, always discuss the departments (or, in the case of large universities, schools) that are particularly strong or weak, while the sections on housing contain information on whether the dorms are co-ed or single-sex and how students get the rooms they want. Other topics, however, such as class size, the need for a car, or the number of volumes in the library, are mentioned only if they constitute a particular strength or weakness at that institution.

We paid particular attention to the effect of the 21-year-old drinking age on campus life. Also, we noted efforts some schools' administrations have been making to change or improve the social and residential life on campuses through such measures as banning fraternities and constructing new athletic facilities.

BEST BUYS

One of the lesser-known facts of life about higher education in the U.S. is that price and quality do not always go hand-in-hand. The college or university with the jumbo price tag may or may not offer a better education than the institution across town with much lower tuition. The relationship between the cost paid by the consumer and the quality of the education is affected by factors ranging from the size of an institution's endowment to judgments by college officials about what the market will bear.

In the face of today's skyrocketing tuition rates, students and families in all economic circumstances are looking for ways to get the best value for their education dollar. Fortunately, there are some bargains to be found in higher education; it just takes a bit of shopping around with a little guidance along the way.

Since its inception nearly two decades ago, the *Fiske Guide* has featured an Index by Price that groups public and private institutions into four price categories, from inexpensive to very expensive. Now we have gone one step further: we have combined the cost data with academic and other information about each college and university, and have come up with 45 institutions—19 public and 26 private—that offer remarkable educational opportunities at a relatively modest cost. We call them Best Buys, and they are indicated by a Best Buy graphic next to the college name. (A list of all 2007 Best Buys appears on page xv.)

All of our Best Buys fall into the inexpensive or moderate price category, and most have four- or five-star academic ratings. But there are bargains to be found among all levels and types of institutions. For example, some of the best values in American higher education are public colleges and universities that have remained relatively small and offer the smaller classes and personalized approach to academics that are typically found only in expensive private liberal arts colleges. Several of these are included as Best Buys.

STATISTICS

At the beginning of each write-up are basic statistics about the college or university—the ones that are relevant to applicants. These include the address, type of location (urban, small town, rural, etc.), enrollment, male/female ratio, SAT or ACT score ranges of the middle 50 percent of the students, percentage of students receiving need-based financial aid, relative cost, whether or not the institution has a chapter of Phi Beta Kappa, the number of students who apply and the percentage of those who are accepted, the percentage of accepted students who enroll, the number of freshmen who graduate within six years, and the number of freshmen who return for their sophomore year. For convenience, we include the telephone number of the admissions office and the school's website and mailing address.

Unlike some guides, we have intentionally not published figures on the student/faculty ratio because colleges use different—and often self-serving—methods to calculate the ratio, thus making it virtually meaningless.

Within the statistics, you will sometimes encounter the letters "N/A." In most cases, this means that the statistic was not available. In other cases, however, such as schools that do not require standardized tests, it means "not applicable." The write-up should make it clear which meaning is the relevant one.

We have included information on whether the school has a chapter of Phi Beta Kappa because this academic honorary society is a sign of broad intellectual distinction. Keep in mind, though, that even the very best engineering schools, because of their relatively narrow focus, do not usually qualify under the society's standards.

Tuition and fees are constantly increasing at American colleges, but for the most part, the cost of various institutions in relation to one another does not change. Rather than put in specific cost figures that would immediately become out of date, we have classified colleges into four groups ranging from inexpensive ($) to very expensive ($$$$) based on estimated costs of tuition and fees for the 2004–2005 academic year. Separate scales were used for public and private institutions, and the ratings for the public institutions are based on cost for residents of the state; out-of-staters should expect to pay more. If a public institution has a particularly low or high surcharge for out-of-staters, this is noted in the essay. The categories are defined as follows:

	PUBLIC	PRIVATE
$$$$	More than $7,000	More than $30,000
$$$	$6,000–$7,000	$27,000–$30,000
$$	$5,000–$6,000	$22,000–$27,000
$	Less than $5,000	Less than $22,000

We also include an index that groups colleges by their relative cost (see Index by Price pages xii–xiv).

SAT and ACT SCORES

A special word needs to be said about SAT and ACT scores. Some publications follow the practice of giving the median or average score registered by entering freshmen. Such figures, however, are easily misinterpreted as thresholds rather than averages. Many applicants forget that if a school reports average SAT–Verbal scores of 500, this means that, by definition, about half of the students scored below this number and half scored above. An applicant with a 480 would still have lots of company.

To avoid such confusion, we report the range of scores of the middle half of freshmen—or, to put it another way, the scores achieved by those in the 25th and 75th percentiles. For example, that college where the SAT–Verbal average was 500 might have a range of 440 to 560. So if you scored within this range, you would have joined the middle 50 percent of last year's freshmen. If your score was above 560, you would have been in the top quarter and could probably look forward to a relatively easy time; if it was below 440, you would have been struggling along with the bottom quarter of students.

The reporting of ranges rather than a single average is an increasingly common practice, but some colleges do not calculate ranges. These are indicated by "N/A." Keep in mind, as well, that score ranges (and averages, for that matter) are misleading at colleges such as Bates, Bowdoin, and Union, which do not require test scores from all applicants. The ranges given for these colleges represent the range of scores of students who choose to submit their test scores, although they are not required to do so.

Unfortunately, another problem that arises with SAT and ACT scores is that, in their zeal to make themselves look good in a competitive market, some colleges and universities have been known to be less than honest in the numbers they release. They inflate their scores by not counting certain categories of students at the low end of the scale, such as athletes, certain types of transfer students, or students admitted under affirmative action programs. Some colleges have gone to such extremes as reporting the relatively high math scores of foreign students, but not their relatively low verbal scores. Aside from the sheer dishonesty of such practices, they can also be misleading. A student whose own scores are below the 25th percentile of a particular institution needs to know whether his profile matches that of the lower quarter of the student body as a whole, or whether there is an unreported pool of students with lower scores.

Even when dealing with a range rather than a single score, keep in mind that standardized tests are an imprecise measure of academic ability, and comparisons of scores that differ by less than 50 or 60 points on a scale of 200 to 800 have little meaning. According to the laws of statistics, there is one chance in three that the 550 that arrived in the little envelope from ETS should really be at least 580 or no more than 520. On the other hand, median scores offer some indication of your chances to get into a particular institution and the intellectual level of the company you will be keeping—or, if you prefer, competing against. Remember, too, that the most competitive schools have the largest and most sophisticated admissions staffs and are well aware of the limitations of standardized tests. A strong high school average or achievement in a field such as music will usually counteract the negative effects of modest SAT or ACT scores.

SCHOLARSHIP INFORMATION

Since the first edition of *Fiske Guide to Colleges* appeared, the problems of financing college have become increasingly critical, mainly because of the rising cost of education and a shift from grants to loans as the basis for financial aid packages.

In response to these developments, many colleges and universities have begun to devise their own plans to help students pay for college. These range from subsidized loan programs to merit scholarships that are awarded without reference to financial need. Most of these programs are aimed at retaining the middle class.

We ask each college and university to tell us what steps it has taken to help students pay their way, and their responses are incorporated in the write-ups. Also indicated is whether a candidate's inability to pay the full tuition, room, and board charges is a factor in admissions decisions. Some colleges advertise that they are "need blind" in their admissions, meaning that they accept or reject applicants without reference to their financial situation and then guarantee to meet the "demonstrated need" of all students whom they accept. Others say they are need blind in their admissions decisions, but do not guarantee to provide the financial aid required of all those who are accepted. Still others agree to meet the demonstrated need of all students, but they package their offers so that students they really want receive a higher percentage of their aid in the form of outright grants than in repayable loans.

"Demonstrated need" is itself a slippery term. In theory, the figure is determined when students and families fill out a needs-analysis form, which leads to an estimate of how much the family can afford to pay. Demonstrated need is then calculated by subtracting that figure from the cost at a particular institution. In practice, however, various colleges make their own adjustments to the standard figure.

Students and parents should not assume that their family's six-figure income automatically disqualifies them from some kind of subsidized financial aid. In cases of doubt, they should fill out a needs-analysis form to determine their eligibility. Whether they qualify or not, they are also eligible for a variety of awards made without regard to financial need.

Inasmuch as need-based awards are universal at the colleges in this guide, the awards generally singled out for special mention in the write-ups in *Fiske Guide to Colleges* are the merit scholarships. We have not mentioned awards of a purely local nature—restricted to residents of a particular county, for example—but all college applicants should search out these awards through their guidance offices and the bulletins of the colleges that are of interest to them. Similarly, we have not duplicated the information on federally guaranteed loan programs that is readily available through both high school and college counseling offices, but we cite novel and often less-expensive variants of the federal loan programs that are offered by individual colleges.

For more information on the ever-changing financial aid scene, we suggest that you consult the companion book to this guide, *Fiske Guide to Getting into the Right College*.

RATINGS

Much of the controversy that greeted the first edition of *Fiske Guide to Colleges* revolved around its unique system of rating colleges in three areas: academics, social life, and quality of life. In each case, the ratings are done on a system of one to five, with three considered normal for colleges included in the *Fiske Guide*. If a college receives a rating higher or lower than three in any category, the reasons should be apparent from the narrative description of that college.

Students and parents should keep in mind that these ratings are obviously general in nature and inherently subjective. No complex institution can be described in terms of a single number or other symbol, and different people will have different views of how various institutions should be rated in the three categories. They should not be viewed as either precise or infallible judgments about any given college. On the other hand, the ratings are a helpful tool in using this book. The core of the *Fiske Guide* is the essays on each of the colleges, and the ratings represent a summary—an index, if you will—of these write-ups. Our hope is that each student, having decided on the kind of configuration that suits his or her needs, will then thumb through the book looking for other institutions with a similar set of ratings. The three categories, defined as follows, are academics, social life, and quality of life.

Academics ✍

This is a judgment about the overall academic climate of the institution, including its reputation in the academic world, the quality of the faculty, the level of teaching and research, the academic ability of students, the quality of libraries and other facilities, and the level of academic seriousness among students and faculty members.

Although the same basic criteria have been applied to all institutions, it should be evident that an outstanding small liberal arts college will by definition differ significantly from an outstanding major public university. No one would expect the former to have massive library facilities, but one would look for a high-quality faculty that combines research with a good deal of attention to the individual needs of students. Likewise, public universities, because of their implicit commitment to serving a broad cross-section of society, might have a broader range of curriculum offerings but somewhat lower average SAT scores than a large private counterpart. Readers may find the ratings most useful when comparing colleges and universities of the same type.

In general, an academics rating of three pens suggests that the institution is a solid one that easily meets the criteria for inclusion in a guide devoted to the top 10 percent of colleges and universities in the nation.

An academics rating of four pens suggests that the institution is above average even by these standards and that it has some particularly distinguishing academic feature, such as especially rich course offerings or an especially serious academic atmosphere.

A rating of five pens for academics indicates that the college or university is among the handful of top institutions of its type in the nation on a broad variety of criteria. Those in the private sector will normally attract students with combined SAT scores of at least 1300, and those in the public sector are invariably magnets for the top students in their states. All can be assumed to have outstanding faculties and other academic resources.

In response to the suggestion that the range of colleges within a single category has been too broad, we have introduced some half-steps into the ratings.

Social Life ☎

This is primarily a judgment about the amount of social life that is readily available. A rating of three telephones suggests a typical college social life, while four telephones means that students have a better-than-average time socially. It can be assumed that a college with a rating of five is something of a party school, which may or may not detract from the academic quality. Colleges with a rating below three have some impediment to a strong social life, such as geographic isolation, a high percentage of commuting students, or a disproportionate number of nerds who never leave the library. Once again, the reason should be evident from the write-up.

Quality of Life ★

This category grew out of the fact that schools with good academic credentials and plenty of social life may not, for one reason or another, be particularly wholesome places to spend four years. The term "quality of life" is one that has been gaining currency in social science circles, and, in most cases, the rating for a particular college will be similar to the academic and/or social ratings. The reader, though, should be alert to exceptions to this pattern. A liberal arts college, for example, might attract bright students who study hard during the week and party hard on weekends, and thus earn high ratings for academics and social life. If the academic pressure is cut-throat rather than constructive, though, and the social system is manipulative of women, this college might get an apparently anomalous two stars for quality of life. By contrast, a small college with modest academic programs and relatively few organized social opportunities might have developed a strong sense of supportive community, have a beautiful campus, and be located near a wonderful city—and thus be rated four stars for quality of life. As in the other categories, the reason can be found in the essay to which the ratings point.

OVERLAPS

Most colleges and universities operate within fairly defined "niche markets." That is, they compete for students against other institutions with whom they share important characteristics, such as academic quality, size, geographic location, and the overall tone and style of campus life. Not surprisingly, students who apply to College X also tend to apply to the other institutions in its particular niche. For example, "alternative" colleges such as Bard, Bennington, Hampshire, Marlboro, Oberlin, Reed, and Sarah Lawrence share many common applications, as do those with an evangelical flavor, such as Calvin, Hope, and Wheaton (IL).

As a service to readers, we ask each school to give us the names of the five colleges with which they share the most common applications, and these are listed in the Overlaps section at the end of each write-up. We encourage students who know they are interested in a particular institution to check out the schools with which it competes—and perhaps then check out the "overlaps of the overlaps." This method of systematic browsing should yield a list of 15 or 20 schools that, based on the behavior of thousands of past applicants, would constitute a good starting point for the college search.

IF YOU APPLY...

An extremely helpful feature is the "If You Apply" section at the end of each write-up. This is designed for students who become seriously interested in a particular college and want to know more specifics about what it takes to get in.

This section begins with the deadlines for early admissions or early decision (if the college has such a program), regular admissions, and financial aid. If the college operates on a rolling-admissions basis—making decisions as the applications are received—this is indicated.

"If You Apply" gives a snapshot of the institution's financial aid policies. It indicates whether the college or university guarantees to meet the demonstrated need of applicants and, if so, the percentage of students whose financial need is actually met. The phrase "guarantees to meet demonstrated need" means that the institution for all practical purposes makes every effort possible to come up with the aid for which all of its students qualify.

Colleges have widely varying policies regarding interviews, both on campus and with alumni, so we indicate whether each of these is required, recommended, or optional. We also indicate whether reports from the person doing the interview are used in evaluating students or whether, as in many cases, the interview is seen only as a means of conveying information about the institution and answering applicants' questions.

This section also describes what standardized tests—SAT, ACT, or achievement—are required, and whether applicants are asked to write one or more essays. In the latter case, the topics are given.

The admissions policies of most colleges are fairly similar, at least among competing clusters of institutions. In some cases, however, a school will have its own special priorities. Some don't care that much about test scores. Others are looking for students with special talent in math or science, while others pay special attention to personal characteristics such as leadership in extracurricular activities. We asked each institution to tell us if its admission policies are in any ways "unique or unusual," and their answers are reported.

CONSORTIA

Many colleges expand the range of their offerings by banding together with other institutions to offer unusual programs that they could not support on their own. These options range from foreign study programs around the world to semesters at sea, and keeping such arrangements in mind is a way of expanding the list of institutions that might meet your particular interests and needs. The final section of the *Fiske Guide* describes 16 of these consortia and lists the member institutions.

MOVING FORWARD

Students will find the *Fiske Guide* useful at various points in the college selection process—from deciding whether to visit a particular campus to selecting among institutions that have accepted them. To make it easy to find a particular college, the write-ups are arranged in alphabetical order in the index. An Index by State and Country and an Index by Price can be found on pages ix and xii, respectively.

While most people are not likely to start reading at Agnes Scott and keep going until they reach Yale (though some tell us they do), we encourage you to browse. This country has an enormously rich and varied network of colleges and universities, and there are dozens of institutions out there that can meet the needs of any particular student. Too many students approach the college selection process wearing blinders, limiting their sights to local institutions, the pet schools of their parents or guidance counselors, or to ones they know only by possibly outdated reputations.

But applicants need not be bound by such limitations. Once you have decided on the type of school you think you want—a small liberal arts college, an engineering school, or whatever—we hope you will thumb through the book looking for similar institutions that might not have occurred to you. One way to do this is to look at the overlaps of schools you like and then check out those schools' overlaps. Many students have found this worthwhile, and quite frankly, we view the widening of students' horizons about American higher education as one of the most important purposes of the book. Perhaps the most gratifying remark we hear comes when a student tells us, as many have, that she is attending a school that she first heard about while browsing through *Fiske Guide to Colleges*.

Picking a college is a tricky business. But given the current buyer's market, there is no reason why you should not be able to find the right one. That's what *Fiske Guide to Colleges* is designed to help you do. Happy college hunting.

Sizing Yourself Up

The college search is a game of matchmaking. You have interests and needs; the colleges have programs to meet those needs. If all goes according to plan, you'll find the right one and live happily ever after——or at least for four years. It ought to be simple, but today's admissions process resembles a high-stakes obstacle course.

Many colleges are more interested in making a sale than they are in making a match. Under intense competitive pressure, many won't hesitate to sell you a bill of goods if they can get their hands on your tuition dollars. Guidance counselors generally mean well, but they are often under duress from principals and trustees to steer students toward prestigious schools regardless of whether the fit is right. Your friends won't be shy with advice on where to go, but their knowledge is generally limited to a small group of hot colleges that everyone is talking about. National publications rake in millions by playing on the public's fascination with rankings, but a close look at their criteria reveals distinctions without a difference.

Before you find yourself spinning headlong on this merry-go-round, take a step back. This is your life and your college career. What are you looking for in a college? Think hard and don't answer right away. Before you throw yourself and your life history on the mercy of college admissions officers, you need to take some time to objectively and honestly evaluate your needs, likes and dislikes, strengths and weaknesses. What do you have to offer a college? What can a college do for you? Unlike the high school selection process, which is usually predetermined by your parents' property lines, income level, or religious affiliation, picking a college isn't a procedure you can brush off on dear ol' Mom and Dad. You have to take some initiative. You're the best judge of how well each school fits your personal needs and academic goals.

We encourage you to view the college selection process as the first semester in your higher education. Life's transitions often call forth extra energy and focus. The college search is no exception. For the first time, you'll be contemplating a life away from home that can unfold in any direction you choose. Visions of majors and careers will dance in your head as you sample various institutions of higher learning, each with hundreds of millions of dollars in academic resources; it is hard to imagine a better hands-on seminar in research and matchmaking than the college search. The main impact, however, will be measured by what you learn about yourself. Piqued by new worlds of learning and tested by the competition of the admissions process, you'll be pushed as never before to show your accomplishments, clarify your interests, and chart a course for the future. More than one parent has watched in amazement as an erstwhile teenager suddenly emerged as an adult during the course of a college tour. Be ready when your time comes.

DEVELOP YOUR CRITERIA

One strategy is to begin the search with a personal inventory of your own strengths and weaknesses and your "wish list" for a college. This method tends to work well for compulsive list-makers and other highly organized people. What sorts of things are you especially good at? Do you have a list of skills or interests that you would like to explore further? What sort of personality are you looking for in a college? Mainstream? Conservative? Offbeat? What about extracurriculars? If you are really into riding horses, you might include a strong equestrian program in your criteria. The main problem won't be thinking of qualities to look for—you could probably name dozens— but rather figuring out what criteria should play a defining role in your search. Serious students should think carefully about the intellectual climate they are seeking. At some schools, students routinely stay up until 3:00 a.m. talking about topics like the value of deconstructing literary texts or the pros and cons of free trade. These same students would be viewed as geeks or weirdos on less cosmopolitan campuses. Athletes should take a hard look at whether they really want to play college ball and, if so, whether they want to go for an athletic scholarship or play at the less-pressured Division III level. Either way, intercollegiate sports require a huge time commitment.

Young women have an opportunity all to themselves—the chance to study at a women's college. The *Fiske Guide* profiles 14 such campuses, a vastly underappreciated resource on today's higher education scene. With small classes and strong encouragement from faculty, students at women's colleges move on to graduate study in significantly higher numbers than their counterparts at co-ed schools, especially in the natural sciences. Males seeking an all-male experience will find two options in the *Fiske Guide*, Hampden-Sydney College and Wabash College.

Students with a firm career goal will want to look for a course of study that matches their needs. If you want to major in aerospace engineering, your search will be limited to schools that have the program. Outside of specialized areas like this, many applicants overestimate the importance of their anticipated major in choosing a college. If you're interested in a liberal arts field, your expected major should probably have little to do with your college selection. A big purpose of college is to develop interests and set goals. Most students change their intentions regarding a major at least two or three times before graduation, and once out in the working world, they often end up in jobs bearing no relation to their academic specialty. Even those with a firm career goal may not need as much specialization as they think at the undergraduate level. If you want to be a lawyer, don't worry yourself looking for something labeled "prelaw." Follow your interests, get the best liberal arts education available, and then apply to law school.

Naturally, it is never a bad idea to check out the department(s) of any likely major, and occasionally your choice of major will suggest a direction for your search. If you're really into national politics, it may make sense to look at some schools in or near Washington, D.C. If you think you're interested in a relatively specialized field, say, oceanography, then be sure to look for some colleges that are a good match for you and also have programs in oceanography. But for the most part, rumors about top-ranked departments in this or that should be no more than a tie-breaker between schools you like for more important reasons. There are good professors (and bad ones) in any department. You'll have plenty of time to figure out who is who once you've enrolled. Being undecided about your career path as a senior in high school is often a sign of intelligence. Don't feel bad if you have absolutely no idea what you're going to do when you "grow up." One of the reasons you'll be paying megabucks to the college of your choice is the prospect that it will open some new doors for you and expand your horizons. Instead of worrying about particular departments, try to keep the focus on big-picture items, such as: What's the academic climate? How big are the freshman classes? Do I like it here? and Are these my kind of people?

KEEP AN OPEN MIND

The biggest mistake of beginning applicants is hyper-choosiness. At the extreme is the "perfect-school syndrome," which comes in two basic forms.

In one category are the applicants who refuse to consider any school that doesn't have every little thing they want in a college. If you're one who begins the process with a detailed picture of Perfect U. in mind, you may want to remember the oft-quoted advice, "Two out of three ain't bad." If a college seems to have most of the qualities you seek, give it a chance. You may come to realize that some things you thought were absolutely essential are really not that crucial after all.

The other strain of perfect-school syndrome is the applicant who gets stuck on a "dream" school at the beginning and then won't look anywhere else. With those 2,200 four-year colleges out there (not counting those in Canada and Great Britain), it is just a bit silly to insist that only one will meet your needs. Having a first choice is OK, but the whole purpose of the search is to consider new options and uncover new possibilities. A student who has only one dream school—especially if it is a highly selective one—could be headed for disappointment.

As you begin the college search, don't expect any quick revelations. The answers will unfold in due time. Our advice? Be patient. Set priorities. Keep an open mind. Reexamine priorities. Again, be patient.

To get the ball rolling, move on to the Sizing-Yourself-Up Survey.

FISKE'S SIZING-YOURSELF-UP SURVEY

With apologies to Socrates, knowing thyself is easier said than done. Most high school students can analyze a differential equation or a Shakespearean play with the greatest of ease, but when it comes to cataloging their own strengths, weaknesses, likes, and dislikes, many draw a blank. But self-knowledge is crucial to the matching process at the heart of a successful college search. The 30-item survey below offers a simple way to get a handle on some crucial issues in college selection—and what sort of college may fit your preferences.

In the space beside each statement, rate your feelings on a scale of 1 to 10, with 10 = Strongly Agree, 1 = Strongly Disagree, and 5 = Not Sure/Don't Have Strong Feelings. (For instance, a rating of 7 would mean that you agree with the statement, but that the issue is a lower priority than those you rated 8, 9, or 10.) After you're done, read on to "Grading Yourself" to find out what it all means.

Fiske's Sizing-Yourself-Up Survey

Size

_____ 1. I enjoy participating in many activities.

_____ 2. I would like to have a prominent place in my community.

_____ 3. Individual attention from teachers is important to me.

_____ 4. I learn best when I can speak out in class and ask questions.

_____ 5. I am undecided about what I will study.

_____ 6. I want to earn a Ph.D. in my chosen field of study.

_____ 7. I learn best by listening and writing down what I hear.

_____ 8. I would like to be in a place where I can be anonymous if I choose.

_____ 9. I prefer devoting my time to one or two activities rather than many.

_____ 10. I want to attend a college that most people have heard of.

_____ 11. I am interested in a career-oriented major.

_____ 12. I like to be on my own.

Location

_____ 13. I prefer a college in a warm or hot climate.

_____ 14. I prefer a college in a cool or cold climate.

_____ 15. I want to be near the mountains.

_____ 16. I want to be near a lake or ocean.

_____ 17. I prefer to attend a college in a particular state or region.

_____ 18. I prefer to attend a college near my family.

_____ 19. I want city life within walking distance of my campus.

_____ 20. I want city life within driving distance of my campus.

_____ 21. I want my campus to be surrounded by natural beauty.

Academics and Extracurriculars

_____ 22. I like to be surrounded by people who are free-thinkers and nonconformists.

_____ 23. I like the idea of joining a fraternity or sorority.

_____ 24. I like rubbing shoulders with people who are bright and talented.

_____ 25. I like being one of the smartest people in my class.

_____ 26. I want to go to a prestigious college.

_____ 27. I want to go to a college where I can get an excellent education.

_____ 28. I want to try for an academic scholarship.

_____ 29. I want a diverse college.

_____ 30. I want a college where the students are serious about ideas.

Grading Yourself

Picking a college is not an exact science. People who are total opposites can be equally happy at the same college. Nevertheless, particular types tend to do better at some colleges than others. Each item in the survey is designed to test your feelings on an important issue related to college selection. Sizing Up the Survey (below) offers commentary on each item.

Taken together, your responses may help you construct a tentative blueprint for your college search. Statements 1–12 deal with the issue of size. Would you be happier at a large university or a small college? Here's the trick: Add the sum of your responses to questions 1–6. Then make a second tally of your responses to 7–12. If the sum of 1–6 is larger, you may want to consider a small college. If 7–12 is greater, then perhaps a big school would be more to your liking. If the totals are roughly equal, you should probably consider colleges of various sizes.

Statements 13–21 deal with location. The key in this section is the intensity of your feeling. If you replied to No. 13 with a 10, does that mean you are going to look only at schools in warm climates? Think hard. If you consider only schools within a certain region or state, you'll be eliminating hundreds of possibilities. By examining your most intense responses—the 1s, 2s, 9s, and 10s—you'll be able to create a geographic profile of likely options.

Statements 22–30 deal with big-picture issues related to the character and personality of the college that may be in your future. As before, pay attention to your most intense responses. Read on for a look at the significance of each question.

Sizing Up the Survey

1. **I enjoy participating in many activities.** Students at small colleges tend to have more opportunities to be involved in many activities. Fewer students means less competition for spots.

2. **I would like to have a prominent place in my community.** Student-council presidents and other would-be leaders take note: It is easier to be a big fish if you're swimming in a small pond.

3. **Individual attention from teachers is important to me.** Small colleges generally offer more one-on-one with faculty both in the classroom and the laboratory.

4. **I learn best when I can speak out in class and ask questions.** Students who learn from interaction and participation would be well-advised to consider a small college.

5. **I am undecided about what I will study.** Small colleges generally offer more guidance and support to students who are undecided. The exception: students who are considering a preprofessional or highly specialized major.

6. **I want to earn a Ph.D. in my chosen field of study.** A higher percentage of students at selective small colleges earn a Ph.D. than those who attend large institutions of similar quality.

7. **I learn best by listening and writing what I hear.** Students who prefer lecture courses will find more of them at large institutions.

8. **I would like to be in a place where I can be anonymous if I choose to be.** At a large university, the supply of new faces is never-ending. Students who have the initiative can always reinvent themselves.

9. **I prefer devoting my time to one or two activities rather than many.** Students who are passionate about one activity—say, writing for the college newspaper—will often find higher quality at a bigger school.

10. **I want to attend a college that most people have heard of.** Big schools have more name recognition because they're bigger and have Division I athletic programs. Even the finest small colleges are relatively anonymous among the general public

11. **I am interested in a career-oriented major.** More large institutions offer business, engineering, nursing, etc., though some excellent small institutions do so as well (depending on the field).

12. **I like to be on my own.** A higher percentage of students live off campus at large schools, which are more likely to be in urban areas than their smaller counterparts.

13. **I prefer a college in a warm or hot climate.** Keep in mind that the Southeast and the Southwest have far different personalities (not to mention humidity levels).

14. **I prefer a college in a cool or cold climate.** Consider the Midwest, where there are many fine schools that are notably less selective than those in the Northeast.

15. **I want to be near the mountains.** You're probably thinking Colorado or Vermont, but don't zero in too quickly. States from Maine to Georgia and Arkansas to Arizona have easy access to mountains.

16. **I want to be near a lake or ocean.** Oceans are only on the coasts, but keep in mind the Great Lakes, the Finger Lakes, etc. Think about whether you want to be on the water or, say, within a two-hour drive.

17. **I prefer to attend a college in a particular state or region.** Geographical blinders limit options. Even if you think you want a certain area of the country, consider at least one college located elsewhere just to be sure.

18. **I prefer to attend a college close to home.** Unless you're planning to live with Mom and Dad, it may not matter whether your college is a two-hour drive or a two-hour plane ride.

19. **I want city life within walking distance of my campus.** Check out the neighborhood(s) surrounding your campus. Urban campuses—even in the same city—can be wildly different.

20. **I want city life within driving distance of my campus.** Unless you're a hardcore urban-dweller, a suburban perch near a city may beat living in the thick of one. Does public transportation or a campus shuttle help students get around?

21. **I want my campus to be surrounded by natural beauty.** A college viewbook will take you only so far. To really know if you'll fall in love with the campus, visiting is a must.

22. **I like to be surrounded by free-thinkers and nonconformists.** Plenty of schools cater specifically to students who buck the mainstream. Talk to your counselor or browse the *Fiske Guide to Colleges* to find some.

23. **I like the idea of joining a fraternity or sorority.** Greek life is strongest at mainstream and conservative-leaning schools. Find out if there is a split between Greeks and non-Greeks.

24. **I like rubbing shoulders with people who are bright and talented.** This is perhaps the best reason to aim for a highly selective institution, especially if you're the type who rises to the level of the competition.

25. **I like being one of the smartest people in my class.** If so, maybe you should skip the highly selective rat race. Star students get the best a college has to offer.

26. **I want to go to a prestigious college.** There is nothing wrong with wanting prestige. Think honestly about how badly you want a big-name school and act accordingly.

27. **I want to go to a college where I can get an excellent education.** Throw out the *U.S. News* rankings and think about which colleges will best meet your needs as a student.

28. **I want to try for an academic scholarship.** Students in this category should consider less-selective alternatives. Scholarships are more likely if you rank high in the applicant pool.

29. **I want a diverse college.** All colleges pay lip service to diversity. To get the truth, see the campus for yourself and take a hard look at the student-body statistics in the *Fiske Guide*'s write-ups.

30. **I want a college where students are serious about ideas.** Don't assume that a college necessarily attracts true intellectuals merely because it is highly selective. Some top schools are known for their intellectual climate—and others for their lack of it.

A Guide for Preprofessionals

The lists that follow include colleges and universities with unusual strength in each of nine preprofessional areas: engineering, architecture, business, art/design, drama, dance, music, communications/journalism, and film/television. We also offer lists covering two of today's hottest interdisciplinary majors: environmental studies and international studies. In compiling the lists, we drew on data from the thousands of surveys used to compile the *Fiske Guide*. We examined the strongest majors at each college as reported in student and administrative questionnaires, and then weighed these against the selectivity and overall academic quality of each institution. After compiling tentative lists in each subject, we queried our counselor advisory group, listed on page 759, for additional suggestions and feedback. To make the lists as useful as possible, we have included some schools that do not receive full-length write-ups in the *Fiske Guide*. Moreover, while the lists are suggestive, they are by no means all-inclusive, and there are other institutions in the *Fiske Guide* that offer fine programs in these areas. Nevertheless, we hope the lists will be a starting place for students interested in these fields.

If you are planning a career in one of the subjects below, your college search may focus largely on finding the best programs for you in that particular area. But we also recommend that you shop for a school that will give you an adequate dose of liberal arts. For that matter, you might consider a double major (or minor) in a liberal arts field to complement your area of technical expertise. If you allow yourself to get too specialized too soon, you may end up as tomorrow's equivalent of the typewriter repairman. In a rapidly changing job market, nothing is so practical as the ability to read, write, and think.

ARCHITECTURE

Private Universities Strong in Architecture
Carnegie Mellon University
Catholic University of America
Columbia University
Cooper Union
Cornell University (NY)
Drexel University
Hobart and William Smith Colleges
Howard University
Lehigh University
Massachusetts Institute of Technology
University of Miami (FL)
New Jersey Institute of Technology
Northeastern University
University of Notre Dame
Princeton University
Rensselaer Polytechnic Institute
Rice University
Temple University
Tuskegee University
Tulane University
Washington University in St. Louis

Public Universities Strong in Architecture
University of Arizona
University of California–Berkeley
University of Cincinnati
Clemson University
University of Florida
Georgia Institute of Technology
University of Illinois–Urbana-Champaign
University of Kansas
Kansas State University
University Maryland
Miami University (OH)
University of Michigan
University of Nebraska
State University of New York–Buffalo
University of Oregon
Pennsylvania State University
Texas A&M University
University of Texas–Austin
Virginia Polytechnic Institute and State University (Virginia Tech)
University of Washington

A Few Arts-Oriented Architecture Programs
Barnard College
Bennington College
Pratt Institute
Rhode Island School of Design
Savannah School of Art and Design
Wellesley College
Yale University

ART/DESIGN

Top Schools of Art and Design
Art Center College of Design
California College of the Arts
California Institute of the Arts
Cooper Union
Kansas City Art Institute
Maryland Institute, College of Art
Massachusetts College of Art
Moore College of Art and Design
North Carolina School of the Arts
Otis Institute of Art and Design
Parsons School of Design
Pratt Institute
Rhode Island School of Design
Ringling School of Art and Design
San Francisco Art Institute
Savannah College of Art and Design
School of the Art Institute of Chicago
School of the Museum of Fine Arts (MA)
School of Visual Arts (NY)

Major Universities Strong in Art or Design
American University
Boston College
Boston University
Carnegie Mellon University
University of Cincinnati

Cornell University
Drexel University
Harvard University
University of Michigan
New York University
University of North Carolina/
   Greensboro
University of Pennsylvania
Syracuse University
Washington University in St. Louis
University of Washington
Yale University

Small Colleges and Universities Strong in Art or Design
Alfred University
Bard College
Brown University
Centre College
Cornell College
Dartmouth College
Furman University
Hollins University
Kenyon College
Lake Forest College
Lewis and Clark
Manhattanville College
Mills College
State University of New
   York–Purchase
Randolph-Macon Woman's College
University of North
   Carolina–Greensboro
Sarah Lawrence College
Scripps College
Skidmore College
Smith College
Southwestern University
Vassar College
Wheaton College (MA)
Willamette University
Williams College

BUSINESS
Major Private Universities Strong in Business
American University
Baylor University
Boston College
Boston University
Carnegie Mellon University
Case Western Reserve University
University of Dayton

Emory University
Fordham University
Georgetown University
Howard University
Ithaca College
Lehigh University
Massachusetts Institute of
   Technology
New York University
University of Notre Dame
University of Pennsylvania
Pepperdine University
Rensselaer Polytechnic Institute
University of San Francisco
Santa Clara University
University of Southern California
Southern Methodist University
Syracuse University
Texas Christian University
Tulane University
Villanova University
Wake Forest University
Washington University in St. Louis

Public Universities Strong in Business
University of Arizona
University of California–Berkeley
University of Cincinnati
University of Connecticut
University of Florida
University of Georgia
University of Illinois–Urbana-
   Champaign
Indiana University
James Madison University
University of Kansas
University of Maryland
University of Massachusetts–Amherst
Miami University (OH)
University of Michigan
University of Missouri
University of North
   Carolina–Chapel Hill
Ohio State University
University of Ohio
University of Oregon
Pennsylvania State University
University of Pittsburgh
Rutgers, The State University of
   New Jersey
University of South Carolina
SUNY–Albany

SUNY–Binghamton University
SUNY–Buffalo
SUNY–Geneseo
University of Tennessee
Texas A&M University
University of Texas–Austin
University of Vermont
University of Virginia
University of Washington
University of Wisconsin
College of William and Mary

Small Colleges and Universities Strong in Business
Agnes Scott College
Babson College
Bucknell University
Calvin College
Claremont McKenna College
Clarkson University
Eckerd College
Fairfield University
Franklin and Marshall College
Furman University
Gettysburg College
Guilford College
Hendrix College
Lafayette College
Lake Forest College
Lehigh University
Lewis and Clark College
Millsaps College
Morehouse College
Muhlenberg College
Oglethorpe College
Ohio Wesleyan University
Presbyterian College
Rhodes College
University of Richmond
Ripon College
Skidmore College
Southwestern University
Stetson College
Susquehanna University
Trinity University (TX)
Washington and Jefferson College
Washington and Lee University
Whittier College
Wofford College
Worcester Polytechnic Institute
Xavier University of Louisiana

COMMUNICATIONS/
JOURNALISM

Major Universities Strong in Communications/Journalism

American University
Arizona State University
Boston University
University of California–Los Angeles
University of California–San Diego
University of Florida
University of Georgia
University of Illinois–Urbana-
   Champaign
Indiana University
Ithaca College
University of Kansas
University of Maryland
University of Michigan
University of Missouri–Columbia
University of Nebraska
University of North
   Carolina–Chapel Hill
Northwestern University
Ohio University
University of Oregon
Pepperdine University
St. Lawrence University
University of San Francisco
University of Southern California
Stanford University
Syracuse University
Texas Christian University
University of Utah
University of Wisconsin–Madison

ENGINEERING

Top Technical Institutes
California Institute of Technology
California Polytechnic Institute–
   San Luis Obispo
Colorado School of Mines
Cooper Union
Florida Institute of Technology
Georgia Institute of Technology
Harvey Mudd College
Illinois Institute of Technology
Massachusetts Institute of
   Technology
Michigan Technological University
Montana Tech of the University of
   Montana
New Jersey Institute of Technology

New Mexico Institute of Mining
   and Technology
Rensselaer Polytechnic Institute
Rochester Institute of Technology
Rose-Hulman Institute of Technology
Stevens Institute of Technology
Worcester Polytechnic Institute

Private Universities Strong in Engineering

Boston University
Bradley University
Brigham Young University
Brown University
Carnegie Mellon University
Case Western Reserve University
Catholic University of America
Columbia University
Cornell University
Drexel University
Duke University
George Washington University
Johns Hopkins University
Northeastern University
Northwestern University
University of Notre Dame
University of Pennsylvania
Princeton University
University of Rochester
Rochester Institute of Technology
Santa Clara University
University of Southern California
Southern Methodist University
Stanford University
Syracuse University
Tufts University
Tulane University
University of Tulsa
Vanderbilt University
Villanova University
Washington University in St. Louis

Public Universities Strong in Engineering

University of Arizona
University of California–Berkeley
University of California–Davis
University of California–Los Angeles
University of California–San Diego
University of Cincinnati
Clemson University
University of Connecticut
University of Delaware

University of Florida
University of Illinois–Urbana-
   Champaign
Iowa State University
University of Kansas
McGill University
University of Maryland
University of Massachusetts–Amherst
University of Michigan
Michigan State University
University of Missouri–Rolla
University of New Hampshire
College of New Jersey
North Carolina State University
Ohio State University
Oregon State University
Pennsylvania State University
Purdue University
Queen's University (CA)
University of Rhode Island
Rutgers, The State University of
   New Jersey
SUNY–Binghamton University
SUNY–Buffalo
Texas A&M University
Texas Tech University
University of Texas–Austin
University of Toronto
Virginia Polytechnic Institute and
   State University (Virginia Tech)
University of Virginia
University of Washington
University of Wisconsin

Small Colleges and Universities Strong in Engineering

Alfred University
Bucknell University
Butler University
Calvin College
Clarkson University
Dartmouth College
Lafayette College
Lehigh University
Loyola University (MD)
University of the Pacific
Rice University
Smith College
Spelman College
Swarthmore College
Trinity College (CT)
Trinity University (TX)

University of Tulsa
Tuskegee University
Union College

FILM/TELEVISION

Major Universities Strong in Film/Television

Arizona State University
Boston University
University of California–Los Angeles
University of Cincinnati
Drexel University
Emerson College
University of Florida
Ithaca College
University of Kansas
Memphis State University
University of Michigan
New York University
Northwestern University
Quinnipiac University
Pennsylvania State University
University of Southern California
Syracuse University
University of Texas–Austin
Wayne State University

Small Colleges and Universities Strong in Film/Television

Bard College
Beloit College
Brown University
California Institute of the Arts
Columbia College (CA)
Columbia College (IL)
The Evergreen State College
Hampshire College
Hofstra University
Hollins University
Occidental College
Pitzer College
Pomona College
Sarah Lawrence College
School of Visual Arts
SUNY–Purchase
Wesleyan University

PERFORMING ARTS—MUSIC

Top Music Conservatories

Berklee College of Music
Boston Conservatory
California Institute of the Arts

Cleveland Institute of Music
Curtis Institute of Music
Eastman School of Music
Juilliard School
Manhattan School of Music
New England Conservatory of Music
North Carolina School of the Arts
Peabody Conservatory of Music
San Francisco Conservatory of Music

Major Universities Strong in Music

Baylor University
Boston College
Boston University
University of California–Los Angeles
Carnegie Mellon University
Case Western Reserve University
University of Cincinnati
University of Colorado–Boulder
University of Denver
Depaul University
Florida State University
Harvard University
Indiana University
Ithaca College
Miami University (OH)
University of Miami (FL)
University of Michigan
University of Nebraska–Lincoln
New York University
Northwestern University
University of Oklahoma
University of Southern California
Southern Methodist University
Vanderbilt University
Yale University

Small Colleges and Universities Strong in Music

Bard College
Bennington College
Bucknell University
Butler University
DePauw University
Furman University
Gordon College
Illinois Wesleyan University
Knox College
Lawrence University*
Loyola University–New Orleans
Manhattanville College
Mills College
Oberlin College*
University of the Pacific

Rice University
St. Mary's College of Maryland
St. Olaf College
Sarah Lawrence College
Skidmore College
Smith College
University of Southern California
Stetson University
SUNY–Geneseo
SUNY–Purchase
Wesleyan University
Wheaton College (IL)

* These two schools are unusual because they combine a world-class conservatory with a top-notch liberal arts college.

PERFORMING ARTS—DRAMA

Major Universities Strong in Drama

Boston College
Boston University
University of California–Los Angeles
Carnegie Mellon University
The Catholic University of America
DePaul University
Emerson College
Florida State University
Fordham University
Indiana University
University of Iowa
Ithaca College
University of Minnesota
New York University
Northwestern University
University of North Carolina–Chapel Hill
University of Southern California
Southern Methodist University
Syracuse University
Texas Christian University
University of Washington
Yale University

Small Colleges and Universities Strong in Drama

Beloit College
Bennington College
Centre College
Colorado College
Connecticut College

Drew University
Ithaca College
Juilliard School
Kenyon College
Lawrence University
Macalester College
Middlebury College
Muhlenberg College
Occidental College
Otterbein College
Princeton University
Rollins College
Sarah Lawrence College
Skidmore College
SUNY–Purchase
Vassar College
Whitman College
Wittenberg University

PERFORMING ARTS—DANCE

Major Universities Strong in Dance
Arizona State University
University of California–Irvine
University of California–Los Angeles
University of California–Riverside
Case Western Reserve University
Florida State University
George Washington University
Howard University
Indiana University
University of Iowa
University Minnesota
New York University
Ohio University
Southern Methodist University
Texas Christian University
University of Texas–Austin
University of Utah
Washington University in St. Louis

Small Colleges and Universities Strong in Dance
Amherst College
Barnard College
Bennington College
Butler University

Connecticut College
Dartmouth College
Goucher College
Hollins University
Juilliard School
Kenyon College
Middlebury College
Mills College
Muhlenberg College
North Carolina School of the Arts
Princeton University
Sarah Lawrence College
Smith College
SUNY–Purchase

ENVIRONMENTAL STUDIES
Allegheny College
College of the Atlantic
Bowdoin College
University of California–Davis
University of California–Santa Barbara
Clark University
Colby College
University of Colorado–Boulder
Dartmouth College
Deep Springs College
Eckerd College
The Evergreen State College
Hampshire College
Hiram College
Hobart and William Smith Colleges
McGill University
Middlebury College
University of New Hampshire
University of New Mexico
University of North Carolina–Asheville
University of North Carolina–Greensboro
Oberlin College
Prescott College
St. Lawrence University
Tulane University
University of Vermont
University of Washington
Williams College
University of Wisconsin–Madison

INTERNATIONAL STUDIES
American University
Austin College
Brandeis University
University of British Columbia
Brown University
Bucknell University
Claremont McKenna College
Clark University
Colby College
Connecticut College
Dartmouth College
Davidson College
Denison University
University of Denver
Dickinson College
Earlham College
Eckerd College
Georgetown University
George Washington University
Goucher College
Hiram College
The Johns Hopkins University
Kalamazoo College
Lewis and Clark College
Mary Washington College
University of Massachusetts–Amherst
Middlebury College
Mount Holyoke College
Occidental College
University of the Pacific
University of Pittsburgh
Pomona College
Princeton University
University of Puget Sound
Randolph Macon Woman's College
Reed College
Rhodes College
University Richmond
St. Olaf College
Scripps College
University of South Carolina
Sweet Briar College
Tufts University
Wesleyan University
College of William and Mary

Learning Disabilities

Accommodation for students with learning disabilities is one of the fastest-growing academic areas in higher education. Colleges and universities recognize that a significant segment of the population may suffer problems that qualify as learning disabilities, and the range of support services offered to such students is increasing. Assistance ranges from counseling services to accommodations such as tapes of lectures or extended time on exams.

Following are two lists—the first of major universities, the second of smaller colleges—that offer particularly strong services for LD students. If you qualify for such support, you should be diligent in checking out the services at each college on your list. If possible, pay a visit to the LD support office or have a phone conversation with one of the administrators. Since many such programs depend on the expertise of one or two people, the quality of the services can change abruptly with changes in staff.

Keep in mind also that many colleges are becoming increasingly skeptical of requests for LD services, especially when the initial diagnosis is made on the eve of the college search.

Strong Support for Students with Learning Disabilities

Major Universities

American University
University of Arizona
University of California–Berkeley
Clark University
University of Colorado–Boulder
University of Denver
DePaul University
University of Georgia
Hofstra University
Purdue University
Rochester Institute of Technology
Syracuse University
University of Vermont
University of Virginia

Small Colleges

Bard College
Curry College
Landmark College
Loras College
Lynn University
Marist College
Mercyhurst College
Mitchell College
Muskingum College
University of New England
St. Thomas Acquinas College (NY)
Southern Vermont College
Westminster College (MO)
West Virginia Wesleyan College

Adelphi University

One South Avenue, Garden City, NY 11530

Situated in a comfortable Long Island suburb within shouting distance of Manhattan, Adelphi lets you taste urban life without being overwhelmed. Strong on preprofessional programs with a grounding in the liberal arts.

Everyone loves a great comeback story. In the mid-1990s, this small Long Island university was strapped for both cash and students because of mismanagement by a free-spending president and a negligent board of trustees. Now, thanks to a revamped mission, Adelphi University is experiencing a renaissance of sorts. Enrollment has increased, new facilities are sprouting up all around campus, and students speak of an almost palpable sense of energy among students and faculty.

Located just 20 minutes from the urgency of Manhattan, Adelphi's campus occupies 75 acres in an attractive residential suburb replete with Gothic cathedrals and stately homes. A new three-story dormitory with 74 rooms opened in 2003, offering students private bathrooms, spacious student lounges, high-speed Internet access, and a communal kitchen.

Adelphi's most popular majors have a decidedly preprofessional bent: business management, nursing, psychology, physical education, and biology. The honors college offers a rigorous liberal arts program for exceptional students, who must complete all the requirements for their major within that department or school and supplement their learning with intensive honors

"Adelphi is a pretty laid-back university."

courses. Recent honors seminar topics included Genetic Disease and Genetic Engineering, The Decline and Fall of Certainty, Censorship and Morality, The Fate of the Earth, and Equality and Inequality. Joint degree programs have been established in a number of disciplines, including physics, dentistry, law, and physical therapy. The combined degree program in engineering with Columbia allows students to earn a BS in physics from Adelphi and a BS in engineering from Columbia in five years or an undergraduate and graduate degree in six years.

The general education curriculum was reorganized in 1999. Students must complete a 24-credit distribution requirement in several areas (arts, humanities and languages, natural sciences and mathematics, and social sciences) as well courses in composition and English, a foreign language, statistics, computer programming, critical thinking, or public speaking. Freshmen take part in an orientation course and a three-credit freshman seminar that introduces students to life at Adelphi.

The academic climate is challenging but not cutthroat. "Adelphi is a pretty laid-back university," says a senior. "There are many competitive classes that challenge students, but the students do not seem to be competing with each other." Nearly two-thirds of all classes have 25 or fewer students, and professors are commended for their accessibility and knowledge. "Professors at Adelphi are excellent," says one student. "They know their material and are intelligent. They are always available during office hours."

"No two students at Adelphi are alike," says a sociology major. "There are students of all backgrounds, cultures, and places around the world." Ninety-one percent of the

Website: www.adelphi.edu
Location: Suburban
Total Enrollment: 4,161
Undergraduates: 4,161
Male/Female: 29/71
SAT Ranges: V 480–590
  M 500–600
ACT Range: 21–26
Financial Aid: 68%
Expense: Pr $
Phi Beta Kappa: Yes
Applicants: 4,379
Accepted: 71%
Enrolled: 26%
Grad in 6 Years: 53%
Returning Freshmen: 79%
Academics: ✍ ✍ ✍
Social: ☎ ☎
Q of L: ★ ★ ★
Admissions: (516) 877-3050
Email Address:
  admissions@adelphi.edu

Strongest Programs:
Nursing
Elementary Education
Biology
Accounting
Performing Arts
Psychology
Physical Education

university's student body hails from New York, and just over half graduated in the top quarter of their high school class. Minority enrollment is consistent with the university's proximity to the Big Apple. Sixteen percent of students are African American, 13 percent Hispanic, and 5 percent Asian American. Political issues don't dominate campus conversations, but students say recent debates include issues of homosexuality, the importance of voting, and the war in Iraq. Adelphi offers more than 700 merit scholarships worth an average of $6,971 to qualified students. Sixty-five athletic scholarships are available in a variety of sports.

Despite "comfortable and well maintained" residence halls, Adelphi remains primarily a suitcase school. Seventy-five percent of students live off-campus, "even if they live close to school," says one student. There are six residence halls, and freshmen and sophomores receive first priority in arranging housing. Though some grumble about the price of food on campus, most admit that there is plenty to choose from. "Adelphi makes attempts to have things for everyone," says a senior. "There are days in which sushi, Caribbean food, and other foods are served. Vegetarians have a good selection, too." Campus security maintains a presence and the university recently installed additional cameras and emergency boxes throughout campus.

"No two students at Adelphi are alike."

Since many students trek home on weekends, they budget their party time for Thursday and Friday nights. "Social life at Adelphi is pretty good," says one student. "There are usually events (parties, lectures, casino nights, bingo nights, poetry contests, etc.) every week." The school sponsors 70 clubs and organizations, including seven sororities and fraternities that attract 4 percent of the women and 2 percent of the men, respectively. Adelphi is a dry campus and students say that the policy is strictly enforced. Still, "As a resident assistant, I know that the 'no alcohol' policies don't work," says a senior. "Students will be tricksters!" The glitz of New York City is just 40 minutes away by train and the Long Island beaches draw crowds when it's warm.

Adelphi fields several competitive teams, including women's soccer, men's and women's basketball, men's and women's lacrosse, and softball. The women's soccer team recently won two consecutive NCAA Division II northeast regional titles and the men's basketball team has made nine straight tournament appearances, including the 2002–2003 season. In addition, the university won the coveted New York Collegiate Athletic Conference Commissioner's Cup, awarded to the most outstanding program, for the last three years. Intramurals are offered in a dozen sports.

"Adelphi has changed tremendously."

"Adelphi has changed tremendously," says one happy student. "It has become more lively and fun." Indeed, this newfound optimism is infectious and seems to permeate the campus. Signs of renewal are everywhere, from the campus facilities to the burgeoning enrollment. Although the university's commuter heritage can leave some wanting for more lively and fun." Indeed, this newfound optimism is infectious and seems to permeate the campus. Signs of renewal are everywhere, from the campus facilities to the burgeoning enrollment. Although the university's commuter heritage can leave some wanting for more social opportunities, many find that this small Northeastern school fits the bill.

Overlaps

Hofstra, St. John's, Long Island University, SUNY–Stony Brook, CUNY–Queens, Pace

If You Apply To ➤

Adelphi: Early action: Dec. 1. Financial aid: Jan. 1 (recommended). Does not guarantee to meet demonstrated need. Campus interviews: recommended, informational. No alumni interviews. SATs or ACTs: required. SAT IIs: optional. Accepts the Common Application and electronic applications. Essay question.

Agnes Scott College

141 East College Avenue, Decatur, GA 30030

Combines the tree-lined seclusion of Decatur with the bustle of Atlanta. More money in the bank than most selective schools, and enrollment is up 50 percent since 1990. Small classes, sisterhood, and a more exciting location than the Sweet Briars of the world.

Agnes Scott College, founded in 1889, offers a small town campus atmosphere and provides women with an intellectually challenging institution—absent the distractions of men. The college is known for its science and math programs, but it also produces skilled writers and artists, and continues to be one of the South's leading women's schools. ASC's climate as a small, single-sex institution leads to close relationships with the faculty and very involved students—both academically and socially. "Consider the benefits of a single-sex institution," advises a first-year. "A woman will learn more here than anywhere else."

The Agnes Scott campus sits on 100 acres in the historic district of Decatur, just outside Atlanta. The well-maintained Gothic and Victorian buildings are surrounded by gardens filled with rare shrubs, bushes, and trees—all evidence of strong alumnae support. A $125 million capital campaign has paid for a new campus center, library expansion and renovation, new tennis courts, and three renovated theme houses in the past few years. The $36.5 million Science Center at Agnes Scott includes an x-ray spectrometer, nuclear magnetic resonance imaging equipment, and a scanning tunneling microscope. The school's Delafield Planetarium has a computer-controlled Zeiss projector, one of only 10 in the United States.

Aside from outstanding instruction in the sciences, Agnes Scott provides students with solid grounding in the liberal arts. First-year students may choose seminars on special topics such as U.S. foreign policy, religion and human rights in Atlanta, or living in Roman Pompeii. To graduate, students must complete one semester of English composition and literature, plus courses in math, historical studies or classical civilization, fine arts, science, social and cultural analysis, and physical

> **"A woman will learn more here than anywhere else."**

education. Students must also attain intermediate-level proficiency in a foreign language and, because ASC is affiliated with the Presbyterian Church, take one course in religion or philosophical thought. Eighty percent of the classes taken by first-years have 25 students or less.

Academically, Agnes Scott excels in biology and math, producing numerous Goldwater scholars in the past four years. The school is also strong in German, with six Fulbright scholars since 1993. A senior says the biology program is "definitely one of the best programs." The college also recently added a dual-degree program in nursing and a new major in economics and management. Those participating in research may attend or present results at an annual conference held in the spring. Entrepreneurs and students interested in nonprofit work may take advantage of the Kauffman and Hubert internship programs. The overall academic climate at ASC is competitive. A biology major says, "As one of the more selective schools in Georgia, ASC's education is challenging and the professors expect the students to work hard and do well."

When Agnes Scott's idyllic campus feels too small, students may enroll in the Atlanta Semester, focusing on women, leadership, and social change, or the Global Awareness and Global Connections programs, which offers a semester of crosscultural study before sending students out around the globe. If it is sun and fun you want, take a term at all-female Mills College in Oakland, California. Engineers and architects may complete their degrees through a 3–2 program with Georgia Tech or a 3–4 program

Website: www.agnesscott.edu
Location: Urban
Total Enrollment: 1,027
Undergraduates: 887
Male/Female: 0/100
SAT Ranges: V 540–680
M 500–620
ACT Range: 22–28
Financial Aid: 63%
Expense: Pr $ $
Phi Beta Kappa: Yes
Applicants: 1,252
Accepted: 59%
Enrolled: 35%
Grad in 6 Years: 71%
Returning Freshmen: 80%
Academics: ✍ ✍ ✍
Social: ☎ ☎
Q of L: ★ ★ ★ ★
Admissions: (404) 471-6285
Email Address:
admission@agnesscott.edu

Strongest Programs:
Astrophysics
Biology
Mathematics
German
Psychology
Economics
English

Varsity sports are improving with the formation of the Great South Athletic Conference, and both of the Agnes Scott tennis and cross-country teams brought home a conference trophy in recent years.

with Washington University in St. Louis. As a member of the Atlanta Regional Consortium for Higher Education*, Agnes Scott shares facilities and resources with 18 other schools in the area through a crossregistration program.

The ASC student body hails mainly from the Southeast; more than half are Georgia natives. One student describes the student body as "inquisitive, bright, involved, activism-oriented, and focused. Sometimes they are characterized as neurotic or too intense." The campus is decidedly liberal, and the "politically conservative students are not well accepted," says a sophomore. Scott students are hard working, but also volunteer in the community. Despite the school's small size, its campus is quite diverse, with 22 percent of the student body African American, more than 4 percent Hispanic, and 6 percent Asian American. An honor system, enforced by a student judiciary, allows for self-scheduled and unproctored exams.

"Students aren't allowed to move off campus, which creates a close campus community."

Agnes Scott awards merit scholarships averaging more than $10,000 annually, based on academic performance, leadership, or musical ability.

Eighty-seven percent of Agnes Scott students live in the dorms, which are linked by tree-lined brick walks. "Students aren't allowed to move off campus, which creates a close campus community, but can be a barrier financially because room and board is so expensive," says a first-year student. Dorms are described as being spacious and well maintained compared to other colleges. Juniors and seniors can live in Avery Glen, the college-owned apartment complex, while first-years are assigned to the two dorms (out of six total). Although it is "girls only," Agnes Scott has no sororities, but the college itself is a close-knit sisterhood. The selection of food at Agnes Scott dining facilities takes every type of diet into consideration, including vegetarian, low-carb, low-fat, and dairy-free. "The food is of good quality and usually there is a lot of options, though, sometimes the food service staff are less than pleasant to students," says one sophomore.

The college is known for its science and math programs, but it also produces skilled writers and artists, and continues to be one of the South's leading women's schools.

ASC has many campus clubs and events, but when the weekend comes, "off-campus is where the party's at," one student says. Convenient public transportation serves cultural landmarks like the High Art Museum and provides access to the social scene in nearby Atlanta. Decatur itself is not really a "college town," but there are some attractions for Agnes Scott students. "There are still nice little venues and coffee shops;

"There are still nice little venues and coffee shops; very hip and fun."

very hip and fun," a student says. A lot of ASC students get involved with community service both on and off campus, with Habitat for Humanity, the DeKalb Rape Crisis Center, Girl Scouts, Hands Across Atlanta, and Best Buddies.

Back on campus, underage students may not imbibe, in accordance with Georgia state law; enforcement falls under the honor code. One student says the restrictions work well, and 21-year-olds can enjoy alcohol in their dorms and at certain functions. But a bulk of the socializing at ASC is off-campus, one student says. "Either you have a clique of friends or hardly any at all and inviting your boyfriend to campus is often difficult because the policies make many men uncomfortable." When traveling, popular road trips include Stone Mountain and Six Flags, or New Orleans for Mardi Gras. Every October, students invite dates to a formal dance known as Black Cat. It follows a week of class competitions and marks the end of new-student orientation. Other quaint old traditions survive, too, such as throwing recently engaged classmates into the alumnae pond. And seniors who get into grad school or find jobs go to the top of the college bell tower, pealing out chimes to share the good news.

Varsity sports are improving with the formation of the Great South Athletic Conference, and both of the Agnes Scott tennis and cross-country teams brought home a conference trophy in recent years. Also strong are soccer, swimming, basketball, and

Overlaps

University of Georgia, Emory, Mount Holyoke, Georgia State, Randolph-Macon Women's College, Wellesley

softball. About 10 percent of students participate in intramural activities, which include the standard roundup of sports plus a few more exotic options, such as Frisbee.

Small but mighty, ASC stands out for the little touches that make students feel part of a close-knit community. "Agnes Scott is distinctive in that it is a bubble of academia in the middle of Atlanta," says a sophomore. Academically, the school offers challenging courses in science and math and supplements its instruction in many other fields with a variety of programs that allow students to explore new opportunities both on campus, in conjunction with other institutions, and abroad.

If You Apply To ➤	**Agnes Scott:** Early decision: Nov. 15. Regular admissions: Mar. 1 (Jan. 15 for scholarship applicants). Financial aid: Feb. 15. Meets demonstrated need of 71%. Campus interviews: recommended, evaluative. Alumni interviews: optional, informational. SATs or ACTs: required. SAT IIs: optional. Accepts the Common Application and prefers electronic applications. Essay question: impact of significant experience, risk or ethical dilemma; issue of personal, local, national or international concern; influential person, fictional character, historical figure, or creative work; topic of your choice.

University of Alabama

Box 870132, Tuscaloosa, AL 35487-0166

"Roll, Tide, Roll" says a lot. Not exactly a hotbed of intellectual energy, 'Bama has been left in the dust by University of Georgia and its Hope Scholarship. Look for pockets of excellence in the professional programs, the Blount Undergraduate Initiative, and honors programs.

Tuscaloosa, Alabama, only looks like a place where time stands still. Sure, the city's landmarks include those that have largely faded from view in other Southern towns: well-preserved antebellum homes, down-home Dreamland barbecue, and world-renowned blues music. And devotion to the University of Alabama and its Crimson Tide football team remains as strong as ever. But Tuscaloosa has also grown to include the only Mercedes-Benz plant outside of Germany, JVC, and other international companies that provide internship opportunities for students. And the state's first university, which dates to 1831, is diversifying itself, updating its facilities, and looking to make the education it offers more global and high-tech while increasing offerings for honors students and undergraduate researchers. And with the number of applications on the rise, it seems someone is taking notice.

'Bama's thousand-acre campus combines classical, revival-style buildings (several of which survived the 1865 burning of the university by Union troops) with modern structures. One of the most stunning in the South, the campus wraps around a shaded quadrangle, the home of the main library and "Denny Chimes," a campanile carillon that rings the Westminster Chimes on the quarter hour. Newer additions to campus include: Shelby Hall, a classroom and research building; a student recreation center, pool, and other athletic facilities; a child development center; and additional student housing.

"The teachers are great. Most of them have real-world experience in the field they are teaching in."

The University of Alabama is organized into eight undergraduate colleges and schools, which together offer 82 undergraduate degree programs. The Culverhouse College of Commerce and Business offers strong programs in marketing and management information systems; with finance and accounting as two of the most popular

Website: www.ua.edu
Location: Small city
Total Enrollment: 17,302
Undergraduates: 14,733
Male/Female: 47/53
SAT Ranges: V 490–620
  M 500–610
ACT Range: 21–26
Financial Aid: 38%
Expense: Pub $
Phi Beta Kappa: Yes
Applicants: 9,106
Accepted: 77%
Enrolled: 37%
Grad in 6 Years: 61%
Returning Freshmen: 83%
Academics: ✎ ✎ ✎
Social: 🍺 🍺 🍺
Q of L: ★ ★ ★
Admissions: (800) 933-2262
Email Address:
  admissions@ua.edu

majors on campus. Nursing, public relations and advertising are also popular. The College of Communication and Information Sciences has one of the country's top 10 journalism schools, while respected programs in the College of Human Environmental Sciences include athletic training and family financial planning. The School of Music is a regional standout, attracting guest artists such as Jean-Pierre Rampal and Midori. The New College allows students to work with faculty to design their own unique program.

The three honors programs, which feature smaller classes, early registration privileges and the opportunity to write a senior thesis, attract nearly 1,700 students. Students of any major—mostly engineers—may participate in the computer-based honors program, which pays them to develop software programs in their field of study. The Blount Undergraduate Initiative is a living/learning program within the College of Arts and Sciences, where freshmen are housed with a faculty director and fellows. Other innovative offerings include 'Bama's Weekend College, the continuing education division, which has attracted a large undergraduate following, and the interim term in May, when students focus on one course in depth.

About 20 percent of Alabama freshmen take part in the Arts and Sciences Mentoring Program, which pairs them with faculty mentors who ease the adjustment to college through informal counseling and enrichment activities such as concerts, movies, or lectures. All students may also enroll in the two-credit Academic Potential Seminar, which covers self-assessment, motivation, personal responsibility, time management, memory, textbook reading, note-taking, and test preparation. The only course 'Bama requires students to take during the first year on campus is a two-term English composition sequence. Before graduation, students must also take courses in writing, natural sciences, math, humanities and social sciences, and either two semesters of a foreign language or one of computer science.

While UA's core curriculum has been streamlined and the math requirement has been reduced, don't expect to party all the time and still pass, students say. Alabama "has an overall laid-back academic climate," but the difficulty of the coursework varies by major, a senior says. In the business fields, "the courses are pretty tough,

"Housing is great and always improving."

but professors are willing to work with you," a senior says. Professors teach lectures and many seminar courses, including some classes for freshmen. "The teachers are great. Most of them have real-world experience in the field they are teaching in," a senior says. "My experience has been filled with quality teachers," notes a junior.

Seventy-eight percent of 'Bama's students are homegrown, 20 percent hail from elsewhere in the United States, and 2 percent are international students representing more than 79 countries. "Most of our students are middle/upper class with Southern values," says one senior. A classmate adds, "This is not the place for really artsy or eclectic people." Alabama is a leader in diversity among Southern flagship universities with more than 14 percent minority enrollment: 12 percent African American, 1 percent Asian American, and 1 percent Hispanic. "The biggest strife is between Greek and non-Greek members," a junior says, noting the "majority of UA is united." 'Bama awards 173 athletic scholarships in nine men's sports and nine women's sports, as well as merit scholarships.

Students of any major—mostly engineers—may participate in the computer-based honors program, which pays them to develop software programs in their field of study.

Most Alabama students live in off-campus apartments in the Tuscaloosa area; only 24 percent remain in campus residence halls, where options range from apartment-style living to private rooms and suites. "Housing is great and always improving," a senior says. New dorms opened recently, but a sophomore still advises that "if a student wants a room for the fall semester, they should apply early in the spring." Another freshman gives high marks to the living/learning communities, some of which are for first-year students and others that bring together students from a particular school or college. Twenty percent of men pledge fraternities and 26 percent of women join sororities, and they may live in chapter houses. 'Bama's campus is safe, thanks to visible school police and a free school escort service.

Much of 'Bama's social life—which students describe as "very active" and "second to none"—revolves around the Greek system and athletic events. Participation has been steady in recent years, despite administrators' efforts to weaken it by prohibiting fraternities and sororities from having parties on campus. Those under 21 can't have alcohol in the dorms—or elsewhere, for that matter, per state law—but a sophomore says, "UA is very lenient compared to other schools." "I think the rules are enforced, but there are plenty of underage people with alcohol," a senior says. Those who don't go Greek, or who don't wish to drink, will find everything from the Society for Creative Anachronism (medievalists) to Bible study groups. City Fest, featuring music, food, beer, and a German theme, is a popular annual event, as is Capstone, a Saturday dedicated to community service. A modern trolley service connects the 'Bama campus to the city's thriving downtown. Tuscaloosa is described as "a grand college town," that is "big enough to always find something to do," but "small enough to not get too lost." Road trips to New Orleans (for Mardi Gras and Greek weekend formals), Atlanta, Nashville, Birmingham, and the Gulf Coast and Florida beaches are popular, too.

'Bama football remains the cornerstone of the university's competitive athletic programs. Following several seasons of struggle, the team finished the 2005–06 season with a top 10 ranking and a post-season bowl win. The annual Auburn–Alabama game—the Iron Bowl, one of the most intense rivalries in college sports—is the highlight of the school year. "Any Alabama football game is a festival," a sophomore says. Alabama competes in Division I, and the women's gymnastics team and men's basketball team brought home sectional championships in 2003. Football, softball and men's baseball, tennis, swimming and outdoor track and field are also competitive.

'Bama's administrators are no longer satisfied with being a purely athletic and social school. (In fact, they brag, the school's debate team has won 14 national championships—two more than the football team!) The emphasis is now on technology, honors programs, global perspectives, and undergraduate research. "We have made great attempts to become a more academically-known school," a senior says. "The number of students enrolled has been steadily growing with every freshman class."

Overlaps

Auburn, University of Georgia, Florida State, University of Tennessee, University of Mississippi, University of Alabama–Birmingham

If You Apply To ➤

'Bama: Rolling admissions: Sept. 1. Financial aid and housing: Mar. 1. Meets demonstrated need of 33%. Campus interviews: recommended, informational. Alumni interviews: optional, informational. SATs or ACTs: required. SAT IIs: optional. Accepts the Common Application and electronic applications. No essay question.

Albertson College

Caldwell, Idaho 83605

Got a map? You'll need a sharp eye to spot Albertson, the *Fiske Guide*'s only liberal arts school other than Colorado College in the interior of the Mountain West. Innovative programs include Leadership Studies and the Center for Experiential Learning.

With an emphasis on technology, education, and experiential learning, Albertson College of Idaho, the state's oldest four-year university, offers students an opportunity to earn a solid liberal arts education through small classes in a small town. "The professors know you by heart, and every face is familiar," a sophomore psychology major says. Outside class, the school's scenic environment allows sports and nature enthusiasts to romp freely before heading back into the classrooms.

The college is in the small town of Caldwell where the atmosphere is calm and serene. For those looking for a little excitement, the state capitol of Boise is a short drive from campus. Also nearby are some of Idaho's most scenic locations such as beautiful mountains, deserts, and whitewater rivers. The school, originally a Presbyterian college, first planted roots in downtown Caldwell in 1891 and then moved to its present site in 1910, where its 21 buildings now inhabit 43 acres. For more than 80 years, it was called the College of Idaho, but officials changed the college's name to honor the Albertson family, which gave $13.5 million for new facilities.

The school's academic schedule is composed of 12-week semesters, spring and fall, separated by a six-week winter session, during which students can assist professors with research, take an internship, volunteer, or travel abroad. The general education requirements include natural sciences, writing, mathematics, civilization, cultural diversity, physical activity, social science, fine arts, and humanities. Freshmen go through a first-year program that includes reading a common book, a junior or senior mentor, a team of adviser, and a weeklong orientation that includes an off-campus overnight stay. First-year students demonstrating leadership potential are invited to a series of seminars to draw them into the leadership studies program, a business minor. The two libraries have 178,000 volumes and are accessible online 24 hours a day.

Biology, English, and history are among the majors recommended by students, and preprofessional majors, such as premed, prevet, and prelaw are also popular and strong. Weaker departments are the smaller ones, such as foreign languages, music, and education. Students can choose such specializations as sports and fitness-center management. Undergraduate research opportunities are available in biology, chemistry, and psychology, and students present their findings at state and regional conferences. It has also overhauled education and is adding a five-year master's degree program. The college cooperates with Columbia University, the University of Idaho, Boise State University, and Washington University in St. Louis to offer a five-year course of study in engineering. The Center for Experiential Learning coordinates out-of-classroom experiences, such as international education and service learning. For those who want to venture abroad (physically or mentally), the International Education Program offers several options, including attending a foreign university, traveling overseas during the summer and winter breaks, and taking international studies on campus. Travel has really taken off, with 25 percent of students accepting opportunities to study in such places as Cuba, Greece, and Germany.

> **"The professors know you by heart, and every face is familiar."**

Most classes at Albertson have 25 or fewer students, and all are taught by full professors. Students agree its small size is the school's strongest asset, allowing students to usually get into the classes they want. "I feel that I'm receiving a great education," says a freshman. "My teachers have all been very knowledgeable."

The school's price tag is lower than that of most private colleges. It offers merit scholarships to nearly all students, as well as 194 athletic scholarships. Not surprisingly, some of those scholarship dollars are set aside for skiers. Seventy-two percent of the students are from Idaho; 74 percent are white. Four percent are Hispanic and Asian Americans add another 3 percent. Only 2 percent hail from foreign nations.

During a six-week winter session, students can assist professors with research, take an internship, volunteer, or travel abroad.

"PC is an issue," says a junior. "Our campus is concerned about environmental issues, and we're evenly divided between conservatives and liberals." Environmental issues also get students riled up.

Fifty percent of students live on campus. Each room in the five residence halls has individual heating and cooling and hookups for Internet access, and each hall has a computer lab. Dorms are "decent-sized, not any better or worse than a typical college," a junior comments. For safety, the college recently implemented a round-the-clock escort system, and there are many emergency stations around campus.

Seven percent of men and 7 percent of women participate in the Greek system, which dominates campus social life. Annual social highlights include Winterfest and Spring Fling and homecoming week. Games against rival Northwest Nazarene also attract attention. Caldwell, with 24,000 people, is not a great spot for college students, but students get involved by helping out the local school district. "Finals breakfasts" offer something for bleary-eyed students to look forward to during finals week. At midnight on Tuesday, faculty and staff cook breakfast for students. Nearby Boise is a popular destination for shopping, dining, cultural events, and volunteering. Many students take advantage of hiking, kayaking, and skiing in the surrounding area, and many hit the road during a weeklong break taken every six weeks.

> **"Our campus is concerned about environmental issues and we're evenly divided between conservatives and liberals."**

Men's basketball is a crowd-pleaser, and the team has made Albertson students proud, chalking up victories in NAIA Division II competition. The women's team was a runner-up in 2001 and advanced to the Cascade Conference Tournament championship game in 2005. The skiing teams have claimed 28 individual or team championships, and men's baseball and soccer are also competitive. For those who enjoy the game but might not make the team, there is an active intramurals program, an outdoors program that offers instruction in areas such as rock climbing and fly fishing, and the large J. A. Albertson Activities Center.

Albertson College has much to offer its "Yotes" (translation: "We are the coyotes"). They enjoy a solid liberal arts education and personal academic attention on a campus striving to keep its offerings on the cutting edge. "The close, intimate nature of ACI is what makes it unique," a sophomore says. "We really are an academic community."

Scholarships are available for skiers, and the skiing teams have claimed 28 individual or team championships.

Overlaps
Boise State, University of Idaho, Linfield, Brigham Young, Idaho State, Reed

If You Apply To ➤

Albertson: Rolling admissions. Early action: Nov. 15. Meets demonstrated need of 17%. Campus interviews: recommended, informational. Alumni interviews: optional, informational. SATs or ACTs: required, writing test required with ACT. SAT IIs: optional. Accepts the Common Application and electronic applications. Essay question: matter you have learned to question; how you would succeed in winter term; more about you and your values.

Albion College

Albion, MI 49224

Next to evangelical Hope and Calvin and out-there Kalamazoo, Albion is Michigan's middle-of-the road liberal arts college. Think Gerald Ford, the moderate Republican president who is the namesake of Albion's signature Institute for Public Service. Future doctors, lawyers, and businesspeople will be well served.

Website: www.albion.edu
Location: Small town
Total Enrollment: 1,548
Undergraduates: 1,548
Male/Female: 45/55
SAT Ranges: V 510–640
    M 520–630
ACT Range: 22–27
Financial Aid: 60%
Expense: Pr $ $
Phi Beta Kappa: Yes
Applicants: 1,297
Accepted: 87%
Enrolled: 40%
Grad in 6 Years: 72%
Returning Freshmen: 86%
Academics: ✏ ✏ ✏
Social: ☎ ☎
Q of L: ★ ★ ★
Admissions: (800) 858-6770
Email Address:
    admissions@albion.edu

Strongest Programs:
Economics and Business
Ford Institute for Public
    Service
Environment Institute
Premed
Prelaw

The Gerald R. Ford Institute for Public Service takes a unique approach for future civic leaders. Students participate in a simulation of city government in which they play the roles of community leaders.

Albion is a small, private college in Michigan whose motto is "Liberal arts at work." The school's motto emphasizes the importance Albion places on combining learning with hands-on experience. Students at Albion often participate in leadership and service-learning seminars. And when the work is through, students here enjoy a close-knit social life. "Albion is where I have built lifetime friendships," admits a senior. Another student says, "Since Albion is a small school, it gives each student personal attention in every aspect of their education."

Founded in 1835 by the Methodist Church, Albion is located near the banks of the Kalamazoo River. In addition to its newer Georgian-style architecture, the college has retained and restored several of its 19th-century buildings. The campus is spacious with statuesque oaks and a beautiful nature center. Robinson Hall, the campus centerpiece, houses myriad departments, including the Ford Institute for Public Service, the Gerstacker Liberal Arts Program in Professional Management, and the Anna Howard Shaw Women's Center. The campus continues to expand with the addition of the Fergusion Student Services Building.

Academically, Albion is as sound as its buildings. It was the first private college in Michigan to have a Phi Beta Kappa chapter (1940) and has produced three Rhodes Scholars. On their journey to becoming Rhodes Scholars, students are required to take core courses distributed among humanities, natural sciences, social sciences, fine arts, and math. They must also satisfy requirements in environmental science and gender and ethnicity studies. Freshmen must take first-year seminars designed to provide a "stimulating learning environment" in a small-class setting, while seniors participate in a capstone experience.

"Albion is where I have built lifetime friendships."

Albion's most distinguishing feature is the emphasis placed on citizenship and service. The Gerald R. Ford Institute for Public Service takes a unique approach for future civic leaders. Students participate in a simulation of city government in which they play the roles of community leaders. Visiting speakers include senators and congressmen, governors and state legislators, and interest group representatives. The premedical and prelaw programs draw dedicated undergrads, and the English and economics departments are well respected. Another option is the Summer Research Program, which allows students to remain on campus during the summer to work with faculty members on different projects.

The academic climate at Albion is described as competitive but not cutthroat. One student says, "The average student who attends is the high achiever who is involved in school." Top-notch academic and career counseling and low student/faculty ratios keep students on track and motivated. Class size varies, but the average class is under 25 students. Professors are interested in students' academic performance and their emotional well-being. While "the courses are carefully prepared and the professors expect diligence from the students, the professors really care and take an interest in the students" and it is not "uncommon to have class at a professor's house with pizza and holiday cookies." The professors seem to know the secret to motivating college students—feed them and they will work. Teaching assistants are used for tutoring, not teaching. Albion's libraries feature computer facilities, an interlibrary loan service, a listening lab for language or music study, and a helpful staff. If you can't find what you need at Albion's libraries, weekly bus trips to the University of Michigan libraries in Ann Arbor provide access to even more resources.

Albion continues to attract an ambitious, involved group of students. Michigan residents make up 90 percent of the student population. Eighty-five percent are Caucasian, 2 percent African American, and 1 percent Hispanic. The remainder comes from abroad. Up to now, there has been little deviation from the white, upper-middle-class norm. In an effort to change this, a new host-family program matches minority students with families from within the community. There are a number of merit scholarships available, based on academic records, extracurricular involvement, and demonstrated leadership abilities. There are no athletic scholarships.

Eighty-nine percent of Albion students call the residence halls home, which are described as "sufficient" and "not exactly modern." The majority of the freshman class inhabits Wesley Hall. During their sophomore year, many students move to Seaton or Whitehouse halls; seniors enjoy apartment-style housing called The Mae. Dorms are co-ed by hall or floor, and the information each student provides in their housing request form is used to assign rooms and roommates. One student claims, "The dorms are extremely well-maintained and have maintenance boards located on every floor so that the students can voice their concerns. Most of the concerns are taken care of by the next day." Other housing options include apartment annexes and fraternity houses. Sororities do not have houses; they hold their meetings in lodges. Two large dining rooms feed campus residents on an "eat all day" meal plan.

Forty percent of Albion men and women belong to one of the school's six national fraternities and seven sororities. Greek parties draw large crowds, composed of Greeks and non-Greeks, making them a primary part of many students' social lives. Controlling the alcoholic intake of students has become a priority of the administration. Students say "underage drinking does happen" but the college "has strict consequences if caught." Those who insist on imbibing can do it at Gina's or Cascarelli's, popular bars in town.

Road trips are a big part of weekends for many students. Ann Arbor, East Lansing, and Canada are frequent destinations. A well-run union board organizes all sorts of activities—films, lectures, plays, comics, and concerts—to keep students occupied in their spare time. Several students report that the town movie theatre shows "free movies if you show a valid student ID!"

Still, students complain that there are not many social outlets available at Albion. Students focus some of their energy with work for groups supported by the Student Volunteer Bureau; in fact, half of the students volunteer on a regular basis. They are

"The average student who attends is the high achiever who is involved in school."

very involved in the community, including "city clean-up day, Habitat for Humanity, and volunteering at nursing homes and schools." Some traditional events that offer a nice break from academics are the Briton Bash, a fair that familiarizes students with clubs and organizations, and the Day of Woden, which is a picnic held in the spring on the last day of class.

The varsity football team has won nine conference championships in the past decade. Recently, the women's soccer team brought home the Conference MIAA Championship. Men's track, baseball, and golf, along with women's swimming, also receive a lot of attention on campus. Hope College is a hated rival, as is Alma College.

At Albion, professors are accessible and interested, and academics are challenging without being overwhelming. Students agree that the "small campus with friendly students, caring faculty, and kind staff members" make this college an appealing place.

The majority of the freshman class inhabits Wesley Hall. During their sophomore year, many students move to Seaton or Whitehouse halls; seniors enjoy apartment-style housing called The Mae.

Overlaps

University of Michigan, Michigan State, Hope, Kalamazoo, Western Michigan

If You Apply To ➤

Albion: Early decision: Nov. 15. Financial aid: Feb. 15. Does not guarantee to meet demonstrated need. Campus interviews: recommended, evaluative. Alumni interviews: optional, informational. SATs or ACTs: required. SAT IIs: optional. Accepts the Common Application and electronic applications. Essay question.

Alfred University

Alumni Hall, Saxon Drive, Alfred, NY 14802-1205

Talk about an unusual combination—Alfred combines a nationally renowned college of ceramics, a school of art and design, an engineering program, and a business school wrapped up in a university of just more than 2,000 students. It takes elbow grease to pry coastal types to the hinterlands of western New York.

Website: www.alfred.edu

Location: Rural

Total Enrollment: 2,235

Undergraduates: 1,863

Male/Female: 50/50

SAT Ranges: V 500–620
   M 520–610

ACT Range: 22–27

Financial Aid: 88%

Expense: Pr $

Phi Beta Kappa: Yes

Applicants: 2,134

Accepted: 77%

Enrolled: 26%

Grad in 6 Years: 65%

Returning Freshmen: 79%

Academics: ✍ ✍ ✍

Social: ☎ ☎ ☎

Q of L: ★ ★ ★

Admissions: (607) 871-2115

Email Address:
   admissions@alfred.edu

Strongest Programs:
Engineering
Art & Design

Alfred University boasts highly respected programs in art and design, as well as ceramic engineering. Innovation not only shapes the curriculum, but also has a profound effect on campus life. Small classes and friendly competition support this diversity while encouraging individuals to succeed. With just under 2,400 students, Alfred isn't a bustling academic factory; it's a quiet, cloistered, self-described "educational village" in a tiny town wholly dedicated to the "industry of learning." Along with being able to handle the academic rigors of the college, students also have to weather brutal winters that dump snow by the foot-load on the region.

Alfred's campus consists of a charming, close-knit group of modern and Georgian brick buildings, along with a stone castle. The Kanakadea Creek runs right through campus, and the town of Alfred consists of two colleges (the other is the Alfred State College) and a main street with one stoplight. There are a few shops and restaurants, but certainly no malls, parking lots, or tall buildings. A new 52-stall equestrian center opened in 2005, and the university is in the process of renovating space for the Fasano Welcome Center, which will house office space and serve as a central location for visitors and alumni to congregate.

The university and its students share a no-nonsense approach to education. Although prospective students apply directly to one of four colleges and declare a tentative major, half of all requirements for a bachelor's degree are earned in the liberal arts college. Requirements are quite different in each school. However, the mix usually includes coursework in oral and written communication, foreign language and culture, social sciences, history, literature, philosophy, and religion.

Alfred, though private, is actually the "host" school for the New York State College of Ceramics, which is a unit of the state university system and comes with a public university price tag. Ceramic engineering (the development and refinement of ceramic materials) is the academic cornerstone and the program that brings Alfred international recognition. All engineering programs have been consolidated into one School of Engineering, and students may choose from six engineering majors. The art department, with its programs in ceramics, glass, printmaking, sculpture, video, and teacher certification, is also highly regarded. The School of Art and Design offers a graphic design major in which students use electronic and computer equipment. The business administration school also gets good reviews from students and provides undergraduates with work experience through a small business institute where students have real clients. There is a liberal arts and sciences school, which offers a fine arts program that one student boasts about. "If you love doing art, but you don't want to do it full time because you're worried about employability, then our program is perfect," the senior says. The computer science major has been dropped, while majors in marketing and finance have been added.

> **"The courses present material in a reasonable amount of time to learn the material."**

Several students described the academic climate of the college as "laid back." "The courses present material in a reasonable amount of time to learn the material," says a biology major. Recently, health planning and management has moved from a major to a career emphasis within the College of Business. The major in foreign language and culture sponsors trips abroad, and exchange programs are available in England, Germany, Italy, France, Japan, China, and the Czech Republic. The Track II program enables students to design their own interdisciplinary majors with personal guidance from top faculty members.

Whatever their major, all students enjoy small classes (average size is 18 students), and the quality of teaching is described as very high. "The teaching has been superb," explains a senior. Most classes are taught by full professors, with graduate students and teaching assistants helping out only in lab sessions. The university stresses its commitment to helping undergrads plan their future, and the academic-advising and career-planning services are strong enough for Alfred to deliver on its promise. Students say faculty members really want to see them succeed, both in class and in the real world. "Most teachers have high expectations, resulting in greater student performance," brags one junior.

Sixty-seven percent of the students at Alfred are from New York State, and 19 percent graduated from high school in the top tenth of their class. Students are mostly white and from public schools. Minority enrollment is growing: 6 percent are African American, 4 percent are Hispanic, and 2 percent are Asian American. Financial aid is available and outstanding students can apply for many merit scholarships ranging from $2,500 to a full ride, and National Merit finalists receive Alfred's Award of Merit. There are no athletic scholarships.

No one seems to mind the two-year on-campus residency requirement because the rooms are large and comfortable, and the dorms are equipped with lounges, kitchens, and laundry facilities. Upper-classmen have a choice of dorms that are co-ed by floor, with single rooms, suites, or apartments. Freshmen enjoy their own

"Campus and AU security will provide rides or walking escorts if you feel unsafe walking home."

housing divided into doubles. Sixty-five percent of all students choose to live on campus, but some juniors and about half of the seniors opt to live off campus. The school has two dining halls and students say the offerings include plenty of selections for vegetarians and vegans. "The dining facilities are very nice and well-equipped and the food is both diverse and edible," says a junior. Campus security is good, according to most students. "There are blue lights all over, campus and AU security will provide rides or walking escorts if you feel unsafe walking alone," a biology major says.

Alfred's location in the Finger Lakes region, almost two hours from Buffalo and an hour and a half from Rochester, is isolated. The other chief complaint is the chilly, snowy weather. Social life is difficult due to the rural atmosphere, but the Student Activities Board brings many events to campus, including musicians, comedians, lecturers, and movies. Favorite road trips are to Letchworth and Stony Brook state parks, and to Ithaca, Rochester, Buffalo, and Toronto. Many students are skiing, hunting, camping, and rock-climbing enthusiasts. Friendly games of hackeysack, Frisbee, football, softball, and other sports can often be found somewhere on campus. Fraternities and sororities, which had been attracting a declining proportion of students in recent years and facing repeated sanctions, were eliminated recently following the death of a fraternity member near the campus. Alfred is a dry campus. The alcohol policy is enforced in the dorms and students say it is respected. "If people want to drink they know it is best not to do it in the dormitory," says a junior.

Because Alfred shares the town with Alfred State University, the dominant student population makes Alfred a good college town. "It is a small town, very close community, but nice," observes a biology major. The downtown scene provides students with an adequate number of movie theaters and eateries. Every spring brings the annual

Overlaps

Rochester Institute of Technology, SUNY–Geneseo, SUNY–Buffalo, University of Rochester, Ithaca

Hot Dog Weekend, a big carnival-like event that fills Main Street with game booths, bands, and lots of hot dog stands. Alfred's Division III Saxons are ominous opponents on the football, soccer, and lacrosse fields, and alpine skiing, equestrian, and men's swimming have all won spots in the top 10 nationally.

Although small and somewhat secluded, Alfred University is a good choice for those students who want to concentrate on the ABCs of arts, business, and ceramic engineering—just be sure to bundle up for the long, snowy winters.

If You Apply To ➤

Alfred: Early decision: Dec. 1. Regular admissions: Feb. 1 (priority). Campus interviews: recommended, evaluative. Alumni interviews: optional, informational. SATs or ACTs: required. SAT IIs: recommended. Accepts the Common Application. Essay question: write article about yourself; build a personal web page; how has technology shaped you; why Alfred?

Allegheny College

520 North Main Street, Meadville, PA 16335

An unpretentious cousin to more well heeled places like Dickinson and Bucknell. Draws heavily from the Buffalo–Cleveland–Pittsburgh area. The college's powerhouse athletic teams clean up on Division III competition. If you've ever wondered what lake-effect snow is, you'll find out here.

Website: www.allegheny.edu
Location: Small city
Total Enrollment: 2,100
Undergraduates: 2,004
Male/Female: 48/52
SAT Ranges: V 550–650
 M 560–650
ACT Range: 23–28
Financial Aid: 74%
Expense: Pr $ $
Phi Beta Kappa: Yes
Applicants: 3,279
Accepted: 74%
Enrolled: 27%
Grad in 6 Years: 66%
Returning Freshmen: 87%
Academics: ✑ ✑ ✑
Social: ☎ ☎ ☎
Q of L: ★ ★ ★
Admissions: (814) 332-4351
Email Address:
 admissions@allegheny.edu

Strongest Programs:
Writing
Sciences

Allegheny College is a down-to-earth Eastern liberal arts school boasting a rich history of academic excellence in an intimate setting. Administrators here understand the importance of providing students with real-world experience to complement their classroom work. The school's innovative May term offers time for internships or other off-campus work and study, and a commitment to civic responsibility has spurred several new programs. Allegheny's small size means students don't suffer from lack of attention, and despite the heavy workload, anyone struggling academically will get help before the situation becomes dire. "The professors are easy to approach and I feel that I have a more eye-level relationship with them," says a sophomore.

Tucked away in Meadville, Pennsylvania, 90 miles north of Pittsburgh, lies Allegheny's 72-acre campus. Founded in 1815, nestled in the Norman Rockwell–esque rolling hills of northwestern Pennsylvania, the campus is home to traditional, ivy-covered buildings and redbrick streets, as well as new apartment-style housing for upperclassmen. A nationally acclaimed science complex supports already-strong programs, and students who wish to pump iron can visit the new fitness center. The college also owns a 182-acre outdoor recreational complex, a 283-acre research reserve, and an 80-acre protected forest.

"Students compete with themselves, not each other."

Students at Allegheny work hard and do well, as evidenced by the fact that 31 percent of a recent senior class immediately went on to graduate or professional school. "Students compete with themselves, not each other. The courses are very rigorous and very rewarding," says a senior. The school's strongest programs are in environmental studies, the sciences, writing, and civic engagement, and students give high marks to English, too. Though the college eliminated its degree program in education some years ago, it enjoys articulation programs with the University of Pittsburgh School of Education and the Columbia University Teachers College, helping graduates get that much sought-after graduate degree. There is a major in biochemistry, a revised chemistry curriculum, and a track for students interested in entrepreneurial and managerial economics. Co-op programs include a 3–1, 3–2, 3–4 option leading to degrees in engineering, nursing, and allied health. The Allegheny College Center for Experiential Learning (ACCEL) is a clearinghouse for internship opportunities, service learning, and overseas study.

(Continued)
Civic Engagement
Environmental Studies

Allegheny has two 15-week semesters each year, and its general education requirements keep students busy. Juniors take a seminar in their major field, and seniors complete an intensive capstone project in their major. All students must take courses in each of three major divisions (humanities and the natural and social sciences) and must finish a divisional minor in a subject area outside their major. Despite Allegheny's small size—71 percent of courses have fewer than 25 students—most of those enrolled graduate in four years.

Students praise Allegheny's faculty for their passion, knowledge, and accessibility. "Most professors will meet you over lunch if there is no other time available," says one education major. You won't find a TA at the lectern in any Allegheny classroom, and the college's honor code allows students to take unproctored exams. Off campus, Allegheny

"Most professors will meet you over lunch if there is no other time available."

offers study in several U.S. cities and abroad, an on-campus independent study option, and semester internships or "externships" (a chance to observe a professional at work during the winter vacation). There's also a three- or four-week Experiential Learning term following spring semester for study abroad and internships not available during the year. The library holds more than 1,009,000 volumes and the campus offers more than 325 computer workstations.

Sixty-five percent of Allegheny's students hail from Pennsylvania, and sizable contingents come from nearby Ohio, New York, and New England. While Allegheny isn't a terribly diverse campus—minority students make up only 7 percent of the total—the school is committed to increasing awareness of and appreciation for diversity. "No one is afraid to express their opinion," claims one senior. The college's new Center for Political Participation engages students by fostering an appreciation for the vital link between an engaged, active citizenry and a healthy democracy. Merit scholarships are available, ranging from $500 to $15,000.

Eleven residence halls and 38 houses (including TV and study rooms) accommodate undergraduates in relative style and comfort with a variety of living situations: all-freshmen dorms; co-ed and single-sex halls; small houses; and single, double, and triple rooms and suites. Dorms are "clean and of reasonable size," says a senior, and "there is no trouble getting a room," says a sophomore. Housing is guaranteed for four years, and 73 percent of students stay on campus. The most popular dorm is the new, townhouse-style College Court complex, which holds 80 students in suites with four single bedrooms each. New furniture was recently added in nearly all dorms, and students will soon have more choices, as more dorms are being built. Students are happy with their on-campus food choices. Officers from campus security are available 24 hours a day, but they aren't much needed. "Meadville is small town with not a lot to do," says a sophomore, but "it's still a lot better than the town of the other college that I looked at."

You won't find a TA at the lectern in any Allegheny classroom, and the college's honor code allows students to take unproctored exams.

Greek organizations draw 26 percent of the men and 29 percent of the women, and provide a great deal of nightlife. Five fraternities have their own houses, while the four sororities are relegated to special dorm suites. There are also two campus theater series, two-dollar movie nights, and comedians, ventriloquists, and live bands provided by the center for student activities. Large-scale philanthropic events like Make a Difference Day and the Month of Service, in March, are also popular. "Campus parties exist but don't dominate social life [neither does Greek life]. There is always something going on and most belong to some club or organization that

The Allegheny College Center for Experiential Learning (ACCEL) is a clearinghouse for internship opportunities, service learning, and overseas study.

hosts special events," says one student. College policy states that students must be 21 to have or consume alcohol on campus, but one student says those who want alcohol can get it, and "as long as you're reasonably responsible, you probably won't get caught." homecoming, Greek Sing, Wingfest in the fall (featuring free wings), Springfest (a day full of bands, activities, and food), and Winter Carnival break up the monotony of studying, and midnight breakfasts served by faculty help ease end-of-semester stress.

Downtown Meadville, lovingly referred to as Mudville, is a 10-minute walk from campus and worlds away from a "college town." It has a four-screen movie theater and several community playhouses, as well as schools, hospitals, children's homes, animal shelters, and other organizations that benefit from the more than 25,000 hours of service students contribute each year. "The students do a lot of volunteer work and help immensely throughout the community," says an economics major. When more time in Meadville is too much to bear, students hit the road, venturing to factory outlets in nearby Grove City, Pennsylvania, or heading toward the bright lights of Pittsburgh, Buffalo, or Cleveland. "What's nice is that even though Meadville is small, larger cities are close by so you can get away if need be," a senior says. Nearby state parks at Conneaut Lake and Lake Erie offer water-skiing and boating in warm weather and cross-country skiing in the winter.

As for Allegheny traditions, there's the somewhat suspect "13th Plank" ritual, which states that all freshman women must be kissed on the 13th plank of the campus bridge by an upperclassman to be considered a "true Allegheny co-ed." Of course, a group of freshmen men steal the plank every year at the beginning of the first semester to prevent that from happening. Athletics play a big role in Allegheny life, although there are no athletic scholarships, and the addition of a $13 million sports and fitness complex gives students reason to cheer. Twenty-five percent of Allegheny students participate in varsity athletics, while 70 percent participate in nine intramural sports, with basketball, soccer and volleyball drawing the most interest. The football, softball, women's soccer and men's track and field—both indoor and outdoor-captured North Coast Athletic Conference championships in 2003–04.

Allegheny College boasts a rich history of academic excellence in an intimate setting, augmented by a new emphasis on extracurricular experiences designed to produce well-rounded alumni. The campus's natural beauty and the genuine affection students feel for it and for each other remain unchanged. As one student says: "There is a sense that Allegheny enables you to do anything you put your mind to—no matter how unusual."

Overlaps

University of Pittsburgh, Washington and Jefferson, College of Wooster, Bucknell, Penn State–University Park, Dickinson

If You Apply To ➤

Allegheny: Early decision: Nov. 15. Regular admissions: Feb 15. Meets full demonstrated need of 46%. Campus interview: recommended, informational. Alumni interviews: optional, informational. SATs or ACTs: required. SAT IIs: optional. Accepts the Common Application and electronic applications. Essay question: significant experience, important issue, or person of significant influence.

Alma College

Alma, MI 48801-1599

The college that put the "Alma" back in "alma mater." As friendly a campus as you'll find, Alma combines the liberal arts with distinctive offerings in health-related fields.

Diversity is an issue and few out-of-staters enroll. If central Michigan drives you stir-crazy, join the hordes who go abroad.

The mission of Alma College, a tiny gem on Michigan's lower peninsula, is fourfold: "To prepare graduates who think critically, serve generously, lead purposefully and live responsibly as stewards of the world they bequeath to future generations." Alma has a wide array of choices for their undergraduates, including distinctive offerings in health-related fields, as well as the opportunity to learn abroad. Alma students have taken part in everything from the U.S. mission to the United Nations to the reclamation of a Jewish cemetery in Poland. And the college's annual Highland Festival, with kilt-wearing bagpipers and competitions, has led some to dub the school "Scotland, USA."

Alma's campus features 25 Prairie-style buildings of redbrick and limestone surrounding a scenic central mall. Alma was founded over a hundred years ago, but most of the buildings have been built or renovated in recent years. There are lots of trees and open places to sit, at least in the warmer months. Administrators are looking at how best to expand toward the Pine River, because the current campus is bound by residential neighborhoods, making it difficult to find room for new academic, athletic, and residential facilities.

> **"The courses will keep students on their toes without making them go crazy."**

The Alma experience begins with the seven-day Preterm Orientation, built around a one-credit academic seminar, which includes readings, discussions, and research, and introduces students to computer resources, on-campus life, and extracurricular activities. Trustee Honors Scholarship recipients are invited to attend a two-credit Freshman Honors Seminar during their first year. To graduate, students must demonstrate proficiency in communication, computation, and foreign language, and must complete 16 credits in each of three areas: arts and humanities, social sciences, and natural sciences. In addition, students must complete a comprehensive series of English courses. "The classes are challenging but not impossible," says one history major. Another student proclaims, "The courses will keep students on their toes without making them go crazy." Administrators candidly admit that weaker programs include the preengineering 3–2 program and classical languages.

Alma's top majors, per student enrollment, are business administration and education. Biology and psychology prepare students for work with wellness intervention programs and public health agencies, or graduate study in medicine, nursing, or physical therapy. Athletic training was recently changed from an area of concentration in the Exercise and Health Sciences program to a major. Alma's Service Learning Program gives students academic credit for work with nonprofit economic development organizations or educational, environmental, and social service agencies. Alma's Model United Nations teams have received the top award for nine of the last 10 years at the world's largest and most prestigious collegiate Model UN conference. Students interested in the Scottish arts find a range of opportunities to work with nationally known instructors of bagpipe and highland dance, or join in seminars offered by award-winning Scottish authors.

Despite Alma's small size and the fact that 95 percent of students are Michigan natives, the terms "provincial" and "insular" just don't apply here. In fact, one of the college's selling points is its wide variety of study abroad opportunities. During the one-month spring term, students enroll in a single intensive course that often includes off-campus study. Past programs have taken students to Australia to study culture and trade in the Pacific Rim, to Paris to learn language and culture, and to Israel for archaeological fieldwork. Alma also offers foreign study programs in

Website: www.alma.edu
Location: Rural
Total Enrollment: 1,199
Undergraduates: 1,199
Male/Female: 42/59
SAT Ranges: V 510-620
  M 490-620
ACT Range: 21–27
Financial Aid: 76%
Expense: Pr $
Phi Beta Kappa: Yes
Applicants: 1,305
Accepted: 84%
Enrolled: 30%
Grad in 6 Years: 70%
Returning Freshmen: 76%
Academics: ✍ ✍ ✍
Social: ☎ ☎ ☎
Q of L: ★ ★ ★
Admissions: (989) 463-7139
Email Address:
  admissions@alma.edu

Strongest Programs:
Business Administration
Education
Biology
History
Psychology
Exercise and Health Science
Music
Sociology and Anthropology

Australia, Bolivia, Ecuador, England, France, Germany, Ireland, New Zealand, Peru, Scotland, South Korea and Spain.

Back on campus, Alma's professors win praise. "I would give the quality of teaching a rating of 10 out of 10. I find that most professors care deeply about the students and truly want us to succeed," claims a music major. None of the classes taken by freshmen have more than 100 students; 54 percent have 25 or fewer. Students say graduating in four years is seldom a problem, except for education majors, who may need a ninth semester to complete their student teaching.

Alma students are quite involved around campus and in the community. "We have a lot of service organizations, service learning courses, and a program called Discovering Vocation that funds service-based programs," says one business major. The campus is 93 percent white, with African Americans and Hispanics comprising 2 percent each. Asians Americans, Native Americans and foreign students make up 1 percent each. "Bursting the Bubble" weekend, which occurs each January around Martin Luther King Jr. Day, is part of the effort to increase diversity. Brainy types can vie for an unlimited number of merit scholarships worth an average of $11,822.

Eighty-four percent of Alma's students take beds on campus. "Dorms are dorms; no more and no less than what you would expect from campus housing," admits one junior. Freshmen are assigned rooms in single-sex and co-ed halls (some co-ed by room, others by floor), while upperclassmen play the lottery and usually get suites. Wright Hall opened in 2005 and is an environmentally friendly residence hall. Other options include an international house, a Model UN house, and a Women's Resource Center. There are fraternities and sororities for the 19 percent of the men and 28 percent of women who go Greek.

"There is not much to do, but there is a large college town only 15 minutes away so it is never an issue."

Everyone buys 14 or 19 meals a week, and chows down at the all-you-can-eat Commons or at Joe's Place, a snack bar. "Yum!" exclaims one student. "There are new choices each day and they always offer a vegetarian item and are always open for suggestions."

Alma students may live in a small town, but "it is very friendly and proud of Alma," according to one student. "There is not much to do, but there is a large college town only 15 minutes away so it is never an issue." Some students go to clubs or the movie theatre but most students claim there is a lot to do on campus, too. Officially, the campus alcohol policy follows Michigan law: No one under 21 can drink. Most students tend to agree that drinking is not a big problem on campus. Underage students caught imbibing are written up and fined.

Town/gown relations at Alma are strong, with students volunteering, taking part-time jobs, and otherwise getting involved in the community. The annual Highland Festival features bagpipers and Scottish dancing; for members of the Alma marching band, who strut in kilts stitched from the college's own registered Alma College tartan, every performance might as well be a festival. Almost all Alma students welcome St. Paddy's Day with Irish Pub, a thunderous celebration sure to rouse the leprechauns for a celebratory toast. Students with wheels will find diversions within easy reach, as Mt. Pleasant, Saginaw, and the East Lansing campus of Michigan State are less than an hour away, and ski slopes are just a bit farther. In the warmer months, the beaches of two Great Lakes, Huron and Michigan, are also two hours away. The Alma softball team has taken first place in the Michigan Intercollegiate Athletic Association since 1997, and in 2004 they finished seventh in the nation in Division III. The volleyball and football teams have also brought home titles in recent years. For nonvarsity types, there is an active intramural program.

Helpful advisors and caring faculty members help Alma students chart a course on campus and in the broader world, allowing them to leave well-prepared for today's

Overlaps

Central Michigan, Grand Valley State, Michigan State, Albion, Western Michigan, Hope competitive job market. Michigan natives and newcomers alike are sure to find a warm welcome and friendly faces at Alma. Confirms one senior, "Everyone here is ridiculously friendly. No where else on earth have I seen so many smiling faces!"

Alma: Rolling admissions. Early action: Nov. 1. Housing: May 1. Meets demonstrated need of 26%. Campus interviews: recommended, informational. No alumni interviews. SATs or ACTs: required (ACT preferred). SAT IIs: optional. Accepts electronic applications. Optional essay question: creatively introduce yourself; discussing something important to you; why Alma is a good fit.

American University

4400 Massachusetts Avenue NW, Washington, DC 20016-8001

If the odds are against you at Georgetown and you can't see yourself on GW's highly urban campus, welcome to American University. The allure of AU is simple: Washington, D.C. American has a nice campus in a nice neighborhood with easy access to the Metro, and the city. It is about a third smaller than GW.

Located just a few miles from where our country's leaders make decisions of national and global impact, American University is a breeding ground for the next generation of reporters, diplomats, lobbyists, and political leaders who will shape domestic and international policy. Alongside these eager buzz hounds is a host of students taking advantage of AU's strong programs in the arts and sciences and business. "American University is a diverse, pulsing, and dynamic school driven by some of the best faculty, staff, scholars, and students in the world," a senior says.

AU's 84-acre residential campus is located in the safe northwest corner of Washington, D.C., in a neighborhood called Tenleytown just minutes from downtown; free shuttle buses transport students to the nearby Metro (subway) station. There's a mix of classical and modern architecture and flower gardens alongside the parking lots. The quads have numerous sitting areas for reflection and study and the campus has gone totally wireless. New additions include the Katzen Arts Center, which provides studio and performing arts spaces as well as galleries.

All AU undergraduates must demonstrate competency in writing and English, either through two courses or an exam; for math or statistics, it's one semester of class or placing out through a test. The general education program requires 30 credit hours from five areas: the creative arts, traditions that shape the Western world, global and multicultural perspectives, social institutions and behavior, and the natural sciences. The requirements are typically completed during the first two years so that upperclassmen can study abroad or participate in an internship or co-op—of which there are many, thanks to the school's relationships with more than 900 private, nonprofit, or government institutions. The school also uses these connections in its Washington Semester* program, which attracts a wide range of majors.

In the classroom, AU has outstanding programs in political science and government, international studies, business, and communications. An honors program offers the top 10 percent of entering students small seminars, special sections of many courses, and designated floors in the residence halls, plus specialized work in the major and a senior capstone experience. There is a new minor in North American studies and certificate programs in Asian studies and European studies.

Website: www.admissions.american.edu
Location: Urban
Total Enrollment: 8,479
Undergraduates: 5,504
Male/Female: 38/62
SAT Ranges: V 580–690 M 570–660
ACT Range: 25–29
Financial Aid: 38%
Expense: Pr $ $
Phi Beta Kappa: Yes
Applicants: 12,211
Accepted: 53%
Enrolled: 20%
Grad in 6 Years: 70%
Returning Freshmen: 88%
Academics: ✍ ✍ ✍ ½
Social: ☎ ☎ ☎
Q of L: ★ ★ ★
Admissions: (202) 885-6000
Email Address: admissions@american.edu

Strongest Programs:
International Studies
Political Science/Government
Justice, Law, and Society
Studio and Performing Arts
Premed

Classes are "challenging but not overwhelming," a senior political science major says. "Courses are extremely demanding, but professors are always willing to work with students if they are struggling," a junior international studies major adds. Although AU has a reputation for bringing in adjunct professors, students see this is a positive move because "they bring real-world experience into the classroom."

Students who attend AU are "preppy" yet "quirky," and "at parties kids talk about politics rather than your average party conversation," a sophomore says. AU prides itself on drawing students from every state and more than 130 foreign countries; just 5 percent hail from the District of Columbia. Six percent of the student body is African American, 5

"At parties kids talk about politics rather than your average party conversation."

percent is Hispanic, and 5 percent is Asian American. Unlike many college campuses where apathy reigns, AU is very active politically—after all, this is Washington, D.C. "Everyone has an opinion on something," notes a junior who says AU is a "pretty liberal campus, but the conservatives make themselves known." AU's hefty price tag draws complaints, but the school offers more than 700 merit scholarships averaging $14,153 and 152 athletic scholarships in six women's and four men's sports.

General education requirements are typically completed during the first two years so that upperclassmen can study abroad or participate in an internship or co-op—of which there are many, thanks to the school's relationships with more than 900 private, nonprofit, or government institutions.

Sixty-eight percent of AU students, mostly freshmen and sophomores, live on campus. "The dorms are roomy, well-maintained, and clean," says a political science major. "South Side dorms are known to be louder and more social than North Side dorms," advises a junior. There is off-campus housing for upperclassmen in newly renovated luxury apartments, and a shuttle bus connects them to campus. "Housing draw is difficult, since it not only goes by current dorm status, but also by credits, making it more difficult for those with fewer credits," says a junior. Students say they generally feel safe on campus, noting public safety officers are visible and "we also sometimes have Secret Service agents on campus since we're so close to the vice president's house."

A good deal of the social life at AU revolves around campus-related functions, such as room and frat parties; 17 percent of men and 18 percent of women go Greek, though the women lament that the bottom-heavy male/female ratio is "a little ridiculous." The immediate area around AU has restaurants and shops, but you need to get a bit farther away for true nightlife in Dupont Circle and Georgetown. While greater D.C. certainly has its share of clubs and bars, they're largely off-limits to students under 21. The AU campus is officially dry, and most students take that seriously. Happily, there is so much other stuff to do in D.C., and much of it is free—from the new art house movie theaters to gallery openings, pro soccer games, museums and monuments, and funky live music. "You just jump on the Metro to get anywhere in the city," says a communication major. Each year, Family Weekend

"The dorms are roomy, well-maintained, and clean."

brings games, rides, and popular bands to campus, along with a carnival on the quad. Homecoming and Founder's Week are also campus favorites. Popular road trips include Baltimore, Annapolis, Williamsburg, Richmond, the Ocean City shore, and nearby amusement parks and outlets.

American competes in Division I, but sports are an afterthought for most students. There's no football team, but students are enthusiastic about Eagles basketball, where games against Bucknell, Holy Cross and the Naval Academy top the schedule. Strong teams include women's volleyball, basketball, field hockey and lacrosse, men's swimming and diving, men's and women's soccer and men's and women's cross-country. AU athletics also earned the distinction of the highest combined GPA in AU history, proving that brains and brawn are not mutually exclusive. There's a slew of intramural and club sports, which are divided into different levels of competitiveness.

AU is heaven on earth for C-SPAN junkies. (AU made headlines of its own last year for the inept way that its board dealt with the university's free-spending former

Overlaps

George Washington, Georgetown, Boston University, NYU, Boston College, University of Maryland—College Park

president.) But even if you are not one, AU and Washington, D.C. are still a top combo for a rich college life. The opportunities for real-world experience—in fields ranging from business to international studies to political science—are outstanding. But AU is small enough to keep students from feeling lost in the fast-paced world inside the beltway. "We are a small campus, which gives the feeling of being out of the city, but yet the city is at our fingertips," a junior says.

Amherst College

Amherst, MA 01002-5000

Original home to the well-rounded, superachieving, gentle-person jock. Compare to Williams, Middlebury, and Colby. Not Swarthmore, not Wesleyan. Amherst has always been the king in its category—mainly because there are four other major institutions in easy reach to add diversity and depth.

Amherst offers a dynamic curriculum in the traditional academic disciplines and in numerous interdisciplinary fields. There are no core curriculum or distribution requirements, so students choose their program based on their own individual interests and plans for the future. Indeed, the focus isn't on racking up high grade point averages. Instead, students focus on becoming people who base their thinking on a strong foundation in the liberal arts. Emphasizing "freedom to explore," the spotlight here is on learning, not competing for grades. "Students encourage others through teamwork and discussion," confirms a senior. "Rarely do you ever hear students boasting about their grades."

Amherst's 1,000 acres overlook the picturesque town of Amherst and the Pioneer Valley and offer a panoramic view of the Holyoke Range and the Pelham Hills. On campus, a plot of open land housing a wildlife sanctuary and a forest shares space with academic and residential buildings, athletic fields, and facilities. While Amherst's predominant architectural style remains 19th-century academia—redbrick is key— everything from a "pale yellow octagonal structure to a garish, modern new dorm" can be found here. Amherst looks like a college is supposed to look, with trees and paths winding through the buildings to offer long, contemplative walks. Of course, the flip side is snowy winters that don't end soon enough when spring break has come and gone. The Amherst College Residential Master Plan (RMP) is well underway and will provide Amherst students with enhanced and updated residential space by 2007.

The most popular majors are English, economics, psychology, law, jurisprudence and social thought, and political science. Students may mix and match among these subjects to form dual-degree programs. About one-third of students pursue double majors, and a few overachievers even triple major. Students may create their own courses of study from Special Topics classes if the subject of their interest is not available. Amherst's unique Law, Jurisprudence, and Social Thought is not a prelaw major. It is instead an interdisciplinary study of the law, drawing on fields as diverse as psychology, history, philosophy, and literature, with a strong theoretical focus.

Website: www.amherst.edu
Location: Small town
Total Enrollment: 1,638
Undergraduates: 1,638
Male/Female: 52/48
SAT Ranges: V 670–780
  M 670–770
ACT Range: 30-33
Financial Aid: 44%
Expense: Pr $ $ $ $
Phi Beta Kappa: Yes
Applicants: 6,284
Accepted: 19%
Enrolled: 37%
Grad in 6 Years: 96%
Returning Freshmen: 98%
Academics: 🖊 🖊 🖊 🖊 🖊
Social: 🍷 🍷 🍷
Q of L: ★ ★ ★ ★
Admissions: (413) 542-2328
Email Address:
  admission@amherst.edu

Strongest Programs:
English
Economics
Psychology

(Continued)
Law, Jurisprudence, and Social
    Thought
Political Science

The dance program is also strong, although it requires courses at each school in the Five College* Consortium. To house all of these programs, Amherst has spent millions of dollars in recent years renovating facilities, upgrading technological capabilities, and improving spaces for studying, exhibits, performances, and sports.

Amherst is home to a rich intellectual environment that centers on a wealth of acclaimed instructors. A freshman boasts, "I've already taken classes taught by deans and world-renowned professors." On such a small campus without graduate students, interaction with professors is encouraged. "The quality of instruction at Amherst is phenomenal and stellar. Professors are not only wise and accomplished but they pursue teaching at Amherst because they are interested in teaching," explains a sophomore.

To graduate, students must take only a first-year seminar, declare a major at the end of sophomore year, fulfill departmental program requirements, pass the requisite number of electives, and perform satisfactorily on comprehensive exams in their major field. First-year seminars, taught by two or more professors, help foster interdisciplinary approaches across topics and are offered in several subject areas. "Amherst's academic climate is conducive to taking intellectual risks," asserts a freshman. "The strongest competition is the internal drive of the students to be as good as the institution knows that they can be, but there is essentially no competition among students."

"I've already taken classes taught by deans and world–renowned professors."

In addition to being one of the Five Colleges*, Amherst also belongs to the Maritime Studies Program* and the Twelve College Exchange*. All-female Smith and Mount Holyoke also add to the social life, and numerous cultural and artistic events at the other schools are open to Amherst students. Each year, about one-third of the junior class spends a semester or year abroad; in the past two years, students enrolled in 72 programs in 35 countries, ranging from a math program in Budapest to analyzing architecture in Rome. Amherst also has a program in Kyoto, Japan, where one of the college's Colonial-style buildings has been duplicated.

Eighty-one percent of Amherst students hail from outside Massachusetts. Eighty-one percent were in the top tenth of their high school class, and, as one junior explains, "Amherst College is populated by nearly every sort of person. Whether you are a geek, jock, hippie, or any other hard-to-define type of human being, you will find kindred spirits." The student body is unusually diverse; 46 percent are Caucasian, 9 percent are African American, 13 percent Asian American, 7 percent Hispanic, and 6 percent foreign. Amherst actively works to educate its community about issues that affect student life. While not a new organization, Residential Life, through its staff of Resident Counselors, sponsors programs that both educate and encourage open discussion about many issues on campus, including race and gender relations, issues of sexual respect, and alcohol/drug abuse. The recently formed Diversity Educators group offers workshops during orientation and in all first-year student dorms, raising student awareness

Any showdown with archrival Williams is inevitably the biggest game of the season, drawing fans from all corners of campus.

"First-year housing is amazing."

about issues pertaining to race. Discussions on political issues and hot topics are common. "Amherst prides itself on its diversity [of] not only color, but nationality, faith, socioeconomic background, interests, ideas, and political thought," says a sophomore.

Housing at Amherst is guaranteed for four years, and 98 percent of students live on campus. "First-year housing is amazing," says a sophomore, "and rooms just get bigger and better as you go up." Everyone who lives on campus, and anyone else who wants to, eats in Valentine Hall, which includes a central serving station and five dining rooms. The selection is diverse but the food overall gets mixed reviews.

Although frats are nothing more than a distant memory, the legacy of beer-drenched partying at Amherst lingers. "Alcohol is not a forbidden fruit at

Amherst," says a junior. "As a result, many students learn from experience that overindulgence is not all they thought it would be. Many avoid imbibing entirely," says a junior. Social activities are conducted almost entirely on campus. They range from quiet gatherings of friends to dorm study breaks to campus-wide parties. The biggest party of the year, thrown in February, is Casino Night, which includes gambling with real money. The weekend-long Bavaria festival in the spring offers a pig roast and big-wheel joust, while a lip-sync contest that offers winners their first pick during room draw usually attracts hilarious entries. The relatively new Campus Center includes outdoor terraces, a formal living room, a game room, a snack bar, a small theater, and a student-run co-op coffeehouse, open three nights a week with live entertainment.

Amherst is "the quintessential college town, full of academics, old hippies, small shops, and cheap restaurants," says an interdisciplinary studies major. "There are tons of places to eat as well as an always-busy town green," concurs a freshman. For the many outdoorsy types, good skiing in Vermont is not far, and Boston (an hour and a half) and New York (a little over three hours) are close enough to be convenient road trip destinations.

Sports are taken seriously, both varsity and intramurals. Amherst's intramural program currently consists of six sports (flag football and soccer in the fall; basketball and volleyball in the winter; and softball and indoor soccer in the spring). Each sport is co-ed and open to all students, staff, and faculty. Amherst competes in Division III, but the strong baseball team takes on Division I opponents as well. Men's soccer is strong, and recent NCAA champions include women's tennis, men's basketball, men's swimming, baseball, track, and the women's lacrosse team. Any showdown with archrival Williams is inevitably the biggest game of the season, drawing fans from all corners of campus.

> "There are tons of places to eat as well as an always-busy town green."

Combine a lack of restrictive requirements with a cadre of professors who are focused on teaching, and it becomes clear why students here so love their institution. Says a proud student: "I see our community as made up of people who are comfortable with themselves and consequently are some of the kindest and most laid-back people I can imagine. Yet this does not deter from the fact that Amherst students are always doing extraordinary things: academically, athletically, artistically, and for the benefit of the world."

Overlaps

Yale, Harvard, Princeton, Dartmouth, Brown, Williams

If You Apply To ➤

Amherst: Early decision: Nov. 15. Regular admissions: Jan.1. Financial aid: Feb. 15. Guarantees to meet demonstrated need. No campus or alumni interviews. SATs or ACTs: required. SAT II: any two subject tests. Accepts the Common Application and electronic applications. Essay question: one Common Application question and respond to one of five quotations.

Antioch College

795 Livermore Street, Yellow Springs, OH 45387

Part Goth, part granola, and part anarchist—with plenty of none-of-the-above mixed in—Antioch is a haven for square pegs. Yet Antioch offers something very practical: the chance for 16-week co-op experiences interspersed with academic study. March and protest, then get a job. Cool.

Come to Yellow Springs, Ohio, and you may think you've stepped out of a time machine. But no, you haven't spun back to 1969—you're simply at Antioch College, where the humanistic messages of that generation are still taken to heart and put into action. The students, many of them products of "alternative" high schools, discuss feminism, gay rights, and nuclear proliferation over vegetarian meals, and they are more likely to take road trips to Washington for an environmental rally than to show up at a neighboring school's fraternity party.

Founded in 1852 by abolitionist and social reformer Horace Mann as its first president, Antioch remains a haven for outspoken and independent students who thrive under the rigors of a refreshingly nontraditional education. Antioch pioneered the idea that students should alternate time in the classroom with jobs in the "real world," and this idea has remained the foundation for Antioch's unique approach to training students. Under the college's famed co-op program, students spend nearly half of their college years out in the real world, be it selling fresh-squeezed orange juice on a street corner in California, studying Buddhism in India, or working in a Fortune 500 company in New York City. Antioch does not use standardized test scores for admission. In classes, written faculty evaluations take the place of grades, and students are required to submit self-evaluations of their class performance.

In completing Antioch's 32-credit general education program, students spend their first year pursuing a core of courses that blends the traditional liberal arts with examination of the "social, historical, philosophical, and economic" nature of work. In addition, there are distribution requirements in the humanities, social and behavioral sciences, natural sciences, and cultural studies. Physical education is also required. "The academic climate at Antioch is what you decide to make it...There are competitive classes, as well as laid-back classes; it all depends on what you are interested in," says one freshman.

Because classes are usually no larger than 20, students must always be prepared to participate. Close relationships often develop between students and faculty; representatives of both groups sit on several of the influential governing committees, including the administrative council, the housing board, and the community council. "Professors at Antioch are some of the best in the country. The teachers are very dedicated to their students and their level of understanding,"

"The academic climate at Antioch is what you decide to make it."

explains a freshman. Each student is assigned a co-op advisor to help with the nearly continuous job hunt, and a network of alumni offering jobs is one major resource that students can depend on in their search. You can't miss with the career counselors. "It's not just counseling; it's cooperative education that teaches you more about yourself than you could imagine. It's the best reason to come to Antioch," says a student.

Antioch's trimester system lasts 15 weeks, with co-op terms lasting 16 weeks. The college helps place students in co-op programs and credit is earned after the student completes a paper or project demonstrating what he or she learned during the co-op experience. Antioch's mission lies in its "commitment to undergraduate experiential learning and to preparing students to face the challenges and opportunities of the 21st century." In order to receive a crosscultural experience, Antioch has all students spend three to 12 months in a significantly different cultural environment. In addition to those offered by the school, study abroad options are available through the Great Lakes College Association.* There is a downside to this: students blame the high attrition rate on the rigors of the co-op program. Friendships and involvement in extracurricular activities at the Yellow Springs campus often suffer because of the on-again, off-again attendance schedules. But the co-op program wouldn't have been there for so long if it didn't have its fans, such as a senior, who

Website: www.antioch-college.edu

Location: Rural

Total Enrollment: 599

Undergraduates: 476

Male/Female: 40/60

SAT Ranges: V 580-670
    M 500-620

ACT Range: 19-29

Financial Aid: 87%

Expense: Pr $ $

Phi Beta Kappa: No

Applicants: 458

Accepted: 59%

Enrolled: 42%

Grad in 6 Years: 45%

Returning Freshmen: 59%

Academics: ✍ ✍ ✍

Social: ☎ ☎

Q of L: ★ ★ ★ ★

Admissions: (937) 769-1100

Email Address: admissions@antioch-college.edu

Strongest Program:
Cultural and Interdisciplinary Studies

says, "The co-op program is the reason to come to Antioch. It's made me as confident and clear about my life goals as can be."

Antioch's traditional academic programs are somewhat uneven. Although there are only eight official majors, each allows a student to in a more specialized area. The major in physical sciences is weak based on current student interests. Concentrations in political science, psychology, and many of the arts offerings are also established strongholds. Environmental and life sciences are excellent, in part because of the proximity of a 1,000-acre forest preserve, Glen Helen, and a nature museum. The communications program benefits from a major public radio station operated by Antioch, which gives students experience in the broadcasting field. Being different may be the only thing Antioch students have in common, and diversity is a given on this campus.

Thirty percent of the students come from Ohio; the rest hail from points throughout the nation. Three percent of students are African American, 1 percent Asian American, 3 percent Hispanic, and 1 percent Native American. A variety of merit scholarships ranging from $5,000 to $10,000 are renewable for four years.

Ninety-eight percent of the students are housed on campus in apartment-style dorms. Co-ed and single-sex dorms are available, and all come equipped with kitchens.

Ninety-eight percent of the students are housed on campus in apartment-style dorms. Co-ed and single-sex dorms are available, and all come equipped with kitchens. Everyone is guaranteed on-campus housing if they want it, and students can choose from a number of special options that include a quiet hall, a moderate-noise hall, and even a substance-free hall, which bars smoking and drinking. "Housing is an issue. Some of the dorms are in disrepair, but most of

"The co-op program is the reason to come to Antioch."

the students live on campus despite this. A strong sense of community draws students here and this is more important than the living conditions," says one student. The Spalt International Center houses 60 students in foreign language living/learning halls. "They are thankfully renovating the dorms," adds one sophomore. Meal plans are available at the Caf, which features vegetarian entrees, a salad bar, and a popcorn machine. One student complains, "The food all seems to be deep fried, extremely cheesy, or lots of potato products. They have normal vegan and vegetarian offerings."

Without Greek organizations, social life tends to be rather spontaneous and limited to on-campus activities—some parties are held at the dance space, a student says. Drinking is said to be less of a problem among students than among the high school students who make the scene at campus parties. There is a student coffeehouse, which "is the best hangout space," while stargazers frequently congregate on the roof of the science building. Each fall, a three-day blues festival hits town. "Community Day" is actually two days a year where everyone takes the day off to mellow out and relax. Many student organizations, including the Anarchist Study Group and Third World Alliance, draw widespread student interest.

The town of Yellow Springs is "quaint, but not for someone craving nightlife. You have to mooch a car and go to Dayton or somewhere for that," says a student. The town hosts a variety of health food stores, a pizza joint that makes its pies with whole wheat crust, and an assortment of bars and restaurants. Yellow Springs may become limiting for some students, but that problem is usually solved by the next co-op trimester. And because they are world-minded, many Antioch students volunteer in the community and care about social issues on campus. "Students at Antioch are encouraged to speak their mind. The issues on campus are influenced by national issues," explains a political science major.

Antioch has all students spend three to 12 months in a significantly different cultural environment.

Traditionally considered taboo, varsity sports have enjoyed a rousing resurgence, thanks to the women's rugby team. Gym classes are offered in kayaking, rafting, and horseback riding. The 1,000-acre nature preserve ("the Glen") across the street is also near John Bryan State Park. A nearby reservoir is a popular place for swimming and windsurfing, and Clifton Gorge offers rock climbing.

For those who think cooperative education would be a "far out" experience, Antioch offers a unique opportunity. Even with an enrollment smaller than many high schools, the college still manages to offer an outside-the-box approach to academics. Horace Mann once implored his students to "be ashamed to die until you have won some victory for humanity." The Antioch community takes this message to heart.

If You Apply To ➤ **Antioch:** Rolling admissions. Does not guarantee to meet demonstrated need. Campus interviews: recommended, informational. No alumni interviews. SATs: optional. SAT IIs: optional. Accepts the Common Application and electronic applications. Essay question: Describe how you would balance freedom with responsibility. Looks for independent, self-directed students who are willing to take risks.

University of Arizona

BEST BUY

Robert L. Nugent Building, Tucson, AZ 85704

Tucson is an increasingly popular destination, and it isn't just because of the UA basketball team. A well-devoted honors program attracts top students, as do excellent programs in the sciences and engineering. Bring plenty of shorts and sunscreen.

Website: www.arizona.edu
Location: Urban
Total Enrollment: 37,036
Undergraduates: 28,482
Male/Female: 47/53
SAT Ranges: V 500–620
  M 500–630
ACT Range: 21–26
Financial Aid: 42%
Expense: Pub $
Phi Beta Kappa: Yes
Applicants: 17,904
Accepted: 88%
Enrolled: 38%
Grad in 6 Years: 58%
Returning Freshmen: 79%
Academics: ✍ ✍ ✍ ½
Social: 🐾 🐾 🐾 🐾
Q of L: ★ ★ ★ ★
Admissions: (520) 621-3237
Email Address:
  appinfo@arizona.edu

Strongest Programs:
Management Information
  Systems
Nursing
Astronomy

With a campus that's encircled by mountain ranges and the beautiful Sonoran Desert, lined with palm trees and cacti, and set against a backdrop of stunning Tucson sunsets, it's no surprise that students at the University of Arizona love to hang out at the mall. Not the shopping center, mind you—but a huge grassy area in the middle of campus where the nearly 35,000 Wildcats gather between classes. Judging by numbers alone, that's enough people to fill a medium-sized town. But students are quick to point out that UA has a strong sense of community and offers a genuinely friendly campus. "Nobody else has a huge central meeting place like we do," says a senior marketing major. "I always see familiar and friendly faces around the mall area." With all the natural beauty that surrounds them, many Wildcats simply purr through four satisfying years.

Architecturally, the UA campus distinguishes itself from the city's regiment of adobe buildings with a design that seems a study in the versatility of redbrick. Old Main, the university's first building, is into its second century, but others verge on high-tech science facilities. Hard hats and heavy machinery have become commonplace on campus; recent construction includes a new student union, facilities for first-year students and learning-disabled students, the Athletic Hall of Fame and weight training facility, a residence hall, and a 1,300-space parking structure.

Sciences are unquestionably the school's forte—the astronomy department is among the nation's best, helped by those clear night skies. Students have access not only to leading astronomers, but also to the most up-to-date equipment, including a huge 176-inch telescope operated jointly by the university and the Smithsonian. A $28 million aerospace and mechanical engineering building has a state-of-the-art subsonic wind tunnel and rocket-combustion test facility. The history and English departments are standouts, as are several of the social science programs. Eager shutterbugs can pore through photographer Ansel Adams's personal collection, and the Center for Creative Photography offers one of the leading photographic collections in the world. Students in the popular business and public administration school can pick racetrack management as their area of expertise, while interested anthropology students can delve into garbage research. Two newer programs are optics and public health. Areas getting low marks from students are the language programs and the journalism department.

Under the core curriculum, students take 10 general education courses in common. They fall under the broad categories of arts, humanities, traditions and cultures, natural sciences, and individuals and societies. In addition, almost everyone gets a healthy dose of freshman composition, math, and foreign language. Academic competition, according to most students, is left up to both the individual and the specific concentration. "The academic program that I have chosen to take part in is a very competitive and challenging program," explains a physiology major. The University Honors Center offers one of the nation's largest and most selective honors programs (students must maintain a grade point average of 3.5 to remain in the program). In addition to offering 200 honors courses per year, the center features smaller classes, personalized advising, special library privileges, and great research opportunities. The Undergraduate Biology Research Program also has a national reputation. Teaching is well regarded, with some freshman courses taught by graduate students. "The quality of teaching here is pretty amazing," a senior says. "Professors are able to combine necessary information while also making the course laid-back."

"Nobody else has a huge central meeting place like we do."

One student describes his peers as "go-getters" who "bleed red and blue." Despite tougher admission standards, the administration cites a sharp increase in freshman applications over the past few years, especially from out-of-staters, who constitute 27 percent of the student body. In addition to various merit scholarships, all the athletic scholarships allowed by the NCAA are available. Hispanics account for 15 percent of the enrollment, African Americans for 3 percent, and Asian Americans for 6 percent, and American Indians 2 percent. A diversity action council, a newly developed student minority advisory committee, and cultural resource centers help students deal with race-relation issues. An active and popular student government runs a free legal service and a tenants' complaint center, and the university has instituted many programs to help those with learning disabilities.

Dorm rooms tend to be small but well-maintained. "In the past, housing was a problem," confides one student, "but three new forms have opened up in the past year." Only 20 percent of undergraduates live in the dorms; 35 percent of freshmen and most upperclassmen flock to the abundant and inexpensive apartments near the school. The best way to enjoy the excellent food service at the student union's seven restaurants is to use the university-issued All Aboard credit card, which helps students take advantage of the wealth of different gustatory options and frees them from carrying cash.

Despite the high percentage of off-campus residents, students stream back onto campus on weekends for parties, sports, and cultural events. Ten percent of the men belong to fraternities and 11 percent of the women belong to sororities. The campus is technically alcohol-free, though some question whether the frats

"The quality of teaching here is pretty amazing."

have realized that yet. Still, most social life takes place off campus. There are a lot of different dance clubs around town, and some do have after-hours for underage people. Those who feel they must go elsewhere need only head to the Mexican town of Nogales (one hour away), where there is no drinking age. Many students are content remaining in Tucson because it offers "the most incredible sunrises and sunsets, and delightful temperatures year-round."

One of the UA's most time-honored traditions is Spring Fling, said to be the largest student-run carnival in the country. Athletics is also somewhat of a tradition here. The basketball Wildcats have been among the nation's leaders in recent years.

(Continued)
Pharmacy
Creative Writing
Aerospace Engineering

Students in the popular business and public administration school can pick racetrack management as their area of expertise, while interested anthropology students can delve into garbage research.

The University Honors Center offers one of the nation's largest and most selective honors programs (students must maintain a grade point average of 3.5 to remain in the program). In addition to offering 200 honors courses per year, the center features smaller classes, personalized advising, special library privileges, and great research opportunities.

Division I football and baseball enjoy national prominence, generate lots of money for other men's and women's sports teams, and provide great weekend entertainment, especially when the opposing team is big-time rival Arizona State. UA's battle cry "Bear Down!" frequently heard at sporting events dates back to the 1930s, when a campus football hero, fatally injured in a car crash, whispered his last message to his teammates: "Tell them, tell them to bear down." More than 60 years later, the enigmatic slogan still appears on T-shirts and in a gym on the central campus.

The University of Arizona offers a wide variety of academic opportunities along with spectacular weather. Prospective students are warned to honestly evaluate how that will affect their ability to concentrate. UA is the place to go to engage in the pursuit of truth, knowledge, and a good tan.

Overlaps

Arizona State, Northern Arizona, UCLA, University of Colorado, UC–Santa Barbara

If You Apply To ➤

Arizona: Early action: Sept. 1. Regular admissions: Apr. 1. Financial aid: Feb. 1. Housing: May 1. Campus interviews: optional, informational. Alumni interviews: optional. SATs or ACTs: recommended. SAT IIs: optional. Accepts electronic applications. No essay question.

Arizona State University

Box 870112, Tempe, AZ 85287-0112

Want to get lost in the crowd? ASU is the biggest university in the Southwest— apologies to UCLA. No matter how appealing the thought of 44,000 new faces, you'd better find the right program to get a good education. Try the professional schools and the honors college.

Website: www.asu.edu
Location: Urban
Total Enrollment: 37,309
Undergraduates: 31,462
Male/Female: 48/52
SAT Ranges: V 490–600
  M 500–620
ACT Range: 21–26
Financial Aid: 42%
Expense: Pub $
Phi Beta Kappa: Yes
Applicants: 20,789
Accepted: 86%
Enrolled: 40%
Grad in 6 Years: 55%
Returning Freshmen: 77%
Academics: ✍ ✍ ✍
Social: 🐦 🐦 🐦 🐦
Q of L: ★★★★★
Admissions: (480) 965-7788

Whether climbing "A" Mountain with a lantern, enjoying water sports on Town Lake or puzzling over the term "dry heat," Arizona State University sits smack in the middle of an oasis in the desert. A very large oasis. With ample educational opportunity and the promise of fun in the sun, it just might be that ASU is the perfect personal challenge. Students can find their niche in a variety of stellar programs, including ASU's anthropology department which is ranked within the top five nationwide. Its Barnett Honors College allows exceptional students to live, work, and study among their peers, and to write a senior thesis, creating a small-school atmosphere on this mammoth campus.

ASU's north Tempe campus offers a beautiful blend of palm-lined walkways, desert landscapes, and public art displays. Architectural styles range from modern to turn-of-the-century historic, as the school renovates and expands Memorial Union to add four restaurants and more seating and program space. Lattie F. Coor Hall, with state-of-the-art classroom space, and the 17,000-square-foot Arizona Biodesign Institute provide lab and office space for research in neural rehabilitation, genomics, molecular biophysics, and neutraceuticals. Other new construction includes Adelphi Commons II, fraternity housing that will replace older houses. Also, a new freshman residence hall is expected to open in the fall of 2006. The campus is officially listed as an arboretum, and ASU groundskeepers tend to more than 115 species of trees that thrive in Arizona's arid climate.

ASU has eight undergraduate schools—business, liberal arts and sciences, engineering and applied sciences, architecture and environmental design, education, fine arts, nursing, and public programs (justice studies, leisure studies, communication, social work, and public affairs)—though students apply to the institution as a whole. The most popular majors are business, psychology, and communication, followed by interdisciplinary studies, a flexible and popular program that includes concentrations such as social welfare, American public policy, international studies, civic education, and Southeast Asian studies. The college of business ranks second in placing graduates with the Big Four accounting firms, while the fine arts college features an innovative child drama program, and nationally recognized majors in art, music, and dance. Engineering programs, especially microelectronics, robotics, and computer-assisted manufacturing, are sure bets; the facility for high-resolution microscopy allows students to get a uniquely close-up view of atomic structures.

The sciences (including solar energy, physical science, geology, and biology) and social sciences also boast first-class facilities, notably the largest university-owned meteorite collection in the world. Planetary science is out of this world; a team of ASU students, faculty, and staff, led by geology professor Philip Christensen, designed the Thermal Emission Imaging System and are conducting research with the system as it orbits Mars. ASU is also a founding member of the NASA Astrobiology Institute, which will focus on studying the origin of life on Earth and elsewhere. Anthropology benefits from its association with the Institute of Human Origins' Donald C. Johannson, who discovered the 3.2-million-year-old fossil skeleton named Lucy. The Walter

"Everything is clean and comfortable, if you are quick enough to get a dorm."

Cronkite School of Journalism and Telecommunication finished first in the annual Hearst writing competition for the second consecutive year. Each year, the legendary CBS newsman visits campus to lecture in individual classes.

Newer options at ASU include global studies, a transdisciplinary major that integrates social and behavioral sciences, humanities, and natural sciences, and a liberal studies option for former students that is distance-based. Regardless of major, students must fulfill requirements in literacy and critical inquiry (including composition), mathematical studies (including college-level algebra or higher), humanities and fine arts, social and behavioral sciences, and natural sciences. Students must also complete courses in three awareness areas: global, historical, and U.S. cultural diversity. An automated phone system helps speed registration. "ASU is competitive enough to drive excellence but laid-back enough to take a breather and relax," says a freshman.

One-quarter of the students at Arizona State come from elsewhere, including many snow bunnies from the Midwest fleeing miserable winters. They must meet tougher standards for automatic admission: While in-state students need to be in the top quarter of their class or have a 3.0 GPA, as well as a total SAT score of 1040 or an ACT score of 22, out-of-staters must meet the same class-rank or GPA requirements and have a cumulative SAT score of 1110 or ACT score of 24. Because ASU draws so heavily from within Arizona, 12 percent of the student body is Hispanic; African Americans contribute 4 percent, Asian Americans 5 percent, and Native Americans 2 percent. The Intergroup Relations Center works to overcome racial, religious, gender, and other differences, including the gulf between Greeks and independents, and athletes and academics. ASU offers merit scholarships to qualified students and awards 351 athletic scholarships annually to male and female athletes. "ASU Advantage" offers families earning less than $18,850 per year a combination of financial resources that includes tuition, fees, books, and room and board.

Only 16 percent of ASU students live in the co-ed dorms, which fill up quickly and are generally available only to freshmen. "Everything is clean and comfortable, if you are quick enough to get a dorm," advises a freshman. After freshman year, students live off campus in nearby apartments and houses. Those lucky enough to get a bed on campus jockey for one of the three residence halls with their own swimming pools

(Continued)
Email Address:
askasu@asu.edu

Strongest Programs:
Business
History
Psychology
Geology
Anthropology
Music
Landscape Architecture
Accountancy

Recent NCAA champions have come from the sports of golf, diving, track and field, and gymnastics.

One-quarter of the students at Arizona State come from elsewhere, including many snow bunnies from the Midwest fleeing miserable winters.

and volleyball courts. No matter where they live, students don't have to buy a meal plan and one student says the "food is great."

ASU's Greek system attracts 10 percent of the men and 9 percent of the women, though the campus is officially dry. The underage are also warned against drinking in student housing: "There is a strict enforcement of a 'three-strikes-you're-out' policy." Perhaps that's why students head off campus on weekends—often way off campus. Many have cars, giving them access to the mountains of Colorado, the beaches of San Diego, the natural beauty of the Grand Canyon, or the bright lights of Las Vegas. Students can fly from Phoenix to San Diego for as little as $60, and they love to follow the NCAA Division I football team to games at the University of Arizona and elsewhere. Arizona State's athletics department is consistently ranked among the nation's best. In 2004, ASU launched the Pat Tillman Scholarship Fund to honor the former football star who died in combat.

> "There is strict enforcement of a 'three-strikes-you're-out' policy."

Arizona State may seem like an overwhelmingly big school to some, but many students come here looking for the enormity of options the campus offers, both academically and socially. "You meet people from all over the world, which definitely adds to your college experience," says a sophomore.

Overlaps

University of Arizona, Northern Arizona, San Diego State, UCLA, University of Southern California, UC–San Diego

If You Apply To ➤

ASU: Rolling admissions. Financial aid: Feb. 15 (priority). Does not guarantee to meet demonstrated need. Campus interviews: optional, informational. No alumni interviews. SATs or ACTs: required. SAT II: optional. Accepts electronic applications. No essay question.

University of Arkansas

200 Hunt Hall, Fayetteville, AR 72701

University of Arkansas rates in the second tier of Southern public universities alongside Alabama, LSU, and Ole' Miss. With traditional strength in agriculture, U of A has also developed programs in business, engineering, and other professional fields. U of A's highest-ranked program takes the field on Saturday afternoons.

Website: www.uark.edu
Location: Small city
Total Enrollment: 17,269
Undergraduates: 11,302
Male/Female: 50/50
SAT Ranges: V 510–650
  M 510–650
ACT Range: 22–28
Financial Aid: 41%
Expense: Pub $ $
Phi Beta Kappa: Yes
Applicants: 5,819
Accepted: 79%
Enrolled: 55%
Grad in 6 Years: 53%

The state of Arkansas is working to transform its flagship public university into a nationally competitive, student-centered research institution in an effort to help stop the flight of the state's young and talented and to jump-start the Arkansas economy. A $300 million cash gift from the family of Wal-Mart founder Sam Walton, the largest ever made to an American public university, put his name on the U of A's business college, and also helped endow the undergraduate Honors College, which will eventually enroll 2,000 of the brightest young scholars on campus. The Walton grant also strengthens and improves the U of A's graduate school. Aspiring politicos might consider Arkansas, as it's the alma mater of Sen. J. William Fulbright and the first employer of one-time law professors Bill and Hillary Clinton. No matter what your aspirations, you're likely to find something to study among Arkansas' 208 academic programs.

The Arkansas campus is nestled among the mountains, lakes, and streams of the Ozarks, in the extreme northwest corner of the state. The community is friendly and safe, and the moderate climate means recreational opportunities abound. Architectural styles range from modern concrete to buildings that date from the Depression.

The center of campus is the stately brick Old Main, which once housed the entire university. There are two new greenhouses for plant science majors and an Innovation Center for engineers, while the Pat Walker Health Facility has been renovated. The $46 million Northwest Quad project includes housing for 600 students, as well as dining areas, classrooms, computer labs, and other amenities.

Established as a land grant institution in 1871, with agricultural and mechanical roots, the U of A includes six colleges and professional schools. U of A's core requirements include six credits each in English and Fine Arts, three credits each in U. S. History and Math, eight in Science and nine in Social Sciences. Students in Fulbright College of Arts and Sciences must also achieve foreign language proficiency. The Walton College of Business offers three of the five most popular majors on campus: marketing, finance, and accounting. Other popular programs are elementary education and data processing; architecture and engineering are likewise strong. The Dale Bumpers College of Agricultural, Food, and Life Sciences, another part of the institution named for a former senator, includes the Poultry Health Center, a national leader in research on poultry epidemics. The master's degree in physical education has been phased out, but undergraduate degrees have been added in landscape architecture, public service, and biomedical engineering.

Students are quick to point out that although the academic climate is generally stress-free, it is competitive at times. "The academic atmosphere is competitive in that students are always trying to beat their friends on the next test. They strive for that sense of pride," explains a junior. Professors are lauded for their teaching skills, but students are also likely to have graduate students leading classes. "I enjoy having graduate students as teachers for some classes," says a freshman, "because often they relate to students better."

A management major claims, "We have students from many nationalities, states, and backgrounds," but the numbers tell a different story: 85 percent of U of A students are homegrown, and minorities comprise less than 15 percent of the student body. African Americans make up 5 percent of the student body, Asian Americans 3 percent, and Hispanics 2 percent. Still, there are commonalities. One student describes classmates as having "a strong sense of school spirit" and being "intelligent, but not snobs." The university is striving to improve race relations, and the chancellor has personally chaired a campus task force to help boost success rates of students from underrepresented minority groups. In addition, increasing diversity is one of the school's top five priorities. Arkansas hands out thousands of merit scholarships each year, worth an average of $6,962. There are also 392 athletic scholarships, representing all U of A sports teams. Additionally, the Good Neighbor program lets students from nearby states with GPAs of 3.0 or higher and ACT scores of at least 24 enroll at in-state rates.

"We have students from many nationalities, states, and backgrounds."

Thirty-one percent of the undergrads at Arkansas live in the dorms, where "it is always too hot or too cold," according to a picky sophomore, who adds, "Sharing a bathroom with that many people is unsanitary." All halls are single-sex, except for one that's co-ed by floor. Students recommend Gregson and Holcombe for freshmen, and note that as part of the First-Year Experience, Arkansas strives to put freshmen in residence halls where peers surround them. A junior recommends "Rock Camp," an optional orientation weekend in Oklahoma. "It is a great way to meet new students, get on email lists, and start making connections." When it comes to chow, you can get everything from salad and burgers to sushi.

Arkansas' 25 Greek chapters attract 17 percent of the women and 14 percent of the men. Aside from the revelry that accompanies Razorback football and basketball, students say Greek parties are pretty much the only game in town on weekends. Dixon Street, the main drag in the town of Fayetteville (population 55,000),

(Continued)

Returning Freshmen: 84%

Academics: ✍ ✍ ✍

Social: 🐷 🐷 🐷 🐷

Q of L: ★ ★ ★

Admissions: (800) 377-8632

Email Address:
uofa@uark.edu

Strongest Programs:
Marketing
Management
Finance
Elementary Education

Eighty-two percent of Arkansas students participate in intramurals, where sports include everything from flag football and soccer to dominoes, putt–putt golf, and trivia. (Who knew using your brain was a competitive sport?)

is full of bars and restaurants; the town also offers drive-in movies, live music at local clubs, and touring Broadway shows at the Walton Arts Center. Those with cars will find Dallas, Tulsa, Oklahoma City, Memphis, and St. Louis all within six hours' drive.

And who could forget Razorback sports? Cries of "Woooooo! Pig sooie!" ring out during football and basketball weekends, and red Razorback logos are all over town—on T-shirts, napkins, book covers, license plates, and on game day, the cheeks of ecstatic fans. "The student section is always packed, and you must arrive one to two hours early to get a seat," says a junior. Men's indoor and outdoor track and field brought home SEC Championships in 2005, and the women's volleyball team has won SEC Western Division titles for the past two years. Eighty-two percent of Arkansas students participate in intramurals, where sports include everything from flag football and soccer to dominoes, putt-putt golf, and trivia. (Who knew using your brain was a competitive sport?)

> **"The student section is always packed, and you must arrive one to two hours early to get a seat."**

The University of Arkansas boasts "fun-loving and free-spirited" students who are "genuinely friendly," says a senior. "If they encounter someone who needs help, they help." This kind of Southern hospitality means poultry science students aren't the only ones flocking to Arkansas for a solid education at a bargain price. Northerners may feel out of their element, and those who dislike football should keep their feelings quiet. Others may look forward to graduation day, when their names will join forever those of 120,000 other alumni, etched into the five-mile network of sidewalks on campus.

Overlaps

University of Central Arkansas, Arkansas State, Arkansas Tech, University of Arkansas–Little Rock, University of Arkansas–Fort Smith, Henderson State

If You Apply To ➢

Arkansas: Rolling admissions: Aug. 15. Early action: Nov. 15. Financial aid: Jun. 30. Does not guarantee to meet demonstrated need. Campus interviews: recommended, informational. Alumni interviews: not available. SATs or ACTs: required. No SAT II. Accepts the Common Application and electronic applications; prefers electronic applications. Essay question.

Atlanta University Center

Atlanta is viewed as the preeminent city in the country for bright, talented, and successful African Americans. It became the capital of the civil rights movement in the 1960s—a town described by its leaders as "too busy to hate."

At the heart of this extraordinary culture is the Atlanta University Center, the largest African American educational complex in the world, replete with its own central library and computing center. The seven component institutions have educated generations of African American leaders. The Reverend Martin Luther King Jr. went to Morehouse College; his grandmother, mother, sister, and daughter went to Spelman College. Graduates spread across the country in a pattern that developed when these were among the best of the few colleges to which talented African Americans could aspire. Even now, when the options are almost limitless, alumni continue to send their children back for more.

The center consists of three undergraduate colleges (Morris Brown, Morehouse, and Spelman) and three graduate institutions (Clark Atlanta University, the Interdenominational Theological Seminary, and the Morehouse College of Medicine) on adjoining campuses in the center of Atlanta three miles from downtown. Students at these affiliated schools can enjoy the quiet pace of their beautiful magnolia-studded campuses or plunge into all the culture and excitement of this most dynamic of Deep South cities. The six original schools—all but the medical school—became affiliated in 1929 using the model of California's Claremont Colleges, but they remain fiercely independent. Each has its own administration, board of trustees, and academic specialties, and each maintains its own dorms, cafeterias, and other facilities. There is crossregistration among the institutions (Morehouse students, for example, go to Spelman for drama and art courses) and with Georgia State and Emory University as well. The governing body of the consortium, the Atlanta University Center, Inc., administers a centerwide dual-degree program in engineering in conjunction with Georgia Tech—and it runs campus security, a student crisis center, and a joint institute of science research. There is also a centerwide service of career planning and placement, where recruiters may come and interview students from all six of the institutions.

Dating and social life at the coeducational institutions tend to take place within the individual schools, though Morehouse, a men's college, and Spelman, a women's college, maintain a close academic and social relationship. The Morehouse–Spelman Glee Club takes its abundance of talent around the nation, and its annual Christmas concert on the Spelman campus is a standing-room-only event.

Morehouse and Spelman (see full write-ups) constitute the Ivy League of historically African American colleges. The following are sketches of the other two institutions offering undergraduate degrees.

Clark Atlanta University (www.cau.edu)

Formed by the consolidation of Clark College, a four-year liberal arts institution, and Atlanta University, which offered only graduate degrees, CAU is a comprehensive coeducational institution that offers undergraduate, graduate, and professional degrees. The university draws on the former strengths of both schools, offering quality programs in the health professions, public policy, and mass communications (including print journalism, radio and television production, and filmmaking). Graduate and professional programs include education, business, library information studies, social work, and arts and sciences. Undergraduate enrollment: 4,000.

Morris Brown College (www.morrisbrown.edu)

An open-admission, four-year undergraduate institution that is related to the African Methodist Episcopal Church, MBC lost most of its students in the spring of 2003 after the college lost its accreditation. A new president and a restructured board of trustees, including the Reverend Jesse Jackson, is working hard to restore its financial and academic viability. Its most popular programs are education and business administration. Morris Brown also offers evening courses for employed adults, as well as a program of co-op work-study education.

Morehouse College

830 Westview Drive, Atlanta, GA 30314

Morehouse's homecoming is a joint effort between Morehouse and Spelman. The queen elected by Morehouse men has traditionally been a Spelman woman, as are the cheerleaders and majorettes.

Along with sister school Spelman, Morehouse is the most selective of the historically black schools. Alumni list reads like a Who's Who of African American leaders. Best known for business and popular 3–2 engineering program with Georgia Tech. Built on a Civil War battlefield, Morehouse is a symbol of the new South.

Founded in 1867, Morehouse College has the distinction of being the nation's only historically African American, four-year liberal arts college for men. If its sister school, Spelman, was once the "Vassar of African American society," Morehouse was the Harvard or Yale, attracting male students from the upper echelons of society around the country. Top students come to Morehouse because they want an institution with a strong academic program and a supportive atmosphere in which to cultivate their success-orientation and leadership skills without facing the additional barriers they might encounter at a predominantly white institution. "Morehouse is a college of young, assertive, ambitious black men," says a psychology major. Notable alumni include the Reverend Martin Luther King Jr., Samuel L. Jackson,

Website:
www.morehouse.edu
Location: Urban
Total Enrollment: 2,970
Undergraduates: 2,970
Male/Female: 100/0
SAT Ranges: V 440–680
M 470–680
ACT Range: 19–32
Financial Aid: N/A
Expense: Pr $
Phi Beta Kappa: Yes
Applicants: 2,079

(Continued)

Accepted: 75%

Enrolled: 36%

Grad in 6 Years: 63%

Returning Freshmen: 83%

Academics: ✍ ✍ ✍

Social: 🐾 🐾 🐾 🐾

Q of L: ★ ★ ★ ★

Admissions: (404) 215-2632
   or (800) 851-1254

Email Address:
   admissions@morehouse
   .edu

Strongest Programs:
Economics
Business
Biology
Political Science
Psychology

Spike Lee, and Dr. Louis Sullivan, current president of the Morehouse School of Medicine and former U.S. Secretary of Health and Human Services.

Located near downtown Atlanta, the 61-acre Morehouse campus is home to 35 buildings, including the Martin Luther King Jr. International Chapel. In a little more than a decade, the college has enriched its academic program, conducted a successful multimillion-dollar national fund-raising campaign, increased student scholarships and faculty salaries, doubled its endowment, improved its physical plant, and acquired additional acres of land.

The general education program includes not only 68 semester hours in four major disciplines (humanities, natural sciences, math, and social sciences), but also the study of "the unique African and African American heritage on which so much of our modern American culture is built." In fact, appreciation of this culture is one of the college's main drawing cards. "Many students are here to get a greater understanding of their heritage and to promote it," attests one student. The academic climate at the House can get intense, with students learning and challenging themselves for the sake of learning and not just to bust a curve. "Morehouse offers an academic structure that is both competitive and rigorous," states a freshman. Counseling, including career counseling, is considered quite strong.

Undergraduate programs include the traditional liberal arts majors in the humanities and social and natural sciences. While the sciences have been traditionally strong at Morehouse, business courses have risen in prominence. The college has obtained accreditation of the undergraduate business department by the American Assembly of Collegiate Schools of Business, and current students are linked to graduates who serve as mentors in the ways of the business world. The most popular major is business administration. Engineering, which trails shortly behind in popularity, is actually a 3–2 program in conjunction with Georgia Tech and other larger universities. The school also runs a program with NASA that allows students to engage in independent research. Programs that receive less favorable reviews from students are English, art, and drama, and the administration admits that physical education and some of the humanities offerings could use some strengthening. Study abroad options include programs offered through the Associated Colleges of the South consortium.* The school also offers courses and additional resources as a member of the Atlanta Regional Consortium for Higher Education.* Newer options include a major in applied physics and minors in public health sciences and telecommunications.

> **"Morehouse offers an academic structure that is both competitive and rigorous."**

Sixty-seven percent of Morehouse students come from outside the state, with a sizable number from New York and California. Sixty-seven percent graduated in the top quarter of their high school class. More than 600 merit scholarships are available, many providing full tuition. There are 121 scholarships for athletes in football, basketball, track, soccer, and tennis.

There's limited housing, leaving half of the student body to find their own off-campus accommodations. For freshmen, students recommend Graves Hall, the college's oldest building, built in 1889. Those who do get campus housing sometimes wish they hadn't. Complaints range from "too small" to "not well-maintained." Most upperclassmen live off campus. The meal plan at Morehouse is mandatory for students living on campus and draws its share of complaints.

Morehouse's homecoming is a joint effort between Morehouse and Spelman. The queen elected by Morehouse men has traditionally been a Spelman woman, as are the cheerleaders and majorettes. The four fraternities, which sign up a very small percentage of the students, hold popular parties; "drinking is not a big deal here," most students concur. Going out on the town in Atlanta is a popular evening activity, and on-campus football games, concerts, movies, and religious programs all draw crowds. In its early years, Morehouse left much to be desired in the area of varsity sports, but it now competes well in NCAA Division II. Track, cross-country, tennis, basketball, football, and soccer are all strong, but it is the strong intramural program that allows students a chance to become the superstar they know is lurking within them. During football season, Morehouse men road trip to follow the games at Howard, Hampton, and Tuskegee universities.

Morehouse is well-equipped to serve the modern heirs of a distinguished tradition. Morehouse students don't just attend Morehouse. They become part of what amounts to a network of "Morehouse Men" who share the bonds of having had the Morehouse experience, and graduates find previous alumni stand ready and willing to help them with jobs and other needs.

Overlaps
Clark Atlanta, Howard, Georgia Tech, Hampton

If You Apply To

Morehouse: Early action: Nov. 1. Regular admissions: Feb. 15. Financial aid: Apr. 1. Does not guarantee to meet demonstrated need. Campus and alumni interviews: recommended, informational. SATs or ACTs: required. SAT IIs: optional. Essay question: greatest influence on your life; why Morehouse?

Spelman College
350 Spelman Lane, Atlanta, GA 30314

The Wellesley of the black college world. Reputation draws students from all corners of the country. Unusually strong in the sciences with particular emphasis on undergraduate research. Wooded 42-acre Atlanta campus offers easy access to urban attractions.

As one of only two surviving African American women's colleges in the United States, Spelman College holds a special appeal for African American women seeking to become leaders in fields ranging from science to the arts. Students flock here for that something special that the predominantly Caucasian schools lack: an environment with first-rate academics where African American women can develop self-confidence and leadership skills before venturing into a world where they will once again be in the minority.

Founded in 1881 by two white women from New England (it was named after John D. Rockefeller's in-laws, Mr. and Mrs. Harvey Buel Spelman), the school was traditionally the starting point for teachers, nurses, and other African American female leaders. Today's emphasis is on getting Spelman grads into the courtrooms, boardrooms, and engineering labs. Honing women for leadership is the main mission, and that nurturing takes place on a classic collegiate-green campus with a $140 million endowment.

These are heady times for Spelman. Although the college finds itself competing head-on with the Seven Sisters and other prestigious and predominantly Caucasian institutions that are eager to recruit talented African American women, the college is holding its own. The college offers a well-rounded liberal arts curriculum that emphasizes the importance of critical and analytical thinking and problem solving. Usually by the end of sophomore year, students are expected to complete 34 credit hours of core requirements, including English composition, foreign language, health and physical education, mathematics, African diaspora and the world,

Website: www.spelman.edu
Location: Urban
Total Enrollment: 2,136
Undergraduates: 2,136
Male/Female: 0/100
SAT Ranges: V 490–590
   M 470–560
ACT Range: 20–24
Financial Aid: 85%
Expense: Pr $
Phi Beta Kappa: No
Applicants: 4,534
Accepted: 39%
Enrolled: 30%
Grad in 6 Years: 75%
Returning Freshmen: 91%
Academics: ✐ ✐ ✐
Social: ☎ ☎ ☎ ☎
Q of L: ★ ★ ★ ★ ★
Admissions: (800) 982-2411

(Continued)

Email Address:
admiss@spelman.edu

Strongest Programs:
Biology
Engineering
Natural Sciences
Premed
Prelaw

African American women's studies, and computer literacy. In addition, freshmen are required to take First Year Orientation, and sophomores must take Sophomore Assembly. Spelman's liberal arts program introduces students to the principal branches of learning, specifically languages, literature, English, the natural sciences, humanities, social sciences, and fine arts.

Spelman's established strengths lie in the natural sciences (especially biology) and the humanities, both of which have outstanding faculties. Over the last decade, the college has greatly strengthened its offerings in math and the natural sciences; extensive undergraduate research programs provide students with publishing opportunities, and many end up attending grad school to become researchers. Students have moved beyond the popular majors of the early '70s—education and the fine arts—in favor of premed and prelaw programs, and these programs remain strong.

"Lectures are tactful and effective." The dual-degree program in engineering (in cooperation with Georgia Tech) is also a standout. The Women's Research and Resource Center specializes in women's studies and community outreach to women.

Individual attention is the hallmark of a Spelman education. About 70 percent of the faculty have doctorates, and many are African American and/or female—and thus, excellent role models, ones the students find very accessible. One political science major reports that the majority of instructors are "very well learned. Their lectures are tactful and effective," and she is "often challenged to put forth the best effort." Except for some of the required courses, classes are small; most have fewer than 25 students. Students who want to spread their wings can venture abroad through a variety of programs, or try one of the domestic exchange arrangements with Wellesley, Mount Holyoke, Vassar, or Mills. The school also offers courses and additional resources as a member of the Atlanta Regional Consortium for Higher Education.*

Extensive undergraduate research programs provide students with publishing opportunities, and many end up attending grad school to become researchers.

Spelman's reputation continues to attract African American women from all over the country, including a high proportion of alumnae children. Three-quarters of the students come from outside Georgia. Students represented here include high achievers looking for a supportive environment and those women with high potential who performed relatively poorly in high school. Only 4 percent of the student body are not African American. Spelman does not guarantee to meet the financial need of all those admitted, but it does offer 120 merit scholarships worth up to $18,015. There are no athletic scholarships.

Fifty-seven percent of students live on campus, and housing is "well kept and quite comfortable," reports a mathematics major. Because Spelman is an old school and has tried to keep up the original buildings, most of the dorms are relatively old. But that certainly can add to the school's historical charm, and students report having little trouble in getting a room. There are 11 dorms, and students recommend that freshmen check out the Howard Harreld dorm. The meal plan is mandatory for campus-dwellers.

Largely because of the Atlanta University Center, students also have plenty of chances for social interaction with other nearby colleges. "Students mingle in the student centers of all four schools all the time, especially on Fridays," a veteran

"No alcohol on campus—period." explains. "Atlanta is a great college town!" gushes one junior. "If there is any place that a student can be academically enriched, it is here." Spelmanites do take advantage of the big-city nightlife; they attend plays, symphonies, and the hot Atlanta nightclubs such as Ethiopian Vibrations and Lenox Mall. Sororities are present but only in small numbers—3 percent of the students go Greek. The attitude on drinking leans toward the conservative. Says one student, "No alcohol on campus—period." The most anticipated annual events include sisterhood initiation ceremonies and the Founders Day celebration. Although varsity sports are not the highlight here, the school boasts fine volleyball, basketball, and tennis teams. Athletic facilities are poor, but there are several organized intramurals, including flag football and bowling.

Spelman College has spent almost 125 years furthering the education and opportunities of African American women. It has adapted its curriculum to meet the career aspirations of today's youth, built up its bankroll, and successfully met the challenge posed by affirmative action in other universities. Still an elite institution in African American society, Spelman is staking its future on its ability to provide a unique kind of education that allows its graduates to compete with anyone.

Overlaps

Clark Atlanta, Howard, Hampton, Georgia State, Florida A&M

If You Apply To ➤

Spelman: Early decision: Nov. 1. Early action: Nov. 15. Regular admissions: Feb. 1. Housing: May 1. Does not guarantee to meet demonstrated need. Campus interviews: optional, informational. Scheduled alumni interviews. SATs or ACTs: required. SAT IIs: optional. Accepts the Common Application. Essay question: personal statement reflecting achievements, interests, personal goal; or issue of personal, local, or national concern. Seeks women who are active in school, church, or community.

College of the Atlantic

105 Eden Street, Bar Harbor, ME 04609

In today's conservative world, COA is as out-there as it gets. A haven for communal, earthy, vegetarian types who would rather save the world than make a buck. Cozy is an understatement; with fewer than 300 students, it is the second smallest institution in the *Fiske Guide*.

The College of the Atlantic attracts rugged individualists troubled by the same issues that so worried the founders of this "mission-oriented" school, notably pollution, environmental damage, and troubled inner cities. The tiny college's curriculum is focused on human ecology—the study of the relationship between humans and their natural and social environments—which is the only major offered. "The interdisciplinary approach that this creates is the most amazing opportunity you can have in an undergraduate program," a sophomore says.

The 31-acre campus, covered in lush flowers, vegetable gardens, and lawns, sits on the island of Mount Desert, along the shoreline of Frenchman Bay and adjacent to the magnificent Acadia National Park. In addition, the college has acquired two offshore island research centers and an 86-acre organic farm, and recently opened the new Witch Cliff residence hall and a zoology lab.

Most courses focus on a single aspect of humans' relationships with the world. Instead of traditional academic departments, the school has three broad resource areas: environmental science, arts and design, and applied human studies. Many students choose to concentrate on more narrowly defined topics within human ecology, such as marine studies, biological and environmental sciences, public policy, visual and performing arts, environmental design, or education. With advisors and resource specialists, each student designs an individual course of study. "I really appreciate the school's encouragement in designing an academic program that suits me," says a junior human ecology/teacher certification student. "You have so much freedom and support here," adds another junior. The natural sciences are stellar, with excellent instruction in ecology, zoology, and marine biology. The arts are catching up, with a more formal video and performance art program created in recent years. COA is

Website: www.coa.edu
Location: Small town
Total Enrollment: 272
Undergraduates: 260
Male/Female: 38/62
SAT Ranges: V 550–680
   M 510–620
ACT Range: 23–31
Financial Aid: 81%
Expense: Pr $ $
Phi Beta Kappa: No
Applicants: 255
Accepted: 67%
Enrolled: 39%
Grad in 6 Years: 57%
Returning Freshmen: 85%
Academics: ✐ ✐ ✐
Social: ☎ ☎
Q of L: ★ ★ ★
Admissions: (800) 528-0025
Email Address:
   inquiry@coa.edu

adding new classes in areas such as marketing, business, and grant writing "to help idealists realize their ideal." An ecological entrepreneurship program was recently developed. Allied Whale, the school's marine study arm, offers hands-on research opportunities, and specializes in training and research in marine mammalogy. Founded in 1972, the non-profit program conducts research into effective methods.

Student life at COA is intense and semi-communal, beginning with a rugged five-day wilderness orientation preceding first trimester. Before graduating, students must also complete a 10-week off-campus internship and 10-week final project. Other requirements are few: freshmen must take a human ecology core course, and two courses are required in environmental sciences, human studies, and arts and design. All students incorporate research of the community into their studies, whether it is a development impact study for the local government or a study on the aggression of fire ants for Acadia National Park.

Some departments only have a professor or two. Since the student body is small, scholars can become close to faculty members. "The teachers are some of the best in their fields," a sophomore says. "The reason professors are here is to teach, that's it. They love teaching and it shows in the quality of the classes." Ninety-nine percent of classes have 25 or fewer students. In lieu of grades, students receive in-depth written evaluations of their work, although they may request grades as well. They must reciprocate with an evaluation of the course and their performance in it. The unusual advising system, a three-person student/faculty team chosen by the advisee, further promotes close contact between students and professors.

Instead of traditional academic departments, the school has three broad resource areas: environmental science, arts and design, and applied human studies.

Students attracted to this quirky academic gem and its unique curriculum tend to be bright and idealistic; many worked with Americorps or traveled the world before beginning school. "There are a tremendous number of students from all over the world, and we all have unique interests," says a junior. COA is predominantly Caucasian, but most students don't report their race. Twenty percent of the students are international students. "Most students get along very well and there is a huge diversity of cultures, religions, countries, beliefs, financial status, and thought," says a freshman. The college's governance system gives students and administrators almost equal voices in how it's run; anyone may voice concerns or vote on policy-change proposals or the hiring of new faculty at the All College Meeting. Students aren't shy about also speaking out on more worldly issues, "from 'students for a free Tibet,' to antiwar protests, to environmental justice, to the global AIDS campaign," says a sophomore. "The whole school is concerned with ongoing environmental and social issues," a sophomore says. "We are moving toward a 'green' campus and are involved in many organizations that work on these issues professionally."

"The reason professors are here is to teach, that's it."

Forty percent of students—freshmen, international students, and upper-class resident advisors—live on campus, while the balance find cozy, inexpensive apartments or houses in the nearby town of Bar Harbor. "The dorms are super comfortable, from the new, spacious Blair/Tyson, to the eccentric, ocean-view, bay-windowed Sea Fox. Peach House houses only eight people—it's a little cabin in the woods," a junior says.

Students attracted to this quirky academic gem and its unique curriculum tend to be bright and idealistic; many worked with Americorps or traveled the world before beginning school.

Though the tiny tourist town of Bar Harbor is packed with visitors during the warmer months, it largely shuts down in the winter. One junior admits, "It's nice to have the town to ourselves." A sophomore adds, "Bar Harbor is nice, but the whole island is one of the best places to go to school in the world." Students get to know the townspeople through the required 30 hours of community service. "People do lots of stuff for local organizations, including work on farms, parks, the Downeast AIDS Network, and the YMCA," says a student. On weekends, few students leave campus, since Portland, the nearest urban center, is three hours away. Campus social functions revolve around nature and the seasons, including biking, hiking, boating, cross-country skiing, skating, and rock climbing, often in Acadia National Park. There are no fraternities or sororities, and students kick back at off-campus house parties, which are generally alcohol-free. There's no drinking on campus, and it's tough for underage students to get served in town. There are no varsity sports, but about half of the students sign up for the intramural program, which offers sports such as cricket, ice hockey, kayaking, and soccer.

The College of the Atlantic is a place where Earth Day really is a cause for celebration, where students ride nude through the cafeteria and on nearby streets during Bike Week, and where everyone from stu- **"We are moving toward** dents to trustees jumps into frigid Frenchman Bay **a 'green' campus."** on the first Friday of the fall term to try to swim from the school's docks to Bar Island. The long snowy winters and shrunken winter population make for an atmosphere that is cozy to some, dreary to others, but the learning opportunities are a bright spot to many. "The whole program is special. You won't find it anywhere else," a sophomore says.

If You Apply To ➤   **COA:** Early decision: Dec. 1, Jan. 10. Regular admissions, financial aid and housing: Feb. 15. Guarantees to meet demonstrated need for four years. Campus interviews: recommended, evaluative. Alumni interviews: optional, informational. SAT I or ACT: optional. SAT IIs: optional. Accepts the Common Application and electronic applications. Essay question: essay on any topic (five suggested topics are provided). Looks for students committed to improving the quality of life on Earth.

Auburn University

202 Mary Martin Hall, Auburn, AL 36849-5111

Sweet Home Alabama, where the skies are so blue and the spirit of football lasts year-round. Auburn was once called Alabama Polytechnic, and today AU's programs in engineering, agriculture, and the health fields are still among its best.

Auburn University may be home to more than 20,000 football-crazy students, but students quickly learn they're here for more than games. Once known as Alabama Polytechnic, Auburn is a public land grant university that still excels in professional and technical fields such as architecture, engineering, and agriculture. But the school also welcomes students with warm and cozy hospitality and charm. "The students at Auburn are extremely friendly. It's one of the things we're known for," says one junior. "In general, students also really care about the university and love being part of the Auburn family."

The town of Auburn, which grew up amid miles of forest and farmland largely to serve the university, is depicted in an Oliver Goldsmith poem as the "loveliest village of the plain." The campus stretches for nearly 2,000 acres, graced by mossy trees, lush lawns, and majestic colonnades. Most buildings are redbrick and Georgian in style with some more modern facilities grouped in a compact central location. Recent additions include the Jule Collins Smith Museum of Fine Art and the 71,500-square-foot Vaughan Large Animal Teaching Hospital. Other recent enhancements include a four-story center for science labs and a new airport terminal building for aviation students. "It's great to see the campus and the student body grow," says one senior, but another adds, "Stop building things and make more parking."

Auburn's core curriculum requires six semester hours of composition; six semester hours each of history, literature, and social sciences; three semester hours each of

Website: www.auburn.edu
Location: Small town
Total Enrollment: 19,720
Undergraduates: 17,416
Male/Female: 52/48
SAT Ranges: V 500-600
M 510-610
ACT Range: 22–26
Financial Aid: 34%
Expense: Pub $
Phi Beta Kappa: Yes
Applicants: 12,827
Accepted: 84%
Enrolled: 33%
Grad in 6 Years: 65%
Returning Freshmen: 85%
Academics: ✑ ✑
Social: ☎ ☎ ☎
Q of L: ★ ★ ★

(Continued)

Admissions: (334) 844-4080
Email Address:
  admissions@auburn.edu

Strongest Programs:
Information Technology
Biological Sciences
Software Engineering
Computer Science
Agriculture

The Samuel Ginn College of Engineering has an excellent aerospace engineering department and has graduated six NASA astronauts.

The Pedestrian Campus Project includes the closing of several streets on campus to vehicular traffic to encourage walking and use of the university transit system.

The College of Veterinary Medicine is home to the Southeastern Raptor Rehabilitation Center.

philosophy and fine arts; three semester hours of math; and eight semester hours of a lab science. "We are very competitive. Most of our academic departments prove to be very challenging," warns a junior. To ease the transition, freshmen undergo the three-day "Camp War Eagle" session and transfer students spend a day in orientation. The academic climate varies by department, and students say it runs the gamut from easy to difficult. "Auburn has a fairly laid-back climate, though certain courses can be rigorous," says a student.

Many Auburn students are eager to get started on their careers, so the co-op program, which provides pay and credit in several professional fields, is increasingly popular. Auburn has also established a first-of-its-kind program in wireless engineering for students who want to design network hardware or software for cell phones and other mobile devices. Students also give high marks to the colleges of human science and of business, though they say the liberal arts suffer from a lack of funding and the perception that they're less useful than other majors after graduation. Seven areas designated as Peaks of Excellence compete for millions of dollars in special funding; these include cell and molecular biosciences, food safety, fisheries and allied aquacultures, and forest sustainability. The quality of teaching varies. "Most freshmen are taught by TAs. The quality of education increases as a student progresses in their curriculum," a junior says.

"The students at Auburn are extremely friendly. It's one of the things we're known for."

Sixty-seven percent of Auburn students are Alabama natives, and many are legacies—the second or third generation in their families to attend the school. African Americans account for 8 percent of the student body, Hispanics and Asian Americans add 1 and 2 percent, respectively, and nearly 2 percent are Native American or foreign. The conservative tone of this Bible Belt campus makes it hospitable for many Christian groups, and Auburn is home to one of the largest chapters in the United States of the Campus Crusade for Christ. Students are also among the friendliest you'll find anywhere, and a public relations major—already using his hard-won knowledge—claims, "Auburn women are probably the best-looking in the South!" Each year, the university awards hundreds of merit scholarships and 361 athletic scholarships in seven men's sports and nine women's sports.

Auburn's 25 dorms are single-sex, and visiting hours are restricted to weekends. Fourteen of the halls have been renovated, but only 16 percent of the students live in them. "Get on a waiting list ASAP," advises a junior. First-year students compete on a first-come, first-served basis with returning students. Eighteen percent of Auburn men join fraternities, and 31 percent of the women join sororities, perhaps because chapters get space in the best dorms. There are food courts at each end of campus and dining facilities in the Foy Student Union as well. Students generally give low marks to the diversity of the menu and accessibility of the facilities, but as one student explains, "You can't accommodate everyone."

"The best road trips are Atlanta, Florida, and the Gulf Coast beaches."

Aside from sporting events and fraternity parties, Auburn sponsors concerts, free movies, and plenty of intramural sports. "Auburn does not have much of a social life," says a junior. "Though there are some fun events that happen on campus, such as Tiger Nights. The best road trips are Atlanta, Florida, and the Gulf Coast beaches." The campus is officially dry, except on game days, and students say the alcohol policy is enforced. Long-standing traditions include the Burn the (Georgia) Bulldogs Parade and Hey Day, when everyone wears a nametag and walks around saying, "Hey!"

Auburn is a football powerhouse, and on fall Saturdays, 86,000 screaming fans turn the place into Alabama's fourth-largest city. The rallying cry "Warrrrr Eagle!"

reverberates each time an Auburn back runs to daylight. Whenever there's a Tiger victory, regardless of the sport, Toomer's Corner (in downtown Auburn) will surely be rolled in toilet paper. The annual Auburn–Alabama football game is known as the Iron Bowl, and "you can't fully understand it until you have been here on game day," says a senior. "It is so much more than a sports event," attracting 150,000 rabid fans, only half of whom actually get into the stadium. The Tigers football squad went undefeated in 2004–05, a rare accomplishment that nearly earned the school a share of the national title. The men's and women's swimming teams brought home SEC championships in 2004 and 2005. The McWhorter Center for Women's Athletics is one of the finest gymnastics training facilities in the country, and intramural programs are numerous and popular.

Auburn is working hard to increase the caliber of its students and academic programs, and especially to achieve a top 20 national ranking for its college of engineering. "Auburn has become more focused on the future," one senior says. But students say certain key characteristics have stayed the same—and that's a good thing. Says one student, "Auburn students believe in the traditions of the university."

If You Apply To ➤ **Auburn:** Rolling admissions. Early decision: Nov. 1. Early action: Aug. 1. Financial aid: Mar. 1. Does not guarantee to meet demonstrated need. Campus interviews: optional, informational. No alumni interviews. SATs or ACTs: required. SAT IIs: optional. Prefers electronic applications. Out-of-state enrollment is capped on a year-to-year basis; there are no set limits. No essay question.

Austin College

900 N. Grand Avenue, Sherman, TX 75090

The second-most famous institution in Texas with Austin in its name. Half the size of Trinity (Texas), runs neck-in-neck with Southwestern to be the leading Texas college with fewer than 2,000 students. Combines the liberal arts with strong programs in business, education, and the health fields.

Not everything in Texas has to be big to be good. Austin College has only 1,300 students, a stark contrast to the Lone Star State's famed focus on enormity. Only an hour away from the 10-gallon hats and gleaming skyscrapers of Dallas, Austin College is a small but warm institution where students know their professors personally and have a broad array of majors to choose from. AC's preprofessional programs, most notably premed, are among the strongest in the state. Professors here even serve students breakfast at 10 p.m. the night before finals. It's just another example of the personal style that is typical of this charming Southern institution.

Austin's 65-acre campus is in a residential area in the city of Sherman. The campus is designed in the traditional quadrangle style and comprises beige sandstone buildings, tree-lined plazas, decorative fountains, and an impressive 70-ton sculptured solstice calendar. Dorms are conveniently located approximately 200 yards from most classrooms, which eases the pain of first-period classes. New additions to campus include the Jackson Technology Center and the Roo Suites residence halls, which house 152 students in four-person suites.

Austin College is "very relaxed," but "the courses demand a high level of self-discipline," a freshman says. Adds a sophomore, "The courses are demanding and rigorous but manageable." The core curriculum begins with a freshman seminar

Website:
www.austincollege.edu
Location: Small town
Total Enrollment: 1,314
Undergraduates: 1,279
Male/Female: 44/56
SAT Ranges: V 570–670
M 570–670
ACT Range: 23–28
Financial Aid: 59%
Expense: Pr $
Phi Beta Kappa: Yes
Applicants: 1,475
Accepted: 69%
Enrolled: 36%
Grad in 6 Years: 74%
Returning Freshmen: 85%

Academics: 🖉 🖉 🖉
Social: ☎ ☎ ☎
Q of L: ★ ★ ★
Admissions: (903) 813-3000
Email Address:
admission@austincollege
.edu

Strongest Programs:
Biology
Chemistry/Biochemistry
Political Science/International
    Studies
Psychology
Business Administration
English
History

The Jordan Language House boards 48 students studying French, German, Japanese, and Spanish, along with a native speaker of each language, and students have to speak the language in all common areas.

called Communication/Inquiry. Each professor who teaches the course becomes the mentor for the 20 freshmen in his or her class. Next is a three-course sequence on the Heritage of Western Culture. Then students select from courses in three categories in humanities, social, and natural sciences. Nearly three-quarters of all classes have 25 students or fewer and no class has more than 100.

Preprofessional areas are Austin College's specialties. When it comes time to apply to grad school, premed and predental students at this little college have one of the highest acceptance rates of any Texas school, and aspiring lawyers also do well. AC's five-year teaching program grants students both a bachelor's and a master's degree. Science and education receive high marks from students, as do international studies, political science and foreign languages, but business administration is the most popular major. The Jordan Language House boards 48 students studying French, German, Japanese, and Spanish, along with a native speaker of each language, and students have to speak the language in all common areas. Students can combine three of the school's 26 majors into an interdisciplinary degree. Students must complete one major and a minor or a double major to graduate. A cooperative engineering program links the college with other schools. Majors in environmental studies and an international relations track of political science have been added while international studies and policy studies majors have been dropped. A minor in Southwestern/Mexican studies has been added.

> "The courses are demanding and rigorous but manageable."

The college also offers its students independent study, directed research, junior year abroad, and departmental honors programs. The Leadership Institute is open to just 15 students of each entering class, and five more can get in after their first year. Participating students enjoy a suite of privileges. Austin also provides three research areas in Grayson County. Students can focus on just one course during the January term, and many use that time to study abroad.

Ninety percent of Austin students hail from the Lone Star State. Hispanics and African Americans comprise 10 and 4 percent of the student body, respectively, and Asian Americans make up 10 percent. Students say there is a wide range of political views on campus. Austin has been tied to the Presbyterian Church in the United States since 1849; this affiliation manifests itself in the emphasis on values in the core courses, participation in service activities, and limited residence-hall visitation hours—a chief complaint of students. AC offers more than 450 merit scholarships worth an average of $8,021.

As for dorm life, there are six residence halls, and 72 percent of undergraduates live in traditional dorm housing. "Dorms are very well kept and you are guaranteed housing for three years, after that it's 'find your own place' or hope someone will not show up," a junior says. One dorm is co-ed, one houses language studies students, one is men-only, and two are women-only. Dean (the only co-ed residence hall) seems to be a popular choice for freshmen, despite (or perhaps because of) its reputation as being loud and social. Others say Clyce is the best bet for freshman women. Residence hall access is computerized, and students say safety is not an issue. Nearly all students take advantage of the three-meal-a-day plan, though not all take advantage of the all-you-can-eat option. "The dining facilities are good, though sometimes the food becomes monotonous," a sophomore says. The Pouch Club, an on-campus joint, serves pizza, burgers, beer and wine for those students 21 and over.

Most of the social life is either on or near campus, with the Greeks taking the lion's share of credit. Thirty percent of the men and 30 percent of the women belong to fraternities and sororities, but the Greeks are not school-funded and are not allowed to advertise off-campus parties without the college's permission. Not everyone depends on the Greek system for a good time. Students get an eyeful during the Baker Bun Run, in which the men of Baker Hall strip to their boxers and cavort around the campus on the Monday night before finals. There are spring and fall festivals, and the Final Blowout party before finals. Students can have alcohol in dorm rooms only if they are 21 or older, and school policy prohibits booze at campus organization events. Popular weekend excursions are a drive to Dallas or to the college's 28-acre recreational spot on Lake

"The dining facilities are good, though sometimes the food becomes monotonous."

Texoma (a half-hour north). Sherman is "quaint" and "historic," and is becoming a better college town, students say. "There are lots of restaurants," a junior says, "but for the most part there is nothing to do late at night."

Dorms are conveniently located approximately 200 yards from most classrooms, which eases the pain of first-period classes.

Even without athletic scholarships, varsity sports are generating increasing support. The school's teams compete in Division III, and the women's volleyball team won a recent division championship. The Robert T. Mason Athletic/Recreation Complex provides facilities for student athletes and the fitness-conscious. There's also an intramural program, with basketball, softball, flag football, and lacrosse proving popular.

"AC is awesome because it's small and comfortable," a senior says. "The professors are incredibly approachable and helpful." The preprofessional programs are among the academic strengths at this college with roots in the Presbyterian Church. And while Sherman may be a sleepy little place, Austin College certainly isn't.

Overlaps

University of Texas–Austin, Southwestern, Baylor, Trinity University, Texas A&M, Texas Christian

If You Apply To ➤	**Austin:** Early decision: Dec. 1. Early action: Jan. 15. Regular admissions: Mar. 1. Financial aid: Apr. 1. Housing: May 1. Campus and alumni interviews: recommended, evaluative. SATs or ACTs: required. SAT IIs: optional. Accepts the Common Application and electronic applications. Essay question: significant experience, achievement, risk, or ethical dilemma; important issue; influential person; influential character, historical figure, or creative work: experience that shows what you would bring to college's diversity or showed you the importance of diversity; topic of your choice.

Babson College

Babson Park, MA 02457-0310

The only college in the *Fiske Guide* devoted entirely to business. Only 14 miles from College Student Mecca, a.k.a. Boston, and tougher to get into now than at any time in its history. The one college in Massachusetts where it is possible to be a Republican with head held high.

The budding corporate leaders who choose Babson College can be summed up in a single word: focused. They're already committed to business careers, and some arrive on campus with their own ventures up and running. Once school starts, they work hard, put their social lives second, and "are determined to be successful," says a sophomore. "Many students are perfectionists, and not easily satisfied." Hands-on experience is the norm; students get school funding to start businesses during their first years, and may hone their stock-picking skills by managing part of the college's endowment. Sound like a four-year stint on Donald Trump's reality show, The Apprentice? For the budding tycoons and entrepreneurs from around the globe who choose Babson, that's the reason they're here.

Founded in 1919, the college sits on 370 acres near the sedate Boston suburb of Wellesley. The tract features open green spaces, gently rolling hills, and heavily

Website: www.babson.edu
Location: Suburban
Total Enrollment: 3,288
Undergraduates: 1,697
Male/Female: 60/40
SAT Ranges: V 560–640
  M 600–690
ACT Range: 26-28
Financial Aid: 40%
Expense: Pr $ $ $
Phi Beta Kappa: No

(Continued)

Applicants: 3,064
Accepted: 36%
Enrolled: 37%
Grad in 6 Years: 85%
Returning Freshmen: 93%
Academics: ✍ ✍ ✍
Social: ☎ ☎
Q of L: ★ ★ ★
Admissions: (781) 239-5522
Email Address:
  ugradadmission@babson
  .edu

Strongest Programs:
Accounting
Economics
Entrepreneurship
Finance
International Business
Marketing
Management

Students say social life at Babson is on campus during the first two years; after that, most students are 21 and have cars, so they head to the clubs and bars of Boston proper, about 20 minutes away.

wooded areas. Buildings are gently shaded and parking lots (filled with expensive foreign cars) are relatively hidden. Architecturally, the campus is mainly neo-Georgian and modern. Several dorms and the admissions office have recently been renovated, and two new dining facilities—Jazzman's Café and Pandini's Italian bistro—provide students with tasty meals.

Although Babson is a business school, about half of students' classes are in the liberal arts, and in 2002, Babson won the Hesburgh Award for curricular innovation. General education requirements emphasize rhetoric (public speaking); ethics and social responsibility; international and multicultural perspectives; and leadership, teamwork, and creativity. In the Foundation Management Experience, students are split into groups of 30 to develop business plans; each group gets up to $3,000 in seed money from the college to get their concept up and running. At year-end, the business is liquidated, and profits go to charity. Recently, FME groups have developed Babsonopoly (a Babson-themed version of Monopoly), opened a Krispy Kreme Doughnuts franchise, and sold customized fleece blankets. "There are 14 businesses all around campus, all trying to sell to the same 1,700 students," says a sophomore. "That's competitive, but it gives us real-world experience."

"Many students are perfectionists, and not easily satisfied."

All Babson students major in business and then select a concentration, such as management, finance, or marketing—or even gender studies or literary and visual arts. (The Sorenson Visual Arts Center has painting, ceramics, and sculpture studios, labs for photography and digital art, a student art gallery, and workspace for artists-in-residence.) The entrepreneurship program is one of Babson's strongest, bringing in venture capitalists and executives (from companies such as Dunkin' Donuts and Jiffy Lube) for how-to lectures. Courses are rigorous and most are small. "Not only textbook: teamwork," says a junior. For projects, students can use more than 250 workstations dotting five computer labs or their brand-new IBM laptops, which are included with tuition. Since the computers are leased, upgrades are guaranteed after two years.

In the classroom, Babson relies on the case-study approach more typically employed by MBA programs. (At 60/40, the school's lopsided male/female ratio is also more similar to those of MBA programs than those at undergraduate business schools.) In the case method, students break into groups or act as officers of pseudo corporations to address specific business situations and solve marketplace problems. Professors teach all courses, and a junior says most have 10 to 20 years of experience in their fields. Accounting students may take graduate classes at Babson in the summer and fall after finishing their bachelor's degrees, letting them sit for the CPA exam about one year earlier than most other programs. Babson offers 30 study abroad programs in 19 countries, as well as the Semester at Sea.* Students can go away for an entire semester or the two-week winter session, and not all programs are business-focused; the London Theatre Program, for example, focuses on arts appreciation.

Babson has partnered with the Posse Foundation to help increase diversity on campus, welcoming 10 Posse scholars from urban public high schools in the Class of 2008. Still, the campus remains largely white and wealthy, with African Americans making up 3 percent of the student body, Hispanics 5 percent, and Asian Americans 7 percent. Foreign students comprise about 17 percent and 44 percent are Caucasian. Twenty-one percent of Babson students are Massachusetts natives. "I call Babson the mini–United Nations because we have representation from so many countries," says a junior. "People are conservative, yet trendy in dress, and very accepting." No one seems to care about politics, but students do want to end the self-segregation of various ethnic and racial groups on campus. Merit scholarships are available but there are no athletic scholarships.

Babson guarantees housing for four years, and 83 percent of undergraduates live on campus, resulting in high demand for singles and suites. Dorms are air-conditioned and carpeted, and most upper-class rooms have their own bathrooms. Most halls are co-ed, but one dorm is reserved for men, and floors and wings of other buildings are reserved for women. After the first year, the large rooms are assigned by lottery, and standing is based on credits earned. "You can easily switch rooms if you are not happy," says a junior. At the main dining hall, you'll find sushi and make your own stir fry stations; every Wednesday is gourmet night, and the menu may include fresh lobster, Italian specialties, or turkey with all the trimmings.

Students say social life at Babson is on campus during the first two years; after that, most students are 21 and have cars, so they head to the clubs and bars of Boston proper, about 20 minutes away. (It helps that many upperclassmen do not have class on Fridays.) For those who aren't of age, or who lack wheels, the Campus Activities Board brings in comedians and organizes parties, as do Greek organizations, which attract 10 percent of the women and men. The school also sponsors trips to Celtics and Red Sox games. If you're caught with booze while underage, or sent to the hospital because of overindulgence, you get one strike; rack up two more, and you're out of the dorms. Popular road trips include the beaches of Cape Cod and Martha's Vineyard, the ski slopes of Vermont and New Hampshire, and the bright lights of New York City and Montreal.

The "very affluent" town of Wellesley has shops and restaurants and there is a subway stop. Students can take the T's Green Line into the city to explore Quincy Market, Fanueil Hall, or the campuses of Harvard, Northeastern, Emerson and Boston University. Wellesley is also home to Wellesley College, and it's not uncommon for Babson students to socialize with Wellesley women; Babson also offers crossregistration at Wellesley, Brandeis, and the Olin College of Engineering. Favorite campus festivals

> **"People are very conservative, yet trendy in dress, and very accepting."**

include homecoming (great networking opportunities), Oktoberfest, and Winter and Spring Weekends, when bands come to play and parties are thrown. April 8 is Founders Day, and classes are cancelled so everyone can celebrate entrepreneurship.

While making money may be the most popular "sport" at Babson, students recognize the importance of keeping their bodies in competitive condition, too. Popular intramural sports include volleyball, rugby and ice hockey, and on the varsity level, the Beavers play in NCAA Division III. Any match against archrival Bentley and soccer games against Brandeis and Colby draw crowds, and the baseball and men's basketball teams brought home conference titles in 2004. In 2002 and 2003, the upper athletic fields were completely renovated and improved.

If Babson College students have one complaint, it's the workload. "However, the benefits far exceed the load and so do the three-day weekends," rationalizes a junior. But perhaps that's the point. After all, learning how to balance work with everything else that's important in life is a prerequisite to climbing the corporate ladder. And thanks to small classes, a laser-like focus on all things financial, and plenty of hands-on experience, students leave Babson well equipped to begin scampering up those rungs—without once being subjected to The Donald's hair.

Although Babson is a business school, about half of students' classes are in the liberal arts, and in 2002, Babson won the Hesburgh Award for curricular innovation.

Overlaps

Bentley, Boston University, Boston College, NYU, University of Pennsylvania, Carnegie Mellon

If You Apply To ➤ **Babson:** Early decision and early action: Nov. 15. Regular admissions: Jan. 15. Meets demonstrated need of 91%. Campus and alumni interviews: recommended, evaluative. SATs or ACTs: required. SAT IIs: recommended (writing and math Ic or IIc). Accepts the Common Application and electronic applications. Essay questions: Common Application essay and a letter to your first-year Babson roommate, explaining what it will be like to live with you, why you chose Babson, and what you most look forward to in college.

Bard College

Annandale-on-Hudson, NY 12504

Welcome to Nonconformity-Central-on-Hudson. Like Reed on the West Coast, Bard combines unabashed individuality with rigorous traditional academics. More selective than Hampshire and with a better male/female ratio than Sarah Lawrence, Bard is an up-and-comer among the nontraditional liberal arts colleges.

Website: www.bard.edu
Location: Rural
Total Enrollment: 1,688
Undergraduates: 1,465
Male/Female: 48/52
SAT Ranges: V 650–750
  M 590–690
Financial Aid: 62%
Expense: Pr $ $ $ $
Phi Beta Kappa: No
Applicants: 3,367
Accepted: 38%
Enrolled: 29%
Grad in 6 Years: 68%
Returning Freshmen: 86%
Academics: ✏ ✏ ✏ ✏
Social: ☎ ☎ ☎
Q of L: ★ ★ ★ ★
Admissions: (845) 758-7472
Email Address:
  admission@bard.edu

Strongest Programs:
Political Science
Economics
Human Rights
Fine Arts
Social Sciences
Literature and Languages

Bard College has come a long way since its 1860 founding, by 12 men studying to enter the seminaries of the Episcopal Church. Those pioneers would no doubt be surprised at the eclectic mix of students now running around Annandale-on-Hudson. "Bard students were the 'weird kids' in high school, and many struggle their first year, when they realize everyone is just as unique as they are, and no one cares what kind of radical statement they are trying to make, because it's not revolutionary when everyone is trying to be different," says a senior. The idea that Bard is strictly a school for artists and social studies majors is slowly disappearing, and the result is a school with lots of intellectual depth—and a higher national profile.

Bard's campus occupies 600 well-landscaped acres in upstate New York's Washington Irving country. There's no prevailing architectural theme, so each ivy-covered brick building stands out—especially the dorms, which range from cottages in the woods to Russian Colonial in style. Renowned architect Frank Gehry designed the $62 million Fisher Center for the Performing Arts, which opened in 2003. The 110,00-square-foot facility includes two theaters, and rehearsal and teaching space for Bard's theater and dance programs. The chemistry department has suffered from a lack of up-to-date facilities, but that should change with a new building on the drawing board from another renowned architect, Rafael Vinoly.

Despite Bard's reputation for nonconformism, the list of requirements is extensive. Freshmen show up three weeks before classes start for the Workshop in Language and Thinking, where they read extensively in several genres, and meet in small groups to discuss reading and writing. (A literature major calls L&T "the best three weeks of my life.") Students then take the two-semester First-Year Seminar, which introduces the intellectual, artistic, and cultural ideas at the core of a liberal arts education. At the end of the second year, students write their educational autobiography and declare a major; the autobiography is more like a proposal, presented for discussion to a board of professors in the relevant area. During the junior year, students take a tutorial to prepare for their senior project—while some students run and report on a scientific experiment, or complete a 100- to 300-page critical review of literary works, others write a play or novel or compose a piece of music, and still others organize a show of their own art, or choreograph a dance performance.

> **"Bard is great for motivated students who take their education into their own hands."**

Bard's academic climate is "intellectual and consistently challenging," says a senior. "Bard is great for motivated students who take their education into their own hands." Ninety percent of classes have 25 or fewer students, and if students want more individual attention, they can devise a syllabus for their own course and find a professor to sponsor it. Bard also considers visual and performing arts as equal to other academic disciplines; as a result, photography is one of the toughest majors to get into. There are no teaching assistants here, and the school "students tend to know who the good professors are and rush to take classes with them." With authors such as John Ashbery, Ann Lauterbach, Mark Danner, and Elizabeth Frank teaching creative writing at Bard, literature is among the school's best programs.

Film and political science also draw praise. Each fall, science majors may take a class on human disease at New York City's Rockefeller University, which also reserves spots for Bard students as Summer Undergraduate Research Fellows. The distinguished-scientist scholars program offers full tuition to top applicants who plan to major in science or math.

Bard has established what administrators believe is the first collegiate program in human rights, which should improve the sociology major, while the new Vinoly building will strengthen the chemistry major. A five-year, dual-degree conservatory program for music students began in 2005; Bard began offering a master of arts in teaching in 2004. Though Bard is far from preprofessional, it does offer combined programs with other schools in engineering, architecture, city planning, social work, public health, business and public administration, forestry, and environmental science. Study abroad is available in Russia, China, Greece, India, Senegal, and South Africa; there are also language programs in France, Germany, Italy, or

"If you like the woods, it's amazing."

Mexico. Those interested in globalization and international affairs may participate in a residential Bard program in New York City, headquartered near Lincoln Center. The Trustee Leader Scholar program provides grants and support for student-run community service projects.

Bardians take pride in diversity, whether racial, geographical (only a quarter are New Yorkers) or ideological, though they admit the latter can be lacking. "Bard students are highly motivated, creative, independent, and intellectual," says a senior. Another student adds, "If you're a Republican or conservative, please come and add some dimension to our conversation. I'm sick of agreeing with everyone." African Americans make up 3 percent of the student body, while Hispanics and Asian Americans add 5 percent each. Bard offers 24 academic scholarships, ranging from $5,000 a year to full tuition, but no athletic awards. Under the Excellence and Equal Cost program, qualified high school students may apply to attend Bard for the price of a public-school education in their home state. About 200 students vie for the program's 25 available slots.

Eighty-one percent of Bard students live on campus, and freshmen are required to do so. Residence halls "vary from small, quiet dorms to large, community-oriented buildings," says a theater major. A classmate adds, "Some are old Victorian mansions, some are new modern buildings that are eco-friendly, one looks like a castle, and others are big cement monsters from the 1950s." Bard still has dorms where smoking is allowed, and the cafeteria, Kline, caters to vegetarians and vegans. Room draw can be chaotic, and since juniors and seniors are not guaranteed beds on campus, many upperclassmen move off campus. To help ease their commute, Bard runs a shuttle to the nearby towns of Red Hook and Tivoli. "Tivoli is home to a variety of restaurants (sushi, Mexican, and Cajun), a few bars (the most popular is the Black Swan), a bookstore and a laundromat," says one student. "Red Hook is home to the Golden Wok (take-out Chinese, a student favorite), the Curry House, grocery stores, Mexican food, and more."

Social life at Bard is almost an afterthought, since New York City is just two to three hours by train. The school does offer concerts and movies, with indie films and alternative rock and hip-hop particularly popular. The Student Activities Board plans Urban Cowboy Night, the Valentine's Day Swing Dance, and Spring Fling, though there are no fraternities or sororities. To the dismay of many, the annual Drag Race party—a celebration of sexuality—has been cancelled, and en masse crossdressing on Parents Weekend is no longer the norm. When it comes to alcohol, policies are focused on safety and respect. "Bard is very liberal," says a student, "but I believe that the administration is trying to stop underage drinking." Bard's hometown of Annandale-on-Hudson is 20 miles from the crafts and antiques meccas of Woodstock and

Despite Bard's reputation for nonconformism, the list of requirements is extensive.

perhaps

A third of the students get involved in intramurals, such as floor hockey, bowling, and table tennis, which emphasize participation and fun.

Rhinebeck, and not much farther from the ski slopes of the Catskills and the Berkshires. Having a car helps to prevent occasional attacks of claustrophobia.

Teams compete in the Division III North East Atlantic Conference. Bard is virtually devoid of dedicated jocks, but one student notes, "There are plenty of pseudo jocks and intellectuals in good shape." A third of the students get involved in intramurals, such as floor hockey, bowling, and table tennis, which emphasize participation and fun. Close to campus, five miles of trails stretch through the woods along the Hudson, perfect for everything from raspberry picking to jogging and hiking. "If you like the woods, it's amazing," sighs an anthropology major. "If you like the city, you'll go stir-crazy."

Bard College isn't for everyone, but thanks to the iconoclastic vision of President Leon Botstein, also erstwhile conductor of the American and Jerusalem symphonies, it now offers strong programs in more than just the arts. "If you show that you have interests, and that you pursue them actively and can explain in an articulate manner what is important to you, Bard will accept you," one student explains. "You don't need perfect grades. You just need an adventurous spirit, an ambitious attitude toward self-improvement, and an ability to evaluate your experiences and capabilities."

Overlaps

NYU, Wesleyan, Oberlin, Vassar, Reed, Sarah Lawrence

If You Apply To ➤

Bard: Early action: Nov. 1. Regular admissions: Jan. 15. Financial aid: March 1. Meets demonstrated need of 90%. Campus interviews: optional, informational. No alumni interviews. SATs and ACTs: optional. SAT IIs: optional. Accepts the Common Application. Essay question: personal, local or national issue of concern; and one of the following: what you do between when school ends in the afternoon and when you go to sleep; the topic and outcome of your last argument; describe a typical meal shared with the people you consider your family.

Barnard College

New York, NY 10027

With applications running double what they were 10 years ago, Barnard has eclipsed Wellesley as the nation's most popular women's college. Barnard women are a little more artsy and a bit more city-ish than their female counterparts at Columbia College. Step outside and you're on Broadway.

Website: www.barnard.edu
Location: Urban
Total Enrollment: 2,287
Undergraduates: 2,287
Male/Female: 0/100
SAT Ranges: V 650–730
    M 620–700
ACT Range: 28–31
Financial Aid: 56%
Expense: Pr $ $ $
Phi Beta Kappa: Yes
Applicants: 4,380
Accepted: 27%
Enrolled: 46%
Grad in 6 Years: 89%
Returning Freshmen: 96%

Barnard students get the best of both worlds—the small, close-knit atmosphere of a liberal arts school, along with the limitless opportunities of Columbia College, the Ivy League research institution just across the street. Whether they are passionate about art and music or urban studies and politics, women seeking a high-energy environment with top-notch academics are likely to find a niche here. "With Barnard women, I can discuss Van Gogh's importance in the scheme of 19th-century art and then move on to debate whether or not Lars Von Trier is misogynistic or not," says one first-year at this New York City women's college.

Barnard's campus is on the Upper West Side of Manhattan, in the Morningside Heights neighborhood. It's just blocks from Riverside Drive, which has a lovely path parallel to the Hudson River for running, biking, or rollerblading. Trees and other greenery shade grand prewar apartment buildings, and grassy medians break up the wide expanse of Broadway itself. Barnard's architecturally diverse buildings are more modern than Columbia's, and in recent years, the college has invested to upgrade labs, classrooms, animal research facilities, and the residence halls with new bathrooms, heat and air-conditioning systems, elevators, and windows. Several classrooms have also been upgraded with multimedia capabilities, a new state-of-the-art organic chemistry lab was built. A campus master plan has been commissioned to focus on future space and building needs.

Barnard's requirements are designed to reflect the changing nature of our technological society, and the fact that graduates are increasingly pursuing law, business, and other professions rather than academic careers. To that end, students take two first-year foundation courses and fulfill nine "area requirements" in reason and value, social analysis, historical studies, cultures in comparison, laboratory science, quantitative and deductive reasoning, language, literature, and the visual and performing arts. Students must also take two physical education courses, though most get plenty of exercise running for the bus or dashing up and down subway stairs.

While curricular requirements guarantee Barnard graduates have intellectual breadth, the mandatory senior thesis project or comprehensive examination ensures academic depth. Barnard students may crossregister at Columbia if they find more courses of interest there, or enroll in graduate courses in any of Columbia's schools. Dual-degree

"I think all departments are strong, and there is a department for everybody."

and joint-degree programs are also available with Columbia and the Jewish Theological Seminary, and music students may also take classes at Juilliard and the Manhattan School of Music. Another innovative program offers women the chance to concentrate on dance, music, theater, visual arts, or writing—while also completing a degree in liberal arts. The school also offers study abroad opportunities at Oxford, Cambridge, the University of London, and other institutions in England, France, Germany, Italy, Japan, and other countries around the world.

Barnard's most popular majors are psychology, English, economics, political science and art history, all of which happen to be among the school's best departments. Also well-subscribed are biology (there's a healthy contingent of premeds) and history. "I think all departments are strong, and there is a department for everybody," says one enthusiastic student. "While renowned for our English and political science departments, even lesser-known areas, such as American studies, have phenomenal professors who truly care about their students," boasts a peer. Women's studies and education also draw praise, though students in these programs must also choose another major. The administration cites statistics and linguistics as weaker programs.

Many students come to Barnard because of its low student/faculty ratio. Seventy percent of classes taken by first-years have no more than 25 students. Another plus: Barnard has no graduate teaching assistants. In fact, Barnard professors enjoy Columbia's proximity almost as much as undergraduates, and each year one-third of the full-time faculty teaches in graduate departments throughout the university. Still, faculty members focus on their teaching responsibilities first. "These are people who, in typical Barnard fashion, are not just amazing educators, but all-around wildly successful people in their individual fields, and are more like Renaissance men (and women) than teachers," says one student. Undergraduate research is also a priority at Barnard. The Centennial Scholars program allows students to conduct extensive research under the guidance of a faculty member for up to three semesters. The innovative Mentor Center program matches students with alumnae who have agreed to help with internships and career advisement.

Thirty-three percent of Barnard students are New York natives, including a sizable contingent from the East Side of Manhattan, and 48 percent attended private high school. A whopping 93 percent ranked in the top quarter of their high school class. Asian Americans make up 17 percent of the student body, while African Americans add 5 percent and Hispanics make up another 7 percent. Barnard now competes head-to-head with Columbia in admissions, an interesting dilemma because Barnard is just another division of Columbia University, similar to the engineering school, the medical school, the business school—or Columbia College. In general, women looking for

(Continued)

Academics: 🖊 🖊 🖊 🖊 🖊

Social: ☎ ☎ ☎

Q of L: ★ ★ ★

Admissions: (212) 854-2014

Email Address:
admissions@barnard.edu

Strongest Programs:
Psychology
English
Economics
Political Science
Art History
Biology

Undergraduate research is also a priority at Barnard. The Centennial Scholars program allows students to conduct extensive research under the guidance of a faculty member for up to three semesters.

a more traditional "rah-rah" experience may prefer Columbia. Those seeking flexibility might do better at Barnard, a hotbed of liberalism where students don't shy away from rallies and protests. "Barnard students are known to be creative thinkers, who think 'out of the box,'" a junior says. "They are socially aware, compassionate, passionate, highly intelligent women." Women's rights, the war in Iraq, and race relations are among the issues that have gotten students stirred up recently. Barnard students do share a first-year orientation program with Columbia, where they mix together in small groups and take tours of the campus and city. Students can also take part in a preorientation backpacking trip.

> **"Barnard students are known to be creative thinkers."**

Ninety percent of Barnard students live in the dorms, which have come a long way since the college's beginning as a commuter school: There's an 18-story Barnard dormitory tower, plus one dorm complex and five off-campus apartment buildings; nonresidents must be signed in by a resident, and entries are always guarded, so students say they feel safe. In addition, Barnard shares two co-ed dorms with Columbia. With New York's notoriously high rents and broker fees, demand for dorm beds remains high. The Quad, which houses all first-years, is pretty well-kept, although individual floors, bathrooms, and common areas are "only as clean as the people who use them," according to one student. Seniors get the best rooms through a lottery system, though an undecided major says, "Res life can be very unorganized and difficult to work with." Housing is guaranteed as long as you stay in the dorms; choose to move out for a year, and you may have difficulty getting back in. Dorm-dwellers must buy a meal plan, which may also be used at Columbia's John Jay cafeteria, though students say Barnard's food is better. "Though by no means gourmet, the variety and availability makes up for the mediocre quality," says a senior. "They make provisions for literally every special taste," another senior adds.

When it comes to social life, students tend to divide their time between on campus and off. "RAs build community programming within the residence halls but usually students opt to explore New York," a junior says. Traditions on campus include Midnight Breakfast, the night before finals begin, when deans and administrators serve up eggs and waffles in the gym. Women in the arts are celebrated in the annual Winterfest, while the Books Etc. series brought Barnard alumnae authors like Jhumpa Lahiri '89 and Anna Quindlen '74 back to campus for lectures in the fall of 2003. Less academic pursuits are available, too. "If you still don't like what you see, you can head out to one of the bars in Morningside Heights," a student says. Fake IDs are easy to come by in Manhattan, and while they often work, Barnard students aren't focused on drinking themselves into oblivion. "Because there is so much else to do in NYC, alcohol is not a primary amusement," explains an English and creative writing double major. Many of the city's offerings are free to students with their ID. Road trips are infrequent—as not many students have cars—but when they happen, destinations range from Washington, D.C., to Boston, easily reached by train and plane, to skiing and snowboarding in Vermont, or spring break on the beaches of South Carolina.

> **"Because there is so much else to do in NYC, alcohol is not a primary amusement."**

Barnard athletes compete alongside their peers enrolled at Columbia, and the field hockey, soccer, lacrosse, archery, and crew teams have the largest number of participants. The fencing team is also strong. Columbia's marvelous gym and co-ed intramurals are also available to Barnard women, but many prefer to exercise their minds.

How do students see Barnard? As an "all women's college, located in a prime city, affiliated with a large research institution, with distinguished faculty, alums, and intelligent and driven students," one proud Barnard woman says. For some, the supportive community created by those students and faculty is what makes this a

Traditions on campus include Midnight Breakfast, the night before finals begin, when deans and administrators serve up eggs and waffles in the gym.

Overlaps

NYU, Columbia, Brown, Yale, Vassar, Harvard

special place. "Barnard is different because although the students here are really intelligent, they are also really down to earth, and are supported by each other and the academic community," another student says.

If You Apply To ➤

Barnard: Early decision: Nov. 15. Regular admissions: Jan. 1. Financial aid: Feb. 1. Housing: Second Friday in June. Campus interviews: recommended, evaluative. Alumni interviews: optional, evaluative. SATs or ACTs: required. SAT IIs: writing or literature and two others required with the SAT I, optional with the ACT. Accepts the Common Application. Essay question: significant experience, achievement, or risk; important issue; influential person or character; experience that illustrates what you would add to diversity of college community; topic of your choice.

Bates College

23 Campus Avenue, Lewiston, ME 04240

Bowdoin got rid of its frats, Bates never had them, and therein hangs a tale. With its long-held tradition of egalitarianism, Bates is a kindred spirit to Quaker institutions such as Haverford and Swarthmore. A month-long spring term helps make Bates a leader in studying abroad.

While Bates, Bowdoin, and Colby share a rugged Maine location, a mania for ice hockey, and popularity among prep-schoolers clad in Patagonia and L.L. Bean, Bates has more in common ideologically with Quaker colleges such as Haverford and Swarthmore. Founded by abolitionists in 1855, Bates takes pride in its heritage as a haven for seekers of guidance, freedom, and justice. Its 4–4–1 calendar offers ample opportunity for study abroad, even for just one month at year's end. The school's small size also means student/faculty interaction is plentiful, and close friendships are easily formed.

The Bates campus features a mix of Georgian and Federal buildings and Victorian homes spread out over grassy lawns in the "recovering mill town" of Lewiston, says a biology major. Lewiston is about two and a half hours from Boston, and very close to Maine's picturesque coast. "You can find stuff to do if you look, but you have to look pretty hard," says a sophomore. "Auburn, across the river, is more of a town, with restaurants and shops," another student says. "Community service and volunteering is huge, with Big Brothers, tutoring, and two hospitals within walking distance."

Bates emphasizes the liberal arts, and to graduate, all students must complete a comprehensive exam in the major field, a senior thesis, or both. The Ladd Library is often crowded, as 85 percent of students write a thesis or produce an equivalent research, service, performance, or studio project. Ladd has almost 600,000 volumes, plus an all-night study room, computer labs, and an audio/visual room with everything from Bach to Bruce Springsteen. In their first year, students must

"Community service and volunteering is huge."

satisfy a physical education requirement through intercollegiate or club sports or two 10-week activity courses. Most take first-year seminars, capped at 15 students each. General education requirements include at least three courses in the natural sciences and another three in the social sciences; at least one course that emphasizes quantitative analysis; and at least five courses in the fine arts, music, theater, or a foreign language. Despite the school's size, and the fact that "some courses are more popular than others," it's usually easy to register for most classes. If the one you need is full, professors will usually "let you in on petition," says a senior.

Website: www.bates.edu
Location: Small city
Total Enrollment: 1,743
Undergraduates: 1,743
Male/Female: 48/51
SAT Ranges: V 630–710
  M 640–710
Financial Aid: 40%
Expense: Pr $ $ $ $
Phi Beta Kappa: Yes
Applicants: 4,098
Accepted: 30%
Enrolled: 38%
Grad in 6 Years: 85%
Returning Freshmen: 96%
Academics: ✑ ✑ ✑ ✑ ½
Social: ☎ ☎ ☎
Q of L: ★ ★ ★
Admissions: (207) 786-6000
Email Address:
  admissions@bates.edu

Strongest Programs:
Economics
Biology
Psychology
History
Political Science

While Bates doesn't require standardized tests for admission, don't expect to coast through. "The academic environment at Bates is rather competitive," says a sociology major. "Students really press each other to do the best they can." A senior gives high marks to political science, biology, economics, and psychology, which also happen to be the four most popular majors, and says art is "small, but quite good." Indeed, the music and art departments benefit from the Olin Arts Center, which houses a performance hall, gallery, recording studio, art studios, and practice rooms. Interdisciplinary programs at Bates include American cultural studies, neuroscience, and women and gender studies. A secondary concentration in African American studies was recently added. Professors teach all courses, including lab and discussion sections, and one senior calls them "some of the most incredible people I've ever met."

Bates offers study abroad opportunities in locations such as China, Japan, Croatia, Chile, and Austria, and more than two-thirds of students take advantage of them. The school also participates in the Washington Semester,* the 10-college Venture Program,* and the American Maritime Studies Program at Mystic Seaport*—all attractive options for students seeking real-world experience. Only two short-term courses are required for graduation, though many students take more. After all, who wouldn't want to spend a month studying the Philosophy of Star Trek? Or how about Cult and the Community, which led two students to a five-week tour with the Grateful Dead? The fall semester study abroad program is even open to first-year students, giving them a chance to acclimate to college through home stays and tours with families in other countries.

> **"Students really press each other to do the best they can."**

Eighty-two percent of Bates students come from outside Maine, many from Massachusetts, Connecticut, and New York. "A Bates student is that person in high school who was really well rounded: involved in sports, clubs, community, and did well in school," says a sophomore. "Batesies are very down-to-earth, great people," says a junior. While the administration is trying to make Bates more diverse, minorities remain a tiny fragment of the student population, with African Americans adding 2 percent, Hispanics 3 percent and Asian Americans 4 percent. "Almost every big political headline creates a stir with Batesies," says a sophomore, noting that most students are "very liberal."

All but 12 percent of Bates students live on campus, where there is "great variety in dorm rooms, from brand-new suite living to immaculately maintained college houses," says a senior. "The school-owned houses directly on and off campus are gorgeous, and dorm rooms are huge," enthuses a freshman. Housing is guaranteed for four years, but awarded by lottery after the first year. Food in the Commons, where everyone eats, is "great, but it gets monotonous," says a biology major. "The food is great," says a student, and choices include "hot meals, a salad bar, sandwich bar, vegan bar, pasta and soup bar," and other options.

> **"Batesies are very down-to-earth, great people."**

Since there's not much to do in Lewiston, parties, concerts, and other weekend diversions mostly occur on campus. Without a Greek system, college alcohol policies are fairly loose, student says, and a ban on hard liquor is often ignored. Barbecues and clambakes are big when the weather is nice, and the annual Winter Carnival includes ice skating, snow sculpting, and a semiformal dance. During the St. Patrick's Day Puddle Jump, students of Irish descent—and all those who want to be Irish for the day—cut a hole in the ice on Lake Andrews and plunge in. Students with cars can easily road trip to the outlet stores in Freeport and Kittery, Maine. Other popular destinations include Bar Harbor in Acadia National Park, or "Portland, for great food," says a senior. Montreal and Boston are not far, and neither are the ski slopes of Vermont and New Hampshire.

Bates' varsity teams compete in Division III, except for the ski team, which is Division I. Everyone gets excited for matches against Bowdoin and Colby, especially when they involve ice hockey. Basketball, football, and lacrosse are also popular among spectators. The intramural program, organized by the students and supervised by faculty members, is "strong and spirited," sparking lively dorm rivalries. Intramural softball is popular, along with ultimate Frisbee, soccer, and basketball.

If you can stand the cold and the silent, starry nights, Bates may be a good choice. With caring professors, a small student body, and a focus on the liberal arts, students quickly become big fans. "Bates feels like home."

Overlaps

Bowdoin, Colby, Middlebury, Williams, Dartmouth, Brown

If You Apply To >

Bates: Early decision: Nov. 15, Jan. 1. Regular admissions: Jan. 15. Financial aid: Feb. 1. Guarantees to meet demonstrated need. Campus and alumni interviews: recommended, evaluative. SATs and ACTs: optional. SAT IIs: optional. Accepts the Common Application and electronic applications. Essay question: Why Bates? Common Application essays.

Baylor University

Waco, TX 76798

BEST BUY

Come to Baylor and Mom can rest easy. Baylor is a Christian university in the Baptist tradition, which means less of the debauchery prevalent at many schools. Dad will like it, too: Baylor is one of the least expensive private universities in the country. Prayers come in handy on the football field, where the team is still praying to beat UT.

Baylor University offers students a solid Christian-influenced education at a bargain price. The university's Baptist tradition fosters a strong sense of community among students and faculty, and the school's 2012 vision plan promises a slew of strategic changes such as lowering the student/teacher ratio and building new residence halls. It's a challenging mission, and one that students here are eager to accept. Without a doubt, success at Baylor requires a healthy dose of faith and fortitude.

The 432-acre Baylor campus, nicknamed Jerusalem on the Brazos, abuts the historic Brazos River near downtown Waco, Texas (population 110,000). The architectural style emphasizes the gracious tradition of the Old South, and the central part of campus, the quadrangle, was built when Baylor moved from Independence, Texas, in 1886. The campus has been witness to a number of renovations and new construction, including a 360,000-square-foot parking structure, the 222,000-square-foot North Village Residential Community, and the Baylor Sciences Building.

Students pursue their major in arts and sciences or one of Baylor's five other schools: business, education, engineering and computer sciences, music, and nursing. Core requirements include four English courses and four semesters of human performance. All students also take two religion courses and two semesters of Chapel Forum, a series of lectures and meetings on various issues or Christian testimonies. The Honors College oversees the honors program (which offers opportunities for course integration and independent research) and the University Scholars Program (which waives most distribution requirements). Students may major or minor in Great Texts, an interdisciplinary program exploring "the richness and diversity of the Western intellectual heritage."

Biology is Baylor's most popular major, followed by psychology, political science, journalism, and forensics. The business school's programs in professional selling (one

Website: www.baylor.edu
Location: Center city
Total Enrollment: 13,003
Undergraduates: 11,162
Male/Female: 42/58
SAT Ranges: V 530–640
    M 550–650
ACT Range: 22–27
Financial Aid: 48%
Expense: Pr $
Phi Beta Kappa: Yes
Applicants: 10,917
Accepted: 73%
Enrolled: 43%
Grad in 6 Years: 70%
Returning Freshmen: 82%
Academics: ✍ ✍ ✍
Social: ☎ ☎ ☎
Q of L: ★ ★ ★
Admissions: (254) 710-3435
Email Address:
    Admissions@baylor.edu

of only two worldwide), and entrepreneurship also draw praise. More unusual options include church-state studies and museum studies, and institutes focusing on environmental studies and childhood learning disorders. The archeology and geology departments benefit from fossil- and mineral-rich Texas prairies. An increasing number of Baylor students are traveling on study abroad programs, which send them to 15 countries, including England, Mexico, and the Netherlands. New undergraduate majors include exercise physiology, and new concentrations include church music, fabric design, and studio art.

One of Baylor's greatest strengths is the sense of campus community, fostered by the emphasis on Christianity and by the administration's efforts to focus faculty members on teaching, rather than on research and other activities, students say. Baylor also strives to keep classes small—students say most have 50 or fewer enrolled. "Baylor's professors are its strongest asset and it takes pride in being a teaching institution above all else," explains a senior. The level of rigor varies with the course. A classmate adds, "Students focus on being well-rounded and stronger individuals through extracurricular activities." Professors teach most courses, but not all instructors are of equal quality, cautions a senior: "While there are a few professors who are less-than-quality, most of the teachers are very intelligent."

Baylor students are largely middle- to upper-middle-class Christians. Eighty-three percent are Texans, and most "tend to be outgoing, involved, friendly, classy, and uphold Christian morals," says a marketing major. Minorities total about one-fourth of the student body, with Hispanics the largest group at 9 percent, Asian Americans at 6 percent, and African Americans at 7 percent. "Baylor is a very conservative and Republican campus," says a sophomore, "especially being in such close proximity to Bush's Crawford ranch." Students vie for numerous merit scholarships and nearly 350 athletic scholarships.

As might be expected on a conservative and religious campus like Baylor's, dorms are single sex and have restrictive visitation privileges, which is a big complaint among students. The dorms "are relatively old but are kept in decent shape," a senior notes. Amenities include lounges, computer labs, and gyms, and 34 percent of the student body resides in campus housing. The dining facilities range from cafeterias to small delis on campus. "The food is very good and offers quite a bit of variety," explains a senior. Upperclassmen look off campus for cheaper housing with private rooms and fewer rules, but there is a push for more students to stay on campus with the construction of a newer residence hall with apartment-style rooms, notes one co-ed. Those who've moved out of the dorms appreciate the presence of 20 fully commissioned police officers patrolling the area on bikes and in patrol cars. "Students feel physically safe on campus," says a prelaw major. "It is well-lit and there are emergency phones placed periodically on campus."

Thirteen percent of Baylor's men and 17 percent of the women belong to a fraternity or sorority, providing a party scene for those who want it, and community service outlets for those who don't participate in the school-sponsored Steppin' Out service days that occur once a semester. With so many students residing off-campus, the social life is rated as decent, but not a party atmosphere. "There are always ways to entertain yourself with a little creativity and effort," a senior concedes. Easy road trips include Dallas, Austin, San Antonio, Bryan/College Station, and beaches at Galveston, South Padre Island, and Corpus Christi. Most destinations are within two-and-a-half hour drive, students say, making a set of wheels a big help, if not a necessity.

When it comes to football, remember: You're in Texas. Freshmen wear team jerseys to games and take the field before the players, then sit together as a pack.

"Baylor's professors are its strongest asset."

Alcohol isn't served on campus or at campus-sponsored events. "Alcohol is much less prevalent at Baylor than at most schools," says a senior. However, another student adds, "Students do drink and Baylor is naive to think otherwise." Highlights of Baylor's social calendar include the weekly Dr. Pepper Hour with free soda floats and the Dia del Oso (Day of the Bear), when classes are cancelled for a day in April in favor of a campuswide carnival. The Fiesta on the River, organized by the Residence Hall Association, lets student-run organizations set up booths to raise funds for the causes they support. The school also has the largest collegiate homecoming parade in the nation.

When it comes to football, remember: You're in Texas. Freshmen wear team jerseys to games and take the field before the players, then sit together as a pack. "It's a very awesome part of the freshman experience," one student says. Baylor is in Division I, and both the men's and women's tennis teams brought home recent championships. Women's track and field also draws fans. For weekend warriors, the McLane Student Life Center offers the tallest rock-climbing wall in Texas. The university maintains a small marina for swimming and paddle boating, and several lakes with good beaches are nearby. Generally, though, religious groups are more popular than the intramural sports program, with chapters of Campus Crusade for Christ and the Fellowship of Christian Athletes very much alive and well.

"The food is very good and offers quite a bit of variety."

The business school's programs in professional selling (one of only two worldwide) and entrepreneurship also draw praise.

While keeping true to its traditional Christian roots, Baylor recognizes it must remain open to new ways of thinking to achieve its goal of becoming a top-tier university by 2012. "Baylor has strengthened its athletic programs and seen increasing admiration for many of its academic programs," praises a senior. Baylor students may party less than their counterparts at other Texas schools. Instead, they focus on academics, spiritual nourishment, community involvement, and finding their vocational calling.

Overlaps
University of Texas–Austin, Texas A&M, Texas Tech, Texas Christian, Rice, Texas State–San Marcos

If You Apply To ➤

Baylor: Rolling admissions. Does not guarantee to meet demonstrated need. SATs or ACTs: required. SAT IIs: optional. Campus interviews: optional, informational. No alumni interviews. Accepts the Common Application and prefers electronic applications. Essay question: Discuss your calling and what role service plays in your life; topic of choice. Looks for students who want a "Christian education with academic excellence."

Beloit College

700 College Street, Beloit, WI 53511

Tiny Midwestern college known for freethinking students and international focus. Has steered back toward the mainstream after its heyday as an alternative school in the '60s and '70s. Wisconsin location makes Beloit easier to get into than comparable schools in sexier places.

Beloit College urges students to "Invent Yourself," encouraging intellectual curiosity and personal initiative by giving students freedom to explore. Known for attracting liberal, freethinkers in the 1960s and '70s, the school is now steering back toward the mainstream. "The joke around campus is you can be anything here but a Republican," says a senior. What hasn't changed is its emphasis on tolerance, understanding, and the world beyond the United States. "We are a very optimistic student body that excels at turning lemons into lemonade," says a junior.

Beloit's 40-acre campus is a Northeastern-style oasis an hour's drive from Madison and Milwaukee and 90 minutes from Chicago. Academic and administrative

Website: www.beloit.edu
Location: Small city
Total Enrollment: 1,290
Undergraduates: 1,290
Male/Female: 40/60
SAT Ranges: V 590–700
    M 570–660
ACT Range: 24–29

Beloit is a bundle of contradictions: a small liberal arts college in the heart of Big Ten state-university country, where the academic program has an East Coast rigor but the laid-back classroom vibe reflects the free-and-easy spirit of the Midwest.

buildings sit on one side, with residence halls on the other. Two architectural themes dominate, says one student: "1850s Colonial and obtuse 1930s." In 2001, the college's Turtle Creek Bookstore opened three blocks away in downtown Beloit. A cozy coffee bar, selection of general books and magazines, and a patio for relaxing, reading, or studying augment the typical stacks of textbooks. Recent campus construction includes a dorm offering apartment-style living for 48 upperclassmen. The school has also renovated two buildings in downtown Beloit to house the Center for Entrepreneurship in Liberal Education at Beloit (CELEB).

All Beloit freshmen complete a First Year Initiative (FYI) seminar led by a faculty member who serves as their advisor until they declare majors the next year. Courses under the recent FYI theme "Departures" included Colonizing Mars: Social Science Fiction and Fact, and London's Dreaming: Pills, Pistols, and Profundities. The FYI program flows into the Sophomore Year Program, which offers a retreat, Exploration Week, and the charting of a Comprehensive Academic Plan for the final two years, which often includes internships, research, and off-campus study. If fact, 80 percent of Beloit students undertake some type of independent project, presenting their findings in the annual Student Symposium.

> "We are a very optimistic student body that excels at turning lemons into lemonade."

All students must also complete three writing courses, at least two units in each of three subject areas (natural science and math, social sciences, and arts and humanities), and a unit of interdisciplinary studies. Students are likewise required to complete at least two units involving a different culture or language, or focusing on relations between nations. "Despite rigorous courses, the general atmosphere is laid-back and encouraging," says a freshman.

Teaching is the faculty's first priority, and 90 percent of classes have 25 or fewer students. "The quality of teaching is incredible," a student says. Another adds that professors are "more than happy to jump in and work with students." English is the most popular major, followed by psychology, sociology, anthropology, and biology. Among more unusual options are a museum studies minor, with hands-on restoration experience, and the rhetoric and discourse major, which asks students to reflect on current nonfiction writing while producing their own prose. Classics is Beloit's one weak spot, administrators say and education majors should be prepared to spend an extra semester because of complexities related to certification.

To satisfy Beloit's experiential learning and global diversity requirements, Venture Grants offer $500 to $1,500 for "entrepreneurial, self-testing activities" that benefit the community; recent awardees presented shows to increase disability awareness, traveled to the Dominican Republic to learn traditional dances, and started an information technology consulting business. An internship program provides up to $2,000 for projects that address a community need, and an exchange program sends five Beloit students and a faculty member to China's Fudan University and brings their counterparts to Beloit. More than half of Beloit's students study or do research abroad through the World Outlook Program, which sends students to 35 countries. The Center for Language Studies complements Beloit's own foreign language programs with intensive summer study in Chinese, Czech, Japanese, Russian, Portuguese, Spanish, and English as a second language. Beloit is also a member of the Associated Colleges of the Midwest* consortium, increasing students' choices.

Beloit's Wisconsin location makes it easier to get into than similar schools in sexier places, but only 20 percent of the student body is homegrown; 80 percent hail from out-of-state, including 9 percent from abroad. Hispanics comprise 3 percent of the total, African Americans are 3 percent, and Asian Americans represent 3 percent. Women's rights, gay rights, and the war in Iraq were hot-button issues in recent months. Liberalism is the norm here, much to the chagrin of some. "We need to discuss conservative ideas before silencing them outright," says a junior. Merit scholarships worth an average of $11,500 are available.

Ninety-three percent of Beloit students live on campus, where they're required to remain for three years. The Haven, Wood, and 815 residence halls boast new carpeting, furniture, and central air-conditioning and heat; one student says other good choices include Chapin and Aldrich. Four fraternities attract 15 percent of the men, and two sororities draw 5 percent of the women; members may live in their chapter houses. Special-interest houses cater to those interested in foreign languages, music, anthropology, and other disciplines.

> **"Despite rigorous courses, the general atmosphere is laid-back and encouraging."**

On-campus movies, concerts, art shows, dance recitals, and parties at the frats and special-interest houses tie up many Friday and Saturday nights at Beloit. "Almost all of our social life takes place on campus. Very few people go home or commute," says a senior. Two all-campus festivals liven up the calendar: the Folk and Blues Fall Music Festival brings jazz, reggae, folk, and blues bands to campus, while on Spring Day, classes give way to concerts and everyone kicks back to enjoy the (finally!) warmer weather. The Beloit Science Fiction/Fantasy Association offers movie marathons, dramatic readings, roleplaying games, board and video games, and other activities for members and nonmembers alike. The school's alcohol policy is lax, students say. "They will treat you as an adult who can make good, responsible choices," explains a junior. "They trust you, but they take action when you are harming yourself or others."

Having wheels here will definitely raise your social standing, as they make it easier to take off from secluded Beloit for Chicago or the college town of Madison, also easily reached through a cheap local bus service. For the outdoors-minded, the nearby Dells offer camping and water parks. "Beloit is the perfect college town in that it encourages students to stay on campus and develop a strong community." That said, the town has basic necessities, such as a few bars (check out the excellent burgers at Hanson's Pub, says a senior), a bowling alley, a movie theater, and a Wal-Mart. "Groups such as Habitat for Humanity, Beloit Interaction Committee, and the Outreach Center work hard to integrate students into the community," says a sophomore.

Beloit's Wisconsin location makes it easier to get into than similar schools in sexier places, but only 20 percent of the student body is homegrown; 80 percent hail from out-of-state, including 9 percent from abroad.

Sports at Beloit are played more for fun than glory. Among the school's Division III squads, standouts include baseball, men's and women's basketball, men's and women's cross-country, and football, especially against rival Ripon College. The women's tennis team won Midwest Conference championships in 2001 and 2002, and intramural Ultimate Frisbee typically draws hundreds of players and spectators. Two-thirds of students participate in the intramural program, with basketball, volleyball, and soccer also popular.

> **"Almost all of our social life takes place on campus."**

Beloit is a bundle of contradictions: a small liberal arts college in the heart of Big Ten state university country, where the academic program has an East Coast rigor but the laid-back classroom vibe reflects the free-and-easy spirit of the Midwest. "Beloit College is not for the student who wants to be told what classes to take," warns a sophomore. "Beloit is for the student who wants to be asked, 'What do you want to do?'"

Overlaps

Oberlin, Macalester, Grinnell, Lawrence, Knox

If You Apply To ➤

Beloit: Early action: Nov. 15, Dec. 15. Rolling admissions: Jan. 15. Financial aid: Jan. 15 (priority), Mar. 1. Guarantees to meet full demonstrated need. Campus interviews: recommended, informational. Alumni interviews: optional, informational. SATs or ACTs: required. SAT IIs: optional. Accepts the Common Application and electronic applications. Essay question: How you heard about Beloit, factors that have led you to apply, and topic of your choice.

Bennington College

Bennington, VT 05201-6003

Known for top-notch performing arts and lavish attention to every student. Arts programs rely heavily on part-time faculty who are practitioners in their field. Less competitive than Bard and Sarah Lawrence, comparable to Hampshire. Enrollment is robust after a dip in the '90s.

Website:
   www.bennington.edu
Location: Rural
Total Enrollment: 820
Undergraduates: 665
Male/Female: 33/66
SAT Ranges: V 580–690
   M 510–610
ACT Range: 23-27
Financial Aid: 66%
Expense: Pr $ $ $ $
Phi Beta Kappa: No
Applicants: 842
Accepted: 73%
Enrolled: 24%
Grad in 6 Years: 67%
Returning Freshmen: 77%
Academics: ✐ ✐ ✐
Social: ☎ ☎ ☎
Q of L: ★ ★ ★ ★
Admissions: (800) 833-6845
Email Address:
   admissions@bennington
   .edu

Strongest Programs:
Literature
Writing
Music
Dance
Sciences

Bennington College is "a crazy bunch of absolutely brilliant geniuses," says one art and Spanish major. A school where architects are teachers, biologists sculpt, and a sociologists might work on Wall Street or in graphic design, it's no wonder they strive to abandon the theory of regimented knowledge. Bennington's focus is on learning by doing, and that's about the only thing that hasn't been tweaked or adjusted since classes began in 1932. Courses are as rigorous as you make them, since faculty members require a personal meeting with each prospective student before they grant a seminar seat. Academic advising is stellar; rather than grades, students get detailed feedback from a self-selected faculty committee that meets as often as once a week. The emphasis on self-direction, field work, and personal relationships with professors sets it apart even from other liberal arts colleges of similar (small) size. "We like to make our own paths and are in a constant state of evaluation and reflection," says one junior.

> **"We like to make our own paths and are in a constant state of evaluation and reflection."**

Bennington sits on 550 acres at the foot of Vermont's Green Mountains. The campus was once an active dairy farm, and a converted barn houses the main classroom and administrative spaces. But don't let the quaint, New England setting fool you. The Dickinson Science Building offers high-tech equipment for aspiring chemists, biologists, environmental scientists, and geneticists. The building is also home to a media lab dedicated to the study of languages, including Chinese, French, German, Italian, Japanese, and Spanish.

Thanks to its focus on experiential learning, Bennington's academic structure differs from that of a typical college or university. Each student designs a major and there are few academic requirements other than a seven-week internship each January and February in a field of interest and a location of the student's choice. "Our professors are so involved in their teaching that students can't help but be sucked in," an architecture major explains. Even without grades, students push themselves to learn, grow, and achieve, says a dance and theatre major. "Bennington is defined by self-motivation and a focus on the individual's learning process and style."

Without academic departments, the faculty works to provide students with a well-rounded academic foundation. Since the school's size limits standard course offerings, more than 175 tutorials fill in the gaps. The most popular area of study is visual and performing arts, followed by social sciences, English, biological/life sciences, and liberal arts. "Students fight tooth and nail for literature classes, but that is due to the fact that they come here for the literature department," says one sophomore. Social and biological sciences are likewise popular. For those undergrads seeking to deepen their understanding of the world, there's the Democracy Project, where students explore and experience democracy in its historical, philosophical, political, cultural, and social dimensions. Led by scholars, the project draws on a curriculum that provides a broad range of perspectives and intellectual orientations.

"Everyone at Bennington is an artist, either in practice or philosophy," says one student. Three percent are from Vermont and another 4 percent are foreign nationals.

One literature major describes students as "vocal, engaged, opinionated, political, artistic, and very individualistic." Curiosity and excitement about exploration and experimentation will take you far here, and if you lean liberal in the voting booth, so much the better. While only moderately active, Bennington students are characterized by one freshman as "mostly anti-Bush, pro-choice, and environmentally conscious." Together, African Americans, Hispanics, and Asian Americans account for 7 percent of the student body. Merit scholarships worth an average of $4,309 are awarded annually; there are no athletic scholarships available.

Given Bennington's rugged location, hiking, rock climbing, caving, camping, and canoeing keep students moving.

As Bennington lacks traditional departments, requirements, and even faculty tenure, it's probably not surprising that the school also lacks dorms. Most students live in one of the college's 18 co-ed houses; 12 are white New England clapboard and three are more modern. Each holds 25 to 30 people with an elected chair to govern house affairs. "Houses are an integral element of life at Bennington," says a senior. "They each have a character and role on the campus." Freshmen and sophomores share rooms—those of the opposite sex may live together if both parties request it—and juniors and seniors are guaranteed singles.

"Students fight tooth and nail for literature classes."

The college food service provides plenty of options, from vegetarian and vegan choices to a salad bar, wok station, and pizza machine. "A large (if not majority) of Bennington students are vegetarian so they are very well taken care of," says one student. When it comes to campus security, students feel very safe, some may even feel that security goes a bit too far.

Although the vibe on Bennington's campus is liberal, sophisticated, and cosmopolitan, the neighboring town of the same name—four miles away—is far more conservative, typical of rural New England. "It's not really a college town at all," sighs an architecture major. "Although if you can become involved in the community, then it is a lovely Vermont town." Students are trying to mend the town/gown rift through volunteer work in local schools and homeless shelters, though such programs can be tough because of the mandatory midyear internship term, which takes many students away from campus.

Each student designs a major and there are few academic requirements other than a seven-week internship each January and February in a field of interest and a location of the student's choice.

Social life centers on rehearsals, performances, films, and lectures. "There is always something going on," assures one freshman. That said, the annual theme parties always draw raves—recent themes have included Gatsby's Funeral and Mods vs. Rockers. The alcohol policies on campus are fairly standard: no one under 21 is allowed to imbibe. "Security randomly walks around and makes sure that minors aren't drinking," says a freshman. Road trips to Montreal and New York are fun but infrequent diversions.

Given Bennington's rugged location, hiking, rock climbing, caving, camping, and canoeing keep students moving. Ski slopes beckon in the winter, when the college turns part of its huge Visual and Performing Arts complex into an indoor roller rink for the Rollerama party. For 12 hours one day each May, the campus celebrates spring with Sunfest, which includes "amazing, crazy bands, a foam pit, sometimes

"There is always something going on."

Jello wrestling, and other games," says a sophomore. Transvestite Night livens things up during Parents' Weekend. And during finals week, the blaring of fire-truck sirens tells weary students to head to the dining hall, where professors and the college president serve up French toast. Sports aren't a big focus, but Bennington does compete in an intramural co-ed soccer league that also includes other Northeastern colleges. The way one student sees it, "Bennington kids prefer going to a dance performance or poetry reading than to playing sports."

As the first school in the nation to grant the arts equal status with other disciplines, Bennington offers a novel, participatory, and hands-on approach. Whether they're painters or writers, musicians or scientists, sculptors, dancers or

Overlaps

Bard, Brown, NYU, Oberlin, Sarah Lawrence

some combination thereof, what Bennington students have in common is self-motivation and a real thirst for knowledge. Crossing disciplines is encouraged, and forget about taking the road less traveled; each student here charts his or her own course. And besides, there's a tree house—and milk and cookies served at every meal. Who says going to college means growing up?

If You Apply To ➤

Bennington: Early decision: Nov. 15. Regular admissions: Jan. 1. Financial aid: Mar. 1. Campus interviews: recommended, evaluative. Alumni interviews: optional, informational. SATs or ACTs: required. SAT IIs: recommended. Accepts the Common Application. Essay question.

Birmingham-Southern College

Box A18, Birmingham, AL 35254

One of the Deep South's best liberal arts colleges. The vast majority of students come from Alabama and the surrounding states. With fewer than 1,400 students, BSC is roughly the same size as Rhodes (Tennessee) and Millsaps (Missouri). Strong fraternity system and a throwback to the way college used to be.

Website: www.bsc.edu
Location: Urban
Total Enrollment: 1,381
Undergraduates: 1,335
Male/Female: 43/57
SAT Ranges: V 550–670
   M 540–640
ACT Range: 24–29
Financial Aid: 45%
Expense: Pr $
Phi Beta Kappa: Yes
Applicants: 1,157
Accepted: 83%
Enrolled: 32%
Grad in 6 Years: 75%
Returning Freshmen: 87%
Academics: ✍ ✍ ✍
Social: ☎ ☎ ☎
Q of L: ★ ★ ★
Admissions: (205) 226-4696
Email Address:
   admission@bsc.edu

Strongest Programs:
Biology
English
Business
Humanities

Once an old-school conservative Southern institution, BSC is now striving to prepare students for all aspects the modern world, with high-tech facilities and a more global curriculum. Birmingham-Southern stresses service, effectively preserving the school's image as a strong liberal arts institution with its own brand of community involvement. More than half the student body participates in community service through Southern Volunteer Services, as well as claiming active membership in fraternities and sororities. Caring and attentive faculty add to a sense of commitment to both personal and community growth. "Our school really cares about the individual students on our campus," a sophomore says. "They try to cater to everyone's needs to make sure our college experience is the best it can be."

Known as the Hilltop for obvious reasons, BSC is the result of the 1918 merger of two smaller colleges: Birmingham College and Southern University. The campus, a green and shady oasis in an urban neighborhood, contains a pleasing hodge-podge of traditional and modern architecture, all surrounded by a security fence for added safety. Recent additions to campus include a new Humanities Building and $7.2 million six-house Fraternity Row.

The courses at BSC are described as rigorous by most. "I've had easy and hard, but you won't get out without having done a lot of writing and analytical thinking," says a business administration major. Each student is assigned a faculty member who serves as his or her academic advisor from freshman convocation to graduation, an arrangement that students praise for its effectiveness. Equal praise goes out to faculty in the classrooms, where 94 percent of classes have 25 or fewer students. "The professors at this college are the best in their fields," reports a history major. Forty-four percent of the students go on to professional or graduate school, something they feel well-prepared for after their time at BSC.

> "Our school really cares about the individual students on our campus."

Business, a division that includes programs ranging from accounting to international issues, is the most popular major, enrolling about a quarter of the students.

Accounting and psychology majors are also popular, and the many premed students cite biology as a major drawing card. English is also one of the school's strongest programs, and The Stephens Science Laboratory gives this program, as well as the chemistry and physics departments, a further boost. The art, drama, dance, and music programs are all among the best in the South. Students stage several major productions each year, often including American and world premieres. A major has been added in English/theatre arts.

(Continued)
Psychology

The Foundations general education program encompasses half of the credits needed to graduate. Students are required to take three first-year courses, five arts units, five science units, one unit in each of the following: creative or performing arts, foreign language and culture, math and writing, an intercultural course, and a Senior Conference course, which can be a scholarly seminar, term project, or independent study. Students also must attend 40 approved intellectual and cultural events, 30 of which must be on campus. BSC, a member of the Associated Colleges of the South* consortium, also offers a wide variety of special programs. The January term allows students to explore new areas of study, from cooking lessons to travel in China. The international studies program offers students the chance to study abroad in several different countries, and the honors program allows 25 exceptional first-year students to take small seminars with one or more professors.

"Our students tend to come from middle to upper class families."

Seventy-eight percent of the students are homegrown Alabamians, and practically all the rest hail from Deep South states, many with family ties to 'Southern. Though moderate by Alabama standards, the student body is quite conservative. Thirty-eight percent of the students belong to the Methodist Church, and the school chaplain heads the personal counseling program. "Our students tend to come from middle- to upper-class families," a junior says. "However, past that everyone is different. It's really pretty cool." Three percent of BSC students are African American, 1 percent are Hispanic, and 3 percent are Asian American. "We have an expanding international student base and multicultural affairs and the beginning of some African American sororities. The college is taking steps to diversify," a student says. BSC offers various merit scholarships to 83 percent of students, with an average grant of more than $11,000. National Merit Scholars who list 'Southern as their first choice receive an automatic scholarship of $500 to $2,000, and up to 10 get full-tuition awards. Athletes compete for scholarships in 14 Division I sports.

Seventy-eight percent of the students are homegrown Alabamians, and practically all the rest hail from Deep South states, many with family ties to '.

Seventy-nine percent of the students live on campus, including many of those whose families reside in Birmingham. Co-ed housing hasn't filtered down to 'Southern yet, so all seven dorms are single-sex with a variety of visitation policies depending on student preferences. Daniel Hall and New Mens are generally the most desired men's residences, while Bruno Hall is the preferred choice for women. Dorms are described as comfortable and convenient. "You can wake up 10 minutes before class, get ready, walk to class, and still have two or three minutes to spare," says a business administration major. Dining facilities get mixed reviews. The quality is decent and special tastes are accommodated, but the food can get repetitive. Campus security is quite visible and students praise its effectiveness in keeping the campus safe.

Forty-eight percent of the men and 65 percent of the women are members of Greek organizations, which means that much of the social activity at BSC revolves around the Greek system. "There are always fraternity parties every weekend, and they are open to everyone," a junior says. As for alcohol, it's not allowed on the quad, and elsewhere it must be in an opaque container, a policy most students find reasonable, described by one senior as a "don't see it, ignore it policy."

The art, drama, dance, and music programs are all among the best in the South. Students stage several major productions each year, often including American and world premieres.

The biggest social event of the year is Southern Comfort, a four-day festival, and freshman take part in a square dance during orientation. Another popular music celebration is E-Fest. When social opportunities on campus dry up, many students take the shuttle to Birmingham for the city's nightlife. There they can find cultural events, bars, and the rather Bohemian (at least for Alabama) South Side. Road trips to Auburn, Nashville, and Atlanta are popular, and beaches and mountains are less than five hours away.

In a state where the late Bear Bryant of 'Bama is practically a saint, BSC is a school without a football team. Men's basketball partially fills the void, as does the

"There are always fraternity parties every weekend, and they are open to everyone."

baseball team, which at one point had 20 winning seasons in a row. The men's and women's soccer teams are also top-notch. Seventy percent of students take part in the intramural program. Basketball, flag football, and soccer are popular, but less traditional sports, such as dodgeball and table tennis, are also offered.

Students at BSC are focused on academics, but balance that with community service and an active social scene. Small classes, a caring faculty, and an expanding menu of academic offerings continue to draw attention to this close-knit liberal arts school. "More and more students are learning about the great things BSC has to offer," a sophomore says. "Our campus gives students a top-notch education and college experience."

Overlaps

Auburn, Millsaps, Rhodes, University of the South, University of Alabama

If You Apply To ➤

Birmingham-Southern: Rolling admissions. Early action: Dec. 1. Financial aid: Mar. 1 (preferred). Meets demonstrated need of 75%. Campus interviews: recommended, informational. Alumni interviews: optional, informational. SATs or ACTs: required. SAT IIs: optional. Accepts the Common Application and electronic applications. Essay questions: topic of interest; two pages of autobiography; choose fictional characters from literature as TV guests.

Boston College

140 Commonwealth Avenue, Devlin Hall, Room 208, Chestnut Hill, MA 02467

Many students clamoring for a spot at Boston College are surprised to learn that it is affiliated with the Roman Catholic church. Set on a quiet hilltop at the end of a "T" (subway) line, BC's location is solid gold. A close second in the pecking order among true-blue Catholics.

Website: www.bc.edu
Location: Suburban
Total Enrollment: 14,500
Undergraduates: 9,059
Male/Female: 47/53
SAT Ranges: V 610–700
   M 630–710
ACT Range: N/A
Financial Aid: 40%
Expense: Pr $ $ $
Phi Beta Kappa: Yes
Applicants: 22,451
Accepted: 32%
Enrolled: 32%

Boston College is a study in contrasts. Both the academics and athletic teams are well respected. The environment is safely suburban, but barely 20 minutes from Boston, the hub of the Eastern seaboard's college scene. The Jesuit influence on the college, one of the largest Roman Catholic schools in the country, provides a guiding spirit for campus life, but the social opportunities still seem endless.

Don't let the name fool you. Boston College is actually a university with nine schools and colleges. It has two campuses: the main campus at Chestnut Hill and the Newton campus a mile and a half away. The dominant architecture of the main campus (known as "the Heights") is Gothic Revival, with modern additions over the past few years, including a new science building. There's lots of grass and trees, not to mention a large, peaceful reservoir (perfect to jog around) right in the front yard.

The college's mission is to "educate skilled, knowledgeable, and responsible leaders within each new generation." To accomplish this goal, the Core Curriculum requires courses in not only literature, science, history, philosophy, social science, and theology, but also writing, mathematics, the arts, and cultural diversity, in addition to specific requirements set by each undergraduate school. "Core Curriculum forces you to take classes you might not want to take but end up enjoying," says a senior. Students in arts and sciences must also show proficiency in a modern foreign language or classical language before graduation. Freshmen are required to take a writing workshop in which each student develops a portfolio of personal and academic writing and reads a wide range of texts. Seniors participate in the University Capstone program, a series of seminars aiming to give a "big picture" perspective to the college experience.

The academic climate is challenging and courses rigorous. "People at BC are extremely driven and ambitious," a junior says. "At the same time, they do not compete against each other." Professors are described as "phenomenal" and "unbelievable," and their classes are called "very interactive and discussion-based." The Jesuits on BC's faculty (about 60 out of 900) exert an influence out of proportion to their numbers. "The philosophy, theology, and ethics departments are the most important in setting the tone of the campus because they keep the students encouraged to be open-minded," says a freshman. Another student says, "Our teachers are dedicated to students and scholarly research, and they are easily accessible through regular office hours."

The schools of arts and sciences, management, nursing, and education award bachelor's degrees. Finance, communications, English, economics, and history are the most popular majors. Future politicians and civic leaders will benefit from the strong political science program. Outside the traditional classroom, at the McMullen Museum of Art in Devlin Hall, students find exhibitions, lectures, and gallery tours. The Music Guild sponsors professional concerts throughout the year, and music students emphasizing performance can take advantage of facilities equipped with Steinways and Yamahas. Theater majors find a home in the 600-seat E. Paul Robsham Theater Arts Center, which produces eight student-directed productions each year.

Students searching for out-of-the-ordinary offerings will be happy at BC. The PULSE program provides participants with the opportunity to fulfill their philosophy and theology requirements while engaging in social-service fieldwork at any of about 35 Boston organizations, and sometimes leads students to major in those areas. Perspectives, a four-part freshman program, attempts to illustrate how great

> "Core Curriculum forces you to take classes you might not want to take but end up enjoying."

thinkers from the past have made us who we are. There's also a Freshman-Year Experience program, which offers seminars and services to help students adjust to college life and take advantage of the school and the city. An honors program allows students to work at a more intensive pace and requires a senior thesis.

Roughly 25 percent of BC students come from the greater Boston area, and Catholics comprise about 70 percent of the student body. African Americans now constitute 6 percent of the student body, while Asian Americans make up another 9 percent and Hispanics 7 percent. "There are many diversity initiatives but these are frivolous since BC is not diverse and minorities stick together," a sophomore says. "All the students here are identical. Most are wealthy and dress up for class daily." Still, the Jesuit appeal for tolerance means that students can find support and interaction even when approaching hot-button issues that Catholicism will not condone, such as homosexuality.

When students are admitted, they are notified whether they will get on-campus housing for three or four years, and most juniors with three-year guarantees live off campus or study abroad in the fourth year. A new dorm houses more than 300 students in six- and eight-person suites. The city of Boston has a fairly reliable bus and subway system to bring distant residents to campus; the few students that drive to school are required to show they need to park on campus. Another lottery system determines where on-campus residents hang their hats. Freshman dorms are

(Continued)
Grad in 6 Years: 87%
Returning Freshmen: 95%
Academics: ✍ ✍ ✍ ½
Social: 🐨 🐨 🐨 🐨
Q of L: ★ ★ ★
Admissions: (617) 552-3100
Email Address:
  ugadmis@bc.edu

Strongest Programs:
Chemistry
Economics
English
Finance
Political Science
Physics
History

The PULSE program provides participants the opportunity to fulfill their philosophy and theology requirements while engaging in social-service fieldwork at any of about 35 Boston organizations, and sometimes leads students to major in those areas.

described as "not great and not very modern," but accouterments in upper-class suites include private baths, dishwashers, and full kitchens. Students pay in advance for a certain number of dining hall meals, served a la carte.

BC students are serious about their work, but not excessively so. There is time and plenty of places to party. Yet BC's reputation as a hardcore party school is diminishing, now that no kegs or cases of beer are allowed on campus grounds. Those of legal age can carry in only enough beer for personal consumption. Bars and clubs in Boston ("THE college town," gushes a junior) are a big draw, along with Fenway Park. On weekends, especially in the winter, the mountains of Vermont and New Hampshire beckon outdoorsy types. The campus is replete with sporting events, movies, festivals, concerts, and plays. As at other Jesuit institutions, there is no Greek system at BC.

Athletic events become social events too, with tailgate and victory parties common. Football games are a big draw—the contest with Notre Dame is jokingly referred to as the "Holy War," and makes for a popular road trip. The football program has been recognized for achieving the highest graduation rate in the College Football Association, and the women's field hockey team made it to the quarterfinals of the NCAA tournament. The Silvio O. Conte Forum Sports Arena is well-attended, and BC meets fierce competition from Atlantic Coast Conference rivals Duke, Miami, Florida State, Virginia Tech, and others. Students even get the day off from classes to line the edge of campus and cheer Boston Marathon runners up "Heartbreak Hill." Intramural sports are huge here. About 4,300 undergrads play on 34 teams—from basketball and volleyball to skiing and golf. Students rave about BC's recreational complex and the new Yawkey Athletics Center.

> "All the students here are identical. Most are wealthy and dress up for class daily."

BC students spend four years fine-tuning the art of the delicate balance, finding ways to make old-fashioned morals relevant to life in the 21st century, and finding time for fun while still tending to their academic performance.

Overlaps

Boston University, Penn, Notre Dame, Yale, Harvard, Georgetown

---

If You Apply To ➤

BC: Early action: Nov. 1. Regular admissions: Jan. 2. Financial aid: Feb. 1. Housing: May 1. No campus or alumni interviews. SATs or ACTs: required, SAT preferred. SAT IIs: A minimum of two subject tests required. Apply to particular schools or programs. Guarantees to meet demonstrated need of all students. Accepts the Common Application.

Boston University

121 Bay State Road, Boston, MA 02215

One of the nation's biggest private universities, but easy to miss amid the bustle of the city. Boston's Back Bay neighborhood is the promised land for hordes of students nationwide seeking a funky, artsy, youth-oriented urban setting that is less in-your-face than New York City.

Website: www.bu.edu
Location: Center city
Total Enrollment: 29,596
Undergraduates: 17,740

Like George Washington University and NYU, Boston University is an integral part of the city it calls home. The school's mammoth collection of nondescript high-rises straddles bustling, six-lane Commonwealth Avenue—and so do thousands upon thousands of students. Whether they're aspiring actors, musicians, journalists, and filmmakers, or wanna-be doctors, dentists, and hotel managers, BU seems to offers something for all of them. "Diversity is very present, but less focused around ethnicity than on personal backgrounds, political views, and social class," says a psychology major. "Generally, BU students are self-motivated and proactive, and they tend to be much more worldly and less insulated" than the students at rival Boston College. Even better, the quality of programs at BU is finally catching up to their quantity.

The BU campus is practically indistinguishable from the city that surrounds it, and while Boston may be America's town, BU is anything but bucolic. A measure of relief is available on the tree-lined side streets, which feature quaint Victorian brownstones. Recent construction includes a 35,000-square-foot Hillel House, a multi-level fitness center, a hockey arena that doubles as a concert hall, and a new life science and engineering building that allows the biology, chemistry, bioinformatics, and biomedical engineering faculty to operate under one roof. The John Hancock Student Village includes a track and tennis center, as well as an apartment-style dorm.

BU's 11 schools include the College of Arts and Sciences, the largest undergraduate division, which caters to the premeds and prelaw students. The College of Communication combines theory and hands-on training—some of it by adjunct professors with day jobs at major newspapers and TV networks. It also houses the nation's only center for the study of political disinformation. The School of Music benefits from its own concert hall and from faculty who also belong to the Boston Symphony Orchestra. College of Fine Arts recently added a dance minor, while the School of Theatre Arts now has a freshman core for its performance and design/production programs. The physical therapy program at the Sargent College of Health and Rehabilitation Sciences now takes six years, culminating in BS and DPT degrees. Students in the School of Education can test their ideas for curricular reform in the public schools of nearby Chelsea, while those in School of Visual Arts may show their work in one of three campus galleries.

The School of Management, regarded as one of BU's top colleges, offers a four-year honors program and minors in law and hospitality administration; the College of Engineering boasts a robotics and biomedical engineering lab. Future employers of students in the School of Hospitality Administration offer paid internships in exotic locales such as Brussels and Britain. (Students in other fields who wish to work abroad may vie for jobs from Australia to Moscow.) Also intriguing is the University Professors Program, which begins with a two-year integrated core focusing on major authors and central themes of Western thought. Juniors and seniors in the program create individualized, interdisciplinary courses of

"Throughout my four years I have had great, caring professors."

study. BU also offers highly competitive seven- and eight-year programs admitting qualified students simultaneously to the undergraduate program and the university's medical or dental school.

Each of BU's schools and colleges sets its own general education requirements, but all students take the two-semester Freshman Writing Program. Students rave about FYSOP, the First-Year Student Outreach Project, which brings freshmen to campus a week early to do community service. For a break from brutal Boston winters, BU offers 44 study abroad programs, including internships, field work, research, language study, and liberal arts programs. There's also a marine science program at the Woods Hole Institute and the Semester at Sea,* a program welcoming students from many schools to spend a term living and studying on a cruise ship as it travels the world.

The academic climate at BU encourages both cooperation and competition. A biochemistry and molecular biology student says, "as a science major, most of my classes are graded on a curve, so I have to compete with my classmates for high grades." Amazingly for such a large school, administrators say that 92 percent of the classes taken by freshmen have 25 or fewer students. "Throughout my four years I

Students rave about FYSOP, the First-Year Student Outreach Project, which brings freshmen to campus a week early to do community service.

(Continued)

Male/Female: 40/60
SAT Ranges: V 600–690
  M 621–700
ACT Range: 26–30
Financial Aid: 46%
Expense: Pr $ $ $ $
Phi Beta Kappa: Yes
Applicants: 28,240
Accepted: 55%
Enrolled: 28%
Grad in 6 Years: 75%
Returning Freshmen: 90%
Academics: 🖉 🖉 🖉 🖉
Social: ☎ ☎ ☎ ☎
Q of L: ★ ★ ★
Admissions: (617) 353-2300
Email Address:
  admissions@bu.edu
International admissions:
  intadmis@bu.edu

Strongest Programs:
Communications
Management
Biomedical Engineering
Natural Sciences
Psychology
International Relations
Fine Arts

have had great, caring professors," says a senior. Students are also thrilled with their new Dean of Students, "who has brought so much life and unity to this campus," says a senior.

More than three-quarters of BU undergrads are from outside Massachusetts and nearly 7 percent come from foreign countries. Asian Americans are the largest minority group on campus, at 13 percent of the total; African Americans add 2 percent and Hispanics 5 percent. Politically, "many students are outspoken democrats and rallied for Kerry," says an English and journalism major. In all, the university offers more than 2,000 merit scholarships each year, with an average value of $13,403. There are also 210 athletic scholarships in seven men's and nine women's sports.

Three-quarters of BU students live in campus housing, which is guaranteed for four years. "Options are vast, from dorms to suites to apartments," says a journalism major. "Since we are on a lottery system it is possible to get a not-so-great room," explains a psychology major, "Freshman/sophomore dorms are fairly typical, but housing gets even better as you get to be a senior." The luxury apartments, known as the Residences at 10 Buick Street, house 814 students on 18 floors, in apartments with four single bedrooms each. Each bedroom is wired for phone and fast Internet service, and each air-conditioned apartment also includes a kitchen, living and dining area, and two full bathrooms. Meal plans are flexible, and one of the six dining halls on campus is Kosher. One junior says the food is "very edible; averagely diverse," but a senior who moved to an apartment this year calls the meal plan choices "awesome" and says, "I made sure to get the limited meal plan (for students in apartments and off campus) because I knew I would miss the food. The burrito bar and BU cookies are widely loved." There's also a food court with chains such as Burger King, Starbucks, and D'Angelo's, a local sub shop.

"Boston is where most people go on weekends."

There are more than 450 student clubs and organizations at BU, and social life is "split about 50/50 between campus and city," says a psychology major. Three percent of the men and 5 percent of the women go Greek, and parties at neighboring schools are an option as well. Owing to Boston's heavily Irish heritage, St. Patrick's Day is also an occasion for revelry. Drinking is fairly common, though not in the dorms, because state laws are strictly enforced, and violators may find themselves without university housing. The Splash party in September, homecoming in October, and Culture Fest in March round out the social calendar. Possible road trips include Cape Cod, Cape Anne, and Providence, Rhode Island, but "Boston is where most people go on weekends," says a senior who calls it "the best college town in the world." The T's Green Line squiggles through the center BU's of campus, putting the entire city within easy reach. Even better, "Fenway Park, downtown, Landsdowne Street, and Boston Common are all within walking distance," says a marine biology major.

By far the most popular intramural sport is broomball, which is like ice hockey on sneakers, with a ball instead of a puck, and a broom instead of a stick. BU has won 26 of 53 titles in the annual Beanpot tournament, which pits BU against Harvard, Northeastern, and archrival Boston College. It's the athletic highlight of the school year, since BU doesn't field a football team. The women's tennis, soccer, and lacrosse teams are all conference standouts, along with men's basketball. All teams compete in NCAA Division I. The Head of the Charles regatta, which starts at BU's crew house each fall, draws college crew teams from across the country.

Boston University urges students to just "Be You" and most are happy to do so, but they warn that coming here is not for the faint of heart. The school is "a great place, with lots of academic and social opportunities, but it's not for the timid student," agrees a geophysics and planetary sciences major. "You have to be proactive about finding out what's going on around campus, so that you can find your niche."

| If You Apply To ⟫ | **BU:** Early decision: Nov. 1. Regular admissions: Jan. 1 (Dec. 1 for the BA/MD and BA/DMD programs and applicants for some scholarships). Financial aid: Feb. 15. Housing: May 1. Meets demonstrated need of 51%. Campus interviews: required, evaluative for BA/MD and BA/DMD programs and some theatre arts programs; not available to other students. Alumni interviews: optional, informational. SATs or ACTs: required (including optional ACT Writing Test). SAT IIs: required (specific tests vary by program). Apply to particular school or program. Accepts the Common Application and electronic applications; prefers electronic to paper applications. Essay question: 500 words on a personally meaningful topic; 500 words on the experiences that have led you to select your professional field and objective; how you became interested in BU. |

Bowdoin College

Brunswick, ME 04011

Rates with Amherst, Williams, and Wesleyan for liberal arts excellence and does not require the SAT. Bowdoin has strong science programs, and outdoor enthusiasts benefit from proximity to the Atlantic coast. Smaller than some of its competitors, with less overt competition among students.

For more than two centuries, Bowdoin College sought to make nature, art, and friendship as integral to the student experience as the world of books. This is, after all, the alma mater of the great American poets Longfellow and Hawthorne. In fact, when they matriculate, new students sign their names in a book on Hawthorne's very desk. Though the New England weather can be brutal ("Be prepared for long, cold winters," warns a junior), students are quick to point out that good food and friendships that "transcend labels" help make campus a warm and friendly place.

Bowdoin's 200-acre campus sits in Brunswick, Maine, the state's largest town. Hidden amid the pine groves and athletic fields are 117 buildings, in styles from German Romanesque, Colonial, medieval, and neoclassical to neo-Georgian, modern, and postmodern. Former fraternity houses now house academic and administrative offices, after Greek groups were phased out. New campus additions include the Schwartz Outdoor Leadership Center, home to the Bowdoin Outing Club, and Kanbar Hall, which houses the psychology, education, and neuroscience departments. Two new dorms also recently opened, allowing the college to renovate first-year dorms and convert triple rooms to doubles.

To graduate, Bowdoin students must complete 32 courses, including two each in natural sciences and math, social and behavioral sciences, humanities and fine arts, and non-Eurocentric studies. New distribution requirements emphasize issues vital to a liberal education in the 21st century and include courses such as Exploring Social Differences; Mathematical, Computational, or Statistical Reasoning; and International Perspectives. Freshmen also have their choice of seminars, capped at 16 students each, which emphasize reading and writing; recent topics included Cultural Difference and the Crime Film, The Cuban Revolution, and The Economics of Art. Academic strengths include the sciences, specifically biology, chemistry, and environmental studies. "The facilities are fantastic," says a sophomore. "The college's Coastal Studies Center and Coleman Farm are great for ecology labs and geology field trips." Bowdoin also offers coursework in Arctic Studies (its mascot is the polar bear), as well as opportunities for Arctic archeological research in Labrador or ecological research at the Kent Island Scientific Station in Canada. Premeds of all persuasions will find top-of-the-line lab equipment and outstanding faculty; the field of microscale organic chemistry was developed and advanced here.

Website: www.bowdoin.edu
Location: Midsize town
Total Enrollment: 1,665
Undergraduates: 1,665
Male/Female: 51/49
SAT Ranges: V 640–740
M 650–720
Financial Aid: 46%
Expense: Pr $ $ $ $
Phi Beta Kappa: Yes
Applicants: 4,853
Accepted: 24%
Enrolled: 40%
Grad in 6 Years: 90%
Returning Freshmen: 99%
Academics: 🖉 🖉 🖉 🖉 🖉
Social: 🍺 🍺 🍺
Q of L: ★ ★ ★
Admissions: (207) 725-3100
Email Address:
admissions@bowdoin.edu

Strongest Programs:
Natural Sciences
Classics
German
Anthropology
Economics
English
Government
Environmental Studies

Students also praise the art history and English departments, and say the popularity of government and economics, the majors with the highest enrollment, is well deserved. The film studies department is tiny, with only one professor. Newer majors include Latin American studies, Eurasian and East European studies, and English and theater. There's also an increasing emphasis on service-learning; 57 percent of Bowdoin students apply their classroom work to real-world problems faced by local community groups. Undergraduate research is a priority, and it's common for juniors and seniors to conduct independent study with faculty members, then publish their results in professional journals.

"Be prepared for long cold winters."

Those same professors teach all Bowdoin classes—there are no graduate students here, and thus no TAs—and their skills in the classroom draw raves. "The department chair taught my introductory physics course," says a chemistry major. "As a freshman, I had a class with one other student taught by a tenured professor," says a junior anthropology major, who adds there are "amazing professors across the board." The recent shift to a plus-minus grading system has made the academic climate more competitive. "There is a bit more emphasis on grades, and students think more about them as they try to figure out where they currently stand," says a biology major. "While there may be a great difference between a B-plus and a B-minus student, it was far simpler and de-emphasized before."

Before school begins, about 70 percent of the entering class takes preorientation hiking, canoeing, or sea kayaking trips, which teach them about the people and landscape of Maine. There's a community service experience in Brunswick for students less interested in the outdoors. The entering class also reads the same book before arriving, to start the year with a common academic experience.

Eighty-two percent of students hail from outside Maine; most are generally hard-working, fun-loving, athletic types. "It's a very friendly campus of mostly white, upper-middle-class students wearing polo shirts with upturned collars and Patagonia fleeces, and carrying Nalgene water bottles," says a sophomore. African Americans make up 5 percent of the student body, Hispanics 6 percent, and Asian Americans add 11 percent. Bowdoin was the first U.S. institution to make SAT I scores an optional part of the admissions process, shifting the emphasis to a student's whole body of work. Merit scholarships worth an average of $1,000 are available to qualified students.

Ninety-three percent of Bowdoin students live on campus, where "freshmen start off in a two-room triple (or if you're lucky, a two-room double), so you'll never be kept up by your roommate typing a paper at 3 a.m.," says a chemistry major.

Students give rave reviews to dining service workers and the food they serve. Students also love the lobster bake that kicks off each school year, and vegans and vegetarians are happy with the options available to them.

"The department chair taught my introductory physics course."

After that, students try their luck with the lottery, although members of the social houses, which have replaced sororities and fraternities, can escape by living with these groups. Upperclassmen may choose four-bedroom quads. Students give rave reviews to dining service workers and the food they serve. Students also love the lobster bake that kicks off each school year, and vegans and vegetarians are happy with the options available to them.

With the Greeks gone, social life at Bowdoin centers around two groups, says a sophomore: sports teams and social houses. "The college does bring in campuswide entertainment, such as hypnotists, bands, and comedians," says a senior. "In addition, there is usually a party open to the entire campus at one or more of the social houses every weekend." While all parties and kegs must be registered, "unless the parties create havoc in the neighborhood by being too loud or rambunctious, security tends not to intrude," says an art history major. Students look forward to homecoming, the BearAIDS benefit concert, and Ivies Weekend, one last blast of fun before spring finals. The latter celebrates the fact that Bowdoin didn't join the Ivy League, with bands and games in the quad.

One student says Brunswick (population 21,000) is "a cute coastal town" with "a funky feel, nice restaurants, and a little shopping." Another says there is an "interesting mix" of retirees, young families, college students, professors and staff. A car comes in handy for the 15-minute drive to the outlets of Freeport (including L.L. Bean's 24/7 factory store) or a quick trip to Portland for a "real" night out. A school shuttle takes students to Boston, less than three hours' away, and ski bums will find several resorts even closer. Habitat for Humanity and various mentoring programs help build bridges between local residents and students. For those who get really stir-crazy, study abroad programs are available in more than 100 countries, including warm ones like Ecuador (a welcomed treat when you consider the normally brutal New England winters). Sixty percent of students take advantage of such programs.

While "the long winters are certainly not a favorite," according to a senior, they do bring out school spirit, with any sporting event against Colby—especially hockey games—inspiring excitement. "That rivalry is almost out of control," says a biology major. "The chanting is brutal, and dead fish have been known to fly onto the ice." Bowdoin's Bears compete in the Division III New England Small College Athletic Conference, and students "get blacked out" to demonstrate support, wearing all black when they attend games. The women's basketball

Undergraduate research is a priority, and it's common for juniors and seniors to conduct independent study with faculty members, then publish their results in professional journals.

"The college does bring in campuswide entertainment such as hypnotists, bands, and comedians."

team fields perennially strong squads and has captured the NESCAC championship for three consecutive years. Students have a big say in the start-up of intramural programs, and about 40 percent play an intramural sport in a given semester.

Outdoorsy types and those who can brave the cold will find warm and inviting academics at Bowdoin, where close friendships with peers and professors are easily forged. "Being able to make friends with my professors is something I'll treasure forever," says an art history major. Agrees a chemistry major: "The outstanding education and the great friends make Bowdoin a special place for me."

Overlaps
Williams, Dartmouth, Middlebury, Brown, Yale, Amherst

If You Apply To ➤

Bowdoin: Early decision: Nov. 15, Jan. 15. Regular admissions: Jan. 1. Financial aid: Jan. 1 (international applicants), Feb. 15 (regular-admissions candidates). Guarantees to meet full demonstrated need. Campus and alumni interviews: recommended, evaluative. SATs or ACTs: optional (SATs preferred). SAT IIs: optional. Accepts the Common Application and electronic applications. Essay question.

Brandeis University

Waltham, MA 02454-9110

Founded in 1948 by Jews who wanted an elite institution to call their own. Now down to 55 percent Jewish and seeking top students of all faiths. Academic specialties include the natural sciences, the Middle East, and Jewish studies. Competes with Tufts in the Boston area.

Brandeis University, founded to provide educational opportunities to those facing discrimination, has always had a reputation for intense progressive thought. Now, it's being recognized as a rising star among research institutions. The only nonsectarian Jewish-sponsored college in the nation, Brandeis continues its struggle to maintain its Jewish identity while attracting a well-rounded, eclectic group of students.

Website: www.brandeis.edu
Location: Suburban
Total Enrollment: 4,518
Undergraduates: 3,145

Set on a hilltop in a pleasant residential neighborhood nine miles west of Boston, Brandeis's attractively landscaped 270-acre campus boasts many distinctive buildings. The music building, for example, is shaped like a grand piano; the theater looks like a top hat. The 24-hour Carl and Ruth Shapiro Campus Center includes a student theater, electronic library and bookstore, and the Rose Art Museum recently received a 7,300-square-foot addition that doubled its exhibition space. The Abraham Shapiro Academic Building houses a state-of-the-art distance-learning classroom, conference rooms, the International Center for Ethics, Justice, and Public Life, the Center for Middle Eastern Studies, the Mandel Center for Jewish Education, and faculty office. A new 34,000-square-foot addition to the Heller School for Social Policy and Management will include classrooms, offices, and a forum for lectures and events, as well as a cafe and grouped lounge seating on several levels.

Biochemistry, chemistry, neuroscience, and physics are top-notch programs, while economics, biology, psychology, and politics enroll the most students. Dedicated premeds are catered to hand and foot, with special advisors, internships, and their own premedical center, with specialized laboratories designed to provide would-be MDs with research opportunities. Grad school acceptance rates are impressive; 80 percent.

With the largest faculty in the field outside of Israel, the university is virtually unrivaled in Near Eastern and Judaic studies; Hebrew is a Brandeis specialty. East Asian studies gives students a broad yet intimate knowledge of the history, politics, economics, art, and language of the major areas of East Asia. A growing number of popular interdisciplinary programs including business, journalism, and legal, environmental, Latin American, peace, and women's and gender studies, add spice to the academic menu. Brandeis also maintains a commitment to the creative arts, with strong theater offerings and a theory-based music program founded by the late Leonard Bernstein. Over two-thirds of the classes have 25 or fewer students. Newer majors include history, politics, and Yiddish and Eastern European Jewish Culture.

The Brandeis core curriculum is rooted in a commitment to developing strong writing, foreign language, and quantitative-reasoning skills and an interdisciplinary and crosscultural perspective. Rising sophomores and juniors now have the opportunity to earn credit through summer internships related to their studies, and more than 250 study abroad programs are offered in 70 countries; 28 percent of each class takes advantage of these opportunities.

Seventeen percent of the Brandeis student population are from Massachusetts and heavily bicoastal otherwise, with sizable numbers of New York, New Jersey, and California residents. The group is also very bright; 89 percent graduated in the top quarter of their high school class, and professors

"Brandeis takes its academic integrity seriously."

want them to continue working hard. Students say the academic climate here is intense. "Brandeis takes its academic integrity seriously," says a creative writing and English major. There is an out for those in need of respite; the Flex 3 option allows students to take three classes one semester if an especially rough course is required, and five the next, to stay on track for four-year graduation.

Though more than half the student body is Jewish, there are three chapels on campus—Catholic, Jewish, and Protestant—built so that the shadow of one never crosses the shadow of another. It's an architectural symbol that students say reflects the realities of the campus community. Muslim students, with an enrollment of over 200, have their own dedicated prayer space. African Americans make up 3 percent of the student body, Hispanics 3 percent, and Asian Americans 9 percent. "Brandeis's character offers a great opportunity to either gain a totally new insight and experience, or to connect in a small community," explains a sophomore. Gays and lesbians have an established presence, and throw some of the liveliest parties. The unofficial fraternities and sororities that have colonized at Brandeis are clamoring for recognition from the school. Other hot-button issues include political correctness, rape awareness, and environmental causes.

Even with one of the highest tuition rates in the country, Brandeis does not guarantee to meet each student's full demonstrated need, but help is generally available to those who apply on time. The level of support remains fairly constant over four years, students report. The university also offers merit scholarships, averaging $17,454. The eight-day freshman orientation program is one of the most extensive in the nation, and includes a broad spectrum of events, such as a Boston Harbor cruise and special programs for minority, international, commuter, and transfer students.

As befits its mold-breaking heritage, Brandeis is the only school in the nation where you can live in a replica of a Scottish castle with pie-shaped rooms and stairways leading to nowhere. More pedestrian housing options include traditional quadrangle dormitories, where freshmen and sophomores live in doubles, and juniors live in singles. The Foster Living Center, or the "Mods," are

"Brandeis students are more focused on grades and academics, and less on big parties or Greek life."

coed, university-owned town houses reserved for seniors. The newest option is The Village, which offers singles and doubles clustered around family-style kitchens, semi-private bathrooms, and lounges. Freshmen and sophomores are guaranteed housing, while upperclassmen play the lottery each spring. Eighty-two percent of students live on campus, and the rest find affordable off-campus housing nearby. Brandeis boasts the best college food in the Boston area, as well as the most appetizing set-ups, students say, thanks to a decision to outsource dining services. Campus meal tickets buy lunch or dinner in a fast-food joint, the pub, a country store, a kosher dining hall with vegetarian selections, or the Boulevard, a cafeteria where "the salad bars are huge."

Social life at Brandeis offers lots of options for those ready to relax. There are 257 campus clubs to keep students busy, but "Brandeis students are more focused on grades and academics, and less on big parties or Greek life," says a student. Weekends begin on Thursday, with live entertainment at the on-campus Stein pub. Students can party at will in the dorms providing they don't get too rambunctious, but suites are officially "dry" unless a majority of the residents are over 21. Major events on the campus calendar include a Tropics Night dance (where beachwear is required in February), the massive Bronstein Weekend festival just before spring finals, and the "Screw Your Roommate" dance, where dormies set up their roommates on blind dates. Also well attended are the homecoming soccer match and the annual lacrosse tilt against crosstown rival Bentley College. The possibilities for off-campus diversion are nearly infinite, thanks to the proximity of Boston and Cambridge, which are accessible by the free Brandeis shuttle bus or a nearby commuter train. (A car is more trouble than it's worth.) And what about Waltham, Brandeis's host town? Waltham receives lukewarm reviews from the students but one global studies major asks, "Who needs Waltham for excitement when Boston is a short shuttle ride away?"

Though the school does not field a football team, Brandeis has developed strong men's baseball and swimming and women's swimming, fencing, and cross-country squads, all of which have taken regional championships in recent years. In 2004, the women's basketball team won the ECAC conference title. The athletic program gets a boost from its membership in the NCAA Division III University Athletic Association, a neo–Ivy League for high-powered academic institutions such as the University of Chicago, Johns Hopkins, and Carnegie Mellon. Brandeis's sports facilities

Rising sophomores and juniors now have the opportunity to earn credit through summer internships related to their studies, and more than 250 study abroad programs are offered in 70 countries.

Social life at Brandeis offers lots of options for those ready to relax. There are 257 campus clubs to keep students busy.

include the 70,000-square-foot Gosman Sports and Convocation Center, which has hosted the NCAA fencing championships three times in the past 10 years.

Few private universities have come as far as Brandeis so quickly, evolving from a bare 270-acre site with the leftovers of a failed veterinary school to a modern research university of more than 100 buildings, a $520 million endowment, and ever-evolving academic opportunities. Landscaping, dining services, health services, and the campus computer network have all been dramatically improved in the past few years, students say, adding to their feelings of pride in the school. One student sums it up this way: "Brandeis is not only an awesome place to get an education, it's also an open, accepting place where anyone can feel at home."

Overlaps

Boston, Brown, NYU, Tufts, Cornell

If You Apply To ➤

Brandeis: Early decision: Jan. 1. Regular admissions: Jan. 15. Financial aid: Jan. 31. Does not guarantee to meet demonstrated need. Campus interviews: recommended, evaluative. Alumni interviews: optional, evaluative. SATs or ACTs: required (SAT I preferred). SAT IIs: required (two different subject areas). Accepts the Common Application and electronic applications. Essay question: Personal statement.

Brigham Young University

Provo, UT 84602

BEST BUY

From the time they are knee-high, Mormons in all corners of the country dream about coming to BYU. Most men and some women do a two-year stint as a missionary. The atmosphere is generally mild-mannered and conservative. Goes absolutely bonkers for its sports teams.

Website: www.byu.edu
Location: City
Total Enrollment: 26,586
Undergraduates: 24,948
Male/Female: 51/49
SAT Ranges: V 550–660
M 570–670
ACT Range: 25–29
Financial Aid: 36%
Expense: Pr $
Phi Beta Kappa: No
Applicants: 9,237
Accepted: 76%
Enrolled: 79%
Grad in 6 Years: 74%
Returning Freshmen: 95%
Academics: ✍ ✍ ✍
Social: ☎ ☎ ☎
Q of L: ★★★★
Admissions: (801) 422-2507
Email Address:
admissions@byu.edu

Brigham Young University's strong ties with the Church of Jesus Christ of Latter-Day Saints means "BYU has high morals and a wholesome environment, which makes students feel safe and comfortable," a senior says. A sense of spirituality pervades most everything at BYU, where faith and academia are intertwined and life is governed by a strict code of ethics, covering everything from dating to academic dishonesty. Indeed, the school's commitment to church values is the reason most students choose it. "The students who attend BYU are unique," says a communication major. "Everyone is clean-cut, shaven, modestly dressed, and proper in their etiquette."

The church's values of prosperity, chastity, and obedience are strongly evidenced on BYU's 557-acre campus, where the utilitarian buildings, like everything else, are "clean, modern, and orderly." The campus sits 4,600 feet above sea level, between the shores of Utah Lake and Mount Timpanogos, with breathtaking sunsets and easy access to magnificent skiing, camping, and hiking areas. Days begin early; church bells rouse students at 8 a.m. with the first four bars of the church hymn "Come, Come Ye Saints." (The same bells also peal every hour throughout the day.) The Joseph S. Smith building, new student housing, an indoor practice facility, and a student athlete building have recently been completed.

The church's influence continues when students set their schedules; students must take one religion course per term to graduate, and offerings include, of course, the Book of Mormon. BYU requires students to demonstrate proficiency in math, writing (first-year and advanced), and advanced languages, a catch-all category that can be satisfied with coursework in a foreign language or in statistics, advanced math or advanced music. Students must also complete an extensive liberal arts core, which includes work in civilization, American heritage, biology, physical sciences, and wellness (three physical education or dance activity courses), and electives in the natural sciences, social and behavioral sciences, and arts and letters. "You have to put in a lot of time in order to succeed," an English major says. "There are few slackers at BYU."

BYU's academic offerings run the gamut, from liberal arts and sciences to professional programs in engineering, nursing, business, and law. Students say the strongest offerings include the J. Rueben Clark Law School and most departments in the Marriott School of Management, especially accounting. New programs include Japanese teaching, music performance, and studio art. Agronomy, botany, conservation biology, and range science performance classes have recently been dropped. Brigham Young also has campuses in Idaho and Hawaii, a center in Jerusalem, and study abroad programs in Vienna, London, and elsewhere.

Freshman are usually taught by full-time professors, who generally get good marks. "The professors are dedicated to helping students learn the material and succeed in their field of study," one senior says. But another senior says "there are so many students in each class that it's hard to have one-on-one contact with the professor." The honors program, open to highly motivated students, offers small seminars with more faculty interaction, and is "an excellent way to get more out of your college experience," one participant says. The strength of the faculty is one reason BYU has more full-time students than any other church-sponsored university in the U.S. Still, with thousands of students to accommodate, registration can be a chore. Approximately 80 percent of the men and 12 percent of the women interrupt their studies—typically after the freshman year—to serve two years as a missionary.

"BYU has high morals and a wholesome environment."

Thirty percent of BYU students are from Utah. Many others hail from California and Idaho, and about 9 percent come from more than 100 other countries, testifying to the effective and far-flung Latter-day Saint missionary effort. Despite the heavy international presence, the student body remains largely white, with Asian American and Hispanic students contributing about 3 percent each, and African Americans and Native Americans less than 1 percent each. Their Honor Code requires students to eschew drinking, smoking, and drugs; a city ordinance in Provo takes care of the "vice" of dancing. Politically, "many of the students have the same views so there is not much activism on campus," says an English major. Tuition for church members is lower than for nonmembers, because Latter-day Saint families contribute to BYU through their tithes. Academic scholarships and 396 athletic scholarships, in several sports, are available.

Twenty percent of BYU students—primarily freshmen—live in the single-sex residence halls, where the "very valuable" Freshman Academy program allows them to take courses and eat meals with fellow dorm-dwellers and professors. "They are so much fun to live in and very social," a senior says. A senior

"You have to put in a lot of time in order to succeed."

says the Helaman Halls are the nicest bet for freshmen. "On-campus housing is limited, however." Upperclassmen typically opt for cheaper off-campus apartments, which are also single-sex (remember the Honor Code?). When it comes to chow, the student dining and frequent fast-food outlets on campus leave some in search of healthier and less greasy options. "The food is good, but let's be honest, you're definitely ready for Mom's home cookin' by Thanksgiving," declares a senior. Concerned with security? "Could you get any safer than BYU? The students don't think so," asserts a senior.

Whether it's work with the homeless or disabled, dances, concerts, plays, or sporting events, most of BYU's social life is organized through or linked to the church. Community service is big, with students visiting patients at hospitals and

(Continued)
Strongest Programs:
Business
Law
Engineering
Languages
Nursing

One of the most popular courses is ballroom dancing, partly because many participants aspire to join BYU's award-winning dance team.

care centers, performing at local festivals, and building and refurbishing houses. Dating is common, within the church's bounds of propriety and is given a light-hearted feeling with groups that encourage "creative dating and lots of dating, period," says a senior. There are no fraternities and sororities to provide housing or parties, which is just fine with most students, since alcoholic and caffeinated drinks are both banned. "There's a reason we're voted the No. 1 Stone-Cold Sober University every year," says a student. Don't be deterred by this as you will still find plenty to do in the social scene. The college does what it can to keep the students too busy to realize that they're still sober, with activities like dances, firesides, and "tons of clubs for every interest," according to a senior. Road trips include Vegas or southern Utah and, with the mountains being so close, you'll find plenty of skiing and camping. Provo itself has plenty of places to eat, shop, and play for those needing a quick getaway from the strict administration enforcing the even stricter honor code. "The town is very supportive of the university, especially the athletic programs," a senior says. "Many of the stores hang up the school flag in the window."

Physical fitness is big here, and the intramural facilities are some of the country's best, with indoor and outdoor jogging tracks; courts for tennis, racquetball, and handball; and a pool. Also important are varsity sports; the church philosophy of obedience has worked wonders

"Could you get any safer than BYU? The students don't think so."

for Cougar teams and the football rivalry against the University of Utah provides some serious end-of-season intensity. One of the most popular courses offered at BYU is ballroom dancing, partly because many participants aspire to join BYU's award-winning dance team. The ESPN television network has dubbed the BYU–Utah rivalry the "Holy War."

To most Americans, BYU probably seems old-fashioned or like a step back in time. But for young members of The Church of Jesus Christ, that may be just what the elder ordered. "BYU's dedicated faculty, devout atmosphere, and beautiful, clean campus set it apart from all other universities," a satisfied senior says.

University of British Columbia: See page 328.

Brown University

45 Prospect Street, Providence, RI 02912

To today's stressed-out students, the thought of taking every course pass/fail is a dream come true. In reality, nobody does, but the pass/fail option, combined with Brown's lack of distribution requirements, gives it the freewheeling image that students love. Bashed by conservatives as a hotbed of political correctness.

Brown University is a perennial "hot college," with an overwhelming number of happy students and many more clamoring to join their ranks. Once here, students not only receive a prestigious and quality education, but a chance to explore their creative sides at a liberal arts college that does not emphasize grades and preprofessionalism and shuns required courses. Brown's environment and policies have drawn both praise and criticism over the years, but its students thrive on this discussion and lively debate. "The freedom of shaping one's own education is both frightening and exhilarating, since the possibilities for good and ill are almost endless," says one student.

Located atop College Hill on the east side of Providence, Brown's 140-acre campus affords an excellent view of downtown Providence that is especially pleasing at sunset. Campus architecture is a composite of old and new—plenty of grassy lawns surrounded by historic buildings that offer students refuge from the city streets beyond. One student describes it as a "melting pot of architecture's finest. We have a building that resembles a Greek temple [and] buildings in the Richardsonian tradition." The neighborhoods that surround the campus lie within a national historic district and boast beautiful tree-lined streets full of ethnic charm. New additions include the English and creative writing department buildings.

Brown's faculty has successfully resisted the notion that somewhere in their collective wisdom and experience lies a core of knowledge that every educated person should possess. As a result, aside from completing courses in a major, the only universitywide requirements for graduation are to demonstrate writing competency and complete the 30-course minimum satisfactorily. (The assumption is that students will take four courses a term for a total of 32 in four years.) Freshmen have no requirements. Those with interests in interdisciplinary fields will enjoy Brown's wide range

"The freedom of shaping one's own education is both frightening and exhilarating."

of concentrations that cross departmental lines and cover everything from cognitive science to public policy. Indeed, there are bona fide departments in cognitive and linguistic sciences and media and modern culture. Students can also create their own concentration from the array of goodies offered. Brown also offers group independent-study projects, a popular alternative for students with the gumption to take a course they have to construct primarily by themselves. Particularly adventurous students can choose to spend time in one of Brown's 57 study abroad programs in 18 countries, including Brazil, Great Britain, France, Tanzania, Japan, Denmark, and Egypt. Closer to home, students can crossregister with Rhode Island School of Design, also on College Hill, or participate in the Venture Program.*

Students can take their classes one of two ways: for traditional marks of A, B, C, or No Credit; or for Satisfactory/No Credit. The NC is not recorded on the transcript, while the letter grade or Satisfactory can be supplemented by a written evaluation from the professor. A habit of NCs, however, lands students in academic hot water. Any fewer than seven courses passed in two consecutive semesters makes for an academic "warning" that does find its way onto the transcript, and means potential dismissal from the university.

The most popular majors are international relations, biology, history, economics, and political science. History and geology are some of the university's best, and students also praise computer science, religious studies, and applied math. Other top-notch programs include comparative literature, classics, modern languages, and the writing program in the English department. Among the sciences, engineering and the premed curriculum are standouts. Future doctors can try for a competitive eight-year liberal medical education program where students can earn an MD without having to sacrifice their humanity. Sociology, psychology, and math receive thumbs down from some students. Fields related to scientific technology have very good

Website: www.brown.edu
Location: City center
Total Enrollment: 7,820
Undergraduates: 5,864
Male/Female: 46/54
SAT Ranges: V 660–760
  M 670–790
ACT Range: 27–33
Financial Aid: 47%
Expense: Pr $ $ $ $
Phi Beta Kappa: Yes
Applicants: 16,911
Accepted: 15%
Enrolled: 57%
Grad in 6 Years: 95%
Returning Freshmen: 97%
Academics: 🎓🎓🎓🎓
Social: ☎☎☎☎
Q of L: ★★★★★
Admissions: (401) 863-2378
Email Address:
  admission_undergraduate@
  brown.edu

Strongest Programs:
History
Geology
Computer Science
Religious Studies
Film and Television
Engineering
Art and Design
Writing
International Relations

facilities, including an instructional technology center, while minority issues are studied at the Center for Race and Ethnicity. New degrees include Commerce, Organizations & Entrepreneurship, Literary Arts, and Science & Society. Biomedical Ethics has been dropped.

Brown prides itself on undergraduate teaching and considers skill in the classroom as much as the usual scholarly credentials when making tenure decisions. Younger professors can receive fellowships for outstanding teaching, and the administration's interest in interdisciplinary instruction and imaginative course design help cultivate high-quality instruction. The size of the faculty ranks is being increased by 20 percent, and investment in university libraries has also risen. The advising system reflects the administration's commitment to treat students as adults. The lack of predetermined requirements is supposed to challenge students, so "no one is going to tell you what to take." The advising system pairs each freshman with a professor and a peer advisor, and resident counselors in the dorms are also available to lend an ear. "As an Asian, I have an Asian advisor as well as a woman's peer counselor, a resident counselor, a minority counselor, and a head counselor who lived on my floor in the dorm," reports one well-advised student. Sophomores utilize special advising resources, upperclassmen are assigned an advisor in their concentration, and a pool of interdisciplinary faculty counselors is on hand for general academic advising problems.

Brown offers more than 100 freshman courses via the Curricular Advising Program (CAP), and the professors in these courses officially serve as academic advisors for their students' first year. This program receives mixed reviews, but some professors are highly praised by students for their abilities and availability. "They are very casual about open office hours, and welcome students to pop in for a chat," one student says. Upper-level classes are usually in the teens, CAP courses are limited to 20, and only 12 percent of introductory lectures have more than 50 students. Especially popular courses are usually jammed with students, and often there aren't enough teaching assistants to staff them effectively. Some popular smaller courses, especially writing courses in the English department and studio art courses, can be nearly impossible to get into, although the administration claims that perseverance makes perfect—in other words, show up the first day and beg shamelessly. Compared with the other Ivies, Brown's academic climate is relatively casual, or at least seems to be. "There is not much competition between students at Brown," one student says. "Everyone is sort of on their own academic path, and the motivation comes from within."

"The students who attend Brown aren't all hippies," chides a junior. "There is no typical Brown student. The jock will do theater, the geek will play ultimate Frisbee, and the average Joe/Jane will do at least two extracurricular activities." With a mere 4 percent of students hailing from Rhode Island, geographical diversity is one of Brown's hallmarks. Brown is one of the few remaining hotspots of student activism in the nation; nary has a semester passed without at least one demonstration about the issue of the day. Students of color account for 29 percent of the population, and foreigners make up 6 percent. Minorities rarely miss an opportunity to speak out on issues of concern. The gay and lesbian community is also prominent. "They throw the best dances on campus," says one science major. Ninety-nine percent of students were in the top quarter of their high school class, and 40 percent hail from private or parochial schools.

Brown admits all students regardless of their financial need, and although it doesn't offer athletic or academic merit scholarships, it does guarantee to meet the full demonstrated need of everyone admitted. Fifteen Starr National Service scholarships, ranging from $1,000 to $2,000, are awarded each year to students who devote

Brown prides itself on undergraduate teaching and considers skill in the classroom as much as the usual scholarly credentials when making tenure decisions.

"Everyone is sort of on their own academic path and the motivation comes from within."

a year or more to volunteer public service jobs. About 120 other "academically superlative" students, called University Scholars, will find their financial aid package sweetened with extra grant money. Brown's use of binding early decision, also used by Princeton, has made some waves.

Freshmen arrive on campus a few days before everyone else for orientation, which includes a trip to Newport, and there is also a Third World Transition Program. About half the freshmen are assigned to one of the eight co-ed Keeney Quad dorms, in "loud and rambunctious" units of 30 to 40 with several sophomore or junior dorm counselors. The other half live in the quieter Pembroke campus dorms or in a few other scattered locations. After the freshman year, students seeking on-campus housing enter a lottery. The lottery is based on seniority, and sometimes the leftovers for sophomores can be a little skimpy, though there are some special program houses set aside to give them a chance to focus their interests in residential halls.

The dorms themselves are fairly nondescript. "There are no fireplaces or engraved wood trim a la Princeton," observes one student, but nevertheless there are many options from which to choose, including apartment-like suites with kitchens, three sororities, two social dorms, and three co-ed fraternities. Brown guarantees housing all four years, and a dorm with suites of singles ensures that there is room for all. A significant number of upperclassmen get "off-campus permission." Places nearby are becoming more plentiful and more expensive as the area gentrifies. Brown's food service, which gets high marks from

"The students who attend Brown aren't all hippies."

students for tastiness and variety, offers meal plans ranging from seven to 20 meals a week. Everyone on a meal plan gets a credit card that allows the student to do what students at every other school only wish they could: use the meal ticket for nocturnal visits to snack bars should they miss a regular meal in one of Brown's two dining halls. Campus security is described as "very good." Says a junior, "I feel safer here than I do at home."

Providence is an old industrial city that recently underwent a renaissance. It is still the butt of student jokes—"Be prepared to wear your proletarian disguise," cautions one—but extensive renovations of the downtown area have had a positive impact. Providence is Rhode Island's capital, so many internship opportunities in state government are available, as are a few good music joints, lively bars, and a number of fine, inexpensive restaurants. For the couch-potato set, there are plenty of good things right in the neighborhood. "Downtown is a 10-minute walk, but why bother when you can buy anything from Cap'n Crunch to cowboy boots on Thayer Street, which runs through the east side of campus?" asks a philosophy major. For a change of scenery, many students head to Boston or the beaches of Newport, each an hour away.

The few residential Greek organizations are generally considered much too un-mellow for Brown's taste (only 12 percent of the men and 2 percent of the women sign up), and hence freshmen and sophomores are their chief clientele. The nonresidential black fraternities and sororities serve a more comprehensive student life function. Tighter drinking rules have curtailed campus drinking somewhat. The university sponsors frequent campuswide parties and plays, concerts, and special events abound. Funk Nite every Thursday night at the Underground, a campus pub, draws a mixed bag of dancing fools. The biggest annual bash of the year is Spring Weekend, which includes plenty of parties and a big-name band. Strong theater and dance programs, daily and weekly newspapers, a skydiving club, political organizations, and "even a Scrabble club and a successful croquet team" represent just a few of the ways Brown students manage to keep themselves entertained. One other is the campus student center, which has been thoroughly renovated. For those interested in community outreach—and there are many at Brown who are—the university's nationally recognized

Among the sciences, engineering and the premed curriculum are standouts. Future doctors can try for a competitive eight-year liberal medical education program where students can earn an MD without having to sacrifice their humanity.

Brown admits all students regardless of their financial need, and although it doesn't offer athletic or academic merit scholarships, it does guarantee to meet the full demonstrated need of everyone admitted.

public service center helps place students in a variety of volunteer positions. The Brown Community Outreach, in fact, is the largest student organization on campus.

Brown isn't an especially sports-minded school, but a number of teams nevertheless manage to excel. Of the 37 varsity teams, recent Ivy League champions include the volleyball, women's crew, men's tennis, and men's soccer teams. The

"Downtown is a 10-minute walk."

women's cross-country squad finished third in the NCAA Regional Championships in 2002. Athletic facilities include an Olympic-size swimming pool and an indoor athletic complex with everything from tennis courts to weight rooms. There's also a basketball arena for those trying to perfect their slam dunks. The intramural program is solid, mixing fun with competitiveness.

Ever since the days of Roger Williams, Rhode Island has been known as a land of tolerance, and Brown certainly is a 20th-century embodiment of this tradition. The education offered at this university is decidedly different from that provided by the rest of the Ivy League, or for that matter, by most of the country's top universities. Brown is content to gather a talented bunch of students, offer a diverse and imaginative array of courses, and then let the undergraduates, with a little help, make sense of it all. It takes an enormous amount of initiative, maturity, and self-confidence to thrive at Brown, but most students feel they are up to the challenge. "You get four years of choice," says one student. "Deal with it."

Overlaps

Harvard, Yale, Stanford, Columbia, Penn, Dartmouth

If You Apply To ➤

Brown: Early decision: Nov. 1. Regular admissions: Jan. 1. Financial aid: Feb. 1 for regular admissions. Does not guarantee to meet demonstrated need. No campus interviews. Alumni interviews: optional, evaluative. SATs or ACTs: required. SAT IIs: required (any three). Accepts electronic applications. Essay question: personal statement.

Bryn Mawr College

101 North Merion Avenue, Bryn Mawr, PA 19010-2899

BMC has the most brainpower per capita of the elite women's colleges. Politics range from liberal to radical. Do Bryn Mawrtyrs take themselves a little too seriously? The college still benefits from ties to nearby Haverford, though the relationship is not as close as in the days when Haverford was all male.

Website: www.brynmawr.edu
Location: Suburban
Total Enrollment: 1,564
Undergraduates: 1,293
Male/Female: 2/98
SAT Ranges: V 620–720
    M 600–690
ACT Range: 25–30
Financial Aid: 54%
Expense: Pr $ $ $
Phi Beta Kappa: No
Applicants: 1,926
Accepted: 47%

Leafy suburban enclaves are a dime a dozen around Philadelphia. But only one is home to Bryn Mawr College, a top-notch liberal arts school. On this campus, students find a range of academic pursuits from archeology to film studies to physics, and a diverse yet community-oriented student body. Founded in 1885, Bryn Mawr has evolved into a place that prepares students for life and work in a global environment. Although students here abide by a strict academic honor code and participate in a host of loopy and long-standing campus traditions, they remain doggedly individualistic.

Bryn Mawr's lovely campus is a path-laced oasis set among trees (many carefully labeled with Latin and English names) and lush green hills, perfect for an afternoon walk, bike ride, or jog. Just a 20-minute train ride to downtown Philadelphia, Bryn Mawr provides a country setting with a vital and exciting city nearby. The predominant architecture is collegiate Gothic, a combination of the Gothic architecture of Oxford and Cambridge Universities and the local landscape, a style that Bryn Mawr introduced to the United States. Ten of Bryn Mawr's buildings are listed in the National Register of Historic Places. The M. Carey Thomas Library, which was named after the school's first dean and second president, a pioneer in women's education, is also a National Historic Landmark. Variations on the collegiate Gothic theme include a sprinkling of modern buildings, such as Louis Kahn's slate-and-concrete residence hall and the redbrick foreign language dormitory. Recent campus additions include a 30,000-square-foot building for the departments of education and psychology and the renovation of four former faculty houses to create a student activity village called Cambrian Row.

Out of respect for their academic honor code, students refrain from discussing their grades, but they freely admit that they work hard. "The atmosphere is intense, and the classes are rigorous, but very interesting," says a political science major. A biology major adds, "Mawrtyrs have a commitment to engaging in intellectually stimulating reading, writing, and discussion." Most departments are strong, especially the sciences, classics, archaeology, art history, and the foreign languages, including Russian and Chinese. The Fine Arts Department, however, is relatively small. Doing serious work in music, art, photography, or astronomy requires a hike over to Haverford, Bryn Mawr's nearby partner in the "bi-college" system. Bryn Mawr handles the theater, dance, creative writing, geology, art history, Italian, and Russian programs for the two colleges, and the departments of German and French are joint efforts. Bryn Mawr also offers a rich variety of special programs. Approximately one-third of students study overseas during their junior year. Projects range from fieldwork in the Aleutian Islands with the Anthropology Department to studying Viennese architecture with the Growth and Structure of Cities Department.

> **"The atmosphere is intense, and the classes are rigorous."**

The general education requirements include two classes in each of the three divisions (social sciences, natural sciences, and the humanities), one semester of "quantitative" work, an intermediate level of competency in a foreign language, and the requirements of a major. Students are also required to take eight half-semesters of physical education and must also pass a swimming test. In addition, all freshmen are required to take two College Seminars to develop their critical thinking, writing, and discussion skills.

The quality of teaching at Bryn Mawr is unquestionably high. "Teachers are very accessible and endlessly interested in their material and in making sure that we learn it and appreciate it fundamentally," a senior says. "The teachers are brilliant and always available," a classmate adds. Freshmen and transfer students are initiated to the Bryn Mawr experience during Customs Week, which includes a variety of seminars and workshops as well as a tour of the campus and town. For those looking ahead to see what the steep tuition will buy in the long term, the campus has a career resource center that offers information on interviewing and building a résumé. It also brings recruiters to campus, offers mock interviews, and keeps students posted on internships.

> **"Students at Bryn Mawr are extremely self-motivated, ambitious, intelligent and confident."**

"Students at Bryn Mawr are extremely self-motivated, ambitious, intelligent, and confident," says a sophomore. African Americans make up 3 percent of the student body, Hispanics 3 percent, and Asian Americans 11 percent. To encourage diversity and harmony on campus, freshmen can take an intensive four-hour session during orientation on pluralism, which teaches students to examine assumptions about class, race, and sexual orientation. "Mawrtyrs are intellectually curious and stimulating," says a biology major, who adds, "We are willing to roll up our sleeves, whether it is to solve a complex math proof or fight poverty. Many of us are idealists, and we

(Continued)

Enrolled: 40%
Grad in 6 Years: 85%
Returning Freshmen: 91%
Academics: 🖊 🖊 🖊 🖊 🖊
Social: ☎ ☎ ☎
Q of L: ★ ★ ★
Admissions: (610) 526-5152
Email Address:
   admissions@brynmawr.edu

Strongest Programs:
Archaeology
Growth and Structure of Cities
Physics
Mathematics
Art History
Classics
Foreign Languages

are not afraid to admit it or stop fighting for what we believe in." Scholarships are not available, but the school does guarantee to meet the demonstrated financial need of every admit.

Another guarantee is quality on-campus housing for all four years. "They usually do a stellar job of placing roommates together freshman year," says a senior. "After that, it is almost always possible to get a single if you want one." Dorm features include hardwood floors, window seats, and fireplaces, says another senior. For good reason, the food service has received a national award from Restaurants and Institutions magazine. "It's not unusual to see the entire baseball team from neighboring Haverford College piling into Bryn Mawr's dining halls in the evenings. "The food is really that good!" says a student. A classmates adds, "I am a vegetarian, and I am in heaven every time I go into the dining hall."

Bryn Mawr is located on suburban Philly's wealthy Main Line (named after a railroad). and the campus is two blocks from the train station. "The town of Bryn Mawr is very much upper-class suburban," says an English major. "Coffee shops, bookstores, and restaurants provide student hangouts, while 'Main Line moms' frequent the gourmet grocery stores and overpriced gyms." A 20-minute train ride provides students with easy access to cultural attractions, as well to social and academic events at the

"Coffee shops, bookstores, and restaurants provide student hangouts."

nearby University of Pennsylvania. Students can also catch a bus to the mall or take a weekend trip to New York, the Jersey Shore, or even Hershey Park. In addition to campus events, students can attend social events at nearby Haverford and Swarthmore colleges. "Much of the co-ed social life takes place on Haverford's campus," says a senior. Aside from being basically a women's college, "the social aspect of Bryn Mawr is very hard at times considering how much work there is," says a political science major, "but that just means students need to take an active role in making a social life for themselves."

Tradition is a very important part of the campus social scene. The Elizabethan-style May Day festivities are held the Sunday after classes end in May. Everyone wears white, eats strawberries, and watches Greek plays. Students are known to skinny-dip in the fountains and drink champagne on the lawn. The presentation of lanterns and class colors to incoming freshmen on Lantern Night, and regal pageants, such as Parade Night, Hell Week, and Step-Sings, fill life with a Gothic sense of wonder and school spirit. Says a student, "They play a big role in uniting all four classes and give students a role in the greater history of the college." As for athletics, Bryn Mawr students are active in 12 intramural sports, including rugby, cross-country, volleyball, and field hockey. And, of course, there's always the champion badminton team. Club sports range from all-female teams, such as rugby, squash, and figure skating, to co-ed teams shared with Haverford College, such as Ultimate Frisbee and fencing.

Bryn Mawr is a study in contrasts: the campus is in suburbia, but steps from a major city. Humanities programs are very strong, but science majors are also enormously popular. The students are independent but revel in college traditions. The result is overwhelmingly positive. Says a sophomore, "When I sit in a math or science course with 15 other women who are smart and eager to learn, I realize that I am surrounded by women who are going places."

Bucknell University

Lewisburg, PA 17837

Bucknell, Colgate, Hamilton, Lafayette—all a little more conservative than the Ivy schools and nipping at their heels. Bucknell is the biggest of this bunch. (Perhaps Lehigh is a better comparison.) The central Pennsylvania campus is isolated but one of the most beautiful anywhere.

The "driven and bright" students at Bucknell University strike a healthy balance between hitting the books and hitting the bars—or the frat houses of their pastoral central Pennsylvania campus. Yes, they tend to be preppy and outdoorsy—"Bucknell students are mostly upper middle class, relatively conservative, and materially conscious; however, they are also highly motivated and eager to succeed." says one junior. With small classes, caring faculty (no TAs!), and not a "bad" dorm to be found, it's no wonder the only complaint is that "four years at Bucknell go by way too fast," says a junior.

In addition to being comfortable and friendly, Bucknell is physically beautiful. Located on a hill just south of quaint Lewisburg, the campus overlooks the scenic Susquehanna River valley. Playing fields, shaded by leafy trees, are sprinkled among the Greek Revival buildings. While some structures date from the 19th century, lending a fairy-tale quality, others are far more modern, including an $8 million engineering building, finished in 2004, with 38,600 square feet of office, lab, and classroom space. Bucknell is also nearing completion of a seven-year effort to renovate and refurbish 82 classrooms and 10 auditoriums. And a $5 million art building is planned for the center of campus, opposite University Center.

Students in Bucknell's College of Arts and Sciences must complete four courses in the humanities, two in social science, three in natural science and math, and a first-year Foundation Seminar, designed to strengthen research, computing, and writing skills. Two of these courses must address "broadened perspectives" on human diversity and on the natural and fabricated world. In the College of Engineering, students have a common first semester, including a special course that introduces them to all five engineering disciplines. Along with major-related requirements, each student completes a capstone project during senior year, and must demonstrate competence in writing in order to graduate. The College of Engineering has added a new MS in environmental engineering as well as the recently added major in biomedical engineering.

> "Bucknell students are mostly upper middle class, relatively conservative, and materially conscious."

After fulfilling Bucknell's many requirements, students select from a variety of courses, including the popular Management 101, where students create and sell a product and donate their profits to charity. About 38 percent of each graduating class studies abroad, and programs staffed by Bucknell professors take them to England, France, and Barbados. Relationships with other colleges and universities enable students—including engineers—to travel to more than 60 other nations, from Japan and Sweden to China, Argentina, and Australia. Independent study is common; in the past five years, 73 percent of chemistry majors have taken at least one research course for credit. The two-summer Institute of Leadership in Technology and Management allows engineering and business students to learn new ways to solve problems, while building their teamwork and communication skills. On-campus study the first summer is followed by an off-campus internship during the second.

Website: www.bucknell.edu
Location: Rural
Total Enrollment: 3,488
Undergraduates: 3,414
Male/Female: 50/50
SAT Ranges: V 600–670
  M 630–710
ACT Range: 27–31
Financial Aid: 51%
Expense: Pr $ $ $ $
Phi Beta Kappa: Yes
Applicants: 8,324
Accepted: 36%
Enrolled: 30%
Grad in 6 Years: 89%
Returning Freshmen: 95%
Academics: ✑ ✑ ✑ ✑
Social: 🐿 🐿 🐿 🐿
Q of L: ★ ★ ★
Admissions: (570) 577-1101
Email Address:
  admissions@bucknell.edu

Strongest Programs:
Humanities
English
Music
Theater
Psychology
Engineering and Natural
  Sciences
Interdisciplinary Studies

Back on campus, 95 percent of courses have fewer than 50 students, and the emphasis is on discussion and group work. "If there is a unifying characteristic of Bucknell students, it is their ability to achieve balance between academics, activities, and a social life," explains a junior. It helps that professors come to Bucknell because they want to teach: "The professors have really challenged me and made me go beyond anything I ever thought that I was capable of achieving," claims a junior. While Bucknell is known for engineering, management, and the natural sciences, students also give high marks to the English major. And administrators highlight programs in animal behavior, which benefits from an outdoor naturalistic primate facility for teaching and research, and in environmental relations, which includes not only science courses, but courses in the humanities, social policy, and civil engineering, too.

Bucknell students describe themselves as outgoing, well-rounded, ambitious and goal-oriented. Thirty percent are Pennsylvanians, and 68 percent went to public high school. Diversity has been slow in coming; Asian Americans are the largest minority group, at 6 percent of the student body, while African Americans add 3 percent and Hispanics 2 percent. Caucasian students comprise 84 percent, Native American less than 1 percent, and foreign 3 percent. The political issues roiling the world and the nation just aren't as significant here. "The campus experiences an atmosphere of political awareness that is stimulating, not stunting," says a Spanish major. Each year, Bucknell awards several merit scholarships, worth an average of $10,222 each, and six athletic scholarships—three each in men's and women's basketball.

Eighty-eight percent of Bucknellians live on campus; all first-years are required to do so, and since upperclassmen must obtain permission to leave, more than 300 live in five college-owned apartment buildings. "There really isn't a bad place to live here," says a junior. "Most dorms are air-conditioned and the furniture is very comfortable," a classmate adds. Beds have loft-style frames, helping students gain space, and though most freshmen live in doubles, students can usually get singles when they return as sophomores. About 25 percent of each entering class affiliates with one of the six intellectually focused "colleges": Arts, Humanities, Environmental, Global, Social Justice, and Society and Technology; a seminar on the theme of their college replaces the required Foundation Seminar that their classmates take. There are four dining halls and two cafes on campus. The Bison, the student snack bar, "offers wraps, burgers, pizza, subs, and Mexican," says a political science major, and it's open all day.

Bucknell's Greek system draws 35 percent of the men and 38 percent of the women, though rush is delayed to the start of sophomore year. And while the Greeks are a driving force in campus social life, there are alternatives. "There is always more than enough to do and see, from comedians and movies to performing arts shows and cultural dinners," says a political science and international relations major. Two student organizations arrange everything from carnivals to hypnotists and religious retreats, while the nonalcoholic, school-run Uptown nightclub offers dancing 'til dawn. When it comes to drinking, a point system hasn't stopped those younger than 21 from drinking, but it does provide for clarity and proportionality when offenses occur. For those who choose not to imbibe, support may be found with CALVIN and HOBBES—that's Creating a Lively, Valuable, Ingenious, and New Habit of Being at Bucknell and Enjoying Sobriety.

Market Street, in downtown Lewisburg, has an old-style movie theatre that serves up first-run flicks and food, as well as "welcoming and warm and perfect for Bucknell students," says one junior. The nearby town of Bloomsburg offers a more ethnic feel, with Indian and Thai cuisine. Through the "I Serve 2" campaign, Bucknell is trying to

Eighty-eight percent of Bucknellians live on campus; all first-years are required to do so, and since upperclassmen must obtain permission to leave, more than 300 live in five college-owned apartment buildings.

"The campus experiences an atmosphere of political awareness that is stimulating, not stunting."

get all students to complete at least two hours of community service each semester. Projects are coordinated through BISON, Bucknellians in Service to Our Neighbors. When students get claustrophobic, New York, Philadelphia, and Washington/ Baltimore are less than three hours away; the main campus of Penn State, in State College, Pennsylvania, is even closer. Bucknell also sponsors road trips to these communities for students who lack wheels. Favorite traditions include Midnight Mania (the official start of the basketball season), House Party Weekend and the formal Chrysalis Ball in the spring, and First Night, "a ceremony congratulating first-year students on the completion of their first semester," says a junior. "They learn the alma mater and serenade the president and his wife." "A great tradition occurs during orientation when the entire first-year class walks through the Christy Mathewson Gates. Four years later, at graduation, you walk through the gates in the opposite direction," says a sophomore.

> "There is always more than enough to do and see."

After fulfilling Bucknell's many requirements, students select from a variety of courses, including the popular Management 101, where students create and sell a product and donate their profits to charity.

Bucknell has captured the Patriot League Presidents' Cup, for the league's all-sports champion, 11 times in 14 years—including the last seven in a row. Men's and women's cross-country and track and field are perennially strong, and men's lacrosse has won four straight league titles. Men's and women's swimming and diving are also notable, while the women's crew team won a gold medal at Philadelphia's Dad Vail Regatta in recent years. Bucknell's biggest rivalries are with Lafayette and Lehigh, though these aren't a tremendous focus. More than 50 intramural sports draw about a third of the students, while others praise the weights and cardio machines at the new Kenneth Langone Athletic and Recreation Center, named for the former Home Depot executive and New York Stock Exchange board member.

Bucknell students get the best of both worlds: excellence in engineering and the liberal arts, abundant research opportunities, and a healthy social life. The school's central Pennsylvania location is lovely but isolated and the preponderance of preppies may seem stifling, but this campus is slowly becoming both more liberal—and more diverse. If you're seeking small classes and professors who really care, in a supportive environment with plenty of school spirit, Bucknell may be a good fit.

Overlaps
Lehigh, Colgate, Boston College, Cornell University (NY), Lafayette

If You Apply To ➤

Bucknell: Early decision: Nov. 15, Jan. 1. Regular admissions and financial aid: Jan. 1. Does not guarantee to meet demonstrated need. Campus and alumni interviews: recommended, informational. SATs or ACTs: required. SAT IIs: optional (foreign language required for any student planning to major in that language). Accepts the Common Application and electronic applications. Essay question: significant experience, achievement, risk or ethical dilemma; issue of personal, local, national or international concern; influential person, fictional character, historical figure, or creative work; or topic of your choice.

California Colleges and Universities

California's three-tiered system of colleges and universities has long been viewed as a model of excellence by other public higher education institutions nationwide and even around the world. Many have attempted to emulate its revered status, which offers a wealth of educational riches, including world-class research universities, enough Nobel Prize winners to fill a seminar room, and colleges on the cutting edge of everything from film to viticulture. Underlying the creation of this remarkable system was a commitment to the notion that all qualified Californians, whatever their economic status, were entitled to the benefits of a college education. In pursuing this ideal, California led the nation in opening up access to higher education for African Americans, Hispanics, and other previously disenfranchised groups.

Unfortunately, in the early 1990s, this golden dream started fading due to the state's recession, population growth, and many other contributing factors. As a result, California's public universities and colleges received reduced tax support, student charges and user's fees shot up, student/faculty ratios increased, fewer classes were offered, and, in some cases, entire academic programs were eliminated. Although it still remained relatively lower than most states, tuition started to climb. The good news is that California has made a brave attempt to counteract this quandary, despite budget deficits, and total enrollment swelling to 60,000 students over the next decade. Tuition increases are a likelihood on the horizon.

The system is composed of the nine combined research and teaching units of the University of California (UC), with a 10th campus, UC Merced, expected to open this year with 1,000 students, and 23 state universities and colleges (CSUC), including the newest CSU campus at Channel Islands, that focus on undergraduate teaching. It also includes 106 two-year community colleges that offer both terminal degrees and the possibility of transferring into four-year institutions.

Admissions requirements to the three tiers and the institutions within them vary widely. Community colleges are open to virtually all high school graduates. The top third of California high school graduates (as measured statewide by a combination of SAT scores and grade point average) may attend units of the state university and college system; all applicants must have taken a course in the fine or performing arts to be considered for admission. In the past, students in the top 12.5 percent of their class have been eligible to attend the University of California. In-state students graduating in the top 4 percent of their high school class will be guaranteed admission to the UC system, although not to a particular campus. The 4 percent proposal is part of a plan to broaden the representation of California applicants and to give more weight to GPA and SAT II subject tests. Out-of-state students continue to face ferocious competition for a limited number of spots, and still pay more.

Although one university system, the nine campuses each offer a full range of academic programs, and each has its own distinctive character. In recent years, UC has moved from relying primarily on statistical academic information to a "comprehensive review" that takes into consideration not only coursework and test scores, but also leadership, special talent, and the educational opportunities available to each student. Despite state laws that prohibit the university from considering race in admission, the system remains dedicated to achieving a diverse student body. The university offers a number of outreach programs designed to assist low-income or educationally disadvantaged students who have promising academic potential with admissions and support services.

To apply for admission to the University of California, complete the electronic application available at UC's PATHWAYS Application Center or submit the printed version to UC's Undergraduate Application Processing Service. Prospective students may apply to as many as eight UC campuses using the same application form. It should be noted that UC does not base admission on the applicant's campus choice, so students cannot request a campus preference. However, it is possible to be accepted at more than one school; in that case, the applicant is free to choose between those campuses. Each of the major undergraduate UC campuses receives a full-length summary in the following pages.

The California State University and College System is totally separate from the University of California; in fact, the two institutions have historically competed for funds as well as students. The largest system of senior higher education in the nation, Cal State focuses on undergraduate education; while its members can offer master's degrees, they can award doctorates only in collaboration with a UC institution. Research in the state-university system is severely restricted, a blow to Cal State's national prestige but a big plus for students. Unlike UC, where the mandate to publish or perish is alive and well, teachers in the state system are there to teach. Cal State's biggest problem is the success of UC, and its frequent lament—"Anywhere else we'd be number one"—is not without justification.

The 23-campus system caters to more than 350,000 students a year. And while most of the campuses serve mainly commuters, Chico, Humboldt, Monterey Bay, San Luis Obispo, and Sonoma stand out as residential campuses. While a solid liberal arts education is offered, the stress is usually on career-oriented professional training. Size varies dramatically, from about 30,000 students at San Diego and Long Beach to fewer than 6,000 at several other branches like San Marcos, Channel Islands, and Monterey Bay. Each campus has its own specific strengths, although in most cases a student's choice of school is dictated by location rather than by academic specialties. For those with a wider choice, some of the more distinctive campuses are profiled below.

Chico (enrollment 14,983), situated in the beautiful Sacramento Valley, draws a large majority of its students from outside a 100-mile radius. The on-campus undergraduate life is strong and the social life is great. Bakersfield (5,594) and San Bernardino (12,000) boast residential villages along with more conventional dorms. The former is in a living/learning center with affiliated faculty members; the latter has its own swimming pool. California Polytechnic at San Luis Obispo is the toughest state university to get into. It provides excellent training in the applied branches of such fields as agriculture, architecture, business, and engineering. Enrollment: 16,735. Fresno, located in the Verdant Central Valley, has the only viticulture school in the state outside of Davis, and undergraduates can work in the school winery. Yosemite, Kings Canyon, and Sequoia national parks are nearby. Enrollment: 18,113.

San Diego State is the biggest and balmiest of the campuses, and since it has a more residential, outdoorsy, and campus-oriented social scene, it appeals more to traditional-age undergraduates. "You could go for the weather alone—some do," says one former student. Contrasted with other state schools, athletics are very important, and the academic offerings are almost as oriented to the liberal arts as at its UC neighbor at San Diego. Enrollment: 30,776.

Humboldt State is perched at the top of the state near the Oregon border in the heart of the redwoods. Humboldt's forestry and wildlife departments have national reputations, and the natural sciences are, in general, strong. Students have the run of excellent laboratory facilities and Redwood National Park. Most in-staters come here to get away from Los Angeles and enjoy the rugged coastline north of San Francisco. Enrollment: 7,475.

California Maritime Academy, located 30 miles northeast of San Francisco with 600 students, specializes in marine transportation, engineering, and maritime technology, and requires summer cruises on the T.S. Gold Bear. Monterey Bay, one mile from the beach with 3,000 students, 65 percent of whom live on-campus, offers an interdisciplinary focus with global perspective and opportunities for internships.

To apply to California State University, complete either the electronic application available at their website, which will be routed to the campus of the applicant's choice, or the paper application, which should be mailed to the admissions office of the campus to which the applicant is applying. It should be noted that Cal Poly and San Diego State require electronic applications. The prospective student can list a first and alternate campus choice on the application. If the first choice can't accommodate the applicant, it automatically sends the application to the alternate campus. However, for competitive campuses and programs, it is wiser to send separate applications to avoid delays.

UC–Berkeley

110 Sproul Hall # 5800, Berkeley, CA 94720-5800

Like everything else, the academic side of Berkeley can be overwhelming. With more than 22,000 undergraduate overachievers crammed into such a small space, it is no wonder that the academic climate is about as intense as you can get at a public university.

Mention Berkeley and even down-to-earth students get stars in their eyes. Students who come here want the biggest and best of everything, though sometimes that ideal runs headlong into budget cuts, tuition increases, and housing shortages. Never mind. Berkeley is where the action is. If you want a quick indicator of Berkeley's academic prowess, look no farther than the parking lot. The campus is dotted with spots marked "NL"—spots reserved for resident Nobel laureates. The last time anyone counted, Berkeley boasted seven Nobel Prize winners, 391 Guggenheim fellows, and a bevy of Pulitzer Prize recipients, MacArthur fellows, and Fulbright scholars. Is it any wonder that this radical institution of the '60s still maintains the kind of reputation that makes the top private universities take note? Engineering, architecture, and business are a few of the best of the fine programs at this mother of UC schools. The social climate is not as explosive as it once seemed to be, but don't expect anything tame on today's campus. Flower children and granola chompers still abound, as do fledgling Marxists, young Republicans, and body-pierced activists.

Spread across 1,200 scenic acres on a hill overlooking San Francisco Bay, the Berkeley campus is a parklike oasis in a small city. The sometimes startlingly wide variety of architectural styles ranges from the stunning classical amphitheater to the

Website: www.berkeley.edu
Location: Urban
Total Enrollment: 33,483
Undergraduates: 22,447
Male/Female: 46/54
SAT Ranges: V 590–710
  M 630–740
ACT Range: N/A
Financial Aid: 49%
Expense: Pub $ $
Phi Beta Kappa: Yes
Applicants: 36,989
Accepted: 27%
Enrolled: 42%
Grad in 6 Years: 87%
Returning Freshmen: 97%

(Continued)

Academics: ✍ ✍ ✍ ✍

Social: 🍷 🍷 🍷 🍷

Q of L: ★ ★ ★

Admissions: (510) 642-3175

Email Address:
ouars@berkley.edu

Strongest Programs:

Engineering

Architecture

Business

Theoretical Physics

Molecular and Cell Biology

Political Science

English

Greeks have become more popular, with 10 percent of the men and 10 percent of the women in a fraternity or sorority.

modern University Art Museum draped in neon sculpture. Large expanses of grass dot the campus and are just "perfect for playing Frisbee or lying in the sun." The oaks along Strawberry Creek and the eucalyptus grove date back to Berkeley's beginnings nearly 140 years ago. Sproul Plaza, in the heart of the campus, is one of the great people-watching sites of the world.

Like everything else, the academic side of Berkeley can be overwhelming. With more than 22,000 undergraduate overachievers crammed into such a small space, it is no wonder that the academic climate is about as intense as you can get at a public university. "Everyone was the top student in his or her high school class so they can't settle for anything less than number one," says one student. A classmate concedes that "it can be a stressful environment, especially during the first years." Another says tersely, "Expect very little sleep." Some introductory courses, particularly in the sciences, have as many as 800 students, and professors, who must publish or perish from the university's highly competitive teaching ranks, devote a great deal of time to research. After all, Berkeley has made a large part of its reputation on its research and graduate programs, many of which rank among the best in the nation.

"Everyone was the top student in his or her high school class."

And while the undergraduate education is excellent, students take a gamble with the trickle-down theory, which holds out the promise that the intellectual might of those in the ivory towers will drip down to them eventually. As a political science major explains, "This system has allowed me to hear outstanding lectures from amazing professors who write the books we read, while allowing far more personal attention by the graduate-student instructors." Another student opines, "It's better to stand 50 feet from brilliance than five feet from mediocrity." Evidence of such gravitation is seen in the promising curriculums designed specifically for freshmen and sophomores that include interdisciplinary courses in writing, public speaking, and the history of civilization, and an offering of small student seminars (enrollment is limited to 15) taught by regular faculty. Despite these attempts at catering to undergraduates, the sheer number of students at Berkeley makes it difficult to treat each student as an individual. As a result, such things as academic counseling suffer. "Advising? You mean to tell me they have advising here?" asks one student.

Each college or school has its own set of general education requirements, which are generally not extensive, and many can be fulfilled through advanced placement exams in high school. All students, however, must take English composition and literature, and one term each of American history and American institutions. Also, undergrads have an American Cultures requirement for graduation—an original approach (via courses offered in several departments) to comparative study of ethnic groups in the United States.

Most of the departments here are noteworthy, and some are about the best anywhere (like engineering and architecture). Sociology, mathematics, physics, chemistry, history, economics and English are just a handful of the truly dazzling departments. Engineering is also strong, and Berkeley offers seven departments and seven interdisciplinary programs in engineering. The biological sciences department integrates several undergraduate majors in biochemistry, biophysics, botany, zoology, and others into more interdisciplinary programs such as integrative biology and molecular and cell biology. Stanley Hall is being rebuilt to serve as the Berkeley headquarters for the California Institute for Quantitative Biomedical Research (QB3). The office and lab complex will support interdisciplinary teaching and research as part of the campus's Health Science Initiative. The College of Natural Resources has streamlined its eight departments into five, and participates in five interdisciplinary research centers.

Special programs abound at Berkeley, though it's up to the student to find out about them. "Our class enrollment system is much like playing a low-risk lottery," opines one undergrad. "Maybe you'll win, or maybe you won't. If anything, adding courses will definitely toughen up any person." Students may study abroad on fellowships at one of 50 centers around the world, or spend time in various internships around the country. If all you want to do is study, the library system, with more than eight million volumes, is one of the largest in the nation and maintains open stacks. The system consists of the main library (Doe-Moffitt) and more than 20 branch libraries, including the newly-completed Hargrove Music Library.

Forty-three percent of the student population is Asian American, 4 percent African American, and 11 percent Hispanic. The Coalition for Excellence and Diversity in Mathematics, Science, and Engineering, which provides women and minorities with undergraduate mentors in these fields, received the Presidential Award for Excellence in Science, Mathematics, and Engineering in 1998. The university also provides a variety of other programs to promote diversity, including Project DARE (Diversity Awareness through Resources and Education), the Center for Racial Education, and a Sexual Harassment Peer Education Program. Despite Berkeley's liberal reputation, the recent trend is away from the legacy of the free speech movement. Business majors and fraternity members increasingly outnumber the young Communists and peaceniks, though the school does produce a large number of Peace Corps volunteers. The main issue concerning every group on campus? Cost. In the past few years, outrageous fee hikes and severe budget cuts had some students wondering if a first-rate, affordable education had gone the way of the dinosaurs.

Though dorms have room for only a quarter of the students, freshmen are guaranteed housing for their first year. After that, the Cal Rentals is a good resource for finding an apartment in town. Many students live a couple of miles off campus, where "apartments are cheaper," says one student. About two-thirds of the university's highly prized dorm rooms are reserved for freshmen, and the few singles go to resident assistants. Three new student housing projects have opened since 2004, offering a variety of rooms in low-rise and high-rise settings. In the absence of a mandatory meal plan, everybody eats "wherever and whenever they wish," including in the dorms.

Though the housing shortage can get you down, the beautiful California weather will probably take your mind off it in time. The BART subway system provides easy access to San Francisco, by far one of the most pleasant cities in the world and a cultural and counter-cultural mecca.

"Expect very little sleep."

The Bay Area boasts myriad professional sports teams, including the Oakland A's and the San Francisco 49ers. From opera to camping, San Francisco has a wide variety of activities to offer. Get yourself a car, and you can hike in Yosemite National Park, ski and gamble in Nevada, taste wine in the Napa Valley, or visit the aquarium at Monterey. But be advised that a car is only an asset when you want to go out of town—students warn that parking in Berkeley is difficult, to say the least.

"Social life at UC–Berkeley is killer!" exclaims one geography major. Weekends are generally spent in Berkeley, hanging out at the many bookstores, coffeehouses, and sidewalk cafes, heading to a fraternity or sorority party, or taking advantage of the many events right on campus. Berkeley is a quintessential college town ("kind of a crazy little town," opines one anthropology major), and of course, there's always the people-watching; where else can an individual meet people trying to convert pedestrians to strange New Age religions or revolutionary political causes on every street corner? Nearby Telegraph Avenue is famous (infamous?) for such antics every weekend. More than 350 student groups are registered on campus, which ensures that there is an outlet for just about any interest and that no one group will ever dominate campus life.

Despite all this activity, many students use the weekend to catch up on studying. Greeks have become more popular, with 10 percent of the men and 10 percent of the women in a fraternity or sorority. Varsity athletics have always been important, with strengths in the men's gymnastics and crew teams. A surge in popularity for the bas-

"Social life at UC–Berkeley is killer!"

ketball team probably has to do with its great performance in the PAC 10. And just about everyone turns out for the "Big Game," (football) where the favorite activity on the home side of the bleachers is badmouthing the rival school to the south: Stanford. Intramurals are popular, and the personal fitness craze is fed by an extensive recreational facility and gorgeous weather year-round.

The common denominator in the Berkeley community is academic motivation, along with the self-reliance that emerges from trying to make your mark among upward of 22,000 peers. Beyond that, the diversity of town and campus makes an extraordinarily free and exciting college environment for almost anyone. "It makes one feel free to dress, say, think, or do anything and not be chastised for being unorthodox," explains a student. "At Berkeley, it is worse to be dull than odd."

If You Apply To ➤   Berkeley: Regular admissions: Nov. 30. Financial aid: Mar. 2. Guarantees to meet demonstrated need of in-state students. No campus or alumni interviews. SATs or ACTS: required. SAT IIs: required (writing, math I or II, and one other). Essay question: personal statement. Apply to particular school or program.

UC–Davis

175 MRAK Hall, Davis, CA 95616

The agricultural and engineering branch of the UC system. Premed, prevet, food science—you name it. If the subject is living things, you can study it here. A small town alternative to the bright lights of UC–Berkeley and UCLA. As is often true of science-oriented schools, the work is hard.

At the University of California–Davis, environmental studies and most everything that has to do with agriculture or biological science is noteworthy. The Aggies' cup truly runneth over. Originally known as the University of California Farm, the campus maintains its sprawling, verdant beauty, replete with native and imported forestry, charming bike paths, and mooing cows. But lest you assume this environmentally oriented university is full of quaint country folk, think again. Davis has become an international leader in the agricultural, biological, biotechnical, and environmental sciences.

Located 15 miles west of Sacramento and 72 miles north of San Francisco, the 6,000-acre campus is in the middle of a stretch of flat farmland that even Dorothy and Toto could mistake for Kansas. It features nearly 1,000 buildings with a blend of architectural styles, from traditional dairy barn to modern concrete. The hub of the university is a central area known as the Quad, one of many grassy open spaces on campus. Newer facilities include the Center for Comparative Medicine and a variety of seismic renovations.

Though it has added programs in many disciplines over the past few years—including Chinese, Japanese, food engineering, and biological systems engineering—its biological and agricultural science departments are still the ones that shine.

Animal science and engineering are strong departments, and the botany program is one of the best in the country. The school is "the No. 1 choice for any prevet," and it's great for premeds, too. The food sciences major is also stellar, and not for the faint of heart or those afraid of chemistry. It was Davis food scientists who gave us the square tomato (better for packing into boxes), as well as more useful things such as the method for creating orange juice concentrate. Studio art, boasting several internationally known artists, is also among the top in the nation, while history and English are generally good but not up to par with the sciences. Noteworthy special programs include the Inter-Disciplinary Electronics Arts (IDEA) Lab, which allows students to create electronically based productions by integrating photography, video, digital editing, and the Internet. Internships and co-op programs are well-established, which is why many students remain for more than four years.

Faculty members here are expected to do top-level research as well as teach, so Davis is charged with both education and research. These two are uniquely blended when undergraduate students contribute to first-class research groups as paid technicians or volunteer interns. Davis also offers the innovative Washington Program, which gives undergraduates academic credits for internships in Congress, at federal agencies, and the like. Many introductory courses are quite large, but Davis also offers 40 freshman seminars taught by the best instructors. The academic advising system gets generally high marks, but you must seek out their assistance. "They helped me plan a four-year college schedule and always kept me on track."

General education requirements stipulate that all students take courses in three broad areas: topical breadth, social–cultural diversity, and writing experience. These areas include courses in the arts and humanities, science and engineering, and the social sciences. Students may elect to take a general education theme option (sets of general education courses that share a common intellectual theme).

The academic demands are intense, and the students are high achievers. Many students describe the atmosphere as competitive if not cutthroat (especially in the biological sciences). "It is not rare to find many students in the library on Saturday night," testifies one student. Another student reports, "Professors expect students to learn vast amounts of information in a 10-week span." For students who still want more, the Davis Honors Challenge is designed for highly motivated, academically talented first- and second-year students who want to enhance their education through special courses. A famous campus saying claims that "Davis students take notes at graduation." Maybe they're taking notes for job interviews: 64 percent of Davis students get jobs after college and 38 percent prefer more class time in graduate school. African Americans account for 3 percent of the students, Asian Americans 35 percent, and Hispanics 10 percent. Students are slightly more conservative than in past years, and most are characterized as "friendly and open-minded." Campus hot topics include fair labor practices and political correctness. In its pledge to fos-

> **"Professors expect students to learn vast amounts of information in a 10-week span."**

ter awareness of diversity issues, the university has established an Office of Campus Diversity and a Crosscultural Center. UC–Davis boasts the highest graduation rate in the UC system. Davis awards merit scholarships, but there are no athletic awards.

Virtually all freshmen inhabit campus housing, which is well-maintained and includes a number of theme houses. The vast majority of upperclassmen live off-campus in nearby houses or apartments. Housing is guaranteed for freshmen and transfer students if applications are received by the deadline. Six different meal plans for the dining halls are available, and one student says, "The dorm food is very good (better than at most colleges)." A variety of nearby eating establishments serve the student clientele, but a car can come in handy if you are looking for a good meal in Sacramento (15 minutes) or a great one in San Francisco (a little more than an hour).

(Continued)

Social: ☎ ☎ ☎
Q of L: ★ ★ ★ ★
Admissions: (530) 752-2971
Email Address:
  thinkucd@ucdavis.edu

Strongest Programs:
Environmental Studies
Botany
Animal Science
Viticulture
Agricultural Sciences
Studio Art
Biological Sciences
Engineering

Many introductory courses are quite large, but Davis also offers 40 freshman seminars taught by the best instructors.

Beaches are a two-hour drive from the campus, and the ski slopes and hiking trails of Lake Tahoe and the Sierra Nevada are a little closer. But if you feel, as most Davis students do, that studies are too important to be abandoned on weekends, the town has restaurants, activities, and entertainment enough to keep the stay-at-homes happy.

In between quizzes and cram sessions, the outlying countryside offers a welcome change of pace. The town of Davis itself is small, about 50,000, and students make up half the population. If some call it a cowtown, others call it peaceful, with its tree-lined streets and quiet nights. The relationship between college and town is one of rare cooperation (partly because the students are a significant voting bloc in local elections). Health and energy consciousness runs high in town and on the vast, architecturally diverse campus, where bicycles are the main form of transportation on the incredible 46 miles of bike paths that crisscross the campus and environs. "Bicycles are the norm at Davis. Don't come without one," advises one psych major. The university has encouraged environmental awareness by sponsoring solar energy projects and promoting such novelties as contests between dorms for the lowest heating and electric bills.

On-campus activities are varied, and many university-sponsored events fill the calendar. One rhetoric major points out that "social functions are hard to avoid at Davis." Active drama and music departments provide frequent entertainment, and there is plenty of room for homegrown talent in the coffeehouses, which offer mellow live entertainment and poetry readings on a regular basis. The

"The dorm food is very good (better than at most colleges)."

1,800-seat Mondavi Center for the Arts features international and local groups. Fraternities and sororities attract 7 percent of the men and 6 percent of the women. Alcohol is allowed in the dorms for those over 21 years old; those too young to imbibe have trouble finding booze, unless it's supplied by peers. Major annual social events include Picnic Day, in which alumni join current students in a massive outdoor shindig; African American Week; and the Whole Earth Festival, "an earthy, tie-dyed sort of event" in celebration of the '60s.

The university's varsity athletic teams compete in Division II and attract relatively scant attention compared to those at most other state universities. Nevertheless, Davis won the Sears Directors' Cup, a trophy symbolic of overall excellence in intercollegiate athletics, and cross-country, basketball, and track and field have brought home NCAA championships. The annual Causeway Classic against rival Sacramento State does create a measure of excitement. Intramurals, however, are much more popular than spectator sports, with 65 percent of students participating. On this outdoor campus, almost everyone does something athletic—jogging, softball, tennis, swimming, or Frisbee—if only to break up the monotony of studies with a different kind of competition.

Proud of its small town atmosphere, Davis is not for the lazy or faint of heart. As one man says, "There's no free ride. You are going to have to work for everything you get." And most students get a lot out of their four or more years at Davis. It's the ideal spot to combine high-powered work in science and agriculture with that famous easygoing California lifestyle.

Overlaps

UC–Berkeley, UCLA, UC–San Diego, UC–Santa Barbara, UC–Irvine

If You Apply To ➤

Davis: Regular admissions: Nov. 30. Financial aid: Mar. 3. Does not guarantee to meet demonstrated need. No campus or alumni interviews. SATs or ACTs: required. SAT IIs: required (writing, math, and one other). Accepts the Common Application and electronic applications. Essay question: personal statement. Apply to particular program.

UC–Irvine

260 ADM, Irvine, CA 92697

Irvine sits in the midst of one of the nation's biggest suburbs, combining funky modern architecture with perhaps the most conservative student body in the UC system. Premed is the featured attraction, along with various other health-related offerings. Not quite as close to the beach as Santa Barbara—but close enough.

On the surface, UC–Irvine's clean, contemporary campus appears to be home to students who study diligently in the busy library, wear sensible shoes to biology lab, and resist that double shot of espresso at the local coffeehouse. But that image starts to dissipate as soon as you hear that bizarre noise: "Zot! Zot! Zot!" Then a UCI student explains that "it's the sound that an anteater supposedly makes when it swipes an ant with its tongue." Hey, any school that has an anteater as a mascot can't be completely straight-laced. The university is, however, straight on its reputation as a school with stellar programs in biology and creative writing. The current academic climate can be quite serious and challenging, but as one UCI student swears, the Anteaters are "also surprisingly cooperative."

Located in the heart of Orange County, UCI (founded in 1965) is among the newest of the UC campuses. Although enrollment is up and the administration has dreams of further expansion, "it is the perfect size," says one English major. UCI is liberally supplied with trees and shrubs from all over the world. Futuristic buildings are arranged in a circle around a large park, "giving it the appearance of a relaxed art school," says one observer. Undergraduates have long quipped that UCI stood for "Under Construction Indefinitely," and current campus construction does little to challenge the moniker.

A "premed mentality" reigns at Irvine, since the School of Biological Sciences is the best and most competitive academic division. The School of Arts offers nationally ranked programs in dance, drama, music, studio art, and musical theatre, as well as a minor in digital arts. The Beall Center for Art and Technology in the Claire Trevor School of the Arts enables students to explore the relationship between digital technology and the arts and sciences. The popular interdisciplinary School of Social Ecology offers courses combining criminology, environmental and legal studies, and psychology and social behavior, and strongly emphasizes teacher/student relationships. Like most of the other UC campuses, UCI is on a 10-week quarter system, so the pace is fast and furious. Students should face registration with the same determination, too; it's a tough fight to get into the science classes of choice as a sophomore.

Languages are strong at UCI, as are the biggest nonbiology majors: economics; information and computer science; psychology; social behavior; criminology, law, and society; and a fiction-writing program that is gaining national recognition. UCI has added a plethora of new programs, including majors in global cultures, literary journalism, biomedical engineering, and German studies.

"UCI is fairly competitive and the courses are moderately rigorous," says a junior. Students may be overwhelmed by the size of most classes. Even seniors find their classes packed with 100 undergrads, which leaves little time for personal attention. "Graduate students teach lower-division writing courses," says one student, adding that "most classes are overcrowded, leaving little room for personal attention." The Center for Health Sciences focuses on five areas of research, including: neuroscience, genetics, cancer,

> **"UCI is fairly competitive and the courses are moderately rigorous."**

Website: www.uci.edu
Location: Urban
Total Enrollment: 23,032
Undergraduates: 19,201
Male/Female: 50/50
SAT Ranges: V 519–620
 M 567–675
ACT Range: N/A
Financial Aid: 49%
Expense: Pub $ $ $
Phi Beta Kappa: Yes
Applicants: 34,417
Accepted: 54%
Enrolled: 22%
Grad in 6 Years: 79%
Returning Freshmen: 92%
Academics: ✍ ✍ ✍ ✍
Social: ☎ ☎
Q of L: ★ ★ ★
Admissions: (949) 824-6703
Email Address:
 admissions@uci.edu

Strongest Programs:
Biological Sciences
Economics
Information and Computer
 Science
Chemistry

Even seniors find their classes packed with 100 undergrads, which leaves little time for personal attention.

infectious diseases, and aging. The university also houses the Reeve-Irvine Research Center, which supports the study of spinal cord trauma and disease with emphasis on finding a cure. The "breadth requirement" means that students must take three courses each in writing, natural sciences, social and behavioral sciences, and humanities in order to graduate. There is also a foreign language requirement, and one in math, statistics, or computer science, as well as requirements in multicultural and international/global issues. Honors programs are available in humanities, economics, psychology, political science, physics, cognitive sciences, anthropology, and mathematics.

Ninety-seven percent of the student body are in-staters, the majority from Southern California and many of those from wealthy Orange County. The students are in general "much more conservative than at the other UC campuses," says one applied math major. Minorities account for well over half the student body, with Asian Americans comprising 49 percent, African Americans 2 percent, and Hispanics 12 percent. "Cultural groups seem to segregate from each other more than I really like," says a senior.

"UCI and the city of Irvine seem like completely different entities."

Condominium-style dorms, both single-sex and co-ed, are "exceptional compared to the high-rise dormitories of other institutions," says one senior. Others agree that the homey campus dwellings provide a good experience for freshmen, though finding a room can be a challenge. "If you really want on-campus housing," warns a student, "you need to make sure you meet the deadlines." Newly added housing, including those with academic themes and ones especially for fraternities and sororities, opens more rooms for students, but most opt to move off-campus after their first year. Currently, 22 percent of freshmen live off-campus—many on the beach—giving the campus a commuter-school atmosphere. One student laments, "You have to find the social life on this campus. It won't find you."

Like most of the other UC campuses, UCI is on a 10-week quarter system, so the pace is fast and furious.

Still, the Greek scene is vigorous, attracting 8 percent of UCI men and women. There are 18 sororities and 18 fraternities, and each has something going on every weekend. As for booze, UCI is a dry campus and students say finding a drink on campus without proper ID is difficult. Irvine touts many festivals that seem to attest to a celebration of diversity: the Rainbow Festival (cultural heritage), Asian Heritage week, Black History month, Cinco de Mayo, and rush week. The one event that brings everybody out is the daylong Wayzgoose, when the campus is transformed into a medieval fair complete with mimes, jugglers, and performers dressed up in medieval costumes.

But if life on campus is slow, life off campus is not. That's because the campus is located just 50 miles from L.A., five miles from the beach, and a little more than an hour from the ski slopes. Catalina Island, with beaches and hiking trails, is a quick boat trip off Newport Harbor; Mexico is two hours away. While some students treasure the quiet setting of Irvine, others lament its "lackluster, homogeneous communities." Notes one student, "UCI and the city of Irvine seem like completely different entities; the former is slightly liberal while the latter is ultraconservative."

Irvine fields 20 athletic teams and competes in Division I of the NCAA. Tennis and crosscountry are perennial Big West powerhouses, and men's water polo has been ranked in the top five nationally for 23 of the last 31 years. There is no football team, but intramurals are extremely popular, as is the 5,000-seat multipurpose gym.

What lures students to UCI is its top-name professors, innovative academic programs, and the chance to be a part of its cutting-edge research. For the students who come here prepared to keep their heads buried in a book for a few years, the reward will be an exceptional education.

Overlaps

UCLA, UC–San Diego, UC–Santa Barbara, UC–Berkeley, University of Southern California

UC–Los Angeles

1147 Murphy Hall, 405 Hillgard Avenue, Los Angeles, CA 90095

Tucked into exclusive Beverly Hills with the beach, the mountains, and chic Hollywood hangouts all within easy reach. Practically everything is offered here, but the programs in arts and media are some of the best in the world. More conservative than Berkeley and nearly as difficult to get into.

With stellar programs in music, film and television, journalism/communication, dance, and drama, you'd think UCLA was some kind of incubator for truly talented and gifted people. Or with alumni such as Kareem Abdul-Jabbar, Troy Aikman, and Arthur Ashe, maybe UCLA's some sort of farm that grows superstar athletes. Well, UCLA is all that and more. A superb faculty, a reputation for outstanding academics, and a powerful athletics program make this university the ultimate place to study.

UCLA's prime location—sandwiched between two glamorous neighborhoods (Beverly Hills and Bel Air) and a short drive away from Hollywood, the Sunset Strip, and downtown Los Angeles—makes it appealing for students who want more from their college experience than what classes offer. The university's beautifully land-scaped 419-acre campus features a range of architectural styles, with Romanesque/ Italian Renaissance as the dominant motif, providing only one of a number of reasons students also enjoy staying on campus. A wealth of gardens—botanical, Japanese, and sculpture—adds a touch of quiet elegance to the campus. New facilities include La Kretz Hall, a certified "green" academic building, and Glorya Kaufman Hall, which houses the Department of World Arts and Cultures and performance venues.

Strong programs abound at UCLA, and many are considered among the best in the nation. The School of Engineering and Applied Science, especially electrical engineering, is generally regarded as the leading department. The School of Film, Theater, and Television is first-rate, and its students have the opportunity to study in Verona, Italy, with the Theater Overseas program. The popular music department offers a course in jazz studies, and the biological sciences are also highly regarded. Global studies is the newest undergraduate major. Research opportunities abound at UCLA, and the university ranks seventh in the nation in federal funding for research. Students say the math department doesn't add up to the sum total of its parts.

Freshmen are encouraged to participate in a three-day summer orientation, which provides workshops, counseling, and a general introduction to the campus and community. Freshmen can also take a yearlong cluster of courses on topics such as The History of Modern Thought, or seminars with titles such as Asian American Youth: Culture, Identity and Ethnicity. During their first two years, most students take required core classes that are sometimes jammed with 300 to 4,000 people. But administrators are quick to point out that nearly two-thirds of all undergraduate classes have fewer than 50 students. Savvy students come to UCLA with advanced courses in their high school backgrounds and test out of the intro courses. First-year students are required to take a course involving quantitative reasoning unless they hit

Website: www.ucla.edu
Location: Urban
Total Enrollment: 37,563
Undergraduates: 24,946
Male/Female: 43/57
SAT Ranges: V 570–690
  M 610–720
ACT Range: 24–30
Financial Aid: 54%
Expense: Pub $ $ $
Phi Beta Kappa: Yes
Applicants: 43,199
Accepted: 23%
Enrolled: 37%
Grad in 6 Years: 87%
Returning Freshmen: 97%
Academics: 🖊 🖊 🖊 🖊 🖊
Social: ☎ ☎ ☎
Q of L: ★ ★ ★
Admissions: (310) 825-3101
Email Address:
  ugadm@saonet.ucla.edu

Strongest Programs:
Music
Engineering
Political Science
Dance
Economics
Psychology
Biology
Film/television

600 or higher on their math SAT, and English composition requirements should also be met during the freshman year. Lab science and a language requirement are also required for a liberal arts degree.

Simply getting into classes here can be a big challenge. Students register by phone in a sequence of two scheduled "passes" based on their class standing.

UCLA's academic environment is extremely intense. "While UCLA provides many challenging academic courses, it also provides a great support system," a junior says. The faculty is also impressive. "My professors, for the most part, have been engaging, excited, and genuinely interested in helping students learn," a junior biochemistry major says. On the other hand, there is a widespread sense here that undergraduate teaching is often sacrificed on

New facilities include La Kretz Hall, a certified "green" academic building, and Glorya Kaufman Hall, which houses the Department of World Arts and Cultures and performance venues.

"We have some very interesting and eccentric students at our school."

behalf of scholarly research. The UCLA library ranks in the top 10 of all research libraries, public or private, and contains more than 7.2 million volumes. The campus newspaper, the Daily Bruin, is the third-largest daily in Los Angeles.

"We have some very interesting and eccentric students at our school," says a freshman. "Most are social, trendy, and tanned." Asian Americans account for 40 percent of UCLA's student population, Hispanics make up 16 percent, African Americans 4 percent, and Native Americans 1 percent. Minority representation, environmental issues and gay and lesbian rights are the largest political issues on campus. UCLA has several student-run newsmagazines, including the feminist Together and the Asian American newsmagazine Pacific Ties. UCLA is one of the few universities in the nation with a gay fraternity and a lesbian sorority. These groups, as well as GALA (Gay and Lesbian Association) and TenPercent, have helped foster a rising feeling of empowerment among the campus's gay and lesbian students and faculty.

Thirty-five percent of the students live in university housing; freshmen and sophomores are guaranteed housing, but for everyone else it's strictly a waiting list. Overcrowding is a concern, though future housing construction should give students a bit more elbow room. The campus is philosophically divided into North and South. North attracts more liberal arts aficionados, while those in math and science tend to favor South. Fifteen dining halls, restaurants, and snack bars serve meals that students rave about.

UCLA has won a nation-leading number of collegiate championships, including 97 NCAA titles, and has produced more than 250 Olympians. The men's football, basketball, baseball, and tennis teams are the undeniable superstars as are the women's gymnastic and water polo teams. Beating crosstown rival USC is the name of the game in any sport; UCLA fans regard

"There is a lot of school spirit, and everyone is very friendly."

their intracity rivals with passionate feelings. Beat 'SC Week, the week leading up to the football game between the two, is an event in itself, featuring a bonfire, concert, and blood drive.

Freshmen can also take a yearlong cluster of courses on topics such as The History of Modern Thought, or seminars with titles such as Asian American Youth: Culture, Identity and Ethnicity.

If you would rather be a doer than a watcher, the opportunities awaiting you are superb. "Whether a fan of the big party scene or more of a Friday-night-movie kind of person, there are opportunities both on and off campus," a sophomore says. The hopping Westwood suburb, which borders the university, has at least 15 movie theaters and scores of restaurants, but the shops cater to the upper class. "There's nowhere to dance and only two bars, but a lot of coffee and cheap food," a junior says. UCLA's Ocean Discovery Center on the Santa Monica Pier is an innovative, hands-on ocean classroom for students and the public. The beach is five miles away, and the mountains are only a short drive. Although public transportation is cheap, it's also inconvenient, making a car almost a necessity for going outside of Westwood. Unfortunately, parking is expensive and difficult to obtain. The easiest solution is to live close to campus and bike it.

With all the attractions of the City of Angels at its doorstep, the campus tends to empty out on the weekends (except when the football Bruins have a home game). Fourteen percent of the men and 11 percent of the women join one of UCLA's 50 fraternities and sororities. The university's alcohol policy is similar to that of other UC schools—open consumption is a no-no. But according to one student, "It is extremely easy for undergrads to be served, especially at fraternities." Top-name entertainers, political figures, and speakers of all kinds come to the campus; film and theater presentations are frequent, and the air is thick with live music. "I met Brad Pitt across the street from campus!" says one excited student.

A leading research center, 190 fields of study, distinguished faculty members, and outstanding athletics make UCLA one of the most prestigious universities in the nation. And despite the large size, students still feel they are part of a tight-knit community. "There is a lot of school spirit, and everyone is very friendly," a junior says.

Overlaps

UC–Berkeley, UC–San Diego, UC–Irvine, UC–Santa Barbara, USC

If You Apply To ➤ **UCLA:** Regular admissions: Nov. 30. Meets demonstrated need of 52%. No campus or alumni interviews. SATs or ACTs: required, ACT with writing component. SAT IIs: required. Apply to particular school or program. Accepts electronic applications. Essay question: how you have taken advantage of educational opportunities; talent or contribution you will bring to UCLA; additional information about you.

UC–Riverside

Riverside, CA 92521

Social life is relatively tame, since so many of the students commute. While some complain of a lack of nightlife in Riverside, they readily agree that activities on campus make up for it. Returning students are welcomed back every year with a campuswide block party, and Spring Splash brings in hot bands.

Lacking the big-name reputation and booming athletic programs of the other UC schools, UC–Riverside has chosen to place its emphasis on something that not all institutions consider to be an important component of higher education: the student. Riverside offers one of the lowest student/faculty ratios in the UC system, strong programs with personalized attention, and a sense of academic community that seems to have been forgotten at other UC schools. "Students are well taken care of and get personal attention," says one satisfied senior. Though part of the UC system, UC–Riverside is a breed apart.

Located 60 miles east of Los Angeles, UCR is surrounded by mountains on the outskirts of the city of Riverside. The beautifully landscaped,1,200-acre campus consists of mainly modern architecture, with a 160-foot bell tower (with a 48-bell carillon) marking its center. Wide lawns and clusters of oaks create "a veritable botanical garden," where students and faculty enjoy relaxing between classes. Acres of citrus groves form a half-circle on the outer edges of campus and perfumes the air. New facilities include residence halls, an international village, a large lecture hall, a plant genomics research center, an entomology building, and science laboratories. Current construction includes a four-level student commons area.

Decades ago, researchers at the Citrus Experiment Station in Riverside perfected the growing methods for the imported navel orange, making discoveries to protect the fruit from disease and pests and saving California's citrus industry. Riverside continues to excel in plant sciences and entomology. But the campus has grown since its

Website: www.ucr.edu
Location: City outskirts
Total Enrollment: 16,622
Undergraduates: 14,555
Male/Female: 47/53
SAT Ranges: V 460–570 M 490–630
ACT Range: 18–23
Financial Aid: 61%
Expense: Pub $ $ $
Phi Beta Kappa: Yes
Applicants: 19,060
Accepted: 75%
Enrolled: 20%
Grad in 6 Years: 65%
Returning Freshmen: 86%
Academics: ✐ ✐ ✐ ½
Social: ☎ ☎
Q of L: ★ ★ ★
Admissions: (951) 827-3411

(Continued)

Email Address:
  discover@ucr.edu

Strongest Programs:
Plant Sciences and
  Entomology
Engineering
Natural Sciences
Social Sciences
Biomedical Sciences
Humanities and Arts
Business
Education
Engineering

founding in 1954 to include excellent programs in engineering, natural sciences, social sciences, humanities, the arts, business, and education. The biomedical sciences program, unique in California, is UCR's most prestigious and demanding course of study, and its most successful students can earn a seven-year BS/MD in partnership with the medical school at UCLA. Students who want a more traditional path can still pursue their graduate studies at a normal pace. The engineering program also is quite selective, more so than the campus as a whole, which generally accepts students who are ranked in the top 12 percent of the state's high school graduates. One of the few undergraduate environmental engineering programs is at UCR, as is an undergraduate program in creative writing, the only one in the UC system.

Graduate programs in the arts are strong, with an MFA in writing for the performing arts and the nation's only doctoral program in dance history and theory. Academic weaknesses include journalism and geography. New undergrad majors include bioengineering, Asian Literatures and Cultures, and interdisciplinary studies. The University Honors Program offers exceptional students further academic challenges in addition to extracurricular activities and special seminars for freshmen. And talented student singers, dancers, and actors can earn stipends for performing in the community through an arts outreach program funded by the Maxwell H. Gluck Foundation.

All students are required to meet extensive "breadth requirements" that include courses in English composition, natural sciences and math, humanities, and social sciences. Some majors include a foreign language requirement. Students do not encounter much difficulty in getting the courses they want. The campus libraries have an impressive two million volumes, an interlibrary loan system within the UC system, and vast electronic databases. A specialized research collection in science fiction is world-class. UCR's museum of photography, located in a downtown Riverside mall and available on the Web, has grown in stature.

Students say the academic climate is cooperative rather than competitive. "Students are more friends than rivals," says a student, unless you are in the biomedical program, where "students are constantly studying, interning, 'labbing,' and trying to one-up their peers." Research is an institutional priority for faculty, but professors continue to dedicate much of their time and attention to their students. "Most of my professors were great at presenting and teaching to me in a relevant, understandable manner," says one junior. Plus, UCR has a tradition of undergraduate and faculty interaction with a wide range of undergraduate research grants available during the academic year. This may be why one in six graduates goes on to get a PhD. State funding woes have not gone unnoticed on campus. "We've lost a lot of core classes and financial aid does not offer as much," grumbles one student.

"Students are more friends than rivals."

Ninety-nine percent of the UCR student body are from California, mainly L.A., Riverside, San Bernardino, and Orange counties. Ninety-four percent of the students graduated in the top tenth of their public high school class. Asian Americans account for 42 percent of the students, and Hispanics and African Americans 24 percent and 7 percent, respectively. As part of the UC commitment to diversity, Riverside upholds policies prohibiting sexual harassment, hazing, and physical and verbal abuses. It supports centers for various ethnicities, for women and for gay and lesbian students. "UCR is one of the most diverse universities in the nation," a political science major says. "Because of this, there is a wide range of students at UCR that make a blended environment of different cultures, nationalities, and social statuses." Numerous merit scholarships, averaging $5,600, are doled out every year, as well as Division I athletic scholarships in baseball, softball, basketball, tennis, volleyball, track, soccer, and golf. Scholarships also are available in specific academic departments.

Athletics is generating more interest on campus since the switch to NCAA Division I competition.

Housing is reasonably priced and relatively easy to obtain, but the quality varies greatly. "While West Lothian looks like a prison, Pentland Hills is like a resort," says one student. Twenty-seven percent of the students live in the well-maintained dorms, where freshmen are guaranteed a spot. Campus dining is described as adequate. "I could eat their tater tots forever," gushes one student. Students feel safe on campus; security measures include an escort service and patrolling security officers.

While some complain of a lack of nightlife in Riverside, they readily agree that activities on campus make up for it. Returning students are welcomed back every year with a campuswide block party, and Spring Splash brings in hot bands. Fraternities and sororities lure 4 percent of men and women

"UCR is one of the most diverse universities in the nation."

on campus. The groups usually hold campuswide parties once a quarter. "There is always something going on, whether it be a concert, lecture, or sorority/fraternity party," one sophomore says. Campus hangouts, including "The Barn," have live bands and comedy nights. Every Wednesday the campus can enjoy a "nooner," where live bands play during lunch. University Village is a commercial center offering a movie theater, restaurants, and an arcade right on the edge of campus. The campus runs a cultural arts program that brings professional shows to campus, such as Laurie Anderson and Margaret Cho.

Riverside weather is temperate except during the summer months, when the heat and haze combine to make a trip to the coast look really inviting. The coast is only about 45 minutes by freeway and the desert is an hour east. Big Bear and numerous ski resorts are also within an hour's drive.

Athletics is generating more interest on campus since the switch to NCAA Division I competition. Successful teams include women's volleyball, men's and women's golf, and men's basketball. A recreational program in men's and women's karate has turned out national champions. A student recreation center offers a health-club atmosphere with sand volleyball, weight and workout machines, and intramural leagues.

All in all, Riverside is growing and improving. Although half the size of some sister UC campuses, it offers more personal attention to its students. UCR is fast becoming a nationally recognized research institution, from which students surely will benefit. "UCR has grown immensely over the past few years," one sophomore says. "The emphasis for the future is to establish a name for UCR, to let the nation know what a wonderful university this is."

The biomedical sciences program, unique in California, is UCR's most prestigious and demanding course of study, and its most successful students can earn a seven-year BS/MD in partnership with the medical school at UCLA.

Overlaps

UC–Irvine, UC–Santa Cruz, UC-Berkeley, UC–Davis, UCLA, UC–Santa Barbara

If You Apply To ➤

Riverside: Regular admissions: Nov. 30. Financial aid: Mar. 1. Housing: Jun. 1. Guarantees to meet full demonstrated need. No campus or alumni interviews. SATs or ACTs: required. SAT IIs: required (writing, math, and one other). Prefers electronic applications. Essay question: personal statement.

UC–Santa Barbara

Santa Barbara, CA 93106

Willpower is the word at UC–Santa Barbara. On a beautiful day with the sound of waves crashing in the distance, it takes willpower to hang in there with pen, paper, and book. Fairly or not, Santa Barbara is known as the party animal of the UC system. In the classroom, science is the best bet.

For students at UC–Santa Barbara, California's famed beaches serve as both classroom and playground. On weekends, sun-worshipping students don surfboards and bikinis and head for the water to have some serious fun. During the week, those same students can likely be found studying technology rather than tan lines. UCSB provides a comfortable mixture of work and play that is unique to the UC system and draws praise from its students. Says a senior, "I love the fact that I am getting a highly rated UC education in such a relaxing location."

Located just a stone's throw from the beach, UC–Santa Barbara's 989-acre campus is bordered on two sides by the Pacific Ocean, with a clear view of the Channel Islands. On the landward side are a nature preserve and the predominantly student community of Isla Vista (IV), and five miles to the north lie the Santa Ynez Mountains. "We are definitely a college town," one senior says. "Isla Vista is almost all college students, and it is a really relaxed atmosphere." The campus itself features mainly 1950s Southern California architecture with a Southern California atmosphere to match. Recent construction includes student housing and the School of Environmental Science and Management.

> **"I love the fact that I am getting a highly rated UC education in such a relaxing location."**

Not surprisingly, the marine biology department capitalizes on the school's aquatic resources and stands out among the university's best. Other favorites include physics, ecology, engineering materials, and chemistry. The accounting program is also very strong, and the courses are geared toward taking and passing the CPA exam, so graduation is usually followed by a mass recruitment by California's big accounting firms. In addition, history, English, communications, and geological sciences are solid, but students say political science and math are considerably weaker. The College of Creative Studies offers an unstructured curriculum to about 400 self-starters ready for advanced and independent work in the arts, math, or the sciences. An interdisciplinary program called the Global Peace and Security Program combines aspects of physics, anthropology, and military science. The National Science Foundation provides funding for the $5.5 million National Center for Geographic Information and Analysis program. The Bren School of Environmental Science and Management is open for business, and the science departments are world-renowned—the college boasts Nobel prize winners in chemistry and physics.

UCSB's general education program requires all students to fulfill four subject areas: writing, non-Western cultures, quantitative relationships, and ethnicity. Other required courses include English reading and composition, foreign languages, social sciences, and art. For those who crave time away, Santa Barbara is the headquarters of the UC system's Education Abroad program, which sends students to any of 100 host universities worldwide. In order to graduate, all students must take courses in English Composition and American History and Institutions, must fulfill a unit requirement, and must also meet the requirements of their individual majors. In addition, students must be registered at UCSB for a minimum of three regular quarters.

> **"Everyone says 'hi' to other students."**

For those who crave time away, Santa Barbara is the headquarters of the UC system's Education Abroad program, which sends students to any of 100 host universities worldwide.

UCSB students are traditionally public-spirited; the fraternities and sororities, which attract 8 percent of men and 10 percent of women, are known for their philanthropy. The students, 94 percent of whom are California residents, are laid-back. "Everyone says 'hi' to other students, we ride bikes around our campus, and people are generally really friendly," one senior says. "Our students differ from students at other UC's because we are probably the most relaxed UC campus." Asian Americans comprise 17 percent of the student body; Hispanics account for 18 percent. "Being of Latino background, I have never felt like a minority on campus," one student says. "I associate with a lot of Latinos. We are a huge family, all know each other, and create great programs that help other Latinos get hyped up for college." The campus's beach locale inspires many students to be environmentally friendly. Merit scholarships and various athletic scholarships are available for those who qualify.

University housing, which includes both dorms and privately run residence halls, is comfortable, well-maintained, and much sought after. "Our on-campus housing is amazing, right in front of the beach" a junior says. "They come fully furnished, with high-speed Internet, cable, telephone lines, and a great atmosphere." Unfortunately, there is a waiting list to get into the dorms—even with the addition of the new Manzanita Village Student Housing. Only 21 percent of the students, most of whom are freshmen, snag on-campus housing. The rest find a home in neighboring Isla Vista, which has welcomed its student population—after all, most of its population is UCSB students. As a result, students are very active in the community. "Community service and maintaining our little community of Isla Vista is very important to students," one film studies/Chicano studies major says. "Isla Vista is the best college town." Meals in the dorms are available to residents and nonresidents alike, and are, according to most students, more than simply edible. "When one thinks of cafeteria food they think of nasty food, but not at UCSB's dining commons," one student says. While all students say they feel extremely safe on campus, one frequently used motto is "four years, four bikes," because of the frequency of bicycle thefts.

Because Isla Vista is predominantly made up of students, it's become what some students consider Party Central. But don't call UCSB a party school—students bristle at what they say is a misnomer. "It's just because we have so many students living in such a small area," one senior says. Alcohol isn't allowed on campus, but many students say the rule is easy to get around. The local bars are off-limits to those under 21, but when the long-awaited birthday arrives, students celebrate with a quaint little ritual known as the State Street Crawl, imbibing at all the numerous establishments up and down the "main drag" of Santa Barbara. Movies and concerts are also available, and the mountains, Los Padres National Forest, and L.A. are all an easy drive away. The annual Extravaganza is an all-day, free concert, and students are known to go wild on Halloween and dress up for the entire weekend.

"Isla Vista is the best college town."

Although the Greeks are strong and growing, there's an ample selection of other organizations from which to choose. A never-ending rotation of intramurals is available on and off the beach. The most successful varsity teams include soccer, water polo, baseball, volleyball, swimming, and basketball. All of UCSB's varsity teams compete in the NCAA's Division I. Ultimate Frisbee is also quite popular, as well as nationally competitive. And students brag their football team has been undefeated since 1992. That was, of course, the last year UCSB had a football team.

UCSB students love to work and play. They rave about their professors and the academic challenges they face. But they also know a good thing when they see it: not everyone gets to spend four years on the beach. "No matter what college you go to, you find people who you relate with," one student says. "At UCSB you find the social, happy, outgoing crowd. I love it here."

Only 21 percent of the students, most of whom are freshmen, snag on-campus housing. The rest find a home in neighboring Isla Vista, which has welcomed its student population—after all, most of its population is UCSB students.

Overlaps

UC–San Diego, UCLA, UC–Irvine, UC–Davis, UC–Berkeley

If You Apply To ➤   **Santa Barbara:** Regular admissions: May 1. Financial aid: Mar. 2. Does not guarantee to meet demonstrated need. Campus interviews: required for dramatic arts and dance, evaluative. No alumni interviews. SATs or ACTs: required. SAT IIs: required (writing). Common application not accepted; College of Creative Studies requires additional application. Essay question: personal statement.

1156 High Street, Santa Cruz, CA 95064

With its flower-child beginnings, UC–Santa Cruz has come back toward the mainstream. The distinctive flavor is still there, but the students are a lot more conventional than in its earlier incarnation, and UCSC is not quite the intellectual powerhouse of yore. Santa Cruz's relatively small size and residential college system give it a homey feel.

Website: www.ucsc.edu
Location: Suburban
Total Enrollment: 14,997
Undergraduates: 13,660
Male/Female: 45/55
SAT Ranges: V 520–640
  M 530–640
ACT Range: N/A
Financial Aid: 44%
Expense: Pub $ $ $
Phi Beta Kappa: Yes
Applicants: 28,582
Accepted: 69%
Enrolled: 20%
Grad in 6 Years: 66%
Returning Freshmen: 87%
Academics: ✍ ✍ ✍ ✍
Social: ☎ ☎ ☎
Q of L: ★ ★ ★ ★ ★
Admissions: (831) 459-4008
Email Address:
  admissions@cats.ucsc.edu

Strongest Programs:
Marine Sciences
Biology
Psychology
Linguistics

UC–Santa Cruz, still a baby in the UC system, was born during the radical '60s when it reigned as the ultimate alternative school. The founding vision of an integrated learning environment remains to this day, and every undergraduate affiliates with one of the residential colleges. The housing crunch has eased thanks to more than 2,000 units of additional on-campus housing. A few years ago, faculty voted to discontinue the Narrative Evaluation System in favor of traditional grades and performance evaluations. Progressive thought continues to flourish, as does a strong academic program that strives to focus on undergraduate education. Students still come to UCSC to do their own thing.

The campus, among the most beautiful in the nation, is set on a 2,000-acre expanse of meadowland and redwood forest overlooking Monterey Bay. Bike paths and hiking trails wind throughout the redwood-tree-filled campus, and the beach is a quick drive away—or a spectacular bike ride or scenic hike. The buildings range from 1860 Cowell Ranch farm structures to the multi-award-winning modern colleges, whose styles range from Mediterranean to Japanese to sleek concrete block. Thanks to a unique building code, nothing may be built taller than two-thirds the height of the nearest redwood tree. Newest additions include a student union, an award-winning second engineering building, an interdisciplinary sciences building, and an expanded bookstore.

The surroundings are deceptive. "Courses are very rigorous, in my experience," warns one undergrad. Santa Cruz's academic offerings range as widely as its architecture and feature both traditional and innovative programs. In an effort to become what one official calls a "near-perfect hybrid" between the large university and the small college, campus life revolves around the residential colleges. Whatever one's specialty, the curriculum can be demanding. Led by marine sciences and biology, the sciences are Santa Cruz's strongest suit, and frequently give students the opportunity to coauthor published research with their professors. Science facilities include state-of-the-art laboratories; the Institute of Marine Sciences, which boasts one of the largest groups of experts on marine mammals in the nation; and the nearby Lick Observatory for budding stargazers. UCSC also includes the Jack Baskin School of Engineering, which was developed to accommodate the growing needs of engineering students. UCSC has recently added majors in bioinformatics, health sciences, and applied physics.

While the majority of students now pursue traditional majors, the possibility is still there for eclectically minded students to pursue "history of consciousness" or just about anything else they can get a faculty member to OK. One of UCSC's most unique features is that professors provide written evaluations for each student in their class and also provide letter grades. UCSC boasts more than the average number of interdisciplinary programs, including environmental, community, and feminist studies; bioinformatics; and creative writing. Field study and internships are encouraged. Overall, the emphasis is on the liberal arts, and students will find few programs with a vocational emphasis.

"Courses are very rigorous, in my experience."

To meet general education requirements, students must complete courses in quantitative methods, U.S. ethnic minorities/non-Western society, arts, writing, humanities and arts, natural sciences, social sciences, and three topical courses. In addition, American History and Institutions and English Composition are required, as is a senior thesis or comprehensive exam. The main library, McHenry, houses more than a 1.5 million books and 25,000 periodicals, and students have access to books at other UC campuses through an online catalog system and interlibrary loans. The science library houses an additional 300,000 volumes.

In an effort to become what one official calls a "near-perfect hybrid" between the large university and the small college, campus life revolves around the residential colleges.

Though the curriculum is demanding and the quarter system keeps the academic pace fast, the atmosphere is emphatically noncompetitive. Such competition as there is tends to be internalized. A majority of the students eventually go on to graduate study. All UC campuses insist on faculty research, but most Santa Cruz professors are there to teach. "I've been very impressed with how accessible professors are," says a sophomore. "Whether it's via email or regular office hours, I feel very comfortable approaching and talking to all of my professors."

Santa Cruz remains the most liberal of the UC campuses, and, according to one student, is "still a school with a social conscience." "Before I came here I was told that UCSC was a 'hippie-dippie' college," says one student, "but this is not true at all." Ninety-four percent of the students are Californians, though Santa Cruz always manages to lure a few Easterners. More than one-third of the students are members of minority groups, with Asian Americans accounting for 18 percent of the students, Hispanics 14 percent, and African Americans 2 percent. "Racial, ethnic, and cultural diversity is celebrated and strongly encouraged by the **"Racial, ethnic, and cultural diversity is celebrated."** majority of the students here," reports a politics major. Santa Cruz offers more than 400 merit scholarships ranging from $1,759 to $2,781, but there are no athletic scholarships.

Forty-five percent of the undergraduate student population lives in university-sponsored housing. Some dorms have their own dining halls with reasonably good food; students may also opt to join a food co-op. Freshmen and transfer students are guaranteed on-campus housing for two years. Upperclassmen can take their chances in the lottery or move off campus.

Santa Cruz remains the most liberal of the UC campuses, and, according to one student, is "still a school with a social conscience."

There are a dozen fraternities and sororities, as well as countless established student groups, to provide an active social life. The beach and resort town of Santa Cruz, with its boardwalk and amusement park, are only 10 minutes away from campus by bike, but pedaling back up the hill takes much longer. Those looking for city lights can take the windy, mountainous highway to San Jose (35 miles away) or the slow, scenic coastal highway to San Francisco (75 miles), or ride a bus to either city. If you have a car, destinations such as Monterrey, Big Sur, the Napa Valley, and the Sierras are easily accessible.

Although Santa Cruz fields only a few varsity teams, students love their school mascot, Sammy the banana slug. In 2003, three-quarters of the varsity teams earned national ranking, and men's tennis coach Bob Hansen was named NCAA Division III Coach of the Year. Participation in intramurals ("Friendship through Competition" is the motto) is widespread, with rugby in particular growing in popularity. Sailing and scuba diving are among the many physical education classes offered, and the student recreation department sponsors everything from white-water rafting to cooking classes.

Santa Cruz is a progressive school with a gorgeous campus and innovative academic programs, where the main priority is the education of undergraduates. Many students are concerned that UCSC is growing too fast, and with population pressures in California's university system, that's likely to continue. Still, as long as UCSC retains its belief in "to each his or her own," it will remain uniquely Santa Cruz.

Overlaps

UC–Santa Barbara, UC–San Diego, UC–Davis, UCLA, UC–Berkeley

<table>
<tr><td>

If You Apply To ➤

</td><td>

Santa Cruz: Regular admissions: Nov. 30. Financial aid: Mar. 2. Housing: May 1. Does not guarantee to meet demonstrated need. No campus or alumni interviews. SATs or ACTs (plus writing): required. SAT IIs: required. Essay question: personal statement.

</td></tr>
</table>

California Institute of Technology

BEST BUY

Mail Code 328-87, 1200 East California Boulevard, Pasadena, CA 91125

If you're a distractedly brilliant techie with a 1600 on the SAT, maybe you'll have a fighting chance of getting into Caltech. With fewer than 1,000 undergraduates, Caltech is a quarter the size of MIT but just as muscular academically. From day one, freshmen have access to the best Caltech has to offer.

Website: www.caltech.edu
Location: Suburban
Total Enrollment: 2,120
Undergraduates: 939
Male/Female: 67/33
SAT Ranges: V 710–780
  M 760–800
Financial Aid: 57%
Expense: Pr $ $
Phi Beta Kappa: No
Applicants: 2,615
Accepted: 21%
Enrolled: 45%
Grad in 6 Years: 85%
Returning Freshmen: 95%
Academics: 🖉🖉🖉🖉🖉
Social: ☎
Q of L: ★★★
Admissions: (626) 395-6341
Email Address:
  ugadmissions@caltech.edu

Strongest Programs:
Engineering
Physics
Applied Sciences

The school counts 27 Nobel Prize winners among its faculty and alumni, and with administrators' permission—which is easy to obtain—students may tap into that brilliance by taking as many classes as they can cram in each semester. Expectations are high; "Techers" are fond of saying that "the admissions office doesn't make mistakes," and it's fairly common to take time off to deal with stress and avoid burnout. "The atmosphere promotes a love of science, learning, and discovery that is truly exhilarating," says a biology major. "There are absolutely no limits as to how much I can push myself academically," agrees a computer science major.

Caltech's 124-acre campus is located in Pasadena, "A wealthy suburban town about 15 miles outside Los Angeles," says a senior. "It's not a college town at all." The distance from downtown means the school is relatively isolated from the glitz, glamour, and good times that many people associate with "La La Land." Outside the classroom, at least, tranquility prevails, with olive trees, lily ponds, and plenty of flowers breaking up clusters of older Spanish-mission style buildings. Leafy courtyards and arcades link these with the more modern, "block institutional" structures. The new Broad Center for the Biological Sciences offers 120,000 square feet of lab, classroom, and office space at the northwest corner of campus. It was designed by Pei Cobb Freed & Associates, the firm behind the U.S. Holocaust Memorial Museum in Washington, D.C.

Caltech's mission, one official says, is "to train the creative type of scientist or engineer urgently needed in our educational, governmental, and industrial development." After all, it was here that Albert Einstein abandoned his concept of a static cosmos and endorsed the expanding-universe model. This is also where physicist Carl Anderson discovered the positron. With these luminaries as their models, students plunge right into the demanding general requirements, which include five terms each of math and physics, three terms of chemistry with lab, one term of biology, two terms of science communication, and courses in the humanities and social sciences to round things out. Students complain about these, "and usually take no more than absolutely required," says a biology major. Still, they can be tough to get into come registration time, says a computer science major, since enrollment is limited "to allow for discussion among a small group." The pass/fail grading system in the freshman year goes a long way toward easing the acclimation period for new arrivals. And the honor system, which mandates that "no one shall take unfair advantage of any other member of the Caltech community," helps discourage competition for grades. Professors give take-home exams, and if violations of the honor code are suspected, "students decide if a violation was indeed made," one student explains.

Caltech made its name in physics, and students say that program remains strong. An economics major also gives high marks to geology, noting that everyone in the major "seems euphoric." Since Caltech is a research institution, "The departments that typically require the most research—as opposed to, say, training for industrial work—are the best," a junior explains, mentioning chemistry, biology, and astronomy as programs that fit the bill. Regardless of major, Caltech students benefit from state-of-the-art facilities, including the Beckman Institute, a center for fundamental research in biology and chemistry, and the Keck telescope, the largest optical telescope in the world. The Moore Laboratory has 90,000 square feet of the latest equipment for engineering and communications majors studying fiber optics and the like. Summer Undergraduate Research Fellowships give 300 undergraduates the chance to get a head start on their own discoveries, with help from a faculty sponsor. Some 20 percent of these students publish results from their endeavors in scientific journals.

The pass/fail grading system in the freshman year goes a long way toward easing the acclimation period for new arrivals.

Despite Caltech's reputation for brilliance, students say the quality of teaching is hit or miss. "At times, you get lucky and get amazing professors," says a computer science major. "Other times, you get professors who either don't care about the class they teach, or are so advanced in their field that they are unable to convey 'simple' concepts." A senior goes farther, calling instruction "not so much poor as nonexistent." Here, the student says, professors in the humanities and social sciences really shine, since they actually want to teach, rather than hole up in a lab with gas spectrometers and computer simulations of atomic fission. Another student calls courses "incredibly rigorous," noting that "if you don't know your stuff, you

"The atmosphere promotes a love of science, learning, and discovery that is truly exhilarating."

won't make it." Perhaps that's why collaboration between students is encouraged and embraced. While teaching assistants do lead some recitation sections affiliated with large lectures, it's not uncommon for professors to lead them, too—even for freshmen, says a sophomore. "If you don't like your TA, switching sections is a breeze," the student says.

Twenty-nine percent of Techers come from California, and the same fraction are Asian American; other minorities are less well-represented, with Hispanics making up 7 percent of the student body and African Americans 1 percent. Students are "brilliant, young, sheltered, driven, interesting, and socially awkward," says a biology major. "The girls aren't catty or ditzy, the guys aren't macho or aggressive. There's room for everyone." Foreign students account for 8 percent of the student body, but even in a year of political strife and war, "social and political issues are not a big deal on campus, period," says a junior. "People live in a Tech bubble, where they care about nothing more than 50 meters from campus," a sophomore agrees. The school awards merit scholarships of $11,000 to $23,000 a year, but "unless you're absolutely at the top of the incoming freshman class—which many think they are, yet most are not even close—you won't get any," a junior says.

Summer Undergraduate Research Fellowships give 300 undergraduates the chance to get a head start on their own discoveries, with help from a faculty sponsor.

Caltech guarantees on-campus or school-affiliated housing for all four years, and 87 percent of students live in the "comfortable and convenient" dorms. While there are no fraternities or sororities, the seven co-ed on-campus houses inspire a loyalty worthy of the Greeks. The four older houses, which have been renovated, offer mostly single rooms, while the three newer dorms have doubles. Freshmen select their house during Rotation Week, after spending an evening of partying at each one, and indicating at week's end the four they like the most. Resident upperclassmen take it from there in a professional-sports-type draft, which places each new student in one of his or her top choices. Business-minded types, for example, may choose Avery House, which focuses on entrepreneurship. Each dorm has a dining hall, and those who live on campus must buy a meal plan, which a junior calls "quite expensive for the quality of food." A vegetarian calls the chow "awful," and says that "by the end of the week, I am often wondering if we're being served the same spinach for five days in a row."

The houses are the emotional center of Caltech life, and the scene of innumerable practical jokes. On Ditch Day, seniors barricade their dorm rooms using everything from steel bars to electronic codes, leave clues as to how to overcome the obstacles, and disappear from campus. Underclassmen spend the day figuring out how to break in, using "cleverness, brute force, and finesse,"

"If you don't like your TA, switching sections is a breeze."

to claim a reward inside, which can range from the edible to…well, anything is possible. Perhaps the best student prank occurred during the 1984 Rose Bowl game, when crosstown rival UCLA played Illinois. A group of Caltech whiz kids spent months devising a radio-control device that would allow them to take control of the scoreboard in the second half, to gain national exposure for Caltech by flashing pictures of their school's mascot, the beaver, and a new version of the score that had Caltech leading MIT by a mile.

While drinking might seem a reasonable escape from the pressure of all that work, Caltech requires any organization hosting a party to hire a professional bartender—"and they card," says a senior. "Ask any local bartender for a Caltech Cocktail and you will get three ounces of straight water," quips a sophomore. Social life at Caltech "is horrible," agrees a junior. "There are occasional parties, but the administration does not allow students from other colleges to attend, unless accompanied by a Caltech student." So students head off-campus—to Old Pasadena, nearby schools like USC, Occidental, and the Claremont colleges, or to downtown LA, now easily reachable on the Metro's gold line. Disneyland and Hollywood are always an option, and road trips to the beach, mountains, or desert—or south of the border, to Tijuana—are options for those with cars. "From yoga studios to death metal concerts, LA has it all," one student says. But some Caltech students still prefer to make their own fun. The annual Pumpkin Drop (on Halloween, of course) involves immersing a gourd in liquid nitrogen, and

"From yoga studios to death metal concerts, LA has it all."

then dropping it from the library roof, so that it shatters into a zillion frozen shards. During finals week, stereos blast "The Ride of the Valkyries" at seven o'clock each morning, just the thing to get you going after that all-nighter.

Caltech fields 18 Division III teams, and the most popular include men's soccer, men's and women's track and field, and men's crosscountry. The school also offers more unusual sports such as water polo and fencing. Perhaps more popular than varsity competition, though, are the intramural matches between the houses, in nine sports every year. Also popular is the annual design competition that's the culmination of Mechanical Engineering 72; it helped inspire the TV shows Battle Bots and Robot Wars.

Caltech students must learn to thrive under intense pressure, thanks to the school's tremendous workload and lackluster social life. But students say they appreciate the freedom to think and explore—and the trust administrators place in them because of the honor code. "The unique student body, how available professors are (I call almost all of them by their first names), and how much we learn make Caltech a special place," says a sophomore. If you're armed with a perfect SAT score, a burning desire to study math, science, or engineering, and some independent research or published papers already under your belt, maybe you'll have a fighting chance of getting into Caltech.

Overlaps

MIT, Stanford, Harvard, UC–Berkeley, UCLA

Caltech: Early action: Nov. 1. Regular admissions: Jan 1. Guarantees to meet demonstrated need. No campus or alumni interviews. SATs: required. SAT IIs: required (writing, math, and either physics, biology, or chemistry). Accepts electronic applications. Looks for math/science aptitude as well as research orientation or unusual academic potential. Essay question: areas of interest; personal statement.

Calvin College

3201 Burton, Grand Rapids, MI 49546

An evangelical Christian institution that ranks high on the private-college bargain list. Nearly half the students are members of the Christian Reformed Church. Archrival of Michigan neighbor Hope and Illinois cousin Wheaton. Best known in the humanities.

Michigan's Calvin College prides itself on being "distinctively academic, strikingly Christian." Though no one is required to attend the school's daily chapel services, classes stop when worship starts, and most students view Christian values as central to the academic experience. Calvin also offers solid preprofessional preparation in engineering, nursing, and education, among other disciplines, though students avoid the religion department, calling the professors "inconsistent" and "painstakingly difficult." Along with Wheaton College in Illinois, Calvin is regarded as one of the country's top evangelical colleges. "We want to actively engage the world and discern it," says a freshman. "People at Calvin are not just numbers or simply students," adds a senior. "They are people looking to grow and develop in all areas of life."

Calvin was founded in 1876, as the educational wing of the Christian Reformed Church in North America. After outgrowing its first home, the college bought a tract of land on the edge of Grand Rapids, and built its present campus. Calvin spreads out over more than 400 beautifully landscaped acres, including playing fields and three ponds. The campus also includes an 80-acre woodland and wetland ecosystem preserve used for classes, research, and recreation. Most facilities are less than 35 years old, and were designed by a student of famed architect Frank Lloyd Wright. The east campus, dedicated in 2002, includes the Prince Conference Center, DeVos Communications Center, Gainey Athletic Facility, and the award-winning Bunker Interpretive Center, powered primarily by student-designed solar energy technology.

Calvin's core curriculum has four components: core gateway, studies, competencies, and capstone courses. All first-year students must take the two linked gateway courses, Prelude and Developing a Christian Mind. Students then tackle the liberal arts core, entitled "An Engagement with God's World," which challenges them to develop knowledge, skills, and Christian character. Studies courses include The Physical World, Societal Structures in North America, and Biblical Foundations. Competencies courses cover foreign languages and Rhetoric in Culture. New programs include majors in international development studies and youth ministry leadership, and integrated science studies in the teacher education program.

Professional programs, such as teacher education, engineering, nursing, and business, tend to be Calvin's best bets, students say—perhaps that's why those programs, along with English, are the college's most popular majors. Biology, chemistry, philosophy, and religion are also regarded as strong, though faculty members in those departments are said to be overly tough. Internships and small-business consulting opportunities are available, whether on campus, or through Calvin's

Website: www.calvin.edu
Location: Suburban
Total Enrollment: 4,042
Undergraduates: 3,969
Male/Female: 55/45
SAT Ranges: V 540–670
  M 540–670
ACT Range: 23–29
Financial Aid: 66%
Expense: Pr $
Phi Beta Kappa: No
Applicants: 1,721
Accepted: 98%
Enrolled: 54%
Grad in 6 Years: 76%
Returning Freshmen: 86%
Academics: ✍ ✍ ✍
Social: ☎ ☎ ☎
Q of L: ★ ★ ★ ★
Admissions: (800) 668-0122
Email Address:
  admissions@calvin.edu

Strongest Programs:
Natural Sciences
Education
Nursing
Engineering
Communication Arts and
  Sciences
English
Philosophy
Mathematics
History

membership in the Christian College Consortium.* Students who receive bachelor's degrees in accounting from Calvin pass the CPA exam at rates 15 to 20 percent higher than the national average.

Academically, Calvin's climate is not competitive. "There is enough pressure around to force you to do your work, and to do your work well, but the pressure is also here to enjoy the ride," one student explains. The school believes that every subject—even the sciences, or mass media and popular culture—can be approached from a Christian perspective, and faculty members work hard to integrate faith and learning. "Calvin profs push students to do their best and focus on students' being able to succeed at the next level," says a speech pathology major.

Almost half of the freshman courses at Calvin have 25 students or fewer students. Faculty members must be committed to Christian teachings, and there are no teaching assistants, so professors are expected to reserve about 10 hours per week for advising and assisting students outside of class. "Much of the quality of instruction comes from knowing that our professors do care," says an English major. "Professors are here to teach, not to do research, so they invest time and energy in us," agrees a special-education major. Students use the interim month of January to pursue a variety of creative, low-pressure enrichment experiences, such as art and theater study in England, language study in Germany, Canada or the Dominican Republic, or courses taught by Calvin profs in other cities and countries.

> "We want to actively engage the world and discern it."

Though Calvin still has a strongly Dutch heritage, the fraction of students who are members of the Christian Reformed Church is now less than half of the student body. "Students are mature, clean-cut, fun, intelligent, mostly friendly people," says a junior. Most students are still white Michigan natives, though—African Americans and Hispanics each make up 1 percent of the total, and Asian Americans add 3 percent. "A sophomore adds, "Students here think for themselves, are open-minded, discern the world, and have purpose in life." President Bush learned about these qualities in May 2005, when, looking for a safe place to give a commencement speech, he was met with a petition signed by more than 100 professors accusing him of violating Christian principles with his Iraq policies. Forty-five percent of Calvin students receive scholarships based on academic merit, ranging from $1,000 to $10,000 each. There are no athletic awards.

Fifty-six percent of Calvin students live on campus in the single-sex dorms. Freshmen and sophomores bunk in suites with two bedrooms, connected by a bathroom, while juniors and seniors move off campus or into the on-campus apartments, "which are nice and being redone," according to one student. Each residence hall and two of the apartment buildings have computer rooms in the basement, along with free washers and dryers. The food gets rave reviews, too—with options such as pizza, cereal, fresh fruit, made-to-order sandwiches, and ice cream and waffles available at every meal.

Calvin has no Greek system, and—owing to its emphasis on Christianity and character—the campus is officially dry. "Students are very creative and do not need alcohol in order to have a good time," says a freshman. "We like to take midnight runs to Meijer, go line-dancing on floor dates, and watch movies as a floor." Downtown Grand Rapids has ice-skating, coffee shops, and occasional concerts by big-name artists

> "Professors are here to teach, not to do research, so they invest time and energy in us."

such as Indigo Girls and Dave Matthews Band. Road trips include the beaches of Lake Michigan (a one-hour drive) or Chicago (three hours distant), and even Florida or California for spring break. A popular annual event is Chaos Day, which brings the dorms together for a day of athletic contests. The Airband lip-sync competition each February is also a favorite, as are athletic contests versus Hope College.

ESPN2 ranked Calvin's rivalry with Hope as one of the top 10 college rivalries in the U.S.; the Calvin men's basketball team went to the Division III Final Four in 2005. "Any game against Hope always turns into a big deal," says a speech pathology major, especially in soccer, volleyball, or women's basketball. Calvin's men's cross-country team is also strong, although the Knights don't field a football squad. The college's intramural program offers classes, leagues, and tournaments in sports from dodge ball to ultimate Frisbee and fantasy football. Thirty to 40 percent of students participate.

The students who come to Calvin College aren't seeking the traditional beer-soaked four years away from home. Instead, they're looking to build community with friends and faculty members who share their already-strong Christian faith. "Calvin has a distinctively Christian character and atmosphere," says a sophomore. "This college, its people, place, and mission, all revolve around a commitment to Christ and the furthering of his kingdom. Faith plays an integral part in the classrooms, offices, and dorm rooms."

If You Apply To ➤ **Calvin:** Rolling admissions. Financial aid: Feb. 15. Housing: May 1. Campus interviews: optional, informational. No alumni interviews. SATs or ACTs: required. ACTs preferred. SAT IIs: optional. Accepts the Common Application and prefers electronic applications. Essay question: why Calvin, and how have your religious beliefs encouraged you to apply; what your community, church, volunteer, school or career activities have taught you about being a steward of your gifts and talents.

Carleton College

Northfield, MN 55057

Less selective than Amherst, Williams, and Swarthmore because of its chilly Minnesota location. Yet Carleton retains its position as the premier liberal arts college in the upper Midwest. Predominately liberal, but not to the extremes of its more antiestablishment cousins.

Minnesota is many things: the land of 10,000 lakes, home to the massive Mall of America, birthplace of lore from Hiawatha to Paul Bunyan, and proud parent of the Mississippi River. Beyond all that history-book stuff, tucked into a small town in the southeastern corner of the state, is Carleton College, arguably the best liberal arts school in the expansive Midwest. Add to this a midwinter carnival complete with human bowling, badminton competitions that raise money to fight cancer, and an expulsion of Coca Cola off campus for human rights violations, and you have one all-around unique institution.

Surrounded by rolling farmland, Carleton's 955-acre campus is in the small town of Northfield, whose one-time status as the center of the Holstein cattle industry brought it the motto "The City of Cows, Colleges, and Contentment." Lakes, woods, and streams abound, and you can traverse them on 12 miles of hiking and crosscountry skiing trails. The city boasts of fragrant lilacs in spring, rich summer greens, red maples in the fall, and glistening blanket of white in winter. There's even an 800-acre arboretum, put to good use by everyone from jogging jocks to bird-watching nature lovers. Carleton's architectural style is somewhat eclectic—everything from Victorian to contemporary, but mostly redbrick. When it's minus eight degrees, the indoor recreation center provides a rock-climbing wall, gym, putting green, sports courts, track, and dance studio.

Website: www.carleton.edu
Location: Small city
Total Enrollment: 1,946
Undergraduates: 1,930
Male/Female: 48/52
SAT Ranges: V 650–750
  M 650–730
ACT Range: 28–32
Financial Aid: 55%
Expense: Pr $ $ $ $
Phi Beta Kappa: Yes
Applicants: 4,737
Accepted: 30%
Enrolled: 20%
Grad in 6 Years: 89%
Returning Freshmen: 97%
Academics: ✍ ✍ ✍ ✍ ✍
Social: ☎ ☎ ☎

(Continued)

Q of L: ★★★
Admissions: (507) 646-4190
Email Address:
admissions@acs.carleton
.edu

Strongest Programs:
Mathematics
Computer Science
Chemistry
Physics
English
History
Economics
Psychology

Carleton's top-notch academic programs are no less varied: the sciences—biology, physics, astronomy, chemistry, geology, and computer science—are among the best anywhere, and scores of Carleton graduates go on to earn PhDs in these areas. Of all the liberal arts schools in the country, Carleton's undergrads were recently awarded the highest number of National Science Foundation fellowships for graduate studies. English, history, economics, and biology get high marks, too. Engineers can opt for a 3–2 program with Columbia University or Washington University in St. Louis, and for geologists seeking fieldwork—and maybe wanting to thaw out after a long Minnesota winter—Carleton sponsors a program in Death Valley. Closer to home at the "arb," as

"Though we only take three courses a trimester, courses are typically very rigorous."

the arboretum is affectionately known, environmental studies majors have their own wilderness field station, which includes a prairie-restoration site. At the opposite end of the academic spectrum, the arts also flourish. Music and studio art majors routinely get into top graduate programs, even though students say the arts are less emphasized, especially music and theatre.

Distribution requirements ensure that a Carleton education exposes students not only to rigor and depth in their chosen field, but also to "a wide range of subjects and methods of studying them," administrators say. All students must show proficiency in English composition and a foreign language while fulfilling requirements in four broad areas: arts and literature; history, philosophy, and religion; social sciences; and math and natural sciences. There's also a Recognition of Affirmation and Difference requirement, under which students must take at least one course dealing with a non-Western culture, and a senior comprehensive project is required in every major field. Carleton offers interdisciplinary programs in Asian, Jewish, urban, African and African American, and women's studies. A concentration in crosscultural studies brings in foreign students to discuss global issues and dynamics with their American counterparts. Approximately 70 percent of students spend at least one term abroad, and many take advantage of programs available either through numerous organizations, including Carleton and the Associated Colleges of the Midwest.* The school's 799,000-volume library is bright, airy, and—much to the delight of caffeine-stoked night owls—open until 1:00 a.m.

With highly motivated students and a heavy workload, Carleton isn't your typical mellow Midwestern liberal arts college. The trimester calendar means finals may be just three months apart and almost everyone feels the pressure. The six-week Christmas vacation is Carleton's way of dealing with the cold winters. "Though we only take

"Anyone who wants to live on campus will get a room on campus."

three courses a trimester, courses are typically very rigorous. But for those who need it, academic support services

are valuable resources," says a student. Ninety-one percent of all classes have fewer than 30 students, so Carls are expected to participate actively. Carleton's faculty members are very committed to teaching. "Office hours are widely available, and the student/faculty relationship is often extended outside of the classroom," says a junior.

Seventy-one percent of Carleton's students hail from outside Minnesota, half are from outside the Midwest, and most attended public schools. "As one of my profs said, 'You can generalize Carleton students until you remember one you know'," recalls an American studies major. Both coasts are heavily represented, and more than 15 foreign countries send at least one student. African Americans and Hispanics account for 9 percent of the total student body, and Asian Americans for another 9 percent. But most Carls have a few things in common, such as being intellectually curious, yet laid-back; individualistic, but concerned about building a community feeling on campus. Their earthy dress and attitude are a sharp contrast from that of their more traditional crosstown cousins at rival St. Olaf College. The Carleton campus is rather left of center, concerned with issues including the environment, multiculturalism, and affirmative action, gay rights, and sexism. "Students are ambitions, aware, and ready to 'save the world'," says a sophomore. Qualified students receive Carleton-sponsored National Merit and National Achievement scholarships every year, and students call financial aid packages "definitely adequate."

Campus accommodations range from comfortable old townhouses to modern hotel-like residence halls. "Dorms are typically comfortable and well-maintained," says a junior. "Anyone who wants to live on campus will get a room on campus." Best of all are the 10 college-owned off-campus "theme" houses, which focus on special interests such as foreign languages, the outdoors, or nuclear-power issues. With the exception of the Farm House, an environmental studies house sitting on the edge of the arb, all the theme houses (including Women's Awareness House) are situated in an attractive residential section of town close to campus. Students who wish to live off campus must apply for a slot. Dorms are co-ed by room, but there are two halls with single-sex floors. Davis is the recommended dorm, although Burton enjoys a "fun" reputation. Everyone who stays on campus must commit to a meal plan, and while "food is not always the greatest, most people have a good sense of humor about it or go to the grocery store," says a freshman. "The dining facilities have also gone through many renovations," says another student.

Absent a Greek system, Carleton's social life tends to be relaxed and informal, and often centers on going out with friends. People go to parties on campus, or if they are of drinking age, bar hop around town. "In a 10-week term, there's not enough time to just go home—so much goes on every weekend between concerts, festivals, carnivals, parties, and cool speakers," says a student. "You really miss out by going away." There are activities for those who pass on imbibing; a group called Co-op sponsors dances and Wednesday socials every two weeks,

> **"The dining facilities have also gone through many renovations."**

free movies, and special events like Comedy Night. Students agree that Carleton makes little more than token efforts to enforce the drinking age. "The administration respects the Carleton students' responsibility to make his/her own decisions about drinking, and the alcohol policy is very relaxed," says a freshman.

Northfield itself is a quaint, history-filled town with a population of about 17,000. There are old-style shops and a beautiful old hotel. "Northfield is a beautiful, small, Midwestern town," a senior sighs. "Enough coffee shops and restaurants for any college student." Students often frequent the St. Olaf College campus and a night spot known as the Reub'n'Stein. Minneapolis–St. Paul, 35 miles to the north, is a popular road trip destination. Since students aren't allowed to have cars on campus, Carleton charters buses on weekends.

About a third of the students play on varsity teams, but about two-thirds play intramurals. The track, swimming, tennis, basketball, and baseball teams are competitive, as are the championship crosscountry ski teams. Popular events include the Winter Carnival, the Spring Concert, and Mai-F'te, a gala celebrated on an island in one of the two lakes on campus. Traditions include the weeklong freshman orientation program, where—during opening convocation—students bombard professors with bubbles as the faculty members process. There's also the annual spring softball game that begins at 5:30 a.m. and runs as many innings as there are years in Carleton's existence. The all-campus 10:00 p.m. scream on the eve of final exams keeps fatigued studiers awake. Notorious outlaw Jesse James failed to rob the Northfield Bank those many years ago, and Northfield still celebrates with a Wild West bank raid reenactment every year. (The robbery was thwarted by brave townsfolk, and the gang broke up immediately afterward.)

It can be cold in Minnesota, in a face-stinging, bone-chilling kind of way. And the classes are far from easy. But Carleton is a warm campus, and the academics are

Overlaps

Macalester, Williams, Brown, Harvard, Middlebury, Swarthmore

challenging without being impossible. Carls toe the line between individuality and community, which makes for personal growth and lifelong friendships. "Get ready to live in rural Minnesota with a bunch of crazy people that like to work hard and have fun," a junior says.

<table>
<tr><td>If You Apply To ➤</td><td>Carleton: Early decision: Nov. 15, Jan. 15. Regular admissions: Jan. 15. Financial aid: Feb. 15. Guarantees to meet demonstrated need. Campus and alumni interviews: recommended, informational. SATs or ACTs: required. SAT IIs: recommended. Accepts the Common Application and electronic applications. Essay question: turning points in your life; influential people; lunch with anyone; integrating classroom learning into daily life; or your own question.</td></tr>
</table>

Carnegie Mellon University

5000 Forbes Avenue, Pittsburgh, PA 15213-3890

Carnegie Mellon is the only premier technical university that also happens to be equally strong in the arts. Applications nearly doubled in the past 10 years, so it must be doing something right. One of the few institutions that openly matches better financial aid awards from competitor schools.

Website: www.cmu.edu
Location: City outskirts
Total Enrollment: 9,756
Undergraduates: 5,337
Male/Female: 64/36
SAT Ranges: V 600–710
  M 680–770
ACT Range: 27–31
Financial Aid: 80%
Expense: Pr $ $ $ $
Phi Beta Kappa: Yes
Applicants: 14,467
Accepted: 38%
Enrolled: 24%
Grad in 6 Years: 81%
Returning Freshmen: 94%
Academics: 🐛 🐛 🐛 🐛
Social: 🐦 🐦 🐦
Q of L: ★ ★ ★
Admissions: (412) 268-2082
Email Address:
  undergraduate-admissions
  @andrew.cmu.edu

Strongest Programs:
Computer Science
Engineering
Drama
Music

Students at Carnegie Mellon don't have to choose between soaking up the high drama of Shakespeare and plunging into the fast-paced dot-com world. The university is known for both its science offerings and strong drama and music programs. But scholars can't be focused on just their own course of study—Carnegie Mellon continues to strive to offer both its technical and liberal arts students a well-rounded education that requires a lot of hard work, but promises great results.

Carnegie Mellon was formed by the merger of Carnegie Tech and the Mellon Institute, resulting in a self-contained 136-acre campus attractively situated in Pittsburgh's affluent Oakland section. Next door is the city's largest park and its major museum, named after—you guessed it—Andrew Carnegie. Henry Hornbostel won a competition in 1904 to design the Carnegie Technical Schools, now Carnegie Mellon University. Hornbostel, who attended the Ecole des Beaux-Arts in the 1890s, created a campus plan that is a modification of the Jefferson plan for the University of Virginia with the Beaux-Arts device of creating primary and secondary axes and grouping buildings around significant open spaces. Buildings are designed in a Renaissance style, with buff-colored brick arches and piers, tile roofs and terra cotta and granite details. Construction was recently completed on New House, a first-year dorm, and the Posner Center, a meeting and display space for art and scientific works.

Carnegie Mellon is divided into six undergraduate colleges: the College of Fine Arts, the College of Humanities and Social Sciences, the Carnegie Institute of Technology, the Mellon College of Science, the School of Computer Science, and the Tepper School of Business. Each has its own distinct character and admission requirements, which applicants may want to contact the admissions office to find out about. All the colleges, however, share the university's commitment to what it calls a "liberal-professional" education, which makes the liberal arts extremely relevant while stressing courses that develop technical skills and good job prospects. Humanities and social science types can major in applied history, professional writing, or information systems, for example, instead of traditional disciplinary concentrations. Under the Science and Humanities Scholars Program, talented undergrads can develop a curricular program based on their interests in the humanities, natural sciences, math, or social sciences. In addition, the Fifth-Year Scholars program provides full tuition for outstanding students who want to remain at Carnegie Mellon for an additional year to pursue more studies that interest them.

(Continued)
Industrial Management
Business
Architecture

Most departments at Carnegie Mellon are strong, but exceptional ones include chemical engineering and electrical and computer engineering. While some humanities courses are praised, most students agree Carnegie Mellon is definitely more of a science-oriented school. Each college requires core work from freshmen; in the College of Humanities and Social Science, for example, students are introduced to computers in a required first-year philosophy course, using the machines to work on problems of logic. Two majors—logic and computation in the philosophy department and cognitive science through the psychology department—combine computer science technology with such fields as artificial intelligence and linguistics. The university created a Department of Modern Languages, and a Bachelor of Science and Arts degree program was added recently along with a Science and Humanities Scholars Program. A program in entertainment technology, spearheaded by a drama professor and a computer science professor, is increasingly appealing to students. One recent faculty hire comes from Disney.

"Expect to work hard if you come here."

As one student bluntly puts it, the courses at Carnegie Mellon are "extremely rigorous with many hours expected outside of the classroom. Expect to work hard if you come here." The College of Fine Arts' drama department, the first and still one of the best in the country, concentrates on performance, and its faculty is made up of highly regarded working professionals. While the program embraces the art of performance, freshmen must take English and history, as well as a basic computer course. After that it's drama all day, every day. Students at CMU work hard, no doubt about it. "Carnegie Mellon is very intense, so lots of time is dedicated to class assignments and group projects," a student says. However, nearly all the classes are small, with fewer than 30 students. Most students agree that the Carnegie Institute of Technology is by far the most difficult college. Professors rate high with most students, who praise their availability and willingness to help. "Most professors are very eager to help and make sure that material is understood," says a sophomore psychology major.

Carnegie Mellon appeals to those yearning for the bright lights of Broadway or the glowing computer screens of the scientific and business worlds.

Carnegie Mellon's professional focus shows through in its internship program. A number of five-year, dual-degree options exist, including a joint BS/MS or an industrial internship co-op program in materials science and engineering, which places students in the industrial environment. Beyond traditional student exchanges with major universities around the globe, Carnegie Mellon has established a campus in the Arabian Gulf nation of Qatar. The campus offers business and undergraduate computer science degrees, and is led by renowned roboticist Charles Thorpe.

Carnegie Mellon remains one of the most fragmented campuses in the nation. Students divide themselves between actors, dancers, and other artsy types and engineers, scientists, and architects. In any case, students are united in their quest for a good job after graduation. Still, many complain about the fact that students will give up sleep to study, and that this kind of academic orientation can often hinder social

"Sometimes there just isn't very much social life, but many students prefer it that way."

life. "Sometimes there just isn't very much social life, but many students prefer it that way," says one student. Every day includes a designated "meeting-free" time for students, allowing them time to study or participate in student activities.

Once a very regional institution, drawing mostly Pennsylvania residents, Carnegie Mellon now counts about 79 percent of its students from out of state. About one-third are from minority groups, including 23 percent Asian American, 5 percent

African American, and 5 percent Hispanic. "We are very diverse and therefore very culturally aware," a biology major says. Some students say a big issue is the nearly two-to-one male/female ratio. The university says it remains committed to need-blind admissions, but it provides larger proportions of outright grants in financial aid packages to "academic superstars." Carnegie Mellon has stopped guaranteeing to meet the financial need of all accepted students, but now offers an early evaluation of financial aid eligibility for interested prospective students. The financial aid office encourages students who have received more generous packages from competing schools to let Carnegie Mellon know so they have an opportunity to match or better them.

Housing, guaranteed for all four years, offers old and newer buildings, the most popular being university-owned apartments. Upperclassmen get first pick, with freshman assignments coming from a lottery of the remainder. "The dorms are generally very comfortable and well-maintained, with ample living space," says one student. The best dorms for freshmen are New House, Donner, Resnik, and Morewood Gardens. Most halls are co-ed, but a few are men-only. Students can remain in campus housing as long as they wish, and about 62 percent do so each year. Meal plans are said to be restrictive and expensive.

With all the academic pressure at Carnegie Mellon, it's a good thing there are so many opportunities to unwind, especially with the entire city of Pittsburgh close at hand. The Greek system provides the most visible form of on-campus social life, and 8 percent of the students belong. For those who choose not to fraternize, coffeehouses, inexpensive films, dances, and concerts in nearby Oakland, plus

"The dorms are generally very comfortable and well-maintained, with ample living space."

downtown Pittsburgh itself (opera, ballet, symphony, concerts, and sporting events just 20 minutes away by bus) provide plenty of alternatives. The administration is desperately trying to curtail underage drinking. Some students say the penalties for being caught are harsh, but others maintain that the rules are "vaguely known."

One event that brings everyone together is the Spring Carnival, when the school shuts down for a day. Students set up booths with electronic games, and student groups race in buggies made of lightweight alloys designed by engineering majors. Students put on original "Scotch and Soda" presentations, two of which—Pippin and Godspell—went on to become Broadway hits. The Jill Watson Festival Across the Arts—named for a former faculty member who died on TWA Flight 800—specifically targets artists who cross boundaries in their work. Carnegie Mellon competes in Division III. Both the women's soccer and volleyball teams recently won tournament championships, and the swim team has earned many AAU honors as well.

Carnegie Mellon appeals to those yearning for the bright lights of Broadway or the glowing computer screens of the scientific and business worlds. And with a broad range of liberal arts and technical courses not only available, but required, there's no doubt students leave Carnegie Mellon with a well-rounded education—and an impressive diploma. "It's driven, but there's no better place to be interacting with people of so many disciplines who are so focused," one satisfied senior says.

Overlaps

MIT, Cornell University, Penn, Princeton, Harvard

If You Apply To ➤

Carnegie Mellon: Early decision: Nov. 15 (Nov. 1 for fine arts applicants). Regular admissions: Jan. 1 (Dec. 1 for fine arts applicants). Financial aid: Feb. 15. Does not guarantee to meet demonstrated need. Campus interviews: recommended, evaluative. Alumni interviews: optional, evaluative. SATs or ACTs: required. SAT IIs: required (varies by college). Essay question: personal statement.

Case Western Reserve University

P.O. Box 128016, Cleveland, OH 44106

The Cleveland Browns always lose to the Pittsburgh Steelers and CWRU is still trying to catch up with Carnegie Mellon. Students may sing its praises, but Cleveland isn't exactly Boston, or even Pittsburgh. On the plus side, students can get an outstanding technical education at Case with solid offerings in other areas.

Cleveland's Case Western Reserve University has long been in the shadow of Pittsburgh's Carnegie Mellon, but the schools also have much in common. Both are the product of mergers between a technical college, known for excellence in engineering, and a more traditional university, focused on the arts and sciences. Both are located in aging rust-belt cities, which have struggled to reinvent themselves. And both tend to attract brainy students more concerned with studying than socializing. Recently, Case has increased its investment in the arts, humanities, and social sciences, with an aim toward helping students connect these disciplines with their technical studies. "We're not a big party school," says a psychology major. "But there are parties, concerts, and cultural and club events every weekend."

Case is located on the eastern edge of Cleveland, at University Circle. This 550-acre area of parks and gardens is home to more than 40 cultural, educational, medical, and research institutions, including the city's museums of art and natural history, its botanical gardens, and Severance Hall, home of the symphony orchestra. Campus buildings are an eclectic mix of architectural styles, and several are listed on the National Register of Historic Places. The Lewis Building, designed by Frank Gehry, is home for the Weatherhead School of Management. It features undulating walls similar to those of Gehry's Guggenheim Museum in Bilbao, Spain, along with offices, classrooms, and meeting rooms on every floor, to encourage informal student/faculty interaction.

The product of the 1967 marriage between Case Institute of Technology and Western Reserve University, Case has four undergraduate schools: the College of Arts and Sciences, the Case School of Engineering, the Bolton School of Nursing, and the aforementioned Weatherhead School; all also offer graduate programs. All Case students participate in a new general education program, SAGES, introduced in the fall of 2005. The acronym stands for the Seminar Approach to General Education and Scholarship, the program emphasizes small seminars, critical thinking, and writing. A student's first seminar focuses on one of four themes: The Life of the Mind; Thinking about the Symbolic World; Thinking about the Natural/Technological World; and Thinking about the Social World. This is followed by more seminars in the sophomore year, then a departmental seminar in the student's major, and a senior project.

Case's strongest programs include engineering, especially biomedical engineering. The school's polymer science major is one of the few such undergraduate programs in the country. Biology, chemistry, physics, and mathematics are all strong. "Humanities have been increasing in reputation," says an anthropology major. Other strengths in the College of Arts and Sciences include music (a joint program with the nearby Cleveland Institute of Music), anthropology (especially medical anthropology), and psychology. Psychology draws the most majors, but many choose it as a second major. Nursing, management, and accounting are also strong. One of the newest majors is Public Health Science, which students may pursue alone or as part of a five-year program leading to a Master of Public Health degree. A program in ethnic studies was recently added, but some students lament the discontinuation of Case's program in communications science. Communications studies are

Website: www.case.edu
Location: Urban
Total Enrollment: 9,095
Undergraduates: 3,243
Male/Female: 60/40
SAT Ranges: V 580–700
  M 620–720
ACT Range: 26–31
Financial Aid: 57%
Expense: Pr $ $
Phi Beta Kappa: Yes
Applicants: 5,493
Accepted: 71%
Enrolled: 20%
Grad in 6 Years: 81%
Returning Freshmen: 90%
Academics: ✐ ✐ ✐ ✐
Social: ☎ ☎
Q of L: ★ ★ ★
Admissions: (216) 368-4450
Email Address:
  admission@case.edu

Strongest Programs:
Engineering
Management
Biology
Chemistry
Music
Nursing
Psychology
Medical Anthropology

now focused on a "communication disorders" program affiliated with the Cleveland Hearing and Speech Center.

Courses tend to be rigorous, but according to a management major, "Students are competitive with themselves, not with one another so much." While professors do focus on their research, "they take time to meet with students individually, and are easily accessible," says a chemistry major. Nearly 40 percent of freshman classes are taught by tenured professors. "It is not uncommon for students to overload to complete a second major," says an electrical engineering student. Even the non-engineers are tech-savvy and focused on life after college. "Students attend Case because they want an education that will empower them to have a fantastic and successful career," one student reasons. Combined bachelor's and master's programs are popular, as is the Preprofessional Scholars program, which gives top freshmen conditional acceptance to Case's law, medical, or dental schools, assuming satisfactory progress through prerequisite courses.

"We are not a big party school."

About 55 percent of Case's students are Ohio natives, and 70 percent come from a public high school. African Americans make up 6 percent of the student body, Asian Americans 15 percent, and Hispanics 2 percent. In addition to need-based financial aid, about half the students at Case receive scholarships based on academic merit, with merit-based awards averaging $12,650. Those attract "smart, self-motivated people," one student notes. "They are very studious and mostly middle class, and largely from the Midwest." Issues that get students riled up are those with a scientific bent, such as fuel cells and stem cell research. Mostly, though, kids at Case are too busy to care about the vagaries of politics, according to a psychology major: "The typical Case student has an opinion on controversial issues, but would never protest or write to the newspaper about it."

Recently, Case has increased its investment in the arts, humanities, and social sciences, with an aim toward helping students connect these disciplines with their technical studies.

Seventy-eight percent of students live on campus; freshmen and sophomores are required to do so. While students give the older dorms mixed reviews, they are awed by the new apartment-based accommodations for upper classmen. The complex houses about 700 upperclassmen in apartment-style suites with two to nine students each. Students enjoy full kitchens, living rooms, single rooms, and double beds. "The new apartments are simply stunning, and the community on campus is unparalleled," says a sophomore. In addition to dishwashers and extra-large windows, the apartments include study rooms, laundry rooms, music practice rooms, a fitness center, and a cyber cafe. Another choice for upperclassmen is off-campus housing, where there are many desirable apartments within walking distance of campus. Among campus meal-plan options, students say the two dining halls are okay but best on weekdays. There are also plenty of quick-service options on campus, such as Starbucks, Subway, and Einstein's Bagels. The Silver Spartan, a classic diner named by students in an online poll, is open seven days, until midnight during the week and until 3 a.m. on weekends.

Cleveland is no Boston—heck, it's not even Pittsburgh—but students seem to love it anyway, especially since Case is located in a quasi-suburban area five miles from downtown. "You have all the luxuries of a big city without the big cost," says

"Humanities have been increasing in reputation."

a sophomore. "Right off campus, you can find Little Italy, home of the best Italian food in Cleveland, and a variety of bars and restaurants in surrounding areas, such as Coventry," says another sophomore. "Downtown, the Flats and the Warehouse District offer upscale dining and numerous clubs that are always packed with students and young professionals." There's also the Rock & Roll Hall of Fame, and—in the warmer months—Cleveland Indians games at Jacobs Field.

On campus, there are dances and fraternity parties (Greek groups draw 31 percent of the men and 23 percent of the women), but "Greek life at Case is atypical," says a senior. "The organizations are well-respected, active, often have high GPAs, and are civic-minded." Community service projects are also big in the Greek community. Having a car is helpful, especially for road trips to Cedar Point (an amusement park about an hour away, in Sandusky), or for longer jaunts to Chicago or Windsor, Ontario, where students under 21 are free to drink and gamble. In Cleveland, students get unlimited bus service for around $25 a semester.

Given the lopsided male/female ratio, when a man at Case pledges his undying love and devotion, it can as easily be to his computer as to a woman. Rationalizes one student: "You may have trouble finding a date on most weekends, but if your computer crashes on a Friday night, it will be up and running by Saturday morning." Popular campus traditions are Greek Week, which includes nearly everyone on campus; the Spring Fest to celebrate the end of classes; and "Study Overs," where students gather during finals week for free food, massages, study groups, and more. The annual sci-fi movie marathon is a rite of passage, while Engineering Week features the Mousetrap Car Race (all cars must run on a one-mousetrap engine) and the Egg Drop (a foolproof protective package for the tossed egg is key).

Issues that get students riled up are those with a scientific bent, such as fuel cells and stem cell research. Mostly, though, kids at Case are too busy to care about the vagaries of politics, according to a psychology major.

Although sports are not a major focus on campus, the Tartans versus Spartans football game against Carnegie Mellon is big, and intramural competition draws 55 percent of undergrads. "Ultimate Frisbee is huge," says a junior. Also popular are intramural soccer, basketball, softball, volleyball, flag football, inner-tube water polo, floor hockey, and other sports. Swimming has been one of the most competitive varsity teams at Case. In recent years, individual swimmers, wrestlers, and track and cross-country athletes have won NCAA and UAA honors. The 26-mile Hudson Relay, held the last week of the spring semester to commemorate Case's relocation from Hudson to Cleveland, pits teams of runners from the four classes against one another, with each person running a half-mile. A class that's victorious four years running gets a steak and champagne dinner. There's also a racquetball and squash complex, and a field house with an Olympic-size pool.

"Right off campus, you can find Little Italy, home of the best Italian food in Cleveland."

If you come to Case, students say, prepare to work hard. Studying takes priority, and one student says his favorite tradition is the Midnight Scream: "The night before you have a final, you go out on the balcony of your dorm, or lean out the window, and scream at midnight. It's great to hear other people screaming, to remind you that you aren't alone." For a student seeking a first-rate technical or premedical education in a friendly and vibrant environment, Case may be just the right fit.

Overlaps

Washington University (MO), Northwestern, Carnegie Mellon, Ohio State, Cornell University (NY), Johns Hopkins

If You Apply To ➤ **Case:** Early action: Nov. 1. Regular admissions: Jan. 15. Housing: May 1. Meets demonstrated need of 89%. Campus interviews: recommended, informational. Alumni interviews: optional, informational. SATs or ACTs: required (including optional ACT Writing Test). SAT IIs: recommended. Accepts the Common Application and electronic applications; prefers electronic applications to paper ones. Essay question: two- to three-page writing sample that provides insight into you as person. Audition required for artists and musicians.

The Catholic University of America

Washington, DC 20064

There are other Roman Catholic–affiliated universities, but this is the Catholic University. Catholics make up 80 percent of the student body here (versus roughly half at nearby Georgetown). If you can't be in Rome, there is no better place than D.C. to work and play. CUA even has a Metro stop right on campus.

Founded in 1887 under a charter from Pope Leo XIII, The Catholic University of America was the brainchild of United States bishops who wanted to provide an American institution where the curriculum was guided by the tenets of Christian thought. Over time, the university has garnered a reputation as a research-oriented school that also provides a strong undergraduate, preprofessional education and an appreciation for the arts.

Catholic's campus comprises 145 tree-lined acres, an impressive layout for an urban university. Buildings range from ivy-covered brownstone and brick to ultra-modern, giving the place a true collegiate feel. Catholic is one of the few colleges in the country that began as a graduate institution (others are Clark University and The Johns Hopkins University), and grad students still outnumber their younger counterparts. Six of its 10 schools (arts and sciences, engineering, architecture, nursing, music, and philosophy) now admit undergrads, while two others (social service and religious studies) provide undergraduate programs through arts and sciences.

"We like students to leave with Catholic values."

Students have excellent options in almost any department at CUA. Apart from politics (which all agree sets the tone on campus), the history, English, drama, psychology, and physics departments are very strong. Philosophy and religious studies are highly regarded and have outstanding faculty members as well. The School of Nursing is one of the best in the nation, and engineering and architecture are also highly regarded. Architecture and physics have outstanding facilities, the latter enjoying a modern vitreous-state lab, a boon for both research and hands-on undergraduate instruction. Also, a high-speed fiber-optic network connects the entire campus to the Internet. For students interested in the arts, CUA's School of Music offers excellent vocal and instrumental training, and there's also a program in musical theater. Students cite communications and business as weaker than others. The library is modest for a school of this size.

Students at CUA need at least 40 courses in order to graduate. In the School of Arts and Sciences, approximately 25 of these must be from a core curriculum spread across the humanities, social and behavioral sciences, philosophy, environmental studies, religion, math and natural sciences, and languages and literature. English composition also is required. The brightest students can enroll in a 12-course interdisciplinary honors program that offers sequences in the humanities, philosophy, and social sciences. CUA's library offers approximately 1.49 million volumes.

Standard off-campus opportunities are augmented by internships at the British and Irish parliaments, NASA, the National Institutes of Health, the Pentagon, and the Library of Congress. The School of Architecture and Planning hosts summer classes for seniors and grad students to study in Italy and a host of European and Mediterranean countries. The Rome study abroad program for design students incorporates design studio, field study, history, theory, and the Italian language. Finally, two students are chosen each year to spend a fall semester at the Fondazione Architetto Rancilio (FAAR) in Milan to study themes including architecture, urban studies, and technology. CUA also offers accelerated degree programs in which students can earn bachelor's and master's degrees in five years, or six years for a joint BA–JD. CUA is part of the 11-university Consortium of Universities of the Washington Metropolitan Area and the Oak Ridge Associated Universities consortium. The latter is comprised of 87 U.S. colleges and a contractor for the federal Energy Department. The program gives students access to federal research facilities.

Although Catholic University is research-oriented, most classes have fewer than 25 students. That means special attention from faculty members. It also means that there's no place to hide. "The teachers push us to work hard but at the same time apply the subjects to everyday living," a history major reports. The faculty is given high marks by students. "The quality of teaching is excellent. Professors are usually very willing to help students," praises a veteran. Clergy are at the helm of certain graduate schools, but the School of Arts and Sciences has a primarily lay faculty, with priests occupying less than 16 percent of the teaching posts. Its chancellor is the archbishop of Washington, and Catholic churches across the country donate a fraction of their annual collections to the university. One downside of being the only Catholic school with a papal charter is that officials in Rome, who do not always warm up to American traditions of academic freedom, keep a sharp eye on the theology department.

The School of Arts and Sciences has a primarily lay faculty, with priests occupying less than 16 percent of the teaching posts.

Catholicism is clearly the tie that binds the student body. Sunday masses are so well attended that extra services must be offered in the dorms. Says one administrator, "We like students to leave with Catholic values, but most of them come here with those values in the first place." Most are from the Northeast, and are primarily white. African Americans and Hispanics comprise 7 and 4 percent of the student body, respectively. Another 4 percent are Asian American, and foreign students account for 3 percent. Ninety percent are from out of state, and 54 percent of freshmen rank in the top quarter of their high school class. Politically, students are fairly conservative, and the big issues on campus include abortion and gay/lesbian rights. "Everyone is basically the same at Catholic—white, upper-middle-class Catholics," says one student. The university recently reversed an effort to block the establishment of a chapter of the National Association for the Advancement of Colored People on campus. Initially, the university rejected the group on the grounds that it would favor abortion rights, but changed its mind when the NAACP agreed not to advocate issues that oppose Catholic's values.

The university maintains a need-blind admissions policy. It does not guarantee to meet the full demonstrated need of all admitted, but 64 percent of aid recipients are offered full demonstrated need. Thirty-one lucky students—one from each archdiocese in the nation—receive a full-tuition merit scholarship. There are 450 additional merit scholarships available ranging from $1,000 to full tuition, along with various types of financial aid. There are no athletic scholarships.

Fifty-eight percent of the students live in the dorms, seven of which are co-ed by floor. The spacious and ultramodern Centennial Village (eight dorms and 600 beds laid out in suites) is available to all students, many of whom flee CUA's strict visitation (no guests past 2:00 a.m.) and alcohol policies and move into apartments of their own. The best dorms for freshmen are Spellman and Flather **"The quality of teaching is excellent."** (co-ed) and Conaty (women). Dorm food is fairly tasty, and there's always the Rathskeller (or "Rat"), the campus bar and grill where students can get a late-night meal or brunch and dinner on weekends. Emergency phones, shuttle buses, and escort services are provided as part of campus security, and students agree that they always feel safe on campus as long as they are careful.

When students want to explore the city, they need only walk to the campus Metro stop and then enjoy the ride. Capitol Hill is 15 minutes away; the stylish Georgetown area, with its chic restaurants and nightspots, is only a half-hour away.

CUA students do indulge in some serious partying. Some of their favorite locales include the Irish Times, Colonel Brook Tavern, the Tune Inn, and Kitty's. It's no wonder most students agree that the social scene is "off-campus at various bars, clubs, and coffeehouses in D.C." Only 1 percent of the men and women join the Greek system. No one under 21 can drink on campus, and most students agree that this policy is effective in curbing underage drinking. Also, alcohol "abuse" has been added as an offense in addition to use, possession, and distribution. For those eager to repent the weekend's excesses, there are student ministry retreats. Annual festivals on the campus calendar include a weeklong homecoming celebration, Beaux Arts Ball, Christmas

Politically, students are fairly conservative, and the big issues on campus include abortion and gay/lesbian rights.

Holly Hop (held in New York City), and Spring Fling. A time-honored winter tradition is sledding down Flather Hill on cafeteria trays.

Sports on campus mean varsity and intramural competition. CUA's athletic teams compete in Division III, and the men's basketball team won the 2001 championship. Other solid men's teams include baseball, swimming, and lacrosse. Volleyball, field hockey, softball, and swimming are the strongest women's teams. Intramural and varsity athletes alike enjoy the beautiful $10 million sports complex. Many students use their strength for community service, including the Christian-based Habitat for Humanity, in which they build houses for needy families.

When discussions first raised the idea of a Catholic university, the man who would become the university's first rector, Bishop John Joseph Keane, argued for an institution that would "exercise a dominant influence in the world's future" with a superior intellectual foundation. Now, more than 100 years later, CUA offers students a wealth of preprofessional courses spanning the arts and sciences. The founders' quest for "a higher synthesis of knowledge" is constantly being realized at CUA, a unique university and a capital destination.

Overlaps

American, Villanova, Loyola (MD), Boston College, Georgetown

If You Apply To ➤ **Catholic:** Early action: Nov. 15. Regular admissions: Feb. 15. Financial aid: Feb. 1. Housing: June 1. Does not guarantee to meet demonstrated need. SATs or ACTs: required. SAT IIs: required (writing and foreign language). Accepts the Common Application and electronic applications. Essay question: local, national, international issue of concern; historical figure to meet. Music applicants must audition.

Centre College

BEST BUY

600 West Walnut, Danville, KY 40422

Centre is college the way it used to be—gentleman scholars, football games, and fraternity pranks (preferably done in the nude). There is also the unparalleled closeness between students and faculty that comes with a student body of just over 1,000. Compare to Sewanee, DePauw, and Kenyon.

Website: www.centre.edu
Location: Small town
Total Enrollment: 1,060
Undergraduates: 1,060
Male/Female: 47/53
SAT Ranges: V 600–700
  M 580–680
ACT Range: 25–30
Financial Aid: 62%
Expense: Pr $
Phi Beta Kappa: Yes
Applicants: 1,604
Accepted: 69%
Enrolled: 27%
Grad in 6 Years: 81%
Returning Freshmen: 90%
Academics: ✑ ✑ ✑ ½

Centre College, the only independent school in Kentucky with a Phi Beta Kappa chapter, has produced two-thirds of the state's Rhodes Scholars over the last 40 years. But the school is not all work and no play. It's also a throwback to the way college used to be, with Friday night parties on fraternity row and Saturday afternoon football games. Centre's small size offers "the ability to get involved and have a direct hand in making improvements," says a biology major. And its liberal arts focus means that despite Centre's Southern location, students are progressive, intellectual, and perhaps more well-rounded than their peers at neighboring schools. "We have an amazing balance of 'northern academics' paired with 'southern hospitalities,'" says a sophomore.

Located in the heart of Kentucky Bluegrass country, Centre's campus is a mix of old Greek Revival and attractive modern buildings. More than 14 of them are listed on the National Registry of Historic Places, a fact that's less surprising when you know that Centre is the 48th oldest college in the U.S. The College Centre, a multi-million-dollar renovation and expansion of library, classroom, faculty offices, and athletic facilities, has been completed.

Speaking of faculty, they receive high marks from students for accessibility and knowledge. "The quality of teaching has been outstanding," says a freshman. "You learn through fascination and intrigue." General education requirements include basic skills in expository writing, math, and foreign language; and two courses in four contexts—aesthetic, social, scientific, and fundamental questions. Students also are required to take a computer seminar. The freshman seminar is offered during the three-week January "CentreTerm." These courses are required and are capped at 15 students each and offer a chance to explore topics such as cloning, baseball in American politics, and coffee and culture.

Centre's most popular majors are economics, biology, history, English, and government; not coincidentally, these are also among the school's best departments. Minors in creative writing and environmental studies were recently added. Art is also strong, and glassblowing enthusiasts will find one of the few fully equipped undergraduate facilities for their pursuit in the nation. No course taken by a Centre freshman has more than 50 students, and more than three-quarters have 25 or fewer. Students report few problems with scheduling, and Centre guarantees graduation in four years. It also promises interested students can study abroad or do internships. "Centre College teaches you to think independently and helps you utilize these skills after graduation," says a psychology major.

Three-quarters of any given class take advantage of Centre's study abroad programs, which offer travel to London, France, Mexico, Japan, and Ireland during the semester, and to New Zealand, Italy, India, Russia, and Cameroon during the January term. Centre also belongs to the Associated Colleges of the South,* through which students may select programs in Central America. A 3–2 program sends aspiring engineers on to one of four major universities, including Columbia and Vanderbilt. About one-fifth of students perform collaborative research with faculty, and the John C. Young Scholars program allows select seniors to participate in a year of guided research.

More than two-thirds of Centre students hail from Kentucky, and three-quarters graduated from public high school. African American, Asian American, and Hispanic students together make up 6 percent of the largely homogeneous student body. "For the most part, Centre students seem open-minded and willing to respect differences whether or not they agree with others' opinions," a junior says. Centre does not offer athletic scholarships, though it does award hundreds of merit scholarships a year, averaging $10,000. Sixty-two percent of students are on financial aid.

"You learn through fascination and intrigue."

Ninety-four percent of students live in Centre's dorms, which are "usually maintained well," says a sophomore. Adds another student: "I love living in the dorms." There are three main clusters of halls on campus—North Side, Old Centre, and the Old Quad—and each has all of the necessities of college life. Freshmen live in single-sex halls, while upperclassmen may choose buildings that are co-ed by floor. Centre has also purchased and remodeled an apartment building to provide additional upperclass housing, though the 38 percent of men and 39 percent of women who go Greek may bunk in one of 10 new fraternity and sorority houses. Everyone eats together in Cowan Dining Commons, and meal plan credits are also good at the Grille in the student union, and the House of Brews coffee shop. While the quality of food is a common complaint, students say it's no better or worse than other college fare. "Food service is beginning to get better," says a sophomore.

Social life at Centre is largely on-campus, and revolves around Fraternity Row. "All parties are open and almost all of campus is there every weekend," a senior says. "The Student Activities Council is always trying to offer alternatives, but the majority of people still go to the frat houses every weekend." When it comes to alcohol, Centre follows federal and state law—no one under 21 can drink. "However, if a student has a beverage in a nonoriginal container, the RAs and department of public safety will

(Continued)
Social: ☎ ☎ ☎
Q of L: ★ ★ ★
Admissions: (800) 423-6236
Email Address:
   admission@centre.edu

Strongest Programs:
English
History
Biology
Biochemistry
Economics
Art

Lexington and Louisville are within an hour's drive, and it's easy to get to the countryside for camping, fishing, and other outdoor pursuits. Students also get free admission to Centre's separately endowed Norton Center for the Arts.

Students report few
problems with scheduling,
and Centre guarantees
graduation in four years. It
also promises interested
students can study abroad
or do internships.

not guess what is in the cup," one student explains. "It is a very lax system." That said, the town of Danville is located in a dry county, and local restaurants only recently won permission to serve alcohol. Thankfully, Lexington and Louisville are within an hour's drive, and it's easy to get to the countryside for camping, fishing, and other outdoor pursuits. Students also get free admission to Centre's separately endowed Norton Center for the Arts, which brings touring musicals, plays, and other performances to campus. Eighty percent of the student body does community service, through the Greek system, Habitat for Humanity, and the Humane Society.

Centre's football team has been around for more than a century, and while it now competes against regional opponents in Division III, that wasn't always the case. In 1921, Centre beat then-powerhouse Harvard, 6–0, a triumph that has been called the greatest sports upset in the first half of the 20th century. They were conference champs in 2003. Men's and women's cross-country and men's basketball are notable teams, and women's volleyball and softball are up-and-comers. One of Centre's divers is ranked 14th in the nation. Over half of the student body regularly takes advantage of the intramural program, with flag football, softball, and soccer drawing a lot of players. Centre's archrival is nearby Transylvania University, but it's other traditions that really get students going. Those include a serenade for the president by senior women clad in bath towels, and faculty Christmas caroling for the freshmen. And don't forget "Running the Flame," which has students dashing from the fraternity houses, around a sculpture, and back—"naked, of course."

"I love living in the dorms."

What Centre College lacks in size, it more than makes up for in quality. With a safe, bucolic campus, an emphasis on academic excellence, and faculty and students who care about forming lasting friendships with each other, this undiscovered gem may be worth a look. "The people and just the feel of the campus were what really won me over," one satisfied junior says.

Overlaps

University of Kentucky, Transylvania, University of Louisville, Vanderbilt, Rhodes

If You Apply To ➤

Centre: Early action: Dec.1. Regular admissions: Feb. 1. Financial aid: Mar. 1. Does not guarantee to meet demonstrated need. Campus interviews: recommended, evaluative. Alumni interviews: optional, evaluative. SATs or ACTs: required. SAT IIs: optional. Accepts the Common Application and electronic applications. Essay question: experience, achievement, or risk you have taken; issue of local, national, or international concern; influential person; or influential fictional character or historical figure.

Chapman University

One University Drive, Orange, CA 92866

The biggest thing to hit The O.C. since a certain racy TV show, Chapman sits at the hub of Orange County and a stone's throw away from L.A. Aspiring actors flock to marquee programs such as film, television, and the arts. Those without showbiz aspirations can opt for biology, journalism, and business.

Website: www.chapman.edu
Location: Suburban
Total Enrollment: 5,554
Undergraduates: 3,520
Male/Female: 42/58

"Lights, camera, Chapman!" Although Southern California has more than its share of budding starlets and Brad Pitt wannabes, it's also home to Chapman University, where future filmmakers and other burgeoning artists flock to hone their crafts under the watchful eye of seasoned faculty. The university offers solid programs in film, television, and music, and sends students out into the world via countless internships. Even those who steer clear of show business find reason to cheer: Chapman has stellar programs in biology and journalism, too.

Founded in 1861, Chapman University is one of the oldest private universities in California. Originally called Hesperian College, the school later merged with California Christian College in Los Angeles. In 1934, the institution was renamed in honor of C.C. Chapman, an Orange County entrepreneur and benefactor of the school. In 1991, the college again changed its name to Chapman University, reflecting its evolution into a comprehensive institution of higher learning. The beautiful residential campus, situated on 75 tree-lined acres, features a mixture of landmark historic buildings and state-of-the-art facilities. It is located in the historic Old Towne district of Orange, near outstanding beaches, Disneyland, and the world-class cultural offerings of Orange County and Los Angeles. It's also home to the largest free-standing marble staircase west of the Mississippi River, as well as the largest piece of the Berlin Wall owned by an American university. New facilities include Oliphant Hall—featuring 14 teaching studios, a 60-seat lecture hall, and an orchestra hall—and Marion Knott Studios, which features a 500-seat theatre, digital arts center, and two full-sized sound stages. Current construction includes the Lastinger Athletics Complex and the 12,500 square-foot Wallace All-Faiths Chapel.

The most popular majors are film, business, music, theatre and dance, and education, and these are among Chapman's best. Budding filmmakers may enter the Dodge College of Film and Media Studies, a comprehensive, production-based program that includes majors in film production, television and broadcast journalism, screenwriting, public relations and advertising, and film studies, as well as internships and other active learning opportunities. Future entrepreneurs and business tycoons can take advantage of a well-stocked portfolio of business programs through the Argyos School of Business and Economics. For more artsy types, Chapman offers solid programs in theater and dance, each with frequent national and international performance components.

Regardless of major, all students must complete series of distribution requirements that includes credits in fine and performing arts, humanities, history, social sciences, and natural sciences. In addition, students are expected to fulfill requirements in quantitative reasoning, world cultures, human diversity, and foreign language, as well as a junior writing proficiency exam. "The climate is generally competitive," says a biology major, but not cutthroat. "The intensity of the classes depends greatly on the type of class and the professor," a junior adds. Freshmen are eased into college life by Chapman's comprehensive first-year program, which provides extensive contact with peers, student mentors, faculty, advisors, as well as an orientation. Freshmen are also assigned a "coach" with whom they meet weekly to discuss goals, plan and organize, and develop critical skills. Finally, new students may take part in the First-Year Experience (FYE), where they "have their own floor in one of the residence halls and participate in special programs aimed at helping them adjust to their first year of college," explains a sophomore.

"The climate is generally competitive."

Ninety percent of classes have 50 or fewer students and the majority have fewer than 25. Freshmen are taught by professors; there are no TAs. "I have had many fantastic professors," says a junior. "They care about students and love the subject they are teaching." The new 144,000 square-foot Leatherby Libraries feature state-of-the-art amenities, including nine discipline-specific libraries, a 24-hour study commons, and Internet-based learning environments.

Chapman attracts a friendly, largely affluent student body. More than two-thirds hail from California and 2 percent are international students. "The students that populate this college are archetypal 'The O.C.' characters for the most part," says a freshman. "Very conservative." African Americans comprise 2 percent of the population, Asian Americans 8 percent, and Hispanics 10 percent. Hot topics center more on national events than campus politics. "The recent election became a heated debate

(Continued)

SAT Ranges: V 540–650
  M 540–660
ACT Range: 22–29
Financial Aid: 60%
Expense: Pr $ $ $ $
Phi Beta Kappa: Yes
Applicants: 3,463
Accepted: 58%
Enrolled: 41%
Grad in 6 Years: 65%
Returning Freshmen: 88%
Academics: ✍ ✍ ✍
Social: ☎ ☎ ☎
Q of L: ★ ★ ★
Admissions: (714) 997-6711
Email Address:
  admit@chapman.edu

Strongest Programs:
Communication Studies
Film Studies
Music
Television and Broadcast
  Journalism
Biological Sciences

Future entrepreneurs and business tycoons can take advantage of a well-stocked portfolio of business programs through the Argyos School of Business and Economics.

on campus," says a public relations and advertising major. Twenty-one percent of undergraduates receive merit scholarships worth an average of $13,364. There are no athletic scholarships.

Half of Chapman students call the five residence halls home and "the dorms are comfortable, with each room getting its own bathroom or sharing with only one other room," according to a theatre major. Braden Hall has 70 rooms that are paired into suites, while Henley Hall features a substance-free community as well as a First Year Experience (FYE) floor for incoming students. Other university-owned options include off-campus houses (for families) and nearby apartments. Dining options are described as "decent, but nothing spectacular." As for safety, students say that campus security is a constant presence. "I've never felt unsafe on campus," says a junior.

Twenty percent of the men join fraternities and sororities attract 35 percent of the women, but the Greeks don't dominate the social scene. Students are apt to hang out with friend on campus or take part in a school-sponsored event. "There are over 60 clubs and organizations that take advantage of the facilities on campus," says a student. "There is always something going on," adds a biology major.

Twenty percent of the men join fraternities and sororities attract 35 percent of the women, but the Greeks don't dominate the social scene.

"There are over 60 clubs and organizations that take advantage of the facilities on campus."

Although alcohol is readily available, "The RAs and Public Safety do a good job of controlling alcohol consumption" by students, according to a theatre major. When students grow weary of campus life, they hit the local shops and bars or take trips to "Mexico, Disneyland, Knottsberry Farm, the mall, and L.A.," according to a film major. Back on campus, students flock to the homecoming celebration and the annual Greek Week festival.

The city of Orange (pop. 135,000) is a college town "by the sole means of being a town in which a college is located," quips one student. It's also home to the usual litany of restaurants and shops, as well as a district known as "Old Towne Orange, the Antique Capital of California." Most of the town closes by midnight and students looking for fun generally head into Los Angeles (40 minutes away).

The Chapman Panthers compete in Division III and the most competitive sports include baseball (2003 national champions) and women's softball (2002 national champions). Intramurals are popular and students can usually be spotted playing Ultimate Frisbee, volleyball, or soccer in the pristine Southern California weather.

At Chapman, the spotlight is definitely on those looking to build careers in film and television, whether it's on a movie set, behind the camera, or on a stage. Students are not only expected to hit the books, but to actively express their creativity through hands-on learning and forays into the real world. All the while, they're encouraged to build relationships with peers and faculty and enjoy themselves, too. "We have a lot of pride," a film major says. "We are a fun school with excellent academic possibilities and opportunities."

Overlaps

Loyola Marymount, University of San Diego, California State, University of Southern California, UC-Irvine, NYU

If You Apply To ➤

Chapman: Rolling admissions. Early action: Nov. 30. Financial aid: Mar. 1. Housing: May 1. Guarantees to meet full demonstrated need. Campus interviews: recommended, evaluative. No alumni interviews. SATs or ACTs: required. SAT IIs: optional. Accepts the Common Application and electronic applications. Essay question.

College of Charleston

Charleston, SC 29424

A public school about half the size of the University of South Carolina that offers business, education, and the liberal arts. College of Charleston compares to William and Mary in both scale and historic surroundings but is far less rigorous academically. Is addressing its housing crunch to help reach the next level.

Whether sampling the traditional Low Country cuisine or delving into the wide range of courses offered at this strong liberal arts institution, students at the College of Charleston know they are getting a solid education based on creative expression and intellectual freedom. Founded in 1770 as Colonial South Carolina's first college, C of C's original commitment to the liberal arts and to the citizens of the region has helped it become a well-respected institution throughout the Southeast. And the location only adds to the experience, providing opportunities for volunteering and interning and a second-to-none social scene. "This place is amazing, unique, cultural, historical, modern, and it feels like home, all at the same time," a senior says.

Located in Charleston's famous Historical District, the campus features many of the city's most historic and venerable buildings. More than 80 of its buildings are former private residences ranging from the typical Charleston "single" house to the Victorian. The wooded area in front of Randolph Hall, known as the Cistern, is a student gathering point and the site of graduation ceremonies. The campus has received countless awards for its design, and has been designated a national arboretum. But the campus is undergoing somewhat of a transformation. In recent years, a new one-million volume capacity library and an apartment-style dorm were opened, a state-of-the-art addition to the business school was completed, and major renovations have been done to other buildings. In addition, the expansion and renovation of the arts complex, construction of a new School of Education facility and athletic center and an upgrade to the baseball stadium are underway. A new multipurpose building, field stations for research and pedestrian paths are being built on an 800-acre property on the Intercoastal Waterway.

C of C has a core curriculum based strongly in the liberal arts and professional programs and focused on the development of writing, computing, language acquisition, and thinking skills. Each student is required to complete six hours in English, history, mathematics or logic, and social science; eight hours in natural sciences; and 12 hours in humanities. Students must also show proficiency in a foreign language. Biology and chemistry are two of the strongest programs; many of the graduates end up at the Medical University of South Carolina a few blocks down the street. Several programs have been awarded with Commendations of Excellence, including all those in the School of Sciences and Mathematics. The most popular major is business administration, and communications, psychology, and education are also popular. Three new majors were recently added: Latin American and Caribbean studies, hospitality and tourism management and discovery informatics (the only one in the country). Many new performing arts majors take advantage of internship opportunities with Spoleto Festival USA, Charleston's annual arts festival. Study abroad options include the International Student Exchange Program and the Sea Semester.* Students say the academic climate at C of C is challenging, but support is easy to find. Professors get high marks in and out of the classroom. "The professors really care about what students have to say and are more than willing to help," a freshman anthropology major says.

> "The professors really care about what students have to say and are more than willing to help."

Website: www.cofc.edu
Location: Urban
Total Enrollment: 10,775
Undergraduates: 9,034
Male/Female: 36/64
SAT Ranges: V 570–640
    M 570–640
ACT Range: 22–25
Financial Aid: 38%
Expense: Pub $ $ $
Phi Beta Kappa: No
Applicants: 8,076
Accepted: 52%
Enrolled: 41%
Grad in 6 Years: 58%
Returning Freshmen: 83%
Academics: ✎ ✎ ✎
Social: 🏨 🏨 🏨 🏨
Q of L: ★ ★ ★ ★
Admissions: (843) 953-5670
Email Address:
    admissions@cofc.edu

Strongest Programs:
Education
Computer Science and
    Information Systems
Geology
Marine Biology
Mathematics
Physics
Languages

More than one-third of the students hail from out of state, and 30 percent graduated in the top tenth of their high school class. Asian Americans and Hispanics each make up 2 percent of the student body, African Americans make up 8 percent and 2 percent are foreign. The college offers hundreds of merit scholarships and athletic scholarships in nine sports.

Lack of dorm space has been one of C of C's biggest challenges as of late, but the campus has invested $35 million to build a new 536-student dorm and renovate eight dorms. The percentage of students living off-campus has slowly increased, and is now near 30 percent. Parking is still reported to be limited. Food is plentiful and there are options for all types of eaters, including "homestyle, grill, deli, salad bar, Greek, dessert, and cereal bar" selections; vegetarian fare is available as well.

No matter where they live, students enjoy Charleston, with its festivals, plays, and scenic plantations and gardens. "Charleston is filled with history, culture, the arts, and wonderful people," a senior says. "No one ever wants to leave!" Students

"No one ever wants to leave!" party off-campus in local clubs and apartments as well as on campus, where 13 percent of the men and 15 percent of the women belong to frats and sororities, respectively. Due to a well-enforced policy on drinking, students report that it is difficult to be served on campus if you are not 21, but off-campus is not a problem. Women far outnumber men, but females looking to beat the odds can always go to the Medical University of South Carolina or the Citadel Military College, both in Charleston.

While Charleston is primarily a historic and tourist town, "The people of Charleston love the students and welcome them back every fall," says one student. On weekends, students can head to beaches such as Folly Beach, Sullivan's Island, and Isle of Palms, which are merely minutes away. For those who don't mind a drive, there's "the Grand Strand," Myrtle Beach, 90 miles north, Savannah and Hilton Head to the south and Atlanta and Clemson University to the West.

The absence of a football team is a common gripe among students, but other athletics are relatively popular. C of C is a Division I school and several teams have claimed recent conference championships, including volleyball and men's basketball. There is a roster of intramural and club sports to choose from, including indoor soccer, tennis, and racquetball.

The College of Charleston has set its sights on becoming the finest public liberal arts and sciences institution in South Carolina, and it seems to be on its way, propelled by an honors college, opportunities to do research and study abroad, and new living and learning facilities. "Our small college feel with large college advantages bring a great atmosphere to C of C," a senior says.

Overlaps

Clemson, USC–Columbia, Georgia, North Carolina, Furman, James Madison

If You Apply To ➤

C of C: Rolling admissions. Early action: Nov. 1. Regular admissions: Apr. 1. Campus interviews: optional, informational (campus visit strongly encouraged). No alumni interviews. SATs or ACTs: required. SAT IIs: optional. Accepts the Common Application and electronic applications. Essay question: something unique you will bring to the college; impact of a significant experience, achievement, or risk; how the college will help you reach your goals; other topic of choice.

University of Chicago

1116 East 59th Street, Chicago, IL 60637

Periodically, the news media reports that students at the University of Chicago are finally loosening up and having some fun. Don't believe it. This place is for true

intellectuals who don't mind working hard for their degrees. Less selective than the top Ivies, but just as good. Social climbers apply elsewhere.

The University of Chicago attracts students eager to move beyond the cliquishness of high school and the superficial trappings of Ivy League prestige—the kids more concerned about learning for learning's sake than about getting a job after graduation, though they're certainly capable of the latter. "We're all nerds at heart," says a senior. Still, administrators have realized that in the 21st century, even the best schools cannot survive on intellectual might alone. To make the U of C more attractive, they've made the core curriculum less restrictive, built a new dorm and sports center, resurrected varsity football, and even opened an office dedicated to fostering school spirit and improved alumni relations. "Everyone came to Chicago despite its reputation as the place where fun comes to die," agrees a freshman. "The fact that college here is a good time just makes us that much happier."

The university's 190-acre tree-lined campus is in Hyde Park, an eclectic community on Chicago's South Side, surrounded by low-income neighborhoods on three sides and Lake Michigan on the fourth. One of 77 city neighborhoods, Hyde Park "is pretty intellectual," says one student, noting that "two-thirds of our faculty live here." Streets are lined with brownstones, row houses, and townhouses, giving way to luxury high rises with beautiful views as you get closer to the lake; the city's Museum of Science and Industry is within spitting distance. The campus itself is self-contained and architecturally magnificent. The main quads are steel-gray Gothic—gargoyles and all—and newer buildings are by Eero Saarinen, Mies van der Rohe, and Frank Lloyd Wright, some of Chicago's favorite architectural sons. The new Ratner Center, designed by Cesar Pelli, features a $60 million gymnasium and swimming pool.

Historically, Chicago has drawn praise for its graduate programs. But administrators and faculty have realized that they must pay attention to undergraduates, too, if Chicago has any hope of staying competitive with schools like Stanford, Harvard, and Princeton. To that end, Chicago remains unequivocally committed to the view that a solid foundation in the liberal arts is the best preparation for future study or work and that, further, theory is better than practice. Thus, music students study musicology, but also learn calculus, along with everyone else. Regardless of major, 15 to 18 of a student's 42 courses fall under general education requirements called the Common Core. (That's down from 21 in years past; the precise number of courses in the core depends on how much foreign language instruction a student needs to reach proficiency.)

Other core requirements include courses in the sciences and math, humanities, social sciences, and European civilization, a recent substitution for a long-standing Western Civ sequence. Sound intense? Students say it is, especially because Chicago pioneered the quarter system. Class material is presented over 11 weeks, rather than the 13 or 14 weeks in a typical semester; the first term starts in late September and is over by Christmas. Practically, this means virtually

"I don't know how professors here could get better."

uninterrupted work through the year, punctuated by a long summer vacation and three exam weeks. "The courses are hard—just plain hard," says one student. "Taking care of the core early in their college career helps students from getting in over their heads," a freshman adds. One good point, says a sophomore, is that you can forget about competition: "Even in the most intense classes, people tend to edit each others' papers, do problem sets together, and study together." Seniors are also encouraged to do final-year projects. "The students here care less about grades and more about learning," says a sociology major. "And they care way less about memorizing things and way more about learning how to think, talk, and write." Helpings students learn those skills are brilliant and distinguished faculty members

Website: www.uchicago.edu
Location: Urban
Total Enrollment: 13,870
Undergraduates: 4,545
Male/Female: 50/50
SAT Ranges: V 670–770
    M 660–760
ACT Range: 28–33
Financial Aid: 41%
Expense: Pr $ $ $ $
Phi Beta Kappa: Yes
Applicants: 8,751
Accepted: 40%
Enrolled: 33%
Grad in 6 Years: 87%
Returning Freshmen: 95%
Academics: ✍ ✍ ✍ ✍ ✍
Social: ☎ ☎
Q of L: ★ ★ ★
Admissions: (773) 702-8650
Email Address:
    collegeadmissions@
    uchicago.edu

Strongest Programs:
Economics
English
Sociology
Anthropology
Political Science
Geography
History
Linguistics

who've won Nobel Prizes, Guggenheim Fellowships (aka "genius grants"), and other prestigious awards. "I don't know how professors here could get better," says a senior. "They make themselves available to students and seem genuinely interested in our ideas."

The economics department, a bastion of neoliberal or New Right thinkers, is Chicago's main academic claim to fame, and the most popular major. Also popular are biological sciences, English, political science—which, along with sociology, was born at Chicago—and math. The university also prides itself on interdisciplinary and area studies programs, such as those focusing on East Asia, South Asia, the Middle East, and the Slavic countries. Undergrads may also take courses in any of the university's graduate and professional schools—law, divinity, social service, public policy, humanities, social sciences, biological and physical sciences, and business. While you may have to fight through a thicket of PhD students to get a professor's attention, you'll be rewarded by an abundance of research assistantships—and opportunities for publication, even before you graduate. When Chicago gets too cold and snowy, students may take advantage of 17 study abroad programs, which reach most corners of the globe.

Seventy-eight percent of Chicago's students come from out of state, including many East Coasters with academic parents; another 8 percent are foreigners. Asian Americans represent 14 percent of the total; Hispanics account for 8 percent, and African Americans add 4 percent. Politically, "the conservative voice is allowed a presence on campus—the effect is to enliven debate and save us liberals from easy self-assurance," says a freshman. "Last year, students wanted to kick Taco Bell off campus because they underpay their tomato pickers in California," adds a junior. Students have fond memories of freshman orientation, known as O Week, an event administrators claim was invented at U of C in 1924. The school hands out merit scholarships each year, worth an average of $9,205. There are no athletic awards.

"The university treats us as responsible adults with common sense."

Though Chicago guarantees campus housing for four years, only 60 percent of undergrads live in the dorms. "Dorms are divided into units of 30 to 100 people called houses," says a junior. "These houses become the center of social life, at least for first-years." Each dorm is different—some house less than 100 people in traditional, shared double rooms without kitchens, while another has 700 beds organized into new and colorful suites. Two dorms used to be hotels, including the Shoreland, the largest and most social dorm, at the edge of Lake Michigan; another used to be a nursing home. All halls are co-ed by room or by floor. Bartlett is the newest dining hall, with restaurant-style service and plenty of options for vegetarians and those who keep kosher.

Chicago's Maroons compete in NCAA Division III, and the school belongs to the University Athletic Association, where rivals include Johns Hopkins and NYU.

Despite its antisocial reputation, Chicago has nine fraternities and two sororities, which attract 10 percent of the men and 5 percent of the women. Aside from frat parties, Chicago, the school, and Chicago, the city, offer what a freshman calls "infinite options: bars downtown, a film festival at DOC, a White Sox game at Comiskey Park, a spoken-word performance at a Belmont coffeehouse, open-mic night at the student center." (Lest you get bored, the city also offers world-class symphony, opera, dance, and theater, along with museums galore, and great shopping and dining on Michigan Avenue.) Though everything is accessible by public transportation, cars are a nice luxury (if you can find a parking place). When it comes to drinking, campus policies are "very, um, accommodating," says one student. "The university treats us as responsible adults with common sense." Off-campus, it's much harder for the underage to imbibe. Road trips are infrequent, but one popular destination is Ann Arbor, about five hours away, for concerts and more traditional collegiate fun at the University of Michigan.

Tradition is a hallmark at Chicago, and each fall, students look forward to Scavenger Hunt, "a pumped-up version of a regular scavenger hunt, with a list of 300 bizarre items," says a sociology major. "If you walked onto campus during those few days, you'd think most people had lost their minds." In the winter, the Midway, site of the 1893 World's Fair, is flooded for skating. Students also celebrate the festival of Kangeiko, which features their naked or semi-naked peers dashing across campus during the Polar Bear Run. The Festival of the Arts features concerts, a fashion show, special lectures, museum exhibits, and "funky installations on the quads." Come summer, students can be found "doing Jello-O wrestling and other carnival activities" as part of Summer Breeze, which also includes a concert. Past artists have included Maroon 5, Bela Fleck and the Flecktones, Talib Kweli, and Method Man.

"Having fun is a form of intelligence."

Chicago remains unequivocally committed to the view that a solid foundation in the liberal arts is the best preparation for future study or work and that, further, theory is better than practice.

Chicago's Maroons compete in NCAA Division III, and the school belongs to the University Athletic Association, where rivals include Johns Hopkins and NYU. Aside from hitting the gridiron or the basketball court, "varsity athletes are Phi Beta Kappa (that is, very smart) and involved with university theater," a junior marvels. In fact, athletes here have a higher overall GPA than the student body as a whole. The wrestling team and women's soccer squad have boasted All-Americans in recent years, and both men's and women's soccer teams have been to the Division III Final Four. Women's softball earned a number one ranking in the Midwest regional in 2005. To everyone's surprise, the football team has also had a couple of winning seasons. When it comes to intramurals, 70 percent of undergraduates participate in sports ranging from the traditional (football, soccer, and broomball) to the offbeat (inner-tube water polo, badminton, and archery).

Robert Maynard Hutchins, who led Chicago from 1929 to 1951, once said, "Having fun is a form of intelligence." A half-century later, it seems his message is finally getting through. While fun has been slow in coming to the U of C, students are beginning to learn that letting their hair down on the weekends can complement, not compromise, the life of the mind. The quarter system is fast-paced, and not everyone will be happy with the high level of intellectualism that prevails here. But for those eager to be in a big city, and to focus on learning for its own sake, Chicago may be worth a look.

Overlaps
Columbia, Harvard, Northwestern, University of Pennsylvania, Yale

If You Apply To >

Chicago: Early action: Nov. 1. Regular admissions: Jan. 1. Financial aid: Feb. 1. Guarantees to meet full demonstrated need. Campus interviews: recommended, informational. Alumni interviews: optional, informational. SATs or ACTs: required. SAT IIs: optional. Essay question.

University of Cincinnati

P.O. Box 210091, Cincinnati, OH 45221-0091

In most states, UC would be the big enchilada. But with Ohio State two hours up the road and Miami U even closer, Cincinnati has to hustle to get its name out there. The inventor of co-op education, it offers quality programs in everything from engineering to art—and a competitive men's basketball team to boot.

Many first-time visitors to Cincinnati are surprised to find an attractive and very livable city. As they traverse the city's hilly roads, they are in for another surprise—

Website: www.uc.edu

UC has taken steps to improve the quality of the undergraduate education by strengthening its general education requirements to focus on critical thinking and expression and expanding its honors program.

its university. Not only is the University of Cincinnati renowned for its extensive research programs, the school's co-op program is also one of the largest of any public college or university in the country.

The compact campus is a mile uphill from Cincinnati's downtown area. Ultra-modern buildings rise up next to traditional ivy-covered Georgian halls. A $233 million construction project to create a "Main Street" in the center of campus and consolidate all student activities was recently completed. The University Pavilion was completed in 2002 and brought student services such as registration and bill paying under one roof. Research is a UC specialty. Campus scientists have given the world antiknock gasoline, the electronic organ, antihistamines, and the U.S. Weather Bureau. UC is also the place where, in 1906, cooperative education was born, allowing students to earn while they learn. Across the Cincinnati curriculum, there is an abundance of co-op opportunities available. More than 3,000 students take advantage of them. In all, 42 programs offer the popular five-year professional-practice option.

The colleges of engineering; business administration; and design, architecture, art, and planning (the schools with the most co-op students) are the best bets at UC. The university's music conservatory, one of the best state-run programs in the field, also offers broadcasting training. The schools of nursing and pharmacy are well known and benefit from UC's health center and graduate medical school. The most popular major is marketing, followed by criminal justice and early childhood education. In addition, education is a strong program. Education students earn two bachelor's degrees: one in education and one in a liberal arts subject. New initiatives include a culinary arts and science degree program offered jointly with Cincinnati State and a series of horticulture therapy classes as part of the human services associate degree.

The academic grind is determined largely by the major. Fields such as engineering, business, and nursing require a substantially larger academic commitment. "Most classes are laid-back until you are admitted to your degree program," says a sophomore. But another student notes "UC harbors a certain competitive spirit." Some courses end up being quite large (in popular design courses, two people to a desk is not unusual), and students say about 20 percent of their classes have up to 100 students. One fine asset is the school's huge library, which has 3 million volumes and is completely computerized.

UC has taken steps to improve the quality of the undergraduate education by strengthening its general education requirements to focus on critical thinking and expression and expanding its honors program. Freshmen must take English and math as well as a contemporary issues class; other requirements vary by college. Additionally, UC has adopted a strategic plan known as UC121 to place students at the center of campus life. A third of the faculty members hold outside jobs, bringing fresh practical experience to the classroom.

Sixteen percent of the student body comes from out of state, which makes the student body fairly heterogeneous. "Students at UC are very diverse, and represent all different levels of academic ability, experience, and interests," says one student. There are art types and business types, liberals and conservatives. African Americans, Asian Americans, and Hispanics comprise 11, 3, and 2 percent of the student body, respectively. Diversity, feminist issues, campus construction, and rising tuition are the hot topics on campus. The

"Most classes are laid-back until you are admitted to your degree program."

school offers over 656 merit scholarships averaging $4,111 and hundreds of athletic scholarships for men and women. While students say they have noticed the budget squeeze in terms of services being cut and the hiring of new personnel curtailed, the school is growing. "Our school is constantly changing," says a triple major who notes a campuswide joke is that UC stands for "Under Construction."

Less than 20 percent of UC students live on campus. Many upperclassmen, especially the older and married students, consider off-campus living far better than dorm life, and expensive apartments can usually be found.

Merchants have turned the area surrounding UC, called Clifton, into a mini college town with plenty to do. Nine nearby bus lines take undergraduates into the heart of the "Queen City" of Cincinnati in minutes. There the students find museums, a ballet, professional sports teams, parks, rivers, hills, and as many large and small shops as anyone could want. On-campus activities include 450 student clubs, with everything from mountaineering to clubs in various majors. Fraternities and sororities are small, but are still the most active places to party on campus, usually opening their functions to everyone. The university sponsors some events, such as WorldFest and Greek Week. The most popular road trips are the city of Cleveland and white-water rafting in West Virginia.

The colleges of engineering; business administration; and design, architecture, art, and planning (the schools with the most co-op students) are the best bets at UC.

"Our school is constantly changing."

In sports, men's and women's basketball, football, and volleyball all have seen recent postseason. Track, soccer, baseball, and women's crew are also popular. Everyone mentions the football rivalry with Miami (of Ohio) as a game you won't want to miss, and the same holds true when the men's basketball squad takes on Xavier University. Weekend athletes also take advantage of UC's first-rate sports center.

Cooperative education is the name of the game at this Ohio school. Students get to take their degrees out for a test drive before graduation thanks to the work-study co-op programs. UC also offers students a lively social scene, both on-campus and minutes away in downtown Cincinnati.

Overlaps

Ohio State, Miami University (OH), Ohio University, Bowling Green State, Wright State, Xavier

If You Apply To ➤

UC: Rolling admissions: varies by college. Does not guarantee to meet demonstrated need. Campus interviews: optional, informational. No alumni interviews. SATs or ACTs: required. SAT IIs: optional. Accepts the Common Application and electronic applications. No essay question. Apply to particular program.

Claremont Colleges

In 1887, James A. Blaisdell had the vision to create a group of colleges patterned after Oxford and Cambridge in England. More than a century later, the five schools that comprise the Claremont Colleges thrive as a consortium of separate and distinct undergraduate colleges with two adjoining graduate institutions, a theological seminary, and botanical gardens. Like families, the colleges coexist, interact, and experience their share of both cooperation and tension. Ultimately, however, the Claremont College Consortium forms a mutually beneficial partnership that offers its students the vast resources and facilities one might only expect to find at a large university.

The colleges are located on 317 acres in the Los Angeles suburb of Claremont, a peaceful neighborhood replete with palm trees, Spanish architecture, and the nearby San Gabriel Mountains. The picture-perfect California weather can sometimes be marred by smog, courtesy of the neighbors in nearby L.A., but the administration claims the smog level has declined dramatically in the past few years.

None of the five undergraduate colleges that make up the Claremont Colleges Consortium—Claremont McKenna, Harvey Mudd, Pitzer, Pomona, and Scripps—is larger than a medium-size dorm at a state school. Each school retains its own institutional identity, with its own faculty, administration, admissions, and curriculum, although the boundaries of both academic work and extracurricular activities are somewhat flexible. Each of the schools also tends to specialize in a particular area that complements the offerings of all the others. Claremont McKenna, which caters mainly to students planning careers in economics, business, law, or government, has eight research institutes located on its campus, while Harvey Mudd is the choice for future scientists. Pitzer, the most liberal of the five, excels mainly in the behavioral sciences, and at the all-women Scripps, the best offerings are in art and foreign languages. The oldest of the five colleges, Pomona ranks as one of the top liberal arts colleges anywhere, and is the one Claremont school that is strong across the board, with the humanities especially superb.

Collectively, the colleges share many services and facilities, including art studios, a student newspaper, laboratories, an extensive biological field station, a health center, auditoriums, a 2,500-seat concert hall, a 350-seat theater, bookstores, a maintenance department, and a business office. The Claremont library system makes more than 1.9 million volumes available to all students, though each campus also has a library of its own. Faculties and administrations are free to arrange joint programs or classes between all or just some of the schools. Courses at any college are open to students from the others (approximately 1,200 courses in all), but each college sets limits on the number of classes that can be taken elsewhere. Perhaps the best example of academic cooperation is the team-taught interdisciplinary courses, which are organized by instructors from the different schools and appeal to a mix of different academic interests.

The Claremont Colleges draw large numbers of students from within California, although their national reputation is growing. These days, about half the students hail from other Western and non-Western states, with a sizable contingent from the East Coast. The tone at Claremont is decidedly intellectual—more so than at Stanford or any other place in the West—and graduate programs in the arts and sciences are more common goals than business or law school. Anyone who is bright and hardworking can find a niche at one of the five schools. Unfortunately, despite their excellence, the Claremonts are also among the most underrated colleges in the nation.

The local community of Claremont is geared more to senior citizens than college seniors. "Quiet town of rich white people—boring," yawns an English major. A sophomore says, "Most of the stores have strange granny knickknacks or cosmic aura trinkets." Still, "the Village," a quaint cluster of specialty shops (including truly remarkable candy stores), is an easy skateboard ride from any campus, though the shades come down and the sidewalks roll up well before sunset. Students report that the endless list of social activities offered at the colleges make up for the ho-hum town of Claremont. For hot times, Hollywood's glamour and UCLA-dominated Westwood are within sniffing distance, and a convenient shuttle bus makes them even closer for Claremont students without cars. Nearby mountains and the fabled surfing beaches make this collegiate paradise's backyard complete. Mount Baldy ski lifts, for instance, are only 15 miles away, and you'll reach Laguna Beach before the end of your favorite CD. For spring break, Mexico is cheap and a great change of pace.

On campus, extracurricular life maintains a balance between cooperation and independence. Claremont McKenna, Harvey Mudd, and Scripps field joint athletic teams, and the men's teams especially are Division III powers, due to the exploits of CMC athletes. Pomona and Pitzer also compete together. Each of the five colleges has its own dorms, and since off-campus housing is limited in Claremont proper, the social life of students revolves around their dorms. "Scripps itself is quiet, but parties at Harvey Mudd and Claremont McKenna can get pretty wild," admits a Scripps student. There are no fraternities, except at Pomona, where joining one is far from de rigueur. All cafeterias are open to all students, and most big events—films, concerts, etcetera—are advertised throughout the campus. Large five-school parties are regular Thursday, Friday, and Saturday night fare. Social interaction among students at different schools, be it for meals or dates, is not what it might be. Pomona is seen as elitist, and its admissions office has been known to try to distance itself from the other colleges. Occasional political squabbles break out between liberal faculty and students at Pitzer and their conservative counterparts at Claremont McKenna. For the most part, students benefit not only from the nurturing and support within their own schools, each of which has its own academic or extracurricular emphasis, but also from the abundant resources the Claremont College Consortium offers as a whole.

Following are profiles of each undergraduate Claremont College.

Claremont McKenna College

890 Columbia Avenue, Claremont, CA 91711

Make way, Pomona—this up-and-comer now has the lowest acceptance rate in the Claremont Colleges and is no longer content with being a social sciences specialty

school. CMC is half the size of a typical liberal arts college and 30 percent smaller than Pomona. Still developing a national reputation.

As a member of the Claremont Colleges consortium, Claremont McKenna College boasts top programs in government, economics, business, and international relations. In addition, CMC has eleven research institutes located on campus, which offer its undergraduates ample opportunities to study everything from political demographics to the environment. The arts and humanities are also available, but Claremont McKenna is better suited to those with high ambitions in business leadership and public affairs.

The fifty-acre campus, located thirty-five miles east of Los Angeles, is mostly "California modern" architecture with lots of Spanish tile roofs and picture windows that look out on the San Gabriel Mountains. Described by one student as "more functional than aesthetic," the physical layout fits right in with the school's pragmatic attitude. Roberts Hall is a state-of-the-art academic center housing classrooms, seminar rooms, a computer laboratory, and faculty offices. New construction includes four additions to the North Quad residence halls and a complete renovation of Collins Dining Hall.

Claremont McKenna offers top programs in economics and government, but the international relations, psychology, and history programs are also considered strong. The biology, chemistry, and physics departments are greatly enhanced through the use of Keck Science Center, an outstanding facility providing students with hands-on access to a variety of equipment. In addition, the eighty-five-acre Bernard Biological Field Station is located just north of the CMC campus and is available to students for field work.

CMC's extensive general education requirements include two semesters in the humanities; three in the social sciences; two in the natural sciences; a semester each in mathematics, English composition and literary analysis, and Questions of Civilization; and a Senior Thesis. The college offers popular 3–2 programs in management engineering, and economics and engineering, and a 4–1 MBA program in conjunction with the Claremont Graduate University. Over 40 percent of Claremont McKenna students take advantage of study abroad programs in Australia, Brazil, Costa Rica, Japan, and other exotic locales around the globe. CMC also offers active campus exchange programs with Haverford, Colby, Spelman, and Morehouse. Another popular program is the Washington Semester program, in which students can intern with E-Span, the State Department, the White House, and lobbying groups.

> "There is a certain experimental spirit on campus."

The academic climate is fairly strenuous at Claremont McKenna, but not overwhelming. "We may be laid-back on Saturday nights," says a student, "but come Monday, it's all about achieving the highest GPA and perfecting the résumé." Professors are described as "outstanding" and praised for their accessibility. "Professors are not only great researchers and writers," says a senior, "but excellent teachers as well."

"There is a certain experimental spirit on campus," says one student. "Students are also very into politics and leadership." The CMC student body is 38 percent Californian, with nearly 20 percent from the east coast. Many attended public high school and 83 percent graduated in the top tenth of their class. "Students here are smart, involved, and always busy," says a student. "We typically have more on our plate than time in the day." The student body is 58 percent white; Asian Americans comprise the largest minority at 14 percent. Hispanics comprise 11 percent, while African Americans make up 4 percent. A junior says, "We are leaders and love to debate politics," says a senior. A classmate adds, "We are about one half liberal and one half conservative with very large Democrat, Libertarian, and Republican clubs." All freshmen take

Website:
www.claremontmckenna.edu

Location: Suburban
Total Enrollment: 1,124
Undergraduates: 1,124
Male/Female: 52/48
SAT Ranges: V 630–720
M 640–720
ACT Range: 28–33
Financial Aid: 67%
Expense: Pr $ $ $
Phi Beta Kappa: Yes
Applicants: 3,528
Accepted: 22%
Enrolled: 37%
Grad in 6 Years: 86%
Returning Freshmen: 97%
Academics: ✍ ✍ ✍ ✍ ½
Social: ☎ ☎ ☎
Q of L: ★ ★ ★
Admissions: (909) 621-8088
Email Address: admission@claremontmckenna.edu

Strongest Programs:
Economics
Government
Psychology
International Relations
History
Sciences

part in a five-day orientation program that includes a beach trip and a reception with the president and department chairs. The school guarantees to meet the demonstrated need of accepted applicants and offers thirty merit scholarships of up to $5,000 a year. There are no athletic scholarships.

Ninety-six percent of CMC students live on campus "because of the social life." The maid service probably doesn't hurt. "They dust and vacuum our rooms and clean our bathrooms! We do nothing (except study, of course)!" declares a happy resident. All the residence halls are co-ed; freshmen are guaranteed a room. Stark Hall, a substance-free dorm, gives students more living options. A cluster of on-campus apartments equipped with kitchen facilities is a popular option for upperclassmen. "The dorms can be like palaces," asserts a junior. "Hot palaces in August and May. Dirty palaces on weekends." Dorm food is said to be quite good, and students can eat in dining halls at any of the other four colleges, though the best bet may be CMC's Collins Dining Hall. "They have a large spread with lots of different options," says one student, including vegetarian, vegan, and organic fare.

Most students agree that the social life at CMC is more than adequate, thanks to the five-college system. One student says, "You could easily lead a full and crazy social life without ever leaving campus." In addition to the usual forms of revelry, a calendar full of annual bashes includes Monte Carlo Night, Disco Inferno, Oktoberfest, Chez Hub, and the Christmas Madrigal Feast. Ponding, another unusual CMC tradition, involves being thrown into one of the two campus fountains on one's birthday. The college sponsors an outstanding lecture series at the Marion Minor Cook Athenaeum on Monday through Thursday nights each week. Before each lecture, students and faculty can enjoy a formal gourmet dinner together and engage in intellectual debates. Road trips to Joshua Tree, San Francisco, Las Vegas, and Mount Baldy are highly recommended by the students.

"We are leaders and love to debate politics."

Athletics are an important part of life at Claremont McKenna and the school has an overflowing trophy case to prove it. Men's and women's cross country, men's and women's track and field, women's basketball, and men's and women's tennis are especially competitive. A third of the students play varsity sports, and CMC students tend to dominate the teams jointly fielded with Harvey Mudd and Scripps. Top rivalries include Pomona, both in athletics and academics, one student claims. "Basketball games rock this campus," another student says.

CMC has embraced its mission to produce great leaders by providing students with ample opportunities for research and study abroad, as well as top-notch programs such as government and economics. "Leadership pervades almost everything that goes on here," says a junior. "Claremont McKenna builds character, fosters a sense of ambition among its students, and drives them to set their sights high."

Overlaps

UC–Berkeley, UCLA, Pomona, Stanford, Georgetown, University of Southern California

If You Apply To ➤ **Claremont McKenna:** Early decision: Nov. 15, Jan.2. Regular admissions: Jan. 2. Financial aid: Feb 1. Guarantees to meet demonstrated need. Campus interviews: recommended, evaluative. Alumni interviews: optional, evaluative. SATs or ACTs: required. SAT IIs: optional. Accepts the Common Application. Essay question: personal statement and discussion of leader. Places "strong emphasis on caliber of an applicant's extracurricular activities."

Harvey Mudd College

301 East 12th Street, Kingston Hall, Claremont, CA 91711

The finest institution that few outside of the science and engineering world have ever heard of. Future PhDs graduate from here in droves. Rivals Caltech for sheer brainpower and access to outstanding faculty. Offers more exposure to the liberal arts than most science- and technology-oriented schools.

A top-ranked technical school, Harvey Mudd College strives to give its students a sense of academic balance. Although it's a leading provider of high-quality programs in science and engineering, it also emphasizes a well-rounded education with knowledge in the humanities. "The academic climate is supportive but intense," says an engineering major. "We work all the time, at all hours of the day (and night). However, we are a tight-knit community, and no Mudder wants another to fail."

HMC's mid '50s vintage campus of cinder-block buildings even "looks like an engineering college; it's very symmetrical and there's no romance." In addition, the buildings have little splotches all over their surfaces that students have dubbed "warts"—not a very attractive picture. The latest campus additions include a new dorm and a new dining hall.

While most technology schools tend to have a narrow focus, HMC has come up with the novel idea that even scientists and engineers "need to know and appreciate poetry, philosophy, and non-Western thought," says an administrator. Students here take a third of their courses in the humanities, the most of any engineering college in the nation. Up to half of them can be taken by walking over to another Claremont school. To ensure breadth in the sciences, students take another third of their work in math, physics, chemistry, biology, engineering design, and computer science. The last third of a student's courses must be in one of six major areas: biology, computer science, chemistry, physics, engineering, or math. And finally, to cap off their HMC experience, all students must complete a research project in their major, as well as a senior thesis in the humanities and social sciences. "We wish we could focus more," complains a math major, but in the end it pays off. "All the hard work makes us the successful people that we are, and there are amazing people at this school," says an engineering student.

Of the six majors, engineering is considered not only the strongest but also the most popular by students, followed by computer science and physics. HMC has one of the nation's top computer science programs and an award-winning math department. In recent years, the number of biology faculty has more than doubled. "The math-bio major is great," says a math student. Students rave about the engineering clinic program, which plops real-life engineering tasks (sponsored by major corporations and government agencies to the tune of more than $30,000 per project) into the laps of students. There's also a Freshman Project that allows neophytes to tackle "some real-world engineering problems." And where else can

> **"The academic climate is supportive but intense."**

you take a freshman seminar in integrated-circuit chip design? The absence of graduate programs means that undergraduates get uncommon amounts of attention even from top faculty. "Professors are always available, and their offices are always open; my robotics professor frequently stays until 3 or 4 a.m.!" says an engineering student. Students love the small-college atmosphere. "The quality of teaching is as good as it gets," asserts one junior. Students strongly support the campuswide honor code.

These budding technology leaders are also top achievers: 93 percent graduated in the top 10 percent of their high school class. "Prospective students should know that

Website: www.hmc.edu
Location: Suburban
Total Enrollment: 718
Undergraduates: 718
Male/Female: 70/30
SAT Ranges: V 670–760
   M 710–800
Financial Aid: 52%
Expense: Pr $ $ $ $
Phi Beta Kappa: No
Applicants: 1,904
Accepted: 38%
Enrolled: 27%
Grad in 6 Years: 86%
Returning Freshmen: 96%
Academics: 🐾 🐾 🐾 🐾 ½
Social: ☎ ☎ ☎
Q of L: ★ ★ ★
Admissions: (909) 621-8011
Email Address:
   admission@hmc.edu

Strongest Programs:
Engineering
Computer Science
Math
Physics
Chemistry

Despite their heavy workload, most HMC students find abundant social outlets, even if it's just joining the parade of unicycles that has overrun the campus.

it can be temporarily damaging to their egos to come to a school with so many bright students," says a junior. Forty-three percent of the students are homegrown Californians. African Americans, Native Americans and foreign students together represent only 3 percent of the student body, but Hispanics account for 6 percent, while Asian Americans weigh in at 18 percent. "Everyone here has interests beyond the sciences," says a chemistry major, "but we share a passion for learning and a talent for technical thinking." A handful of merit scholarships help with the hefty tuition bill, but as an NCAA Division III college, Mudd offers no athletic scholarships.

Ninety-six percent of undergrads live on campus, and "the rooms are fairly big and comfortable and very well maintained," says a junior. Five older dorms and two newer, more modern ones are all co-ed and mix the classes. "They are definitely the engineering-school type—functional and efficient," notes a freshman. They range from Atwood ("study hard, party hard") to North ("way cool, so very"). The dorms are also ideal for computer whizzes: all are wired for online access to the HMC mainframe.

Despite their heavy workload, most HMC students find abundant social outlets, even if it's just joining the parade of unicycles that has overrun the campus. The college has no Greek life, and most social life takes place in and around the dorms, where there are parties every weekend.

"Professors are always available, and their offices are always open."

"People tend to know each other, so there is plenty of social life," says an engineering major. A student describes the town of Claremont as "a wonderful place if you're married or about to die." However, most students say there is always fun to be had on one of the five Claremont college campuses. Down-and-dirty types often frequent the Mudd Hole, a pizza/pinball/Ping-Pong hangout. Underage drinking is "compliments of a peer over 21," as one student puts it.

Students here take a third of their courses in the humanities, the most of any engineering college in the nation.

Mudd celebrated its 50th birthday in 2005, and for a school so young, it is rife with tradition. In the annual "pumpkin caroling" trip on Halloween, students serenade professors' homes with doctored-up Christmas carols. Another night of screwball fun is the Women's Pizza Party, in which men don dresses and crash a meeting of the Society of Women Engineers. There is also an annual Five Class competition among the four classes and the handful of fifth-year students, complete with amoebae soccer and relay races that include unicycles (backward), peanut butter and jelly, and slide-rule problem solving. Engineering pranks are popular but must be reversible within 24 hours.

Mudd fields varsity sports teams together with Claremont McKenna and Scripps, and mainly because of all the CMC jocks, the teams do extremely well. The men's and women's teams in cross country, track, swimming, tennis, and basketball have all won recent championships. Not long ago, some enterprising Mudders stole archrival Caltech's cannon, elevating the Mudd–Caltech rivalry to include a soccer game dubbed the Cannon Bowl. Intramurals, also in conjunction with Scripps and CMC, are even more popular. Traditional sporting events include the Black and Blue Bowl, an interdorm game of tackle football, and the Freshman–Sophomore Games, which climax in a massive tug-of-war across a pit of vile stuff.

"People tend to know each other, so there is plenty of social life."

A common student complaint is "too much work," and students would welcome more time to reflect on what they are learning, but the work tends to pay off in grad school and in the job world. HMC is right on the heels of Caltech as the best technical school in the West. Mudd doesn't promise you'll end up with a hot job in Silicon Valley, but some students certainly do, and the college offers a gem of a technical education perfectly blended with a dash of humanities and social sciences. HMC's intimate setting also offers something bigger schools can't: a sense of family.

Overlaps

MIT, Caltech, Stanford, UC–Berkeley, Rose-Hulman

<table>
<tr><td>**If You**
Apply
To ></td><td>**Harvey Mudd:** Early decision: Nov. 15. Regular admissions: Jan. 15. Guarantees to meet full demonstrated need. Campus and alumni interviews: recommended, informational. SATs: required (ACT not accepted). SAT IIs: required (math II, and one other). Accepts the Common Application and prefers electronic applications. Essay question: fun, cool, or interesting things about yourself; recent moral, ethical, or personal decision decision; what troubles you about the world around you?</td></tr>
</table>

Pitzer College

1050 North Mills Avenue, Claremont, CA 91711

Offers a haven for the otherwise-minded without the hard edge of nonconformity at places like Evergreen and Bard. Traditional strengths lie in the social and behavioral sciences. Still nearly 60/40 female, but much more selective than it was 10 years ago.

As the most laid-back of the Claremont colleges, Pitzer College offers students a creative milieu, abundant opportunities for intellectual exploration, and a sense of fierce individualism. Founded in the '60s, this small school has changed with the times but continues its emphasis on progressive thought, social responsibility, and open social attitude.

Even the campus is, well, different. The classroom buildings are modernistic octagons, and the grass-covered "mounds" that distinguish the grounds "are perfect for sunbathing and Frisbee," says one student. The college is in the first phase of construction of new, environmentally friendly dorms.

In keeping with Pitzer's philosophy of student autonomy, each student has the maximum freedom to choose which classes he or she would like to take. A lively freshman seminar program sharpens students' learning skills, especially writing. Students select from 40 majors in sciences, humanities, arts, and social sciences. Almost anything in the social and behavioral sciences is a sure bet, especially psychology (the most popular major), anthropology, sociology, political science, and biology. Most courses in Pitzer's weaker areas can be picked up at one of the other Claremont schools. New offerings include majors in organismal biology/ecology and molecular biology. A minor in art history has been added as well.

> **"The student body is relatively liberal and politically aware. The school is very untraditional."**

The academic climate is laid back, but "encourages intellectual growth and inquiry," says a senior. "Group study sessions are common and if you miss a class, students will share their notes." Interdisciplinary inquiry is encouraged and original research is common. Class size is generally small, promoting close interaction between students and faculty. "People work together with their professors to create a classroom climate that is supportive and engaging," says a psychology major. "Professors are very accessible at all hours," says a politics major, who adds, "They are really great people."

Individualism is a prized characteristic among Pitzer students. Fifty-six percent are from California and the college has a substantial minority community: African Americans comprise 5 percent of the student body, Hispanics 15 percent, and Asian Americans 10 percent. A sophomore says, "The student body is relatively liberal and politically aware. The school is very untraditional." Lest anyone get the idea that Pitzer students are too far out in left field, many of them eventually go on to graduate or professional school. Pitzer offers merit scholarships worth an average of $8,125.

Website: www.pitzer.edu
Location: Suburban
Total Enrollment: 911
Undergraduates: 911
Male/Female: 41/59
SAT Ranges: V 570–680
  M 560–660
ACT Range: N/A
Financial Aid: 40%
Expense: Pr $ $ $ $
Phi Beta Kappa: No
Applicants: 3,251
Accepted: 39%
Enrolled: 39%
Grad in 6 Years: 70%
Returning Freshmen: 88%
Academics: ✍ ✍ ✍
Social: ☎ ☎ ☎
Q of L: ★ ★ ★
Admissions: (909) 621-8129
Email Address:
  admission@pitzer.edu

Strongest Programs:
Psychology
Sociology
Political Studies
Media Studies
English
Biology

Seventy-three percent of students live on campus. "The dorms are starting to get old but are well maintained," says a student Boarders can choose from a variety of meal plans in the dining hall (which never fails to have a vegetarian plate). Campus security is ever-present; a student says, "Pitzer seems to be more safe than other campuses because campus security is so effective." One interesting campus curiosity is Grove House, a California craftsman-style house students saved from the wrecking ball nearly two decades ago and moved to campus. It houses a dining room, study areas, and art exhibits.

And what about the social scene? "Most students stay on campus to attend events or go to parties," says a senior. Pitzer has no Greek organizations, nor does it want any, and social life tends to be fairly low-key. Kohoutek is the big party: "A weeklong art/music fest celebrating the comet that never came," says a senior. Activities include bands, food, and a "whole week of hoopla." The college enforces the 21-year-old drinking age, and all parties that serve alcohol must be registered. Dances, cocktail parties, and cultural events do much to occupy students' leisure time, but without a car things can get claustrophobic.

According to one student, Pitzer "doesn't have enough athletic spirit," but the Pomona–Pitzer football team—"The Sagehens"—has had winning seasons and the school fields a variety of teams within the Southern California Intercollegiate Athletic Conference. Students play a large role in Pitzer's community government and sit on all policy committees, including those on curriculum and faculty promotion.

Pitzer attracts open-minded students looking for the freedom to go their own way. Notes one student: "Pitzer is the only Claremont school that can claim to be genuinely different, in terms of race, religion, sexual orientation, and political belief. Pitzer is an amalgamation of every color of the spectrum."

Overlaps

Occidental, UC-Santa Barbara, UC–San Diego, UC-Santa Cruz, UCLA, Pomona

If You Apply To ➤

Pitzer: Regular admissions: Jan. 1. Does not guarantee to meet demonstrated need. Campus interviews: recommended, informational. Alumni interviews: optional, informational. SATs or ACTs: optional. SAT IIs: optional (English and two others). Accepts the Common Application and electronic applications. Essay question: Common Application.

Pomona College

333 North College Way, Claremont, CA 91711

The great Eastern-style liberal arts college of the West. Offers twice the resources of stand-alone competitors with its access to the other Claremonts. Location an hour east of LA would be ideal except for the choking smog that hangs over the area during the warmer parts of the year.

Website: www.pomona.edu
Location: Suburban
Total Enrollment: 1,562
Undergraduates: 1,562
Male/Female: 50/50
SAT Ranges: V 690–770
   M 680–760
ACT Range: 30–34

Pomona College, located just 35 miles east of the glitz and glamour of Hollywood, is the undisputed star of the Claremont College Consortium and one of the top small liberal arts colleges anywhere. This small, elite institution is the best liberal arts college in the West, and its media studies program (film and television) gets top billing. But the school's prestigious reputation doesn't get to the heads of Pomona's friendly students. "Students here are very open about different types of people—[Pomona] prides itself on its diverse community," chirps one Sage Hen (the school's mascot).

The architecture is variously described as Spanish Mediterranean, pseudo-Italian, or, as a sophomore puts it, "a perfect mix of Northeastern Ivy and Southern California

Modern." The administration building, Alexander Hall, is described as "postmodern with Mediterranean influences," and one notices more than one stucco building cloaked in ivy and topped with a red-tile roof on campus, as well as eucalyptus trees, canyon live oaks, and an occasional "secretive courtyard lined with flowers." By virtue of its location and beauty, Pomona's campus has served as the quintessential collegiate milieu in various Hollywood movies. New construction includes the Seaver Life Sciences Building and the Lincoln and Edmunds buildings, which will add 93,000 square feet of space for a variety of academic departments.

Economics, English, biology, politics, and math are the most popular majors at Pomona. Although no specific course or department is prescribed for graduation, students must take at least one course in each of five areas: creative expression; social institutions and human behavior; history, values, ethics and cultural studies; physical and biological sciences; and mathematical reasoning. The Critical Inquiry seminar emphasizes thoughtful reading, logical reasoning, and graceful writing through subjects such as "Living With Our Genes" and "Penguins, Polar Bears, People and Politics." Student must also complete foreign language and physical education requirements.

Educational opportunities abound at Pomona. Students can spend a semester at Colby or Swarthmore, pursue a 3–2 engineering plan with the California Institute of Technology, or spend a semester in Washington, D.C., working for a congressperson. Nearly one-half of the students take advantage of study abroad programs offered in 24 foreign countries, and many others participate in programs focusing on six cultures and languages at the Oldenborg Center. In addition, the Summer Undergraduate Research Program (SURP) provides students with the opportunity to conduct funded research with a faculty member in their area of study.

Classes at Pomona are challenging. "Introductory classes are usually not very work-intensive," says one student. However, "Upper-level courses are very rigorous as the professors is attempting to teach a great deal of difficult material in a short period of time." Students often form study groups in an effort to help one another through the demanding curriculum. One undergrad estimates the average student spends 20 to 30 hours a week studying outside the classroom.

Classes are small at Pomona—the average is 14 students—and the faculty makes a point of being accessible. It's not uncommon for professors to hold study sessions at their houses. "I've had some really incredible professors who have taught me a lot," a neuroscience major says. An ever-popular take-a-professor-to-lunch program gives students free meals when they arrive with a faculty member in tow, and there is even a prof who leads aerobics classes open to all interested parties. Better still, "We do not have graduate students or TAs teaching class," says a senior. "Thus, students do not have to wait until they are upperclassmen to enjoy the benefits of working with and learning from brilliant professors."

Pomona students "tend to be high-achieving, confident, verbal students with a fairly liberal political ideology," says a senior. "You'll find people who are really into sports, people who are very artsy, computer geeks, talented musicians, people who like to party every night, or people who like to study on the weekends." Thirty-four percent of the students are Californians, and a growing percentage venture from the East Coast. Pomona is proud of its diverse student body: 7 percent are African American, 9 percent are Hispanic, and 14 percent are Asian American. There is a healthy mix of liberals and conservatives on campus, though the leftists, especially the feminist wing, are much more vocal. One interesting way students voice their issues is by painting the Walker Wall. Anyone is allowed to paint any message they want on the wall, and four-letter words and descriptions of alternative sexual practices show up on a regular basis. The student government is active, and the administration is credited with respecting students' opinions.

(Continued)

Financial Aid: 53%
Expense: Pr $ $ $
Phi Beta Kappa: Yes
Applicants: 4,927
Accepted: 20%
Enrolled: 41%
Grad in 6 Years: 92%
Returning Freshmen: 99%
Academics: ✍ ✍ ✍ ✍ ✍
Social: ☎ ☎ ☎
Q of L: ★ ★ ★ ★
Admissions: (909) 621-8134
Email Address:
  admissions@pomona.edu

Strongest Programs:
English
International Relations
Economics
Neuroscience
Foreign Languages
Media Studies
Chemistry
Politics

Students at Pomona often spend Friday afternoons relaxing with friends over a brew at the Greek Theater. Social life begins in the dorms, where barbecues, parties, and study breaks are organized.

Pomona is need-blind in admissions and meets the full demonstrated need of all those who attend. Admissions officers are on the lookout for anyone with special talents and are more than willing to waive the usual grade-and-score standards for such finds. A five-day freshman orientation program divides the new arrivals into groups of six to 12 students headed by a sophomore. "We provide a great deal of support in acclimating students to a college environment," says a senior.

The vast majority of Pomona students (98 percent) live on campus all four years. The dorms are co-ed, student-governed, and divided into two distinct groups. Those on South campus are family-like, fairly quiet, and offer spacious rooms, and those on the North end have smaller rooms with a livelier social scene. "At Pomona, living on campus is an integral part of the college experience," says a student. The open courtyards and gardens are popular study spots. A handful of students isolate themselves in Claremont proper, where apartments are scarce and expensive. Boarders must buy at least partial meal plans. The food is good, with steak dinners on Saturday and ice cream for dessert every day. Students with common interests can occupy one of the large university houses; there is a vegetarian group and a kosher kitchen, both of which serve meals to other undergraduates. Pomona has a well-established language dorm with wings for speakers of French, German, Spanish, Russian, and Chinese, as well as language tables at lunch. Students generally feel safe on campus. "The worst that usually happens is bike thefts," says a junior. "We're in a pretty nice suburb, so there really aren't many problems with crime."

> **"Students here are very open about different types of people."**

Students at Pomona often spend Friday afternoons relaxing with friends over a brew at the Greek Theater. Social life begins in the dorms, where barbecues, parties, and study breaks are organized. There are movies five nights a week, and students also enjoy just tossing a Frisbee on the lawn. One student wanted to be sure that incoming freshmen and transfers knew of the Coop's (student union) "best milkshakes west of the Mississippi" and its "game room, with pool, Ping-Pong, pinball, and assorted video games." "I appreciate the diversity and depth that the Five-College community brings to the social life," says a student. "You are guaranteed to meet new and interesting people whenever you step off campus." Five-college parties happen nearly every weekend. During midterms and finals, however, the campus is a "social ghost town." Of more concern is the poor air quality, described by a junior as "oppressive on hot days during the fall semester." Most students are willing to live with the smog, but at least one student complains, "I'd prefer to breathe clean air."

Pomona is unique among the Claremont Colleges in that it has three non-national fraternities (two co-ed; there are no sororities), each with its own party rooms on campus. There is "no peer pressure to join frats," and no fraternity rivalry. As for booze, "I haven't noticed any pressure to drink here," reports one student, but "alcohol is definitely present in the social scene." Harwood dorm throws the five-college costume party every Halloween, and interdorm Jell-O fights keep things lively. Freshman

> **"I've had some really incredible professors who have taught me a lot."**

orientation gets interesting, too. "First-years have to run through the gates of Pomona with blue and white carnations while upperclassmen throw water balloons and shoot water at them," says a student.

There was a time when Pomona was an athletic powerhouse; the football team even knocked off mighty USC on Thanksgiving Day back in 1899. Currently, women's basketball, tennis, soccer, and swimming, and men's football, baseball, soccer, track, and water polo are strong programs. Intense rivalry exists between the colleges in the Claremont consortium; basketball games between Pomona, Pitzer, and

Educational opportunities abound at Pomona. Students can spend a semester at Colby or Swarthmore, pursue a 3–2 engineering plan with the California Institute of Technology, or spend a semester in Washington, D.C., working for a congressperson.

CMS are "particularly heated." Intramurals, including hotly contested inner-tube water polo matches, attract many participants, and Pomona's $14 million athletic complex makes its facilities the best of the Claremonts.

"Pomona offers a unique and desirable juxtaposition of rigorous academics and comfortable social atmosphere," says a student. Another student says, "Once you take advantage of the five-college system, you realize how cool it is." The strongest link in an extremely attractive chain, Pomona continues to symbolize the rising status of the Claremont Colleges—and the West in general—in the world of higher education. There are few regrets about coming to Pomona. Says a senior, "We're in California. The sun is always shining. What's the problem?"

Overlaps

Stanford, Yale, Harvard, UC–Berkeley, UCLA, Brown

If You Apply To > | **Pomona:** Early decision: Nov. 15, Dec. 28. Regular admissions: Jan. 2. Financial aid: Feb. 1. Guarantees to meet full demonstrated need. Campus and alumni interviews: recommended, evaluative. SATs or ACTs: required. SAT IIs: required. Accepts the Common Application and electronic applications. Essay question.

Scripps College

1030 Columbia Avenue, Claremont, CA 91711

Scripps is a tiny, close-knit women's college with co-ed institutions literally right next door. Only Barnard and Spelman offer the same combination of single-sex and co-ed. Innovative Core Curriculum takes an interdisciplinary approach to learning.

Scripps College offers the best of both worlds—a close-knit women's college, where traditions include weekly tea and fresh-baked cookies, and the size and scope of a major research institution, thanks to its membership in the Claremont Colleges.* Founded in 1926 by newspaper publisher Ellen Browning Scripps, the college continues to pursue her mission: "To educate women by developing their intellects and talents through active participation in a community of scholars." Students tend to be outgoing, articulate, and serious about their studies, though they still know how to have fun. "The atmosphere is helpful, not competitive and scary," says one student. "It is impossible to be depressed in this beautiful place."

Indeed, Scripps's scenic 30-acre campus, listed on the National Register of Historic Places, offers a tranquil, safe, and comfortable environment. The architecture is Spanish and Mediterranean, with tiled roofs and elegant landscaping. A performing arts center opened in 2003, with permanent space for the Claremont Concert Orchestra and Concert Choir. In addition to a 700-seat theater, the center offers a music library, recital hall, practice rooms, faculty offices, and classrooms.

The academic experience at Scripps emphasizes cooperation. "Even in science classes, it's not uncommon to find students working together on labs and problem sets," a freshman says. Everyone takes the Core Curriculum in interdisciplinary humanities, focusing on ideas about the world, and the methods used to generate them. Other requirements include courses in fine arts, letters, natural and social sciences, women's studies, race and ethnic studies, foreign language, and math. Professors "are amazing and dedicated," says a senior. "They are bright and love to teach." Classes average 12 to 15 students each; one student says her Calculus II class had four people, while her Introduction to European History course had seven. "Professors know their students by name and face," says one student.

Website:
   www.scrippscollege.edu
Location: Suburban
Total Enrollment: 899
Undergraduates: 878
Male/Female: 0/100
SAT Ranges: V 650–740
   M 620–710
ACT Range: 28–31
Financial Aid: 48%
Expense: Pr $ $ $
Phi Beta Kappa: Yes
Applicants: 1,836
Accepted: 46%
Enrolled: 28%
Grad in 6 Years: 84%
Returning Freshmen: 88%
Academics: ✍ ✍ ✍ ½
Social: ☎ ☎ ☎
Q of L: ★ ★ ★ ★
Admissions: (909) 621-8149
   or (800) 770-1333
Email Address: admission@
   scrippscollege.edu

(Continued)

Strongest Programs:
Politics/International Relations
English
Studio Art
Biology
Psychology
Foreign Languages
Music

The Scripps Humanities Institute offers seminars and lectures open to the general public, along with fellowships for juniors; recently, the institute explored how and why empathy is a shared focal point in disciplines as broad as neuroscience, literary criticism, and legal studies.

The Scripps cross-country, tennis, and swimming, and diving teams brought home conference championships in 2004–05.

Overlaps

Claremont McKenna, Occidental, Pomona, UC-San Diego, University of Southern California, Smith

Popular and well-regarded majors at Scripps include psychology, English, politics and international relations, art, and music. The Millard Sheets Art Center offers a state-of-the-art studio and freestanding museum-quality gallery for aspiring painters and sculptors. Premeds benefit from the Keck Science Center, a joint facility for students at Scripps, Claremont McKenna (CMC), and Pitzer (the other Claremont Colleges are Pomona and Harvey Mudd). The Scripps Humanities Institute offers seminars and lectures open to the general public, along with fellowships for juniors; recently, the institute explored how and why empathy is a shared focal point in disciplines as broad as neuroscience, literary criticism, and legal studies. While Scripps doesn't offer business, students can take economics courses at the college, and accounting across the street at Claremont McKenna.

> **"The atmosphere is helpful, not competitive and scary."**

Forty-three percent of Scripps women are from California. African Americans account for 3 percent of the student body, Hispanics 6 percent, and Asian Americans make up another 13 percent. "The majority of girls at Scripps are liberal," a history major says. "Students are very aware of current events and what is happened in the world around them," another student agrees. "Scripps encourages positive change and discourages ignorance." SCORE, the Scripps Communities of Resources and Empowerment, provides support and funding to organizations that further promote social and political awareness, with respect to issues of class, ethnicity, gender, race, religion, sexuality, and sexual orientation. There are no athletic scholarships, though more grant money has been made available for students with financial need, so that each student has to take out no more than $4,000 in loans each year.

Ninety-six percent of Scripps students live in one of the eight "beautiful" dorms, where options range "from singles to seven-person suites, apartment-style living arrangements to charming Spanish Mediterranean residence halls built in the 1920s." Many dorms have reflecting pools and inner courtyards; some rooms have balconies and are furnished with antiques and beautiful rugs, and juniors are guaranteed single rooms. The cafeteria garners rave reviews as well: "This is not traditional college food," says a bioethics major. "The salad bar is gourmet, the bread comes from a local bakery, and the pizza is made in a wood-fired brick oven. Don't get me started about the hot cookies!"

Social life at Scripps centers around the residence halls, which take turns throwing parties. The school's alcohol policy complies with state law—those under 21 can't drink—but also specifies that if an underage student is drunk at a party, she will be helped and kept safe, rather than written up and punished. Students also receive daily emails detailing what's going on at all of the Claremont institutions, organized by

> **"You're appreciated for who you are and what you stand for."**

"things to do" and "music, art, lectures, theater, film, and dance." The town of Claremont also offers a farmer's market on Sundays, with fresh fruit, flowers, and gifts. For students with cars, popular road trips include Pasadena, Mt. Baldy, San Diego, and even Las Vegas and Mexico; students without wheels can hop on the MetroLink commuter train and get to and from Los Angeles for less than $5.

Athletic rivalries aren't the focus here, but Scripps does field joint teams with CMC and Harvey Mudd, and when those teams face off against Pomona and Pitzer, students pay attention. All of the teams compete in Division III, and the Scripps cross-country, tennis, and swimming and diving teams brought home conference championships in 2004–05. Intramural sports are also played jointly, and popular options include inner-tube water polo, soccer, flag football, volleyball, rugby, and lacrosse. Traditions are also important at Scripps, including the Matriculation ceremony at the start of each year, and the signing of the "graffiti wall" by each class before graduation.

Scripps offers a winning combination of outstanding academics and personal attention, with a cooperative, non-threatening feel. And should the women-only environment of Scripps begin to feel claustrophobic, the other Claremont Colleges beckon, with parties, intramural sports and cross-registration privileges. Scripps students want to achieve great things, but not if that requires stepping on their classmates' toes. "A very common passion is empowering women of all ages, ethnicities and backgrounds," says a freshman. "You're appreciated for who you are and what you stand for."

Clark University

950 Main Street, Worcester, MA 01610-1477

If Clark were located an hour to the east, it would have become the hottest thing since Harvard. Worcester is not Boston, but Clarkies bring a sense of mission to their relationship with this old industrial town. Clark is liberal, tolerant, and world-renowned in psychology and geography.

A classic Clark University poster distills the school's philosophy into a single photograph: A normal green peapod, filled with multicolored peas. "Categorizing people," the poster says, "isn't something you can do here." And indeed, it's not. "At Clark you have to be prepared to be open-minded and accepting since there are so many different types of people and ideas," says a junior. Clark started as an all-graduate school, excelling in disciplines including psychology and geography, and now welcomes undergraduates of all backgrounds and interests, with small classes and no shortage of faculty attention.

Clark's compact, 50-acre campus has "enough ivy, tall maples, and collegiate brick buildings to make a traditionalist happy," even though it's located in the gritty Main South section of Worcester. Buildings range from remodeled Victorian-era residences, former homes of prosperous merchants, to the award-winning Robert Hutchings Goddard Library. Clark is always renovating something, and careful restoration has brought a renewed sense of history to the area. Clark is the only American university where famed psychoanalyst Sigmund Freud lectured, and a statue of him marks the spot in the center of campus where he spoke. A new building for the biological sciences recently opened, and the biophysics building is being renovated. Other new additions include the Traina Center for the Arts and a new home for the International Development, Community, and Environment Department.

While Clark now serves primarily undergraduates, its history of graduate education is evident in its classrooms. Most courses are seminars, and more than two-thirds have 25 or fewer students. First-year seminars are even smaller, limited to 16 students each. They permit students to explore issues in depth in their first or second semesters, and the faculty member teaching the course acts as an academic advisor until students declare a major. "It is a nice way to immediately meet people and continue having contact with them throughout the semester, and your advisor gets to

Website: www.clarku.edu
Location: Center city
Total Enrollment: 2,636
Undergraduates: 1,996
Male/Female: 39/61
SAT Ranges: V 550–660
  M 540–645
ACT Range: 22–28
Financial Aid: 58%
Expense: Pr $ $ $
Phi Beta Kappa: Yes
Applicants: 4,239
Accepted: 62%
Enrolled: 20%
Grad in 6 Years: 69%
Returning Freshmen: 86%
Academics: 🖉 🖉 🖉 🖉
Social: ☎ ☎ ☎
Q of L: ★ ★ ★
Admissions: (508) 793-7431
Email Address:
  admissions@clarku.edu

Strongest Programs:
Psychology

know you better," a junior communication and culture major says. A newer program for incoming students, Clark Trek, is an optional orientation program held outdoors.

The foundation of a Clark education is the Program of Liberal Studies, which promotes the habits, skills, and perspectives essential to lifelong learning. Each student must complete eight courses: one in verbal expression, one in formal analysis, and six in perspectives—aesthetic, comparative, historical, language, scientific, and values. International Studies Stream students take courses in those areas with an international focus. Interdisciplinary programs are popular, and students may design their own majors. Those who finish with a grade point average of 3.25 or better may take a fifth year for free to obtain a master's degree.

Clark's historically strong psychology and geography departments continue to burnish their national reputations, the latter having churned out more PhDs in the field than any other school in the nation, plus four members of the National Academy of Science (the most of any geography program). Clark is the birthplace of the American Psychological Association, and the concept of adolescence as distinct from childhood. Also strong are the sciences and programs in management, government and international relations, and communication and culture. A major in Global Environmental Studies was added in spring 2004, along with a concentration in bioinformatics—a burgeoning field that brings together math, computer science, and life sciences. Concentrations in environment and society, and cultural identities and global processes, are no longer offered.

"There are a lot of hippies and people who love to speak their minds and protest."

Regardless of major, Clark encourages students to take internships, through the university itself or the 14-school Colleges of Worcester Consortium.* More than 20 percent of all Clark students spend at least one semester studying abroad at one of 15 programs in 10 countries. Even those who don't go abroad can get a taste of foreign culture by taking courses or attending international research conferences at the Clark University Center in Luxembourg. Back on campus, faculty members really make an effort to get to know their students, says a senior: "I had a professor who, for our first assignment, asked us to bring in a picture and a paragraph describing ourselves. In a class of 150, this biology professor takes the time to learn the names of every single student." About 40 percent of students participate in undergraduate research.

Thirty-seven percent of Clark students are from Massachusetts, and international students from about 90 countries make up another 8 percent. African Americans account for 3 percent of the student body; Hispanics and Asian Americans combine for another 7 percent. Clarkies are "laid-back, chill, friendly, liberal, and from the Northeast," a senior says. The university has a collaborative educational program with historically African American Howard University in Washington, D.C. Politically, "there are a lot of hippies and people who love to speak their minds and protest," a sophomore says. Many Clark students do community service, and the Community Engagement and Volunteering Center is a hub for the many social activism groups. Clark also offers merit scholarships averaging $9,620 annually plus special "Making a Difference" scholarships for students interested in community service, worth $44,000 each.

Students who finish with a grade point average of 3.25 or better may take a fifth year for free to obtain a master's degree.

Freshmen and sophomores at Clark are required to live in the dorms, and all except one are co-ed by floor or wing. In all, 77 percent of the student body bunks on campus. "Dorms are fairly spacious and comfy to live in, although a few are due for new carpet and some paint," a junior says. The rest of the students—mostly juniors and seniors—find apartments and group houses nearby. After the first year, students must play the lottery to get rooms. Campus dwellers must buy the meal plan, which always offers student favorites, along with vegan, vegetarian, and kosher options. "There is one big dining facility on campus. I like this because everyone eats here, and it is a social scene and builds community," a senior says.

Clark has no Greek life, but 80 student-run organizations offer "concerts, dances, karaoke nights, ice cream socials, and other events," says a junior. "Clark is not a big party school, but there is always something to do," one junior says. First-year dorms are dry, and mixed-class halls "are dry if you are under 21," says a Spanish major. "It's quite common for students to get caught" with beer or liquor that they shouldn't have.

Worcester and the vicinity host 14 colleges, but the area's history—a manufacturing and industrial hub that's fallen on hard times—means it's hardly a "college town," students say. That said, Worcester does have movie theaters, restaurants with every conceivable type of cuisine, and small clubs where bands can play, as well as the Centrum, a 13,000-seat arena. "Main South Worcester is not the prettiest, quietest locale for a college, but it's got flavor and spice, and you'll either love it or hate it," a junior biology major says. Students mix with the townspeople through volunteer programs such as Clark University Brothers and Sisters. "If you like volunteering someplace that needs it, or fighting for human rights, this is your school," a junior says. To get away, Clarkies head to the larger cities of Boston and Providence, or the rural wilds of Vermont, New Hampshire, and Maine—all easily reachable by car or public transit.

Coping with the frigid New England winters includes quaffing cups of hot chocolate and dreaming about Spree Day—which one student describes as "better than your birthday and Christmas combined." On Spree Day, classes are spontaneously cancelled one spring day, and everyone celebrates spring with a carnival on the green, including food, music, and games (with prizes!). Completely different is Academic Spree Day, which celebrates undergraduate research. Clark competes in the Division III, and the men's basketball team reached the Elite Eight of the NCAA tournament in 2001 and 2002, and won the conference championship in those years and 2003. The women's basketball team won the conference championship in 2004 and advanced to the NCAA tournament for the ninth time. Also competitive are women's field hockey, crew, soccer, and softball, and men's basketball and crew. About half of the students participate in intramural sports, which range from soccer and flag football to ultimate

> "Clark is not a big party school, but there is always something to do."

Frisbee and volleyball. The Dolan Field House opened in May 2003, providing facilities and locker rooms for spring and fall teams, plus lighted outdoor fields. The crew team has a new boathouse on Lake Quinsigamond, and the cross-country teams recently broke in a new course.

Clark started out differently, serving only graduate students. Though it now caters mainly to undergraduates, the school continues to challenge convention, pioneering new teaching methods, pursuing new fields of knowledge, and finding new ways to connect thinking and doing. "Its urban location gives it a distinct identity," a senior says. "It is also fairly progressive, making room for students to satisfy a wide variety of interests."

Clark is the only American university where famed psychoanalyst Sigmund Freud lectured, and a statue of him marks the spot in the center of campus where he spoke.

Overlaps

University of Massachusetts–Amherst, Boston University, George Washington, Brandeis, Wheaton (MA), American

If You Apply To ➤

Clark: Early decision: Nov. 15. Regular admissions, financial aid, housing: Jan. 15. Meets demonstrated need of 66%. Campus and alumni interviews: recommended, evaluative. SATs or ACTs: required. SAT IIs: optional. Accepts the Common Application and electronic applications. Essay question: significant experience, achievement or risk and its impact on you; issue of personal, local, national, or intellectual concern; influential person, fictional character, historical figure, or creative work; what you would bring to the diversity of a college community; or a topic of your choice.

Clarkson University

Holcroft House, Box 5605, Potsdam, NY 13699

You know you're in the north country when the nearest major city is Montreal. Clarkson lies over the river and through the woods. With an informal and close-knit atmosphere, Clarkson is one of the few small, undergraduate-oriented technical universities in the nation. Compare to Lehigh, Bucknell, and Union.

Website: www.clarkson.edu
Location: Small town
Total Enrollment: 3,067
Undergraduates: 2,719
Male/Female: 76/24
SAT Ranges: V 520–630
  M 570–660
ACT: 23–28
Financial Aid: 85%
Expense: Pr $ $
Phi Beta Kappa: No
Applicants: 2,473
Accepted: 86%
Enrolled: 31%
Grad in 6 Years: 69%
Returning Freshmen: 86%
Academics: ✍ ✍ ✍
Social: ☎ ☎
Q of L: ★ ★ ★
Admissions: (315) 268-6479
Email Address:
  admission@clarkson.edu

Strongest Programs:
Engineering
Chemistry
Business

At Clarkson University, engineering and ice hockey reign supreme. About half of the student body is enrolled in the engineering program, and the hockey team is a perennial contender for top honors. Students at this tiny school get a quality technical education in a small town environment that offers plenty to do, especially during the sled dog days of winter.

The village of Potsdam, New York, is cloistered away between the Adirondacks and the St. Lawrence River. The "hill campus," where most freshmen and sophomores live and take classes, relies mainly on modern architecture and lots of woods and wildlife. Recent additions to campus include the Adirondack Lodge, the headquarters for student outdoor recreation.

Engineering isn't the only academic offering at Clarkson, but it certainly gets top billing; 49 percent of the students are in the program, and it claims four of the five most popular majors. The combined programs in electrical/computer engineering and mechanical/aeronautical engineering earn the highest marks from students. Clarkson's School of Business has several majors to choose from, and all first-year business students actually start and run a business. Project Arete allows students to earn a double major in management and a liberal arts discipline. The engineering offerings recently got even bigger, with the addition of a bachelor's program in environmental engineering; a major in digital arts and sciences is also new. Physics and chemistry are the strongest offerings in the sciences, and would-be doctors have the benefit of a joint program combining biology and—you guessed it—engineering. The liberal arts and humanities are cited by students as weaker.

As part of their Foundation Curriculum requirements, all students at Clarkson are required to take six liberal arts courses; two in mathematics; two in science; and one each in computing, engineering, and business. Freshmen are required to take a personal wellness course, which covers topics such as fitness, stress management, and sexuality. About 30 freshmen are invited to participate in the honors program, which offers specially developed courses and research experiences. Study abroad opportunities are available at 20 different schools in 12 countries.

Clarkson prides itself on intimacy and personalized instruction; 40 percent of classes taken by freshman have 25 or fewer students, and three-quarters have 50 or fewer. Eighty percent of the Foundation courses are taught by full-fledged faculty members, and nearly 200 students conduct research with a faculty mentor each year.

> **"The professors are excited by the subjects they teach, and it shows."**

"The professors here are very intelligent, readily available, and willing to help their students in any way they can," says an environmental science and policy major. Another student adds, "The professors are excited by the subjects they teach, and it shows." Some students say Clarkson isn't the academic pressure cooker that many technical institutes are, but others disagree. "The climate is very academic-oriented and very competitive," a senior says. "The courses are hard, and every grade received is well-earned." But another senior adds, "Students mainly help each other out and have a laid-back demeanor." The bottom line of a Clarkson education is getting a job after graduation, and students uniformly praise the career counseling office and proudly note Clarkson's high placement rate.

At Clarkson, the students are friendly, serious-minded, and down-to-earth; radicals are notably absent. Seventy-three percent of the students graduated in the top quarter of their class. Seventy-three percent are New Yorkers, and 2 percent hail from abroad. Clarkson has trouble luring minorities to its remote locale; African Americans, Hispanics, and Asian Americans each make up 2 percent of the student body and Native Americans another 1 percent. "Our campus definitely needs more minority students," says a senior. Many applicants demonstrating financial need are offered some aid, but not necessarily enough to meet full need. Clarkson awards a handful of merit scholarships each year, averaging nearly $10,000. Thirty athletic scholarships are offered, but only to ice hockey players.

Seventy-seven percent of students live in campus housing. Students are required to reside on campus all four years, unless exempted to live in a Greek house. Most dorms are centrally located and are cleaned every day. "The dorms are comfortable and very well maintained," says a student, but another notes "there is a constant dorm shortage." Four of the dorms are all-men and the rest are co-ed by floor. All freshmen are housed with students in their major areas of study and in some instances in their department, giving them the chance to study and learn together. Many underclassmen are housed in conventional dorms, but university-owned townhouse apartments offer more gracious living. "The dorm situation is handled by the lottery, and housing improves based on your class year," a senior reports.

> **"The dorms are comfortable and very well maintained."**

In keeping with Clarkson's "come as you are" atmosphere, the social scene is low key. "There are activities, such as comedians, picnics, and other types of entertainment on campus," says one senior. "However, a good deal of socializing also takes place off campus." Sixteen percent of the men and 13 percent of the women join the Greek system. Fraternity beer blasts are the staple of weekend life, and those not into the Greek scene (and over 21) can head to the handful of bars in downtown Potsdam. Nearby SUNY–Potsdam is also a source of social life, especially for men frustrated by Clarkson's three-to-one male/female ratio. Drinking is prohibited on campus, but students report that it's still easy to imbibe and for underage students to get served off campus. For those who crave the bustle of city nightlife, Ottawa and Montreal are each about an hour and a half away by car.

When it comes to sports, hockey is first and foremost in the hearts of Clarkson students—the only one in which the university competes in Division I. The team has been ECAC champ in recent years, and contends for the national championship with other blue-chip teams like archrivals Cornell and St. Lawrence. A Division I women's ice hockey program has been initiated. In addition, Clarkson offers 19 Division III sports, and men's lacrosse, basketball, and baseball have been successful of late. The men's and women's Nordic skiing teams brought home national titles in 2004. About three-quarters of students take advantage of the intramural program, with soccer and volleyball proving popular. For weekend athletes, an abundance of skiing and other outdoor and winter sports is within easy driving distance.

While other majors are offered, Clarkson's bread and butter are its technical programs, particularly its slew of engineering majors. Students here gain exposure to the ever-growing variety of specialties in the field. And the extended snowy winters in Potsdam are great for ice hockey fans or ski bunnies looking for fresh powder.

The already strong engineering offerings recently got even bigger, with the addition of a bachelor's program in environmental engineering; a major in digital arts and sciences is also new.

The men's and women's Nordic skiing teams brought home national titles in 2004.

Overlaps

Cornell, Rensselaer Polytechnic, Rochester Institute of Technology, Syracuse, Worcester Polytechnic, University of Buffalo

Clarkson: Rolling admissions. Early decision: Dec. 1, Jan 15. Does not guarantee to meet demonstrated need. Campus interviews: recommended, informational. Alumni interviews: optional, informational. SATs: required. SAT II: optional. Accepts the Common Application and electronic applications. Essay question: optional essay.

Clemson University

Clemson, SC 29634

Clemson is a technically oriented university in the mold of Georgia Tech, Virginia Tech, and North Carolina State. Smaller than the latter two and more focused on undergraduates than Georgia Tech, Clemson serves up its education with ample helpings of school spirit and small town hospitality.

Website: www.clemson.edu
Location: Small town
Total Enrollment: 17,016
Undergraduates: 14,740
Male/Female: 55/45
SAT Ranges: V 550–630
  M 570–660
ACT Range: 24–29
Financial Aid: 38%
Expense: Pub $ $ $ $
Phi Beta Kappa: No
Applicants: 11,419
Accepted: 61%
Enrolled: 40%
Grad in 6 Years: 72%
Returning Freshmen: 89%
Academics: ✍ ✍ ✍
Social: ☎ ☎ ☎ ☎
Q of L: ★ ★ ★ ★
Admissions: (864) 656-2287
Email Address:
  cuadmissions@clemson.edu

Strongest Programs:
Engineering
Architecture
Landscape Architecture
Economics
Genetics

Nestled in the foothills of the Blue Ridge Mountains, Clemson University is a place where Southern spirit continues to flourish. The campus occupies terrain that once was walked by John C. Calhoun, former Southern senator and a Civil War–era rabble-rouser of the first degree. Today Clemson features quality academics in technical areas such as engineering and biology, and big-time athletics supported by strong school spirit.

CU's 1,400-acre campus is situated on what was once Fort Hill Plantation, the homestead of Thomas Green Clemson. The campus is surrounded by 17,000 acres of university farms and woodlands and offers a spectacular view of the nearby lake and mountains. Architectural styles are an eclectic mix of modern and 19th-century collegiate. Newer additions to the campus include an on-campus research facility for biotechnology and the McAdams Hall annex for computer science. Renovations have also been completed on Hardin Hall, with the addition of new "smart classrooms" and the student recreation facility, featuring a fitness center focusing on health education. The Campbell Graduate Engineering Center and the research facility for advanced materials are currently under construction.

Electrical engineering is the university's largest department, and computer engineering is among the nation's best in research on large-scale integrated computer circuitry and robotics. The College of Architecture, one of the school's most selective programs, offers intensive semesters at the Overseas Center for Building Research and Urban Study in Genoa, Italy. A fantastic resource for science enthusiasts and history buffs is the library's collection of first editions of the scientific work of Galileo and Newton. Because of the prevailing technical emphasis, most students interested in the liberal arts head "down country" to the University of South Carolina. Undergraduate teaching has always been one of Clemson's strong points, and for students interested in pursuing a liberal arts curriculum, the school has degrees in fine arts, philosophy, and languages and enjoys a strong regional reputation for its history program. Most students agree that engineering and architecture are the school's strongest programs, but also give high marks to business and agriculture. Highly motivated students should consider Calhoun College, Clemson's honors program—the oldest in South Carolina—open to freshmen who scored 1200 or above on their SATs and ranked in the top 10 percent of their high school graduating class. Clemson also offers exchange programs in Mexico, Scotland, Ecuador, Spain, England, Australia, and Italy.

General education requirements have recently been reorganized. They include courses in advanced writing, oral communications, mathematical, scientific, and technological literacy, social sciences, arts and humanities, crosscultural awareness, and science and technology in society. An electronic portfolio pilot was instituted in 2004; freshmen build their portfolio, demonstrating changes in competencies throughout their experiences at Clemson. Academically, the level of difficulty varies. "Students may get more competitive over co-op opportunities than over classes," one junior says. Professors run the gamut from average to stellar. "The quality of teaching varies," says a junior. "The best advice is to choose classes based on the professor's reputation, which is easy to find out." Students report some problems finishing a degree in four years, and class registration can be a hassle.

"Students may get more competitive over co-op opportunities than over classes."

Clemson's student body has a decidedly Southern air, as 78 percent of the undergrads hail from South Carolina, with most of the rest from neighboring states. The average Clemson student is friendly and conservative, and though, as a public institution, the school isn't affiliated with any church, there is a strong Southern Baptist presence on campus. Forty-two percent were in the top tenth of their high school graduating class. African Americans make up 7 percent of the student body, and Hispanics account for 1 percent and Asian Americans 2 percent. The university offers over 4,100 merit scholarships and nearly 400 athletic scholarships. Parking is the overwhelming complaint among the students.

Housing gets positive reviews, and 46 percent of the students live on campus, usually during their first two years. Most of the dorms are single-sex, though co-ed university-owned apartment complexes are also an option. "Apartment housing is competitive, but rooms on campus are usually available," says a student. Clemson House and Calhoun Courts, the co-ed halls, are considered the best places to be. "The west campus high-rise dorms are awesome," raves a junior. The dining facilities have been improving according to students. "They have specials and even ask students to contribute recipes," according to one student. Upperclassmen can cook for themselves, and each dorm has kitchen facilities.

Electrical engineering is the university's largest department, and computer engineering is among the nation's best in research on large-scale integrated computer circuitry and robotics.

After class, many students hop on their bikes and head to nearby Lake Hartwell. The beautiful Blue Ridge mountain range is also close by for hiking and camping, and beaches and ski slopes are both within driving distance. Atlanta and Charlotte are only two hours away by car, and Charleston is four hours away on the coast. Aside from the sports teams, fraternities and sororities provide most of the social life. Sixteen percent of Clemson men and 30 percent

"The west campus high-rise dorms are awesome."

of women go Greek. The town itself is pretty small, with a few bars and movie theaters, but some students love it. "Downtown is across the street from campus and has many bars," a student affairs major says.

Sports still help make the world go 'round at Clemson, and on weekends (when the Tiger teams are playing) there are pep rallies, cookouts, dances, and parties for the mobs of excited fans. The roads leading to campus are painted with large orange pawprints, an insignia that symbolizes great enthusiasm for Clemson sports. So, too, are half the fans at an athletic event, making the stands look like an orange grove. Football fever starts with the annual First Friday Parade, held before the first home game, and on every game day the campus dissolves into a sea of Tiger orange. Clemson has regained its former gridiron glory under the leadership of Coach Tommy Bowden. Hordes of Tiger fans cram "Death Valley" for every game and are especially rowdy when the reviled University of South Carolina Gamecocks are in town. Other very competitive athletic teams include basketball, baseball, and men's track.

No haven for carpetbaggers or liberals, Clemson is best at serving those whose interests lie in technical fields. School spirit is contagious, fueled by a love of

Overlaps

South Carolina, UNC–Chapel Hill, Georgia, Georgia Tech, Duke, Charleston

big-time college sports, and becomes lifelong for many Clemson students. Everyone can become part of the Clemson family, from Southern belle to Northern Yankee, as long as they're friendly, easygoing, and enthusiastic about life in general and the Tigers in particular.

If You Apply To ➤

Clemson: Early action: Dec. 1. Regular admissions: May 1. No campus or alumni interviews. SATs or ACTs: required. SAT I preferred. SAT IIs: optional. No essay question.

Colby College

Waterville, ME 04901

The northernmost outpost of private higher education in New England. Colby's picturesque small town setting is a short hop from the sea coast or the Maine wilderness. No frats since the college abolished them 20 years ago. A well-toned, outdoorsy student body in the mold of Middlebury, Williams, and Dartmouth.

Website: www.colby.edu
Location: Small city
Total Enrollment: 1,821
Undergraduates: 1,821
Male/Female: 53/47
SAT Ranges: V 640–720
    M 640–710
ACT Range: 27–31
Financial Aid: 39%
Expense: Pr $ $ $ $
Phi Beta Kappa: Yes
Applicants: 4,065
Accepted: 37%
Enrolled: 34%
Grad in 6 Years: 88%
Returning Freshmen: 92%
Academics: ✍ ✍ ✍ ✍½
Social: ☎ ☎ ☎
Q of L: ★★★★
Admissions: (800) 723-3032
Email Address:
    admissions@colby.edu

Strongest Programs:
Art
Economics
Government
English
International Studies

Colby College draws students who like to work hard and play harder, whether in the classroom or on the ski slopes. The nearby town of Waterville, Maine (population 20,000), offers few distractions, and close friendships with peers and professors help ward off the winter chill. Colby's top study abroad program offers students an opportunity to explore the world, and even those who don't spend a semester or year away can get a taste during the month of January, when Jan-Plan trips send Colby students far and wide. "Colby allows me to explore educational possibilities and experiences of all kinds, from taking a class with a top U.S. economist, to sea kayaking, to mentoring needy children in local schools," says a sophomore. "The setting is picturesque, and the faculty and students alike are friendly and warm."

Colby sits high on a hill, with beautiful views of the surrounding city and countryside. Its 714 acres include a wildlife preserve, miles of crosscountry trails, and a pond used in winter as an ice-skating rink. Georgian architecture predominates, and the oldest buildings are redbrick with white trim, ivy, and brass nameplates above their hunter-green doors. The more contemporary buildings lend a touch of modernity. One of the most iconic Colby buildings is the library tower, which is topped with a blue light. A $44 million plan to renovate Colby's residence halls and three dining halls continues, with Averill Hall gutted and renovated in recent years. The trustees have approved a campus expansion, which will add four buildings in the next decade, centered on the new Colby Green.

As a small college with a history of innovation and educational excellence, Colby encourages students to learn for learning's sake, rather than for a good grade. "Colby's academic climate is a well-balanced mix of work and enjoyment," says a sophomore. Students must complete distribution requirements in English composition, foreign language, "Areas" (one course each in arts, historical studies, literature, quantitative reasoning and social sciences, and two courses in natural sciences), "Diversity" (two courses focusing on how diversity has contributed to the human experience), and "Wellness" (five supper seminars over the first two semesters). Freshmen eager to fulfill that language requirement can ship off to Salamanca or Dijon to take care of it, delaying on-campus enrollment until the second semester.

Popular and well-regarded programs include economics and government, followed closely by English, international studies, environmental studies, and all of the natural sciences. A major in science, technology, and society has been added, while majors in Geology have been restructured.

Colby's faculty is unusually devoted to undergraduate teaching. "The faculty are the best part of Colby. They are here because they enjoy teaching and are concerned with your development as a whole person. Most professors encourage you to continue classroom discussions during office hours or over meals," says a senior. Nearly 60 percent of all classes have 25 or fewer students, allowing those highly lauded profs to spend more time with each student.

Colby was the first college to establish a special January term, back in 1962, and students must take three such terms for credit to graduate. Motivated students might use the month off to serve an internship, study abroad, or prepare an in-depth report. Less serious types head for the ski slopes or Southern beaches, and write a quick

> **"Colby allows me to explore educational possibilities and experiences of all kinds."**

paper at the end of the month. The school also sponsors Jan-Plan trips to everywhere from Nicaragua to Vietnam, including Bermuda (for biology). Other programs include Connecticut's Mystic Seaport (for marine biology), Kyoto, Japan, and the great cities of Europe. For would-be engineers, there is a joint 3–2 program with Dartmouth, and others may take exchange programs with Clark Atlanta and Howard. With all of these options, perhaps it's no wonder that 65 percent of Colby students spend some time abroad taking advantage of more than 50 approved international programs and another four of Colby's own, encompassing every continent except Antarctica. A high proportion of graduates enter the Peace Corps and the Foreign Service.

Only 12 percent of Colby students are Mainers; the rest learn to act like natives during the COOT program (Colby Outdoor Orientation Trips). These four-day excursions by bicycle, canoe, or foot introduce them to the beauty of the Maine wilderness or to service or theater experiences. The administration is striving to make Colby more diverse, sometimes even a bit too much for some tastes, as one senior complains: "The school has approached this problem by overemphasizing it in every area so as to stigmatize students from diverse backgrounds." African Americans account for 1 percent of the student body, Hispanics 3 percent, and Asian Americans contribute 5 percent. There are no athletic or merit scholarships available.

Ninety-three percent of Colby students live on campus, where residence halls have live-in faculty members. Newly renovated dorms are described as "very nice" to "beautiful" and offer single, double, and triple occupancy, with even some suites available. About 100 seniors live off campus each year in new apartment-style buildings. Dining halls cater to the various tastes, lifestyles, religions, and even holidays throughout the year. "The three dining halls do a wonderful job of providing delicious food and unique atmospheres. Students are free to eat at whichever one they want," states a senior.

When the weekend comes, you'll find most Colby students staying close to campus. "Waterville is not much of a college town; however, for dining there are a few hidden treasures," confides a sophomore. Although fraternities were abolished 20 years ago in response to rising alcohol use, students maintain an active party life. In response to student requests, administration has insti-

> **"The three dining halls do a wonderful job of providing delicious food and unique atmospheres."**

tuted a program allowing a glass of wine or beer at dinner on Friday nights in Dana dining hall for students of legal age. Still, there are options for those who choose not to imbibe, including "parties, shows, plays, talks, and concerts," according to a

As a small college with a history of innovation and educational excellence, Colby encourages students to learn for learning's sake, rather than for a good grade.

Only 12 percent of Colby students are Mainers; the rest learn to act like natives during the COOT program (Colby Outdoor Orientation Trips). These four-day excursions by bicycle, canoe, or foot introduce them to the beauty of the Maine wilderness or to service or theater experiences.

junior. Popular road trips include Augusta, Portland, and Freeport, Maine (home to the L.L. Bean factory and store). Also easy to reach are the bright lights of Boston and Montreal, and the slopes of Sugarloaf, Maine.

The Colby administration likes to share two "big secrets" about Maine winters: they're beautiful, and they're a lot harsher in the telling than in the living. Still, an enthusiasm for chilly weather and outdoor sports are the major nonacademic credentials needed to find contentment here. Everyone looks forward to football, lacrosse, and hockey games, as well as the annual winter carnival and snow-sculpture contest. Athletics have come a long way since the first intercollegiate croquet game, played at Colby in 1860, and in 2004–05 alone, Colby produced 22 All Americans in eight sports. Nonvarsity athletes are eager participants in 10 club teams and six intramural sports.

Colby's traditional New England liberal arts college vibe extends far beyond its small town setting and historic, ivy-covered buildings. It permeates the air, punctuated by the long-standing traditions, abundant school spirit, and caring faculty members who focus on developing their students' minds.

Overlaps

Bowdoin, Middlebury, Bates, Dartmouth, Colgate, Hamilton

If You Apply To ➤ **Colby:** Early decision: Nov. 15, Jan. 1. Regular admissions: Jan. 1. Financial aid: Feb. 1. Campus and alumni interviews: recommended, informational. SATs or ACTs: required. SAT IIs: optional. Accepts the Common Application and electronic applications. Essay questions: choose from quotes and relate to personal experience, issue, or thoughts on the future.

Colgate University

13 Oak Drive, Hamilton, NY 13346

At less than 3,000 students, Colgate is smaller than Bucknell and Dartmouth but bigger than Hamilton and Williams. Like the other four, it offers small town living and close interaction between students and faculty. Greek organizations and jock mentality are still well entrenched despite administrative efforts to neutralize them.

Website: www.colgate.edu
Location: Rural
Total Enrollment: 2,799
Undergraduates: 2,796
Male/Female: 48/52
SAT Ranges: V 630–710
   M 640–720
ACT Range: 28–32
Financial Aid: 42%
Expense: Pr $ $ $ $
Phi Beta Kappa: Yes
Applicants: 6,551
Accepted: 33%
Enrolled: 34%
Grad in 6 Years: 89%
Returning Freshmen: 94%
Academics: ⚏ ⚏ ⚏ ⚏ ½

Colgate University offers small town living, super skiing, and close student/faculty interaction. While you may see the same North Face or Patagonia fleece coming and going (and coming and going) as you stroll across campus, all students here aren't spun from the same recycled soda bottles. "There are the athletes, the bookworms, the partiers, the all-around kids, the preppy kids, the neat freaks, the drama kinds and queens, the activists—the list goes on and on," says a computer science and physics major. "But there are two things which all the students share: An enjoyment of learning for the sake of learning, and acquiring knowledge because it is intriguing and interesting." From the herbarium to the Devonian fossils to the 16-inch reflecting telescope, it's clear that Colgate has more to offer than just its picture-postcard setting.

Colgate's 13 founders started the school with 13 prayers and 13 dollars. Their prayers were answered in 1880, when toothpaste mogul William Colgate gave $50,000 to the fledgling university, enough to get the name changed from Madison to his own. Today, the 515-acre campus sits on a hillside in rural New York, overlooking the village of Hamilton. Ivy-covered limestone buildings peek out from tree-lined drives; lush green spaces are perfect for rugby, Frisbee, or other outdoor diversions, at least in the warmer months. Rolling hills and farmland surround the campus, making for stunning vistas during the snowy season, which stretches from mid-October to mid-March. The O'Connor Campus Center recently underwent a nearly $6 million renovation, and new student townhouses have been completed as well.

Aside from blazing a trail to rural New York, Colgate has led its peers in emphasizing interdisciplinary study. The faculty first established an interdisciplinary core program in 1928, and it's been a foundation of the curriculum ever since. Even now, all freshmen take a first-year seminar that introduces liberal arts topics, skills, and ways of learning. The seminars are capped at 18 students each, and there are more than 40 topics, ranging from the history of rock and roll to the advent of the atomic bomb. The seminars focus on individual needs and strengths, learning from classmates, and learning from resources beyond the classroom; academic advising also comes from the seminar instructor, since students don't declare majors until the sophomore year. Students also complete two courses from each of Colgate's three academic divisions: natural sciences and

"There are no TAs, so you will always have an actual professor."

math, social sciences, and humanities. Four courses in the liberal arts core—on Western traditions, the challenge of modernity, cultures, and scientific perspectives—round out the requirements and equip students to contemplate the issues they will face throughout their lives. Aside from a major (or two), Colgate also mandates foreign language proficiency, four physical education classes, and a swim test.

Students give high marks to the natural and social sciences, including economics, political science, and history, all of which are also among the most popular majors. English is likewise strong, and sociology and anthropology round out the list of programs with the highest enrollments. Befitting Colgate's rugged location, there are four concentrations within environmental studies: environmental biology, geography, geology, and economics. Classrooms and labs devoted to foreign language study help students gain comfort with another tongue—a good thing, since more than half participate in Colgate's off-campus study programs. Aside from programs led by faculty members in foreign locales, from England, Japan, and Nigeria to Russia and Central America, there are three domestic programs, such as one at the National Institutes of Health, in Bethesda, Maryland. Colgate also participates in the Maritime Studies Program* and the Semester at Sea.*

Classes at Colgate are small, and 97 percent of those taken by freshman have 50 or fewer students. Even better, "There are no TAs, so you will always have an actual professor, and all the professors hold office hours every week," says a freshman. Since most of the faculty lives within 10 miles of campus, "It is not uncommon for the professors to have a class over to their house for dinner, either to continue the conversation, or just to get to know you as people," adds an economics and political science major. While courses are challenging, students report that most people work together and help one another. Undergraduate research also wins raves, and each summer, more than 100 students work under faculty members as research assistants. The three-quarters of students who go straight into the workforce credit Colgate's strong and loyal alumni network with helping them land their first job.

"Colgate students are very active, whether in sports, volunteer work, student government, academic pursuits, or—most likely—a combination of all of these," says a neuroscience major. They're also overwhelmingly white graduates of public high schools, though only about a third are New Yorkers. African Americans and Hispanics each make up 4 percent of the student body, and Asian Americans add 6 percent—better than in the past, but still insufficient, students say. There are no merit scholarships, but Colgate now offers a varying number of awards in five men's and nine women's sports. Politically, this is a "generally apathetic campus," says a Chinese major. "I have seen about three protests in my time at Colgate: one to save a fraternity, one for gay, lesbian, bisexual and transgender issues, and one regarding the environment," agrees an economics and political science major.

(Continued)

Social: ☎ ☎ ☎
Q of L: ★ ★ ★
Admissions: (315) 228-7401
Email Address:
   admission@mail.colgate.edu

Strongest Programs:
Biology
Economics
Foreign Language and
   Literature
History
Philosophy
Political Science

The faculty first established an interdisciplinary core program in 1928, and it's been a foundation of the curriculum ever since. Even now, all freshmen take a first-year seminar that introduces liberal arts topics, skills, and ways of learning.

Ninety percent of Colgate students live in the dorms, which range from traditional buildings with fireplaces to newer facilities that seem more like hotels. "Even as a freshman, I lived in a spacious four-person room, with two doubles and a common room," says a sophomore. "Options range from one to five people per room

"Colgate students are very active."

the first year, to up to six as a sophomore (as well as a sophomore house on Broad Street), to theme housing, Greek housing, and apartment living as a junior or senior." About 250 upperclassmen are allowed to live off campus each year. Three of the four dining halls serve buffet-style, and the other is a la carte, with salad and sandwich bars, soup, cereal, and bagels always available; take-out food is provided at the campus center, known as the Coop. Campus chefs are also happy to make your favorite recipes and to deliver healthy snacks: "My roommates asked for carrot and celery sticks, and they appeared at the salad bar the next day!" says one student. "I had no trouble gaining the Freshman 15," another sighs.

Befitting Colgate's rugged location, there are four concentrations within environmental studies: environmental biology, geography, geology, and economics.

Hamilton is "the epitome of a college town—small, quaint, and very much a part of the university," says a junior. "We have three delis, two pizza places, two fancy places, and a coffee shop, as well as a number of small stores," a classmate adds. "When school is in session, the population more than doubles; the town really caters to the students, and vice versa." The town is within walking distance of campus, but there's also a free bus that cycles through every half-hour, especially nice in the dead of winter. Students enjoy free "Take Two" movies on Friday and Saturday nights, a cappella concerts featuring their friends, and open mic nights at Donovan's Pub or the Barge Canal Coffee Company, which Colgate opened in a downtown storefront. The coffeehouse is open to all, including townspeople, and has become very popular. "The atmosphere is terrific, and there are games, puzzles, magazines, and books to occupy your hours," gushes a senior. The Palace draws crowds with music, dancing, a bar, and a Mexican restaurant; it's also located downtown.

Back on campus, 37 percent of the men and 30 percent of the women join the Greek system, while debates (and lawsuits) continue over the proper balance between academics and social life. In an effort to cut down on alcohol consumption, hazing, and other problems that regularly get out of hand at Colgate, the administration forced fraternities and sororities to sell their off-campus houses to the university, resulting in an ongoing legal battle. For the outdoorsy, "Base Camp can direct you to campgrounds and other facilities to try out, and they will also rent you any

"The town really caters to the students and vice versa."

gear you might need," says a computer science and physics major. In addition to the required four-day orientation program, freshmen may also participate in Wilderness Adventure, where groups of six to eight canoe and hike in the Adirondacks, or in Outreach, which involves three days of community service in the surrounding area. Colgate students remain involved in the community through work as tutors, mentors, and student teachers, on Habitat for Humanity projects, and with the elderly. For those with wheels, skiing is 45 minutes away in Toggenburg, and the malls and city lights of Syracuse and Utica are roughly the same distance. Everyone looks forward to Spring Party Weekend, a last blast before finals, which celebrates the thaw with a carnival, barbecues, fireworks, and multiple bands. Winterfest is a traditional field day... played in two feet of snow.

While Colgate students participate in intramurals ranging from bowling to ultimate Frisbee, their most fervent cheers are reserved for Division I-AA football against Bucknell, and Division I men's lacrosse against Cornell. The women's basketball and lacrosse teams and the football and men's water polo squads all competed in their national championship tournaments recently, and softball and men's hockey won league titles. Even weekend warriors may take advantage of the Sanford Field House, the Lineberry natatorium, and the nationally recognized Seven Oaks golf course. There's also a trap-shooting range, a quarry for rock-climbing, miles of trails for running and cycling, and sailing and rowing facilities at Lake Moraine, five minutes away.

Colgate has come a long way. The school has led the way in interdisciplinary work and continues to do so now, both literally—with torchlight processions for incoming freshmen and graduating seniors—and figuratively, through its first-year seminar program. What else has remained constant? "Colgate seeks students who are eager to be a part of the community, who will add energy to the campus," says a sophomore.

If You Apply To ➤ **Colgate:** Early decision: Nov. 15, Jan. 15. Regular admissions and financial aid: Jan. 15. Guarantees to meet full demonstrated need. Campus and alumni interviews: optional, informational. SATs or ACTs: required. SAT IIs: optional. Accepts the Common Application and electronic applications. Essay question: personal statement.

Colorado College

14 East Cache La Poudre Street, Colorado Springs, CO 80903

The Block Plan is CC's calling card. It is great for in-depth study and field trips but less suited to projects that take an extended period of time. The Rockies draw outdoor enthusiasts and East Coasters who want to ski. CC is the only top liberal arts college between Iowa and the Pacific.

CC is one of few U.S. schools offering block scheduling, also known as the "One-Course-At-A-Time" method. For more than a century, CC's focus on creative approaches to academics and its breathtaking location in the heart of the Rocky Mountains have drawn liberal-leaning liberal arts enthusiasts who also like to go out and play.

Founded in 1874, the college campus lies at the foot of Pike's Peak, in the politically conservative town of Colorado Springs. The surrounding neighborhood is on the National Register of Historic Places, as are many CC buildings, including its first, Cutler Hall (1879), and Palmer Hall, named after town founder William J. Palmer, a major force behind the establishment of the college. The prevailing architectural styles are Romanesque and English Gothic, with some more modern structures thrown in. The Western Ridge dorm complex opened in fall 2002, offering apartment-style living for 290 students. A 54,000-square-foot building for the psychology, math, and geology departments, and the environmental sciences program, was finished in 2003. The Cornerstone Arts Building, with teaching and performance space, is being built.

CC requires students to take 32 courses, at least 18 outside their major department. Within those 32 courses, two must focus on the Western tradition; three on the non-Western tradition, minority culture, or gender studies; and two on the natural sciences, including lab or field study. Foreign language proficiency is also required, and students must complete either a six-course thematic minor, which examines an issue or theme, cultural group, geographic area or historical era, or six social sciences courses outside their major. What really defines the academic climate, though, is the block schedule (also see Cornell College in Iowa). Students take eight courses between early September and mid-May, but focus on each one, in turn, for three-and-a-half weeks. Some courses, such as neuroscience, are two blocks long. Four-and-a-half-day

Website:
www.coloradocollege.edu
Location: Urban
Total Enrollment: 2,044
Undergraduates: 2,011
Male/Female: 47/53
SAT Ranges: V 600–690
M 610–690
ACT Range: 25–30
Financial Aid: 47%
Expense: Pr $ $ $
Phi Beta Kappa: Yes
Applicants: 4,172
Accepted: 44%
Enrolled: 32%
Grad in 6 Years: 84%
Returning Freshmen: 91%
Academics: ✐ ✐ ✐ ✐
Social: ☎ ☎ ☎ ☎
Q of L: ★ ★ ★ ★
Admissions: (800) 542-7214
Email Address: admissions@ coloradocollege.edu

breaks separate the terms. The plan helps students stay focused, eliminating the temptation to let one course slide so that they can catch up in another. But there are trade-offs. Students say it can be hard to integrate material from courses taken one at a time. There's also the danger of burnout, because so much material is crammed into such a short span. Still, prevailing vibe is low-key. "You decide how rigorous the course is by how much effort you give," explains a freshman. "The only person you are ever really competing with is yourself." The First Year Experience program, with a student mentor and two advisors, helps students adjust.

Students at Colorado tend to be bright and independent; they say the school's best programs include the sciences and English. "Writing and hands-on experience are strong priorities," says a biology major. The block schedule permits some classes at unique times and in unique places—for instance, astronomy at midnight, or coral

Students say it can be hard to integrate material from courses taken one at a time. There's also the danger of burnout, because so much material is crammed into such a short span.

"You decide how rigorous the course is by how much effort you give."

biology work in the Caribbean. The college's popular program in Southwest studies includes time at its Baca campus, 175 miles away in the historic San Luis Valley. Other interesting interdisciplinary programs include Asian studies, studies in war and peace and American-ethnic studies. CC also offers study abroad in locations ranging from France and Germany to Japan, China, Tanzania, and Zimbabwe. Yet more options are available through the Associated Colleges of the Midwest.* More than half of the class of 2005 spent time abroad. And for students who want to see more of the U.S., there are arts and urban studies programs in Chicago, a Washington Semester for budding politicos, and a science semester at Tennessee's Oak Ridge National Laboratory.

Back on campus, the average class size is 13. Required courses aren't hard to get, since spots are secured with an auction system. At the beginning of each year, students get 80 points to "bid" on the classes they want. Those who bid the most for a particular class get a seat. And if you're going to take only one class at a time, it helps to like the teacher. Students say that's no problem here. "The professors are very accessible, and it is easy to have a good working relationship," says a history and political science major.

Just 29 percent of Colorado College students are in-staters; 3 percent are foreign, and the rest are from elsewhere in the U.S. "Most students come from families that are well-off, but are trying to defy societal norms," says a German major. "The school could definitely be classified as 'hippie,'" agrees a freshman. "The students tend to be incredibly smart, but grades don't matter that much to them." Minorities account for about 16 percent of the student body—2 percent are African American, 7 percent Hispanic, 4 percent Asian American, 1 percent American Indian, and 2 percent other minorities—and the school is trying to attract more. The Queer Straight Alliance; the Feminist Collective; the College Republicans; the Jewish Chaverim; and the Black Student Union also provide support to students of varied backgrounds and viewpoints. "It's a very liberal campus; most are outdoor, tree-hugging types," says a biology major. The admissions office places great weight on students' high school records, class rank, and essay. Only seniors are permitted to live off campus at Colorado College, so the other 73 percent of the student body bunks in the dorms. And while seniors don't have to move, a junior says it's easy to see why they do: "There's housing for about 80 percent of our study body, but a lot of

Students take eight courses between early September and mid-May, but focus on each one, in turn, for three-and-a-half weeks. Some courses, such as neuroscience, are two blocks long. Four-and-a-half-day breaks separate the terms.

"Writing and hands-on experience are strong priorities."

it sucks." Architecturally, dorms range from large brick halls to small houses; some are for freshmen only, others are same-sex, and still others offer a language or cultural theme. Campus residents give the dining hall chow a universal thumbs-down: "There is a good variety of food, but almost all of it is horrible," quips a freshman. "Many times, it can make you physically ill, and it just doesn't taste good." The dining options include an organic café, coffee bar, traditional dining hall, and a coffee house that showcases student music, poetry, and other talent.

When the weekend comes, students stay on campus for parties in friends' rooms or events sponsored by the "low-key" Greek system, which attracts 10 percent of the men and 16 percent of the women. Officially, no one under 21 is permitted to have alcohol, in the dorms or elsewhere, but students say enforcement is lax. "It's fairly easy to get alcohol from an upperclassman," says a biology major. For those who don't, won't, or can't imbibe, Herb 'n' Farm offers great smoothies. Each spring, the outdoors Llama-palooza festival features bands from on and off campus. For those seeking a bit of urban culture, Denver and Boulder are a short drive away. Most CC students love heading off campus to ski or hike, either at nearby resorts, or in Utah, New Mexico, or the Grand Canyon area. (Freshman Outdoor Orientation Trips help out-of-staters sort out the options, from backpacking and hiking to rafting, bicycling, and wind-surfing. Students may even reserve a college-owned mountainside cabin.) Service trips are sponsored during block breaks, and 84 percent of students do some type of community service.

> **"It's a very liberal campus; most are outdoor, tree-hugging types."**

When it comes to sports, most Colorado College teams compete in Division III, except for women's soccer and men's ice hockey, which are Division I. Men's ice hockey reached the playoffs in 2005, and women's lacrosse and volleyball, men's soccer, and men's and women's track and field all have made national tournament appearances in recent years. There's a huge rivalry with the University of Denver.

The block plan made Colorado College what it is today, and the school continues to build on this reputation. While CC is intense, and the schedule is not for everyone, "I really enjoy the people and the unique learning environment," a freshman says. "It's small and conducive to the way I learn."

Overlaps

University of Colorado, Middlebury, University of Denver, Whitman, Colby

---

If You Apply To ➤

Colorado College: Early action: Nov. 15. Regular admissions: Jan. 15. Financial aid: Feb. 15. Housing: June 20. Guarantees to meet demonstrated need. Campus interviews: optional, informational. No alumni interviews. SATs or ACTs: required. No SAT IIs. Accepts the Common Application and electronic applications. Essay questions: why Colorado College, and design your own three-and-a-half week intellectual adventure.

University of Colorado at Boulder

BEST BUY

Office of Admissions, 552 UCB, Boulder, CO 80309-0552

Boulder is a legendary place that draws everyone from East Coast ski bums to California refugees. The scenery is breathtaking and the science programs are first-rate. The University of Arizona is the only public university of similar stature in the Mountain West. Check out the residential academic programs.

Wild buffalo may be all but extinct on America's Great Plains, but they're in boisterous residence, proudly wearing gold and black, at the University of Colorado at Boulder. A raft of scholars' programs, learning communities, and academic neighborhoods give the campus a community feel, and stress is no problem thanks to the active social scene, which emphasizes nature, fitness, sports, and outdoor pursuits. With more than 300 days of sunshine a year, is it any wonder students here are a happy lot?

Website: www.colorado.edu
Location: Suburban
Total Enrollment: 29,258
Undergraduates: 24,710
Male/Female: 53/47

(Continued)

SAT Ranges: V 530–630
   M 550–650
ACT Range: 23–28
Financial Aid: 32%
Expense: Pub $
Phi Beta Kappa: Yes
Applicants: 19,360
Accepted: 85%
Enrolled: 31%
Grad in 6 Years: 66%
Returning Freshmen: 84%
Academics: ✍ ✍ ✍ ✍
Social: 🏆 🏆 🏆 🏆 🏆
Q of L: ★ ★ ★
Admissions: (303) 492-6301
Email Address: N/A

Strongest Programs:
Physics
Psychology
Geography
Applied Mathematics
Biology
Physiology
Music

Boulder has tried to make its mammoth campus seem smaller through "academic neighborhoods" focusing on topics such as leadership, diversity, natural or social sciences, international studies, engineering, music, and the American West.

Tree-shaded walkways, winding bike paths, open spaces, and an incredible view of the dramatic Flatirons rock formation makes CU's 600-acre Boulder campus a haven for students from both coasts and for Colorado residents eager to pursue knowledge in a snowy paradise. Campus buildings, in a rural Italian style, are Colorado sandstone with red tile roofs. In fact, the campus tends to look and feel a bit Ivy League, which is not surprising when you know that CU's architect also worked for Yale and Princeton. The 45,000-square-foot Discovery Learning Center gives engineering students nine labs in which to tackle society's challenges with video-conferencing and other high-tech capabilities. The University Memorial Center has received a $27 million facelift and expansion, and Folsom Stadium has a 125,000-square-foot addition. The Williams Village residence hall complex has added 1,900 apartment-style beds and the most recent addition is the ATLAS Center which houses modern technology-enhanced teaching, learning, and research facilities.

Entering freshmen at CU choose from four colleges and one school: arts and sciences (the easiest), architecture and planning, music, engineering and applied science (the hardest, students say), and business. Transfers may apply to two additional schools: journalism and education. Each has different entrance standards and requirements; music, for example, requires an audition. General education requirements for the 70 percent of students who enroll in arts and sciences are designed to provide a broad background in the liberal arts to complement their major specialization. The requirements cover four skills-acquisition areas—writing, quantitative reasoning and math, critical thinking, and foreign language—and seven content areas: historical context, culture and gender diversity, U.S. context, natural sciences, contemporary societies, literature and the arts, and ideals and values.

In a typical semester, CU–Boulder may offer 2,500 undergraduate courses in 100 fields. Among the best choices is molecular, cellular, and developmental biology, which takes advantage of state-of-the-art electron microscopes. CU–Boulder also receives the second-most NASA funding of any university in the nation, leading to unparalleled opportunities for the design, construction, and flight of model spacecraft—and to 17 CU alumni having worked as astronauts. CU distinguished professor Carl Wieman and adjunct professor Eric Cornell of the National Institute of Standards and Technology

> "The faculty at Boulder is extremely knowledgeable on their subject matter."

won the Nobel Prize for Physics in 2001. Business, engineering, sociology, and psychology are likewise strong. Students say the quality of teaching is very good. "The faculty at Boulder is extremely knowledgeable on their subject matter," says a junior. "Most importantly, they are always more than willing to share their knowledge with all students." A new department, aimed at preparing undergrads for careers in health care, his quickly become the second most popular on campus.

Boulder has tried to make its mammoth campus seem smaller through "academic neighborhoods" focusing on topics such as leadership, diversity, natural or social sciences, international studies, engineering, music, and the American West. Through these programs, students take one or two courses, each limited to 25 students, in their residence halls. "The Residential Academic Program for freshmen is essential for gaining a well-rounded experience at CU," advises a senior. The Presidents Leadership Class is a four-year scholarship program that exposes the most promising students to political, business, and community leaders through seminars, work and study trips, and site visits. The Undergraduate Academy offers special activities and advising for 150 to 200 of CU's most "intellectually committed" students, chosen for their excitement about learning and academic success.

Sixty-eight percent of CU's student body comes from Colorado, and by state regulation that fraction can be no lower than 55 percent, on average, over a three-year period. "I cannot characterize CU as a very diverse campus," laments one philosophy major. Hispanics and Asian Americans each comprise 6 percent of the total, and African Americans make up 2 percent. CU leans liberal, and important campus issues include environmental awareness, ethnic issues, and the war in Iraq. Sixteen percent of undergrads receive merit scholarships worth an average of $5,496, and 232 athletes receive scholarships as well.

First-year students are required to live on campus, where rooms get good ratings. "The dorms on campus are very comfortable, well maintained, and well supervised," says one student. Most sophomores, juniors, and seniors, however, find off-campus digs in Boulder. Those who want to stay on campus are advised to make early reservations for Farrand, Sewall, or Kittredge halls. All rooms come with microwaves, refrigerators, cable TV, and high-speed Internet hook-ups.

"I cannot characterize CU as a very diverse campus."

Generally, students say campus is safe, helped by 30 emergency telephones along walkways and paths, and 16 more in the parking structures. CU also offers walking and riding escorts at night. An alternative to the dining hall is the student-run Alferd Packer Memorial Grill, which provides fast food under innocent auspices. Boulder students and trivia buffs know, however, that Packer was a controversial 19th-century folk figure known as the "Colorado Cannibal." Bon appetit.

Eight percent of CU men and 11 percent of women go Greek, though fraternity and sorority parties have changed dramatically since CU's chapters became the first in the nation to voluntarily make their houses dry. On campus, the ban on alcohol is taken seriously, and dorms are officially "substance-free." Get caught with booze two times while underage, and you'll be booted from school housing. Even if you don't drink, though, you'll surely find something to do. "Social life is great because Boulder is one of the best college towns in America," says a biochemistry major. "Only in Boulder can you go skiing, hiking, boating and to a play, all in the same day," boasts another student. For the culturally minded, the university and the city of Boulder offer films and plays, the renowned Colorado Shakespeare Festival, and concerts by top rock bands. Even better, Denver is only 30 miles southeast, reachable by a free bus service. Day trips to ski resorts like Breckenridge, Vail, and Aspen largely replace weekend getaways here, but for those who've got to get out of the cold, Las Vegas isn't so far, says one student. For a drive to the slopes, the Eldora ski area—with 12 lifts, 53 trails, runs up to two miles long, and a vertical drop of as much as 1,400 feet—is just a half hour from campus.

Aside from skiing, exercise is the leading extracurricular activity at CU. The school's Triathlon Club has won the USA Triathlon National Challenge for seven years running, and CU-Boulder has also captured national titles in cycling and mountain biking. Just $150 a year gives students access to the Student Recreation Center, with swim-

"CU–Boulder is energy."

ming pools, basketball and tennis courts, three weight rooms, an indoor rock climbing gym, and an ice-skating rink. (Over 90 percent of CU students use the facility regularly.) The football program, which competes in the Big 12, has had its share of success on the field but is still reeling from a national scandal involving allegations of sexual assault and recruiting violations that raised embarrassing questions about the university's real values. Each year, fans flock to Denver for the game against Colorado State, and any showdown with Nebraska is sure to get students riled up. Ralphie, the live buffalo who acts as CU's mascot, doesn't miss a game—and neither do many students.

"CU–Boulder is energy. Every student, teacher and department always has something new and exciting going on. It would be very hard to get bored here," claims one senior. If you want to exercise your body as well as your mind, forget the ivy-covered bricks and gray city skies endemic to so many Eastern institutions, and consider going west instead.

Entering freshmen at CU choose from four colleges and one school: arts and sciences (the easiest), architecture and planning, music, engineering and applied science (the hardest, students say), and business.

Overlaps

Colorado State, UCLA, University of Arizona, University of Illinois, University of Minnesota, University of Northern Colorado

If You Apply To ➤

CU–Boulder: Rolling admissions: Sept. 9. Regular admissions: Jan. 15. Financial aid: Apr. 1. Housing: May 1. Campus interviews: optional, informational. No alumni interviews. SATs or ACTs: required. SAT II: optional. Apply to one of four colleges and one school. Accepts electronic applications. Essay question: optional.

Colorado School of Mines

1811 Elm Street, Golden, CO 80401-1842

The preeminent technical institute in the Mountain West. Twice as big as New Mexico Tech, but one-tenth the size of Texas Tech. Best-known for mining-related fields but strong in many areas of engineering. Men outnumber women three to one, and Golden provides little other than a nice view of the mountains.

Website: www.mines.edu
Location: Small town
Total Enrollment: 3,666
Undergraduates: 2,770
Male/Female: 77/23
SAT Ranges: V 540–650
  M 630–690
ACT Range: 25–29
Financial Aid: 74%
Expense: Pub $ $ $
Phi Beta Kappa: Yes
Applicants: 3,168
Accepted: 79%
Enrolled: 34%
Grad in 6 Years: 67%
Returning Freshmen: 84%
Academics: ✑ ✑ ✑ ½
Social: ☎ ☎ ☎
Q of L: ★ ★
Admissions: (303) 273-3220
Email Address:
  admit@mines.edu

Strongest Programs:
Geology/Geophysics
Mining Engineering
Petroleum Engineering
Metallurgy and Materials
  Engineering
Chemical Engineering
Engineering Physics

If you're a bit of a geek whose only dilemma is what type of engineer to become, and you want to spend your scarce free time hiking, biking, and skiing with friends, then Colorado School of Mines may be the school for you. The school's small size and rugged location endear it to the mostly male students who shoulder heavy workloads to earn their degrees—and truly enjoy starting salaries averaging $52,000 a year. "There are often fun and entertaining conversations that could only be possible with the types of students here," says a sophomore mechanical engineering major. Just down the road from Coors Brewing Co., which taps the Rockies for its legendary brews, students at Mines learn to tap the same mountains for coal, oil, and other natural resources.

CSM's 373-acre campus sits in the shadow of the spectacular Rocky Mountains in tiny Golden, Colorado. Architectural styles range from turn-of-the-century gold dome to present-day modern, and native trees and greenery punctuate lush lawns. The traditional dorms recently received $4 million in renovations, and $3 million has been spent to build three new sorority houses. Another $6 million was spent to build new student apartments and recreation fields. Next on tap are a $25 million Student Wellness Center and a $2.5 million expansion of a classroom building. A $10 million research building was completed in 2003.

Academics at Mines are rigorous. All freshmen take the same first-year program, which includes chemistry, calculus, physical education, physics, design, earth and environmental systems, quantitative chemical measurement, nature and human values, and the Freshman Success Seminar, an advising and mentoring course designed to increase retention. Because of CSM's narrow focus, the undergraduate majors—or "options," as they're called—are quite good. There's plenty of variety, as long as you like engineering; programs range from geophysical, geological, and petroleum to civil, electrical, and mechanical. Courses in a student's option start in the second semester of sophomore year, after yet more calculus, physics, and differential equations. Mines offers the only BS degree in economics in of Colorado. Physics has grown, now enrolling 8 percent of undergraduates, and the school has been investing more in humanities and social sciences.

Pass/fail grading is unheard of at Mines, but failing grades are not. "A lot of students come in expecting to excel like they did in high school, but this really does not happen very often," a junior says. Professors are well-qualified and usually helpful, but a junior warns that "once in a while, you will have professors that cares more about their research." Adjunct professors, who work in the fields they teach, draw raves for bringing real-world application into the classroom. Forty-five percent of freshman classes have fewer than 45 students, but 4 percent are packed with more than 100 students. The required two-semester EPICS program—the acronym stands for Engineering Practices Introductory Course Sequence—helps develop communications, teamwork, and problem-solving skills with weekly presentations and written reports. Students say teamwork helps soften the load a bit. "Because the courses are so difficult, the students tend to help each other rather than compete. In my experience, as long as everyone passes a course, we all won," one student says.

CSM supplements coursework with a required six-week summer field session, enabling students to gain hands-on experience. About 120 undergraduates participate in the McBride Honors Program in Pubic Affairs, which includes seminars and off-campus activities that encourage them to think differently about the implications of technology. CSM also offers the opportunity to live and study at more than 50 universities in Europe, Australia, Latin America, Asia, and the Middle East, though only 5 to 7 percent of students take part. Each year, 60 to 80 undergraduates participate in research with faculty members or on their own.

CSM is a state school, making it a good deal for homegrown students, who comprise 80 percent of the student body. "Not only do we all share the same classes, but most of the same interests," a sophomore says. "Since the students here are all science and engineering majors, we all have a lot in common." A classmate is

> "Because the courses are so difficult, the students tend to help each other rather than compete."

more blunt, saying Mines attracts "a lot of nerds." Hispanics comprise 6 percent of the student body, Asian Americans 5 percent, and African Americans and Asian Americans each add 1 percent. More than 250 merit scholarships averaging $5,000 are available to qualified students, and student-athletes may vie for 175 athletic scholarships.

Forty-five percent of CSM students—mostly freshmen—live in the residence halls. Most buildings are co-ed, though the preponderance of men results in a few single-sex dorms. "All the residence halls have been refurbished and are looking better than ever," a sophomore says. Most upperclassmen move to fraternity or sorority housing, college-owned apartments, or off-campus condos and houses. There's only one cafeteria, and a sophomore says "food tends to be very repetitive and mostly from frozen sources."

There is life outside of the library here. "There is a lot that goes on on campus," a junior says. "There is always a club putting together an event or just students throwing parties." CU–Boulder offers more partying 20 minutes away. Mines also has an active Greek system, with fraternities and sororities attracting 18 percent of the men and 22 percent of women. Still, rush is dry, and, owing to Mines' small size, those serving the alcohol almost always know the age of those trying to obtain it, making it tough for the underage to imbibe. Social life also includes comedy shows, homecoming, and Engineering Days—a three-day party with fireworks, a pig roast, tricycle races, taco-eating contests, and 25-cent beers. The celebration includes the M-climb, in which freshmen hike up Mount Zion lugging a 10-pound rock, "and white-

> "There is always a club putting together an event or just students throwing parties."

wash it, and each other," says one participant. The rock is added to an M formation atop the mountain, then "seniors return to take down a rock, completing the cycle."

CSM's location at the base of the Rockies means gorgeous Colorado weather (make sure to bring sunscreen) and easy access to skiing, hiking, mountain climbing, and biking. Denver is also nearby, and aside from its museums, concerts, and sports teams, the city is home to many government agencies and businesses involved in natural resources, computers, and technology, including the regional offices of the U.S. Geological Survey and Bureau of Mines. Golden hosts the

The traditional dorms recently received $4 million in renovations, and $3 million has been spent to build three new sorority houses. Another $6 million was spent to build new student apartments and recreation fields.

Physics has grown, now enrolling 8 percent of undergraduates, and the school has been investing more in humanities and social sciences.

National Earthquake Center, the National Renewable Energy Laboratory, and, of course, the Coors Brewery. (The 3,000-foot pipeline that runs from the Coors plant to campus is there to convert excess steam from the brewery into heat for the school—not to supply the frats with the foamy stuff.) The biggest complaints are too much homework and not enough girls. Road trips to Las Vegas or Texas provide some respite.

Despite the abundance of wacky school traditions, CSM competes in Division II, so there aren't many true athletic rivalries. In 2004, the football team reached the second round of the NCAA playoffs. Men's and women's basketball are competitive, and women's soccer was added as a varsity sport in 2005. The intramural program has grown dramatically, with 70 percent of students now participating.

While time spent in the classroom at Mines may not be fun, for those who are focused on engineering, educational options don't get much better than those offered here. "Professors are extremely smart and more than willing to help," a junior math and computer science major says. But that doesn't mean academics are the only thing CSM has to offer. "Our school is academically challenging, but it has all the social events and an environment like any college."

Overlaps

University of Colorado, Colorado State, MIT, Texas A&M, University of Texas, USAF Academy

If You Apply To ➤

CSM: Rolling admissions. Regular admissions: Jun. 1. Financial aid: Mar. 1. Housing: May 1. Guarantees to meet demonstrated need. Campus and alumni interviews: optional, informational. SATs or ACTs: required. SAT IIs: optional. Accepts and prefers electronic applications. No essay question.

Columbia College

212 Hamilton Hall, New York, NY 10027

Columbia may soon leave Yale in the dust as the third most selective university in the Ivy League. Applications have doubled in the past 10 years for one simple reason: Manhattan trumps New Haven, Providence, Ithaca, and every other Ivy League city, with the possible exception of Boston. The heart of Columbia is still the core.

Website: www.columbia.edu
Location: Urban
Total Enrollment: 17,405
Undergraduates: 5,661
Male/Female: 54/46
SAT Ranges: V 670–760
  M 670–780
ACT Range: 28–33
Financial Aid: 40%
Expense: Pr $ $ $ $
Phi Beta Kappa: Yes
Applicants: 18,125
Accepted: 13%
Enrolled: 58%
Grad in 6 Years: 92%
Returning Freshmen: 98%

Though students entering Columbia College will, of course, expect the rigorous academic program they'll encounter at this Ivy League school, there's no room here in the heart of Manhattan for the bookish nerd. Students must be streetwise, urbane, and together enough to handle one of the most cosmopolitan cities in the world. "It's an Ivy League school with a campus in the leading cultural center of the United States," says a sophomore. CC lets its students experience life in the Big Apple, but serves as a refuge when it becomes necessary to escape from New York; ideally, Columbians can easily be part of the "real world" while simultaneously immersing themselves in the best academia has to offer.

Although Columbia is among the smallest colleges in the Ivy League, its atmosphere is far from intimate. With a total universitywide enrollment of 21,000 students, says one, "It's easy to feel lost." Still, the college is the jewel in the university's crown and the focus is "unquestionably oriented toward undergraduate education," reports a classics major. Columbia's campus has a large central quadrangle in front of Butler Library and at the foot of the steps leading past the statue of Alma Mater to Low Library, which is now the administration building. The red-brick, copper-roofed neoclassical buildings are "stunning," and the layout, says an undergrad, "is well thought out and manages to provide a beautiful setting with an economy of space."

Columbia is an intellectual school, not a preprofessional one, and even though 60 percent of the students aspire to law or medical school (they enjoy a 90 percent acceptance rate), "we are mostly content to be liberal artists for as long as possible," says an English major. Even the 30 percent of undergraduates who enroll in the School of Engineering and Applied Sciences pursue "technical education" with a liberal arts base. Almost all departments that offer undergraduate majors are strong, notably English, history, political science, and psychology. Chemistry and biology are among the best of Columbia's high-quality science offerings. The Earth and Environmental Science department owns 200 acres in Rockland County, home to many rocks and much seismographic equipment. There are 35 offerings in foreign languages, ranging from Serbo-Croatian to Uzbek to Hausa. The fine arts are not fabulous, but are improving, thanks to departmental reorganization, new facilities, and joint offerings with schools such as the Juilliard School of Music. And while the administration admits that the economics and computer science departments are geared too much toward graduate students, at least the comp-sci undergrads benefit from an abundance of equipment. Columbia offers many challenging combined majors such as philosophy/economics and biology/psychology. The East Asian languages and cultures department is one of the best anywhere. There is also an African American studies major and a women's studies major that delves into topics from the Asian woman's perspective to the lesbian experience in literature.

The kernel of the undergraduate experience is the college's renowned core curriculum. While these courses occupy most of the first two years and can become laborious, students generally praise them as worthwhile and enriching: "You learn how to read analytically, write sharply, and speak succinctly, and you are exposed to the greatest ideas in Western art, music, literature, and philosophy," exclaims an

"It's an Ivy League school with a campus in the leading cultural center of the United States."

enlightened sociology major. The value of the Western emphasis of the core, however, is a subject of perennial debate. "Why should we study the Western tradition when it represents sexism, racism, imperialism, and exploitation?" asks one incensed student. "The canon is composed almost exclusively of dead European males." Yet, as it has since World War I, the college remains committed to the core while at the same time expanding the diversity of the canon and requiring core classes on non-Western cultures.

Two of the most demanding introductory courses in the Ivy League—Contemporary Civilization and Literature Humanities—form the basis of the core. Both are yearlong and taught in small sections, generally by full profs. "Nearly everything I'd grown up believing was questioned in one way or another. They forced me to examine my life and to ponder how I fit into the big picture," states an art history major. LitHum (as it is affectionately called) covers about 26 masterpieces of literature from Homer to Dostoyevsky, usually with some Sappho, Jane Austen, and Virginia Woolf thrown in for alternative perspectives. CC examines political and moral philosophy from Plato to Camus, though professors have some leeway in choosing 20th-century selections. One semester each of art and humanities is required and, while not given the same reverence as their literary counterparts, are eye-opening all the same. Foreign language proficiency is required, as are two semesters of science; two semesters of "extended core" classes dealing in cultures not covered in the other core requirements; two semesters of phys ed; and logic and rhetoric, a one-semester, argumentative writing class that first-year students reportedly "either love or hate."

Columbia is tough, and students always have something to read or write. Student/faculty interaction is largely dependent on student initiative. Additional

(Continued)

Academics: 🎓 🎓 🎓 🎓 🎓
Social: ☎ ☎ ☎
Q of L: ★ ★ ★ ★
Admissions: (212) 854-2522
Email Address: ugrad-admiss@columbia.edu

Strongest Programs:
English
History
Political Science
Economics
Dance
Drama
Chemistry
Biology

Social life on campus is best described as mellow. Rarely are there big all-inclusive bashes, the exceptions being fall's '60s throwback, Realityfest, and spring's Columbiafest.

interaction stems from professorial involvement in campus politics and forums and from the faculty-in-residence program, which houses professors and their families in spruced-up apartments in several of the residence halls. First-year students are assigned an advisor and receive a faculty advisor when they declare a major at the end of sophomore year. Columbia students can take classes at Barnard, which maintains its own faculty, reported to be "more caring and involved than Columbia's."

"You learn how to read analytically, write sharply, and speak succinctly."

As at Barnard, students can also take graduate-level courses in several departments, notably political science, gaining access to the resources of the School of International and Public Affairs and its multitude of regional institutes. For students wishing to spend time away from New York, there are summer, semester, and one-year programs at the Reid Hall campus in Paris; other programs include opportunities with Kyoto University in Japan, Howard University in Washington, D.C., Oxford or Cambridge in England, and The Free University of Berlin. Columbia University engineering students suffer through the core, too—they take almost all of their classes with CC students during their first two years.

To call Columbia diverse would be "a gross understatement," says a sophomore. "We make Noah's Ark look homogeneous." In fact, Columbia has the largest percentage of students of color in the Ivy League; 8 percent are African American, 8 percent are Hispanic, and 22 percent are Asian American. Twenty-seven percent of the students come from New York. Socially, the campus is also diverse. In a city such as New York, "diversity is assumed," says one student.

Almost all departments that offer undergraduate majors are strong, notably English, history, political science, and psychology. Chemistry and biology are among the best of Columbia's high-quality science offerings.

Columbia remains one of the nation's most liberal campuses. "Columbia has always been known for its tradition of social and political activism," says a junior. "Students are not afraid to protest to get what they want." No one group dominates campus life. Although 15 percent of the men and 9 percent of the women go Greek, Columbia is hardly a Hellenocentric campus, namely because, as a junior argues, "the frats are chock-full of athletic recruits, the organizations—even the co-ed ones—are deemed elitist and politically incorrect, and there are too many better things to do in NYC on a Friday night than getting trashed in the basement of some random house." The advent of co-ed houses has raised interest in Greek life as has the arrival of sororities open to both Columbia and Barnard women.

With the New York housing market out of control, 98 percent of Columbia students live in university housing, which is guaranteed for four years. Security at the dorms is rated as excellent by students, and every person entering has to flash an ID to the guard on duty at the front door or be signed in by a resident of the building. One exciting aspect of Columbia housing is that many rooms are singles, and it is possible to go all four years without a roommate. Carman Hall is the exclusively first-year dorm and "the fact that you get to meet your classmates compensates for the noise and hideous cinder-block walls," says a music major. First-year students can also live in buildings with students of all years. "Living with upperclasspeople was great. They knew the ins and outs of the university and the neighborhood. It wasn't the blind leading the blind," offers a junior. First-year students are automatically placed on a 19-meal-a-week plan and take most of those meals at John Jay, an all-you-can-eat "binge-a-rama with salad bar, deli, grill, and huge dessert bar." Many soon-bloated students scale down their meal plans or convert to points, a buy-what-you-want arrangement with account information stored electronically on student ID cards. Several dorms have kitchens, allowing students to do much of their own cooking. Some students dine at the kosher dining hall at Barnard.

"We make Noah's Ark look homogeneous."

The kernel of the undergraduate experience is the college's renowned core curriculum.

Social life on campus is best described as mellow. Rarely are there big all-inclusive bashes, the exceptions being fall's '60s throwback, Realityfest, and spring's

Columbiafest. "The social scene here is well-balanced between school events, concerts, and dances, and the variety of activities the city offers," says a senior.

Columbia athletics don't inspire the rabid loyalty of, say, a Florida State, because "Columbia students are individualists," according to one sophomore. "This is not a school that rallies together at football games." Still, the fencing teams are superlative, and men's soccer and basketball are also strong. As an urban school, Columbia lacks team field facilities on campus; however, a mere 100 blocks to the north are the modern Baker Field, home of the football stadium, the soccer fields, an Olympic track, and the crew boathouse. On campus, the Dodge Gymnasium, an underground facility, houses four levels of basketball courts, swimming pools, weight rooms, and exercise equipment. The gym is often crowded and not all the stuff is wonderful. "It does the job, as well as providing for the best pickup basketball this side of Riverside Park," notes a sophomore. Intramural and club sports are popular, with men's and women's Ultimate Frisbee both national competitors.

> "Columbia students are individualists."

Columbians are proud that they are going to college in New York City, and most would have it no other way. Explains an art history major: "Choosing to isolate oneself in the middle of nowhere for four years isn't what college is about. It's about taking one's place as an adult in an adult society. Columbia is the perfect place for that."

Overlaps
Harvard, Yale, MIT, Princeton, Stanford, University of Pennsylvania

If You Apply To ➤

Columbia: Early decision: Nov. 1. Regular admissions: Jan. 1. Financial aid: Jan. 15. Guarantees to meet full demonstrated need. Campus interviews: not available. Alumni interviews: optional, evaluative. SATs or ACTs: required. SAT IIs: required (any two). Essay: personal statement.

University of Connecticut

Tasker Building, 2131 Hillside Road, Unit 3088, Storrs, CT 06269-3088

Squeezed in among the likes of Yale, Brown, Wesleyan, Trinity, and UMass—all within a two-hour drive—UConn could be forgiven for having an inferiority complex. But championship basketball teams, both men and women, have ignited Husky pride, and the university's mammoth rebuilding project is boosting its appeal.

UConn, the top public university in New England, has seen billions of dollars poured into improving and expanding its facilities in the past decade. Couple the new buildings with the glow of two championship basketball teams, a wealth of research opportunities, and more than 250 clubs and organizations, and it's clear why students who in the past might have dismissed it as a "cow college" are choosing UConn, even when they have other options. "It's the perfect atmosphere to go to college in," says a communications major. "The academics are challenging and interesting, and the social setting is fun and diverse."

UConn's 4,000-acre campus is about 23 miles northeast of Hartford. Building styles range from collegiate Gothic and neoclassical to half-century-old redbrick. Dense woods surround the campus, which also boasts two lakes, Swan and Mirror. Ongoing renovations are the norm, sparking jokes about the "University of Construction," but the results are impressive: an expanded and renovated student union, the newly expanded Neag School of Education, a new School of Pharmacy, a

Website: www.uconn.edu
Location: Rural
Total Enrollment: 18,653
Undergraduates: 14,752
Male/Female: 48/52
SAT Ranges: V 530–630
    M 550–640
Financial Aid: 48%
Expense: Pub $ $ $ $
Phi Beta Kappa: Yes
Applicants: 18,466
Accepted: 50%
Enrolled: 35%

(Continued)

Grad in 6 Years: 71%

Returning Freshmen: 90%

Academics: ✍ ✍ ✍ ✍

Social: 🐾 🐾 🐾

Q of L: ★ ★ ★

Admissions: (860) 486-3137

Email Address:

beahusky@uconn.edu

Strongest Programs:

Biosciences

Communication Sciences

Business

Education

Engineering

Pharmacy

Psychology

Physical therapy

state-of-the-art biophysics building, a new five-story Information Technologies Engineering Building, a 40,000-seat football stadium, new student housing (with more on the way), and other projects.

Students say UConn's strongest offerings are preprofessional, including business, engineering, education, pharmacy, and allied health, including nursing and physical therapy. Also notable are basic sciences, history, linguistics, psychology, and, of course, agriculture. (UConn was founded more than a century ago as a farm school; it's where America learned to get more eggs per chicken by leaving the lights on in the coops.) In addition to new buildings, UConn has been adding new curricula, including a program that combines biodiversity and conservation biology with public policy. There are also new multi-disciplinary programs in neurosciences, cognitive science, American studies, aquaculture, survey research, coastal studies, urban and community studies, and human rights. Engineering is demanding, and, as at many schools, it has a relatively high attrition rate, with many students switching to the less-rigorous major in management information systems. UConn is also the only public university in New England to offer majors in environmental engineering, computer engineering, computer science, and metallurgy and materials engineering. New majors in engineering physics and biomedical engineering bring the total number of undergraduate engineering specialties to 14. A special program in medicine and dentistry allows students to earn bachelor's degrees in any of UConn's more than 100 disciplines, and guarantees admission to the School of Medicine or Dental Medicine if they meet all criteria. Administrators candidly admit that fine arts are a weak spot.

UConn's core requirements include courses in four basic areas: arts and humanities, social sciences, diversity/multiculturalism, and science and technology. Also required are two foreign language courses, waived if a student has studied three years of a single language in high school—and competency in computer technology and information literacy. Seminar-style writing classes are available to all freshmen, and 75 percent also take one or more First Year Experience courses focusing on time management, how to use the library, and other useful skills. The Academic Center for Exploratory Students helps freshmen and sophomores who still need to decide on a major. Students applaud the enthusiasm of their professors—and the graduate teaching assistants who administer tests, collect assignments, and run labs and discussion groups. "Quality teaching is the trademark of a UConn education. With the top research and academic faculty, students receive quality educations," a junior finance major says. "I had over half my freshman year classes taught by full professors," says an education major.

"It's the perfect atmosphere to go to college in."

UConn's engineering, business, pharmacy, and honors students are required to undertake research projects, and each year two teams of finance majors run the $1 million student-managed investment fund. Students who aspire to graduate school in academic fields, rather than professional certification, may win grants to work independently under faculty members through the undergraduate summer research program. The 7 percent of students who qualify for the honors program gain access to special floors and dorms; several programs for disadvantaged students are also available. In addition, about 300 students a year participate in the study abroad program, which offers programs in 65 countries. UConn's five campuses around Connecticut offer the first two years of the undergraduate program and some four-year degree programs. Students who satisfactorily complete work at these schools are automatically accepted at the Storrs campus for their last two years.

Three-quarters of UConn students are from Connecticut, and about 16 percent are minorities—5 percent African American, 4 percent Hispanic, and 7 percent Asian American. "There are students who take academics seriously and those who

In 2004, both the men's and women's basketball teams won the ultimate prize: the NCAA national championship—the first time any university has pulled off this feat.

do not; personally, all the students I know are very serious about their undergraduate studies," says a sophomore majoring in classic and ancient Mediterranean studies. Twenty percent of UConn students receive merit scholarships averaging about $5,600, and 371 athletic scholarships are available, too, in seven men's sports and 11 women's sports. There are cultural centers for African American, Asian American, Latin American, and Puerto Rican students, as well as the new Rainbow Center, a resource for gay, lesbian, bisexual, and transgender students. Hot topics on campus recently have ranged from the war in Iraq to parking difficulties.

"Quality teaching is the trademark of a UConn education."

Seventy-two percent of the students live in university housing, which is available to all undergraduates. "Halls are clean and spacious," says one student. "I love my dorm," says another. Though a few dorms are single-sex, most are co-ed by floor. In addition, "We have awesome suites and on-campus apartments," says a secondary education major. Nearly all campus housing has high-speed Internet, cable, data networking service in the rooms, not just in student lounges. Eleven dining halls offer plenty of choices, even for vegetarians and vegans, though many students would just as soon visit the snack bar for some ice cream, freshly made with help from the cows grazing nearby.

The freshman dorms are officially dry, and other students are allowed to possess no more than a six-pack of beer, one bottle of wine, or a small bottle of liquor. Students under 21 who are caught with booze may be evicted from campus housing. Late-night activities at the student union and other campus events provide a lot of alternatives to alcohol use. On weekends, there are busses to Hartford (only 30 minutes away), Boston, New Haven, New York, and Providence. Cape Cod and the Vermont ski slopes are within weekend driving distance.

Closer to home are the Buckland Hills Mall and Wal-Mart. A new shopping center is under construction a stone's throw from campus, but "honestly, everything you would need can be found right on campus," says a sophomore. Fraternities attract 10 percent of the men, and sororities claim 7 percent of the women; members can live in chapter housing at the new Husky Village.

The town of Storrs "is no college town, but it's rural and we're proud of it," says one student. The university provides transportation for students who volunteer in area schools and hospitals. Legend also holds that UConn also offers one diversion most other colleges can't:

"Honestly, everything you would need can be found right on campus."

cow tipping—that is, sneaking up on unsuspecting cows, who sleep standing up, and tipping them over. The administration contends that this is a myth, though students always claim to "know someone who did it."

UConn's teams are known as the Huskies (Get it? Yukon!), and basketball is by far the most popular sport. In a state without professional sports teams, the UConn women's team routinely sells out the Hartford Civic Center. In 2004, both the men's and women's basketball teams won the ultimate prize: the NCAA national championship—the first time any university has pulled off this feat. The field hockey, football, men's and women's soccer, and women's volleyball teams are also recent award-winners. Intramurals are offered at three levels, from recreational to competitive. Popular offerings range from underwater hockey and inner-tube water polo to basketball, volleyball, and flag football. Favorite annual campus events include the mud volleyball tournament, carnival-style "UConn Late Nights," Midnight breakfasts during finals, homecoming, Winter Weekend, and Midnight Madness—the first official day of basketball practice. In addition to cheering for the Huskies, "it is good luck to rub the nose of the bronze statue of our mascot, Jonathan," says a sophomore.

UConn has been adding new curricula, including a program that combines biodiversity and conservation biology with public policy. There are also new multi-disciplinary programs in neurosciences, cognitive science, American studies, aquaculture, survey research, coastal studies, urban and community studies, and human rights.

Overlaps

Northeastern, Boston University, University of Massachusetts, University of Delaware, Boston College

Despite the school's agricultural roots, UConn students aren't "cowed" by the plethora of offerings. Those seeking greener pastures will be hard-pressed to find a more dynamic public institution. "We are a well-rounded campus with students from every background," a junior pharmacy student says. And with the campus undergoing a complete facelift, a student says it's an exciting time to be at UConn.

Connecticut College

270 Mohegan Avenue, New London, CT 06320-4196

Like Vassar and Skidmore, Connecticut College made a successful transition from women's college to co-ed. The college is strong in the humanities and renowned for its study abroad programs. It is also an SAT I–optional school. New London does not offer much, but at least it is on the water.

Website:
www.connecticutcollege.edu
Location: Suburban
Total Enrollment: 1,807
Undergraduates: 1,777
Male/Female: 40/60
SAT Ranges: V 630–720
M 620–700
ACT Range: 25–29
Financial Aid: 45%
Expense: Pr $ $ $ $
Phi Beta Kappa: Yes
Applicants: 4,503
Accepted: 34%
Enrolled: 32%
Grad in 6 Years: 85%
Returning Freshmen: 92%
Academics: ✍ ✍ ✍ ✍
Social: ☎ ☎ ☎
Q of L: ★ ★ ★ ★
Admissions: (860) 439-2200
Email Address:
admission@conncoll.edu

Students at Connecticut College follow the example of their mascot, the camel—they take pride in drinking up and storing knowledge. The student-run honor code means finals are not proctored; they're even self-scheduled, whenever students prefer, during a 10-day window. Thanks to the code, students also feel comfortable leaving doors and bikes unlocked. Utopian? Perhaps. Still, "there really isn't much to complain about," a sophomore says. "The location is right between Boston and New York, the campus is beautiful, the people are extremely friendly, and the teachers are great."

Placed majestically atop a hill, the Conn College campus sits within a 750-acre arboretum with a pond, wetlands, wooded areas, and hiking trails. It offers beautiful views of the Thames River (pronounced the way it looks, not like the "Temz" that Wordsworth so dearly loved) on one side and Long Island Sound on the other. The granite campus buildings are a mixture of modern and collegiate Gothic in style, with some neo-Gothic and neoclassical architecture thrown in for good measure. A new recital hall and recording facility was recently completed.

Conn was founded in 1911 as a women's college, and since then, it's been dedicated to the liberal arts, broadly defined. The general education requirements are aimed at fostering intellectual breadth, critical thinking, and acquisition of the fundamental skills and habits of minds conducive to lifelong inquiry, engaged citizenship, and personal growth. To that end, students are required to complete a series of at least seven courses that introduce them to the natural and social sciences, humanities, and arts. Academics are definitely the focus here. "The academic climate here can be quite rigorous and demanding, though I find it challenging and intellectually stimulating," says a senior, who adds that "professors have a genuine interest in helping you pursue your goals."

Conn's dance and drama departments are superb, and it's not uncommon for dancers to take time off to study with professional companies. Aspiring actors, directors, and stagehands may work with the Eugene O'Neill Theater Institute, named for New London's best-known literary son. Chemistry majors may use high-tech gas chromatograms and mass spectrometers from their very first day, and students say Conn also offers excellent programs in biology and physics. The Ammerman Center for Arts and Technology allows students to examine the connections between artistic pursuits and the worlds of math and computer science. The most popular majors are English, economics, psychology, government, and history; not coincidentally, students give all of those departments high marks. The teacher certification program also wins raves. To escape Conn's small size and occasionally claustrophobic feel, the Study Away/Teach Away initiative allows groups of 15 to 30 Conn students and two faculty members to spend a semester living and working together at an overseas university, in locations as far-flung as Egypt, Ghana, Tanzania, and Vietnam. Conn also participates in the Twelve-College Exchange* bringing the total number of foreign study programs to more than 40. A gift from Conn helps students secure extraordinary sum-

"All of the dorms are beautiful, comfortable, and well-maintained."

mer internships; everyone is guaranteed one $3,000 grant during his or her four years to help cover housing or other costs incurred while gaining real-world work experience.

Only 18 percent of Conn College students come from Connecticut, and half graduated from public high schools. African Americans and Asian Americans each make up 4 percent of the student body, and Hispanic students add 5 percent. Freshmen must attend a session on issues of race, class, and gender, run by a panel of peers representing different cultures, socioeconomic backgrounds, sexual orientations, and physical disabilities. "We treat each other as equals. I can sit down with anyone in the cafeteria and start a conversation," says a junior. Efforts to improve diversity have been helped by the school's decision to emphasize high school transcripts, rather than the SAT I, as a measure of achievement and potential in the admissions process. There are no merit or athletic scholarships; admissions decisions are need-aware.

Ninety-nine percent of Conn College students live on campus, where "there's something for everyone." Dorms house students of all ages, and are run by seniors who apply to be "house fellows." Roommates tend to be well matched because incoming students complete a three-page questionnaire about personal habits before coming to campus, says a sophomore. "All of the dorms are beautiful, comfortable, and well-maintained," says a freshman. "The amenities are plenty, and the facilities are spectacular." Among the seven specialty houses are Earth House (environmental awareness), the Abbey House co-op (where students cook their own meals), Unity House (fostering relationships across ethnic and racial boundaries), and houses dedicated to

The Conn Camels compete in NCAA Division III, and men's ice hockey games against rival Wesleyan draw crowds, though students say Conn doesn't really have any true athletic rivals.

"If you want to be a number, Conn is not the place for you."

substance-free living, quiet lifestyles, and international languages. The campus dining hall offers traditional main courses, as well as "fast food, stir-fry, pizza, pasta, vegetarian options, deli sandwiches, salad bars, and an ice cream bar," says a psychology major.

Because Conn lacks a Greek system, most activities—including co-ed intramural sports—revolve around the dorms, which sponsor weekly keg and theme parties. Also keeping students busy are movie nights, comedy shows, student productions, and dances—sometimes with out-of-town bands and DJs. The alcohol policy falls under the honor code, so those under 21 can't imbibe at the campus bar, and students take that prohibition seriously. Conn is helping to revitalize New London, where defense-contractor General Dynamics and drug maker Pfizer both have operations. Students volunteer at the local schools, aquarium, youth community center, and women's center; a college van makes it easy to get to and from work sites. When students get the urge to roam, the beaches of Mystic and other shore towns are 20 minutes from campus, and the Mohegan Sun casino is also very close. Trains go to

Roommates tend to be well matched because incoming students complete a three-page questionnaire about personal habits before coming to campus.

Providence, Rhode Island, New York City, or Boston, while Vermont and upstate New York offer camping, hiking, and skiing. Conn's traditions include October's Camelympics, which pit dorms against each other in a 24-hour marathon of games from Scrabble to Capture the Flag; the winter Festivus ("the festival for the rest of us"); and Floralia, an all-day music festival the weekend before spring finals, recently headlined by the Dave Matthews Band.

The Conn Camels compete in NCAA Division III, and men's ice hockey games against rival Wesleyan draw crowds, though students say Conn doesn't really have any true athletic rivals. A T-shirt brags that Conn football has been undefeated since 1911; of course, Conn—as a former women's college—has never had a team. About 200 students participate in intramurals, and Ultimate Frisbee and broomball are some of the most popular IM sports. Between classes or at the end of the day, all students may use the natatorium's pool and fitness center, and the rowing tanks and climbing walls at the field house.

On its friendly campus, Conn College fosters strong student/faculty bonds and takes pride in its ability to challenge—and trust—students, both in and out of the classroom. But getting the most out of the Conn experience depends on being receptive—and on taking initiative, students say. "If you want to be a number, Conn is not the place for you."

<table>
<tr><td>Overlaps</td></tr>
<tr><td>Brown, Vassar, Tufts, Wesleyan, Skidmore, Trinity College</td></tr>
</table>

If You Apply To ➤ **Conn College:** Early decision: Nov. 15, Jan.1. Regular admissions: Jan.1. Financial aid: Feb. 1. Guarantees to meet demonstrated need. Campus interviews: recommended, evaluative. Alumni interviews: optional, evaluative. SAT Is: optional. SAT IIs: required (any two or the ACT). Accepts the Common Application (and Connecticut College Supplement). Prefers electronic applications. Essay question: why Connecticut College?

Cooper Union

BEST BUY

30 Cooper Square, New York, NY 10003

As college costs skyrocket, so does the popularity of Cooper Union's free education in art, architecture, and engineering. Expect Ivy-level competition for a place in the class here. Instead of a conventional campus, Cooper Union has the East Village—which is quite a deal.

Website: www.cooper.edu
Location: Urban
Total Enrollment: 907
Undergraduates: 870
Male/Female: 65/35
SAT Ranges: V 510–760
  M 510–780
Financial Aid: 40%
Expense: Pr $
Phi Beta Kappa: No
Applicants: 2,216
Accepted: 13%
Enrolled: 69%
Grad in 6 Years: 80%

Some say the best things in life are free. In most cases, they're probably wrong. But not in the case of the Cooper Union for the Advancement of Science and Art. If you manage to get accepted into this top technical institute, you get a full-tuition scholarship and some of the nation's finest academic offerings in architecture, engineering, and art. With cool and funky Greenwich Village in the background and rigorous studying in the forefront, college life at Cooper Union may seem to be faster than a New York minute. Whatever the pace, though, no one can deny that a CU education is one of the best bargains around—probably the best anywhere. The only problem is that its acceptance rate is comparable to the Ivies.

The school was founded in 1859 by entrepreneur Peter Cooper, who believed that education should be "as free as water and air." With hefty contributions from J.P. Morgan, Frederick Vanderbilt, Andrew Carnegie, and various other assorted robber barons, the school was able to stay afloat in order to recruit poor students of "strong moral character." Today, students must pay a few hundred dollars for nonacademic expenses, but tuition is still free.

In place of a traditional collegiate setting are three academic buildings and one dorm plunked down in one of New York's most eclectic and exciting neighborhoods. The stately brick art and architecture building is a beautiful historic landmark. Built of brick and topped by a classic water tower, the dorm blends right in with the neighborhood. The Great Hall was the site of Lincoln's "Right Makes Might" speech and the birthplace of the NAACP, the American Red Cross, and the national women's suffrage movement. Wedged between two busy avenues in the East Village, Cooper Union offers an environment for survivors. One mechanical engineering major describes the climate as "a tropical rain forest. Only the truly dedicated should come here."

"We all feed off each other and strive for our best."

The academic climate is intense, yet cooperation is critical, according to students. "We all feed off each other and strive for our best, but rivalry is low," says an architecture major. A junior adds, "You don't know the meaning of stress until you've been through Cooper." The curriculum is highly structured, and all students must take a sequence of required courses in the humanities and social sciences. The first year is devoted to language and literature and the second to the making of the modern world. In some special circumstances, students are allowed to take courses at nearby New York University and the New School for Social Research. The nationally renowned engineering school, under the tutelage of the nation's first female engineering dean, offers both bachelor's and master's degrees in chemical, electrical, mechanical, and civil engineering as well as a bachelor of science in general engineering. "Architecture and engineering are the most acclaimed, but then, these occupations are more mainstream, and graduates get big money and success," reflects an art major. "It's harder to measure success in the art school." The art school offers a broadbased generalist curriculum that includes graphic design, painting, sculpture, photography, and video but is considered weak by some students. The architecture school, in the words of one pleased participant, is "phenomenal—even unparalleled." Requirements for getting into each of these schools vary widely—each looks for different strengths and talents—hence the differences in test-score ranges.

The Cooper Union library is small (90,000 volumes), but contains more than 100,000 graphic materials. Classes are small and, with a little persistence, are not too difficult to get into. Professors are engaging and accessible. "One of the best aspects of this college is that everyone is taught by full professors," reports a junior. A professional counseling and referral service is available, as is academic counseling, but the school's small size and its rigorously structured academic programs set the

"One of the best aspects of this college is that everyone is taught by full professors."

classes the students take and eliminate a lot of confusion or decision making. Reactions to career counseling vary between "horrible" from an art major to "excellent" from an engineering major. Students "tend to talk to other students, recommending or insulting various classes and profs around registration time," notes a senior.

Strong moral character is no longer a prerequisite for admission, but an outstanding high school academic average most certainly is. Prospective applicants should note, however, that art and architecture students are picked primarily on the basis of a faculty evaluation of their creative works. For engineering students, admission is based on a formula that gives roughly equal weight to the high school record, SAT scores, and the SAT IIs in mathematics and physics or chemistry.

"The students here tend to be incredibly driven people," says one student, noting that some classmates have spent "literally 24 hours at the drafting desk." Sixty-one percent of the students are from New York State, and more than half of those grew up in the city. Most are from public schools, and many are the first in their family to attend college. Forty-four percent of the students are from minority groups, most

(Continued)
Returning Freshmen: 90%
Academics: ✎ ✎ ✎ ½
Social: ☎
Q of L: ★ ★ ★
Admissions: (212) 353-4120
Email Address: N/A

Strongest Programs:
Architecture

The combination of intense workload and CU's location means that campus social life is limited, though the administration hopes the dorm will promote more on-campus social activities.

of them Asian Americans (27 percent); 6 percent are African American, and 8 percent are Hispanic. One student attests that diversity is not an issue at CU: "We are a racially mixed student body that stays mixed. There's no overt hostility and rare self-segregation. One of the officers of the Chinese Student Association is a large black man from Trinidad. Need I say more?" The campus is home to ethnically based student clubs, but, according to one student, membership is not exclusive: "In other words, you can be white and be a member of Onyx—a student group promoting black awareness." According to one senior, CU is a very liberal place: "If you can't accept different kinds of people, you shouldn't come here." For students who demonstrate financial need, help with living expenses is available.

Students love the dorm, a 15-story residence hall that saves many students from commuting into the Village or cramming themselves into expensive apartments. It is noteworthy that housing here is guaranteed only to freshmen. The facility is composed of furnished apartments with kitchenettes and bathrooms complete with showers or tubs and is "in great condition and well-maintained," states one resident. A less enraptured dweller notes, "Rooms are barely big enough to fit a bed, a table, and a clothes cabinet." Still, each apartment does have enough space for a stove, microwave, and refrigerator. So you can cook for yourself or eat at the unexciting but affordable school cafeteria or at one of the myriad nearby delis and coffee bars.

The combination of intense workload and CU's location means that campus social life is limited, though the administration hopes the dorm will promote more on-campus social activities. "Many students will say that Cooper social life is dead," notes a junior. "In many ways they are right." On the other hand, as one senior puts it, "The East Village is great place to be young, with tons of bars and culture." About 20 percent of the men and 10 percent of the women belong to professional societies. Drinking on campus is allowed during school-sponsored parties for adult students—otherwise, no alcohol on campus. But as one student puts it, "This is New York; one can be served anywhere."

"If you can't accept different kinds of people, you shouldn't come here."

The intramural sports program is held in several different facilities in the city, and the games are popular. Students organize clubs and outings around interests such as soccer, basketball, skiing, fencing, Ping-Pong, classical music, religion, and drama. And of course, the colorful neighborhood is ideal for sketching and browsing. McSorley's bar is right around the corner, the Grassroots Tavern is just down the block, and nearby Chinatown and Little Italy are also popular destinations. The heart of the Village, with its abundance of theaters, art galleries, and cafes, is just a few blocks to the west. The Bowery and SoHo's galleries and restaurants are due south; all of midtown Manhattan spreads to the northern horizon.

Getting into Cooper Union is tough, and once admitted, students find that dealing with the onslaught of city and school is plenty tough as well. But most students like the challenge. "The workload, living alone in New York, and the administrative policies force you to act like an adult and take care of yourself," explains a senior. Surviving the school's academic rigors requires talent, self-sufficiency, and a clear sense of one's career objectives. Students who don't have it all can be sure that there are six or seven people in line ready to take their places. That's quite an incentive to succeed.

Overlaps

NYU, Columbia, Cornell University, MIT, Carnegie-Mellon

If You Apply To ➤ **Cooper Union:** Rolling admissions (for art applicants, by invitation). Early decision (for art and engineering applicants): Dec. 1. Regular admissions: Jan. 1 (architecture), Jan. 10 (art), Feb. 1 (engineering). Financial aid and housing: May 1. All students receive full-tuition scholarships. No campus or alumni interviews. (Portfolio Day strongly recommended for art applicants.) SATs: required. SAT IIs: required for engineering (math and physics or chemistry). Apply to particular program. Essay question: varies by school.

Cornell College

600 First Street West, Mount Vernon, IA 52314-1098

One-course-at-a-time model is Cornell's calling card. Cornell's main challenge: trying to lure students to rural Iowa. With a student body of about 1,000, Cornell lavishes its students with personal attention. Though primarily a liberal arts institution, Cornell has small programs in business and education.

Cornell College attracts a unique type of student that seeks an intense yet flexible, self-designed program and a liberal, progressive atmosphere in which to solidify strict habits and routines. If you're not satisfied with easy answers, don't mind heading to the rural Midwest, and want loads of personal attention while you focus on one class, Cornell College may be worth a look. "This has been hands-down the best experience of my life," says a junior. "I plan on sending my children to Cornell someday."

Aside from its distinctive schedule, Cornell has one of only two U.S. college or university campuses listed in its entirety on the National Register of Historic Places. The majestic bell tower of King Chapel offers an unparalleled view of the Cedar River valley. A pedestrian mall runs through campus, and other recent additions include an eight-lane, all-weather track and an outdoor amphitheater. A state-of-the-art, 280-seat theatre has been added to the performing arts building, and a new coed residence hall is on the way.

Cornell awards the Bachelor of Arts (BA) in more than 40 academic majors, as well as an extensive group of preprofessional programs, resulting in a variety of degrees. The college also offers the Bachelor of Special Studies, which administrators describe as "an opportunity which permits students to combine courses in an individualized fashion and to broaden or deepen their studies beyond the traditional framework of the Bachelor of Arts. The BSS has no general education requirements and no restrictions as to either the number of courses that may be taken in any one department or the level of such courses, or even that a student complete traditional course work." The One-Course method can be problematic here because "it is difficult to learn a language in three and a half weeks," a junior says. Another sums it up. "OCAAT: You either love it or hate it." Also available are the bachelor's degree in special studies, which 16 percent of students pursue, and the bachelor of music degree, which attracts just 2 percent of students. Interdepartmental majors in archeology and medieval and early modern studies are new as is Dimensions, a science program for those interested in healthcare fields.

Block scheduling makes it easier for some students to graduate early; others use the flexibility to finish with a double major. If that sounds intimidating, it can be. But administrators say it also improves the quality of Cornell's liberal arts education, by helping students acclimate to the business

> **"This has been hands-down the best experience of my life."**

world, where "what needs to be done needs to be done quickly and done well." The One-Course method also helps in academic advising—with grades every four weeks, signs of trouble are quickly apparent. Block scheduling does have drawbacks, though. "Courses are completed in 18 days, so each class is pretty intense," says a junior biology and Spanish major.

The most popular programs are psychology, elementary and secondary education, economics and business, English, and history, and other strong options include biology, philosophy, politics, and theater. Weaker areas include German, Latin American studies, and medieval and early modern studies. Classes usually have fewer than 25 students, and most have around 15; you won't find graduate students

Website:
www.cornellcollege.edu
Location: Rural
Total Enrollment: 1,134
Undergraduates: 1,134
Male/Female: 43/57
SAT Ranges: V 560–660
  M 570–670
ACT Range: 23–29
Financial Aid: 73%
Expense: Pr $ $
Phi Beta Kappa: Yes
Applicants: 1,716
Accepted: 64%
Enrolled: 27%
Grad in 6 Years: 65%
Returning Freshmen: 82%
Academics: ✍ ✍ ✍
Social: ☎ ☎ ☎
Q of L: ★ ★ ★
Admissions: (319) 895-4477
Email Address: admissions@ cornellcollege.edu

Strongest Programs:
Art
Biology
Education
English
Philosophy
Psychology
Politics
Theater

at the lectern, since Cornell doesn't hire them. "Professors are friendly, knowledgeable, and very accessible," says a senior. "The teaching I have received has been of the highest quality," a junior adds.

When Mount Vernon gets too small, Cornell students may choose from study programs around the world, such as Marine Science Research in the Bahamas, Advanced Spanish in Spain and Mexico, or Greek Archaeology in Greece. They can also spend a semester at sea or in one of 36 countries through the Associated Colleges of the Midwest* consortium. During the short breaks between courses, students can take advantage of symposia, Music Mondays, carnivals, and athletic events. The school's Cole Library is also the town of Mount Vernon's public library, one of only two such libraries in the country.

One of Cornell's biggest challenges is drawing students to its rural Iowa campus, but administrators are doing well on that score: only a third of a recent freshman class were homegrown. African Americans represent 3 percent of the student population, Hispanics 3 percent, and Asian Americans 1 percent. Three percent hail from other nations. Politically, Cornell leans liberal; hot topics have included the 2004 presidential candidates (since the Iowa caucuses are the campaign's first)

"Many students knit themselves into the community."

and President Bush's actions in Iraq. "The social and political issues on campus reflect the issues of society as a whole," another student explains. Merit scholarships are offered to qualified students; there are no athletic awards.

Eighty-eight percent of students live on campus, where "the dorms are historic buildings and are not the best maintained, though some of the housing is beautiful and spacious," says a sociology major. Nearly 10 percent of students participate in living/learning communities. The largest co-ed residence hall, which houses Cornell's living/learning communities, has been renovated. Everyone eats together in the Commons, which is also being renovated. Sodexho Marriott runs the kitchen, and the food is "not great but the most complaints are about lack of variety," a senior says. Vegetarian options are always available.

On campus, the fraternities draw 30 percent of the men and 32 percent of the women, though they are not associated with national Greek systems. Some dorms and floors are substance-free; on the others, only students over 21 may have alcohol. "They treat underage drinkers as children and aim to punish but this does not reduce underage drinking," says a senior. Mount Vernon itself is "small, but very welcoming," says a physical education major. "Many students knit themselves into the community, whether it be with jobs downtown or going to the local churches," a junior agrees. Students either love the town's idyllic pace—a few local bars, an acclaimed restaurant, some funky shops, and a lot of peace, quiet, and safety—or long for more excitement. The latter is available in Cedar Rapids (home of archrival Coe College) or Iowa City (home to the University of Iowa), each less than half an hour away. Chicago is less than four hours away.

On the field or on the court, Cornell's competition with Coe "is intense, and the entire student body is involved," says one student, especially when it comes to football or basketball. "Every time a rival plays us at home in men's basketball, it's a tradition that we throw rolls of toilet paper out on the floor after we score our first basket," adds another—perhaps to show how Cornell plans to "clean up" its opponent. The baseball field was upgraded recently, and the Meyer Strength Training Facility helps student-athletes improve their speed and power. Cornell teams compete in the Iowa Intercollegiate Athletic Conference and have been to the NCAA men's basketball tournament five times. Recently, the women's tennis team and track teams brought home conference championships. Forty-four percent of students, and some faculty and staff, participate in intramural sports.

Cornell offers a top-notch education and a supportive community—if you can take the bitter winters and relative isolation of rural Iowa. And while the curriculum requires students to focus on just one course at a time, "It is the most practical and interesting way to learn," declares a senior. Indeed, life here allows them to explore just about anything.

If You Apply To ➤

Cornell: Early action: Dec. 1. Regular admissions: Mar. 1. Meets demonstrated need of 50%. Campus interviews: recommended, informational. Alumni interviews: optional, informational. SATs or ACTs: required. SAT IIs: optional. Accepts the Common Application and electronic applications. Essay question: significant experience, achievement, risk or ethical dilemma; important issue; your room; influential character; topic of your choice.

Cornell University

Ithaca, NY 14850

Cornell's reputation as a pressure cooker comes from its preprofessional attitude and "we try harder" mentality. Spans seven colleges—four private and three public—and tuition varies accordingly. Strong in engineering and architecture, world-famous in hotel administration. Easiest Ivy to get into.

Cornell has a long tradition for being the lone wolf among the Ivy League universities. So it should come as no surprise that Cornell has taken another huge step away from its Ivy League counterparts by announcing its intention to become the finest research university for undergraduate education in the nation. Cornell's president recently unveiled a $400 million, 10-year plan to improve undergraduate education by combining education and research and having all freshmen live in the same residential area. And the mixture of state and private, preprofessional, and liberal arts at one institution provides a diversity of students rare among America's colleges.

Aside from the great strides in undergraduate education, Cornell also has its stunning campus to lure students to upstate New York. Perched atop a hill that commands a view of both Ithaca and Cayuga lakes, the campus is breathtakingly scenic; or, as the saying goes, "Ithaca is gorges." Ravines, waterfalls, and parks border all sides of the school's campus. The Cornell Plantation, more than 3,000 acres of woodlands, natural trails, streams, and gorges, provides space for walking, picnicking, or contemplation.

At the undergraduate level, Cornell has four privately endowed colleges: architecture, art, and planning; arts and sciences; engineering; and hotel administration. "Architecture and hotel administration are two of the best programs in the country," confirms one senior. Cornell is also New York State's land grant university. Therefore, Cornell operates three other colleges under contract with New York State: agriculture and life sciences, human ecology, and the school of industrial and labor relations (ILR). Thirty-seven percent of the students in these state-assisted colleges are New York State residents who pick up their Ivy League degrees at an almost-public price (as tuition at these schools is slightly steeper than SUNY rates).

The College of Arts and Sciences boasts considerable strength in history, government, and just about all the natural and physical sciences. The English program has turned out a number of renowned writers, including Toni Morrison, Thomas Pynchon, and Richard Farina. Foreign languages, required for all arts and sciences students, are also strong, and the performing arts, mathematics, and most

Website: www.cornell.edu
Location: Small city
Total Enrollment: 19,518
Undergraduates: 13,625
Male/Female: 51/49
SAT Ranges: V 630–730
   M 660–760
ACT Range: 28–32
Financial Aid: 49%
Expense: Pr $ $ $ $
Phi Beta Kappa: Yes
Applicants: 20,822
Accepted: 29%
Enrolled: 50%
Grad in 6 Years: 92%
Returning Freshmen: 96%
Academics: ✑ ✑ ✑ ✑ ✑
Social: ☎ ☎ ☎ ☎
Q of L: ★ ★ ★
Admissions: (607) 255-5241
Email Address:
   admissions@cornell.edu

Strongest Programs:
Biology
Physical Science/Math
English
Economics/Business

social science departments are considered good. Among the state-assisted units, the agriculture college is solid and a good bet for anyone hoping to make it into a veterinary school (there's one at Cornell with state support). The School of Hotel Administration is top-notch, and ILR is also well-regarded. Hotel's wine tasting course draws students from across the university. Human ecology is among the best in the nation in human service related disciplines, and the Department of Applied Economics and Management offers an undergraduate business major. The Johnson Museum of Art, designed by IM Pei, has been rated as one of the 10 best university museums in America. Students enjoy the $22 million theater arts center, designed specifically for undergraduates.

Student/faculty relations at Cornell are a mixed bag, but for the most part students do have a lot of respect for their professors. A junior muses, "It's always entertaining when your professor wrote the book for the class." First-year courses in the sciences and social sciences are generally large lectures, though many are taught by "charismatic profs" who try to remain accessible. The largest course on campus, Psych 101, packs in more than 1,000, but students report that scintillating lectures make it a well-loved rite of passage. Some undergrads complain that it is difficult to get into popular courses unless you are a major. "Students joke about the 'Big Red Tape' because it can be daunting trying to navigate Cornell's bureaucracy," explains one senior. The administration, however, is hoping that the decision to make undergraduates a priority will improve

"It's always entertaining when your professor wrote the book for the class."

most of the problems in the lower-level courses. For now, first-year students do have access to senior faculty members through mandatory First-Year Writing Seminars.

The Fund for Educational Initiatives gives professors money to implement innovative approaches to undergraduate education, which have included a visual learning laboratory and a course on electronic music. Cornell was early among universities to add women's studies to the curriculum and continues to be an innovator, with programs in Asian American studies and by offering its students programs like its Sea Semester.*

Cornell academics are demanding and foster an intensity found on few campuses. "The easiest Ivy to get into; the toughest to get out of," quips one student. "Students at Cornell take college life from the work hard, play hard perspective." Another student adds, "While it's hard to ignore the prestige of attending an Ivy League school, most Cornellians seem to have checked their attitudes at the door." Eighty-five percent of Cornell students ranked in the top tenth of their high school class, so those who were the class genius in high school should be prepared for a struggle to rise to the top. To cope with the anxieties that the high-powered atmosphere creates, the university has one of the best psychological counseling networks in the nation, including an alcohol-awareness program, peer sex counselors, personal-growth workshops, and EARS (Empathy, Assistance, and Referral Service).

The library system is superb. Cornell students have access to more than seven million volumes, 63,000 journals, and 1,000 networked resources in the 20 libraries comprising Cornell's library system. The resources are available to a wide range of students, faculty, staff, and, in some cases, the community. Also, the digital initiative has made many resources and collections available online. Within the beautiful, underground Carl A. Kroch Library, students study in skylit atriums and reading rooms and move about the renowned Fiske Icelandic Collection and the Echols Collections, the finest Cambodian collection on display.

Cornell offers more than 4,000 courses in a wide range of pursuits. A co-op program is available to engineering students, and Cornell-in-Washington, with its own dorm, is popular among students from all seven undergraduate colleges. Students looking to study abroad can choose from more than 200 programs

Cornell is need-blind in admissions and guarantees to meet the demonstrated need of all accepted applicants, but the proportion of outright grants—as opposed to loans that must be repaid—in the financial aid package varies depending on how eager the university is to get students to enroll.

and universities throughout the world, including those in Indonesia, Belgium, Ireland, and Nepal. Research opportunities are outstanding at Cornell, and students can take part in some of the most vital research happening in the nation. Recent research findings include solving the mystery of how Jupiter's rings are formed and discovering a new technology to make computer software less vulnerable to bugs.

Prospective students apply to one of the seven colleges or schools through the central admissions office, and admissions standards vary by school. City slickers and country folk, engineers, and those with an artsy flair all rub shoulders here. Fifty-five percent of Cornell's students are out-of-staters; another 8 percent are foreign. African Americans and Hispanics each account for 5 percent of the student body, and Asian Americans comprise 16 percent. Cornell offers many workshops and discussion groups aimed at increasing tolerance. The state-assisted schools draw a large number of in-staters, as well as many students from New Jersey, Pennsylvania, and New England, while arts and sciences and engineering draw from the tristate metropolitan New York City area, Pennsylvania, Massachusetts, and California. Whatever their origin, students seem self-motivated and studious. Upon graduation, 35 percent of Cornell students take jobs, and 34 percent continue to graduate and professional schools.

"While it's hard to ignore the prestige of attending an Ivy League school, most Cornellians seem to have checked their attitudes at the door."

Cornell is need blind in admissions and guarantees to meet the demonstrated need of all accepted applicants, but the proportion of outright grants—as opposed to loans that must be repaid—in the financial aid package varies depending on how eager the university is to get you to enroll. The Cornell Installment Plan (CIP) allows students or their parents to pay a year's or semester's tuition in monthly interest-free installments. The university also takes pride in its Cornell Tradition fellowship programs that recognize leadership and academic excellence, work and service, and research and discovery. Tradition students may receive up to $4,000 in loan replacement each year in addition to other financial rewards.

Cornell housing has undergone a few changes recently. North Campus has two new residence halls and a dining room and is the home of all freshmen. A few students are housed in two dorms on the edge of Collegetown, the blocks of apartments and houses within walking distance of the campus. There are dorms devoted to everything from ecology to music, and cultural houses include the International Living Center, Latino Living Center, Ujamaa Residential College, and Akwe:kon, a program house focusing on American Indian

"Just make sure that you turn in your housing form on time."

culture (the only facility of its kind in the nation). "Just make sure that you turn in your housing form on time," warns a senior psychology major. Also available are a small number of highly coveted suites—six large double rooms with kitchens and a common living area. Just under half of Cornell's students live in university housing, though many try their luck in Collegetown, where demand keeps the housing market tight and rents high. Cornell's food service is reputedly among the best in the nation. There are eight residential meal plan dining halls that function independently, so, one student enthuses, "the food is fantastic and incredibly diverse." Milk products and some meats come right from the agriculture school, and about twice a semester a crosscountry gourmet team—the staff of a famous restaurant—prepares its specialties on campus.

Despite the intense academic atmosphere—or maybe because of it—Cornell social life beats most of the other Ivies hands down. Once the weekend arrives, local parties and ski slopes are filled with Cornell students who have managed to strike a balance between study and play. Collegetown bars offer good eats and drinks, but those under 21 are barred. "Social life can be found on or off campus.

There is always something going on and I've always felt socially stimulated." With 28 percent of men and 22 percent of women pledging, fraternities and sororities also play a significant role in the social scene. Big events include Fun in the Sun (a day of friendly athletic competition), Dragon Day (architecture students build a dragon and parade it through campus), and Springfest (a concert on Libe Slope). Students celebrate the last day of classes—Slope Day—by hanging out at Libe Slope. There are also innumerable concerts and sporting events. In addition, there are more than 600 extracurricular clubs ranging from a tanning society to a society of women engineers.

Hockey is unquestionably the dominant sport on campus (the chief goal being to defeat Harvard), and camping out for season tickets is an annual ritual. Cornell boasts the largest intramural program in the Ivy League; it includes more than a dozen sports, including 100 hockey teams organized around dorms, fraternities, and other organizations. The aforementioned "four seasons of Ithaca" can make walking to class across the vast and hilly campus challenging, but with the first snow of the winter, "traying" down Libe Slope becomes the sport of choice for hordes of fun-loving Cornellians. Ithaca boasts "wonderful outdoor enthusiast stores," says one student. It also hosts Greek Peak Mountain for nearby skiing, Cayuga Lake for boating and swimming, and lots of space for hiking and watching the clouds roll by.

"Cornell is a world unto itself."

One junior sums it up: "Cornell is a world unto itself. It has the academic rigor of an Ivy League university, but the size and diversity of a large state school. The city and surrounding geography is beautiful and unique, which fosters a love of this place that is unmatched." Like most other Ivy League universities, Cornell is a premiere research institution with a distinguished faculty and outstanding academics. What sets it apart is the university's willingness to stray from the traditional Ivy League path. Cornell University is a pioneer in the world of education, and students unafraid to blaze their own trail will feel at home here.

Overlaps

Harvard, Princeton, Stanford, University of Pennsylvania, Yale

If You Apply To ➤

Cornell: Early decision: Nov. 1. Regular admissions: Jan. 1. Financial aid: Jan. 1. Housing: May 1. Campus interviews: not available. Alumni interviews: recommended, informational (varies by program). SATs or ACTs: required. SAT IIs: required (varies by program). Accepts Common Application and electronic application. Essay question: Common Application. Apply to individual programs or schools.

University of Dallas

Irving, TX 75062

Bulwark of academic traditionalism in Big D. Despite being a "university," UD has fewer than 1,200 undergraduates. Except for the Business Leaders of Tomorrow program, the curriculum is exclusively liberal arts. The only outpost of Roman Catholic education between Loyola of New Orleans and University of San Diego.

Website: www.udallas.edu
Location: Suburban
Total Enrollment: 3,005
Undergraduates: 1,174
Male/Female: 47/53

While many universities around the nation have reexamined their Eurocentric core curriculums, the University of Dallas—the best Roman Catholic college south of Washington, D.C.—remains proudly dedicated to fostering students in "the study of great deeds and works of Western civilization."

UD's 744-acre campus occupies a pastoral home in a Dallas suburb on top of "the closest thing this region has to a hill." Texas Stadium, home of the Dallas Cowboys, is right across the street. A major portion of the campus is situated around the Braniff Mall, a landscaped and lighted gathering place near the Braniff Memorial Tower, the school's landmark. The primary tone of the buildings is brown, and the architecture, as described by one student, is "post-1950s, done in brick, typical Catholic-institutional." While it may not be a picture-perfect school, it does have a beautiful chapel and a state-of-the-art science building. The Art Village has five buildings and each art major has private studio space. The new Dominican Priory was recently completed, as was the extension and renovation of the Maher Athletic Center, which includes a gym, weight room, and aerobics equipment.

Students characterize the academic climate as respectfully competitive. "The Catholic Christian environment, however, takes any excessive edge off of competition," says a theology major. "That is, people realize there are more important things in life, and that grades don't determine how good of a person you are or whether you're going to heaven or hell." And appropriately for a Roman Catholic school, much of the focus is on Rome, where most of the sophomore class treks every year. The unique and intense program focuses on the art and architecture of Rome, the philosophy of man, classical literature, Italian, and the development of Western civilization.

English is the most popular major, followed by business leadership, biology, politics and theology. The business leadership program, which is fairly new, "draws on the learning opportunities in the Dallas Metroplex to develop responsible and competent managers through classroom and industry experiences." Political philosophy is also a popular major, although students claim that most courses tend to be slanted toward the conservative side. Students can also participate in an accelerated BA-to-MBA five-year plan. Premed students are well served by the biology and chemistry programs, and 80 percent of UD graduates go on to grad school.

The Rome semester is part of UD's four-semester Western Civilization core curriculum. Included in the core are philosophy, English, math, fine arts, science, American civilization, Western civilization, politics and economics, as well as a serious foreign language requirement. Two theology courses (including Scripture and Western theological tradition) are also required of all students. Those inclined toward the sciences may take advantage of the John B. O'Hara Chemical Science Institute, which offers a hands-on nine-week summer program to prepare new students for

"As a current senior, I have taken only one class that was not taught by a full professor."

independent research and earns them eight credits in chemistry. Due to a decline in popularity, the computer science major is no longer offered as a major, but is still available as a concentration.

Students report the academic pressure and the workload can be intense. The university uses no teaching assistants, and professors are easy to get to know. "As a current senior, I have taken only one class that was not taught by a full professor," one student says. Getting into the small, personal classes is rarely a problem, and counseling receives high marks. "Even if you aren't the best in the class or the course isn't your favorite, they value your input and are looking for ways to improve," claims one junior. Seventy-eight percent of classes taken by freshmen have 25 or fewer students.

Two-thirds of UD students are Catholic, and many of them choose this school because of its religious affiliation. Fifty-three percent are from Texas, and 16 percent of the student body is Hispanic. Six percent are Asian American and 1 percent is African American.

UDers tend to lean to the right politically, with topics such as abortion and homosexuality leading the discussions. "While most of the students agree on these issues, we certainly have our 'dissenters,' but I don't think they feel alienated or

(Continued)

SAT Ranges: V 560–670
  M 540–650
ACT Range: 23–28
Financial Aid: 63%
Expense: Pr $
Phi Beta Kappa: Yes
Applicants: 815
Accepted: 87%
Enrolled: 34%
Grad in 6 Years: 65%
Returning Freshmen: 86%
Academics: ✎ ✎ ✎
Social: ☎ ☎
Q of L: ★ ★ ★
Admissions: (800) 628-6999
Email Address:
  ugadmis@udallas.edu

Strongest Programs:
English
Biology
History
Politics
Philosophy
Pre-med

The business leadership program, which is fairly new, "draws on the learning opportunities in the Dallas Metroplex to develop responsible and competent managers through classroom and industry experiences."

looked down upon," says one student. "In fact, I think there are probably some people who go too far in making sure that these people don't feel offended or despised." UD offers various merit scholarships, averaging $10,000, but no athletic scholarships.

Tradition and religion govern conduct. Everyone under 21 who doesn't reside at home with their parents must live on campus in single-sex dorms, "where visitation regulations are relatively strict," one student reports. As for the dorms, they "aren't huge," but are "clean and updated," according to one student. The most popular dorms are Jerome (all-female) and Madonna (all-male). At Gregory, the dorm reserved for those who like to party, the goings-on are less than saintly. In addition to a spacious and comfortable dining hall with a wonderful view of North Dallas, there is the Rathskeller, which serves snacks and fast food (and great conversation). A car is a must for off-campus life because there is virtually no reliable public transportation in the Dallas/Fort Worth Metroplex.

With no fraternities or sororities at UD, the student government sponsors most on-campus entertainment. Three free movies a week, dances, and visiting speakers are usually on the agenda. Church-related and religious activities provide fulfilling social outlets for a good number of students. Annual events include Mallapalooza,

> **"Generally speaking, they're the best people I've ever met and probably the best I ever will."**

a spring music festival, and Groundhog, a party on Groundhog's Day weekend. Then there's Charity Week in the fall, when the junior class plans a week's worth of fundraising events. Each year, students dread Sadie Hawkins Day and the annual Revenge of the Roommate dance—dark nights of the soul, each. The university can be vigorous in enforcing restrictive drinking rules and, as a result, it is difficult for a minor to drink at campus events.

Students describe Irving as "a suburb, just like any other," but the Metroplex offers almost unlimited possibilities, including a full agenda for bar-hopping on Lower Greenville Avenue, about 15 minutes away. The West End and Deep Ellum offer a taste of shopping and Dallas's alternative music scene. And for the more adventurous, New Orleans isn't too far away.

The University of Dallas is unusual for a Texas school in that its entire population does not salivate at the sight of a football or basketball. But baseball, men's basketball and women's soccer are still competitive. Men's basketball and women's soccer recently reached the NCAA Division III tournaments in two consecutive years, and women's soccer won the Collegiate Athletic Association Championship in 2002 and 2003. Intramural sports are well organized and very popular, with volleyball attracting the most players. Chess is also a favored activity.

UD appeals to those students who pride themselves on being the "philosopher kings of the 21st century," but whose roots go back to the Roman thinkers of an earlier era. The mix of religion and liberal arts can serve a certain breed of students well. In the words of one senior, "Generally speaking, they're the best people I've ever met and probably the best I ever will."

Overlaps

University of Texas–Austin, Texas A&M, Notre Dame, Baylor, University of Texas–Arlington

If You Apply To ➤

Dallas: Rolling admissions: Aug. 1. Early action: Nov. 1. Priority admissions: Jan. 15. Financial aid: Mar. 1. Housing: Apr. 10. Meets demonstrated need of 22%. Campus interviews: recommended, informational. No alumni interviews. SATs or ACTs: required (SAT preferred). SAT IIs: optional. Accepts the Common Application and electronic applications. Essay question: describe a character in fiction, a historical figure, or a creative work (as in art, music, science, etc.) that has had an influence on you, and explain that influence; favorite joke; your activities; why you want to attend UD and what you expect to gain.

6016 McNutt Hall, Hanover, NH 03755

The smallest Ivy and the one with the strongest emphasis on undergraduates. Traditionally the most conservative member of the Ivy League, it has been steered leftward in recent years. Ivy ties notwithstanding, Dartmouth has more in common with places like Colgate, Williams, and Middlebury. Great for those who like the outdoors.

Unlike the other seven members of the Ivy League, which trace their roots to Puritan New Englanders or progressive Quaker colonists, Dartmouth College was founded in 1769 to educate Native Americans. The student body has always been the smallest in the Ancient Eight, and the school's focus on undergraduate education differentiates Dartmouth from its peers, though the college does offer graduate programs in engineering, business, and medicine. Dartmouth's campus is probably the most remote of the Ivies, and its winters may be the coldest, with the possible exception of those at Cornell. The Big Green compensates with the warmth of community, keeping sophomores on campus for the summer to build closeness, and using intensive language training and study abroad to emphasize the importance of global ties.

While tradition is revered at Dartmouth, the school also continues to grow, change, and evolve. That's the legacy of former president James Freedman, hired in the 1980s to "lead Dartmouth out of the sandbox" and make it a more hospitable place (especially for women and minorities) with a more scholarly feeling. Freedman said he wanted students "whose greatest pleasures may not come from the camaraderie of classmates, but from the lonely acts of writing poetry, or mastering the cello, or solving mathematical riddles, or translating Catullus." (The reference to the Latin poet Catullus may have been the president's little joke, as Catullus wrote erotic, sometimes obscene, verse on topics such as his passion for his mistress Lesbia, a boy named Juventius, and the sexual excesses of Julius Caesar.) Today's Dartmouth hardly resembles the college of yesteryear, whose rowdy Greek scene inspired the movie Animal House. The school still attracts plenty of hiking and skiing enthusiasts, and the most popular extracurricular organization is the Dartmouth Outing Club, the oldest collegiate outdoors club in the nation. But these days, students are just as apt to join a hip-hop dance group called Sheba, or to spend a vacation doing Dartmouth-sponsored community service in South America.

Set in the "small, Norman Rockwell town" of Hanover, New Hampshire, which is bisected by the Appalachian Trail, Dartmouth's picturesque campus is arranged around a quaint green. It's bounded by the impressive Baker Library at one end, and by the college-owned Hanover Inn at the other. Architectural styles range from Romanesque to postmodern, but the dominant theme is copper-topped Colonial frame. The nearest big city, Boston, is two hours away, but major artists like Itzhak Perlman routinely visit Dartmouth's Hopkins Center for the Creative and Performing Arts, adding a touch of culture. The avant garde dance troupe Pilobilus was formed by Dartmouth alumni, and a graduate student says she was pleasantly surprised to find that she could see the group for $5 at the Hop, a fraction of what she had paid in New York.

Dartmouth's status as a member of the Ivy League means academic excellence is a given. But that doesn't mean students have complete freedom when it comes to choosing courses. First-years must take a seminar that involves both independent research and small-group discussion; about 75 are offered each year. The seminars "ensure that every student's writing is up to par," while supplementing the usual introductory survey courses available in most disciplines, and offering a glimpse of

Website: www.dartmouth.edu
Location: Rural
Total Enrollment: 5,460
Undergraduates: 3,996
Male/Female: 50/50
SAT Ranges: V 670–770
  M 690–780
ACT Range: 28–34
Financial Aid: 51%
Expense: Pr $ $ $ $
Phi Beta Kappa: Yes
Applicants: 11,734
Accepted: 19%
Enrolled: 50%
Grad in 6 Years: 95%
Returning Freshmen: 98%
Academics: ✍ ✍ ✍ ✍ ✍
Social: 🎉 🎉 🎉 🎉 🎉
Q of L: ★ ★ ★
Admissions: (603) 646-2875
Email Address:
  admissions.office@
  dartmouth.edu

Strongest Programs:
Biological Sciences
Computer Science
Engineering
Economics
Languages
Psychological and Brain
  Sciences

the self-directed scholarship expected at the college level. Students must also demonstrate proficiency in at least one foreign language. And they must take three world culture courses (one non-Western, one Western and one Culture and Identity), and 10 courses from various distribution areas: the arts, literature, systems and traditions of thought, meaning, and value, international or comparative studies, social analysis, quantitative and deductive science, natural or physical science and technology or applied science. In addition, Dartmouth has a senior culminating activity—a thesis, public report, exhibition, seminar, production, or demonstration—which allows students to pull together work done in their major, with a creative and intellectual twist of their own. "The whole campus is one giant, interactive, constant learning community," says a senior.

Though Dartmouth students work hard, the climate is far from cutthroat. "You are much more likely to see students cooperating, studying together, and helping each other out with labs than competing," says a religion and environmental studies major. "I'm a senior and I still don't know my friends' GPAs. It's not important to us, and we don't talk about it. And that's the norm." The most popular majors are economics, government, history, English and psychology. The languages are also well-regarded, and students benefit from the Intensive Language Model developed by Professor John Rassias. Computer science offerings are among the best in the nation, thanks in no small part to the late John Kemeny, the former Dartmouth president who coinvented time-sharing and the BASIC language. Indeed, computing is a way of life here; well before the Internet, all of Dartmouth's dorm rooms were networked, and students would "Blitzmail" each other to set up meetings, discussions, or meals. Now, a Voice over Internet Protocol phone system also lets students use their laptops as telephones, which means long-distance calls home are free.

Professors get high marks at Dartmouth, perhaps because of the school's focus on undergraduates. The isolated location also helps; faculty make a conscious choice to teach here, leaving behind some of the distractions afflicting their peers at more urban schools. "I've been in classes with eight people before," says a senior. "The teachers are honored and excited to be here, and to engage with the students." Ninety-one percent of classes taken by freshmen have 25 or fewer students. The Presidential Scholars Program offers one-on-one research assistantships with faculty, and the Senior Fellowship Program enables 10 to 12 students a year to pursue interdisciplinary research projects, and to pay no tuition for their final term. The Women in Science Project encourages female students to pursue courses and careers in science, math, and engineering, with mentors, speakers, and even research positions for first-years. The Montgomery Fellowships bring well-known politicians, writers, and others to campus for periods ranging from a few days to several months, while the Visionary in Residence program invites notable thinkers to campus to share their talents and insights.

> "The whole campus is one giant, interactive, constant learning community."

The school's most notable eccentricity is the Dartmouth Plan, or "D Plan"—four 10-week terms a year, including one during the summer. Students must be on campus for three terms during the freshman and senior years, and also during the summer after the sophomore year, but otherwise, as long as they're on track to graduate, they can take off whenever they wish. More than half of the students use terms away for one of Dartmouth's 44 study abroad programs, where they may focus on drama in London or the environment in Zimbabwe; other students pursue part-time jobs, internships, or independent travel. The college also participates in the Twelve College Exchange* and the Maritime Studies Program.*

Dartmouth went co-ed in 1972, and women now make up half of the student body. Ethnic minorities also comprise a substantial chunk, with African Americans making up 7 percent, Asian Americans 13 percent and Hispanics 6 percent. Another

The school attracts plenty of hiking and skiing enthusiasts, and the most popular extracurricular organization is the Dartmouth Outing Club, the oldest collegiate outdoors club in the nation.

3 percent of the students are Native Americans. No matter their background, "students have an amazing ability to effectively balance being intellectually engaging and academically motivated with being down-to-earth and fun and social," says a religion major. "They are outgoing, love a good time, enjoy the outdoors, engage in intellectual conversations outside of class, care deeply about their peers, and love their school." Admissions are need-blind, even for students who get in off the waitlist, and the school guarantees to meet each student's demonstrated need for all four years. The college has added about $4 million in scholarship funds over the past few years, enabling students to borrow less for their education. It's also sold tax-exempt bonds through a state authority to help fund low-interest loans for students and their families. Dartmouth is also trying to lure more middle-class students by offering bigger grants to those whose parents earn less than $60,000 a year. No merit or athletic scholarships are awarded; the Ivy League prohibits the latter.

Eighty-two percent of Dartmouth students live on campus in one of 34 dorms, which have been grouped into 11 clusters to help create a sense of community. "The dorms are spacious and comfortable and very well-maintained," says an environmental studies major. "You can live in a single, double, triple, or quad, with anywhere from one to three rooms of different shapes and sizes." First-year students may choose freshman-only housing, or dorms where all classes live together. Sophomores may get squeezed during the housing lottery (and because construction work on a new dorm is behind schedule), but because of the D Plan, people are always coming and going; it may be easier to find a new room or roommate than at schools on the semester system. "Students routinely leave their doors unlocked and laptops out in the open because this is an incredibly trusting environment," says one student. Still, "the college installed locks on the doors to dormitories in the past five years—before, they were open to everyone." Dining facilities are open until 2:30 a.m., for those needing sustenance during late-night study sessions. Seniors may move off campus, into group houses, and many choose to do so.

Dartmouth's Greek system attracts 39 percent of the men and 34 percent of the women; it's "big, but not exclusive—all parties are open to everyone," says a junior. The Greeks have become less of a force in campus social life because of the Student Life Initiative, a steering committee that developed more-rigorous behavior standards. Parties and kegs must also be registered, and the houses where they're being held are subject to walk-throughs by college safety and security personnel. Alcohol policies are aimed at keeping booze away from those under 21. "I suppose they work," a senior sighs, noting that they're the source of some frustration. Indeed, recognizing that the nickname of its hometown has long been **"I've been in classes with eight people before."** "Hangover," Dartmouth was one of the first schools to develop a counseling and educational program to combat alcohol abuse. And students say a campus bar called the Lone Pine Tavern is more likely to be the scene of Scrabble and chess tournaments than hardcore drinking games. Popular road trips include Montreal or Boston, for a dose of bright lights and the big city, or the White Mountains for camping. (Dartmouth has a 27,000-acre land grant in the northeast corner of New Hampshire, where cabins may be rented for five dollars a night.) But in truth, students don't leave campus very often, "because no one wants to miss a weekend in Hanover," says a religion major.

Those weekends include traditions such as a 75-foot-tall bonfire at homecoming, and Winter Carnival, which includes ski racing at the college's bowl, 20 minutes away, as well as snow-sculpture contests, and partiers from all over the Eastern seaboard. Spring brings mud as the snow slowly melts, and also Green Key weekend, which one student calls "an excuse to drink under the guise of community service." (The school is striving for 100 percent participation in community service by

The Senior Fellowship Program enables 10 to 12 students a year to pursue interdisciplinary research projects, and pay no tuition for their final term.

During the summer term, the entire sophomore class heads to the Connecticut River for "Tubestock," a day of lazy, floating fun in the sun.

graduation, "and we're close," says one student. "I've traveled twice to rural Nicaragua on a Dartmouth-sponsored, student-organized crosscultural education and service program; we provide medical assistance to villagers and construct clinics, compostable latrines, and organic farms.") During the summer term, the entire sophomore class heads to the Connecticut River for "Tubestock," a day of lazy, floating fun in the sun.

Love of the outdoors at Dartmouth extends to varsity athletics. The women's ice hockey team is a perennial powerhouse, winning the Ivy League championship in 2003–2004 and an Eastern Collegiate Athletic Conference championship the year before. Women's lacrosse, men's and women's soccer, and women's basketball also make Big Green fans proud. Hanover residents support the basketball teams, and few Dartmouth students miss a trip to Cambridge for the biennial Dartmouth–Harvard football game. The school's sports facility boasts a 2,100-seat arena, a 4,000-square-foot fitness center, and the only permanent three-glass-wall squash court in North America.

"You can live in a single, double, triple, or quad." The $3 million Scully-Fahey Field offers an Astroturf surface for soccer, field hockey, and other team sports. Each winter, 1,500 students join one of the 85 intramural ice hockey teams. "I've played intramural soccer (2003 champs!), ice hockey, and softball," says one student. "I've also walked onto the varsity crew team and played club rugby. One year into my involvement with rugby, I was playing in the national tournament in California." Nonathletes beware: Dartmouth does have a non-timed swim test and a physical education requirement for graduation; you can fulfill the latter with classes such as fencing or ballet, or participation in a club or intramural sport.

Dartmouth attracts outdoorsy, down-to-earth students who develop extremely strong ties to the school—and each other—during four years together in the hinterlands. It seems as if every other grad has a title like deputy assistant class secretary, and many return to Hanover when they retire, further cementing their bonds with the college, and driving local real-estate prices beyond the reach of most faculty members. You'll have to be made of hardy stock to survive the harsh New Hampshire winters. But once you defrost, you'll be rewarded with lifelong friends, and a solid grounding in the liberal arts, sciences, and technology.

Overlaps

Harvard, Yale, Princeton, Brown, Stanford, Duke

If You Apply To ➤ **Dartmouth:** Early decision: Nov. 1. Regular admissions: Jan. 1. Financial aid: Feb. 1. Housing: July 1. Guarantees to meet demonstrated need. Campus and alumni interviews: optional, evaluative. SATs or ACTs: required (including optional ACT Writing Test). SAT IIs: required (any two). Accepts the Common Application and electronic applications; prefers electronic applications. Essay question: significant experience, achievement, risk or ethical dilemma; issue of personal, local, national or international concern; influential person, fictional character, historical figure or creative work; what you would bring to diversity of college; topic of your choice.

Davidson College

P.O. Box 1737, Davidson, NC 28035

Has always been styled as "The Dartmouth of the South." Goes head-to-head with Washington and Lee (VA) for honors as the most selective liberal arts college below the Mason-Dixon Line. At just over 1,700 students, it is slightly bigger than Rhodes and Sewanee and slightly smaller than W&L.

Website: www.davidson.edu

Davidson College boasts the Southern tradition and gentility of neighbors like Rhodes and Sewanee, with the athletic and academic prowess more common to

Northern liberal arts powerhouses such as Dartmouth and Middlebury. Often overlooked because of its small size and sleepy location, Davidson is one of the most selective liberal arts colleges below the Mason-Dixon Line. The school's size, honor code, and strong interdisciplinary, international, and preprofessional programs distinguish Davidson from many of its contemporaries. "Davidson offers one of the best undergraduate experiences and is the liberal arts school of the South," says a senior economics major.

Located in a beautiful stretch of the North Carolina Piedmont, Davidson's wooded campus features Georgian and Greek Revival architecture. The central campus is designated as an arboretum, and college staff lovingly maintain a collection of the woody plants that thrive in the area. In fact, the arboretum serves as an outdoor laboratory for students, with markers identifying the varieties of trees and shrubs. Davidson retains its original quadrangle, which dates from 1837, plus two dorms and literary society halls built in the 1850s. Chambers Building, the school's main academic building, was renovated in 2004.

Davidson's honor code allows students to take exams independently and to feel comfortable leaving doors unlocked. "Because of an honor code that works, Davidson students are able to walk around campus feeling safe and can leave their belongings anywhere without worrying that they will be stolen," says a senior. Another student adds, "It is not uncommon to see money taped to a bench or a pole, saying it was found there." Every entering freshman agrees to abide by the code, and all work submitted to professors is signed with the word "pledged." Core requirements include one course each in fine arts, literature, and history, and two courses each in religion and philosophy, natural sciences and math, and social sciences. Students must also take classes with significant writing and discussion in the first year to satisfy the composition requirement. Four physical education classes are required, as is proficiency in a foreign language equal to three semesters of work. Many requirements, including in-depth or comparative studies of another culture, may be met through the two-year interdisciplinary humanities program.

Davidson's academic climate is rigorous, but not grueling. "The college places a lot of emphasis on well-roundedness," a senior says. "Students at Davidson are self-actualized people who are able to appreciate the ideas, talents, and interests of their fellow students," adds a senior religion major. The most popular majors are English, economics, political science, psychology and history. Professors are highly lauded for being friendly and accessible. "The high quality of teaching at Davidson is one of the hallmarks of the college. It is not unusual for a professor to invite his or her students to their home for a study break or a meal."

"The college places a lot of emphasis on well-roundedness."

For those whose academic interests lie outside the mainstream, Davidson's Center for Interdisciplinary Studies allows students to develop and design their own majors, with faculty or on their own. Environmental studies majors may apply to the School for Field Studies to spend a month or a semester studying environmental issues in other countries or to work and conduct research at Biosphere 2. Aspiring diplomats can tap into the Dean Rusk Program for International Studies, named for the Davidson alumnus who served as Secretary of State to Presidents Kennedy and Johnson. The South Asia Studies program focuses on India, Pakistan, Bangladesh, Sri Lanka, Nepal, and Bhutan; study abroad is also available in countries from France, Germany, and England to Cyprus and Zambia, and more than 65 percent of the students go abroad. A 3–2 engineering program is available with five larger universities. A Sloan Foundation grant is helping Davidson integrate technology into the liberal arts, with courses such as From Petroleum to Penicillin, and Sex, Technology, and Morality. On campus, class size is restricted; you won't find a room other than the cafeteria with more than 50 students.

(Continued)
Location: Small town
Total Enrollment: 1,714
Undergraduates: 1,702
Male/Female: 49/51
SAT Ranges: V 630–730
   M 640–710
ACT Range: 26–31
Financial Aid: 34%
Expense: Pr $ $ $
Phi Beta Kappa: Yes
Applicants: 4,154
Accepted: 27%
Enrolled: 42%
Grad in 6 Years: 89%
Returning Freshmen: 95%
Academics: ✍ ✍ ✍ ✍ ½
Social: ☎ ☎ ☎
Q of L: ★ ★ ★ ★
Admissions: (800) 768-0380
Email Address:
   admission@davidson.edu

Strongest Programs:
Biology
Psychology
English
Political Science
Theatre
Chemistry
International Studies
History

The eating clubs are the center of social life on campus. All but one are in Patterson Court, which freshmen are not allowed to enter for the first three weeks of school.

Most Davidson students come from affluent Southern families, though only 18 percent are native North Carolinians. Many students are Presbyterian, and the school has ties to the Presbyterian Church. Their parents are doctors, lawyers, and ministers and as well as premed and prelaw preparation, Davison has a number of courses appropriate for students who aim to become clergy. Six percent of the student body is African American, with 4 percent Hispanic and 2 percent Asian American. Gushes one senior, "Students are compassionate, motivated, goal-oriented, friendly, dynamic, enthusiastic, reliable, and very hard working." Modest, too. Davidson lures top students with merit scholarships, averaging about $7,700 a year. One hundred eighty-five athletic scholarships are available.

Ninety-one percent of Davidson's students live on campus in co-ed or single-sex dorms. "Dorms are comfortable and centrally located," a senior says. Freshmen are housed together in two five-story halls and they eat in Vail Commons, where the "food is great—all you can eat, and lots of options, though it's hard to be a vegan at Davidson." Upperclassmen may live in the dorms, off campus, or in college-owned cottages on the perimeter of campus, which hold about 10 students each. Seniors get apartments with private bedrooms. Most upperclassmen take meals

"Dorms are comfortable and centrally located."

at one of the 11 eating clubs—six for men, four for women; one coed eating club has opened for the adventurous. These Greek-like groups have their own cooks and serve meals family style.

The eating clubs are the center of social life on campus. All but one are in Patterson Court, which freshmen are not allowed to enter for the first three weeks of school. The dues charged by these clubs cover meals, as well as parties and other campuswide events. The fraternities, which claim 40 percent of Davidson's men, are not much different from the eating clubs, and freshmen simply sign up for the group they want to join on Self-Selection Night, with no "rushing" allowed. There are no sororities on campus. And even if you don't join up, don't despair; Davidson requires that most parties-"at least two per weekend" at the eating clubs—be open to the entire community. Alcohol policies comply with North Carolina law; officially, no one under 21 can be served. But one student says, "The administration won't run after people to catch them; it's a good idea to be discreet."

Davidson's five-day freshman orientation includes a regatta, scavenger hunt, and the Freshman Cake Race. The program helps introduce students to the cozy town of Davidson, which has coffee shops and cafes, nearby Lake Norman for sailing, swimming, and waterskiing, and plenty of volunteer opportunities. The equally quaint town of Cornelius is only a 10-minute drive from campus, so it's a common destination for dinner and a movie or a relaxed night out. When those diversions grow old, North Carolina's largest city, Charlotte, is just 20 miles away, with clubs and other attractions. A car definitely helps here, as Myrtle Beach and skiing are several hours from Davidson, in different directions. Intramural and club sports are varied and popular. The men's basketball squad brought home the 2005 Southern Conference championship, as did the women's cross-country team in 2003.

Davidson has strengthened its position among liberal arts colleges, attracting more top students to its charming neck of the woods and improving facilities. "Sure, we live in a bubble," admits a physics major, "but we are all genuinely happy to be here." From study abroad and independent research to a strawberries-and-champagne reception with the college president for graduating seniors, students here combine tradition with forward thinking, to make great memories, friends, and intellectual strides.

Overlaps

**Duke, Wake Forest,
UNC–Chapel Hill,
University of Virginia,
Vanderbilt**

University of Dayton

Dayton, OH 45469-1323

Among a cohort of second-tier Midwest Roman Catholic institutions that includes Duquesne, Xavier (OH), U of St. Louis, and DePaul and Loyola of Chicago. Drawing cards include business, education, and the social sciences. The city of Dayton is not particularly enticing and UD's appeal is largely regional.

Anyone who thinks college students of today subscribe to postmodern cynicism ought to take a peek at Dayton, where optimism and Christian charity are alive and well. "If you used one word to describe UD students, it would be friendly," a senior says. "Everyone on campus is very welcoming. We smile and say hi to people we don't know and hold the doors open for each other." There's good reason for the cheery disposition: Applications recently hit a record level for the fourth year running.

Founded by the Society of Mary (Marianists), Dayton continues to emphasize that order's devotion to service. The majority of UD students volunteer their time in 30 different public service areas. Christmas on campus, where UD students "adopt" local elementary students for a night of crafts, games, and a visit with Santa, is one of the most student-involved activities. "We bring in about 1,000 inner-city Dayton school kids and walk them around campus which is transformed into a winter wonderland," says one student.

The parklike campus is on the southern boundary of the city, secluded from the traffic and bustle of downtown. The more historic buildings make up the central core of the campus and blend architectural charm with modern technological conveniences. A new $25 million fitness and recreation complex, dubbed the "RecPlex," opened in 2006. It houses classrooms, a climbing wall, basketball and volleyball courts, a juice bar, and many other sports-related facilities. A $22 million expansion of Sherman and Wohlleben Halls will provide 55,000 square feet of new science facilities, and five new five-person houses were recently added to the student housing lineup. A new 400-bed residence hall with amenities such as a post office and credit union is in the heart of campus. ArtStreet, a $9 million arts-centered living/learning complex, includes six two-story townhouses and five loft apartments above performance spaces, art studios, the campus radio station, and a recording studio.

UD students take full advantage of the strong offerings found in business, education, communications, and the social sciences—the most popular majors. Weaker offerings include theater and physical education. Most students agree the academic climate varies between demanding and laid back depending on the degree, but that all departments provide challenging curriculum. "It's not so difficult you feel overwhelmed or spend all your time studying, but it's not a breeze either," says a senior communication management major.

Dayton's general education requirements include courses in five "domains of knowledge": arts, history, philosophy and religion, physical and life sciences, and

Website: admission.udayton.edu
Location: City outskirts
Total Enrollment: 10,495
Undergraduates: 6,671
Male/Female: 50/50
SAT Ranges: V 510–620 M 520–640
ACT Range: 23–27
Financial Aid: 60%
Expense: Pr $
Phi Beta Kappa: No
Applicants: 8,156
Accepted: 80%
Enrolled: 28%
Grad in 6 Years: 76%
Returning Freshmen: 87%
Academics: ✍ ✍ ✍
Social: ☎ ☎ ☎ ☎ ☎
Q of L: ★ ★ ★
Admissions: (800) 837-7433
Email Address: admission@udayton.edu

Strongest Programs:
Education
Communication
Marketing
Finance
Psychology

The Interdepartmental Summer Study Abroad Program is a popular ticket to the world's most exciting cities, while the Immersion Program in Third World countries is much praised by participants.

social sciences. Students must also complete the humanities base and a thematic cluster. Faculty members in the College of Arts and Sciences have developed a 12-course core curriculum that satisfies the general education requirements through an interdisciplinary program that clumps mandatory classes into sequences pertinent to academic disciplines. Women's studies, a minor since 1978, has been expanded into a major. The prestigious Berry Scholars program includes seminars, study abroad opportunities, service and leadership projects, and a major independent research project. Students with at least a 1300 combined SAT score or a 30 ACT score and who place in the top 10 percent of their graduating class or have a 3.7 GPA may join the University Honors Program, which provides guest speakers in small classes and requires an honors thesis project.

The Interdepartmental Summer Study Abroad Program is a popular ticket to the world's most exciting cities, while the Immersion Program in Third World countries is much praised by participants. The University of Dayton Research Institute (UDRI) is one of the nation's leading university-based research organizations. All students purchase a notebook computer upon entering UD. Students speak enthusiastically about the quality of teaching, stating that professors are "passionate" about their courses. "They are so knowledgeable, friendly and encouraging," a senior says. New students unsure of their majors can take advantage of First Year Experience, a structured program where students are required to meet with their advisors once a week.

"It's not so difficult you feel overwhelmed or spend all your time studying."

"Most of our students are from middle-class families and about 70 percent are Catholic," says a senior. Two-thirds of Dayton's students are from Ohio, and minorities make up just 7 percent of the student population; 4 percent are African American, 2 percent are Hispanic, and 1 percent are Asian American. The Task Force on Women's Issues, the Office of Diverse Student Populations, and an updated sexual-harassment policy demonstrate UD's growing sensitivity to campus issues. More than three-quarters of incoming students rank in the top half of their high school class, and the school is becoming more selective. Dayton's athletic scholarships go to athletes in six men's sports and seven women's sports. There are also many merit awards, averaging nearly $5,000.

Women's studies, a minor since 1978, has been expanded into a major.

Seventy-eight percent of students are campus residents; those who live off-campus generally live adjacent to it. "All first-year students live in one of four traditional residence halls," a senior explains. "Sophomores opt to live in suites or apartments, while upperclass students live in university-owned houses, apartments or town-houses." Students say the dorms are well-maintained yet somewhat outdated. Sophomores have an opportunity to live in Virginia Kettering, a residence hall whose amenities evoke luxurious apartments. The food in the dining halls that dot the campus is generally well-received; one dining hall is located in one of the first-year dorms, another in the sophomore complex, the third is centrally located in the student union, and a fourth is in the newly built Marianist Hall. A food emporium is in the newest dorm on campus, and a cafe is in the new ArtStreet complex.

"The Xavier game is our biggest rivalry and attracts the attention of most students."

The student neighborhood (aka "the Ghetto") serves as a sort of continuous social center. A lit porchlight beckons party-seeking students to join the weekend festivities. Because the university owns most of the properties, a 24-hour campus security patrol keeps watch over the area. The more adventurous weekend excursions are trips to Ohio State University, Ohio University, Indianapolis and the restaurants, shops, and sports arenas in Cincinnati. But the best road trip is the Dayton-to-Daytona trip after spring finals, a 17-hour trek that draws loads of students each year. Partying on campus is commonplace and controlled, but parties have sized down due to the university's enforcement of the 21-year-old drinking age. "There is a 'no keg policy' that most students ignore," admits one student. Still, "There is a 'three strikes, you're out' policy regarding drinking," which students say makes them cautious. Greek organizations draw 15 percent of UD men and 19 percent of the women, with all chapters playing an active role in the community service and social life.

More important, though, are sports, particularly basketball. "The Xavier game is our biggest rivalry and attracts the attention of most students," says a student. The men's basketball team were Atlantic 10 conference champions in 2003. The football team, which is Division I-AA, plays in the Pioneer Football League; UD is in the Atlantic 10 for Division I athletics in all other sports. Women's soccer has won seven regular season titles and four tournament crowns. In 2003 and 2004, the women's volleyball team won the Atlantic championship and played in the NCAA championships. When students aren't cheering, they can participate in an intramural program that offers 45 sports. Other activities in the city include a minor-league baseball team, an art institute, an aviation museum, and a symphony and ballet are in the new Schuster Performing Arts Center. Two large shopping malls are also easily accessible.

The success of Dayton's attempts to provide its students with a high quality of life and a sense of cohesiveness is reflected in many of the students' comments about the terrific social life and family-like atmosphere among both students and faculty. As a midsize university where the undergraduates come first, Dayton has managed to maintain an exciting balance of personal attention, academic challenge, and all-American fun. "We're a community. We live together, learn together and socialize together," a senior says. "UD isn't just a school. It's a family!"

More than three-quarters of incoming students rank in the top half of their high school class, and the school is becoming more selective.

Overlaps

Miami (OH), Ohio, Xavier (OH), Ohio State, Notre Dame, Marquette

If You Apply To > **Dayton:** Rolling admissions: Jan. 1 (priority). Financial aid: Mar. 31 (priority). Housing: varies. Campus interviews: recommended, informational. Alumni interviews: optional, informational. SATs or ACTs: required. SAT II: optional. Requires electronic applications. Essay question: personal statement on an achievement, experience, or risk and its impact on you.

Deep Springs College

Deep Springs, CA. Mailing address: Dyer, NV 89010-9803

BEST BUY

Picture 25 Ivy League–caliber men living and learning in a remote desert outpost— that's Deep Springs. DS occupies a handful of ranch-style buildings set on 50,000 acres on the arid border of Nevada and California. Most students transfer to highly selective colleges after two years.

If the thought of spending countless hours under the fluorescent lights of the classroom makes you grimace, you may consider getting your hands dirty at Deep Springs College. This two-year institution doubles as a working ranch. Bonding is easy here, and students enjoy a demanding and individualized education supplemented by the challenges and lessons of ranch life. Both, it seems, demand the same things: hard work, commitment, and pride in a job well done. Deep Springs College students are also rewarded for their efforts in other ways: tuition is free and so is room and board. Students pay only for books, travel, and personal items; the average cost of one year at Deep Springs is $500.

Many of the men who work, study, and live at this college have shunned acceptance at Ivy League schools to embrace the rigors of a truly unique approach

Website:
  www.deepsprings.edu
Location: Rural
Total Enrollment: 26
Undergraduates: 26
Male/Female: 100/0
SAT Ranges: V 718–800
  M 685–780
Financial Aid: N/A
Expense: Pr $

(Continued)

Phi Beta Kappa: No
Applicants: 160
Accepted: 11%
Enrolled: 86%
Grad in 6 Years: N/A
Returning Freshmen: 93%
Academics: ✐✐✐✐½
Social: ☎
Q of L: ★★★
Admissions: (760) 872-2000
Email Address:
apcom@deepsprings.edu

Strongest Programs:
Humanities
Liberal Arts
Environmental Studies
Philosophy

to learning. Deep Springs students tend to be of the academic Renaissance-man variety with wide-ranging interests in many fields. Almost all transfer to the Ivies or other prestigious universities after their two-year program, and 70 percent eventually earn a PhD or law degree.

California's White Mountains provide a stunning backdrop for the Deep Springs campus, set on a barren plain 5,200 feet above sea level, near the only water supply for miles around. The campus is an oasis-like cluster of trees and a lawn with eight recently renovated, ranch-style buildings that were built from scratch by the Class of 1919. Deep Springs is 28 miles from the nearest town, a thriving metropolis known as Big Pine, population 950. The focal point of campus is the Main Building, a venerable ranch house that includes a computer room and offices. Dorm rooms are now housed in the new, spacious Student Residence. Faculty houses and the dining facilities are grouped around the circular lawn a few yards away, and the trappings of farm life surround the tiny settlement. The college has 170 acres under cultivation, mostly with alfalfa, and an assortment of barnyard animals. Once threatened with extinction (thanks to meager financial resources), the college launched a capital campaign that generated $18 million in six years. True to its practical spirit, the school used much of the money to enhance facilities and put itself back on track to a long future.

Founded in 1917 by an industrialist who made a fortune in the electric-power industry, Deep Springs today remains true to its charter "to combine taxing practical work, rigorous academics, and genuine self-government." Ideals of self-government, reflectiveness, frugality, and community activity have weathered more than 85 years of a grueling academic climate. "The academic climate is vibrant, alive, almost explosive," says one student. "Study anything. Study it well, and seriously,

> **"The academic climate is vibrant, alive, almost explosive."**

and if you're psyched, you'll find others to get psyched about it, too. Get a professor psyched and you've got yourself an independent study—a one person class." Academic learning is the primary activity here, but students are also required to perform 20 hours per week of labor, which can include everything from harvesting alfalfa to cooking dinner. When asked which are the best majors, one wit exclaims, "Dairy is the most popular, but many students swear by irrigation."

Students' input carries a lot of weight at this school. The student body committees are an essential part of the self-governance pillar at DS. There are four committees: the student-run Applications Committee, which is made up of nine students, a faculty member, and a staff member, the Curriculum Committee, the Review and Reinvitations Committee, and the Communications Committee. They help choose the college's faculty and even elect two of their own to be a voting member on the board of trustees. They play a determining role in admissions and curricular decisions. And they abide by a spartan community code that bans all drugs, including alcohol, and forbids anyone to leave Deep Springs Valley (the 50 square miles of desert surrounding the campus) while classes are in session, except for medical visits and college business. Lest these rules sound unnecessarily strict, keep in mind that these are all decided on and enforced by the student body, not the administration.

Like almost everything else about it, Deep Springs has an unorthodox academic schedule: two summer terms of seven weeks each, and a fall and spring semester of 14 weeks each. Between seven and 10 classes are offered every term. The faculty consists of three "permanent" professors (they sign on for two years, but can stay for up to six), plus an average of three others who are hired on a temporary basis to teach for a term or two. The quality of particular academic areas varies as professors come and go. "Teaching is better than a mixed bag, but not as good as it could be," says one student. "They're always available, they're always committed, but they're not always the best teachers." Although the curriculum is altered yearly, students predict that literary theory and philosophy will always remain superior. The students control the academic program and quickly replace courses—and faculty—that do not work out. Foreign language offerings are still sparse, and lack of high-tech lab equipment puts a damper on chemistry and physics courses, though administration points out the acquisition of "some very fine new microscopes and telescopes." Currently, the only required courses are public speaking and composition.

Deep Springers aren't much for the latest conveniences, but computers have taken the campus by storm; whether provided by DS or brought from home, almost every student room has one, plus several in a common area. With class sizes ranging from two to 14, there is ample opportunity for close student/faculty interaction. Close living arrangements have fostered a kind of kinship between faculty and students. Students routinely visit their mentors in their homes, sometimes to confer on academic matters and sometimes to play soccer with their children.

Deep Springers can truly boast of being hand-picked to attend; of the approximately 200 applications received each year, only 11 or so students are accepted. Most DS students are from upper-middle-class families and typically rank in the top 3 percent of their high school class. A freshman says his peers are "willing to take responsibility to manage a cattle ranch, to teach themselves what they don't know, to fix things that break, and clean up after themselves and others." Many Deep Springers are transplanted urbanites; the rest hail from points scattered across the nation or across the seas. Political leanings run the gamut, and there is diversity even among this small population: 76 percent of the student body is white, Asian Americans make up 20 percent, and Hispanics account for 4 percent. Though as any statistics student will tell you, the numbers are so small, that statistics are meaningless. "My peers are the smartest people I've ever met in my life," says one student. "They're a little eccentric, very compassionate, and full of a camaraderie that's hard to find outside of sports teams."

Dorm selection and maintenance is entirely the responsibility of the students. "Dorms are gigantic and very comfortable. Some are full of old furniture and art. One is filled with Greek busts and another has a mural on the ceiling," says a student. "The nicest rooms I have ever seen; anywhere. Too nice for us actually, some students like to sleep out in the desert.'" Students all pitch in preparing the meals, from butchering the meat to milking the cows to washing the dishes. "We eat lots of beef; well, we are a cattle ranch," says a student. Given the sequestered location of DS, crime is not an issue. Safety, however, is another matter. "Sometimes we get charged by bulls," admits one student. Another adds, "What security issues? A pack of coyotes?"

Social life can be a challenge. "The lack of women, alcohol, and nightlife can at times be frustrating," reports one student. And loneliness can be an issue. Still, "despite work, fatigue, and over-philosophizing, spirits are generally high." When the moon is full, students go out en masse in the middle of the night to frolic in the 700-foot-high Eureka Sand Dunes with Frisbees and skis. "We slide down the Eureka Valley sand dunes au naturel," says one student. As for "recent technological advancement," they used to have

"Teaching is better than a mixed bag, but not as good as it could be."

one telephone line for the whole school; now they have six. Perhaps the most popular social activity on campus is conversation over a cup of coffee in the dining hall, where the chatter is usually lively until the wee hours of the morning. Other common activities are road trips to nearby national parks, hikes in the nearby mountains, and horseback riding. The Turkey Bowl, the potato harvest, the two-on-two basketball tournament, and Sludgefest, an annual event involving cleaning out the reservoir, are only some of the time-honored Deep Springs traditions.

Critics of Deep Springs charge that DS cultivates arrogance and social backwardness among students who were too intellectual to be in the social mainstream during high school. They argue that students who come here are doomed to be misfits for

"My peers are the smartest people I've ever met in my life."

life, citing a survey that shows many Deep Springers never marry. While that charge is debatable, even supporters of Deep Springs confess to a love-hate relationship with the college. Although the interpretations may vary, one common thread winds through the DS mission from application to graduation: training for a life of service to humanity.

Perhaps more than any other school in the nation, Deep Springs is a community where students and faculty interact day-to-day on an intensely personal level. Though the financial commitment is small, the school demands an intense level of personal commitment. All must quickly learn how to get along in a community where the actions of each person affect everyone. "We are oriented towards serving humanity," says a freshman, "and we try to understand what service means in a nuanced and original way." Urban cowboys who dream of riding into the sunset are in for a rude awakening. For a select few, however, the camaraderie and soul-searching fostered in this tight-knit community can be mighty tempting—just stay clear of those bulls.

Overlaps

Harvard, Yale, University of Chicago, Columbia, Stanford, Swarthmore

If You Apply To ➤

Deep Springs: Regular admissions: Nov. 15. Campus interviews: required, evaluative. No alumni interviews. SATs: required. SAT IIs: optional. Accepts electronic applications. Essay questions: describe yourself; critical analysis of book or other work of art; and why Deep Springs?

University of Delaware

116 Hullihen Hall, Newark, DE 19716

Plenty of students dream of someday becoming Nittany Lions or Cavaliers–even Terrapins–but not many aspire to be Blue Hens. The challenge for UD is how to win its share of students without the name recognition that comes from big-time sports. Less than half the students are in-staters.

Website: www.udel.edu
Location: Small city
Total Enrollment: 17,628
Undergraduates: 15,109
Male/Female: 42/58
SAT Ranges: V 540-630
  M 560-650
ACT Range: 24-28
Financial Aid: 38%
Expense: Pub $ $ $
Phi Beta Kappa: Yes
Applicants: 22,208
Accepted: 45%
Enrolled: 35%
Grad in 6 Years: 76%

The University of Delaware is a manageable-sized public gem that boasts more than 124 solid academic programs, from engineering to education. Though lacking in a big-time sports program, UD attracts its share of students who are looking for solid academics and a friendly atmosphere. It all adds up to "the small-school feel with the opportunities of a larger university," as one junior says.

Delaware's 1,000-acre campus has an attractive mix of Colonial and modern geometric buildings, set among one of the nation's oldest Dutch elm groves. The hub of the campus is a grassy green mall, flanked by classic Georgian buildings. Mechanical Hall has undergone a $4.6 million renovation and is now a climate-controlled art gallery and home to the Paul R. Jones collection. Hotel and restaurant management students benefit from a recently-opened Courtyard by Marriott right on campus, which doubles as a learning and research facility. A performing arts center is the newest campus addition.

Delaware's academic menu includes more than 125 majors, ranging from the liberal arts and sciences to more professional programs such as apparel design and fashion merchandising. To graduate, students must pass freshman English (critical reading and writing) and earn at least three credits of discovery-based or experiential learning, such as an internship, research, or Study Abroad. Other requirements vary by college; Delaware has seven colleges, and all except the College of Marine Studies award undergraduate degrees. Business and psychology are the most popular majors, followed by English, biology, and teacher education. New majors include agriculture, finance, human services, landscape horticulture, marketing, natural resource management, sport management, and landscape design.

Engineering, especially chemical engineering, is one of UD's specialties, and the school benefits from the close proximity of DuPont, which developed Lycra spandex. The music department is another attraction, with a 350-member marching band and several faculty members holding impressive professional performance credits. UD created the nation's first study abroad program in 1923, and more than 70 study abroad programs are available on all seven continents. Journalism students can take a winter-term trip to Antarctica aboard a Russian icebreaker ship. Each year, about 600 UD students hold research apprenticeships with faculty members; in fact, the Carnegie Endowment Reinvention Center at SUNY–Stony Brook has called Delaware a "national model" for undergraduate research.

As UD has grown in popularity, academic standards have become more rigorous. Delaware routinely gets the highest number of nonresident applications for state-affiliated U.S. institutions. "In the last few years, Delaware has become more competitive and more expensive," says a senior. "Particularly, the out-of-state tuition has become a topic of dissent." About 500 new students enter the University Honors Program each year, which offers interdisciplinary colloquia, priority seating in "honors" sections of regular courses, along with talented faculty, personal attention, and extracurricular and residence hall programming.

Forty-two percent of students at Delaware hail from the First State; many of the rest are from the Northeast. Minority enrollment has been increasing; 6 percent of the student body is African American, 4 percent is Hispanic, and 3 percent are Asian American. In spite of these advancements, "The racial divide needs to be addressed. It's getting better, but it

"Particularly, the out-of-state tuition has become a topic of dissent."

still has a ways to go," a finance major says. Merit scholarships average more than $4,000 each, and athletic scholarships are offered in five men's and nine women's sports. The university maintains a search program to ensure that deserving Delaware students are aware of the scholarships for which they are eligible.

Forty-five percent of students live on campus, including all freshmen—except those commuting from home. After that, dorm housing is guaranteed and awarded by lottery, though many juniors and seniors move into off-campus apartments. Those who stay on campus find a range of accommodations: co-ed and single-sex halls with single and double rooms, as well as suites and apartment-style buildings. LIFE (Learning Integrated Freshman Experience) is a popular program that allows freshmen to live with others in the same major. Honors students also live together in designated residence halls. Campus dwellers must buy the meal plan, which offers "lots and lots of selection, though some complain about how limited the vegan, kosher, and other options are," says a junior.

When the weekend comes, Delaware students know how to let loose, though a ban on alcohol at campus parties has really taken things down a notch. "The three-strike policy works fairly well, especially in the freshman dorms," says a student. (First two strikes: fines and meetings. Third strike: suspension.) Fraternities attract 13 percent of the men and sororities 13 percent of the women. Greek groups often throw parties, but there are plenty of other options, from concerts and plays on campus to casual gatherings in friends' rooms or apartments. "It's an awesome social life—lots of on-campus activities and off-campus parties," says an English major.

(Continued)
Returning Freshmen: 89%
Academics: ✐ ✐ ✐
Social: 🐷 🐷 🐷 🐷 🐷
Q of L: ★ ★ ★
Admissions: (302) 831-8123
Email Address:
  admissions@udel.edu

Strongest Programs:
Chemical Engineering
Business Administration
Biological Sciences
Music
Nursing
English
Animal Sciences
International Relations
Teacher Education

About 500 new students enter the University Honors Program each year, which offers interdisciplinary colloquia, priority seating in "honors" sections of regular courses, along with talented faculty, personal attention, and extracurricular and residence hall programming.

Main Street, the heart of downtown Newark (pronounced "NEW-ark"), "practically runs right through campus," one student says. "It's easy walking distance from anywhere, and there are tons of coffee shops, pizza places, restaurants, a movie theater, a bowling alley, bookstores, and shops—anything you could possibly want." For

"The three-strike policy works fairly well, especially in the freshman dorms."

those seeking further excitement, New York, the Washington/Baltimore area, and Philadelphia are all within a two-hour drive. When the weather is warm, the beaches of Rehoboth and Dewey beckon, and in chilly months, the Pennsylvania ski slopes aren't too far. Mall-stock is the annual spring bacchanal, bringing music and a carnival to the central campus green.

Delaware's Blue Hens compete in Division I, and on Saturdays in the fall, watch out. "Football is big," says one student. "Now that our football team won the NCAA IAA championship, it is getting more popular. The cheerleaders are also very good." Tailgate picnics are popular before and after the game. The Blue Hens are recent champs in field hockey, women's basketball, and men's lacrosse, and spectators also love to cheer for the soccer and women's crew squads. Delaware's sports center has space for 6,000 to cheer; intramural sports are popular.

Aspiring engineers and educators, and practically everyone in-between, can find something to delve into at the University of Delaware. With a challenging and stimulating academic environment, an increasingly smart student body, a healthy social scene, and up-and-coming athletic teams, UD offers a blend of strengths that would make many schools envious—and leads to many happy Blue Hens.

Overlaps

Penn State, University of Maryland, Rutgers, University of Connecticut, Boston University, James Madison

If You Apply To ➤ **Delaware:** Early decision: Nov. 1. Regular admissions: Jan. 15 (Dec. 15 for scholarships) Financial aid: Feb. 1. Housing: May 31. Does not guarantee to meet demonstrated need. Campus and alumni interviews: optional, evaluative. SATs or ACTs: required. SAT IIs: recommended. Accepts the Common Application and electronic applications. Essay question: describe a life-changing experience; how your ethnic or cultural heritage has shaped your worldview; or use your imagination to surprise or entertain the admissions officers.

Denison University

Granville, OH 43023

Denison shut down its Frat Row in an effort to shift the spotlight from partying to academics. Not quite as selective as Kenyon, it draws more Easterners than competitors such as Wittenberg and Ohio Wesleyan. Denison has a middle-of-the-road to conservative student body and one of the most beautiful campuses anywhere.

Website: www.denison.edu
Location: Small town
Total Enrollment: 2,099
Undergraduates: 2,099
Male/Female: 44/56
SAT Ranges: V 570–670
  M 570–660
ACT Range: 25–30
Financial Aid: 49%
Expense: Pr $ $ $

Denison University, tucked into the "quaint, small, and beautiful" hamlet of Granville, draws "bright and laid-back, engaging and interesting, athletic, good-looking, generally privileged and ambitious students", says an immodest senior. Thanks to Denison's small size, there's ample opportunity to interact (and do research with) professors, and to form close relationships with peers, as everyone focuses on the liberal arts. "Our experience is a much more holistic one," an English major explains.

Denison's campus is set atop rolling hills in central Ohio. Huge maples shade the sloping walkways, which offer a panoramic view of the surrounding valley. And don't be surprised if you're reminded of New York's Central Park—Denison retained park architect Frederick Law Olmsted for its first master plan back in the early 1900s.

The Georgian style of many buildings—redbrick with white columns—also evokes shades of New England and its private liberal arts colleges. Higley Hall has been renovated for the departments of economics, communication, and service learning, after the biology department moved to the new Samson Talbot Hall. The chemistry department's Ebaugh Laboratories have been renovated and student offices in Slayter Hall were recently improved.

Denison has overhauled its general education requirements, moving from an inquiry-based to a division-based program and reducing the minimum number of required credits to 11 from 14. Students now take two first-year seminars, and then during their four years, two courses each in the fine arts, the sciences (one with lab), the social sciences, the humanities and a foreign language. Some courses may be double-counted to fulfill oral communication and quantitative reasoning requirements. Students must also complete a course focusing on interdisciplinary and world issues. Administrators hope that with fewer mandates and more opportunities to fulfill them, Denisonians will take more responsibility for—and ownership of—their individual academic programs.

Students say that some of the best majors are unique to Denison. The PPE major is effectively a triple major in philosophy, political science, and economics. The economics department is nationally ranked among undergraduate institutions. "Geology, astronomy, philosophy, and psychology offer a thinking person's alternative to the more technically demanding sciences," advises a senior. The environment is more collaborative than competitive. "Students tend to enjoy each other in class and aim for individual success," says a student. Denison's 350-acre biological reserve is a boon for environmental studies majors. The school encourages students to pursue independent research or to work with faculty members on their projects, and gives 125 students summer stipends of $3300 plus housing and research support for supplies and travel each year. The Honors Program offers up to 50 courses per year, and also sponsors a "Chowder Hour," where students and faculty gather for an informal presentation while dining on a faculty member's culinary specialty.

Classes are small, and individual attention is the norm, says a recent graduate. "Professors here love teaching as much as research. Their office doors are always open and they will drop their sandwich if you stop by during lunch in order to answer your academic or personal questions," comments one senior. When Granville gets too small, internships and off-campus studies are available through the Great Lakes Colleges Association* and the Associated Colleges of the Midwest.* Those considering a run for office may be interested in the Richard G. Lugar Program in American Politics and Public Service, which includes political science courses on campus and culminates in a House or Senate internship in Washington. (The Senator happens to be a Denison grad.) As a participant in the Denison Internship Program, formerly known as May Term, students select from more than 250 internships around the country.

"Our experience is a much more holistic one."

Geographically, 40 percent of Denison's population is homegrown, and 4 percent come from abroad. The Posse Program funds 10 full-tuition scholarships per class for multicultural student leaders from Chicago and Boston public high schools, which has helped boost diversity on campus. African Americans now constitute 5 percent of the student body, while Hispanics and Asian Americans combine for 6 percent. "The environment, social justice, and fair trade are the largest issues on campus. The percentage of liberal students on campus is relatively high despite the somewhat conservative and wealthy backgrounds of many students," explains a student. A senior agrees, "Social justice is a major concern for a lot of students at Denison. Students are always discussing current events and how they relate to what they are learning in class." Fifty-six percent of students receive merit scholarships, including the Wells,

(Continued)
Phi Beta Kappa: Yes
Applicants: 4,947
Accepted: 44%
Enrolled: 28%
Grad in 6 Years: 77%
Returning Freshmen: 90%
Academics: 📖 📖 📖 ½
Social: 🍸 🍸 🍸 🍸 🍸
Q of L: ★ ★ ★
Admissions: (740) 587-6276
Email Address:
  admissions@denison.edu

Strongest Programs:
Natural and Social Sciences
Philosophy
Theatre
Creative Writing
Geology
International Studies
Computer Science

Dunbar, and Faculty Achievement awards, which cover full tuition. The average non-need-based award is more than $11,500, though there are no athletic scholarships.

Ninety-nine percent of Denison students live on campus; the only ones allowed to live elsewhere are those commuting from home. (One exception is the dozen Homesteaders, who live in three student-built solar-paneled cabins on a farm a mile away, and grow much of their own food.) Options range from singles to nine-person suites, and housing is guaranteed for four years. That said, "The only frustration that students at Denison generally share is over housing. Rooms are guaranteed to all students and a lottery is held each spring for the coming year and students are often unhappy with their assignment," says a senior. That will change, as the school's fifth and sixth apartment-style dorms become available. Crawford Hall, the freshman dorm, offers counseling, entertainment, and other assistance on the premises. Former fraternity houses now focus on common interests, such as service-learning (Morrow House) or honors courses (Gilpatrick House), while Stone Hall, Curtis East, and Smith Hall have been upgraded in recent years. Entrees in the two dining halls change daily.

"Students tend to enjoy each other in class and aim for individual success."

When the weekend comes, "Denison does a wonderful job at providing a ton of events for students to choose from," says a psychology major. "The only problem I ran into was deciding which to attend." Options include movie screenings, comedy shows, and concerts at the student union, where guest artists have included Bela Fleck and the Flecktones, Edgar Meyer, Ani di Franco, Bobby McFerrin, George Clinton and the P-Funk All-Stars, and Joshua Bell, to name a few. The school also runs trips to the local mall and to Meijer, a Midwestern superstore similar to Wal-Mart, and the student government has even been known to hold fireworks shows. Alcohol policies are less punitive and more focused on ensuring safety. "Alcohol consumption is common and frequently high. Thankfully, everything at Denison is within walking distance, so it is far more likely to find drunken underclassmen nursing tacos or pizza in the student union than crumpled around a highway divider," says one student. Though the Greek system is now nonresidential, 32 percent of the men and 43 percent of the women still join up. Students also look forward to two blowout parties each year—November's D-Day, which recently featured Third Eye Blind, and Festivus, on the last day of spring classes, headlined in the past by Dave Matthews Band, Guster, Rusted Root, and the Samples.

The tiny town of Granville "is a gorgeous slice of small town Americana," says one student. "Granville in spring is a sight to behold, with a seemingly endless supply of blooming, fragrant flowers," enthuses a senior. There are four churches on the corners of the town's main intersection, along with "two bars, a coffee shop, a bank, a greasy spoon restaurant, a library, and gift shops," says another student. Most stores and restaurants close by 8 p.m., though students appreciate the feeling of safety and security that results. The Denison Campus Association frequently sends students into Granville and nearby Newark to provide tutoring, mentoring, and environmental cleanup. Popular road trips include Ohio University, Ohio State (in the state capital, Columbus), and Miami University in Oxford, Ohio. Pittsburgh, Cleveland, Cincinnati, and Dayton are also close by.

"The only frustration that students at Denison generally share is over housing."

Denison students are enthusiastic supporters of the Big Red, and men's lacrosse games against Ohio Wesleyan always draw large crowds. The school competes in the North Coast Athletic Conference and has won the All Sports Championship for eight years running. Denison posted top-five finishes in 21 of 22 sports. In its history of participation in the NCAA, 37 students have received NCAA Post-Graduate Scholarship awards, the third largest number in Division III sports. Enthusiasm

Ninety-nine percent of Denison students live on campus; the only ones allowed to live elsewhere are those commuting from home.

The economics department is nationally ranked among undergraduate institutions.

reaches a fevered pitch during homecoming weekend, when the all-campus gala always includes a chocolate volcano.

Denison University is a school on the move, aiming to graduate independent thinkers who become active citizens of a democratic society. The school continues to value tradition—woe to the student who steps on the school seal in front of the chapel, for doing so will cause him to fail all his finals—while growing and evolving to emphasize academics and the life of the mind. A recent graduate says, "Denison is distinctive for its commitment to preparing its students to be life-long learners. The liberal arts tradition at Denison teaches students how to become analytical and critical thinkers—something valued in nearly any field of work."

If You Apply To ➤

Denison: Early decision: Nov. 1, Jan. 1. Regular admissions: Jan. 1. Financial aid: Jan. 15. Housing: Jun. 1. Meets demonstrated need of 59%. Campus and alumni interviews: recommended, evaluative. SATs or ACTs: required. SAT IIs: optional. Accepts the Common Application and electronic applications; prefers electronic applications. Essay question: paragraph or two describing reasons for applying to Dennison.

University of Denver

2199 South University Boulevard, Mary Reed Building, Denver, CO 80208

The only major midsized private university between Tulsa and the West Coast, DU's campus in residential Denver is pleasant but uninspiring. Brochures instead tout Rocky Mountain landscapes. DU remains a haven for ski bums and business majors.

The oldest private university in the Rocky Mountain region, the University of Denver is where Secretary of State Condoleeza Rice earned her BA in political science at age 19 and later returned for a PhD in International Studies. Her mentor was Soviet specialist Joseph Korbel, father of former Secretary of State Madeline Albright. Thus, it's not surprising that DU boasts strong programs in political science, international studies, and public affairs. However, many students opt for DU's business program, and the campus location offers ample opportunities for networking, skiing, and taking in the beautiful Colorado landscape. "Academics are high, social life is awesome, friendships are easily formed, and it's four years of unforgettable memories," a junior says.

DU's 125-acre main campus is located in a comfortable residential neighborhood only eight miles from downtown Denver and an hour east of major ski areas. The north campus is home to several programs, including the Women's College, but a multiyear, $380 million project is underway to unite all university programs onto the same campus. Architectural styles vary, and include Collegiate Gothic, brick, limestone, Colorado sandstone, and copper. Nearby Mount Evans (14,264 feet) is home to the world's loftiest observatory, a DU facility available to both professors and students. The 2,000-seat Peter Barton Lacrosse Stadium opened in 2005 as the nation's first campus facility devoted to the sport. A new building to house the School of Hotel, Restaurant, and Tourism Management also functions as a student-operated conference center.

DU is known for its business school—especially the hotel, restaurant, and tourism management offerings—and for its innovative core curriculum. Pre-professional programs are feeders for graduate schools in business, international studies, engineering, and the arts. Chemistry, atmospheric physics, music, psychology, and

Website: www.du.edu
Location: City outskirts
Total Enrollment: 6,132
Undergraduates: 4,188
Male/Female: 48/52
SAT Ranges: V 510–630
    M 520–630
ACT Range: 22–27
Financial Aid: 78%
Expense: Pr $ $
Phi Beta Kappa: Yes
Applicants: 3,787
Accepted: 87%
Enrolled: 34%
Grad in 6 Years: 69%
Returning Freshmen: 86%
Academics: ✍ ✍ ✍
Social: ☎ ☎ ☎ ☎
Q of L: ★ ★ ★ ★
Admissions: (303) 871-2036
Email Address:
    admission@du.edu

computer science have solid reputations. Undergrads can opt for a five-year program toward a master's degree in business, international studies, or law. The academic climate is relatively relaxed. "My classes are somewhat challenging and require some hard work, but the classes aren't too difficult," says a biology major. Professors receive high marks for their intelligence and passion. "Many of the professors are invested in the lives of students and are genuinely concerned for them and their education," says a senior.

All undergraduates must take courses in English, natural science, a foreign language, arts and humanities, social sciences, math and computer science, and creative expressions, in addition to core curriculum courses in communities and environments, self and identities, and change and community. A freshman orientation program brings new students onto campus a week early, during which they spend 10 hours with a small group of students and a professor discussing a collection of essays by prominent writers. Freshmen also take a first-year seminar limited to 15 students. "I really appreciated the orientation program and the first-year program," says a junior."

University rules stipulate that all core courses must be taught by senior faculty. "At first I thought, 'Who wants to take these science, art, and English classes?'" explains a business major. "But now that I've completed the core, I feel better about myself and my world knowledge. Now I can speak of Goya, Berlioz, and define my favorite artists with a knowledge of the period, styles, and works." A rigorous honors program is available, as are numerous study abroad options. All juniors and seniors have the chance to study abroad at no extra cost. Writing offerings have been expanded to include small classes focused on helping students write effectively within their field.

For the most part, students come from fairly affluent families. One student jokes that "the stereotypical DU student drives a brand-new SUV, wears only Abercrombie and Gap clothing, and skis every weekend." Another says, "They work hard, ski hard, and drink hard." Fifty-five percent of the students are from Colorado; ethnic minorities account for 16 percent of the student body. Because it is one of the few private colleges in the West, DU is also among the most expensive in the region. In a nod to the diminishing importance of standardized test scores and GPAs, the university now conducts personal interviews of every candidate for undergraduate admissions, either in person or by phone. There are hundreds of merit and athletic scholarships available.

> "Now that I've completed the core, I feel better about myself and my world knowledge."

Students are required to live their first two years on campus in the residence halls. "The dorms are comfortable enough," says a sophomore. "They have a beautiful view of the mountains, and at sunset or during lightning storms, students often crowd around lounge windows to watch." The Johnson-McFarlane hall ("J-Mac") is supposed to be the best place for freshmen, though another student says that the Towers are a much quieter on-campus option. "Dorms are very well-maintained and provide a sense of closeness for activities," says a junior. Greeks can live and dine together in their houses. Most juniors and seniors opt for the decent quarters found within walking distance of campus.

A new building to house the School of Hotel, Restaurant, and Tourism Management also functions as a student-operated conference center.

With consistently beautiful sunny weather and great skiing, hiking, and camping less than an hour away in the Rockies, many DU students head for the hills on weekends. "During the winter weekends, the campus is empty because everyone is skiing," a senior says. Besides various ski areas, one can explore Estes Park, Mount Evans, and Echo Lake. Additionally, DU is not far from Moab, Albuquerque, and Las Vegas. Since Denver is not primarily a college town, many students with cars head for Boulder (home of the University of Colorado), about 30 miles away. For those staying home, the transit system makes it easy to get to downtown Denver. The options there are tremendous and include great local restaurants, bars, and stores, many of which cater to students. Students gripe about the lack of a student union. Twenty percent of the men and 19 percent of the women belong to a fraternity or sorority, and Greeks tend to dominate the social life. Drinking policies abound, and although DU enforces the law, students say drinking is prevalent. "Drinking is abundant in the dorms. I've seen mini-kegs in dorm rooms," notes a senior.

All types of students unite when the DU hockey team, a national powerhouse, skates out onto the ice, especially against archrival Colorado College. The team brought home the NCAA championship in 2004–2005. That same year, the skiing team also captured the conference champi-

"In my three years here I have found a wide variety of people."

onship, along with women's golf and men's lacrosse, basketball, and golf. Intramural and club sports are varied and popular. Each January, academics are put aside for the three-day Winter Carnival. Top administrators, professors, and students all pack off to Steamboat Springs, Crested Butte, or another ski area to catch some fresh powder and see who can ski the fastest, skate the best, or build the most artistic ice sculptures. In the spring, the whole campus turns out for the annual Chancellor's Barbecue. May Daze, held the first week of May, includes events on the lawn such as a musical festival.

Students like DU for its modest size and friendly atmosphere. And while there remain some moneyed students with attitude problems, plenty of others are more down-to-earth. "In my three years here I have found a wide variety of people," a senior says. As the school pushes for a more ethnically diverse student body and improves its curriculum and facilities, the University of Denver is striving to become better known for its intellectual rigor than its gorgeous setting in the Rocky Mountains.

If You Apply To ➤

DU: Early action: Nov. 1. Regular admissions: Jan. 15. Financial aid: March 1. Housing: May 1. Does not guarantee to meet demonstrated need. Campus and alumni interviews: required, informational. ACTs or SATs: required. SAT IIs: optional. Accepts the Common Application and electronic applications. Essay question: Open-ended question.

DePaul University

Chicago, IL 60604

Gets the nod over Loyola as the best Roman Catholic university in Chicago. DePaul's Lincoln Park setting is like New York's Greenwich Village without the headaches. Especially strong in business and the performing arts. The student body is about half Roman Catholic.

While there is no refuting that DePaul is the largest Catholic university in the nation, students claim its diversity and liberal leanings set it apart from rival institutions. Based in the heart of Chicago, DePaul is a feeder to Chicago's business community. A spate of campus construction has transformed it from the "little school under the tracks" to Chicago's version of NYU.

DePaul has two residential campuses. The Lincoln Park campus, with its state-of-the-art library and new student center, is home to the College of Liberal Arts and Sciences, the School of Education, the Theatre School, and the School of Music, as well as residence halls and academic and recreational facilities. Lincoln Park itself is a fashionable Chicago neighborhood with century-old brownstone homes, theaters, cafes, parks, and shops. The Loop, or "vertical" campus, 20 minutes away by elevated train in downtown Chicago, houses the College of Law, the School for New Learning, the College of Commerce, and the School of Computer Science, Telecommunications, and Information Systems in four high-rise buildings. The DePaul Center, a $70 million teaching, learning, and research complex, is the cornerstone of this campus. A new residence hall shares space with Columbia College and Roosevelt University. As of June 2005, the Barat College campus is in Lake Forest, north of Chicago, is no longer affiliated with DePaul.

DePaul's name is closely associated with Midwestern business and law, and undergraduates can find internships with local legal and commercial institutions. The School of Accountancy draws many majors and is reported to be the most challenging department in the College of Commerce, which has added majors in e-business and management information systems. Programs in music and theater are renowned, while the School of Computer Science, the School of Education, and several of the science departments (including biology, chemistry, and physics) have been rejuvenated, and a new digital cinema program has been added. DePaul's academic climate is demanding but not overwhelming. "Some courses are difficult and rigorous, but others are easy-going," says an education/sociology major.

> "Some courses are difficult and rigorous, but others are easy-going."

Courses at DePaul are small—75 percent have fewer than 25 students—and professors teach at all levels. The administration appoints student representatives from each school and college to faculty promotion and tenure committees. Social activities bring undergraduates and faculty members together, and students receive a phone book with all the profs' home numbers. "Especially during freshman year, professors really take care to make sure that students become well acclimated to college life," says a communications and American studies double major. All freshmen take a course called Discovering Chicago or its alternative, Exploring Chicago. "This class is one of the best things about DePaul. It's really fun and valuable," says a senior. Other common core courses include composition and rhetoric as well as quantitative reasoning for freshmen, a sophomore seminar on multiculturalism in the U.S.; and a junior-year program in experiential learning. Students also complete a series of "learning domains," consisting of arts and literature, philosophical inquiry, religious dimensions, scientific inquiry, social science, and history. To earn a BA, students must take three foreign language courses. The highly selective honors program includes interdisciplinary courses, a modern language requirement, and a senior thesis. Nearly a quarter of students participate in study abroad programs.

> "There are student organizations to represent all different faiths, ethnicities and backgrounds."

DePaul's president is a priest, and priests teach some courses and hold (voluntary) Mass every day. In addition, the University Ministry hosts other religious services and leads programs to teach students about other faiths. Seventy-five percent of DePaul students hail from Illinois. Hispanics represent 13 percent of the student body, African Americans 10 percent, and Asian Americans 9 percent. DePaul hopes to boost those figures by reaching out to disadvantaged inner-city students with high academic potential. "The students at DePaul are very diverse," says a sophomore. "There are student organizations to represent all different faiths, ethnicities, and backgrounds." DePaul has a reputation for being liberal, and it has become more liberal in recent years," says a junior. "The anti-Coke movement is huge. So is Fair Trade Coffee," says a senior. Athletic and merit scholarships are available to qualified students.

One student complains, "Weekends can be boring because many students go home." Traditionally, DePaul has been a commuter school, but 30 percent of students

Courses at DePaul are small—75 percent have fewer than 25 students—and professors teach at all levels.

now live in university housing. Students find the dorms comfortable and well-maintained, but they advise applying early to secure a bed, especially after sophomore year. "Housing is in high demand around here," says a junior. The Lincoln Park campus includes eight modern co-ed dorms, several townhouses and apartments; and a new residence hall opening in fall 2006. At the Loop campus, a 1,700-student residence hall includes a rooftop garden, fitness center, and music, art, and study rooms. Although students like campus housing, some find the food overpriced and limited. "I'm a vegan, and there is not a large or good variety," says a junior. While Chicago may have a high-crime reputation, students say campus security is visible, with officers patrolling in cars and on foot, emergency blue lights on campus, and dorms requiring students to swipe ID cards at two or three places before allowing entrance.

DePaul's name is closely associated with Midwestern business and law, and undergraduates can find internships with local legal and commercial institutions.

Fraternities and sororities draw just 3 percent of DePaul men and 2 percent of women. Not surprisingly, with the school's proximity to Chicago's clubs (especially on Rush Street), sporting events, and bars, most social life occurs off-campus. In the warmer months, the beaches of Lake Michigan beckon downtown students, while the huge annual outdoor Fest concert attracts large crowds from both campuses. "Chicago is the ultimate college town," says a music major. "There is everything to do here." On campus, the alcohol policy forbids beer for underage students, but students say that enforcement doesn't always work.

"Chicago is the ultimate college town."

On the sports scene, men's basketball is the headline story, beginning with the Midnight Madness of each fall's first practice in October. Recently, they were conference USA champions. The game against Notre Dame always draws a capacity crowd, though Loyola is DePaul's oldest rival. Women's basketball is also strong, as is DePaul's solid intramural program.

DePaul's student body has become more diverse while increasing in size, an admirable achievement. The administration credits the school's "increased academic reputation" for growth, but students say DePaul's popularity is due as much to the special bonds they feel with fellow Blue Demons. "DePaul University provides students a unique atmosphere in which to learn and grow," says a sophomore. "The campus and its students are friendly, open, and always inviting."

Overlaps
University of Illinois–Urbana Champaign, Loyola University, Marquette, Illinois State, Northern Illinois

If You Apply To ➤ **DePaul:** Rolling admissions: Jan. 1. Early action: Nov. 15. Regular admissions: Feb. 1. (Music/Theatre: Jan. 15) Financial aid: Mar. 1. Campus interviews: optional, evaluative. No alumni interviews. SATs or ACTs: required. SAT IIs: optional. Accepts the Common Application and electronic applications. Essay questions: who or what influenced your decision to apply to DePaul; impact of a recent failure or achievement.

DePauw University

315 South Locust Street, P.O. Box 37, Greencastle, IN 46135

DePauw is a solid Midwestern liberal arts institution in the mold of Illinois Wesleyan, Ohio Wesleyan, Denison, and Dickinson. Its Greek system is among the strongest in the nation and full of students destined for Indiana's business and governmental elite.

DePauw University offers a liberal arts education with an orientation toward experiential learning. Art history, creative writing, and music are solid, as are (more surprisingly) computer science and economics. Indeed, students here are career-oriented and happy to take advantage of the rigorous classwork and ample real

Website: www.depauw.edu
Location: Small town
Total Enrollment: 2,391

(Continued)

Undergraduates: 2,349
Male/Female: 46/54
SAT Ranges: V 550–660
  M 570–660
ACT Range: 23–29
Financial Aid: 50%
Expense: Pr $ $
Phi Beta Kappa: Yes
Applicants: 3,485
Accepted: 69%
Enrolled: 27%
Grad in 6 Years: 75%
Returning Freshmen: 90%
Academics: ✎ ✎ ✎ ½
Social: ☎ ☎ ☎
Q of L: ★ ★
Admissions: (800) 447-2495
Email Address:
  admission@depauw.edu

Strongest Programs:
Chemistry and Biochemistry
Biology
Economics and Management
Communications and Theatre
English and Creative Writing

DePauw's first-year program helps students transition to college by combining academically challenging coursework with co-curricular activities and programs.

world experiences. And with an undergraduate population of 2,300 students, close ties to classmates and faculty is a given.

DePauw is set amid the gently rolling hills of west-central Indiana. The lush green campus has a mix of older buildings and more modern redbrick structures, centered around a well-kept park with fountains and a reflecting pool. Newer additions include a $15 million art building, which provides studio space, a digital image library, classrooms, and galleries; a $36 million technology and physical science center, which offers 200,000 square feet of classrooms and labs; and a new set of residence life units collectively known as Rector Village.

DePauw's first-year program helps students transition to college by combining academically challenging coursework with co-curricular activities and programs. When they arrive, students are assigned to mentor groups with 10 to 12 peers, plus an upperclassman advisor and a faculty member who will teach their first-year seminar and serve as their academic advisor. By graduation, students must demonstrate competence in writing, quantitative reasoning, and oral communication. And they must fulfill distribution requirements in six areas: natural science and math, social and behavioral sciences, literature and the arts, historical and philosophical understanding, foreign language, and self-expression through performance and participation.

Academically, the DePauw student body is as career-oriented as they come. Aspiring business leaders benefit from courses, speakers, and internships offered through the McDermond Center for Management and Entrepreneurship. Future reporters, editors, anchors, and producers will find a home in the Pulliam Center for Contemporary Media, which supplements DePauw's strong student-run newspaper, TV station, and radio stations. And DePauw's School of Music is also worth a mention, offering all students the chance to take lessons, join ensembles, and perform, in genres from orchestra to jazz to opera. For exceptionally motivated students, five programs of distinction offer the chance to focus on an area of interest, such as media, management, scientific research, or information technology. The latter program includes real-world work experience, both in IT departments at DePauw and with off-campus employers. Recent additions to the curriculum include courses in statistics and Middle Eastern studies. A new major in education studies qualifies students for a fifth-year program in teaching

"I am aided by professors with years of experience."

with a master's degree and certification. Interdisciplinary studies at DePauw range from long-established programs in Asian studies, women's studies, and black studies to new programs in biochemistry, conflict studies, film, Jewish studies, and courses focusing on Latin America, the Caribbean, and Europe.

True to its focus on experiential learning, the DePauw curriculum includes a January term, during which first-year students remain on campus for a focused, interdisciplinary course, while upperclassmen pursue independent study or off-campus study or service in the U.S. or abroad. Approximately 40 percent of DePauw students spend a semester off campus, and when the January term is included, that fraction rises to more than 80 percent. The school offers its own programs as well as those arranged by the Great Lakes Colleges Association.* Students say that DePauw's classes are rigorous but well-supported. "I am aided by professors with years of experience," says a junior, one of whom "actually came to see my theater production!"

One student describes her peers at DePauw as "intellectually curious, philanthropically minded, and socially active." The minority presence has grown, thanks in part to recruitment of Posse Foundation students from New York and Chicago. African Americans now account for 5 percent of the student body, with Hispanics adding 3 percent, and Asian Americans 2 percent. Nearly three-quarters of students receive a merit scholarship, and the average award is more than $12,000. Three-quarters of DePauw students volunteer with area churches and social service agencies, which can also help them qualify for scholarships.

Ninety-five percent of DePauw students live in university housing, which is guaranteed for four years. Overcrowding is a thing of the past, since the school has opened 17 new duplexes and renovated another 46 apartments in recent years. The homey buildings have computer labs, common areas, and TV lounges; students recommend Humbert Hall for freshmen because of its hotel-like atmosphere. Only a few students are allowed to move off campus, a privilege doled out by lottery. A whopping 75 percent of DePauw's men and 74 percent of the women go Greek, though they must wait until sophomore year to move into their chapter houses.

Perhaps because of the prevalence of Greeks on campus, these groups have worked hard to change the stereotypes of fraternities and sororities. They've devised a risk-management policy and instituted a community council to review conduct violations. In addition, rush is delayed until second semester so freshmen can first get their feet on the ground academically. Fraternities still maintain the old custom of having "house moms." Still, students say it's easy for underage drinkers to imbibe, especially at fraternity parties. Off campus, ,however fake IDs "get confiscated quicker than you can take them out," one student warns.

The town of Greencastle has a movie theater, bowling alley, and several pizza places, but it "lacks an atmosphere," says a recent grad. "It is fine for sustaining day-to-day living, but doesn't offer many alternatives to the university." In good weather, several state parks offer hiking trails and a lake for the sailing club; Indianapolis is only a 45-minute drive, and St. Louis, Chicago, and Cincinnati make for good road trips. Another cherished tradition is a takeoff on Indiana University's famed Little 500 bike race, itself a takeoff on the Indianapolis 500 auto race. DePauw's version pits Greeks against independents on a 40-mile course.

"The university, the faculty, and the staff are all amazing and will give you stepping stones with which to build your path."

Aside from Greek parties, social life at DePauw revolves around varsity athletics, especially the annual football game against Wabash College. The Wabash–DePauw rivalry is the oldest west of the Alleghenies, and the winner of each year's content gets the much-cherished Monon Bell, hence the popular T-shirt: "Beat the bell out of Wabash." Several teams have recently played in NCAA Division III championship games, including women's soccer and golf, men's and women's cross-country and tennis, and men's golf. Swimming, track, baseball, and women's basketball are also strong. Intramural sports attract some 90 percent of students.

For a small school, DePauw offers a multitude of opportunities, balancing strong academics with a healthy dose of school spirit and a wealth of opportunities to lead—whether in one of the abundant extracurricular activities or by blazing a trail through study abroad. "The university, the faculty, and the staff are all amazing and will give you stepping stones with which to build your path," says a junior. "Don't overlook or discount any of these opportunities, because there will never be another one just like it."

True to its focus on experiential learning, the DePauw curriculum includes a January term, during which first-year students remain on campus for a focused, interdisciplinary course, while upperclassmen pursue independent study, off-campus study or service in the U.S. or abroad.

Overlaps

Indiana, Miami University (OH), Purdue, Notre Dame, Vanderbilt

If You Apply To ➤

DePauw: Early decision: Nov. 1. Early action: Dec. 1. Regular admissions: Feb. 1. Financial aid: Feb. 15. Meets demonstrated need of 95%. Campus interviews: recommended, evaluative. No alumni interviews. SATs or ACTs: required. SAT IIs: optional. Accepts the Common Application and electronic applications. Essay question: teacher who has had the greatest impact, or copy of an English paper.

Dickinson College

P.O. Box 1773, Carlisle, PA 17013

Dickinson occupies an historic setting in the foothills of central Pennsylvania. Known foremost for study abroad and foreign languages, Dickinson's curriculum combines liberal arts with a business program that picks up the international theme. Competes head-to-head with nearby Gettysburg.

Website: www.dickinson.edu

Location: Small town

Total Enrollment: 2,352

Undergraduates: 2,352

Male/Female: 44/56

SAT Ranges: V 600–700
   M 600–680

ACT Range: 26–30

Financial Aid: 58%

Expense: Pr $ $ $ $

Phi Beta Kappa: Yes

Applicants: 4,784

Accepted: 49%

Enrolled: 27%

Grad in 6 Years: 84%

Returning Freshmen: 89%

Academics: ✑ ✑ ✑ ✑

Social: ☎ ☎ ☎

Q of L: ★ ★ ★

Admissions: (717) 245-1231

Email Address:
   admit@dickinson.edu

Strongest Programs:
Political Science
Foreign Languages
English
Biological Sciences
International Business and
   Management

Dickinson College won its charter just six days after the Treaty of Paris recognized the United States as a sovereign nation, and this small liberal arts school has been blazing trails ever since. Though it has occupied the same central Pennsylvania plot for more than 200 years, location is one of the few constants in Dickinson's history. The school asks students to challenge what is safe and comfortable, to meet the future with a voice that reflects America and engages the world. To that end, its 40 study abroad programs in 24 countries draw well over half of the student body. Now, administrators are focused on diversity, global education, and attracting the best and brightest academic talent. "This is a school where one can find abundant resources to develop their academic skills as well as a variety of people to develop friendships," says a biochemistry major.

Almost all of Dickinson's Georgian buildings are carved from gray limestone from the college's own quarry, which lends a certain architectural consistency. Even the three-foot stone wall that encloses much of the wooded 90-acre Dickinson yard is limestone. The campus is part of the historic district of Carlisle, an economically prosperous central-Pennsylvania county seat nestled in a fertile valley. The newly renovated Community Studies Center fosters interdisciplinary hands-on learning in the social sciences and humanities, including taped interviews, surveys, and videotapes produced by students and faculty engaged in field work.

Dickinson is best known for its workshop approach to science education, for its outstanding and comprehensive international education program, and for the depth of its foreign language program—a total of 12 languages are offered, including Chinese, Japanese, Hebrew, Portuguese, and Italian. A 3–3 program with Penn State's Dickinson School of Law allows students to obtain undergraduate and JD degrees in six years. The international business and management major includes coursework in economics, history, and financial analysis, as well as internships and overseas education. Regardless of major, about half of all Dickinson students complete internships, where they may learn about stock trading at a brokerage firm, assist a judge in a common pleas court, or work with the editorial staff of a magazine. Recently added majors include women's studies, policy management, neuroscience, and archeology; there's also a new minor, in creative writing. A certificate program in law and public service is now a full major, renamed law and policy.

"The academic climate of Dickinson College is competitive."

The required First Year Seminar Program introduces new students to college-level study and reflection, with interdisciplinary courses such as Law, Justice and the Individual, and Physics or Philosophy? The Debate over "Intelligent Design." To help students understand how the liberal arts fit into the broader world, Dickinson requires distribution courses in the arts and humanities, social sciences, and laboratory sciences; writing intensive and a quantitative reasoning course; cross-cultural studies courses include comparative civilization, U.S. diversity, and foreign language courses through the intermediate level. Academics are rigorous, but not cutthroat. "The academic climate of Dickinson College is competitive. There has been a noticeable transition in the general attitudes of students in regard to academic pursuit and I attribute this to a shift in the incoming classes boasting higher SAT scores and high school GPAs, therefore having a more pronounced dedication towards academics," explains a junior.

Dickinson is trying to recruit more minority and international students, especially through partnerships with New York's Posse Foundation and the Philadelphia Futures Foundation. For now, though, "you have your wealthy preppy kids and your artsy kids and your scholarship academic kids and every combination," says an English major. Nearly a third of the student body hails from the Keystone State, and many of the rest are white, middle-class, or upper-middle-class, coming from elsewhere in the Northeast. What else do they have in common? According to one junior, "We are very active and extremely dedicated to our co-curricular activities in addition to our studies." Recent events, such as the war in Iraq, drew out opinions from all corners of the campus. African Americans and Asian Americans each make up 4 percent of the student body, and Hispanics add 3 percent. Dickinson awards three types of merit scholarships worth an average of $12,000; the school does not offer athletic scholarships.

Only seniors are allowed to live off campus, and Dickinson guarantees housing for four years, so 92 percent of students remain in the dorms. First-Year students have their own halls and upperclass students live in traditional dorms, which are co-ed by floor, or in townhouses with eight-person suites. The college transformed an abandoned factory into a combination of art studios and loft-style apartments, with 118 beds for juniors and seniors, and also recently renovated Morgan Hall, the largest dorm on campus. All Greek houses are owned and maintained by the college, and special interest housing includes areas devoted to French, Spanish, volunteerism, cultural diversity, and the environment.

"There is no tolerance for underage drinking, but where there is a will..."

Most social life at Dickinson occurs on campus. Fraternities and sororities attract 19 percent of the men and 24 percent of the women, and though they throw open parties at their houses, "you will not find many large, raging, house parties, but if you know where to look, you can find some," says an international studies major. At the Quarry, a former frat house, you can grab a cup of coffee, play some video games, or bust a move on the dance floor. When it comes to booze, Dickinson follows Pennsylvania state law, so you must be 21 to drink; monitors check IDs at parties. Kegs aren't permitted in any college housing, and four underage drinking incidents will get you expelled. "There is no tolerance for underage drinking, but where there is a will...." says a first year student. Another adds, "the alcohol policy deters neither drinking nor stupidity." There's a big concert each semester, where The Roots and Guster have played, and Hub-All-Night includes "music, food, and lots of free stuff," says a political science and economy major. Each fall brings an arts festival, and a spring carnival gives students one last blast before finals. One English major concludes, "on campus, if you can't find something to do, you live in a closet."

Carlisle is 20 miles from the Pennsylvania state capital of Harrisburg, and has "every fast-food restaurant you could want, as well as a Wal-Mart," says an international studies major. For those seeking more of a college town vibe, Amy's Thai and Pomfret Street Books are good bets. Big Brother–Big Sister programs, the Alpha Phi Omega community service fraternity, and programs like Adopt-a-Grandparent help bring the school and community together. In the spring and early fall, Maryland and Delaware beaches beckon; they're just a two- to three-hour drive. Come winter, good skiing is a half-hour away. Nature lovers will enjoy hiking the Appalachian Trail, just 10 minutes away. For those craving urban stimulation, the best road trips

Most social life at Dickinson occurs on campus. Fraternities and sororities attract 19 percent of the men and 24 percent of the women.

Dickinson is best known for its workshop approach to science education, for its outstanding and comprehensive international education program, and for the depth of its foreign language program.

are to Philadelphia, New York, and Washington, D.C. All are accessible by bus or train—a good thing, since first years can't have cars.

Dickinson students get riled up for any match against top rival Franklin and Marshall; the schools battle it out each year for the Conestoga Wagon trophy. Dickinson also squares off with Gettysburg College each year for the Little Brown Bucket. Football, the women's basketball team, cross-country team and indoor and outdoor track and field squads have won Centennial Conference championships in the past two years. About three-quarters of the men and half the women take part in intramurals, where dodgeball, basketball, floor hockey, and soccer are most popular. The soccer, softball, baseball, and varsity football fields sit within a 30-acre park, and they're lighted for night games. A 116,000 square foot synthetic turf field was installed in 2004. There is an outdoor track, jogging trails, and an indoor rock climbing wall. Students may also organize club teams to compete with other schools in sports like ice hockey, where Dickinson doesn't field varsity squads.

Dr. Benjamin Rush founded Dickinson more than two centuries ago, after signing the Declaration of Independence, and some things haven't changed since then. Seniors still share a champagne toast before graduation. And the steps of Old West, the first college building, are still used only twice a year—in the fall, at the convocation ceremony that welcomes new students, and in the spring, for commencement. But Dickinson continues to honor Rush's global vision, with its wealth of study abroad options and its demand that students cross the traditional borders of academic disciplines to grasp the interrelated nature of knowledge. One student sums it up: "A Dickenson education is finding that there are an infinite number of ways to think and be."

Overlaps

Gettysburg, Franklin and Marshall, Lafayette, Muhlenberg, Bucknell, Kenyon

Drew University

Madison, NJ 07940-4063

From Drew's wooded perch in suburban Jersey, Manhattan is only a 30-minute train ride away. That means Wall Street and the UN, both frequent destinations for Drew interns. Drew is New Jersey's only prominent liberal arts college and one of the few in the greater New York City area.

Website: www.drew.edu
Location: Suburban
Total Enrollment: 2,675
Undergraduates: 1,569
Male/Female: 40/60
SAT Ranges: V 560–670
M 540–650
ACT Range: 22–29
Financial Aid: 50%
Expense: Pr $ $ $

Some schools take the idea of a liberal arts education to the max. To wit: Drew University sends its students abroad for month-long educational ventures, promotes internships on Wall Street, and encourages theater and the arts to thrive. Founded more than a century ago as a Methodist university, Drew has grown into a place where an emphasis on hands-on learning, research, independent studies, and internships are just as important as performance in the classroom. And the changes keep coming. Robert Weisbuch, Drew's new president, came up with the idea of dropping the SAT and ACT requirement for entrance, and the response has been overwhelmingly positive.

The school occupies 186 acres of peaceful woodland in the upscale New York City suburb of Madison and is known as "The University in the Forest." Fifty-six campus buildings peek through splendid oak trees and boast classic and contemporary styles, a physical reflection of Drew's respect for both scholarly traditions and progressive education. The school is currently sprucing up the atmosphere through a reforestation project and the opening of the $20 million Dorothy Young Center for the Arts for the theater and studio arts departments.

Political science is Drew's strongest undergraduate department, and future politicos can take advantage of off-campus opportunities in Washington, D.C., London, Brussels, and the United Nations in New York City. Other popular majors include behavioral science, economics, English, and psychology. The Dana Research Institute for Scientists Emeriti offers opportunities for students to do research with distinguished retired industrial scientists, and recently won the lofty Merck Innovation Award for Undergraduate Science Education for fresh thinking and imaginative use of resources. Even more impressive is a program whereby students can earn a BA and MD from Drew and the University of Medicine and Dentistry of New Jersey/New Jersey Medical School in seven years. Future financiers can follow in the footsteps of the school's founder and take advantage of Drew's Wall Street Semester, an on-site study of the national and international finance communities. Other recent program additions include Pan-African studies, Chinese studies, and business studies majors.

Drew's commitment to liberal arts education includes the lofty goal of universal computer literacy. In fact, tuition for full-time students includes a notebook computer and supporting software, which students take with them when they graduate. The school's campuswide fiber-optic network links all academic buildings and many residence halls.

General education requirements, which take up a third of each student's total program, involve coursework in natural and mathematical sciences, social sciences, humanities, and arts and literature. Students must also show competency in writing, and each first-year student enrolls in seminars limited to 16 people, 80 percent of which are taught by senior faculty. The theater arts department works closely with the Playwrights Theater of New Jersey (founded by faculty member Buzz McLaughlin) to produce plays that are written, directed, and designed by students. Drew has long been a proponent of study abroad programs, including the Drew International Seminar program, where students study another culture in-depth on campus, then spend three to four weeks in that country. "These seminars are a great way of learning firsthand about a country and experiencing a once-in-a-lifetime chance to put your education into practice," says one student.

Maintaining a rigorous study schedule is key, according to many upperclassmen. A cast of highly praised, interactive faculty who generate enthusiasm and ambition fuels the industrious grind of hard work. "The best teachers that I have ever had are at Drew. They care about their students and go out of their

"The best teachers that I have ever had are at Drew."

way to make sure that you understand the material," says a sophomore. Some students complain that professors can be less than enthusiastic about teaching introductory classes, but students will only find teaching assistants in the science labs. Drew's library complex, a cluster of three buildings, contains more than 450,000 titles and offers ample study accommodations, though some students complain that some collections are outdated.

Fifty-six percent of Drew's students are from New Jersey, and most attended public high schools. The school continues to work on increasing its racial diversity—62 percent of the students are white, 6 percent are Asian American, and 4 percent are African American. Hispanics comprise 6 percent, Native Americans 1 percent, and foreign students 1 percent. And the differences extend past heritage: "My favorite thing about Drew is that although people are politically and socially

(Continued)
Phi Beta Kappa: Yes
Applicants: 3,266
Accepted: 70%
Enrolled: 18%
Grad in 6 Years: 75%
Returning Freshmen: 90%
Academics: ✍ ✍ ✍
Social: ☎ ☎ ☎
Q of L: ★ ★ ★
Admissions: (973) 408-3739
Email Address:
  cadm@drew.edu

Strongest Programs:
Political Science
English
Biology
Psychology
Theater

Robert Weisbuch, Drew's new president, came up with the idea of dropping the SAT and ACT requirement for application, and response has been overwhelmingly positive.

active, they are more interested in listening to what others have to say than in projecting their own opinions," says a senior. Merit awards average $11,781 and there are other scholarships available.

Eighty-eight percent of the students live in university housing, which includes both single-sex and co-ed dorms and six theme houses. Themes have included Earth House, Umoja House, Womyn's Concerns, Asia Tree House, and Spirituality Home. Some students lament their quality, but the school is renovating many dorms. Several housing options are available to upperclassmen, from dorm rooms of all sizes to suites and townhouses. A lottery gives housing preference to seniors and juniors, and most freshmen reside in dorms situated at the back of campus, which aren't the best. Still, most students live on campus because housing prices in Madison are out of reach for collegians. Although the dorms have kitchenettes, everyone must buy the meal plan, which students say is improving and offering a wider range of eating options.

"There is always a concert, play, or lecture."

The Dana Research Institute for Scientists Emeriti offers opportunities for students in biology, chemistry, physics, mathematics, and computer science to do research with distinguished retired industrial scientists.

There is no Greek system, but social life mostly takes place on campus. Officially, nobody under 21 is allowed to drink, but alcohol is said to be easy to come by. There is a 21-and-over pub on campus, but there are also two on-campus coffeehouses. On-campus social programming is extensive. "With more than 100 clubs on campus and the Student Activity Board, there is always a concert, play, or lecture," a psychology major says. New York City's Pennsylvania Station is less than an hour away by commuter train, and Philadelphia, the Jersey Shore, and the Delaware River are close by.

The First Annual Picnic, held on the last day of classes and numbered like Super Bowls (FAP XVII), provides an opportunity to enjoy live music and food. On Multicultural Awareness Day, students are excused from one day of classes to celebrate cultural diversity by attending lectures, workshops, and social events. Drew also launched an initiative to give all students and staff opportunities to participate in diversity training.

The commuter town of Madison tends to get discouraging reviews as a college town by students who feel its wealthy residents don't take too kindly to Drewids, as they affectionately call themselves. However, Community Day—designed to bring students and residents together—has become an annual event, and approximately 50 percent of students volunteer in activities such as Mentors at Drew and The Honduras Project, in which a group of Drew students travel to Honduras to help at an orphanage. Madison does provide several unique shops and restaurants within walking distance of campus, though the town "is a nice college town according to my parents, but not to students. Everything closes up pretty early." Nearby Morristown is more of a college place. The New Jersey Shakespeare Festival is in residence part of every year and offers both performances and internships. If that doesn't float your boat, NYC is a short train ride away.

Students used to seem more interested in intramural sports than in the school's Division III varsity teams, but interest has grown as the teams have become more successful. The $15 million athletic center is a 126,000-square-foot state-of-the-art facility that seats 4,000 and is used by varsity sports teams and intramural programs. The fencing team has done exceptionally well, too.

From a tight-knit campus to far-flung study abroad programs, Drew offers its small body of students a wide range of opportunities in a classic liberal arts structure. "It's easy to get involved, make friends, and feel like you make a difference," says a senior. Not too bad for a school in the forest.

Overlaps

Rutgers, College of New Jersey, NYU, Boston University, Skidmore, Muhlenberg

Drexel University

3141 Chestnut Street, Philadelphia, PA 19104

Drexel is a streetwise, no-nonsense technical university in the heart of Philadelphia. Go to school, work an internship, go to school again, work again—that's the Drexel way. Like Lehigh, Drexel also offers programs in business and arts and sciences, and its most distinctive offering is a College of Media Arts and Design.

For career-minded students who want to bypass the soul-searching of their liberal arts counterparts, Drexel University offers both solid academics and an innovative co-op education that combines high-tech academics with paying job opportunities. "If you want a good job, you go to Drexel and you do co-op." It's easy to see why Drexel University is nicknamed "the Ultimate Internship."

"Drexel's campus is impressive for its downtown Philadelphia location, with gardens and greenery on every block," says a student, "but the campus is woven tightly into the fabric of the city." The buildings are simple and made of brick; most are modern and in good condition. Sitting just west of the city center and right across the street from the University of Pennsylvania, the campus is condensed into about a four-block radius. Students are encouraged to use a shuttle bus between the library and dorm at night, and access to dorms, the library, and the physical education center is restricted to students with ID, so most feel safe on campus.

Cooperative education is the hallmark of the curriculum, which alternates periods of full-time study and full-time employment for four or five years, providing students with six to 18 months of money-making job experience before they graduate. And the co-op possibilities are unlimited: students can co-op virtually anywhere in this country, or in 11 foreign countries, and 98 percent of undergraduates choose this route. Freshman and senior years of the five-year programs are spent on campus, and the three intervening years (sophomore, prejunior, and junior) usually consist of six months of work and six months of school. A pre-cooperative education course covers such topics as skills assessment, ethics in the workplace, résumé writing, interviewing skills, and stress management. Each co-op student has the opportunity to earn from $7,000 to $30,000 while attending Drexel. And although some students complain that jobs can turn out to be six months of make-work, most enjoy making important contacts in their potential fields and learning while earning. "It starts out laid-back, but after a while you begin to feel the competitiveness," mentions one sophomore. "Keep in mind Drexel works on trimesters, so it keeps you on your toes."

To accommodate the co-op students, Drexel operates year-round. Flexibility in requirements varies by college, but in the first year everyone must take freshman seminar, English composition, mathematics, and Cooperative Education 101; engineering majors must also complete the Drexel Engineering Curriculum, which integrates math, physics, chemistry, and engineering to make sure that even techies enter the workforce well-rounded and able to write as well as they can compute and design. Students enjoy the 700,000-volume library, which offers good hours, and

Website: www.drexel.edu
Location: City center
Total Enrollment: 13,128
Undergraduates: 10,582
Male/Female: 63/37
SAT Ranges: V 520–620
  M 540–640
Financial Aid: 78%
Expense: Pr $ $
Phi Beta Kappa: Yes
Applicants: 10,355
Accepted: 65%
Enrolled: 34%
Grad in 6 Years: 54%
Returning Freshmen: 87%
Academics: ✍ ✍ ✍
Social: ☎ ☎
Q of L: ★ ★
Admissions: (215) 895-2400
Email Address:
  enroll@drexel.edu

Strongest Programs:
Engineering
Graphic Design
Architecture
Film and Video

lots of room for studying. Professors receive high praise from most, and are noted for their accessibility and warmth. Says one student, "They take a great interest in the students and are always willing to offer assistance or direction outside of class."

Drexel's greatest strength is its engineering college, which churns out more than 1 percent of all the nation's engineering graduates, BS through PhD. The electrical and architectural engineering programs are particular standouts. The College of Arts and Sciences is well-recognized for theoretical and atmospheric physics; chemistry is also recommended. The futuristic Center for Automated Technology complements the strong computer science program. Students mention that the biology and chemistry departments are weak, primarily due to lack of organization and foreign teachers, who are hard to comprehend. One film and video major says, "The dramatic writing major is lacking in popularity due to its placement under the College of Design rather than Arts and Sciences."

The performance-oriented student body is 64 percent Pennsylvanian, with another large chunk of students from adjacent New Jersey. The foreign student population is 13 percent, while Asian Americans and African Americans account for 20 percent of the student body. Twenty-three percent of Drexel undergrads graduated in the top tenth of their high school class, and the student body tends to lean right politically. "This is a science and technology school full of conservative students who don't really have the time to worry about liberal issues," says a student. In addition to need-based financial aid, a wide range of athletic and merit scholarships (the latter in amounts up to $10,000 per year) is offered.

Freshmen live in one of six co-ed residence halls, including a luxurious high-rise, but many upperclassmen reside in nearby apartments or the fraternities, which are frequently cheaper and more private than university housing. Overall, 28 percent of the

"It's hard to get people involved because of the amount of schoolwork and co-ops."

students live in the dorms; another third commute to campus from home. The cafeteria offers adequate food and plenty of hamburgers and hot dogs, but it's far away from the dorms. While on-campus freshmen are forced to sign up for a meal plan, most upperclassmen make their own meals; the dorms have cooking facilities on each floor. If all else fails, nomadic food trucks park around campus providing quick lunches.

With so many students living off campus and the city of Philadelphia at their disposal, Drexel tends to be a bit deserted on weekends. A student notes, "In a single weekend, I may play paintball in the Poconos, swim at the Jersey shore, see an opera in Philadelphia, and go mountain biking in nearby Wissahickon Park." Friday-night flicks are cheap and popular with those who stay around, and dorms sponsor floor parties. The dozen or so fraternities also contribute to the party scene, especially freshman year, but a handful of smaller sororities has little impact. Still, Greek Week is well-attended by members of both sexes, as is the spring Block Party, which attracts four or five bands. The Greeks recruit 7 percent of the men and women. Drinking is "not a big deal to everyone," and campus policies are strict; dorms require those of age to sign in alcohol and limit the quantities they may bring in.

The co-op program often undermines any sense of class unity, and can strain personal relationships. Activities that depend on some continuity of enrollment for success—music, drama, student government, athletics—suffer most. "It's hard to get people involved because of the amount of schoolwork and co-ops," says one woman. There is no football team, but men's basketball and soccer are strong. "Our biggest rivalry is our feud with Delaware," admits one frenzied student. "We delight in sacrificing blue plastic chickens!" Men's and women's swimming and women's volleyball also generate interest. An extensive intramural program serves all students, and joggers can head for the steps of the Philadelphia Art Museum, just like Rocky did in the movies. Students take full advantage of their urban location by frequenting clubs, restaurants, cultural attractions, and shopping malls in Philadelphia, easily accessible by public transportation.

Aspiring poets, musicians, and historians may find Drexel a bit confusing. But for future computer scientists, engineers, and other technically oriented minds, the university's unique approach to learning inside and outside the classroom could give your career a fantastic jumpstart. As one satisfied customer explains, "The terms are intense, the activities unlimited, but Drexel graduates are surely among the most capable and motivated individuals I have ever met. When I graduate, I will be prepared and proud of it."

Overlaps

Penn State, Temple, Villanova, Rutgers, LaSalle

If You Apply To ➤

Drexel: Rolling admissions. Financial aid: May. 1. Does not guarantee to meet demonstrated need. Campus interviews: recommended, informational and evaluative. No alumni interviews. SATs: required. SAT IIs: optional. Accepts electronic applications. Apply to particular schools or programs.

Duke University

2138 Campus Drive, Durham, NC 27708

What fun to be a Dukie—face painted blue, rocking Cameron Indoor Stadium as the Blue Devils score again. Duke is the most prestigious private university in the South—similar to Rice in selectivity, but not as tough for out-of-staters to get into as public archrival UNC. Duke is strong in engineering as well as the humanities and offers public policy and economics rather than business.

Duke University is one of the few elite U.S. colleges where strong academics and championship-caliber sports teams manage to coexist. It might be south of the Mason-Dixon Line, and may seem a bit wet behind the ears compared to the nation's oldest and most prestigious Northeastern schools, but Duke is competing with them and winning its fair share of serious students as well as superb athletes. A rising star in the South, Duke is on even footing with the Ivies and Stanford.

Founded in 1838 as the Union Institute (later Trinity College), Duke University is young for a school of its stature. It sprouted up in 1924, thanks to a stack of tobacco-stained dollars called the Duke Endowment. Duke's campus in the lush North Carolina forest is divided into two main sections, West and East, and, with 8,300 acres of adjacent forest, offers enough open space to satisfy even the most diehard outdoors enthusiast. West Campus, the hub of the university, is laid out in spacious quadrangles and dominated by the impressive Gothic chapel, a symbol of the university's Methodist tradition. Constructed in the 1930s, West includes Collegiate Gothic residential and classroom quads, the administration building, Perkins Library (with 4.2 million volumes, nearly 8.9 million manuscripts, and two million public documents), and the student union. East Campus, built in the 1920s, consists primarily of Georgian redbrick buildings. Most of Duke's arts facilities are here, as are dorms that house all first-year students together "for a sense of class unity, which works quite well," says a freshman. East and West are connected by shuttle buses, though many students enjoy the mile-or-so walk between them along wooded Campus Drive. The Nasher Art Museum opened in 2005, and the Center for Interdisciplinary Engineering, Medicine, and Applied Science is currently under construction.

Website: www.duke.edu
Location: Small city
Total Enrollment: 12,085
Undergraduates: 6,092
Male/Female: 52/48
SAT Ranges: V 660–750
  M 670–780
ACT Range: 29–34
Financial Aid: 39%
Expense: Pr $ $ $ $
Phi Beta Kappa: Yes
Applicants: 16,749
Accepted: 23%
Enrolled: 43%
Grad in 6 Years: 94%
Returning Freshmen: 97%
Academics: ✐ ✐ ✐ ✐ ✐
Social: ☎ ☎ ☎ ☎
Q of L: ★ ★ ★ ★
Admissions: (919) 684-3214
Email Address: undergrad-admissions@duke.edu

(Continued)

Strongest Programs:
Biology
Ecology
Neuroscience
Political Science
Public Policy
Economics
Literary/Cultural Studies
Engineering

Duke includes two undergraduate schools: The Pratt School of Engineering and Trinity College of Arts & Sciences (the latter resulted from a merger of the previously separate men's and women's liberal arts colleges). The school's engineering programs—particularly electrical and biomedical—are national standouts. Natural sciences, most notably ecology, biology, and neuroscience, are also first-rate. The proximity of the Medical Center enhances study in biochemistry and pharmacology.

Duke's Sanford Institute of Public Policy offers an interdisciplinary major—unusual at the undergraduate level—that trains aspiring public servants in the machinations of the media, nonprofit organizations, government agencies, and other bodies that govern public life. Internships and apprenticeships are a big part of the program. Additionally, Duke offers more than 100 interdisciplinary courses, bolstered by the John Hope Franklin Center for International and Interdisciplinary Studies. Duke is looking to double the number of undergraduates participating in mentored research, improve science and engineering even more and increase its interdisciplinary offerings. More than 40 percent of Duke students study abroad, and there are also opportunities for those who want a break from campus without leaving the country. An architecture concentration was recently added within the art history major, and Duke has added a certificate program in politics, philosophy, and economics. Certificate programs were also added recently in documentary studies and policy, as well as in journalism and media studies. Economics attracts the most majors, followed by public policy, psychology, political science, and biology.

"Kids complain about the core curriculum, but I haven't found it hard to complete."

Trinity College's curriculum, part of the traditional undergraduate coursework known as Program I, requires courses in five general areas of knowledge: arts, literature, and performance; civilizations; social sciences; natural sciences; and quantitative studies. Students must also fulfill requirements in six modes of inquiry, including foreign language, writing, research, and ethical inquiry. The requirements get mixed reviews from students. "Kids complain about the core curriculum, but I haven't found it hard to complete. In fact, it's helped make my academic experience a diverse one," says a junior. All students also must complete three Small Group Learning Experiences: one seminar course during the freshman year—offered in topics such as Imagining Dinosaurs and The Psychology of Social Influence—and two more as upperclassmen. Students must finish 34 courses to graduate; those who wish to explore subjects outside and between usual majors and minors may choose Program II, to which they are admitted after proposing a topic, question, or theme, for which they plan an individualized curriculum with faculty advisors and deans. "Students are given considerable freedom, and with it, responsibility," says a student.

When college counselors say Duke is hot, they're not referring to the temperatures in the South. Duke is up there with the Ivies and the select few other colleges that compete with them for students. Courses here are rigorous and the academic atmosphere has become more intense, particularly in the sciences and engineering. "Classes are difficult and require large amounts of study time and out-of-the-box thinking, approaching problems from new and different perspectives," a freshman biomedical engineering student says. In recent years, the university has focused resources on undergraduate education, reducing the number of nonprofessors who teach incoming students and having senior professors teach more classes. The new president, lured from Yale, has made the expansion of interdisciplinary work—already part of the Duke culture—a priority for faculty and students alike. "Certainly not all professors desire out-of-classroom interaction, but students don't have to look far to find ones that do," a senior English major says.

"Only seniors may live off campus, and an increasing number of them are choosing to do so."

The nationally recognized FOCUS program offers groups of seminars with 15 or fewer students clustered around a single broad theme such as Biotechnology and Social Change, and Humanitarian Challenges at Home and Abroad. It is "an incredible opportunity to engage with the university's top professors," a senior says. Despite Duke's relatively large undergraduate population, 73 percent of courses have 25 or fewer students.

Only 15 percent of Duke students are from North Carolina, although a large fraction of the student body hails from the South, and the Northeastern corridor sends a fair-sized contingent. Not quite 60 percent of students come from public high schools. Eleven percent of students are African American, 7 percent are Hispanic, and 13 percent are Asian American. Students of different ethnicities and races tend to "self-segregate," students say, producing little tension, but also little interaction. Overcoming these self-imposed barriers has been an ongoing quest for students and administrators, who conduct a diversity orientation program each year. There is also a new student-run Center for Race Relations.

Duke's Southern gentility is reflected in campus attire, which is generally neatly pressed on guys and maybe a bit outfitty on women, in contrast to the thrown-together antistatus uniform of jeans and sweats that dominates on some other campuses. Duke is also a culturally active campus; theater groups thrive, and the Freewater Film Society shows classic movies each week. During the summer, Duke is home to the splendid American Dance Festival. Undergraduates use the school's cable television system to make and broadcast parodies of game shows and other entertainment.

Despite the imprimatur of wealth evident here, Duke admits students without regard to financial need and guarantees to meet all accepted applicants' full demonstrated need for four years. Four percent of students receive merit scholarships averaging $22,000. There are a number of scholarships earmarked for outstanding African Americans. Like most other NCAA Division I universities, Duke hands out athletic scholarships annually, offering them in seven men's sports and eight women's sports.

Eighty-five percent of Duke undergrads live on campus, and each student is loosely affiliated with one of 60 "living groups," ranging in size from 14 to 250 students (in a nod to the college- or house-based living units at some Ivy League schools). On East Campus, the university operates freshman dorms led by a faculty member and his or her family. "Housing is excellent there," says a junior. The decision to have all freshman live on the dry East Campus was aimed at making it easier to adjust to academic life and insulating them from the wilder aspects of Duke's social scene, which attracted national attention following a scandal involving off-campus behavior of members of the lacrosse team. A new housing plan requires all sophomores to live on West Campus. There are also special interest dorms focused on themes such as women's studies, the arts, languages, and community service. University-owned apartment buildings popular with upperclassmen are located on two nearby satellite campuses. "Only seniors may live off campus, and an increasing number of them are choosing to do so," says a junior. Students say the dining choices are excellent. "There are over 20 eateries to choose from, plus off-campus restaurants on our meal plan," says a student. Unused "money" from prepaid meal cards is refunded at the end of the semester, an unusual and much-appreciated policy.

Durham is "urban and not very student-friendly as a whole," says a junior. "As a college town, it has several of the requisite bars and pizza places, but compared to a place like Madison, Ann Arbor, or Boston, or even Chapel Hill, it's pitiful." Fraternities and sororities attract 29 percent of men and 42 percent of women, respectively. Fraternity parties are open to everyone, and the free shuttle bus service that connects the school's various dorm and apartment complexes runs until 4 a.m.,

All students also must complete three Small Group Learning Experiences: one seminar course during the freshman year—offered in topics such as Imagining Dinosaurs and The Psychology of Social Influence—and two more as upperclassmen.

"There are over 20 eateries to choose from."

making it easy to socialize in rooms or suites. "Alcohol, it seems, is quite easy to find," says a freshman, and students report that the Greek scene has been pushed off campus. During the basketball season, men's games always sell out, and the town is proud of its Durham Bulls, the local minor-league baseball team, which coined the term "bullpen." Durham offers bars and clubs aplenty to feed and water students, as well as the beloved Durham Bulls, the local minor-league baseball team,

"Duke-Durham relations are tenuous at best."

which coined the term "bullpen." Popular road trips include nearby Chapel Hill, home of archrival UNC, and Raleigh, the state capital and home of North Carolina State University. In warm weather, the broad beaches on North Carolina's outer banks are two to three hours away, while ski slopes are three to four hours distant in winter. The popular Oktoberfest and Springfest bring in live bands and vendors peddling local crafts and exotic foods each fall and spring, and concerts are being brought back to Cameron Indoor Stadium.

"Duke–Durham relations are tenuous at best," says a student dismayed by the contrast between the school's wealth and the economic depression afflicting Durham. However, another student adds, "Community service is huge, and there has been a recent emphasis on the Duke-Durham partnership," which includes tutoring in local schools. (No one misses the irony of the fact that Durham, once known as the "City of Tobacco," now bills itself as the "City of Medicine.") Durham is about 15 minutes from Research Triangle Park, the largest research center of its kind in the world. Duke, North Carolina State, and the University of North Carolina at Chapel Hill created the park for nonprofit, scientific, and sociological research. Many Silicon Valley technologies companies have East Coast outposts in the park, which has helped make the Raleigh–Durham area one of the most productive regions in the nation, with the highest percentage of PhDs per capita in the U.S.

Duke's official motto is Eruditio et Religio only to a few straight-laced administrators; everyone else knows it as "Eruditio et Basketballio," which translates more or less as "To hell with Carolina"—the University of North Carolina, Duke's archrival for supremacy in the Atlantic Coast Conference. At games, students get the best courtside seats, where they make life miserable for the visiting team. Their efforts paid off in 2001 when the Blue Devils won the national Division I men's basketball championship for the third time in a decade. "By far, basketball season brings out the best of student support," a senior says. Sports-crazed Blue Devils erect a temporary "tent city" to vie for the best seats. This is far from "roughing it"—students form groups to hold their places so that some fraction can go to class and keep their peers on track academically, while those who hold down the fort may check their email thanks to lampposts with Internet jacks. "Basically, the line for the Duke-UNC men's game starts two to three months in advance," says one fan. The women's basketball team has come on strong and is the perennial winner in the ACC and a regular presence in the Final Four. In 2004, the women's golf team was also the best in the conference. Football is, to put it kindly, rebuilding. For part-time jocks, there are two intramural leagues, one for competitive types and one for strictly weekend athletes, which draw heavy participation from the Greeks and guys.

Meandering around Duke's up-to-date campus, you can see the latest technology, but also can hear the whisper of the Old South through those big old trees. "If you come here, there isn't a chance in the world that you won't fall in love with it, with its possibilities and opportunities and people and beauty," one student says. In addition to blending old and new, Duke also does an amazing job combining sports and academia, producing students who almost define the term "well-rounded." "It's attracting better students, shifting the focus away from basketball and fraternities, and trying to create a more intellectual environment on campus," says a junior.

Courses here are rigorous and the academic atmosphere has become more intense, particularly in the sciences and engineering.

Overlaps

UNC-Chapel Hill, Washington University, Northwestern, University of Virginia, Cornell, Penn

If You Apply To >

Duke: Early decision: Nov. 1. Regular admissions: Jan. 2. Financial aid and housing: Feb. 1. Guarantees to meet full demonstrated need. Campus interviews: optional, evaluative. Alumni interviews: recommended, evaluative. SATs or ACTs: required. SAT IIs: required. Accepts the Common Application and electronic applications. Essay question: help you got on essay; why Duke; how you responded to someone doing something wrong, most profound or surprising intellectual experience, or a matter of importance to you.

Earlham College

Richmond, IN 47374

BEST BUY

Earlham is a member of the proud circle of liberal colleges in the Midwest that includes Oberlin, Kenyon, Grinnell, and Beloit, to name a few. Less than half the size of Oberlin and comparable to the other three, Earlham is distinctive for its Quaker orientation and international perspective.

Earlham is a study in contradictions—a top-notch liberal arts institution in a conservative city that few could place on a map, and an institution that even in the 21st century remains true to the traditions of community, peace, and justice that are hallmarks of its Quaker heritage. Earlham's curriculum and programs "really do engage students with the world," says faculty, by exposing them to classmates from 46 countries and offering more than 200 academic courses that incorporate an international perspective. Its variety of study abroad programs offer close faculty involvement and a thoughtful focus on cross-cultural perspectives.

Earlham's 800-acre campus sits in the small, quintessentially Midwestern city of Richmond, just a short distance from Cincinnati and Indianapolis. Georgian-style buildings dominate, surrounded by mature trees and plantings, while the Japanese gardens symbolize the college's long friendship and closeness with Japan. Recent additions to campus include a suite-style residence hall and the $13.3 million Landrum Bolling Center for Interdisciplinary Studies and Social Sciences. It offers the latest classroom technology as well as meandering hallways where comfortable seating alcoves encourage spontaneous discussion.

To graduate, students must satisfy general education requirements in the arts, analytical reasoning, wellness, scientific inquiry, foreign language, and, not surprisingly, diversity. Biology is the most popular major, followed by psychology, sociology/anthropology, politics, and business and non-profit management. A wide range of interdisciplinary offerings includes such programs as peace and global studies, legal studies, Quaker studies, Latin American studies, and Japanese studies, a field in which Earlham is a national leader. Challenged to think and meet high academic expectations, students see themselves as capable and eager to learn. "More than that, professors expect students to expect a lot out of themselves," says a politics major.

Class discussion, rather than lecture, is the predominant learning style here. Earlham faculty members are selected for their excellence in teaching and their ability to cross disciplinary lines. "The quality of teaching at Earlham is one of its best attributes," states a freshman. "Not only are most professors very experienced and knowledgeable in their field, they are also very approachable and easy to talk to." While profs are available, class outlines demand the individual to "figure things out" by taking the initiative to take their work seriously.

About three-quarters of students eventually pursue postgraduate study, often after taking some time off for a job or to participate in volunteer or service programs. During their undergrad years, 66 percent of Earlham students participate in

Website: www.earlham.edu
Location: City outskirts
Total Enrollment: 1,200
Undergraduates: 1,145
Male/Female: 42/58
SAT Ranges: V 580–690
   M 530–650
ACT Range: 24–29
Financial Aid: 67%
Expense: Pr $ $
Phi Beta Kappa: Yes
Applicants: 1,518
Accepted: 72%
Enrolled: 31%
Grad in 6 Years: 70%
Returning Freshmen: 89%
Academics: ✑ ✑ ✑ ✑
Social: ☎ ☎ ☎
Q of L: ★ ★ ★ ★ ★
Admissions: (765) 983-1600
Email Address:
   admission@earlham.edu

Strongest Programs:
Biology
English
Psychology
Interdisciplinary Studies

at least one off-campus study experience. Earlham offers study abroad programs in 25 countries, including Mexico, India, Senegal, Martineque, Northern Ireland, East Africa, and the Far East. In a Border Studies program, students live with families in El Paso or Ciudad Juarez and take courses focusing on U.S.-Mexico border issues. Programs are managed by the college, not by an outside consortium; students first receive preparation for a multicultural experience, and most programs have an onsite director.

Earlham may be small, but its student body is exceptionally diverse. Only 28 percent of the students are Hoosiers; 7 percent hail from abroad, representing 46 different countries. Another 7 percent are African American, with Hispanic students adding 3 percent and Asian Americans 2 percent. With a strong emphasis on conversation, the campus is full of well-intentioned activists blazing their own trails through life, albeit on "Earlham Time" (a tardy-favorable clock widely accepted in this laid-back climate). "There is also a huge feeling of community here, and students care more about their fellow students instead of being only concerned for one's self and one's own pursuits," says a peace and global studies major. Merit scholarships are available for qualified students; there are no athletic scholarships.

Earlham students are strongly encouraged to live on campus, and 88 percent do. Single, double, and triple rooms are available in the two older dorms, which connect with the new East Hall, set to open in fall 2006. It features a cyber café, two-to-four bedroom suites sharing private baths, and, on each floor, a kitchen, study, laundry, and, yes, entertainment

"The quality of teaching at Earlham is one of its best attributes."

facilities. Dorm space is reserved for first-years, and upperclassmen enter a lottery for the remaining rooms or petition to live together. All residence halls and academic buildings provide access to the campus computer network, and students may also tap into more than 50 databases from any of six public computer labs, one of which is open 24 hours. Most students eat in the college dining hall, which offers an impressively diverse selection for special diets. "At a liberal school like Earlham, there are plenty of vegetarians and vegans, so the dining hall is always prepared for special needs," says a junior.

Quaker beliefs and Indiana's liquor laws prohibit alcohol on campus, making Earlham a dry campus, at least technically. While any college has its dissenters on alcohol policy making it more realistically a "damp campus," Earlham oddly seems to embrace its policy well enough. "There are a significant number of students who adamantly support the policy," says a junior. "Alcohol is kept quiet and is a significantly less crucial aspect of EC's social scene than at other schools." The atmosphere this creates is very respectful of nondrinkers' decisions and avoids pressure.

With no fraternities or sororities at Earlham, gatherings and parties on weekends may be at a minimum and quiet when they do happen, but on-campus activities abound. Students enjoy improv comedy, a cappella music, equestrian programs, a lip synch competition, fall and spring festivals, concerts, and sports. "Very little of the social life of Earlham students takes place off campus," says a freshman, "simply because students don't need to seek outside sources of entertainment." Student organizations include numerous cultural, ethnic, and religious groups as well as left-of-center organizations such as Amnesty International and the Earlham Progressive Union. Apart from day trips to Cincinnati, Indianapolis or Columbus, students stick with a laid-back

"Very little of the social life of Earlham students takes place off campus."

social atmosphere of visiting with others or checking out one of the musicians, speakers, or other groups that Earlham brings to campus.

Richmond and the surrounding county offer standard American as well as Mexican restaurants, movie theaters, bowling alleys, roller skating, and golf. Students fan out into the city racking up nearly 50,000 hours of volunteer service a year. Guaranteed to impress, outreach programs are truly getting students involved in their community and building a close relationship with the city. "Volunteerism is an important value of many Earlham students, and despite class work and other commitments, many students still make time to volunteer," says a freshman.

Indoor and outdoor soccer, basketball, Ultimate Frisbee, and the wiffleball tournament are especially popular intramurals. The school's 16 varsity teams include nearly a third of the student body and compete in Division III sports, including lacrosse, soccer, rugby, track, cross-country, and more. Women's soccer and men's basketball are among the school's strongest squads.

Although Earlham students are based in the Midwest, they graduate ready to take on the world, thanks to the school's cooperative, can-do spirit, international perspective, and caring student/faculty community.

If You Apply To ➤

Earlham: Early decision: Dec. 1. Early action: Jan. 1. Regular admissions: Feb. 15. Financial aid: Mar. 1. Campus and alumni interviews: recommended, evaluative. SATs: required. SAT I preferred. SAT IIs: optional. Accepts the Common Application and electronic applications. Essay (five options).

Eckerd College

4200 54th Avenue South, St. Petersburg, FL 33711

There are worse places to go to school than the shores of Tampa Bay. Eckerd's only direct competitor in Florida is Rollins, which has a business school but is otherwise similar. Marine science, environmental studies, and international studies are among Eckerd's biggest draws.

Attending Eckerd College demands a special sort of willpower. Why? In the words of an international business major: "We are right on the water, and it is like going to college in a resort." With free canoes, kayaks, boats, coolers, and tents always available for student use, it's a wonder anyone studies. But study they do, as administrators continue to lure capable students to Eckerd with small classes, skilled professors, renovated housing, and a reinvigorated social scene. "The standard of education and competition has improved dramatically," says a computer science major.

Founded in 1958 as Florida Presbyterian College and renamed 12 years later after a generous benefactor (of drug store fame), Eckerd considers itself nonsectarian. Still, the school maintains a formal "covenant" with the major Presbyterian denomination, from which it receives some funds. The lush, grassy campus is on the tip of a peninsula bounded by the Gulf of Mexico and Tampa Bay, with plenty of flowering bushes, trees, and small ponds—and it's not unusual to spot dolphins frolicking in the adjacent waters. Campus buildings are modern, and none are taller than three stories. New additions to campus include the Peter H. Armacost Library.

Freshmen arrive three weeks early for orientation and take a one-credit seminar on the skills required for college-level work. First-years also take a yearlong course called Western Heritage in a Global Context, which focuses on influential books, and students must meet composition, foreign language, information technology, oral communication, and quantitative skills requirements. Also required are one course in each of the four academic areas—arts, humanities, natural sciences, and

(Continued)

Email Address:
admissions@eckerd.edu

Strongest Programs:
Marine Science
Biology
Psychology
International Relations
Creative Writing and Literature
Management and International
    Business
Environmental Studies

social sciences—plus one course each in environmental and global perspectives. The capstone senior seminar, organized around the theme "Quest for Meaning," asks students to draw on what they've learned during college to find solutions to important issues. Popular departments include marine biology, business management, international business, environmental studies, and human development.

Watery subjects such as marine science are especially strong. "If you are only interested in swimming with dolphins, don't be a marine sciences major," says a junior. The program is "very rigorous." The college was granted a Phi Beta Kappa chapter in 2003, making it the youngest private college ever to receive the honor. Eckerd pioneered the 4–1–4 term schedule, in which students work on a single project for credit each January. Every student has a faculty mentor, and there are no graduate assistants at the blackboards. "Teaching is excellent," a junior says. "Professors are also available outside the classroom to help students." The academic climate is very laid-back, students say. "Students are friendly and helpful academically. We

> **"We are right on the water, and it is like going to college in a resort."**

often study for tests together and I don't even know my class rank," says a senior majoring in creative writing and psychology. A major in interdisciplinary art and a minor in film studies have been added to the curriculum. A Freeman Foundation grant has funded significant new coursework in the Chinese and Japanese languages, and there are new opportunities to study in India, Vietnam, China, and Japan.

While St. Petersburg isn't a college town (a senior says it "is closer to a retirement community" and closes up by 10 p.m.) a side benefit to the school's location is the Academy of Senior Professionals, a group of senior citizens who mentor undergrads. Academy members, who come from all walks of life, take classes with students, work with professors on curriculum development, help students with career choices, and lead workshops in their areas of expertise. About half of Eckerd's students study abroad, in countries ranging from Austria and France to Bermuda and China. The school also has its own campus in London. Marine science programs include a Sea Semester* and the Eckerd College Search and Rescue, which performs more than 500 marine rescues annually and inspires a popular campus T-shirt that tells students to "GET LOST! Support Eckerd Search and Rescue."

Eckerd's president once referred to students as "intellectuals in sandals," says a junior. "I like the quote and it really works for the students." Another student says his classmates are "barefoot and brainy" and feel at home in an academically challenging, aesthetically pleasing atmosphere. About two-thirds of the student body

> **"If you are only interested in swimming with dolphins, don't be a marine sciences major."**

hails from out of state, with a large contingent coming from the Northeast; 7 percent are foreign. Hispanics are the largest minority group at 4 percent, African Americans comprise 3 percent, and Asian Americans account for 2 percent. Ten athletic scholarships are awarded annually, and merit scholarships are available to qualified "barefoot and brainy" types.

Seventy-nine percent of students live in one of eight housing quads, separated from the rest of campus by the imaginatively named Dorm Drive. Rooms are fairly large and air-conditioned, and waterfront views and beach access are in-your-face—and free. Two trendy townhouse- and apartment-style residence halls provide suite living and other dorms have been renovated to add computer labs and kitchens in lounges. "Dorms are old but well-maintained, though they are very utilitarian," says a sophomore. Adds a junior: "Dorms also build an amazing community that makes Eckerd."

There are no Greek organizations at Eckerd, and a strict alcohol policy—no kegs on campus, no alcohol at university events—means wristbands at campus parties,

Off campus, students can take in the nightclubs and bars of Latin-flavored Ybor City about 30 minutes away.

even for those over 21. The policy has been relaxed a bit to allow students of drinking age to imbibe at the campus bar, the Triton Pub, and to drink in public areas of the dorms. Students say those who are underage still manage to get booze and consume it in their rooms, away from prying eyes. Off campus, it's next to impossible for underage students to be served at bars and restaurants, students say—though they do enjoy the new Baywalk shopping complex, about 15 minutes from campus, with a stadium-seating movie theater, bars, and restaurants.

On-campus, students can partake in concerts, lectures, shows, and games arranged by the student activity board. At the Festival of Hope, seniors present their Quest for Meaning social work. The Kappa Karnival offers rides and games galore. Off campus, students can take in the nightclubs and bars of Latin-flavored Ybor City about 30 minutes away. Tampa and St. Pete also offer a Salvador Dali museum—which

"Dorms are old but well-maintained."

Eckerd students get into for free—and professional baseball, football, hockey, and soccer teams. Tempting road trips include Orlando's Walt Disney World and Islands of Adventure theme parks, Miami's South Beach, and that hub of debauchery on the delta, New Orleans.

Eckerd doesn't have a football team, but popular intramurals include flag football, soccer, baseball, softball, and the assassin game, in which students try to shoot their peers with dart guns. Varsity teams compete in NCAA Division II, and the men's basketball squad recently competed in the final Elite Eight, and was NCAA conference champs in 2004. "Men's basketball is the only sport that attracts lots of fans and spectators," a senior says, and a night of Midnight Madness helps kick off the season. The co-ed sailing team has claimed several recent divisional and regional championships.

"I love what I'm learning," says a junior marine biology student. Eckerd is striving to add "experiential, service, and international learning" to the traditional classroom experience and attract a higher caliber of students. That mission, combined with new facilities and the fun to be had in the Florida sun, makes Eckerd a standout.

Overlaps
University of Tampa, University of Miami, Stetson, Rollins, College of Charleston, Florida State

---

If You Apply To ➤

Eckerd: Rolling admissions. Does not guarantee to meet demonstrated need. Campus and alumni interviews: recommended, evaluative. SATs or ACTs: required. SAT IIs: optional. Accepts the Common Application and prefers electronic applications. Essay questions: significant concern and how you'll address it in college; significant experience; book or author that's impacted you.

Elon University

2700 Campus Box, Elon, NC 27244

A rapidly rising star among liberal arts colleges in the Southeast and an emerging name nationwide. With a welcoming environment and a supportive faculty, Elon is good at taking average students and turning them on to the life of the mind. Strong emphasis on global perspectives and hands-on learning in the classroom.

Elon University derives its name from the Hebrew word for "oak," which is fitting when you consider the many ways in which the school is growing. It seems everything is changing here—from the name and the mascot, to the buildings, academic majors, and programs. With an emphasis on undergraduate research, group work, service learning, and study abroad, the university also provides its students with

Website: www.elon.edu
Location: Small town
Total Enrollment: 4,796
Undergraduates: 4,622

(Continued)

Male/Female: 39/61

SAT Ranges: V 540–620
  M 550–630

ACT Range: 22–27

Financial Aid: 35%

Expense: Pr $

Phi Beta Kappa: No

Applicants: 8,063

Accepted: 41%

Enrolled: 37%

Grad in 6 Years: 74%

Returning Freshmen: 88%

Academics: ✍ ✍ ✍

Social: 🐘 🐘 🐘 🐘

Q of L: ★ ★ ★ ★ ★

Admissions: (336) 278-3566
  or (800) 334-8448

Email Address:
  admissions@elon.edu

Strongest Programs:
Business
Communications
Performing Arts
Psychology
Political Science
Biology
Education

Elon may just have one of the best living-learning residential life programs in the nation.

plenty of opportunities to grow—intellectually and socially. "Each student is a part of his or her education. Nowhere else will students have the opportunity to learn and grow with such a dedicated and experienced faculty," says a sophomore.

Elon was founded in 1889 and occupies a 575-acre campus set in the woods of North Carolina's Piedmont region. It is arguably the most architecturally consistent campus in the nation. Buildings are Georgian-style brick with white trim, and newer buildings have been adapted to modern architectural lines while maintaining this classic collegiate feel. At the center of campus is Lake Mary Nell, home to an abundance of geese and ducks. Academic buildings are organized in two clusters: an arts and sciences quad near a fountain in the older section of the campus, and a newly constructed "academic village," complete with a colonnade and rotunda. There has been a building boom along with a spate of renovations in recent years. Newer facilities include an honors pavilion, the Belk Library (which remains open 24 hours a day), a political science pavilion, and the Phoenix sports club.

All of the new facilities have been designed to support Elon's highly interactive academic programs. The university offers over 40 undergraduate degrees, with strong programs in business, communications, psychology, education, and biology (which also happen to be the most popular). The School of Communications—where the curriculum was recently completely revamped—is nationally recognized and benefits from two ultramodern digital television stations that broadcast seven hours of live programming each week. The communications and business schools were recently accredited, and chemistry and education curricula have been revised as the university strives for accreditation in those areas. Majors in computer information systems and performing arts and design were added recently, along with minors in global information systems, art history, and multimedia authoring.

"Each student is a part of his or her education." Weaker academic areas include nonviolence studies and Asian-Pacific studies. Students agree the academic climate is rigorous but varies greatly depending on your major. "The academic climate here is definitely under a state of transition, becoming much more competitive and demanding," a junior says.

Elon has an elaborate support system designed to ensure that first-year students don't fall through the cracks. Students begin general studies with a first-year course called The Global Experience, a seminar-style interdisciplinary class that investigates challenges facing the world. First-year orientations include Move-In Day, in which faculty members literally help students lug their belongings from their cars to their new rooms, and an optional experiential learning program that partners 120 freshmen with returning students for activities ranging from whitewater rafting to volunteer work. Elon 101 is taken by all first-years; students meet weekly in groups of no more than 16 during the first semester and discuss academic, social, and personal concerns with a faculty member and an upper-level student.

Students must complete a core that includes English, mathematics, wellness, eight courses in liberal arts and sciences, three courses at the advanced level, an experiential learning component, and a general studies interdisciplinary seminar. The university places a big emphasis on service learning and service research. Ten percent of undergrads are engaged in research work with faculty. Nearly two-thirds study abroad, thanks to the 4–1–4 academic calendar and the Honors Program offers a series of demanding courses that focus on writing and critical thinking skills, and the university offers a variety of prestigious fellows programs.

More than three-quarters of all classes have 25 or fewer students, and professors are highly praised. "The environment in class is cooperative, geared towards collective learning and application. I have developed some very meaningful relationships with the professors at the university," explains an economics major. Elon prides itself on attracting students who may not have been academic stars in high school (but who have leadership potential) and turning them on to the life of the mind. "Academics are always a priority, but it does not inhibit an Elon student's desire to be involved," a senior says. "Often, the most social place on campus during the semester is the library." Nearly 70 percent come from outside North Carolina. Eighty-nine percent of Elon's student body are Caucasian, 7 percent African American, 1 percent Hispanic, 1 percent Asian American and 1 percent foreign. Students can vie for hundreds of merit scholarships averaging $3,713, and there are 147 athletic scholarships available.

Fifty-nine percent of students reside on campus and are required to for their first two years. "The rooms are large and spacious with big windows," says a senior. "Other universities that I visited had dorm rooms that made it feel like I was in a prison cell." Options include traditional residence halls, an academic village complex where students and faculty live and study together, and university-owned apartments. Campus dining gets mixed reviews, but most agree that there are a variety of options for the discerning palette.

"The academic climate here is definitely under a state of transition."

When it's time to let off steam, students generally turn to the active Greek scene-which attracts 25 percent of the men and 44 percent of the women-or countless activities on campus. "There is always a lot going on. I like to have fun on the weekends and have rarely been bored here," a junior says. "I believe in working hard and playing hard, and at Elon, you can have a healthy balance." Students say that while alcohol is ever-present, there is little pressure to drink. Says a student: "Elon's alcohol policy focuses on education not prohibition. They encourage students to make wise decisions and optimize their time at Elon." Road trips to the beach (three hours), the mountains (one hour), and Washington, D.C. (five hours) are popular diversions.

The tiny town of Elon is virtually indistinguishable from the university, which even owns the two main restaurants. Students take an active role in the community through volunteer projects both "through certain classes as well as on their own time," says a student. Back on campus, popular events include the Festival of the Oaks, homecoming, and a weekly College Coffee, where students and faculty mingle over free breakfast and coffee.

And let's not forget the road trip to rival Furman University. "Six to eight chartered buses are filled and we tailgate at the university before the game," a student says. Elon competes in the Division I Southern Conference, and offers eight women's sports and seven men's. There's also an intramural program covering 20 sports, which almost half of students participate in, and a successful club sports program that lets students compete with those at other schools.

Without a doubt, Elon University has come a long way in recent years. "Elon is truly an up-and-coming school. The leadership of the university continually strives toward excellence and is taking Elon to a new level of national prominence. Our programs of study are getting better and better and the campus is growing by leaps and bounds," a communications major reports. By steadily ramping up its educational offerings, growing and improving its facilities, and upping its admissions standards, this quality liberal arts university is quickly outgrowing its local reputation and making a name for itself across the country.

"I believe in working hard and playing hard, and at Elon, you can have a healthy balance."

Overlaps

UNC-Chapel Hill, James Madison, Furman, North Carolina State, Wake Forest, College of Charleston

Emerson College

120 Boylston Street, Boston, MA 02116-4624

Emerson is strategically located in the heart of Boston's theatre district and within walking distance of the city's major attractions. Media production/film heads the list of strong programs. With roughly 2,900 undergraduates, Emerson is a smaller alternative to neighboring giants Northeastern and Boston U.

Website: www.emerson.edu
Location: Urban
Total Enrollment: 3,777
Undergraduates: 2,976
Male/Female: 42/58
SAT Ranges: V 580–670
   M 540–640
ACT Range: 24–28
Financial Aid: 53%
Expense: Pr $ $
Phi Beta Kappa: Yes
Applicants: 4,584
Accepted: 45%
Enrolled: 32%
Grad in 6 Years: 68%
Returning Freshmen: 86%
Academics: 🎓🎓🎓
Social: ☎☎
Q of L: ★★★
Admissions: (617) 824-8600
Email Address:
   admission@emerson.edu

Strongest Programs:
Media Production-Film
Writing, Literature, &
   Publishing
Performing Arts
Journalism
Marketing Communication

Those who aspire to a career in Hollywood or Manhattan may want to start with a four-year stint in Boston. There they will find Emerson College, a small liberal arts school that offers strong programs in communications and the performing arts. Here, students take notes from professors who also happen to be working directors, producers, actors, and writers. It's an approach that helps talented students find their voice and prepare for the spotlight.

Founded in 1880, Emerson is located on Boston Common in the middle of the city's theatre district and features a mix of traditional and modern high-rise buildings. Much of the surrounding city is accessible by foot, including the historic Freedom Trail and the Boston Public Garden. The new 11-story Tufte Performance and Production Center includes rehearsal space, a theatre design and technology center, costume shop, makeup lab, and television studios. When most of the college was relocated to Boston's cultural district, part of that purchase included the historic Majestic Theatre, which in 2003 was reopened after being fully restored to its original 1903 appearance. Emerson's newest addition is a 13-story residence hall on a choice Boston Common site. It includes a campus center with new athletic facilities and offices for student services. Now, the college is restoring Boston's Paramount Theater complex to create new student residences, a cinema, and performing arts space.

Emerson was founded with an emphasis on communication and performance, and the school still offers a plethora of strong programs in this vein. Undergraduates may choose from more than a dozen majors, including acting, broadcast journalism, print and multimedia journalism, film, communication sciences, television/radio, political communication, and theatre design/technology. General education requirements consist of a combination of interdisciplinary seminars and traditional courses. All students must take courses in three areas: foundations, which includes courses in writing, oral communications, and quantitative reasoning; perspectives, which includes courses in aesthetics, ethics and values, history, literature, and scientific, social, and psychological perspectives; and multicultural diversity, which includes classes in global and U.S. diversity. Interdisciplinary seminars of no more than 20 students stress the interrelationships between different communication fields; recent seminars include Minds and Machines, The City, Ways of Knowing: Philosophy and Literature, and Words, Imagination, Expression.

> **"EC students tend to be very passionate about the course material."**

The most popular major is media production-film, followed closely by a major that combines writing, literature, and publishing. Performing arts, journalism, and marketing communication are also popular. Courses can range from demanding and competitive to laid-back and relatively easy. "EC students tend to be very passionate about the course material," says a film major. Faculty and students often develop tight relationships, and "students receive individual attention from day one," says a senior. In visual and media arts, new production courses focus on animation, screenwriting, and digital media. The college also provides students with access to state-of-the-art equipment and facilities—including digital editing labs, Avid composers, recording studios, and fully-equipped television studios—and the campus is home to the oldest noncommercial radio station in Boston.

For those seeking a spotlight and stage in a different setting, Emerson offers a semester-abroad program at Kasteel Well (the Netherlands), where students are housed in a restored 13th-century castle complete with moats, gardens, a gate house, and peacocks. Film students may attend a summer program in Prague, and each year about 200 students spend a semester at Emerson's Los Angeles Center. There, they can participate in internships with companies such as Interscope Records, CNN, Warner Bros., Dreamworks, and NBC. Back on campus, students may cross register with nearby Suffolk University and the six-member Boston ProArts Consortium.

Social life on campus includes plays and film shoots that take place on a regular basis.

Nearly two-thirds of all classes have fewer than 25 students, and professors receive high marks for their knowledge and accessibility. "Most of the faculty still work in their respective fields, so I feel I'm really getting prepared," says one student. Another student says that in recent conflict between administrators and full-time faculty, students have strongly supported the faculty. Though adjunct professors teach a large portion of freshman classes, students seem to appreciate their real-world advice—especially considering the competitive nature of a career in the arts. The library holds 200,000 volumes and other media, mostly related to communication and performing arts. Students may also take advantage of more than 700,000 volumes in the collections of 10 nearby academic and museum libraries.

Emerson students are "very open-minded, creative, and driven," according to a television/video major. Nearly two-thirds hail from outside of Massachusetts, and 76 percent come from public high schools. African Americans account for only 3 percent of the student body, Hispanics 5 percent, and Asian Americans another 4 percent. Hot campus issues include politics, government and the war in Iraq. One acting student says, "Emerson is a model for an active student body. Most students and faculty march

"Most of the faculty still work in their respective fields, so I feel I'm really getting prepared."

in rallies, protest outside the state house, and some even get arrested for disturbing the peace." Emerson offers 202 merit scholarships to qualified applicants, ranging from $5,000 to a half-ride. There are no athletic scholarships.

Forty-eight percent of students live on campus, some in dorms with special theme floors, including the Writers' Block (cute, huh?), and the Digital Culture floor. Freshmen are guaranteed on-campus housing, and the new residence hall is helping to bring more upperclassmen back to campus. The current residence halls are "the nicest I've seen at any school in Boston," says one junior. Others seem to agree that the dorms are spacious and well-maintained. Campus dining is not only about eating but also, according to one sophomore, "the social mecca for kids on campus." The food rates well, with lots of options for vegans, vegetarians, and those with special diets. Students feel safe on campus. Each building requires an ID to enter, and public safety officers regularly patrol the streets outside the buildings.

Social life on campus includes plays and film shoots that take place on a regular basis. More than 60 student clubs, organizations and performance groups offer

Students take notes from professors who also happen to be working directors, producers, actors, and writers.

students ample opportunity for involvement, including two radio stations, six humor and literary journals, 10 performance troupes, and six production organizations. "Most of the social life is off campus," says a theatre major who finds that students are "so immersed in their independent projects, they don't have time to party." Party animals can be found among performing arts majors who "use substances to thrive," according to one student, and among members of the Greek scene, which attracts 5 percent of Emerson men and 4 percent of the women. Though the campus is considered "dry," parties at off-campus apartments make it possible for students to drink. However, "Alcohol is not a huge problem," says a sophomore.

When students tire of on-campus events, they can rush headlong into Boston, arguably the best college town in the nation. One student says, "There are so many colleges in the Boston area that this city is crawling with young people." Another gushes, "Emerson students live, study, work, and volunteer in almost every major neighborhood and area of the city." There are plenty of

"Most of the social life is off campus."

diversions, including museums, the Franklin Park Zoo, Freedom Trail, the Boston Symphony Orchestra, and major league baseball at Fenway Park. Back on campus, students enjoy poetry slams and comedy sketches. Popular festivities include EVVY Awards, the largest student production/organization in the country. There is also Hand-Me-Down Night (during which outgoing club officers "hand down" their positions to incoming officers), Greek Week, and the New Student Revue.

Emerson fields 12 Division III athletic teams, and the Lions compete as a member of the Eastern College Athletic Conference and the Great Northeast Athletic Conference. Men's basketball, women's soccer, men's tennis, and the cross-country team are perennial GNAC conference finalists. Emersonians also enjoy a strong intramural program and take advantage of their new athletic field and 10,000-square-foot fitness center featuring state-of-the-art fitness equipment, classes, and wellness workshops.

While you are not guaranteed to become the next Julia Roberts, Spike Lee, or Brad Pitt, the possibility for stardom exists at Emerson. And even if a lifestyle of fame is not for you, the excellent education, small classes, and attentive professors may teach you how to be the "star" of your own life.

Overlaps

New York University, Boston University, Northeastern, USC, Ithaca, Syracuse

If You Apply To ➤

Emerson: Regular admissions: Jan. 5. Financial aid: Mar. 1. Housing: May 1. Meets demonstrated need of 80%. Campus interviews: optional, informational. No alumni interviews. SATs or ACTs: required. SAT IIs: recommended. Accepts electronic applications. Essay question: personal statement.

Emory University

200 Boisfeuillet Jones Center, Atlanta, GA 30322-1950

Often compared to Duke and Vanderbilt, Emory may be most similar to Wash U in St. Louis. Both have suburban locations in major cities and both tout business and premeds as major draws. If the campus is uninspiring, the suburban Atlanta location is unbeatable.

Website: www.emory.edu

Emory University may lack the liberal arts prowess of the Northeastern schools with which it competes, but it's a favorite of preprofessional students from both U.S.

coasts. They come for its size (big, but not too big), location (beside bustling Atlanta), and reputation (increasingly prominent on the national stage)—and yes, for the balmy weather, too. Popular majors include psychology, English, biology, and political science. "There aren't any no-no departments," says a neuroscience and behavioral biology major.

Debate, discussion, and political organizations are popular at Emory. "Students have strong social and political beliefs, and all sides are represented on campus," says an economics major. Though most students are clean-cut and career-oriented, a freshman says the population ranges "from preppy, to Northeast and very designer-oriented, to hippie, and everything in between." Regardless of how they're dressed, students are challenged, not coddled, in the classroom; they form study groups and work together to succeed. An atmosphere of friendliness and southern hospitality enhance the vibrant campus life.

Atlanta also beckons with volunteer and mentorship programs, arts, concerts, professional sports, and a lively club and bar scene. "Atlanta is far enough away that the campus feels very campus-like, but close enough that there are lots of opportunities for great shopping, food, and internships," says a sophomore.

Set on 631 acres of woods and rolling hills, in the Druid Hills area of Decatur, Emory's campus spreads out from an academic quad of marble-covered, red-roofed buildings. Contemporary structures dot the periphery of the lush, green grounds. In recent years, the campus has gained a new performing arts center, new computer labs, and a new business school. The 90,000-square-foot Schwartz Center for Performing Arts, completed in 2002, includes an 825-seat concert hall, 135-seat theater lab, and 135-seat dance studio. The central campus is now closed to all car traffic except for Emory shuttles.

Emory's distribution requirements aim to develop competence in writing, quantitative methods, a second language, and physical education, and include exposure to the humanities, social sciences, and the natural sciences. Other required coursework helps broaden students' perspectives on national, regional, and global history and culture. Finally, students take two seminars—one as freshmen (50 to 60 are available each term, limited to 18 students each) and one at an upper level. Entering freshmen seeking a smaller environment may want to consider Emory's two-year Oxford College, where 600 students earn associate's degrees in a "small town" atmosphere, and transfer to the main campus to finish up. Emory also belongs to the Atlanta Regional Consortium for Higher Education, which lets students take courses at other area schools. The Center for International Programs Abroad (CIPA) offers study in more than 70 locations around the world. Participants earn Emory credit and Emory grades, and they can receive Emory financial aid, scholarships and grants

> "Atlanta is far enough away that the campus feels very campus-like."

Just as Emory has invested in its physical plant, the school has spent lavishly to add star faculty members to key departments, such as Archbishop Desmond Tutu in the school of theology. Chemistry and biology benefit from physical proximity to the federal Centers for Disease Control, while many political science professors have ties to the Carter Center (named for the former president, who holds a town hall meeting on campus each year), and serve as regular guests on nearby CNN. The most popular majors are business, psychology, economics, political science, and biology, followed closely by neuroscience and behavioral biology, a favorite of premeds. A 4–2 program allows students to earn bachelor's degrees at Emory, then a master's in engineering at Georgia Institute of Technology. New programs include Chinese studies, American studies, and Irish studies. Emory has received a significant portion of Nobel laureate Seamus Heaney's archive, and its Irish studies program is said to rival those of Notre Dame and Boston College.

(Continued)
Location: Suburban
Total Enrollment: 12,134
Undergraduates: 5,625
Male/Female: 44/56
SAT Ranges: V 640–730
  M 660–740
ACT Range: 29–33
Financial Aid: 52%
Expense: Pr $ $ $
Phi Beta Kappa: Yes
Applicants: 12,011
Accepted: 36%
Enrolled: 29%
Grad in 6 Years: 88%
Returning Freshmen: 95%
Academics: ✑ ✑ ✑ ✑
Social: ☎ ☎ ☎
Q of L: ★ ★ ★ ★
Admissions: (800) 727-6036
Email Address: admiss@
  learnlink.emory.edu

Strongest Programs:
Business
Psychology
Natural Sciences
Political Science
English
History
Art History

Just as Emory has invested in its physical plant, the school has spent lavishly to add star faculty members to key departments, such as Archbishop Desmond Tutu in the school of theology.

Only 20 percent of Emory students are Georgians, and a little over half are from the Southeast. New York, New Jersey, California, and Florida are also well-represented. "The students tend to be academically competitive, and upper-middle to upper class," says a junior. "There is a large Jewish student population, which is not found at [some of] our rival schools," adds a senior. African Americans make up 10 percent of the student body, Asian Americans 16 percent, and Hispanics 3 percent. Merit scholarships range from two-thirds of tuition to a full ride; there are no athletic scholarships.

Seventy percent of Emory students live on campus; freshmen and sophomores are required to do so. Lucky juniors, seniors, and graduate students may hang their hats in the one- to four-bedroom Clairmont Campus apartments, which boast private bedrooms with full-size beds, kitchens and baths, and a washer-dryer in each unit. Clairmont residents also get an activity center with basketball, volleyball and tennis courts, a heated, outdoor, Olympic-sized pool, and weight-training facilities. Housing is guaranteed for four years, and students can request to live in a building that is co-ed by floor, co-ed by room, or single sex. They can also request a specific roommate. "Emory has dining options for even the pickiest eaters," says a satisfied junior. In addition to the dining halls, there are small cafés, grills, and a food court on campus.

Fraternities and sororities attract 31 percent of Emory's men and 33 percent of the women. While Greek parties are a big part of the social scene, "so is just hanging out in the dorms," says a junior. Upper classmen enjoy the Atlanta bar scene. Other options include college nights at local dance clubs and concerts organized by the Student Programming Committee, which recently brought Usher, Guster, and Dave Matthews Band to campus. Popular road trips include: Stone Mountain for hiking or a picnic; the cities of Athens and Savannah for concerts, beaches, or big-time college sports; Florida and the Carolinas. Atlanta also offers a multitude of diversions, from Braves baseball, Thrashers hockey, and Hawks basketball to plays at the Fox Theatre, exhibits at the High Museum of Art, and shopping at Underground Atlanta or the Lenox Mall, to which Emory provides a free shuttle every Saturday. Alcohol isn't allowed in the freshman dorms, though "if you want to drink, it is possible," a sophomore says. A very popular highlight of the social calendar is Dooley's Week, a spring festival in honor of Emory's enigmatic mascot, James W. Dooley, a skeleton who reportedly escaped from the biology lab almost 100 years ago. If Dooley walks into your class, the class is dismissed, and the week culminates with a costume ball in his honor. Freshman halls also have Songfest, a competition where residents make up spirit-filled song-and-dance routines.

"Emory has dining options for even the pickiest eaters."

Emory doesn't field a varsity football team, though students show their spirit with T-shirts that proudly proclaim: "Emory Football: Still Undefeated (since 1836)." Last year, the women's tennis team and women's swimming and diving team both finished first nationally in NCAA Division III, while men's tennis and swimming and diving both placed second, women's volleyball placed sixth, and men's golf placed fifth. Men's basketball competes in the University Athletic Association, against such academic powerhouses as the University of Chicago, Johns Hopkins, and Carnegie Mellon. All around, Emory's athletic program is exceptionally strong, ranking eighth in the nation last year in the NACDA Director's Cup standings. Most students join at least one intramural sports team at either a competitive or a recreational level. Popular intramurals include flag football, volleyball, soccer, basketball, water polo, and ultimate Frisbee.

While many Southern schools suffer from a regional provincialism, that isn't true at Emory, which blends a focus on teaching and research to nurture creativity, generate wisdom, instill integrity and honor in its students, and graduate leaders who are highly sought after in the working world—and by postgraduate law, medical,

Overlaps

Duke, Washington University (MO), University of Pennsylvania, Vanderbilt, Georgetown, Northwestern

and business programs. "It is an awesome environment for academics and athletics and social life," says a junior. "You make some life-long friends."

Eugene Lang College—The New School for Liberal Arts

(formerly New School for Social Research)
65 West 11th Street, New York, NY 10011

Eugene Lang College is home to more than 800 street-savvy, freethinking students. New York City is the campus, and Lang offers little sense of community. In keeping with the New School's traditional ties to Europe, an internationalist perspective is predominant. Strong in the arts and humanities.

Students seeking a typical college experience—large lectures, rowdy football games, and rigid academic requirements—would do well to avoid Eugene Lang College. That's because Lang has no required courses, seminars instead of traditional lectures, and not a single varsity sport. Instead, this small, urban liberal arts college offers individualized academic programs, small classes, and a campus that reflects the quirky and kinetic atmosphere of Greenwich Village. "We don't want to become business leaders, but instead teachers, community organizers, thinkers, professors, and writers," a junior says. "Students here want to change the world—and I think in many ways we are."

Lang fits right in amid the brownstones and trendy boutiques of one of New York's most vibrant neighborhoods. The majority of Lang's classrooms and facilities are in a single five-story building between Fifth and Sixth Avenues on West 11th Street, although The New School occupies 16 buildings along Fifth Avenue. NYU and the excitement of Greenwich Village and Washington Square Park are just a few blocks away.

The New School was founded in 1919 by a band of progressive scholars that included John Dewey, Charles Beard, and Thorstein Veblen. A decade and a half later, it became a haven for European intellectuals fleeing Nazi persecution, and over the years it has been the teaching home of many notable thinkers, including Buckminster Fuller and Hannah Arendt. Created in 1978, the undergraduate college was renamed in the late '80s for Eugene Lang, a philanthropist who (surprise, surprise!) made a significant donation to the school.

The two most distinctive features of Lang College are the small classes—fewer than 16 students—and undergraduates designing their own path of study with no required courses. As freshmen, students choose from a broad-based menu of seminars, and as sophomores they select from 11 new paths of study: cultural studies and media; literature; writing; the arts (including dance and theater); philosophy; psychology; science, technology and society; social and historical inquiry; urban studies; religious studies; and education studies. In their final year, students take on advanced "senior work" through a seminar or independent project which synthesizes their educational experience. The standard courseload is at least four seminars

Website: www.newschool.edu
Location: Urban
Total Enrollment: 860
Undergraduates: 860
Male/Female: 32/68
SAT Ranges: V 540–660
  M 470–590
ACT Range: 20–26
Financial Aid: 61%
Expense: Pr $ $
Phi Beta Kappa: No
Applicants: 854
Accepted: 68%
Enrolled: 27%
Grad in 6 Years: 55%
Returning Freshmen: 76%
Academics: ✎ ✎ ✎
Social: ☎
Q of L: ★ ★ ★
Admissions: (212) 229-5665
Email Address:
  lang@newschool.edu

Strongest Programs:
Writing
Fine Arts
Education Studies
Cultural Studies

Freshmen choose from a broad-based menu of seminars, and sophomores select from 11 new paths of study.

a semester, with topics such as From Standup to Shakespeare and the History of Jazz. All first-year students must take one year of writing and workshops focusing on nonacademic concerns and library research skills. Cooperation, not competition, is the norm. "The courses are rigorous in the way that they ask for mental, emotional, and intellectual energy from each student," a junior says. "Students are usually excited about what they are taking, so the rigor takes a back seat to the excitement involved in learning," another student adds.

Lang's top offerings include political and social theory, writing, history, literature, and literary theory. Its city location lends strength to the urban studies and education programs. Writing is highly praised, especially poetry, and theater is strong. The natural sciences and math are weak, though courses are offered through an arrangement with nearby Cooper Union. While introductory language courses are plentiful, upper-level language offerings are limited. And the college has beefed up its offerings on the history and literature of Third World and minority peoples, which were already better

> "Students here want to change the world —and I think in many ways we are."

than those at most colleges. The professors at Lang are well-versed and engaging, according to many students. "Getting lectured is rare, and I appreciate the way that class discussions are so well-planned and thought out," says one student.

The main academic complaint is the limited range of seminars, but outside programs offer more variety. After their first year, students may enroll in a limited number of approved classes in other divisions of The New School. A joint BA/BFA with Parsons The New School for Design has proven very popular. There's also a BA/BFA program in jazz and a BA/MA in media studies with The New School for General Studies's communications department. A newer addition is the exchange program with Sarah Lawrence College, established to provide motivated students with additional academic opportunities. The New School's library is small, but students have access to the massive Bobst Library at nearby New York University.

Lang College attracts a disparate group of undergraduates, but most of them can be described as idealistic and independent. "We are nontraditional college students who relish in this difference and exciting uniqueness that sets us apart from conforming NYU students," a junior says. Some are slightly older than conventional college age and are used to looking after themselves. Eleven percent are African American or Hispanic, another 3 percent are Asian American, and 2 percent are foreign. A junior says "the freedom involved with concentrations, as opposed to majors, attracts the type of student that really wants to just learn things." Forty-two percent of Lang's students are from New York City and many cite the school's location as one of its best features. "Whatever is desired can be found somewhere in New York City," says a junior. "It's a nice place to be if you want to party or be a stone-cold intellectual." Lang College admits students regardless of their finances and strives to meet the demonstrated need of those enrolled. However, the school does not guarantee to meet the demonstrated financial need of all admits. A deferred-payment plan allows students to pay tuition in 10 installments, and there are various loan programs available. There are a handful of merit scholarships, but no athletic awards.

A joint BA/BFA with Parsons The New School for Design has proven very popular. There's also a BA/BFA program in jazz and a BA/MA in media studies with The New School for General Studies's communications department.

> "Getting lectured is rare, and I appreciate the way that class discussions are so well-planned and thought out."

Dorm life at Lang engages only about 30 percent of the student body, though the rooms are in good shape. One student offers this assessment: "Union Square is comfortable and fun to live in. Loeb Hall is the newest and is mostly for freshman. Marlton Hall is in sort of a drab location...and is just old and generally uncomfortable." Off-campus dwellers live in apartments in the Village, if they can afford it, or in Brooklyn or elsewhere in the New York City area. Eighty percent of freshmen live on campus. A meal plan is available, but most students opt for the hundreds of delis, coffee shops, and restaurants that line Sixth Avenue.

The social network at Lang is quite small, and like many things, is left up to the student. "Our lack of campus kind of makes all activity 'off campus,' though we do have dances and club activities within the school facilities themselves," a junior says. The social activities found on campus generally involve intellectual pursuits such as poetry readings and open-mic nights, as well as typical college activities like the student newspaper and the literary magazine. Occasionally, students organize dances and parties, like the Spring Prom, a catered affair with live music that is "a satirical offshoot of the high school tradition." Students generally avoid drinking on campus, and when they do imbibe, alcohol is "far from the central focus of activity," says a junior. With no intramural or varsity sports, another junior says "the most popular sports including 'chopstick using' and 'car dodging.'"

> **"Whatever is desired can be found somewhere in New York City."**

Students relish the freedom and independence they have at Eugene Lang College. For a student who yearns for four years of "traditional" college experiences, Lang would likely be a disappointment. But for those desiring an intimate education in America's cultural capital, Lang offers all the stimulation of the city it calls home.

If You Apply To ➤ **Eugene Lang:** Early decision: Nov. 15. Regular admissions: Feb.1. Meets demonstrated need of 80%. Campus interviews (or by telephone): required, evaluative. No alumni interviews. SATs or ACTs: required; SAT preferred. SAT IIs: recommended. Students taking the ACT must take the Writing Test. Accepts Common Application and electronic applications. Essay question: explain how your community has affected your thinking; discuss a social, economic, or political issue of personal importance; and personal statement. Seeks "independent" students.

The Evergreen State College

Olympia, WA 98505

There's no mistaking Evergreen for a typical public college. Never mind the way-out garb favored by its students. Evergreen's interdisciplinary, team-taught curriculum is truly unique. To find anything remotely like Evergreen, you'll need to go private and travel East to places like Hampshire or Sarah Lawrence.

In "La Vie Boheme," the anthem of Jonathan Larson's rock opera *Rent*, one of the characters asks, "Anyone out of the mainstream / Is anyone in the mainstream?" At Evergreen State College, the answer has always been a vehement "No!" The school's unofficial motto is *Omnia Extares*, Latin for "Let it all hang out." Founded in 1967 as Washington State's experimental college, Evergreen lacks grades, majors, and even departments. This system may sound strange, but it works: Alumni include Matt Groening, creator of *The Simpsons*, *Futurama*, and *Life in Hell*. "The character of the school is openly artistic, earth-friendly, musically open, and a place to truly be an individual," says a freshman. "Students are free to explore and be whoever they want to be," agrees a sophomore.

Evergreen lies in a fir forest at the edge of the 90-mile-long Puget Sound. The peaceful, thousand-acre campus includes a 24-acre organic plant and animal farm, as well as 3,300 feet of undeveloped beach. Most of Evergreen's buildings are boxy concrete-and-steel creations, though the Longhouse Education and Culture Center is designed in the Native American style typical of the Pacific

Website: www.evergreen.edu
Location: City outskirts
Total Enrollment: 4,410
Undergraduates: 3,593
Male/Female: 46/54
SAT Ranges: V 530–600
  M 480–600
ACT Range: 19–27
Financial Aid: 53%
Expense: Pub $
Phi Beta Kappa: No
Applicants: 1,534
Accepted: 95%
Enrolled: 33%

Northwest. Seminar II, a five-building, 160,000-square-foot complex, opened in 2004, the first new academic building to be built on campus in more than 25 years. The complex incorporates "green" design concepts, construction methods, and materials, and houses classrooms, workshop spaces, lecture halls, art studios, and offices.

At first glance, Evergreen's wide-open curriculum looks like Easy Street: It's based on five "planning units"—culture, text, and language; environmental studies; expressive arts; scientific inquiry and society; and politics, behavior and change—which means no required classes and few traditional exams to slog through at the end of each 10-week quarter. And instead of signing up for unrelated courses to fulfill distribution requirements, students enroll in a coordinated "program," team-taught by multiple professors. One recent program, Problems Without Solutions, looked at AIDS and homelessness from the perspective of political science, philosophy, anthropology, economics, statistics, and writing. Still, there is some structure at the college. Freshmen select an interdisciplinary core program, while upperclassmen concentrate in more specialized areas, often writing a thesis or fulfilling an Individual Learning Contract developed in partnership with a faculty sponsor.

Students praise Evergreen's environmental science major, which offers classes in ornithology, marine biology, and wetlands studies. To supplement their coursework, environmental scientists may also study marine animals while sailing in Puget Sound, spend seven weeks at a bird sanctuary in Oregon, or trek to the Grand Canyon or the tropical rainforests of Costa Rica. Various arts programs—dance, writing, visual arts and media arts—also get high marks. Foreign languages tend to be weaker. And regardless of what they study, students warn that—while the integrated approach to learning may improve comprehension and deepen understanding—it likewise means a lot of work. "You get out of Evergreen what you put into it," explains a student pursuing an emphasis in psychology. "Students here are not competitive with each other; they are motivated, though."

Because Evergreen attracts many nontraditional students, and students who are older than the typical college freshman, administrators take advising and career counseling seriously. They've also asked faculty members to do more to help students adjust to life on campus. "It's not about teaching—it's more like guidance through a subject," a junior says. "If students want to understand the subjects, they must motivate

Seminar II, a five-building, 160,000-square-foot complex, opened in 2004, the first new academic building to be built on campus in more than 25 years. The complex incorporates "green" design concepts, construction methods, and materials, and houses classrooms, workshop spaces, lecture halls, art studios, and offices.

"Students here are not competitive with each other; they are motivated, though."

to do more on their own." Another bonus: Because Evergreen doesn't award tenure, there's less pressure for professors to conduct research and publish their findings—and less to distract them from teaching undergraduates.

Seventy-eight percent of Evergreen's students are Washington natives; African Americans, Hispanics and Native Americans each account for 5 percent of the student body, while Asian Americans add 4 percent. Most are "environmentally conscious and socially aware," says an arts major. Other adjectives used to describe Greeners: "Laid-back, political, respectful, liberal, active in the community, and overall just pretty chill," says another student. Hot topics on campus include gender and sexuality, the Washington Public Interest Research Group, and "issues of government, the local community, and synergy with the college," says a sophomore. Evergreen awards 22 merit scholarships a year, averaging $4,100 each, along with athletic scholarships in four sports. Special admissions consideration is given to applicants 25 years of age and older, as well as Vietnam-era veterans and applicants whose parents are not college graduates.

Twenty percent of Evergreen students, mostly freshmen and sophomores, live on campus, where there are "nine different types of housing," says one student. "It is not difficult to apply and get a room." The school's apartment complexes have single bedrooms, shared bathrooms—with bathtubs, not just shower stalls—and full kitchens, another adds. Still, because campus housing can be expensive, most upperclass students live off campus. There's an efficient bus system to get nonresidents to class on time, though it helps to have a car. Evergreen's food service offers a wide variety of dishes, including vegetarian and vegan options; some choices are organic, too. That said, opinions on the quality of campus chow are mixed.

Not surprisingly, Evergreen lacks a Greek system, but students say the housing office organizes plenty of weekend events—including open mic nights, soccer and other field games, performances and parties. Nearby Olympia (the state capital) doesn't really qualify as a college town, but it's progressive and open-minded, with art walks through local galleries, coffee shops, clothing stores, co-ops, and lots of live music. Even better, "Evergreen is 10 minutes from theaters, parks, and recreation, an hour or so from skiing, hiking, or the beach, and about an hour from Seattle," says a student concentrating in sociology. The college offers all types of outdoor equipment for rent, from backpacks and skis to kayaks and sailboats. Its large College Activities Building houses a radio station, the student newspaper, along with space for student gatherings. Portland and the rugged Oregon coast (three to four hours away) provide other changes of scenery for students with wheels; everything is kept green and lush by the (interminable) rain, which stops in time for summer break and resumes by October.

You may chuckle at Evergreen's mascot, an eight-foot clam named "Gooeyduck," for the large geoduck clams found in Puget Sound, but the school is getting more serious about organized sports. Its basketball, cross-country, soccer, and women's volleyball teams compete in the NAIA Region I. While those squads haven't brought home any titles yet, Evergreen has produced two All-American swimmers and one All-American men's basketball player.

> "Evergreen is 10 minutes from theaters, parks, and recreation, an hour or so from skiing, hiking, or the beach, and about an hour from Seattle."

And 9 percent of students participate in recreational or intramural sports, which include Frisbee, volleyball, skiing, tennis, basketball, and sailing.

Evergreen isn't for everyone; indeed, this remains one of the best choices for students who think they were born 40 years too late. Freed from requirements and grades, Greeners delight in exploring the connections between disparate disciplines at their own pace. Succeeding in that endeavor, however, requires an incredible ability to focus; while some students would find the task burdensome, students here welcome the challenge. "It's up to us to learn what to believe in, not some instructor telling us what it's going to be," says a satisfied math and computer science student.

Evergreen's basketball, cross-country, soccer, and women's volleyball teams compete in the NAIA. While those squads haven't brought home any titles yet, Evergreen has produced two All-American swimmers and one All-American men's basketball player.

Overlaps

Western Washington, University of Washington, Lewis and Clark, Washington State—Pullman, UC—Santa Cruz

If You Apply To ➢

Evergreen: Rolling admissions: Mar. 1. Financial aid: Mar. 15. Housing: Jun. 1. Guarantees to meet full demonstrated need. Campus interviews: optional, informational. No alumni interviews. SATs or ACTs: required. SAT IIs: optional. Accepts electronic applications. Essay question: academic preparation and why you're ready for college-level studies at Evergreen, along with a description of educational and career goals, and how Evergreen will help you reach them.

Fairfield University

Fairfield, CT 06824

Fairfield is one of the up-and-coming schools in the Roman Catholic school scene. Undergraduate enrollment has grown in recent years. Strategic location near New York City is a major attraction. Lack of big-time sports keeps Fairfield from enjoying the visibility of Boston College/Holy Cross.

Website: www.fairfield.edu
Location: Suburban
Total Enrollment: 5,060
Undergraduates: 3,305
Male/Female: 43/57
SAT Ranges: V 540–630
  M 560–650
ACT Range: 23–27
Financial Aid: 49%
Expense: Pr $ $ $
Phi Beta Kappa: Yes
Applicants: 7,136
Accepted: 64%
Enrolled: 19%
Grad in 6 Years: 78%
Returning Freshmen: 91%
Academics: ✑ ✑ ✑
Social: ☎ ☎ ☎ ☎
Q of L: ★ ★ ★ ★
Admissions: (203) 254-4100
Email Address:
  admis@mail.fairfield.edu

Strongest Programs:
Art History
Communication
Religious Studies
Accounting
Finance
Management
Marketing
Nursing

No doubt about it, Fairfield University is moving into the same class as older, more revered East Coast Jesuit institutions. The school provides a well-rounded education, combining solid academics, real-world opportunities in and outside of the classroom, and an abundance of community service projects.

The physical beauty of the university's scenic, tree-lined campus just 90 minutes from Manhattan is a source of pride. The administration takes pains to preserve a lush atmosphere of sprawling lawns, ponds, and natural woodlands. Buildings are a blend of collegiate Gothic, Norman chateau, English manor, and modern. Students enjoy a 24-hour computer lab, Geographic Information Systems lab, wireless 125-person computer lab in the School of Nursing and wireless area in the Barone Campus Center. The north wing of the Bannow Science Center recently opened, along with the Ignatian Residential College and a trading floor in the Dolan School of Business.

Students may have difficulty finding time to enjoy the beautiful facilities. A demanding class schedule requires everyone to complete the liberal arts core curriculum over four years, with two to five courses from each of five areas: math and natural sciences; history and social and behavioral sciences; philosophy, religious studies, and applied ethics; English and visual and performing arts; modern and classical languages. The core constitutes almost half of a student's total courseload. "This pretty much means that a student is taking at least 15 credits a semester. Being a major in the sciences increases that load," says a senior physics major who has taken up to 21 credits at a time. Fairfield's main academic strengths are business (accounting, finance, and management), art history, communication, and religious studies. "Fairfield is mainly known by reputation as a liberal arts school, but I believe their biology program is underrated," says one biology major. Upperclassmen can design their own majors.

Fairfield's academic climate is not cutthroat, but challenging nevertheless. "There are opportunities to develop a challenging courseload that is competitive

"There are opportunities to develop a challenging courseload that is competitive and engaging."

and engaging or you can choose courses that will let you skate through them," a senior politics major reports. Recent additions to the curriculum include minors in information systems; operations management; classical studies; Irish studies, which has strong ties to the University of Galway; and Italian studies, which maintains strong ties to the Lorenzo de'Medici Institute in Florence. Engineering, nursing, and business curricula have been revamped, and a major in new media, television has been added. Neuroscience, legal studies and environmental science have been dropped. Engineering students may enroll in joint five-year programs with the Rensselaer Polytechnic Institute, Columbia University, the University of Connecticut or Stevens Institute of Technology. MBA candidates can now have a concentration in e-business or minor in information systems or operations management. Since 1993, 33 Fairfield students have been awarded Fulbright Scholarships for studies abroad. About 8 percent are part of the four-year honors program.

Students looking to travel abroad without committing a full semester can take a trip with one of several professors who lead educational summer tours for credit. About 225 students study abroad each year, through their choice of more than 100 programs in 50 nations. Sophomores can join the Ignatian Residential College; afterward, they can continue on to the new Companions program, which includes cultural activities and mentoring.

Freshmen are introduced to Fairfield with a thorough orientation program. A formal academic convocation in the first week of classes includes a speaker chosen to reflect the school's Jesuit values. There are no teaching assistants at Fairfield; 70 percent of classes have fewer than 25 students, and none have more than 50. "The professors are well-educated, well-informed, and engaging," a senior says. "Professors constantly encourage students to put their ideas on the line so that they have to truly believe what they are arguing," a junior art history major says.

The vast majority of Fairfield's students come from Roman Catholic families, and approximately half from Connecticut. Minority enrollment is small, with African Americans constituting 2 percent of the student body, Hispanics 5 percent, and Asian Americans another 3 percent. "The students at Fairfield are largely white, upper-middle class or upper-class and from the Northeast," a senior says. "The diversity of opinion and ethnicity is not great." Minority recruiting efforts include programs in Latin American, Asian, Women's, Judaic, and Black studies. To help students with Fairfield's steep price, the school offers merit scholarships annually, ranging from $10,000 to $15,000, as well as 158 athletic scholarships in six men's sports and eight women's sports.

Fairfield's "comfortable and well-maintained" residence halls house 80 percent of the student body. The school recently built a new upperclassman apartment village, and four of the traditional halls have been renovated. "Though we joke that they are not luxury suites, the dorms, townhouse,s and apartments are always clean and become home to many students," one student says. In one of the

"Community members are not often comfortable participating in university events, and vice versa."

more unusual housing arrangements in American higher education, upperclassmen can move off-campus to nearby beach houses. Meal plan options are available to all students, and many say the food is constantly improving.

Fairfield's proximity to the beaches of the Long Island Sound, a quick five-minute drive from campus, provides students with a scenic social space for everything from romantic retreats to rowdy parties. Still, students say much of the social life takes place on campus, where sponsored events range from dances to hanging out at the coffeehouse and on-campus pub to concerts with stars such as Blues Traveler and Third Eye Blind. Harvest Weekend at the end of October and Dogwoods Weekend at the end of April provide relief from the stress of studying. Road trips to New York (an hour by train) and Boston (two hours away) are popular. The college recently instituted a new program for alcohol misuse or abuse. "Students always find ways around the policies and drink in dorms, in upperclass housing and off-campus," one senior reports. Although Jesuits are very much in evidence and often live in the dorms, students say they do not hinder the social scene. The Campus Ministry draws a large following, with daily masses, retreats about three times a semester, and regular community service work, including two weeks of programs in the Caribbean and Latin America. But one student complains "our Jesuit identity needs to be expressed more clearly and something more must be done to excite students about the spiritual life."

As for the surrounding area, some students say the quaint, wealthy Fairfield area can feel a bit "snobby," though there are plenty of shopping outlets and restaurants that fit college-student budgets. Beach residents don't always approve of beach-apartment students and their activities. "Community members are not often

Living up to the Jesuit motto of sound mind and body, about three-quarters of students play on one of 25 intramural teams.

Recent additions to the curriculum include minors in Irish studies, which has strong ties to the University of Galway, and Italian studies, which maintains strong ties to the Lorenzo de'Medici Institute in Florence.

comfortable participating in university events, and vice versa," a student says. Volunteerism abounds, much of it in the nearby city of Bridgeport. "The influence of Bridgeport on my Fairfield experience has been profound," a student says.

Athletics have come of age at Fairfield, with a number of women's sports leading the way. Men's basketball went to nationals in 2003, and men's lacrosse reached the first round of the NCAA tournament in 2005. Women's lacrosse, soccer, and softball captured conference championships that year, as the women's tennis team did in 2004. Men's and women's basketball both draw crowds, and the boisterous home-court fans, who come to games in full Fairfield regalia, have been dubbed the "Red Sea." The university recently moved varsity football and men's ice hockey into club sports as a budget-cutting move. Living up to the Jesuit motto of sound mind and body, about three-quarters of students play on one of 25 intramural teams, whose exploits are copiously chronicled in the campus newspaper. "Many students sign up and create teams with their friends, and have a great time playing during the weekends," one student says. The school also takes pride in its high graduation rate for athletes, regularly one of the highest rates in the country.

Fairfield University has combined several traditions to create a rich undergraduate experience, including close bonds with faculty, an emphasis on community involvement, challenging academics, modern facilities, and, of course, big fun on the beach. "Fairfield seeks to help people realize that there is more to life than your marketing degree," a satisfied student says. "Students are taught to open their eyes and see the real world."

Overlaps

Boston College, Villanova, Providence, Loyola (MD), Fordham, College of Holy Cross

If You Apply To ➤

Fairfield: Rolling admissions. Early action: Nov. 15. Regular admissions: Jan. 15. Financial aid: Feb. 1. Meets demonstrated need of 25%. Campus and alumni interviews: optional, informational. SATs or ACTs: required. SAT IIs: optional. Accepts the Common Application and electronic applications. Essay question: from Common Application and a personal statement.

University of Florida

Gainesville, FL 32611

BEST BUY

It should come as no surprise that UF is a world leader in citrus science. Throw in communications, engineering, and Latin American studies to the list of renowned programs. Among Deep South public universities, only the University of Georgia rivals UF in overall quality.

Website: www.ufl.edu
Location: City center
Total Enrollment: 47,373
Undergraduates: 31,217
Male/Female: 47/53
SAT Ranges: V 560–660
   M 580–680
ACT Range: 24–29
Financial Aid: 49%
Expense: Pub $
Phi Beta Kappa: Yes

Set on 2,000 acres of rolling, heavily forested terrain in north-central Florida, the University of Florida is an athletic powerhouse, and administrators are working hard to gain the same level of national recognition for their academic offerings. The school is massive and continues to grow, and in this case, bigger does seem to be better. While some students certainly get lost in the shuffle, those who can navigate the bureaucratic red tape will find ample resources at their fingertips, including the second-largest academic computing center in the South and a micro-Kelvin laboratory capable of producing the coldest temperature in the universe.

UF's central campus has 21 buildings on the National Register of Historic Places. Most are collegiate Gothic in style—redbrick with white trim. They're augmented by more modern facilities, including a 173,000-square-foot complex for nursing, pharmacy, and the health professions; and an honors dorm complex, which offers suite-style living, a computer lab, classrooms, and a full-time honors staff in residence. UF's research capabilities and equipment are likewise impressive, and a boon to aspiring physicians. The school has one of the nation's few self-contained intensive care hyperbaric chambers for treatment of near-drowning victims, and a world-class, federally funded brain institute. Media types flock to the school's public TV and radio stations, and to its two commercial radio stations.

Academically, UF's strongest programs are those with a preprofessional bent, including engineering, tax law, and pharmacy. Popular majors include business administration, finance, elementary education, and advertising. Students also give high marks to the College of Journalism and Communications, the first in the nation to offer students an electronic newsroom. Students mention foreign languages and math as weaker, saying they rely too much on teaching assistants. Fine arts and music also suffer, probably because they're perceived as less helpful in the eventual job search. Students with high school GPAs of 3.9 or higher and SAT scores of at least 1350, gain access to the Honors Program, where classes are limited to 25 students. The program offers honors sections in standard academic subjects, and interdisciplinary courses such as masterworks of music, writing and love, and the history of rock and roll. The University Scholars Program offers $2,500 stipends to 175 students each year for one-on-one research with a faculty member. (Results must be published in the online Journal for Undergraduate Research.) Even if you don't qualify for those options, you should find something of interest, since only Ohio State and the University of Minnesota offer more degree programs on one campus than UF, the nation's fourth-largest university.

"The dorms are comfortable and clean."

To balance students' preprofessional coursework, UF's general education program requires credits in composition, math, humanities, social and behavioral sciences, and physical and biological sciences. Students must also take six credits in the humanities, or social or physical sciences that focus on themes of internationalism or diversity. Internships abound, along with volunteer and leadership opportunities, and foreign study in Latin America, Asia, the Middle East and more than a dozen cities in Eastern and Western Europe. UF has recently added a major in women's studies and an accelerated bachelor of science degree in nursing for students already holding BA or BS degrees in another field. New minors include family, youth, and community sciences; urban and regional planning; aerospace studies and military science (for students in Air Force or Army ROTC); information technologies in agriculture; and organizational leadership for nonprofits.

"UF is very competitive," says a senior. "It is competitive to get into, and students are challenged by teachers in an environment conducive to gaining knowledge and achieving success." While UF offers programs in every conceivable discipline, like many super-sized schools, it also forces students to climb a mountain of bureaucracy to get the courses and credits they need. Occasionally, for example, lectures in the College of Business Administration have to be videotaped and rebroadcast on the campus cable network, so that everyone can see them. Still, administrators are working to fix these problems, moving course registration to a telephone system and reserving some seats in many courses for first-year students. Professors often have deep professional experience, and bring enthusiasm to their work, though academic pressure varies by major and student. "Most general education course I have had have either been taught by a graduate student or have been massive lecture hall settings where there is little personal attention," grumbles a journalism major. "There is no doubt the quality of teaching significantly improves when students begin taking courses in their major."

UF is one of Florida's three state universities, and 92 percent of students here hail from the Sunshine State. Despite the geographical homogeneity, they're an ethnically

(Continued)
Applicants: 22,973
Accepted: 52%
Enrolled: 55%
Grad in 6 Years: 77%
Returning Freshmen: 92%
Academics: ✍ ✍ ✍ ✍
Social: ☎ ☎ ☎ ☎
Q of L: ★ ★ ★ ★
Admissions: (352) 392-1365
Email Address:
  freshman@ufl.edu

Strongest Programs:
Business
Engineering
Journalism/Communications
Citrus Science
Latin American studies

UF is one of Florida's three state universities, and 92 percent of students here hail from the Sunshine State.

diverse bunch, with African Americans adding almost 9 percent of the study body, Asian Americans nearly 7 percent, and Hispanics 12 percent. UF has established the Latino-Hispanic Cultural Center to serve the largest minority on campus, and many African American students belong to historically African American fraternities and sororities. The multicultural celebration known as People Awareness Week has grown into a popular campus event, but students say that, unfortunately, while there's no hostility between ethnic groups, there's also not much mixing. UF offers more than 200 athletic scholarships and 3,100 merit scholarships. National Merit Scholars automatically qualify if they list UF as their first choice.

Twenty-two percent of Florida's undergrads live on campus, and students say rooms are tough to come by if you're not a first-year student. "The dorms are comfortable and clean," says a senior, "and there is a great sense of community." Doubles, triples, and suites in the co-ed dorms are awarded by lottery, based on Social Security numbers, and there just isn't enough room for everyone. Dorm-dwellers buy the campus meal plan or use kitchens in their residence halls. Fifteen percent of men and the same fraction of women go Greek; rush is held before classes start in the fall and again in the spring. The 22 traditional fraternities and 16 Panhellenic Council sororities have privately owned houses in Gainesville, which also offer meal service. Nine historically African American Greek groups and seven culturally based Greek organizations also recruit at various times during the year; they don't offer housing.

Students say Gainesville, a city of about 125,000 between the Atlantic Ocean and the Gulf of Mexico, is a great college town. "Gainesville revolves around UF," a student says. There are plenty of stores, restaurants, and bars, as well as a sports arena and the Center for Performing Arts, which brings in world-class symphony orchestras, Broadway plays, opera, and large-scale ballet productions. The university owns a nearby lake, which is "great for lazy Sundays" and more vigorous water sports, and there's a plethora of parks, forests, rivers, and streams for backpacking, camping, and canoeing. Beaches are also a popular destination.

Sports are a year-round obsession here, and students say best road trips are to UF away football games, especially against in-state rivals or the University of Georgia. The annual homecoming extravaganza, known as "Gator Growl," boasts a half-million-dollar budget and annual attendance averaging 78,000. Other sports are not forgotten, though; the university has one of the top intercollegiate programs in the nation, with varsity competition for men and women in 16 sports, including nationally ranked teams in baseball, track, golf, tennis, gymnastics, volleyball, and swimming, and diving. Men's and women's basketball are also powerhouses, and the school has built a new women's softball stadium. Intramural sports are popular, and for those who don't want to join a team, the 60,000-square-foot fitness park offers aerobics classes, martial arts, strength training equipment, and squash and racquetball courts.

"UF is a school with an impressive history."

For some students, Florida's sheer size is overwhelming. For others, it's a drawing card. "UF is a school with an impressive history," says a senior, "and its students and alumni remain proud of that." Combine great weather with nationally recognized programs in engineering and business, and nationally ranked athletic teams, and it's easy to see why Sunshine State natives clamor to study here.

If You Apply To ➤ **Florida:** Early decision: Oct. 1. Rolling admissions: Jan. 12 (for fall semester). Financial aid: Mar. 15. Campus interviews: optional, evaluative. No alumni interviews. SATs or ACTs: required. SAT IIs: required for placement in some programs. Accepts the Common Application and electronic applications; students apply to a particular school within UF. Essay question (choose two): meaningful activity, interest, experience, or achievement; how family history, culture, or environment has influenced you; qualities or unique characteristics.

Florida Institute of Technology

Melbourne, FL 32901-6975

FIT is practically a branch of the nearby Kennedy Space Center, so it should come as no surprise that aeronautics and aviation are popular specialties. The Atlantic Ocean is close at hand, also making the school an ideal spot for marine biology. With a total enrollment of about 2,300, FIT is the smallest of the major technical institutions in the Southeast.

Students at the Florida Institute of Technology can explore the endless depths of the ocean or shoot for the stars. Located just 40 minutes from one of NASA's primary launch pads, FL Tech grew out of the nation's space program. The school's subtropical setting is perfect for scientific research and study in oceanography, meteorology, marine biology, and environmental science. It comes as no surprise that some of the most cutting-edge work in space and water-related sciences happens here. The combination of academic excellence and a convenient central Florida location—just an hour from the dizzying bustle of Walt Disney World—draws students to this unique and innovative school.

Founded in 1958 to meet the needs of engineers and scientists working at what is now the Kennedy Space Center, Florida Tech's contemporary 130-acre campus features more than 200 species of palm trees and botanical gardens in a tropical setting. Campus architecture ranges from modern to Georgian Gothic. Newer facilities include the state of the art F.W. Olin Engineering Complex, F.W. Olin Life Sciences Building, Charles Ruth Clemente Center for Sports & Recreation, and the Columbia Village Residence Hall complex.

If you're considering Florida Tech, the only independent technological university in the Southeast, make sure you have a strong background in math and science, especially chemistry and physics. Few students major in the less practical sciences. Though many students grouse that Florida Tech is too expensive for their tastes, those who plan their education well are able to get high-paying technical jobs as soon as they graduate. Sixty-three percent of students go into the workforce, and another 29 percent move on to graduate school. Prospective aviation students can major in aviation management, aviation meteorology, or aviation computer science, as well as aeronautics with or without a flight option. The flight school has a modern fleet of 30 airplanes and three flight-training devices, and the precision-flying team regularly wins titles. The most popular majors are aviation management, business administration, computer science, electrical engineering, and marine biology. Newer programs include software engineering, aviation meteorology, business accounting, business information systems, environmental studies, forensic psychology, and mathematical sciences.

The academic climate at FIT is challenging. "The atmosphere is not disastrously competitive, students are more than willing to help each other out," says an senior. A junior reports "the focus is on getting the grade rather than beating your classmates." Graduate teaching assistants are not overused. **"It's like traveling the world in four years."** All majors offer co-op programs and senior independent research at the Indian River Lagoon or on the RV Delphinus, a 60-foot research boat the school owns. Recent marine research includes manatee preservation, beach erosion, and sea turtle studies. Everyone must take courses in communication, physical or life science, math, humanities, and social sciences, and be proficient in using computers.

Fifty-one percent of Florida Tech students are out-of-staters, while 17 percent hail from outside the country. "It is a microcosm of intelligent people representing

Website: www.fit.edu
Location: Small city
Total Enrollment: 2,823
Undergraduates: 2,220
Male/Female: 68/32
SAT Ranges: V 500–630
  M 550–660
ACT Range: 22–28
Financial Aid: 56%
Expense: Pr $ $
Phi Beta Kappa: Yes
Applicants: 2,481
Accepted: 83%
Enrolled: 27%
Grad in 6 Years: 54%
Returning Freshmen: 79%
Academics: ✍ ✍ ✍
Social: ☎ ☎ ☎
Q of L: ★ ★ ★
Admissions: (321) 674-8030
Email Address:
  admission@fit.edu

Strongest Programs:
Computer Science
Marine Science
Electrical Engineering
Aerospace Engineering
Computer Engineering
Mechanical Engineering
Aviation Management

97 countries," says a sophomore. "It's like traveling the world in four years." The student body is 56 percent white, yet political correctness and diversity-related issues seem to be taken in stride. African Americans comprise 4 percent of the student body, Native Americans 1 percent, and Hispanics 6 percent. "There is no 'typical' Florida Tech student," explains one junior. Florida Tech offers merit scholarships that average $7,059, and 45 athletic scholarships in nine sports. Incoming freshmen are welcomed with a weeklong orientation program highlighted by trips to Disney World and the beach, just three miles away. On campus, freshmen may take part in the University Experience Program, which helps first-years adapt to college life.

The growing selection of dorms at Florida Tech is modern, air-conditioned (whew!), and well maintained. Fifty-two percent of students make their home on campus, though some complain about the price of it. Still, the rooms are well received. "Residence Life takes a holistic approach to making every resident feeling right at home," says a junior. Freshmen are required to live on campus in large double rooms. Four-student apartments are available to a small percentage of qualifying upperclassmen by lottery. Students who live off campus are drawn by cheap rent and not much else, because Melbourne is "quiet and is not a typical college town," reports an aerospace engineering major. The meal plan is an open, unlimited arrangement, and students report the food is improving every year.

"If you don't have a car of your own it may be hard because public transportation is limited."

Most Florida Tech students who don't have cars choose bikes as their favorite mode of transportation. "If you don't have a car of your own it may be hard because public transportation is limited," cautions one student. Diversions can be found in Orlando (with Epcot, MGM Studios, and Animal Kingdom abutting Disney World) or at the Kennedy Space Center. Students also hit the road for other Sunshine State cities, including Tampa, Key West, Miami, Daytona, and St. Augustine. Watching space shots from campus with a trained eye and a cold brew is a treasured pastime. The campus bar, the Rat, is a popular hangout. Otherwise, campus social life is predictably hampered by the low male/female ratio. Fraternities and sororities are slowly becoming more popular at Florida Tech, claiming 16 percent of the men and 10 percent of the women. While the campus is officially dry, every frat party has beer that the underage eagerly guzzle, students say. Besides partying, students spend their downtime surfing, fishing, hanging out at the beach, shopping, or going for a "Sunday drive" (in the sky) with a flight school student. Every April, students brace for the invasion of other collegians on spring break. Techies also look forward to Greek Week and intramural sports competitions. Florida Tech is in Division II, and with so much water around, it's not surprising that crew is popular and awesome.

Whether it's surveying marine coral 50 feet below the sea or the sky 30,000 feet above, students at Florida Tech get hands-on experience that serves to sharpen the school's already specialized, high-quality academics. The administration continues to focus on capital improvements, sponsor cutting-edge research, and embrace diversity. And with beaches and amusements close at hand, students can have some real fun in the sun while they prepare for high-flying—or low-lying—careers.

Overlaps

University of Florida, Embry-Riddle, University of Central Florida, University of Miami, Georgia Tech, MIT

If You Apply To ➤

Florida Tech: Rolling admissions. Campus interviews: recommended, informational. Alumni interviews: optional, informational. SATs or ACTs: required. SAT IIs: optional. Accepts the Common Application. No essay question.

Florida State University

A2500 University Center, Tallahassee, FL 32306-2400

With an assist from its football program, FSU's popularity has burgeoned in recent years. Not that there weren't some quality programs to begin with. The motion picture school is among the best around, and business and the arts are also strong. So long as the football team beats the hated Gators, all is well.

Florida State University has long been synonymous with football, but students at this Sunshine State university enjoy success off the gridiron, too. Here, you could have a Nobel laureate for a professor, study in one of the finest science facilities in the Southeast, or network at the state capitol. The choices are plentiful at FSU, and the pace of life makes it possible to taste a little of everything: a wide array of academic choices, Florida sunshine, and plenty to do, from football to Tallahassee hang-outs.

FSU is located in the "Other Florida": the one with rolling hills, flowering dogwoods and azaleas, and a canopy of moss-draped oaks. Glistening Gulf of Mexico waters are only half an hour away. The main campus features collegiate Jacobean structures surrounded by plenty of shade trees, with some modern facilities sprinkled in. Situated on 450 compact acres, the campus is the smallest in the state university system—it's just a 10-minute walk from the main gate on the east side to the science complex on the west side. Bicycling and skating are popular forms of transportation, and a free shuttle bus circles campus for those without wheels. Recent campus improvements include a medical school complex, new dining halls, and renovated residence halls.

FSU has outstanding programs in music, drama, art, and dance; it's moving up fast in the sciences, thanks to strong faculty and some cutting-edge research. The College of Medicine, which focuses on serving the elderly and underserved communities, graduated its first class in 2005. Communications, statistics, and business (especially accounting) have strong reputations in the Southeast. The English department and the School of Motion Picture, Television, and Recording Arts have consistently won an impressive array of national and international awards. For gifted students, the honors program offers smaller classes, closer faculty contact, and has been revamped to include service and research

> **"It is a place I can consider almost like my home."**

components. Certain students can even earn their degrees in three years. Directed Individual Study courses offer undergraduates the chance to participate in independent research projects with faculty direction. Internships and political jobs abound for tomorrow's politicians, since the state capitol and Supreme Court are nearby.

Students report the academic climate is somewhat laid back but that "the courses are rigorous." Freshman can take advantage of the First-Year Experience (FYE), Living/Learning Communities, and Freshmen Interest Groups. FYE is an extended orientation that introduces students to campus organizations, events, and activities; students who enroll in FIGs attend classes with the same group of peers, who have similar academic interests.

Within FSU's liberal studies program, students must also complete six hours of multicultural understanding coursework focusing on diversity within the Western experience and crosscultural studies. Freshmen must take math and English, and may find a TA at the helm in these courses. But overall, faculty members do teach. "The quality of teaching is excellent," a senior says. For those with wanderlust, FSU offers extensive study abroad options. They include a branch campus in Panama, year-round programs in Italy, England, and Spain, and summer programs in Greece,

Website: www.fsu.edu
Location: City outskirts
Total Enrollment: 38,886
Undergraduates: 30,015
Male/Female: 43/57
SAT Ranges: V 530–630
  M 540–630
ACT Range: 24–28
Financial Aid: 65%
Expense: Pub $
Phi Beta Kappa: Yes
Applicants: 22,541
Accepted: 62%
Enrolled: 44%
Grad in 6 Years: 65%
Returning Freshmen: 86%
Academics: ✍ ✍ ✍
Social: ☎ ☎ ☎
Q of L: ★ ★ ★ ★
Admissions: (850) 644-6200
Email Address:
  admissions@admin.fsu.edu

Strongest Programs:
Accounting
Biological sciences
Meteorology
Oceanography
Music
Dance
Theatre
Film

The English department and the School of Motion Picture, Television, and Recording Arts have consistently won an impressive array of national and international awards.

Upperclassmen generally forsake the housing rat race and move into nearby apartments, houses, or trailers, where they take advantage of the city and campus bus systems to get to school.

Vietnam, Switzerland, France, Costa Rica, Russia, the Czech Republic, Ireland, Japan, Belize, Brazil, and China. The university is making strides in the world of distance learning, allowing some students with an associate's degree to earn their bachelor's degree online. Four undergrad and seven master's majors are online.

Perhaps not surprisingly, FSU's student body has a distinctly Floridian flavor: in-staters comprise 87 percent of the group. Nearly two-thirds of the student body are white, 12 percent are African American, and 11 percent are Hispanic. There's little evidence of racial tension on the diverse campus. Seminoles are a mixture of friendly small-towners and city dwellers, and political tastes tend toward the conservative. While tuition is a hot topic of campus conversation, so are issues like voter registration, the environment, and student government concerns.

Fourteen percent of FSU's undergrads live in the university dorms, all of which are air-conditioned and wired for Internet access. Students may opt for typically spacious older halls or newer ones that tend to be more cramped. The dorms get mixed reviews from students, and the number who can live in them is limited, so rooms are assigned on a first-come, first-served basis. Upperclassmen generally forsake the housing rat race and move into nearby apartments, houses, or trailers, where they take advantage of the city and campus bus systems to get to school. The dorms are equipped with kitchens; meal plans that offer "good but expensive" food are also available.

When they're not studying, plays, films, concerts, and dorm parties keep FSU students busy. "The social life is fine," a freshman says. Those with a valid ID can head for one of Tallahassee's bars or restaurants, which fall somewhere between "college hangout" and "real world." Generally, though, students give the area a thumbs-up. As for Greek life, 15 percent of the men and 16 percent of the women join fraternities and sororities, which constitute another important segment of the social scene.

In sports, the big-time Seminole football team won two national titles in the '90s and has dominated the Atlantic Coast Conference. Coach Bobby Bowden is the all-time leader in wins in major college football. Going to games is an integral part of the FSU social scene, especially when games are against FSU's two most hated rivals: the University of Florida and the University of Miami (now a member of the ACC). FSU's baseball team also draws an enthusiastic following, as do women's basketball, volleyball, soccer, and softball teams.

Florida State remains a solid choice for those seeking knowledge under the blazing Florida sun. FSU students take pride in their school and what it has to offer. "It is a place I can consider almost like my home," says a business major.

Overlaps

University of Florida, University of Central Florida, University of Georgia, University of North Carolina, University of South Florida, Florida International

If You Apply To ➤

Florida State: Regular admission: Mar. 1. Financial aid: Feb. 1. Guarantees to meet demonstrated need of 31%. No campus or alumni interviews. SATs or ACTs: required. SAT IIs: optional. Accepts the Common Application and electronic applications. Essay question: personal experience; family history; personal qualities.

Fordham University

Rose Hill Campus: 441 East Fordham Road, Bronx, NY 10458
Lincoln Center Campus: 113 West 60th Street, New York, NY 10023

New York City's Fordham has climbed a few notches on the selectivity scale. There is no better location than Lincoln Center in Manhattan, where the performing arts programs are housed. The Bronx location is less appealing but better than the horror stories you may hear.

The Jesuit tradition pervades all aspects of life at Fordham University, from the quality of teaching, to the emphasis on personal relationships, to the pursuit of both "wisdom and learning," which also happens to be the school's motto. Students benefit from three campuses: the suburban Marymount College in Tarrytown, New York; the gated Bronx community of Rose Hill; and the Lincoln Center facility, just a short subway ride away in the heart of midtown Manhattan. Small classes provide individual attention, and though a majority of students are from New York, there's plenty of variation in ethnic background and in students' political and social views. Fordham is "more diverse than Boston College, less funky than NYU," says a German and English double-major. "We have an even mix of preppy, athletic types and independent, Manhattan types, the latter more so at the Lincoln Center campus."

The 85-acre Rose Hill campus is an oasis of trees, grass, and Gothic architecture; it's close to the New York Botanical Garden and Yankee Stadium and had cameo appearances in films such as A Beautiful Mind. Rose Hill is home to Fordham College, the largest liberal arts school at the university, as well as the undergraduate schools of business administration and liberal studies. The Lincoln Center campus benefits from its proximity to the Juilliard School, to the CBS and ABC television studios between Tenth and Eleventh Avenues, and to Lincoln Center itself, Manhattan's performing arts hub. This campus has its own undergraduate college, and also houses Fordham's law school and other graduate programs. Started as an alternative-style urban institution with no grades, the Lincoln Center campus has become more traditional over the years, and now uses the same 18-course core curriculum as Rose Hill.

> **"We have an even mix of preppy, athletic types and independent, Manhattan types."**

No matter where at Fordham you study, humanities are a good choice. Strengths at Rose Hill include history, philosophy, psychology, and economics, while at Lincoln Center, the forte is, appropriately, drama (music isn't bad, either). The BFA in dance is offered in with the Alvin Ailey American Dance Theater; students must be accepted by both Fordham and by the Ailey audition panel. Fordham's public radio station, WFUV, offers hands-on experience for aspiring deejays and radio journalists, and there are TV production studios in both Manhattan and Rose Hill, but so far, no university-sponsored station. Both colleges offer interdisciplinary majors, such as African American and Latin American studies, as well as 3–2 engineering programs with Columbia and Case Western Reserve, a 3–3 program with Fordham Law School, and a teacher-certification program. The latter may include a fifth year, culminating in a master's degree in education.

Popular and well-regarded majors include business, history, communications, psychology, and English. Helped by alumni connections, business students often obtain internships on Wall Street or elsewhere in the Manhattan financial community; some of these positions lead to jobs after graduation. The GLOBE Program in International Business includes an international internship or study abroad assignment, two

---

Website: www.fordham.edu
Location: Urban
Total Enrollment: 14,861
Undergraduates: 6,725
Male/Female: 40/60
SAT Ranges: V 550–650
   M 540–640
ACT Range: 23–28
Financial Aid: 62%
Expense: Pr $ $ $
Phi Beta Kappa: Yes
Applicants: 14,261
Accepted: 50%
Enrolled: 24%
Grad in 6 Years: 78%
Returning Freshmen: 90%
Academics: ✍ ✍ ✍
Social: ☎ ☎ ☎
Q of L: ★ ★ ★
Admissions: (800) FORDHAM
Email Address:
   enroll@fordham.edu

Strongest Programs:
Business
Theatre
Psychology
English
Philosophy
Theology
History

courses with an international focus, and proficiency in a foreign language. New academic programs include entrepreneurship, electronic business, Catholic American studies, and new foreign language offerings, including Arabic. When it comes to teaching, "I have had amazing professors who speak on CNN," says a student majoring in international political economy. "The professors foster an environment that stimulates discussion and continuously challenges the students to think," adds a classmate. "Many of the lower level core courses are taught by adjunct professors, but I have never had a bad experience with a professor," says a sophomore. Core requirements include English, social and natural sciences, philosophy, theology, history, math/computer science, fine arts, and foreign languages. Marymount, which Fordham took over in 2002, continues to offer the traditional Roman Catholic women's college experience, augmented by the academic and administrative resources of a major university.

> **"I have had amazing professors who speak on CNN."**

New academic programs include entrepreneurship, electronic business, Catholic American studies, and new foreign language offerings, including Arabic.

Fifty-seven percent of the students at Fordham are from New York state, and many of the rest are Catholics from elsewhere on the East Coast, even though the school is independent of the church. "Abortion is a big issue on campus—on either side," says a junior. The atmosphere is less intellectual than at nearby Columbia and NYU, but students are driven to do well academically and to get good jobs after graduation, says a senior. African American and Asian American students each comprise nearly 6 percent of the student body, and Hispanics make up 11 percent. In the Jesuit tradition of "men and women for others," students travel as far away as Romania and Belize during vacations for intensive study and service projects. There are hundreds of merit scholarships worth an average of $8,276, and 115 athletic scholarships as well. Students willing to commute from home are eligible for a $5,000 Metro Grant.

Fifty-nine percent of Fordham students live in the dorms, and they are guaranteed university housing for four years. Those lucky enough to snag rooms in the 20-story, 850-bed residence hall near Lincoln Center are saved from the borough's unscrupulous brokers and unconscionable rents. At Rose Hill, "Dorms are spacious, and community bathrooms are cleaned daily." says a senior. Students must sign in to gain admission to dorms other than their own, and Rose Hill has its own security personnel, but the Bronx "is very much an eye-opener for all the suburban white kids," one student quips. "It's a good experience if you have the common sense to keep a low profile among the locals." The dining facilities have been renovated. "While you have many choices, they are the same every day of the week," says a sophomore. Then again, with New York's many ethnic communities at your doorstep, plenty of other options are available, at all hours of the day or night.

> **"Many students go to Manhattan weekly, if not more."**

Fifty-six percent of the students at Fordham are from New York, and many of the rest are Catholics from elsewhere on the East Coast, even though the school is independent of the church.

Fordham's social life is an embarrassment of riches. "Most night-time socializing takes place off-campus and in downtown Manhattan, which offers endless choices for things to do," says a marketing major. "Many students go to Manhattan weekly, if not more. On campus, there are also many activities going on." Fordham sponsors an intramurals program in Central Park, as well as movies and concerts on both campuses; recent guest artists include Wyclef Jean, Busta Rhymes, and Mos Def. There's a "huge bar scene, both in the Bronx and in Manhattan," one student says—presumably aimed at students over 21, but this being New York, fake IDs are easy to come by, and sometimes they work. Off-campus parties also provide another opportunity to imbibe, if students are interested. The Rose Hill campus backs up against the Bronx Zoo and it's around the corner from Arthur Avenue, another Little Italy. Both provide welcome weekend diversions. Students look forward to homecoming, Fall Fest, Fordham Week, Spring Weekend, and Senior Week, as well as to the Columbia–Fordham football game and the Irish v. Italian rugby match. "The 10 o'clock scream," a Thursday night ritual in which everyone leans out their window and screams for one minute, is a favored stress reliever.

The marvelous Lombardi Memorial Athletic Center (named for Vince, an alumnus) supports club sports and intramurals, including ultimate Frisbee and tae kwon do, as well as "grandstand athletes," who root for the varsity basketball team. With a new head coach and strong recruiting classes, basketball is poised for increasing competitiveness. The football team has also improved markedly, winning the Patriot League Championship in 2002. Fordham competes in Division I and the Atlantic 10 Conference, and its location on the Hudson River has also helped to produce the women's rowing Metropolitan Champs.

Consistent with its Jesuit tradition, Fordham fancies itself a family. Indeed, students are often so happy with what they find that they preach the gospel to younger siblings, who obligingly follow them to one of the school's three campuses. Some things are changing at Fordham—including its admission and academic standards, which are slowly creeping up, and its national profile, which is also far higher than in years past. What hasn't changed is the idea that diversity and community can coexist, instilling confidence and pride in Fordham students and loyalty in the expanding alumni base.

> ### Overlaps
> **NYU, Boston College, Boston University, Villanova, George Washington, Fairfield**

If You Apply To ➤ **Fordham:** Early action: Nov. 1. Regular admissions: Jan. 15. Financial aid: Feb. 1. Meets demonstrated need of 15%. Campus and alumni interviews: optional, evaluative. SATs or ACTs: required. SAT IIs: recommended. Apply to particular school or program. Accepts the Common Application and electronic applications. Essay question: significant life experience; literary character with whom you identify; important political, social or cultural issue.

Franklin and Marshall College

637 College Avenue, Lancaster, PA 17604-3003

F&M is known for churning out hard-working preprofessional students. Faces tough competition from the likes of Bucknell, Gettysburg, Lafayette, and Dickinson for Pennsylvania-bound students. Known for natural sciences, business, and internships on Capitol Hill.

At Franklin and Marshall College, set in the serene hills of Pennsylvania's Amish country, you might come nose-to-nose with a horse and buggy, but you can still enjoy the perks of being in one of the country's 50 largest metro areas. While the city has modernized beautifully, parts of this historic town and many of its residents look much the same as they did when two acclaimed but struggling colleges decided to pool their resources. Marshall College (named for Chief Justice John Marshall) merged with Franklin College (started with a 200 English pound donation from Ben himself) in Lancaster. These days, F&M is trying to modernize too, particularly by bringing a more international bent to the curriculum.

F&M's 125-acre campus is surrounded by a quiet residential neighborhood shaded by majestic maple and oak trees. The campus itself is an arboretum and boasts 47 buildings of Gothic and Colonial architecture. The College Square complex appeals to students seeking a study respite. Recent additions to the campus include the Roschel Performing Arts Center, with a main-stage theater and dance performance spaces, the Writers House, and a bookstore/cafe.

> **Website:** www.fandm.edu
> **Location:** Small city
> **Total Enrollment:** 1,933
> **Undergraduates:** 1,933
> **Male/Female:** 54/46
> **SAT Ranges:** V 580–670
>   M 590–690
> **Financial Aid:** 40%
> **Expense:** Pr $ $ $ $
> **Phi Beta Kappa:** Yes
> **Applicants:** 4,231
> **Accepted:** 4%
> **Enrolled:** 31%
> **Grad in 6 Years:** 82%

(Continued)

Returning Freshmen: 92%

Academics: ✍ ✍ ✍ ✍

Social: ☎ ☎ ☎

Q of L: ★ ★ ★

Admissions: (717) 291-3953

Email Address:

  admission@fandm.edu

Strongest Programs:

Biology

Chemistry

Geosciences

Physics

Business

Government

English

Although there are no required courses freshman year, nine out of 10 students enroll in First-Year Residential Seminars. Participating students live together in groups of 16 on co-ed freshman floors and study a major theme or concept within a discipline. General education requirements include writing and language requirements, one course in three different "Foundation" areas (Mind, Self, and Spirit; Community, Culture, and Society; and Natural World), and one course each in the arts, humanities, social sciences, natural sciences, and non-Western cultures. Collaborations are optional opportunities to get course credit for an experience that includes working with others. F&M has long been known for being strong in the natural sciences, and the school is now placing more emphasis on courses with a service learning component. Majors have been added in dance, environmental studies and environmental science, along with a minor in literary studies. All majors can be combined with an international studies concentration that requires students to study abroad and become proficient in a foreign language. About 70 percent of F&M students have the chance to work one-on-one with a professor on a project. A pre-professional college in line with Lafayette and Bucknell, F&M has an excellent reputation for preparing undergrads for medical school, law school, and other careers.

Students uniformly describe the coursework as strenuous and demanding, but say the environment remains more cooperative than competitive. "F&M is a very rigorous place academically, but without the cutthroat competition of other institutions," a senior says. Students rate the quality of teaching as outstanding, and the relatively small student body and intimate class sizes help create a strong sense of community between students and professors. "The quality of teaching defines the F&M experience," says a senior. "You will have one, if not more, professors that will change your life." One student adds, "It's rewarding to know that you will be prepared when you leave." F&M offers cross-registration with two other small Pennsylvania colleges-Dickinson and Gettysburg-and several domestic-exchange and cooperative-degree programs. In the summer, the college sends students to countries such as Japan and Russia, and nearly 25 percent study in locations around the world during the junior year. Others participate in the Sea Semester.*

"F&M is a very rigorous place academically."

Seventy-seven percent of students rank in the top quarter of their graduating high school class, and almost half rank in the top tenth. Only 31 percent hail from Pennsylvania. Asian American students comprise 4 percent of the student body, African Americans 2 percent, and Hispanics 3 percent. The student body has been diversifying, but remains fairly homogeneous, students say. "F&M is characterized by popped collars and Audis," claims a freshman. An occasional political debate may waft through the murmurs of light social exchanges during dinner, but according to one student, the big issue on campus is the lack of issues on campus. Fummers do, however, take an interest when it comes to extracurricular activities and social opportunities. The 115 clubs on campus attest to that, as does an unusually high level of participation in community service activities.

Approximately 50 Marshall and 75 Presidential scholars are named each year. Marshalls receive a $12,500 tuition grant, a Macintosh computer, and the chance to apply for up to $3,000 in research travel funds. Presidential scholars receive a $7,500 tuition grant. F&M also offers two Rouse scholarships worth full tuition, books, and fees, and about 40 Buchanan community service grants of $5,000 each. The school also offers merit-based financial aid to outstanding students of ethnic backgrounds that have been traditionally underrepresented in higher education. There are no athletic scholarships.

Student housing, all co-ed, ranges from campus dorms to theme houses and private apartments near the campus. Although dorm rooms can vary greatly, student

The college has a good selection of intramural sports, which include popular co-ed competitions, and about 40 percent of nonvarsity athletes take part.

reports are mixed. "Dorms are livable and they are maintained," says one senior. But another describes them as, "fairly dismal." One freshman, though, "finds the dorms to be very comfortable and promoting of a family atmosphere, though," they add, "some complain about the lack of independent living options on campus." All dorms also have heating, air-conditioning, carpet, hard wiring, and cable. Every student is guaranteed housing and about two-thirds of the student body takes advantage; freshmen and sophomores are required to live on campus, while many juniors and seniors live off campus in houses and apartments. Boarders eat most of their meals in the campus cafeteria under a flexible meal plan, but students are issued debit cards that they may use

"You will have one, if not more, professors that will change your life."

at a number of different food stops on campus. Food has been a common complaint in the past but a total revamping of the dining facilities last summer has one student commenting that, "the result is tons of choices even if the food still isn't spectacular." Another student has a different complaint, "A certain scone offered at Jazzmans Cafe has 3,000 calories! Three thousand calories in a very little pastry; the freshman 15 is history, try the freshman 45!"

Regarded by the college as independent social organizations, the seven fraternities attract 35 percent of men, and two sororities attract 20 percent of women. They are integral to much of the nightlife, although the residence halls and special-interest groups offer a range of alternatives, including concerts, comedians, and Ben's Underground, a popular student-run nightclub. Hildy's, a tiny local bar, is a favorite campus meeting place. In recent years, the student-run and college-funded College Entertainment Committee has brought the Gin Blossoms, Rusted Root, Live, Ben Folds Five, and Vertical Horizon to the campus.

All majors can be combined with an international studies concentration that requires students to study abroad and become proficient in a foreign language.

Lancaster is a historical and well-to-do city of 60,000 people located in a larger metro area of more than 400,000. Lancaster offers a 16-screen cinema, scores of shops, a farmer's market, brick-and-cobblestone streets (with hitching posts for the Amish horses and buggies that are almost never used), and a plethora of quaint restaurants and cafes. Students have a measured, realistic appreciation of its urban amenities and rural ambiance. A senior business major explains, "Lancaster is certainly not a college town, but there are things for students to do." Another agrees, "This is the downfall to a city college." The Amish culture draws the interest of some students, and many frequent the charming farmer's market to shop for handmade quilts. Those with a hankering for contemporary action take road trips to Philly, Baltimore, Washington, D.C., and New York City. The biggest annual event is Spring Arts, held the weekend before finals, which includes student air-band contests, live concerts, art

"Lancaster is certainly not a college town, but there are things for students to do."

exhibits, games, booths, and barbecues. Other highlights include the freshman Pajama Parade, the Sophomore Sensation, the Senior Surprise, International Day, Black Cultural Arts Weekend, and Flapjack Fest (when professors serve pancakes to students) and Fum Follies, a faculty-produced play.

The college has a good selection of intramural sports, which include popular co-ed competitions, and about 40 percent of nonvarsity athletes take part. In addition to competing in Division I in wrestling, F&M boasts recent Centennial Conference championships in men's swimming, football, baseball, and women's swimming. Varsity squads are called the Diplomats, a name that is irresistibly abbreviated to "the Dips." The annual football game against Dickinson for the Conestoga Wagon trophy is always a crowd-pleaser.

"Franklin and Marshall may fly under the radar but we get a solid education from the professors while cultivating an idiosyncratic character that defies an easy label," boasts a student. "We are both laid-back and spirited, liberal and conservative,

Overlaps

Dickinson, Bucknell, Lafayette, Gettysburg, Penn State, Colgate

athletic and artsy; you get a great mix here." The school's true illustrious namesakes, who are spoofed on the admissions office website, would be proud.

Franklin W. Olin College of Engineering

BEST BUY

Olin Way, Needham, MA 02492

The new kid on the block among engineering schools. Olin opened its doors in 2006 with an innovative curriculum, a personalized approach to instruction, and the best students that money can buy. Every accepted student gets a full-ride merit scholarship. Clearly the best-kept secret in U.S. higher education—but not for long.

Website: www.olin.edu
Location: Urban
Total Enrollment: 216
Undergraduates: 216
Male/Female: 55/45
SAT Ranges: V 710–770
   M 710–800
ACT Range: 31–34
Financial Aid: 46%
Expense: Pr $
Phi Beta Kappa: No
Applicants: 546
Accepted: 25%
Enrolled: 14%
Grad in 6 Years: N/A
Returning Freshmen: 100%
Academics: ✍ ✍ ✍
Social: ☎ ☎ ☎
Q of L: ★ ★ ★
Admissions: (781) 292-2222
Email Address: info@olin.edu

Strongest Programs:
General Engineering
Electrical and Computer
   Engineering
Mechanical Engineering

Founded in 1997, the Franklin W. Olin College of Engineering admitted its inaugural freshman class in 2002 and held its first graduation ceremony earlier this year. Sure, the college lacks the rich tradition and reputation of more established institutions. But that doesn't seem to bother the 200 students who call this campus home. Instead, they've embraced the college's innovative engineering curriculum and are working hard to create history of their own. In the past five years, Olin "has built its campus, opened its doors to its first students, and developed into the most dynamic engineering school in the nation," says a junior. What's more, the college aims to lure superbright students away from MIT and Caltech with full-ride scholarships. Says one happy senior: "Olin has quite literally gone from a hole in the ground to a home."

Olin's 70-acre campus is located adjacent to Babson College in a pleasant suburb less than 20 miles west of Boston. The campus design is an innovative blend of the traditional and futuristic. Five buildings curve around a central green space, creating a sense of community and echoing the design of the traditional New England college. The entire campus is wired for high-tech communications, and designed for easy updating to stay on the cutting edge. The classrooms make use of state-of-the-art instructional media, while the residence halls offer unparalleled desktop connectivity. There is also plenty of meeting and public space to encourage the kind of collaboration called for in modern-day engineering. Newer facilities include East Hall, a residence hall that features single- and double-occupancy rooms, as well as music practice rooms, an exercise room, study rooms, and lounge areas.

Olin's innovative curriculum is based on the "Olin Triangle," which emphasizes science and engineering, business and entrepreneurship, and the liberal arts. Students choose from three majors—general engineering, electrical and computer engineering, and mechanical engineering—and a number of concentrations including bioengineering, computing, materials science, and systems. In addition, students must complete 30 credits of math and science (10 of which must be in math) and 28 credits of arts, humanities, social science (AHS), and entrepreneurship, 12 of which must be in AHS. Every student also completes a major, yearlong senior capstone project known as SCOPE (Senior Consulting Program for Engineering).

Because the academic menu is so narrowly focused, weak programs are virtually nonexistent. "While there are individual professors who are unpopular, there is no specific subject area which students avoid," says a senior. While the courses are demanding, students say that the intellectual environment fosters cooperation rather than competition. "Our college is based solidly on teamwork, which makes for a rigorous but friendly academic climate," a mechanical engineering major says. A junior adds, "Courses at Olin College are like lateral thinking puzzles: some are simple, some are difficult, but all the answers are deep and all the thinking is outside the box." All classes have fewer than 25 students and are led by professors. "These professors dedicate so much of their time to teaching and to nurturing their students that the quality of teaching is almost comparable to private tutoring," says one student.

"Olin has quite literally gone from a hole in the ground to a home."

First-year students have an opportunity to participate in an interactive weeklong orientation program that includes teambuilding exercises, meetings, and meals with faculty and advisors, as well as a trip into Boston. The college also encourages students to engage in "Passionate Pursuits," by enabling them to pursue artistic or humanistic interests via non-degree credit projects. Recent student projects include trapeze lessons, exploring Kung Fu, video game design, and conversational Arabic.

Olin students are "hardworking and passionate," says an engineering major. "Our students are well-rounded people that bring with them a passion for activities that are not strictly academic. Such passions could include music, entrepreneurship, or even something like origami." Only 9 percent hail from Massachusetts, and a whopping 94 percent graduated in the top tenth of their high school class. African Americans comprise 3 percent of the student body, Asian Americans 9 percent, and Hispanics 4 percent. "Politically, Olin is rather balanced," says a senior. Hot-button issues include environmental awareness, homosexuality, abortion, and the war in Iraq. Every accepted student receives a merit-based scholarship—valued at more than $130,000— that covers tuition for all four years.

Every accepted student receives a merit-based scholarship—valued at more than $130,000—that covers tuition for all four years.

All Olin students live on campus and "housing is given on a seniority basis," says a senior. "The worst rooms on campus are doubles with a private bath, so getting a low room draw pick isn't that bad." The two dorms are "beautiful and well furnished" and feature "a host of resources from wireless to high-speed Ethernet," says a junior.

"Politically, Olin is rather balanced."

The dining hall provides students with a tasty—if not repetitive—meal selection that includes "a fresh salad and cold cuts bar, pizza and pasta, and usually two or three entrees for every meal." Campus security is described as "unbelievable" and "officers are amazingly quick to respond to any call," according to a junior. "One look at the campus crime statistics will show you that there's not much to worry about."

When students aren't laboring over the latest engineering project or Structural Biomaterials assignment, they "spend most of their free time on campus simply because there is so much to do," says a junior. A senior adds, "Our student activities board plans a large event for pretty much every weekend." There are no Greek organizations, and students say the social scene does not revolve around alcohol. "The campus alcohol policies are quite reasonable," says a student, "relying largely on student responsibility." When the campus scene grows tiresome, students often travel to nearby Babson or Wellesley to mingle. There are also frequent roadtrips to Boston ("the best college town in the nation"), Vermont, or the beaches of Maine.

Olin's innovative curriculum is based on the "Olin Triangle," which emphasizes science and engineering, business and entrepreneurship, and the liberal arts.

One student describes the surrounding town of Needham as "a quaint bedroom community that tries to be a college town." An engineering major says, "It has few inexpensive restaurants and even fewer locations for late-night dining." Still, students take advantage of volunteer opportunities and "we also try to have some sort of larger event with the Needham community every month or so," says a student. Such events have included a Halloween labyrinth for local school children and "an event where Olin students auctioned off their skills or services to community members for charity."

Although Olin does not offer varsity sports, "a number of pick-up leagues have evolved for soccer, Frisbee, football, and basketball," says a junior. "Some students also play on teams at Babson or Wellesley for sports such as lacrosse, rugby, and cross country." Other popular intramural sports include Ultimate Frisbee, soccer, volleyball, and dodgeball.

For those who have what it takes, Olin College offers a top-notch engineering degree at a bargain price. Olin students have watched their school grow up before their eyes. "Five years ago we had no students, no buildings, no classes, and no curriculum," says a senior. "Olin now has 300 students, over 30 faculty, two residence halls, an innovative curriculum, and a supportive, enthusiastic community." Says a student, "Olin College is really about change, creativity, and people."

If You Apply To ➤

Olin: Regular admissions: Jan. 6. Meets full demonstrated need. Campus interviews: recommended, evaluative. No alumni interviews. SATs or ACTs: required. SAT IIs: required (math, science, and one other). Prefers electronic applications. Essay question: how will you contribute; what are your passions?

Furman University

3300 Poinsett Highway, Greenville, SC 29613-5245

Furman's campus is beautiful, and the swans are definitely a nice touch. At just under 3,000 total enrollment, Furman is nearly twice the size of Davidson and half the size of Wake Forest. As befits its Baptist heritage, Furman is a conservative place and still a largely regional institution.

Furman University has been called the "Country Club of the South." And if you're Southern, white, Christian, and conservative, y'all are likely to love it here. As a political science major says, "One of the biggest issues on campus is the distribution of condoms. Students here tend to be sheltered and ignorant of real world issues. They are very image-conscious and our gym stays busier than most others." Beyond the lush lawns lie small classes led by caring faculty, and plenty of opportunities for independent research, all part of what administrators call "engaged" or "active" learning.

Furman's 750-acre campus is one of the country's most beautiful, featuring tree-lined malls, fountains, a formal rose garden and Japanese garden, and a 30-acre lake filled with swans and ducks. Flowering shrubs dot the well-kept lawns, which surround buildings in the classical revival, Colonial Williamsburg, and modern architectural styles. Many have porches, pediments, and other Southern touches, such as handmade Virginia brick. The library is undergoing renovations that will double its current size.

Furman considers itself a new type of liberal arts institution, in that it prepares students for life in a rapidly changing society by placing an emphasis on experiential learning outside of the classroom. While this is hardly novel, few other schools make it their core emphasis. As such, general education requirements include freshman composition, four other humanities courses, one to three courses in math, two courses each in natural sciences and social sciences, and one course each in fine arts, health and exercise science, and the Asian-African program. Students must also achieve foreign language proficiency and attend nine events a year from the Cultural Life Program. High marks go to the departments of psychology, chemistry, and music, but students reserve their most vocal praise for political science. "The department promotes the most involvement, through debate clubs, opportunities for foreign travel, and summer internships in D.C.," says one student. The academic calendar enables students to focus on topics in greater depth, with three courses each during the fall and spring terms, and two courses during the eight-week winter term. Neuroscience has been added to the list of majors; none have been dropped.

Perhaps because of the calendar, students say Furman's academic climate is intense. "Grades, grades, grades; that's what matters the most," says one student. Almost three-quarters of the classes taken by freshman have fewer than 25 students, and virtually none of the rest has more than 50, helping students get to know faculty members well. "Classes are small and interactive, and professors are nurturing and passionate," says a communication major. The Furman Advantage program helps fund research fellowships and teaching assistantships for more than 120 students a year. Furman also typically sends one of the largest student delegations to the annual National Conference of Undergraduate Research. More than 250 students study abroad each year, through one of 13 Furman-sponsored programs on five continents, including a special exchange with Japan's Kansai-Gaidai University. Furman also belongs to the Associated Colleges of the South.* Entering freshmen have the opportunity to travel in small groups to an island off the coast of Charleston, the mountains of NC, or even China during the summer before they enroll.

Furman broke with the South Carolina Baptist Convention in 1992 after 166 years, but it remains in South Carolina, where religion ranks second only to football. Furman is trying to diversify, but those efforts have been slow to bear fruit. African Americans make up 7 percent of the student body, and Hispanics and Asian Americans add 1 and 2 percent, respectively. Students are "well off and this changes the aspects of similar people. Furman students have a successful air about them," observes one junior. There's also a lot of competition for leadership positions among this resume-conscious bunch. Each year, Furman awards a number of merit scholarships (averaging about $10,000), plus 245 athletic scholarships.

Ninety-two percent of students live on campus as Furman has a four-year residency requirement.

Ninety-two percent of students live on campus as Furman has a four-year residency requirement. "The dorms are quite comfortable and well-maintained, and the housing lottery is fair." Furman is a dry campus and the policy is strictly enforced in freshman and sophomore dorms, where underage students shouldn't be imbibing anyway. The university has recently changed its policy. Having been a dry campus for 177 years, Furman now allows alcohol to be served to those of legal age in designated places on campus, which does

"Grades, grades, grades; that's what matters the most."

not include residence halls or academic buildings. The atmosphere is more relaxed in North Village, a newer university-owned apartment complex of 10 buildings. If there are no noise complaints, students close the doors of their suites and do what they wish. All dorms are equipped with telephone, cable TV, and Internet access, and students enjoy the camaraderie that results from a residential campus. Meal plan credits can be used in the dining hall or food court, which always offers student favorites like hamburgers and hot dogs. "There is always something to eat. Whether or not you'll like it is the question," quips a freshman political science major. Campus security helps provide a relatively safe environment.

When the weekend comes, Furman's Student Activities Board sponsors "free movies, weekend trips, restaurant deal, huge concerts, and basically always something to do," says a communication major. Fraternities claim 35 percent of the men and sororities 40 percent of the women, and off-campus Greek parties draw crowds. "I am increasingly becoming a fan of Greenville," says a political science major. The Peace Center for the Performing Arts, located downtown, brings in touring casts of Broadway shows and other top-rated acts. More than 60 percent of Furman's students

Fraternities claim 35 percent of the men and sororities 40 percent of the women, and off-campus Greek parties draw crowds.

devote spare time to the Collegiate Educational Service Corps, which provides volunteers to 85 community agencies and organizes the annual May Day-Play Day carnival, converting the campus into a playground for underprivileged kids. However, one freshman remarks, "A good amount of students volunteer, yes, but most are content to simply live out their privileged lives in the peace of the Furman bubble." The best road trips are to the mountains of Asheville (only 45 minutes away), Atlanta (for the big city and shopping, about two hours), and Charleston or Myrtle Beach (four hours).

Furman's athletic teams compete in the Southern Conference, and in recent years, the men's rugby and women's tennis and golf teams have brought home conference titles. Furman also fields a handball team, which was the runner-up in the national collegiate tournament in a previous year. Students happily yell out the school's tongue-in-cheek cheer ("F.U. one time, F.U. two times, F.U. three times, F.U. all the time!") during football games against archrivals Wofford and Georgia Southern. Almost 65 percent of the student body competes for the coveted All Sports Trophy by participating in intramurals, which range from flag football to horseshoes.

> **"There is always something to eat. Whether or not you'll like it is the question."**

Furman may call itself a university, but its educational approach is closer to that of a liberal arts college, emphasizing problem solving, projects, and experience-based learning. More than a decade after severing its religious ties, the school continues to evolve, drawing more academically capable students from increasingly diverse backgrounds.

Overlaps

Wake Forest, Vanderbilt, Clemson, Davidson, University of Georgia, Duke

If You Apply To ➤ **Furman:** Early decision: Nov. 15. Regular admissions and financial aid: Jan. 15. Meets demonstrated need of 45%. Campus and alumni interviews: optional, informational. SATs or ACTs: required. SAT IIs: optional. Accepts the Common Application and electronic applications. Essay question: personal statement.

George Mason University

4400 University Drive, Fairfax, VA 22030-4444

Located in one of the richest suburbs in America, GMU is poised to become a major university. Though still mainly a commuter school, campus housing continues to grow. The presence of prominent conservatives such as Walter Williams has added cachet to economics and public policy.

Website: www.gmu.edu
Location: Suburban
Total Enrollment: 28,874
Undergraduates: 16,888
Male/Female: 44/56
SAT Ranges: V 480–580
M 490–590
ACT Range: 19–23
Financial Aid: 37%
Expense: Pub $ $

Located smack in the middle of greater Washington, D.C.'s budding high-tech corridor, George Mason University is a leading center of conservative political and economic thought. The urban campus and symbiotic relationship with the surrounding region contrast starkly with Virginia's two other major universities, which have held classes for a hundred years in the relative isolation of Charlottesville and Blacksburg. With just 30 years on its Fairfax campus—and only 45 years of life experience—GMU is clearly the new kid on the block.

Founded as a sleepy outpost of the University of Virginia, GMU sits on a 583-acre wooded campus in the Washington, D.C., suburb of Fairfax, Virginia. Campus architecture is modern and nondescript; most structures were erected after the mid-seventies. GMU's 10,000-seat arena, the Patriot Center, hosts both sporting and entertainment events. In addition, a new aquatic and fitness center, featuring two pools, a whirlpool, and co-ed saunas, was recently completed. And although GMU's campus doesn't have the Colonial ambiance or tradition of William and Mary or UVA, its namesake does have the same Old Virginia credentials. George Mason drafted Virginia's influential Declaration of Rights in 1776, and he later opposed ratification of the federal Constitution because there was no Bill of Rights attached.

Mason's general education requirements stipulate that all students take the equivalent of two courses in English composition, humanities, social sciences, and math and sciences. Students who prefer to find their own way can design a major under the Bachelor of Individualized Study program. The academic climate is intense but manageable. "I find the courses to be quite stimulating," says a sophomore. "Our professors are innovative and challenge students to succeed without overwhelming them." If they do fall behind or need guidance, academic counseling is likely to put them back on course. Advisors "have been so helpful and really supportive," says a marketing major.

Mason has grown by leaps and bounds for most of the past two decades; recent additions to the curriculum include degree programs in classical studies, international transactions, computational sciences, public policy, and urban systems engineering. Another option is the New Century College degree program, which teams small groups of faculty and undergraduates on projects that can be easily connected to the world outside GMU.

"I find the courses to be quite stimulating."

Though it is growing up fast, Mason's youth shows in a number of ways. First, programs taken for granted at more established universities are just hitting their stride here. Next, GMU's relatively small endowment means almost constant tuition increases. Last, some of the school's facilities are just plain inadequate for its more than 20,000 students. The library, for example, has fewer than 700,000 volumes, though it now subscribes to more than 300 online databases and allows students to borrow books from all eight members of the Washington Research Library Consortium.

The lack of resources in the library may present less of a problem for GMU's career-focused students, who seem to like learning on the job: 70 percent enter the working world after graduation, and just 20 percent proceed to graduate and professional schools. Psychology tops the list of popular majors, and economics—which boasts its own Nobel laureate—is probably the strongest department. Other well-regarded majors include computer science, nursing, engineering, and English; not surprisingly, given the school's location, the public policy department also receives accolades. The drama department, once a weak sister, is now part of the Institute of the Arts, created to make the arts an intrinsic part of every student's GMU experience. The institute includes a professional theater company, which hosts actors and playwrights in residence.

Eighty-six percent of GMU students are homegrown, and Mason's student body is fairly diverse, likely due to the diversity of the surrounding area. Minorities make up 28 percent of the student population—9 percent African American, 6 percent Hispanic, and 13 percent Asian American. Students are politically aware and tend to lean rightward. That said, racial tensions haven't been a problem, perhaps thanks to the four-year-old Stop, Look, and Learn program. The program attempts to increase campus discussion on prejudice, discrimination, and harassment. Athletic and merit scholarships are available to those who qualify.

George Mason has been a commuter school for much of its short existence, but there is on-campus housing, and 19 percent of undergrads choose this option. Another several thousand live around campus in university-sponsored housing. The administration admits that room and board costs are inflated because the university's entire housing stock dates from 1978 or later, which means the buildings are

(Continued)
Phi Beta Kappa: No
Applicants: 14,857
Accepted: 68%
Enrolled: 39%
Grad in 6 Years: 48%
Returning Freshmen: 76%
Academics: ✍ ✍ ✍
Social: ☎ ☎
Q of L: ★ ★
Admissions: (703) 993-2400
Email Address:
  admissions@gmu.edu

Strongest Programs:
Economics
Engineering
Public Policy
Nursing
Government
English
Communications
Information Technology

George Mason has been a commuter school for much of its short existence, but there is on-campus housing, and 19 percent of undergrads choose this option. Another several thousand live around campus in university-sponsored housing.

Mason has grown by leaps and bounds for most of the past two decades; recent additions to the curriculum include degree programs in classical studies, international transactions, computational sciences, public policy, and urban systems engineering.

modern and air-conditioned—but still being paid for. And though the dorms are comfortable and well-maintained, there's still a lot of building to do. "The demand and production of housing has skyrocketed, and more and more students are moving on campus," says a student. Freshmen live together in Presidents Park, while other students get rooms on a first-come, first-served basis based on class status. Those looking for an active social life should definitely consider a stint in the dorms, particularly in Presidents Park or the Freshman Center, but freshman dorms are dry, and you can get the boot if you're caught having a party with alcohol.

GMU's University Center, with its food court, movie theater, classrooms, computer labs, and study areas, has become the center of on-campus social life. The center is a convenience and a lure for students who commute to school and have gaps between classes. On the weekends, students find a predictable assortment of malls and shopping centers in Fairfax, just

> "The demand and production of housing has skyrocketed, and more and more students are moving on campus."

southwest of D.C., but off-campus parties and the sights and sounds of downtown Washington, Georgetown, and Old Town Alexandria beckon when the sun goes down. Best of all, these are only a short commute away via a free shuttle bus to the subway. Those searching for a more lively collegiate scene take road trips to other local schools, including James Madison and UVA.

With barely a generation of history under its belt, Mason is notably lacking in traditions and annual events: "Come here and invent one!" a student urges. Patriots Day and Mason Day are the two major bashes, in addition to homecoming, Greek Week, and International Week. GMU competes in Division I, and basketball dominates the sports scene because there's no football team. Any game against James Madison University draws a big crowd. Other successful teams include women's soccer, men's and women's track, and women's volleyball. Intramurals are catching on now that many games are held in the Patriot Center.

The name of George Mason may not have the cachet of George Washington, James Madison, or the other luminaries of Virginia history who have had universities named for them, but with improving academics, a growing and improving physical campus, and the rich cultural and economic resources of Washington, D.C., Mason's namesake looks like it's set to follow in those other schools' fine footsteps.

Overlaps

Virginia Tech, James Madison, Mary Washington, University of Virginia, University of Maryland

If You Apply To ➤

Mason: Regular admissions: Feb. 1. Meets demonstrated need of 40%. Campus interviews: required, informational. Alumni interviews: optional, informational. SATs or ACTs: required. SAT IIs: optional. Accepts the Common Application. Essay question: personal statement.

George Washington University

Washington, DC 20052

Ten years ago, GW was a backup school with an 80 percent acceptance rate that was maligned for its lack of identity. But the allure of Washington, D.C.'s opportunities coupled with an intellectually stimulating educational environment has proved to be a strong drawing card, and GW now accepts less than half who apply. The nation's leader in internships per capita.

Like Washington itself, George Washington University draws students from all over America—and around the world. Upon arrival, they find a bustling campus in the heart of D.C., enriched with cultural and intellectual opportunities. Students have easy access to the Smithsonian Institution museums, the Folger Shakespeare Library, the Library of Congress, and other national treasures. GW also offers top political officials as guest speakers and visiting professors. Since Congress chartered GW in 1821, perhaps it's not surprising that the school has learned well from nearby government agencies how to create red tape. "The bureaucracy is annoying," a junior laments.

Today, George Washington University is comprised of two campuses—the main, older campus in the Foggy Bottom neighborhood on Pennsylvania Avenue near the White House, and the new Mount Vernon campus three miles away with five residence halls and some classroom buildings. The Foggy Bottom campus has a mix of renovated federal row houses and modern buildings, while the wooded Mount Vernon campus spans 26 acres near Georgetown, and also includes athletic fields, tennis courts, and an outdoor pool. Formerly a women's college, Mount Vernon now permits all GW students to take classes and attend activities, though certain programs and academic initiatives are geared toward women. At the Mount Vernon campus, three new science laboratories and a computer lab have opened, and 379-bed residence hall will open later this year.

Aside from the Elliott School, freshmen may enroll in the School of the Engineering and Applied Science, the School of Business and Public Management, the School of Media and Public Affairs, and the Columbian College of Arts and Sciences, which is the largest undergraduate division. During freshman year, all undergraduates take English composition. Other requirements vary by school. To graduate, students fulfill requirements covering seven areas of knowledge: literacy, quantitative and logical reasoning, natural sciences, social and behavioral sciences, creative and performing arts, humanities, and foreign languages and cultures.

"Students care deeply about their work and put in long hours to get the most out of their classes."

For highly motivated and capable undergraduates seeking a challenge, GW's honors program offers special seminars, independent study, and a university symposium on both campuses. The intensive Enosinian Scholars Program culminates with a written thesis and oral examination. The School of Engineering also offers an honors program in which students work with professors on research projects; a team recently collaborated with America Online to create a wireless technology lab. GW's political communications major, which combines political science, journalism, and electronic media courses, is one of the few undergraduate programs of its kind and benefits from its Washington location. A BS in pharmacogenomics has been added, as have several combined degree programs and a transportation engineering option.

Many GW students describe the academic climate as competitive and rigorous. "Students care deeply about their work and put in long hours to get the most out of their classes," says one sophomore. Sixty-nine percent of the classes taken by freshmen have 25 students or less; professors handle lectures and seminars, and TAs facilitate discussion or labs. "They bring valuable outside experiences with them," says one political science major. "They also use Washington D.C.'s resources in their lectures and assignments." Almost half of GW's faculty members divide their time between the halls of academia and the corridors of power, with many holding high-level government positions. "Avoid the 'super-profs,'" says a junior history major. "They tend to cancel classes more for things like an appearance on CNN." Then again, those connections allow students tremendous access to the bigwigs of D.C.— prominent figures such as President Bush, Virginia Governor Mark Warner, the Dalai Lama, and Larry King have all addressed GW students.

Website: www.gwu.edu
Location: Urban
Total Enrollment: 15,481
Undergraduates: 9,716
Male/Female: 44/56
SAT Ranges: V 590–690
    M 590–680
ACT Range: 25–30
Financial Aid: 39%
Expense: Pr $ $ $ $
Phi Beta Kappa: Yes
Applicants: 20,159
Accepted: 38%
Enrolled: 35%
Grad in 6 Years: 79%
Returning Freshmen: 92%
Academics: ✍ ✍ ✍ ½
Social: ☎ ☎ ☎
Q of L: ★ ★ ★
Admissions: (202) 994-6040
Email Address:
    gwadm@gwu.edu

Strongest Programs:
Astronomy
Biology
Chemistry
Computer Science
Media and Public Affairs

For highly motivated and capable undergraduates seeking a challenge, GW's honors program offers special seminars, independent study, and a university symposium on both campuses.

Given GW's location and its improved academic reputation, students "are from diverse economic, religious, racial, ethnic, and social backgrounds," says a freshman. A sophomore adds, "They are very involved and dedicated with strong beliefs, no matter the topic." Six percent of the students are African American, 5 percent are Hispanic, 9 percent are Asian American, and 4 percent hail from foreign countries. "The diversity of the campus sets it apart," says a senior. As you might expect, political issues important on the national stage are also important here. "Students are politically minded and aware," says an international affairs major. "Students at GW are very liberal, with the College Democrats being the largest student organization on campus," claims another student. Merit scholarships worth an average of $12,744 are awarded annually and student-athletes vie for 160 awards. The university has recently adopted a fixed-rate tuition plan that guarantees fees will not increase for up to five years of full-time undergraduate study. Students who receive need-based grant aid for their first year are guaranteed the same amount of aid for four years.

> "The diversity of the campus sets it apart."

Sixty-seven percent of GW students live in campus housing, where freshmen and sophomores are guaranteed housing. Dorms are "primarily converted hotels and apartment buildings, so housing is very plush," says a junior. "Almost every room has private bathrooms and excellent closet space," says another. Those who move off-campus typically find group houses in Foggy Bottom or go to nearby neighborhoods like Dupont Circle and Georgetown, just a short walk from campus. Some also choose the Maryland or Virginia suburbs, where housing stock is newer, a little more affordable, and just a short subway ride away. Many freshmen are assigned to suites with up to four roommates in Thurston Hall, the biggest and rowdiest dorm on campus. They may also choose one of 24 Living and Learning Communities, groups of students who share similar interests. These groups have gone to the Kennedy Space Center for a rocket launch and to New York City to tour the United Nations.

Fifteen percent of GW men and 13 percent of the women go Greek, and students say it does not dominate the social scene. "Parties occur in residence halls, fraternity houses, and the Hippodrome, the top floor of our student center, which has a bowling alley and pool tables," says one sophomore. That said, a D.C. police crackdown on underage drinking has made it extremely difficult for those under 21 to be served at off-campus restaurants and pubs. Major annual events include the Fall Fest and Spring Fling carnivals, with free food and such nationally known entertainment as The Roots and Busta Rhymes. Popular road trips include the beaches of Ocean City, Maryland, and Virginia Beach, Virginia. Philadelphia and New York City are easily accessible by bus or train, a boon because most GW students don't have cars.

> "Almost every room has private bathrooms and excellent closet space."

GW doesn't field a football team, but its men's and women's basketball teams, men's soccer squad, and baseball team have won Atlantic 10 conference championships in recent years. The gymnastics squad is also strong, and the men's and women's rowing teams compete on the Potomac River, right in GW's backyard. Approximately 20 percent of undergraduates participate in the intramural sports program, which offers more than 30 events throughout the year. The school's unofficial mascot is the hippopotamus.

A popular GW T-shirt proclaims: "Something Happens Here." Something certainly has happened on both of the school's campuses in the past five years, says a junior. "GWU has become a much more well-known institution," a sophomore says. "Standards are higher and admission criteria is much more competitive." For students interested in urban living in the heart of the nation's political establishment, GW may fit the bill.

Major annual events include the Fall Fest and Spring Fling carnivals, with free food and such nationally known entertainment as The Roots and Busta Rhymes.

Overlaps

Boston University, NYU, Georgetown, American, University of Maryland, Boston College

If You Apply To ➤	**GW:** Early decision: Dec. 1. Second early decision: Jan. 15. Financial aid: Jan. 31. Housing: Jul. 1. Campus and alumni interviews: optional, evaluative. SATs or ACTs: required. SAT preferred. SAT II: recommended. Accepts the Common Application. Prefers electronic applications. Essay question: why GW; media and public affairs applicants must answer one concerning political communication, electronic media, or journalism. Freshmen must answer about an experience or design their own monument.

Georgetown University

37th and O Streets, NW, Washington, DC 20057

For anyone who wants to be a master of the political universe, this is the place. Only a small handful of schools are tougher to get into than Georgetown. In the excitement of studying in D.C., students may pay little attention to the Jesuit affiliation, which adds a conservative tinge to the campus.

As the most selective of the nation's Roman Catholic schools, Georgetown University offers students an intellectual milieu that is among the nation's best. With unparalleled access to Washington D.C.'s corridors of power, aspiring politicos benefit from the university's emphasis on public policy, international business, and foreign service. The national spotlight shines brightly on this elite institution, drawing dynamic students and athletes from around the world.

From its scenic location just blocks from the Potomac River, Georgetown affords its students an excellent vantage point from which to survey the world. The 104-acre campus reflects the history and growth of the nation's oldest Jesuit university. The Federal style of Old North, home of the school of business administration, which once housed guests such as George Washington and Lafayette, contrasts with the towers of the Flemish Romanesque–style Healy Hall, a post–Civil War landmark on the National Register of Historic Places. The newer Southwest Quadrangle includes a student residence hall, dining facility, underground parking garage, and Jesuit community residence.

"The majority of my courses have been taught by full professors."

Although Georgetown is a Roman Catholic university (founded in 1789 by the Society of Jesus), the religious atmosphere is by no means oppressive. Just over half of the undergraduates are Catholic, but all major faiths are respected and practiced on campus. That's partially due to the pronounced international influence here. International relations, diplomatic history, and international economics are among the hottest programs, as evidenced by former Secretary of State Madeline Albright's return to the School of Foreign Service. Through its broad liberal arts curriculum, GU focuses on developing the intellectual prowess and moral rigor its students will need in future national and international leadership roles. The curriculum has a strong multidisciplinary and intercultural slant, and students can choose among several programs abroad to round out their classroom experiences.

Would-be Hoyas may apply to one of four undergraduate schools: Georgetown College for liberal arts, the School of Nursing and Health Studies, McDonough School of Business, and the Walsh School of Foreign Service (SFS), which gives future diplomats, journalists, and others a strong grounding in the social sciences. Prospective freshmen must declare intended majors on their applications, and their secondary school records are judged accordingly. This means, among other things, intense competition within the college for the limited number of spaces in Georgetown's popular premed program.

Website:
  www.georgetown.edu
Location: Center city
Total Enrollment: 13,233
Undergraduates: 6,522
Male/Female: 46/54
SAT Ranges: V 640–740
  M 640–730
ACT Range: 27–32
Financial Aid: 43%
Expense: Pr $ $ $ $
Phi Beta Kappa: Yes
Applicants: 14,855
Accepted: 22%
Enrolled: 47%
Grad in 6 Years: 93%
Returning Freshmen: 97%
Academics: ✎ ✎ ✎ ✎ ½
Social: 🍷 🍷 🍷 🍷
Q of L: ★ ★ ★ ★
Admissions: (202) 687-3600
Email Address: guadmiss@
  georgetown.edu

Strongest Programs:
Government
Chemistry
Philosophy
Business
International Relations
Diplomatic History
International Economics

Georgetown's liberal arts program is also very strong: The most popular programs include international relations, finance, government, English, and psychology. Of course, the theology department is also strong. The School of Foreign Service stands out for its international economics, regional and comparative studies, and diplomatic history offerings. SFS also offers several five-year undergraduate and graduate degree programs in conjunction with the Graduate School of Arts and Sciences. The business school balances liberal arts with professional training, which translates into strong offerings in international and intercultural business as well as an emphasis on ethical and public policy issues. A new major, operations and information management, prepares students to understand business processes and the information systems that support them. The School of Nursing and Health Studies runs an integrated program combining the liberal arts and humanities with professional nursing theory and practice, and offers majors in nursing and health studies. The Faculty of Languages and Linguistics, the only undergraduate program of its kind nationwide, grants degrees in nine languages, as well as degrees in linguistics and comparative literature. There are few weak spots in the university's programs, and "the appeal of a department is mainly due to the professors," says a student.

"Washington is an ideal place to spend your college years."

All students must complete requirements in humanities and writing, philosophy, and theology; other requirement are specific to each school. Recently, Georgetown College has added new interdisciplinary programs and the School of Business has introduced a major in Operations and Information Management. That GU views most subjects through an international lens is evidenced by the 38 percent of students who study abroad. University-sponsored study programs in 90 countries—in Asia, Latin America, Poland, Israel, France, Germany, and at the university's villas in Florence, Italy, and Alanya, Turkey—attract the culturally curious. First-years read the same novel during the summer and the author visits campus during the first few weeks for a daylong seminar. There are no special academic requirements for the freshman year, but about 30 Georgetown College freshmen are accepted annually into the liberal arts colloquium.

Georgetown likes to boast about its faculty, and well it should. "The majority of my courses have been taught by full professors," says a senior, providing "a rich and supportive quality of teaching that operates in accordance with Georgetown's Catholic and Jesuit identity." The academic climate can be rigorous, but students are quick to point out that competition is friendly and community-oriented, with study groups the norm.

The GU community includes students from all over the United States, and 6 percent of the student body comes from abroad. African Americans make up 7 percent of undergrads, Hispanics 6 percent, and Asian Americans comprise 9 percent. More than half the students come from private or parochial schools. A student committee works with the vice president for student affairs to improve race relations and develop strategies for improving inclusiveness and sensitivity to issues of multiculturalism. About two-thirds of graduates move directly into the job market after graduation, and a quarter of the graduating class heads straight to graduate or professional school. Georgetown offers no academic merit scholarships, but it does guarantee to meet the full demonstrated need of every admit, and 157 athletic scholarships draw male and female athletes of all stripes.

Just over half of the undergraduates are Catholic, but all major faiths are respected and practiced on campus.

University-owned dorms, townhouses, and apartments accommodate 78 percent of undergrads, and "with the recent completion of the Southwest Quadrangle, campus housing offerings have drastically improved," says a history and government major. All dorms are co-ed, and some have more activities and community than others. "All have great amenities like Ethernet and landscaping," says one student. Two dining halls serve "passable" food, but the popular student-run coffee shop offers more palatable options. GU students feel relatively safe on campus, thanks to the school's ever-present Department of Public Safety and its walking and riding after-dark escort services.

Jesuits, who know a thing or two about secret societies, frown upon fraternities and sororities at their colleges, and so there are none at Georgetown. The university's strict enforcement of the 21-year-old drinking age has led to a somewhat decentralized social life, which is not necessarily a bad thing. Alcohol is forbidden in undergrad dorms, and all parties must be registered. The dozens of bars, nightclubs, and restaurants in Georgetown—Martin's Tavern and the Tombs are always popular—are a big draw for students who are legal, but they can get pricey. The Hoyas, a campus pub in the spectacular student activity center, is a more affordable alternative. Popular annual formals such as the Diplomatic and the Blue/Gray Ball force students to dress up and pair off.

Washington offers unsurpassed cultural resources, ranging from the museums of the Smithsonian to the Kennedy Center. "Washington is an ideal place to spend your college years," says a student. "The city has everything students could want, including culture, shopping, museums, monuments, social life, and the clean and convenient Metro for transportation." Indeed, given the absence of on-campus parking, a car is probably more trouble than it's worth.

Should you notice the hills begin to tremble with a deep, resounding, primitive chant—"Hoya...Saxa...Hoya...Saxa"—don't worry; it's probably just another Georgetown basketball game. Hoya is derived from the Greek and Latin phrase hoya saxa, which means, "What rocks!" Some say it originated in a cheer referring to the stones that formed the school's outer walls. The Hoya men's basketball team has a long history of prominence; in 2004–05 it advanced to the NIT Quarterfinals and defeated Boston University and Cal-State Fullerton earlier in that tournament. The Hoyas are especially competitive in men's and women's lacrosse and sailing; the women's lacrosse team has won five straight Big East Championships. The thrill of victory in intramural competition at the superb underground Yates Memorial Field House is not to be missed, either.

For anyone interested in discovering the world, Georgetown offers an outstanding menu of choices. Professors truly pay attention to their undergrads and the diverse students who are "hard-working, diligent, caring individuals," says one sophomore. "Georgetown is a place where students of all backgrounds, all traditions, and all faiths come together for a common purpose of educating each other and making an impact on the world."

International relations, diplomatic history, and international economics are among the hottest programs.

Overlaps

Boston College, Duke, NYU, University of Pennsylvania, George Washington, University of Virginia

If You Apply To ➢ **Georgetown:** Early action: Nov. 1. Regular admissions: Jan. 10. Financial aid: Feb. 1. Campus interviews: not available. Alumni interviews: required, evaluative. SATs or ACTs: required. SAT IIs: recommended. Apply to particular schools or programs. Essay question: personal statement plus one additional question for each school.

University of Georgia

212 Terrell Hall, Athens, GA 30602-1633

What a difference free tuition makes. Top Georgia students now choose UGA over highly selective private institutions. Business and social and natural sciences head

the list of strong and sought-after programs. The college town of Athens boasts great nightlife and is within easy reach of Atlanta.

Website: www.uga.edu

Location: Small city

Total Enrollment: 33,405

Undergraduates: 25,019

Male/Female: 43/57

SAT Ranges: V 560–660
M 570–660

ACT Range: 24–28

Financial Aid: 26%

Expense: Pub $

Phi Beta Kappa: Yes

Applicants: 13,267

Accepted: 62%

Enrolled: 55%

Grad in 6 Years: 74%

Returning Freshmen: 93%

Academics: ✍ ✍ ✍

Social: ☎ ☎ ☎ ☎ ☎

Q of L: ★ ★ ★

Admissions: (706) 542-8776

Email Address:
undergrad@admissions.uga
.edu

Strongest Programs:
Life Sciences
Ecology and Environmental
Studies
Agriculture
International and Public Affairs
Business
Education
Journalism/Mass
Communication

College-aged Georgians hit the jackpot when the state began using lottery receipts to fund the Hope Scholarship program. The program covers tuition, books, and most fees at the University of Georgia for all four years for students who finish high school in the state with a B average and maintain that average in college. In fact, the scholarship has made it much tougher to get into to UGA, which not long ago was known mostly for its dynamite football team and raucous parties. The university has moved aggressively to challenge its new and brainier breed of students, but some things haven't changed. "While we are academically competitive, we are not pretentious," a senior says. "We are very welcoming."

Founded in 1785, Georgia was the nation's first state-chartered university. Its attractive 706-acre campus is dotted with greenery and wooded walks. The older north campus houses the administrative offices and law school, and features 19th-century architecture and landscaping. The southern end of campus has more modern buildings and residence halls. A dining hall and four new dorms opened 2004, along with the $34 million Complex Carbohydrate Research Center, which has specialized labs for chromatography, computer graphics, and plant and animal cell culture. A $40 million facility under construction will house the new Biomedical and Health Sciences Institute.

UGA's core curriculum includes 9 to 10 credit hours of essential skills and 4 to 5 hours of institutional options selected with an academic advisor. Also required are 6 hours in arts and humanities, 10 to 11 hours in science, math, and technology, 12 hours in social sciences, and at least 18 hours in the major field. Finally, students must demonstrate proficiency in written and oral communication, computer skills, and reading comprehension, and pass an exam on the U.S. and Georgia constitutions. Before the semester starts, freshmen may spend a month on campus to learn their way around, meet new friends, and even earn six hours of credit. Don't want to stay for an entire month? Choose the Dawg Camp weekend retreat, which promotes networking and leadership skills, and includes programs on time and stress management, diversity, and "What It Means to Be a Georgia Bulldog." During the year, freshman seminars allow first-year students to study under a senior faculty member in a small, personalized setting while earning an hour of academic credit.

"We are very welcoming."

Students give high marks to UGA's Terry College of Business, Grady College of Journalism, the School of Public and International Affairs, and the colleges of education and of agriculture and environmental sciences. New majors include water and soil resources, environmental resource science, dance, avian biology, and environmental chemistry. Majors in crop science and textile science have been dropped. "The campus has a laid-back feeling with a competitive edge," says a political science and journalism major. As you might expect, large lecture classes are common. But "teaching assistants do just that," says a senior. "They assist the professor in break-out sessions, and the monitoring and grading of exams." A computerized registration system helps students sign up for courses; first pick usually goes to the 2,500 honors students and to UGA's varsity athletes, with everyone else prioritized by class standing. (That's become more important as recent cuts in state funding leave hundreds of faculty and staff positions unfilled. Classes are larger, some programs have stopped enrolling new students entirely, and students report more difficulty getting into the classes they want.) The Center for Undergraduate Research Opportunities allows students to conduct a research or service project, write a thesis, or develop a creative work with close faculty supervision. About 15 percent of Bulldogs study abroad, through 75 programs in more than 30 countries. UGA operates year-round residential study abroad programs of its own in Oxford, England; Avingon, France; and Cortona, Italy; and the school has an ecological research center in Costa Rica.

Eighty-five percent of UGA students are Georgian, and 86 percent graduated in the top quarter of their high school class. "Students tend to be either suburban kids from Atlanta or from more affluent south Georgia rural backgrounds," says a broadcast news major. African Americans and Asian Americans each make up nearly 5 percent of the student body, and Hispanics add another 2 percent. Politically, the school tends to veer right, but as a junior notes, "UGA students tend not to care too much if it does not directly relate to them." Hence, the biggest issues on campus are not foreign or domestic policy, or sexual orientation, but "the misunderstanding of Greek vs. non-Greek," a senior says. Merit scholarships are available, worth nearly $1,900 on average, and UGA also gives out 386 athletic scholarships. As many as 100 top undergraduates are named Foundation Fellows, netting a full scholarship plus stipends for international travel and research.

Twenty-seven percent of Bulldogs live in the dorms, and freshmen are required to do so. After freshman year, it's much harder to get a room, students say. Most keep their meal cards even after moving off campus. "The meal plan is one of the best things about UGA!" says an accounting major. "You can eat all you want, all day long, for a flat, per-semester fee," adds a political science

"The meal plan is one of the best things about UGA!"

and journalism major. There are four campus dining halls – each with its own specialty cuisine — and a snack bar, and the excellence of UGA's food service program has been recognized with the Ivy Award.

When the weekend comes, students know how to have a good time. "Most student GPAs suffer because of the social aspect of UGA," says a junior. There are over 500 student organizations, including 18 sororities and 23 fraternities, which attract 15 percent of the men and 18 percent of the women, respectively. More significant than Greek life is the funky mix of shops, restaurants and clubs and various cultural events found in downtown Athens, a 10-minute walk from most residence halls. "Athens is the ultimate college town, with an amazing music scene. It gave Widespread, R.E.M., John Mayer, and many others their start," says a psychology major. Many clubs in Athens cater to UGA students and admit those under 21, as long as they get a stamp saying they can't drink. Alcohol is prohibited in the dorms, but as at most schools, the determined manage to imbibe anyway. Athens is also "far enough away from Atlanta to maintain the college community, yet close enough to provide an escape," a senior says. Other popular road trips include the Florida and Carolina beaches, and anywhere the Bulldogs are playing on a fall Saturday.

Indeed, Athens residents worship UGA's perennially fierce football team, which made another post-season bowl appearance in 2006. The Georgia–Florida rivalry is particularly notable: "The game takes place on neutral ground in Jacksonville, and since it coincides with fall break, 90 percent of the students go," says an accounting major. In 2004–05, the women's equestrian team, gymnastics team and swimming and diving team won national championships, and the men's tennis doubles team won the NCAA championship. Women's softball and men's golf and baseball are also competitive. For the weekend warrior, there are intramural teams in 15 sports and the Oconee River Greenway, a 13-mile paved trail.

UGA's sheer size means you could coast through four years here as nothing more than a number. But with a little effort, that doesn't have to happen. Freshman seminars, research projects, study abroad, and honors courses offer the opportunity to graduate with a solid background in any number of areas and fond memories of Saturdays spent cheering on the Bulldogs—along with 92,000 of your closest friends. "UGA is a land of opportunity," a senior says. "Of course you have academic

Overlaps

Georgia Tech, UNC–Chapel Hill, Auburn, Vanderbilt, Emory

opportunity, but the relationships you form here are more valuable than anything you learn from a book."

Georgia Institute of Technology

Atlanta, GA 30332-0320

As the South's premier technically oriented university, Ma Tech does not coddle her young. That means surviving in downtown Atlanta and fighting through a wall of graduate students to talk with your professors. Architecture and big-time sports supplement the engineering focus.

Website: www.gatech.edu
Location: City center
Total Enrollment: 16,841
Undergraduates: 11,546
Male/Female: 72/28
SAT Ranges: V 600–690
   M 650–740
ACT Range: 25–32
Financial Aid: 17%
Expense: Pub $
Phi Beta Kappa: No
Applicants: 8,561
Accepted: 70%
Enrolled: 43%
Grad in 6 Years: 72%
Returning Freshmen: 92%
Academics: 🐾 🐾 🐾 🐾 🐾
Social: ☎ ☎
Q of L: ★ ★
Admissions: (404) 894-4154
Email Address:
   admission@gatech.edu

Strongest Programs:
Engineering
Computer Science
Architecture

If you're looking for lazy days on the college green and hard-partying weekends, look elsewhere. You won't find those at Georgia Institute of Technology, the South's premier tech university. What you will find are challenging courses that prepare you for a high-paying job as an engineer, architect, or computer scientist. "Tech is tough," reasons a graduate student. "You have to want to be here." Still, even those who want to be here are happy to finally arrive at graduation day. What makes Tech a special place? "The fact that I survived it and got out with a degree," says a computer science major, only partially joking.

Located just off the interstate in Georgia's capital city, Tech's 330-acre campus includes seven residence halls, an aquatic center, a sports performance complex, and an amphitheater. Reflective of the history of Georgia Tech, the building styles include the Georgian Revival and Collegiate Gothic of the historic Hill District (listed on the National Register of Historic Places) and surrounding area, the International Style buildings constructed from the 1940s into the 1960s, the modernist structures of the 1970s and '80s, the postmodern facilities of the '90s, and the recently constructed high-tech facilities. All these styles coexist comfortably on a tree-filled and landscaped campus seen as a green oasis in the midst of a dense urban environment. The ambitious Campus Master Plan resulted in the opening of more than two million square feet of new and renovated space at a cost of nearly $500 million. Recently completed facilities include the Technology Square complex, a new management building, the Global Learning Center, a hotel and conference center, a campus Barnes & Noble and other retail outlets, a new science and technology building, and new biomedical engineering building, renovation expansion of the stadium, and several other projects.

Courses at Tech are "extremely rigorous," says a senior, at least in the sciences and engineering. "Grading on a curve creates hypercompetitive situations because your absolute grade is largely irrelevant—you just have to do better than most of the others." Strong programs include math and computer science ("It's hard to have a life and be a CS student," one major quips) as well as most types of engineering, especially electrical, computer, and mechanical. Tech also offers materials, ceramic, chemical, and nuclear engineering. Tech has plenty of liberal arts courses, but a grad student says history, philosophy, and English aren't the reasons why most students enroll. "International affairs, while it has some interesting classes, seems to be a haven for people that can't hack the engineering stuff," another student adds. The newest undergraduate programs include a BS in science, technology & culture with a gender studies option; and a multidisciplinary degree in computational media.

Aside from the technical fare, Tech's management college is increasingly popular, and its school of architecture has done pioneering work in historic preservation and energy conservation. Among the architecture program's alumni are Michael Arad, whose winning design for the September 11 memorial in lower Manhattan was selected from a field of more than 5,200. The prelaw certificate is a boon to aspiring patent attorneys, as is the minor in law, science, and technology. As most courses need computers, the school requires students to bring their own desktops or laptops.

Regardless of major, students must complete nine semester hours of social sciences, eight hours each of math and science, six hours each of English and humanities and fine arts, and three hours each of computer science and U.S. or Georgia history. As students move from those core and required courses to upper-level options within their majors, the quality of teaching improves. "It's absolutely horrible for things like freshman math classes," says a computer science major. "You're typically taught by TAs (grad students), maybe half of whom have only the slightest grasp of English. Things get better as you progress and get to know professors." That's because those professors are indeed exceptional; some have worked on projects such as the Star Wars missile-defense system and the space shuttle. Still, classes are big—18 percent of those taken by freshmen have more than a hundred students—and the problem has been getting worse rather than better. "Students are generally stressed and tired," sighs a grad student. "Not working hard is not an option here."

In fact, Tech's demanding workload means it's common to spend five years getting your degree. There's also the frustrating course selection process: "Sleep through your registration time ticket, and you may blow your semester because you won't get into anything," warns a senior. Also contributing to delayed graduation dates is the popular co-op program, through which more than 3,000 students earn money for their education while gaining on-the-job experience. Those eager to experience another culture or environment can tap into the courses and resources of the Atlanta Regional Consortium for Higher Education,* or choose Tech study abroad programs in Paris, London, Australia, or England's Oxford University. By graduation day, around 60 percent of Tech students have jobs and at least 13 percent are admitted to graduate school.

Nearly two-thirds of Georgia Tech's mostly male students come from Georgia, and most are too focused on school or their co-op jobs to care about politics, causes, or any of the issues that get their peers riled up on nearby campuses. "There are a lot of left-brain types here—high on the introspection and thinking, low on the social skills," says a senior. And though they may be

"Grading on a curve creates hypercompetitive situations."

united in their pursuit of technical expertise, the campus is hardly homogenous: African Americans account for 8 percent of the student body, Hispanics 3 percent, and Asian Americans 15 percent. To limit burgeoning enrollment, out-of-state applicants must meet slightly higher criteria than their Georgia counterparts. The university awards merit scholarships to 22 percent of students, awards averaging $3,249. Another 220 students receive 372 athletic scholarships.

Fifty-three percent of Tech students live in the dorms, where freshman are guaranteed a room. A senior says that despite the new construction and renovation that took place before 1996, when Tech was transformed into the Olympic Village, the quality of residence halls varies widely. "Some dorms are new, apartment-style, and

When the weekend comes, students throw off their lab coats and pocket protectors and become wild members of the "Rambling Wreck from Georgia Tech."

nice," the student says. "Others are foul dungeons." Many dorms have full kitchen facilities, though, and while most halls are single-sex, visitation rules are lenient. Off-campus housing is generally comfortable, but parts of the surrounding neighborhood are unsavory. "Far too many cars are broken into or stolen," says one student. "There's usually a couple of armed robberies (at least) a semester." The campus dining halls offer "little variety and less quality," according to another student.

Fortunately, even if mystery meat is on the day's menu at Tech, the school is smack-dab in the middle of "Hot-Lanta," with its endless supply of clubs, bars, movie theaters, restaurants, shopping, and museums, both in midtown Atlanta and the Buckhead district. "Atlanta is not a college town," reasons a computer science major. "However, it is the best thing going in Georgia," with friendly, young residents, good cultural activities, beautiful green spaces, and a booming economy. The city also offers plenty of community service opportunities. Fraternities draw 21 percent of Tech's men and 24 percent of the women, and members may live in their chapter houses. Alcohol flows freely at frat parties, but otherwise, students say, Tech's policies against open containers and underage drinking are strictly enforced. "There's not much in the way of social life here outside of the frats," says a

"Some dorms are new, apartment-style, and nice."

senior. "You have your group of friends and you do your own thing." The best road trips include Florida's beaches, which are a half-day's drive, and Athens, Georgia, for basketball or football games against the University of Georgia.

Tech's varsity sports have become as big-time as any in the South, and when the weekend comes, students throw off their lab coats and pocket protectors and become wild members of the "Rambling Wreck from Georgia Tech." In the past two years, 15 of 17 Tech varsity teams have qualified for postseason play, and the men's golf, women's softball, and women's indoor track teams have brought home conference championships. Unfortunately, the university is in the midst of a two-year probation due to NCAA eligibility violations. Among Tech's many other traditions are "stealing the T," in which students try to remove the huge yellow letter "T" from the tower on the administration building and return it to the school by presenting it to a member of the faculty or administration. The addition of alarms, motion sensors, and heat sensors on the T has made the task more difficult, but "certainly not impossible for a Georgia Tech engineer," says an electrical engineering major. And then there's the Mini 500, a 15-lap tricycle race around a parking garage with three pit stops, a tire change, and a driver rotation.

Forget fitting the mold; the engineers of Georgia Tech are proud to say they make it. Self-direction, ambition, and motivation will take you far here, as will dexterity with a graphing calculator and a fondness for highly complex software algorithms. And despite their complaints about the workload, the social life (or lack thereof), the safety of their surrounding neighborhood, and the impact of budget cuts, Tech students do have a soft spot for their school. Says one student, "I love a good challenge, and Tech is perfect for that."

Overlaps

MIT, Stanford, Duke, Emory, University of Georgia, University of Virginia

If You Apply To ➤

Georgia Tech: Regular admissions: Jan. 15. Financial aid: May 1. Housing: Jul. 1. Does not guarantee to meet demonstrated need. No campus or alumni interviews. SATs or ACTs: required. SAT IIs: optional. Accepts the Common Application and electronic applications. Essay question: the personal experience that gave you the feeling of greatest achievement or satisfaction because of the challenges you met. Looks for high math and science aptitude.

Gettysburg College

300 North Washington Street, Gettysburg, PA 17325-1484

The college by the battlefield is strong in U.S. history—that's a given. The natural sciences and business are also popular, and political science majors enjoy good connections in D.C. and New York City. Students can also take courses down the road at Dickinson and Franklin and Marshall.

Mention the word "Gettysburg," and patriotic heart palpitations and echoes of the "Battle Hymn of the Republic" are likely to result. Whether the reference is to the Pennsylvania town steeped in Civil War history or the small, high-caliber college located in the famed battlefield's backyard, a certain pride and reverence are immediately evident. This feeling is not lost on students at Gettysburg College, who come to southeastern Pennsylvania to acquaint themselves with American history while gearing up for the future.

Situated in the midst of gently rolling hills, Gettysburg's 200-acre campus is "a historical treasure," an eclectic assemblage of Georgian, Greek, Romanesque, Gothic Revival, and modern architecture, plus several styles not easily categorized. One campus building—Penn Hall—was actually used as a hospital during the Battle of Gettysburg. Rumor has it that ghostly soldiers can still be seen walking the grounds. The new 86,000-square-foot Science Center provides a new home and state-of-the-art equipment for the sciences, and the departments of English and Asian studies have new facilities.

Indoors, the English department, home of the Gettysburg Review, is among the strongest at Gettysburg, as are the natural sciences, which are well-endowed with state-of-the-art equipment. The fine psychology department offers opportunities for students to participate in faculty research. The management major is the most popular. Also popular, of course, is the excellent history department, which is bolstered by the school's nationally recognized and prestigious Civil War Institute. The library system boasts nearly 400,000 volumes, a library/learning resource center, and an online computer catalog search. "Students here take academics seriously," says a sociology major, "and do quite a bit of outside work related to their classes." Still, the climate is cooperative rather than competitive. "Students tend to support each other," says a junior.

The small class sizes make for close student/faculty relationships. "The profs are phenomenal here," gushes a senior. A junior adds, "The professors are very friendly and willing to work with students outside of the classroom." Advising draws praise from students. "Academic counseling here helped me through any speed bumps I might have encountered," says one happy undergrad. The academic honor code contributes to the atmosphere of community and mutual trust. The popular first-year seminars explore topics such as "Why Do People Dance?"; participants live in the same residence hall and are in the same first-year residential college program. Another popular program is the Area Studies Symposium, which focuses each year on a different region of the world and offers lectures and films for the whole campus, in addition to academic credit for participating students. There are disciplinary programs such as environmental studies, Latin American studies, and biochemistry and molecular biology. Japanese studies and anthropology are the two newest majors, and minors are offered in neuroscience and peace studies.

Gettysburg sponsors a Washington semester with American University, a United Nations semester through Drew University in New Jersey, and cooperative dual degree programs in engineering and forestry. Most departments offer structured

Website: www.gettysburg.edu
Location: Small town
Total Enrollment: 2,597
Undergraduates: 2,597
Male/Female: 54/52
SAT Ranges: V 600–670
  M 600–670
Financial Aid: 61%
Expense: Pr $ $ $ $
Phi Beta Kappa: Yes
Applicants: 5,017
Accepted: 46%
Enrolled: 30%
Grad in 6 Years: 77%
Returning Freshmen: 92%
Academics: ✍ ✍ ✍ ½
Social: ☎ ☎ ☎
Q of L: ★ ★ ★
Admissions: (717) 337-6100
Email Address:
  admiss@gettysburg.edu

Strongest Programs:
English
History
Psychology
Natural Sciences
Business
Political Science

internships, and the chemistry department offers a summer cooperative research program between students and professors in which most majors participate and work on a joint publication. Through the Central Pennsylvania Consortium, students may take courses at two nearby colleges—Dickinson and Franklin and Marshall. Outstanding seniors may participate in the Senior Scholar's Seminar, with independent study on a major contemporary issue, but all students have a chance to do independent work and/or design their own majors. Study abroad programs are global and popular with more than half of the students taking part during their college career.

"Students here take academics seriously."

The student body is 91 percent white and mostly middle- to upper-middle-class. Terrorism and the war in Iraq led to campuswide discussions. "Students are ambitious and energetic," says a junior. "They are well-rounded and tend to participate in a variety of different programs and clubs." African American, Asian American, and Hispanic enrollment accounts for just 8 percent of the student body. Students are so interested in public service that the school set up a Center for Public Service to direct their community activities. Seventy percent of the students come from public high school and nearly two-thirds were in the top tenth of their high school class. No athletic scholarships are available, but academic scholarships run from $7,500 to $12,500.

Campus housing is guaranteed all four years, and students can choose from apartment-style residence halls, special interest halls, and the Quarry Suites. The top scholars in each class get first crack at the best rooms. Student rooms have been added in renovated historical properties (some reputed to be haunted) on campus, and there are more options for interesting housing and suite living. Off-campus apartments lure 8 percent of the student body while freshmen are required to remain in the residence halls. There are a variety of dining options, including the ever popular Cafe 101, the campus snack bar and grill room where many students take their regular meals. Kitchens are also available in the residences for upperclassmen. In a word, "Dining facilities are fantastic!" says a French major.

Social life at the 'Burg involves the Greek system and other activities. Forty-four percent of the men belong to the dozen fraternities; the seven sororities draw 26 percent of the women. Greek parties are open and attract crowds eager to dance the night away, although students insist they're not the only source of fun on campus. A Student Activities Committee provides alternative social events, including concerts, comedians, bus trips to Georgetown, movies, and campus coffeehouses. "Students spend their weekends doing community service, going to sporting events, hanging out in town, going to campus special events, or just hanging out in their dorms," says a senior. Officially the campus is dry, but like many such campuses, drinking can be done, albeit carefully, students report. The orchards and rolling countryside surrounding the campus are peaceful and scenic, and there is a small ski slope nearby. Students also get free passes to the historic attractions in town. Many participate in the November 19 Fortenbaugh Lecture by noted historians commemorating the Gettysburg Address and in the yearly wreath-laying ceremony in front of the Eisenhower Admissions Office to commemorate the general's birthday. Tourist season is a common complaint among students. But those who want to escape can do so—the campus is within an hour and a half of Washington, D.C., and considerably closer to Baltimore, where students enjoy the scenic Inner Harbor area.

"Dining facilities are fantastic!"

About a quarter of Gettysburg's students earn varsity letters, and the college boasts a strong athletic program. Thirty-seven teams have gone to the Division III playoffs over the past five years. The annual football game against Dickinson draws a good turnout, and the Little Brown Bucket, mahogany with silver handles, is passed to the team that wins. Both track and swimming frequently produce All

About a quarter of Gettysburg's students earn varsity letters, and the college boasts a strong athletic program.

The English department, home of the Gettysburg Review, is among the strongest at Gettysburg, as are the natural sciences, which are well-endowed with state-of-the-art equipment.

Overlaps

Dickinson, Bucknell, Franklin and Marshall, Lafayette, Muhlenberg

Americans. The college is a 10-time winner of the President's Cup, awarded to the top overall athletic program in the Centennial Conference.

At Gettysburg, students stay true to their slogan: "Work Hard, Play Smart." "Gettysburg is in a league of its own," a music/political science double major says. Students wanting personal attention from professors, solid academics, and an area rich with history might consider getting their education with a Gettysburg address.

If You Apply To > | **Gettysburg:** Early decision, regular admissions and financial aid: Feb. 15. Guarantees to meet demonstrated need. Campus interviews: strongly recommended, informational. No alumni interviews. SATs or ACTs: required. SAT IIs: optional. Accept Common Application and electronic applications. Essay question: Common Application questions.

Gordon College

255 Grapevine Road, Wenham, MA 01984

Gordon is the most prominent evangelical Christian college in New England and competes nationally with Wheaton (IL) and Calvin without all those strict rules. Not quite in the Boston area, but close enough.

Christian values color almost all aspects of life at this Evangelical school, where faith and spirituality are actually required courses of study. But while Gordon emphasizes moderation in life, it doesn't skimp when it comes to its liberal arts education. The college, founded as a missionary training school, is always evolving, sharpening its offerings across the board from neuroscience to music education and looking to increase its diversity. The students revel in the atmosphere. "When I think of Gordon students, I think of curious, well-rounded, critical thinkers who have love for God and for owning the truth," says one sophomore.

Gordon is located on Massachusetts's scenic North Shore, three miles from the Atlantic Coast and 25 miles from Boston. The campus sits on hundreds of forested acres with five lakes. Academic buildings and dorms are clustered in one small section. Most structures are Georgian-influenced traditional redbrick, except for the old stone mansion that houses administration and faculty offices. The college opened a 162-student residence hall, along with an athletic complex with facilities for tennis, soccer, lacrosse, and track and field. Many college offices recently moved to a nearby corporate park, alleviating a space crunch.

Because religious commitment is seen as an enhancement to, not a threat against, serious academic inquiry, Gordon's core curriculum includes 46 hours of instruction distributed among religion, the fine arts, humanities, social and behavioral sciences, natural sciences, math, and computer science. Freshmen also take a first-year Christianity, Character, and Culture seminar to help them learn how to integrate faith into their academic experience. The City Scholars Program provides inner-city students with mentoring and support both on campus and at home. The most popular major is English, followed by psychology, business, communications, history, and Biblical studies. Finance was recently added as a major—a rarity at small Christian colleges—and theatre was spun off from communications to become its own major. Some students complain that some of the science departments, such as chemistry and physics, lack modern equipment, and administrators admit this limits the programs' strength.

Website: www.gordon.edu
Location: Suburban
Total Enrollment: 1,634
Undergraduates: 1,579
Male/Female: 35/65
SAT Ranges: V 550–670
   M 540–650
ACT Range: 23–29
Financial Aid: 67%
Expense: Pr $
Phi Beta Kappa: No
Applicants: 987
Accepted: 81%
Enrolled: 82%
Grad in 6 Years: 70%
Returning Freshmen: 88%
Academics: ✍ ✍ ✍
Social: ☎ ☎
Q of L: ★ ★ ★ ★
Admissions: (866) 464-6736
Email Address: admissions@ hope.gordon.edu

Strongest Programs:
Education
Psychology
English
Biblical/Theological Studies

Gordon's faculty receives high marks; a junior psychology major calls the quality of teaching "outstanding." "I have experienced professors who genuinely care about the students and want to see them succeed. I am blown away by the brilliant, yet humble nature of each professor," a sophomore raves. Off-campus opportunities include stints in Washington, D.C., for aspiring politicos, in Michigan for environmentalists, in Los Angeles for filmmakers, and trips abroad through the Christian College Consortium.* The college also has its own program in Orvieto, Italy, focused on the country's history, art, and language, Aix-En-Provence in France, and at Oxford University in England, and partners with programs elsewhere around the world, from Africa to Israel.

Hard-working Christians come to Gordon from all over the United States. "Unlike other college students, Gordon students have a higher calling which drives them to succeed academically and spiritually."

Hard-working Christians come to Gordon from all over the United States. "Unlike other college students, Gordon students have a higher calling which drives them to succeed academically and spiritually." Still, the regional diversity doesn't translate into ethnic diversity, something the college is trying to change. "Most of the students are white, middle-class New Englanders," says a sophomore. African Americans constitute 1 percent of the campus, while Asian Americans, international students and Hispanics each comprise 2 percent. Gordon students face the same campus issues as their peers at most colleges—homosexuality and tolerance, for example—but are required to sign a Statement of Faith promising acceptance of racial and gender equality, and moderation in behavior. "The student body is mostly split between Democrat and Republican," says a Bible studies and English major, "which is very unusual in Massachusetts." Merit scholarships worth an average of $8,000 are available, but there are no athletic scholarships.

> "I am blown away by the brilliant, yet humble nature of each professor."

Eighty-eight percent of Gordon students live in the co-ed dorms, where men and women live in separate wings of the same buildings—separated by a lobby, a lounge, and a laundry room. Persons of the opposite sex may traverse these barriers only at specified times. That policy draws some complaints from students, and the Student Council has been trying to extend the hours. Permission to move off-campus is granted only after the dorms are filled. "I really love living on campus," raves a sophomore, "because spending time outside of classes with people makes college so much richer."

Social life at Gordon is "fairly quiet. The academic rigors keep everyone pretty busy." Another student agrees, but adds, "The social life at Gordon is well-balanced by students with their academic life." As drinking and smoking are forbidden on campus (and may result in suspension or expulsion), students focus on other activities. "There is always something to do on campus," a junior reports, "whether it be going to one of the varsity games, seeing a play, or going to a dance or talent show." Those who are 21 or older may drink off campus, but are expected to do so responsibly. Other options include weekend excursions to Boston (25 miles away by a five-minute walk to the T, the city's public transit system), the beach, church-related functions, movies, and an occasional square dance.

> "The social life at Gordon is well-balanced by students with their academic life."

Because religious commitment is seen as an enhancement to, not a threat against, serious academic inquiry, Gordon's core curriculum includes 46 hours of instruction distributed among religion, the fine arts, humanities, social and behavioral sciences, natural sciences, math, and computer science.

Everyone looks forward to homecoming, the Winter Ball formal (held at the Danversport Yacht Club), and the Last Blast spring party. Each year, the most popular guys in each class face off in the "hilarious" Golden Goose talent show, where the winner is crowned "Mr. Gordon." Gordon has no Greek system—so drunken toga parties are out. For outdoorsy types, Gordon's setting on rugged Cape Ann is ideal, and it attracts its share of tourists. The campus has cross-country ski trails and ponds for swimming, canoeing, and skating. The ocean is a quick bike ride away, nice beaches are available on Cape Cod and in Maine, and students frequently ski

New Hampshire's nearby White Mountains. Having a car is essential. Volunteering through prison ministry and in soup kitchens and local churches is popular, and missionary road trips take students to Tennessee, Florida, and Washington, D.C.

When it comes to sports, Gordon competes in NCAA Division III, and "a good portion of the student body comes out to the games" when the opponent is rival Endicott College, says a history major. Another adds: "The basketball games are standing-room-only when we play them." The men's and women's lacrosse teams brought home Commonwealth Coast Conference championships in recent years with women winning in 2005. Other popular sports are men's and women's soccer. Intramural sports draw a lot of players.

For many students, Gordon's combination of Christian values, strong academics, and relaxed setting is a winning one. "Gordon wants to graduate men and women of academic excellence and high Christian character." And as the school tries to attract students of different backgrounds, those here already find it welcoming. "I don't need to be anything I'm not. I have the respect and acceptance of my peers," says another junior. "Gordon is a Christian community where students from all different backgrounds can come together and learn from each other with freedom within a framework of faith."

If You Apply To ➤

Gordon: Early decision: Dec. 1. Rolling admissions: Mar. 1. Financial aid: Mar. 1. Does not guarantee to meet demonstrated need. Campus interviews: required, evaluative. No alumni interviews. SATs: required. SAT IIs: recommended. Accepts the Common Application and prefers electronic applications. Essay question: Do you consider yourself a Christian?; Why are you interested in Gordon?; Your response to a meaningful educational experience or achievement, or a pressing issue in American life.

Goucher College

Baltimore, Maryland 21204

This is not your grandmother's Goucher. Once a staid women's college, Goucher has added men and a more progressive ambience, similar to places like Skidmore and Sarah Lawrence. Strategically located near Baltimore and not far from D.C., Goucher offers an excellent internship program.

Goucher is the kind of place where a student starts off with a dance class, then dashes to a lab to use a nuclear magnetic resonance spectrometer, and finally wraps up the afternoon chatting with a professor about studying abroad in Ghana. The school's mission is to prepare students for a life of inquiry, creativity, and critical and analytical thinking. According to students, the atmosphere is academically challenging and competitive but not uptight. A sophomore says it succinctly: "We're a family."

Goucher, once a woman's college that went co-ed in 1987, has a long-standing history of excellence. Phi Beta Kappa established a chapter on campus only 20 years after the college was founded, and the college ranks among the nation's top 50 liberal arts colleges in turning out students destined for PhDs in the sciences. Set on 287 landscaped acres in the suburbs of Baltimore, Goucher's wooded campus features lush lawns, stately fieldstone buildings (the fieldstone is mined from local quarries), and rare trees and shrubs from all corners of the globe. A new residence hall opened in 2005 and among its other features, it incorporates two faculty apartments designed for use by visiting scholars.

Website: www.goucher.edu
Location: Suburban
Total Enrollment: 1,460
Undergraduates: 1,322
Male/Female: 32/68
SAT Ranges: V 560–660
  M 530–630
ACT Range: 23–27
Financial Aid: 55%
Expense: Pr $ $
Phi Beta Kappa: Yes
Applicants: 2,870
Accepted: 68%
Enrolled: 21%
Grad in 6 Years: 69%

A rigorous general education program forms the foundation of every Goucher student's education. The core curriculum requires a first-year colloquium (Frontiers), one course in each of the humanities, social sciences, and mathematics, a lecture/lab course in the natural sciences, computer proficiency, a writing class, completion of the intermediate level of a foreign language, a one-credit Connections course, and two physical education courses. Of Goucher's offerings, the science departments are arguably the strongest, with a nuclear magnetic resonance spectrometer and scientific visualization lab available for student use. Other facilities include dedicated research space, a greenhouse, and an observatory with a six-inch refractor telescope. The dance department is especially strong. Administrators acknowledge that psychology and communications, ironically two of the most popular majors, are the weakest programs due to their large size and lack of full-time faculty. Administrators have recently revamped the programs and predict that they will emerge among the strongest majors.

"We're a family."

An honors program has been dropped, but an international scholars program has been added. There's also a German minor offered through Loyola College (MD), and future engineers can take advantage of the 3–2 program offered in conjunction with the Whiting School of Engineering at Johns Hopkins University. A curriculum change has transformed the Intercultural studies major into the new International Portfolio Program. Goucher students may take courses at nearby Johns Hopkins and seven smaller area colleges. The campus library houses 280,000 volumes and draws complaints from some students, mainly because it closes at 6 p.m. on Saturdays. However, Goucher students have free access to the libraries at Hopkins and other nearby schools.

Faculty members here devote most of their time and energy to undergraduate teaching and have a good rapport with students. "Professors are eager to help you learn and the one-on-one [interaction] really improves grades and general attitude," says one student. Each freshman has a faculty advisor to assist with the academic and overall adjustment to college life, which is made easier by Goucher's trademark small classes and individual instruction. "Goucher has small classrooms and the professors always keep their office doors open if you need help," says one sophomore.

In addition to their academic work, all Goucher students are required to do a three-credit internship or off-campus experience related to their major. Popular choices include congressional offices, museums, law firms, and newspapers. Another option is the three-week-long Public Policy Seminar in Washington, D.C., where students meet informally with political luminaries. Goucher also hosts College Summit, a nonprofit organization for economically challenged high school students. It offers summer mentoring workshops where members of the campus community serve as writing coaches. Study abroad is no longer an option: it's mandatory. Students are required to take a three-week course abroad, but may elect to stay longer. The college has pledged to provide every student with a $1,200 voucher to offset the cost.

The administration hosts "campus conversations" with students, faculty, and the college president to discuss various issues.

Thirty-three percent of Goucher's students are homegrown, and most of the rest hail from Pennsylvania, Virginia, New York, and New Jersey. African Americans make up 5 percent of the student body, Hispanics, 3 percent, Asian Americans 3 percent, foreign students 1 percent, and Caucasian 65 percent. The administration hosts "campus conversations" with students, faculty, and the college president to discuss various issues. Newer, more intensive programs such as the Study Circle on Diversity and the peace studies dialogue sessions have also been implemented to address diversity issues. "A lot of students hold forums, discussions, and workshops to talk about the issues," says one sophomore. Goucher offers merit scholarships for those who are qualified, some providing full tuition, room, and board each year.

Eighty percent of students live on campus and this figure promises to increase as students fill the new residence hall. Freshmen double up in spacious rooms, while upperclassmen select housing through lotteries; the available singles usually go to juniors and seniors, though a lucky sophomore may occasionally get one. "Housekeeping is friendly and most students get the rooms that they want. It's a very family-like atmosphere," says a sophomore. Campus dining options include vegan and vegetarian fare. One satisfied sophomore claims it's the "best homemade campus food" anywhere.

The social life on campus is improving, though it is often up to students to make their own fun. One student says, "Most students go off-campus at least one night a weekend," so access to a car is a virtual necessity because many students travel to nearby universities (Loyola and Towson State) or Baltimore's Inner Harbor for entertainment. The CollTown Network, however, provides transportation to nearly 20 colleges in the area. Students who are of age frequent restaurants and bars in Towson, the small but bustling college town a five-minute walk away. Goucher has no sororities or fraternities, but the close-knit housing units hold periodic events, and the college hosts weekend movies, concerts, and lectures. Major annual

Of Goucher's offerings, the science departments are arguably the strongest, with a nuclear magnetic resonance spectrometer and scientific visualization lab available for student use.

"A lot of students hold forums, discussions, and workshops to talk about the issues."

social events include Rocktoberfest, Spring Fling, and the Blind Date Ball each fall. Biggest of all is GIG, Get-into-Goucher Day, when classes are canceled and the whole campus celebrates. Popular road trips include Ocean City, New York, Philadelphia, and Washington, D.C.

As Goucher was a women's college for so long, women's athletics are more highly developed than those at many co-ed schools. The women's lacrosse team is popular, along with men's basketball and lacrosse. The genteel sport of horseback riding is popular, thanks to the indoor equestrian ring, stables, and beautiful wooded campus trails. Goucher also has several tennis courts, a driving range, practice fields, a swimming pool, and saunas.

Goucher is far from a stagnant place. Indeed, it is constantly rethinking its mission and redirecting its resources to broaden student experiences. With self-designed interdisciplinary majors, an emphasis on experiential learning, and several partnerships with other top schools, Goucher students find themselves sampling from a buffet of options. As one student sums it up, at Goucher, "no one is unoriginal."

Overlaps

American, NYU, Skidmore, Towson, University of Maryland–College Park, Vassar

If You Apply To ➤ **Goucher:** Early action: Dec. 15. Regular admissions: Feb. 1. Financial aid: Feb. 15. Housing: May 1. Guarantees to meet full demonstrated need. Campus and alumni interviews: recommended, informational. SATs or ACTs: required. SAT IIs: optional. Accepts the Common Application and prefers electronic applications. Essay questions (choose one): ability to contribute to global learning academic community; important issue of personal, local, national, or international concern; expectations of a Goucher experience; topic of own choosing.

Grinnell College

Grinnell, IA 50112

BEST BUY

Iowa cornfields provide a surreal backdrop for Grinnell's funky, progressive, and talented student body. At just under 1,500 students, Grinnell is half the size of Oberlin. That translates into tiny classes and tutorials of 13 students or fewer. Grinnell's biggest challenge is simply getting prospective students to the campus.

Website: www.grinnell.edu
Location: Small town
Total Enrollment: 1,540
Undergraduates: 1,540
Male/Female: 46/54
SAT Ranges: V 640–760
  M 650–730
ACT Range: 28–32
Financial Aid: 50%
Expense: Pr $ $
Phi Beta Kappa: Yes
Applicants: 2,284
Accepted: 51%
Enrolled: 29%
Grad in 6 Years: 85%
Returning Freshmen: 93%
Academics: 🖊🖊🖊🖊½
Social: ☎☎
Q of L: ★★★
Admissions: (800) 247-0113
Email Address:
  askgrin@grinnell.edu

Strongest Programs:
Foreign Languages
Biology
Chemistry
History

"Go West, young man, go West," Horace Greeley said to Josiah B. Grinnell in 1846. The result of Grinnell's wanderings into the rural cornfields, 55 miles from Des Moines and 60 miles from Iowa City, is the remarkable college that bears his name, and is second only to Carleton as the best liberal arts college in the Midwest. Despite its physical isolation, Grinnell is a powerhouse on the national scene. Ever progressive, it was the first college west of the Mississippi to admit African Americans and women, and the first in the country to establish an undergraduate political science department. It was once a stop on the Underground Railroad, and its graduates include Harry Hopkins, architect of the New Deal, and Robert Noyce, inventor of the integrated circuit, two people who did as much as anyone to change the face of American society in the 20th century.

The school's 108-acre campus is an attractive blend of collegiate Gothic and modern Bauhaus academic buildings and Prairie-style houses. (Architecture buffs should take note of the dazzling Louis Sullivan bank facade just off campus.) The Noyce Science Center, a technological showpiece, recently underwent a $15.3 million renovation (Phase II is expected to be completed in 2008), and a 75,000-square-foot addition to the Fine Arts Center—including gallery, studio, performing, and rehearsal space—has opened.

True to its liberal arts focus, Grinnell mandates a first-semester writing tutorial, modeled after Oxford University's program, but doesn't require anything else. The more than 30 tutorials, limited to 12 students each, help enhance critical thinking, research, writing, and discussion skills, and allow first-year students to work individually with professors. When it comes to declaring a major, students determine their own course of study with help from faculty. Strong departments include the natural sciences and foreign languages, including German and Russian, bolstered by an influx of research grants, including one from the National Science Foundation. Beware of language courses if you aren't planning to major in the field, though: "I took an intermediate class in Spanish first semester freshman year, and I spent three hours in class as well as about eight hours outside of class on homework, and two hours in Spanish lab," says a drained sophomore. The chemistry department draws majors with independent research projects, and English, anthropology, sociology, and economics are popular, too.

Grinnell's standards are high—94 percent of students were in the top quarter of their high school class—and 30 percent of graduates move on to graduate and professional schools. Students who don't mind studying, even on weekends, will be happiest here. "Despite Grinnell's strong academic reputation and rigorous course-loads," explains a senior, "students tend to approach their education as an opportunity for self-improvement and not an opportunity to outperform their class-

"Students tend to approach their education as an opportunity for self-improvement."

mates." During finals, perhaps to help ease the stress, costumed superheroes run around the library giving out candy, says a sociology major. Teaching is the top priority for Grinnell faculty members, and because the college awards no graduate degrees, there are no teaching assistants. "Classes are very small, which allows for discussion-based instruction that is more engaging and challenging," reports one senior. A junior adds, "The professors are personable and always willing to talk to students outside of class. I love my professors and will miss them after next year."

Academic advising is also well regarded, as students are assisted by the professor who leads their first-year tutorial, and then choose another faculty member in their major discipline. It's rare to find classes with more than 50 students, and 94 percent of classes have 30 or fewer. When the urge to travel intrudes, students may study abroad in more than 100 locations, through the Associated Colleges of the Midwest* consortium and Grinnell-in-London. Fifty percent of students spend some time away from campus, and financial aid extends to study abroad, administrators say, and there are opportunities for research across disciplines. Co-ops in architecture, business, law, and medicine, and 3–2 engineering programs are also available.

Grinnell is a bit of Greenwich Village in corn country. Despite the rural environment, the college attracts an urban clientele, especially from the Chicago area. Only 13 percent are from Iowa, and 11 percent are foreign. "Students who attend Grinnell are a fun-loving, hardworking crowd. They have a wealth of ambition and academic curiosity and are able to maintain these qualities without impeding other students' efforts." The student body is 4 percent Hispanic, 5 percent Asian American, 4 percent African American, and 68 percent Caucasian. Women's rights, gay rights, labor rights, human rights, globalization, the environment, and groups such as PAFA (the Politically Active Feminist Alliance), GEAR (Grinnell Escalating AIDS Response), and Fearless (formed to combat gender-based violence) set the tone. Grinnell benefits from a hefty endowment, considering the school's size, thanks to portfolio managers who are among the best in the country.

The college guarantees four years of campus housing and 88 percent of students take advantage of the dorms, each of which has kitchen facilities, cable television, and a computer room. All but two dorms are co-ed, and after freshman year, students participate in a room draw, which can be stressful but usually works out. One senior remembers, "Dorm life is fun, fostering a great sense of community." Another says, "You're even allowed to pick your room and your roommate after the first year." Students who move off campus, mostly seniors, live just across the street. There are two dining halls, one on each side of campus, and meal plans range from full board to just dinner. Special family-style dinners are served every other Wednesday. "I feel safe on campus, but less so in the town at night," cautions a senior.

> "Students who attend Grinnell are a fun-loving, hardworking crowd."

That town, Grinnell (population 9,100), is "a quaint, rural town that students find to be very friendly and laid back. It holds a variety of stores and facilities that, unfortunately, many students do not discover because there is so much to do on campus." Community service helps bridge the town/gown gap, with some students serving as tutors and student teachers at the local high school and others participating in mentoring programs and community meals, among other projects. Outdoor recreation is popular, and nearby Rock Creek State Park lends itself to biking, running, camping, kayaking, and cross-country skiing, as well as other pursuits sponsored by the Grinnell Outdoor Recreation Program, or GORP. There are a few bars and pizza joints downtown, but for those craving bright lights, Iowa City and Des Moines are within an hour's drive, and the college runs a shuttle service to them. Chicago and Minneapolis are each about four hours distant.

With no fraternities or sororities, intramurals and all-campus parties revolve mainly around the dorms. Each dorm periodically sponsors a party using wordplay from its name in the title. For instance, Mary B. James Hall puts on the Mary-Be-James party, for which everyone comes in drag. As for alcohol, a senior reports, "Grinnell is not a dry campus, but there are no bars on campus and there is no peer pressure to drink or culture of problematic drinking. There are liberal limits on how much alcohol can be served at parties and these events always have trained servers who check ID." Nondrinkers need not sit home, however. Grinnell's social groups and activities range from the Society for Creative Anachronism and the Black Cultural Center to improvisational workshops, poetry readings, symposia, concerts, and movies. Highlights of the campus calendar include semiformal Winter and Spring Waltzes, where "most people wear formals and look very nice, not a common occurrence at a school where comfort is the usual standard and women rarely wear

With no fraternities or sororities, intramurals and all-campus parties revolve mainly around the dorms. Each dorm periodically sponsors a party using wordplay from its name in the title.

Grinnell is a bit of Greenwich Village in corn country. Despite the rural environment, the college attracts an urban clientele, especially from the Chicago area.

academic challenges ranging from cinema studies to neuroscience, Obies thrive on higher thinking and exploring their myriad talents.

Oberlin's attractive campus features a mix of Italian Renaissance buildings (four designed by Cass Gilbert), late-19th- and early-20th-century organic stone structures, and some less interesting 1950s barracks-type dorms. The buildings rise over flatlands typical of the Midwest, which do little to stop brutal winter winds. The Allen Memorial Art Museum, sometimes mentioned in the same breath as Harvard's and Yale's, is one of the loveliest buildings on campus, with a brick-paved, flower-laden courtyard and a fountain. The Oberlin College Science Center offers state-of-the-art classrooms, wireless Internet areas, a science library, and laboratory space.

Oberlin has been a leader among liberal arts colleges seeking to promote their science offerings; biology and chemistry are two of the college's strongest departments, and undergraduates may major in interdisciplinary programs like neuroscience and biopsychology. Students also flock to the English, politics, and history departments. Other popular majors include religion and environmental studies; computer science and anthropology attract relatively few majors. Oberlin students rave about their faculty. "The professors are all here because they love to teach, so in general their classes are really spectacular," says a music history major. Oberlin's conservatory of music holds a well-deserved spot among the nation's most prominent performance schools; the voice, violin, and TIMARA (Technology in Music and Related Arts) programs are especially praised. Interdisciplinary and self-created majors, such as black, Latin American, Russian, Third World, and women's studies, are popular.—not surprisingly at such a liberal school. East Asian studies have long been outstanding at Oberlin. About 40 percent of students

> "The professors are all here because they love to teach, so in general their classes are really spectacular."

study abroad; students are sorry to have lost the Oberlin in London program, a victim of a recent budget cuts that have also included slight reductions in the number of faculty and students.

Oberlin's students are as serious about their schoolwork as they are about politics, justice, and other social causes. Courses are rigorous; heavy workloads and the occasional Saturday morning class are the norm. "The atmosphere is intense and laid-back at the same time," says a sophomore. "The courses are challenging, and students work very hard, but the atmosphere here is anything but competitive. Students really support each other." A credit/no-entry policy allows students to take an unlimited number of grade-free courses (if they can get in). Recognizing that students at Oberlin are gifted and want to challenge themselves, most departments offer group and individual independent study opportunities and invite selected students to pursue demanding honors programs, especially during their senior year. "Professors are very demanding, yet very understanding and always willing to help," says a politics/creative writing double major.

There are no requirements for freshmen at Oberlin, but general education requirements include proficiency in writing and math and nine credit hours in each of the three divisions—arts and humanities, math/natural sciences, and social sciences—plus another nine credit hours in cultural diversity courses, including a foreign language. Students are also required to take one-quarter of the semester hours needed to graduate outside their major's division; those who shy away from math and science can satisfy distribution requirements by taking interdisciplinary courses such as "Chemistry and Crime." Students must also participate in three January terms, during which they pursue month-long projects, traditional or unique, on or off campus. About 60 different first year seminar classes are available, with enrollment limited to 14 students each, and though the majority of all other classes are limited to 25 students, the computerized registration system makes it easy to get in.

(Continued)
Undergraduates: 2,807
Male/Female: 45/55
SAT Ranges: V 640–730
  M 610–710
ACT Range: 26–31
Financial Aid: 60%
Expense: Pr $ $ $ $
Phi Beta Kappa: Yes
Applicants: 5,824
Accepted: 39%
Enrolled: 32%
Grad in 6 Years: 79%
Returning Freshmen: 93%
Academics: ✐ ✐ ✐ ✐ ½
Social: 🐾 🐾 🐾 🐾
Q of L: ★ ★ ★ ★
Admissions: (440) 775-8411
Email Address: college.
  admissions@oberlin.edu

Strongest Programs:
Neuroscience
Environmental Studies
Creative Writing
East Asian Studies
Biology
Chemistry
Politics
Music

Oberlin's students are as serious about their schoolwork as they are about politics, justice, and other social causes.

One of Oberlin's more unusual offerings is EXCO, an experimental college that offers students and interested townsfolk the chance to learn together. Most classes are taught by students, and topics can range from Fairy Tales to Knitting, Salsa Dancing, X-Files Lovers, and much more. Hot spots on campus include the Mudd Library, with more than 2.1 million volumes – a superb facility for research and studying or socializing; the famous A-level is the place to be on weeknights. Even more special are the music conservatory's 150 practice rooms, substantial music library, and Steinway pianos—one of the world's largest collections. Each year, 25 to 35 students enter the dual degree program, which allows them to earn both a BM and a BA in as little as five years. Dual-degree students must be admitted to both the college and the music conservatory.

"We tend to be left-leaning, although we have a growing number of conservative students."

Obies are "diverse—not just in terms of race or ethnicity—but across the board," says one student, while another adds, "The only word that really encompasses the majority of Oberlin students is the word 'passionate.' Everyone here is passionate about something." Eighty-three percent of students are from out of state, hailing primarily from the Mid-Atlantic States. African Americans account for 6 percent of the student body, Asian Americans 8 percent, Hispanics 5 percent, and foreign students 6 percent. Initiatives to increase diversity at Oberlin include advisors from various ethnic and racial backgrounds and a multicultural resource center with a full-time director. The Israeli-Palestinian conflict is one of the biggest political issues on campus; also hot are issues of sexuality, race, and gender. "We tend to be left-leaning, although we have a growing number of conservative students," says a senior. A popular annual event is the Drag Ball, in which half the student body shows up in full drag. "It's very Oberlin, because it's all about challenging social norms," says a student. Ten percent of undergrads receive merit scholarships worth an average of nearly $12,000.

Seventy-three percent of Oberlin's students live on campus in 24 dorms, including co-ops, several of which focus on foreign languages. Students are guaranteed housing, but choices are widest for upper-classmen. Only one dorm is single-sex; all dorms are four-class except Barrows, which is reserved for freshmen. The best dorms are said to be the program houses, including French House, African Heritage House, Russian House, and Third World House. Seniors and lucky juniors can land the preferred singles (thanks to their standing or good lottery numbers), but many move into cheaper off-campus apartments, although only a fraction are allowed off the college's meal plan. Students may eat in any of seven dining rooms. Appetizing alternatives to institutional fare can be found at the six co-ops that comprise the Oberlin Student Cooperative Association (OSCA), a more than $2-million-a-year corporation run entirely by students. Co-op members plan and prepare their own meals, and though

"The town is very supportive of us and manages to be quaint and cosmopolitan at the same time."

only 6 percent of the student body actually live in these houses, nearly 23 percent take their meals there, enjoying everything from homemade bread to whatever's left in the pantry before the next food shipment arrives.

Social life, like so much of the Oberlin experience, is what you make of it, students say. Almost all social events are on campus, and students find more than enough to do. Even in the middle of the day, "It's hard to walk across campus without becoming distracted by a pick-up game of Frisbee, the construction of a snow fort, or some students dancing contact improvisation on the lawn," says a senior. House parties, plays, movies, and conservatory performances are planned every other night. And since there's no Greek system, nothing is exclusive. As for drinking, underage students can finagle booze, and of-age students are allowed to imbibe in their rooms.

When the need to wander strikes, Cleveland is only 30 miles away, but students enjoy their small town. "The town is very supportive of us and manages to be quaint and cosmopolitan at the same time," says one student. Another student adds, "Pretty much all of the restaurants downtown are used to working until at least 2 a.m., delivering pizza to hungry late-nighters or having special offers for college students." And Obies are very enthusiastic about giving back to the community through volunteer activities at local schools, hospitals and nursing homes. "Our motto is "Think one person can make a difference? So do we!" says a student.

Oberlin's new athletic director has taken charge of what many consider to be a lukewarm athletics program, with an eye on reversing the school's losing ways and building a loyal fan base. Oberlin College is an NCAA Division III member institution and a charter member of the North Coast Athletic Conference. As for intramural sports, "As soon as the rain stops in the spring, there are students on every green area between the dorms playing Ultimate Frisbee," says a sophomore. Fencing, Aikido, soccer, and women's rugby also have loyal followings.

Oberlin may be small in size, but its emphasis on global learning, undergraduate research, and a vibrant liberal arts education helps it bust those statistical seams. Students are more likely to discuss local poverty than the quality of cereal choices in the dining halls, and can be found playing a Steinway or plugging away at astronomy. One Obie sums it up this way: "Oberlin is all about thinking critically and creatively in order to make a difference. Unconventionality is prized, as is challenging commonly held beliefs and norms."

> ### Overlaps
>
> **Wesleyan, Brown, Vassar, Carleton, Macalester, Yale**

If You Apply To ➤ **Oberlin:** Early decision: Nov. 15, Jan. 2. Regular admissions: Jan. 15. Financial aid: Feb. 15. Guarantees to meet demonstrated need. Campus interviews: recommended, evaluative. Alumni interviews: optional, evaluative. SATs or ACTs: required. SAT IIs: recommended. Accepts the Common Application and electronic applications. Essay question: Why Oberlin?

Occidental College

1600 Campus Road, Los Angeles, CA 90041

Oxy is a diverse, urban, streetwise cousin to the more upscale and suburban Claremont Colleges. Plentiful internships and study abroad give Oxy students real-world perspectives. Oxy's innovative diplomacy and world affairs program features internships in Washington and at the UN.

Occidental College is one of a handful of small colleges located in a big city, in this case LalaLand. But unlike the sprawling and impersonal City of Angels, Oxy emphasizes a strong sense of community and a decidedly diverse student population.

Set against the backdrop of the San Gabriel Mountains, Occidental's self-contained Mediterranean-style campus is a secluded enclave of flowers and trees between Pasadena and Glendale, minutes from downtown Los Angeles. New facilities include the $16-million science center, and renovations to many campus buildings, including Fowler Hall.

Inside this urban oasis resides a thriving community of high achievers who don't for a moment believe that the liberal arts are dead, or even wounded. Required first-year cultural studies seminars include topics in human history and culture, with an emphasis on writing skills. Each seminar has 16 students who also share the

> **Website:** www.oxy.edu
> **Location:** Urban
> **Total Enrollment:** 1,887
> **Undergraduates:** 1,866
> **Male/Female:** 42/58
> **SAT Ranges:** V 590–690
>   M 580–670
> **Financial Aid:** 65%
> **Expense:** Pr $ $ $
> **Phi Beta Kappa:** Yes
> **Applicants:** 4,837

(Continued)

Accepted: 45%

Enrolled: 23%

Grad in 6 Years: 75%

Returning Freshmen: 92%

Academics: 🖉 🖉 🖉 🖉

Social: ☎ ☎ ☎

Q of L: ★ ★ ★ ★

Admissions: (800) 825-5262

Email Address:
  admission@oxy.edu

Strongest Programs:
Economics
English
Music
Chemistry
Biology
Diplomacy and World Affairs

same residence hall; it's called the Learning Communities Program. In addition, all Oxy students must show proficiency in a foreign language and complete 12 units of world cultures courses, a fine arts course, preindustrial-era coursework, and 12 units of science and math. Many of Occidental's academic departments are excellent, with English, music, chemistry, and an innovative diplomacy and world affairs program among the strongest, and psychology the most popular. A biochemistry major says, "Most courses are intellectually challenging and have adequate work loads, but there is still a sense that Oxy students enjoy learning, not just getting grades."

Occidental encourages diverse learning experiences through internships, independent study, and study abroad—including the only undergraduate program to offer internships with the United Nations Secretariat and the U.S. Mission. Over the past decade, more than a thousand students have engaged in summer research projects or academic year independent projects, and in 2004–05, 16 Occidental students were accepted for the National Conference on Undergraduate Research. The student-managed Charles R. Blyth Fund allows students to invest about $150,000 of the college's endowment. No new majors have been added, but environmental science and environmental studies are no longer available.

Faculty members are readily available in and out of the classroom, and students say the teaching, in general, is excellent. "The quality of teaching here is good overall, but it is important to talk to current and more experienced students to find out who is worth having," says a junior. The great majority of classes have 25 or fewer students, and as academic advisors are responsible for about four students per class (16 total), personal relationships develop quickly. "I had in-home lunch, dinner, museum outings, and hour-long office discussions with my professors," explains one senior. Students also broaden their horizons in study abroad programs in Western Europe, Japan, China, Mexico, Nepal, Hungary, Costa Rica, and Russia. For

"Social life is largely contained on campus."

politicos, there's Oxy-in-Washington and Oxy-at-the-UN. There are also 3–2 engineering programs with Caltech and Columbia University, exchange programs with Spelman and Morehouse colleges in Atlanta, and cross-registration privileges with Caltech and Pasadena's Art Center College of Design. Students may also take advantage of a 4–2 biotechnology program with Keck Graduate Institute (of the Claremont Colleges).

Half the students at Occidental are from California, and 3 percent are foreign. African Americans make up 7 percent of the student population, Hispanics 15 percent, and Asian Americans 11 percent. Economic diversity is reflected in the fact that since 1999, an average of 24 percent of Occidental students qualified for Pell Grants. The college's financial aid staff even visits local high schools to help families fill out applications, offering sessions in English, Spanish, and Vietnamese. Perhaps not surprisingly, students tend to be liberal. "Many are active in Democratic politics and liberal social causes," says a philosophy major. "The students here are very diverse economically and racially. They tend to be outspoken politically and environmentally active and community-oriented." Since 1989, students here have won three Rhodes scholarships, five Marshall scholarships, six Truman scholarships, nine Fulbright fellowships, and dozens of other significant awards. Administrators say "excellence and equity in education" is Oxy's top priority, though admission is not need-blind. Nearly 20 percent of students receive merit scholarships each year, averaging $17,370. There are no athletic scholarships.

Fraternities and sororities, though declining on the Oxy social ladder, attract 3 percent of men and 8 percent of the women, but they are neither selective nor exclusive; students choose which to join, rather than being chosen, and the frats must invite everyone to their functions.

Upperclassmen on the "O-team" plan freshman orientation the week before school starts. Freshmen are required to live on campus and eat in the dining hall (tip from a junior: don't try anything that has an unusual name, like "Mayan tofu.") Dining hall food is available throughout the day, and there are also plenty of hole-in-the-wall eateries nearby, including Burger Continental (BC's), Senor Fish, and Tommy's.

The 11 residence halls are small—fewer than 150 students each—and co-ed by floor or room. Students say they are quite comfortable and well-maintained. Seventy percent of students live on campus, but what you get depends on your luck in the housing lottery. Students from all four classes live together, many in special-interest houses like the Multicultural Hall, the Women's Center, or the Substance-Free Quad. Those who move off campus by senior year tend to stay within a three-block radius of the college. A student characterizes the surrounding neighborhood of Eagle Rock as "most definitely a family-oriented town that does not cater to the college student, but provides a wonderful array of diverse foods and activities." Another student describes it as a working-class Hispanic community.

While the bright lights of L.A. often beckon on weekends, "social life is largely contained on campus," says a junior. "There are always one or two things happening on the weekends," Fraternities and sororities, though declining on the Oxy social ladder, attract 3 percent of men and 8 percent of the women, but they are neither selective nor exclusive; students choose which to join, rather than being chosen, and the frats must invite everyone to their functions. As for alcohol, "like most other colleges, there is underage drinking even though this is illegal," says another junior. The Senior Smack offers graduates-to-be the chance to smooch whomever they've

"You can find almost anything except snow."

wanted to during the past four years. Other big events include parties such as Love on the Beach and Da Getaway—a Roaring Twenties bash where students gamble with fake money and Charleston 'til they drop. "Winter Formal is probably my favorite," says a theatre major, Here's a tip: Keep your birthday a secret, or on that unhappy day a roaring pack of your more sadistic classmates will carry you out to the middle of campus and mercilessly toss you in the Gilman Fountain. It's a tradition, after all.

When students become weary of the incestuous social life in the 60 percent female "Oxy fishbowl," they head for the bars, restaurants, museums, and theaters of downtown Los Angeles and Old Pasadena, where, one student notes, "You can find almost anything except snow." But the ski slopes of the San Gabriel Mountains are not far away, and neither is Hollywood nor the beautiful beaches of Southern California. When they tire of California, students try their luck in Las Vegas—or trek south of the border, into Tijuana. A car (your own or someone else's) is practically a necessity, though the college runs a weekend shuttle service to Old Town Pasadena. The weather is warm and sunny, but the air is often thick with that infamous L.A. smog.

Oxy's sports teams compete in Division III and draw a modest following. Football is the most popular (Oxy's team won the Southern California Intercollegiate Athletic Conference championship in 2004), followed by men's basketball and soccer. And don't forget that L.A. is home to the NBA's Lakers, the NHL's Kings, and baseball's Dodgers. Oxy has a small intramural program; popular club sports include rugby, lacrosse, and Ultimate Frisbee.

Occidental's creative, motivated, and diverse students are not here for the bright lights and beautiful people of Los Angeles; those are just fringe benefits. Instead, students are drawn to this intimate oasis of learning by professors who hate to see anyone waste one whit of intellectual potential. And students here are only too happy to live up to these lofty expectations.

Overlaps
USC, UCLA, UC-Berkeley, Pomona, Claremont–McKenna, Stanford

If You Apply To ➤ **Oxy:** Early decision: Nov. 15. Regular admissions: Jan. 10. Financial aid: Feb. 1. Guarantees to meet full demonstrated need. Campus interviews: recommended, evaluative. Alumni interviews: optional, informational. SATs or ACTs: required. SAT IIs: recommended. Accepts the Common Application and prefers electronic applications. Essay question: what generates passion in your life; what person or character best represents your generation; ask and answer an important question.

Oglethorpe University

4484 Peachtree Road NE, Atlanta, GA 30319

Small wonder that brochures for Oglethorpe trumpet Atlanta as the college's biggest asset. In a region where most liberal arts colleges are in sleepy towns, Oglethorpe has the South's most exciting city at its fingertips. With only 945 undergraduates, Oglethorpe puts heavy emphasis on community.

Website: www.oglethorpe.edu
Location: City outskirts
Total Enrollment: 1,029
Undergraduates: 945
Male/Female: 35/65
SAT Ranges: V 540–660
   M 530–640
ACT Range: 24–29
Financial Aid: 55%
Expense: Pr $
Phi Beta Kappa: No
Applicants: 746
Accepted: 66%
Enrolled: 23%
Grad in 6 Years: 61%
Returning Freshmen: 87%
Academics: ✍ ✍ ✍
Social: ☎ ☎ ☎
Q of L: ★ ★ ★ ★
Admissions: (404) 364-8307
   or (800) 428-4484
Email Address:
   admission@oglethorpe.edu

Strongest Programs:
Biology
Accounting
Business Administration
English
Psychology

Each Christmas, students at Oglethorpe University take part in a unique tradition. The Boar's Head Ceremony celebrates a medieval scholar who halted a stampeding wild boar by ramming his copy of Aristotle down the animal's throat. Though some may find it boorish, students at this small Southern school explain that it fosters a sense of family.

Founded in 1835, the school is named for the idealistic founder of the state of Georgia, James Edward Oglethorpe. Its 118-acre campus is located near suburban Buckhead, a ritzy area about 10 miles north of downtown Atlanta. The heavily wooded, slightly rolling terrain is perfect territory for walks or long runs, and the beautiful campus has served as the backdrop for several movies and TV shows. Oglethorpe's academic buildings and some residence halls are in the English Gothic style; the campus is also home of the Georgia Shakespeare Festival.

Oglethorpe's strengths are business administration, English, biology, accounting, psychology, and communications. Weaker bets are the fine arts and foreign language departments, though the latter does offer courses in Japanese, German, French, and Spanish. And whatever isn't offered at Oglethorpe can usually be taken through crossregistration at other schools in the Atlanta area.

Aspiring engineers may take advantage of 3–2 dual-degree programs with Georgia Tech, the University of Southern California, Auburn, and the University of Florida. The school also offers courses and additional resources as a member of the Atlanta Regional Consortium for Higher Education.* Oglethorpe also offers a wide variety of study abroad programs, including a semester at Seigakuin University in Japan and sister-school exchanges in Argentina, the Netherlands, Germany, France, Russia, and Monaco. According to administrators, Oglethorpe "emphasizes the preparation of the humane generalist" and "rejects rigid specialization." That doesn't mean the curriculum's a cakewalk, though. "The academic climate is pretty laid-back," explains one junior. "However, there are always those few students that try to make things competitive. The courses are rigorous and I have to study every day."

The university's guiding principle is the Oglethorpe Idea, which says students should develop academically and as citizens. This philosophy is based on the conviction that education should help students make both a life and a living. All students take the sequenced, interdisciplinary Core Curriculum program at the same point in their college careers, providing them with a model for integrating information and gaining knowledge. In addition to the ability to reason, read, and speak effectively, the core asks students to reflect on and discuss matters fundamental to understanding who they are and what they ought to be. The core requires Narratives of the Self (freshmen), Human Nature and the Social Order (sophomores), Historical Perspectives on the Social Order (juniors), and Science and Human Nature (seniors), plus a fine arts core course in music and culture or art and culture, and coursework in modern mathematics or advanced foreign language.

Oglethorpe's faculty may be demanding, but they're also friendly and helpful. "All classes are taught by full professors and the quality is excellent. Most strive to make themselves available to teach on and off campus, in and out of the classroom," says one biopsychology major. Classes are generally small, and most students notice few problems at registration. Advising services are said to be helpful. The library's holdings are minuscule, though—just over 131,000 volumes.

What's an Oglethorpian like? The vast majority are smart, semiconservative off-spring of middle- and upper-middle-class Southern families. Sixty-six percent ranked in the top quarter of their high school class; most come from public schools and more than half are native Georgians. "Our campus is pretty small, however, cliques do form. The students are usually extremely personable and cordial." Oglethorpe prides itself on being one of the first Georgia colleges to admit African American students, and today 30 percent of the students are members of minority groups: roughly 20 percent are African American, 3 percent are Asian American, 3 percent are Hispanic, and 3 percent hail from abroad. There's a level of comfort with racial differences, students report. Some students complain that their peers can be rather cliquish, but say that all in all, everyone gets along well.

> **"The academic climate is pretty laid-back."**

Fifty-four percent of Oglethorpe's students choose to live on campus—and love it. "The dorms are big and have nice furniture," says an accounting major. Most rooms are suites with private bathrooms, and some singles are available. Some students commute to campus; a quarter live in Atlanta—not a college town, but where the wild life is. "Some weekends, everyone stays around and life is great, and then there are others when campus is deserted," one student explains. Fraternities and sororities, which claim 33 percent of the men and 25 percent of the women, throw parties that draw big numbers. Officially, the campus is dry, but underage students can find alcohol if they try, students agree. It's rumored that Oglethorpe barflies do more hopping than Georgia bullfrogs, and bars, clubs, and cafes abound within 10 minutes of campus.

Those who tire of the Oglethorpe scene can find excitement on the campuses of the dozen or so other colleges in the area or in downtown Atlanta, which one student describes as "the heart of Atlanta and a few minutes from Buckhead, a party district, and two great malls." Atlanta proper offers everything you can imagine—arts, professional sports (including basketball's Hawks, football's Falcons, and baseball's Braves), and entertainment (ride the Great American Scream Machine at Six Flags). Facilities built for the 1996 Olympics also provide a diversion. Oglethorpe always has a big contingent going to Savannah for St. Patrick's Day and to New Orleans for Mardi Gras. The campus celebrates its origins once a year during Oglethorpe Day. Students looking for warmer weather, though, head down to sunny Florida.

Intramurals are important at Oglethorpe, sometimes more so than varsity sports. Perhaps Atlanta's diversions or the relatively small number of students on campus cause varsity sports to be a weak draw. Still, the Stormy Petrels men's golf team has brought home a Southern Collegiate Athletic Conference title, and basketball games against crosscity rival Emory are popular. The Georgia landscape makes possible a plethora of outdoor activities, including hiking at nearby Stone Mountain and boating or swimming in Lake Lanier (named for Georgia poet Sidney Lanier—Oglethorpe Class of 1860).

> **"The dorms are big and have nice furniture."**

Though Oglethorpe may lack widespread name recognition, its students get all the attention they need from a caring faculty on a close-knit campus. And being in a large city like Atlanta provides anything else that might be lacking, ranging from great nightlife to internships and postgraduate employment with big-name corporations. In a sea of large Southern state schools, Oglethorpe stands out as a place where students come first.

Intramurals are important at Oglethorpe, sometimes more so than varsity sports. Perhaps Atlanta's diversions or the relatively small number of students on campus cause varsity sports to be a weak draw.

Aspiring engineers may take advantage of 3–2 dual-degree programs with Georgia Tech, the University of Southern California, Auburn, and the University of Florida.

The university's guiding principle is the Oglethorpe Idea, which says students should develop academically and as citizens.

Overlaps

University of Georgia, Emory, Georgia State, Georgia Tech, Mercer

Oglethorpe: Rolling admissions. Early action: Dec. 5. Financial aid: Mar. 1. Does not guarantee to meet demonstrated need. Campus interviews: recommended, evaluative. Alumni interviews: optional, informational. SATs or ACTs: required. SAT IIs: optional. Accepts the Common Application. Essay question: more about you.

Ohio State University

3rd floor, Lincoln Tower, 1800 Cannon Drive, Columbus, OH 43210

Ohio State may be the biggest university in the Big Ten, but it is far from the best. OSU has never achieved the reputation of a Michigan or a Wisconsin—partly because it has three major in-state rivals (Miami, Cincinnati, and Ohio U) that siphon off many top students.

Website: www.osu.edu
Location: City center
Total Enrollment: 50,731
Undergraduates: 37,605
Male/Female: 55/45
SAT Ranges: V 520–630
   M 590–660
ACT Range: 23–28
Financial Aid: 40%
Expense: Pub $ $ $ $
Phi Beta Kappa: Yes
Applicants: 20,122
Accepted: 72%
Enrolled: 44%
Grad in 6 Years: 62%
Returning Freshmen: 86%
Academics: ✐ ✐ ✐
Social: 🐿 🐿 🐿 🐿
Q of L: ★ ★ ★
Admissions: (614) 292-OHIO
Email Address:
   askabuckeye@osu.edu

Strongest Programs:
Business
Premed
Engineering
Education
Geography
Industrial Design
Linguistics
Psychology

Think big. Think very big. Think very, very big. Envision a school with almost 50,000 students and too many opportunities to count. What might come to mind is Ohio State University, located in the heart of the state's capital, offering 19 colleges and more than 10,444 courses in 175 undergraduate majors. If those numbers aren't staggering enough, consider the fact that OSU has 34 varsity teams, 44 intramural sports, and 51 sports clubs. While students cite the school's size as both a blessing and a curse, all seem to agree that at OSU, the sky is the limit for those with a desire to sample its academic and other resources.

This megauniversity stands on 3,200 wooded acres rubbing the edge of downtown Columbus on one side. On the other side, across the Olentangy River, is farmland associated with the College of Agriculture. OSU's architectural style is anything but consistent, yet it's all tied together in one huge redbrick package. "One part of the campus maintains a nostalgic air while another is relatively modern," observes a student. The grounds are nicely landscaped, and a centrally located lake provides a peaceful setting for contemplation.

Business, education, geography, industrial design, and engineering are among the school's most celebrated departments. OSU bills itself as the place to go for computer graphics and has a supercomputer center to back up its claim. It also boasts the largest and most comprehensive African American studies program anywhere and turns out more African American PhDs than any other university in the nation. Furthermore, the university has the nation's only programs in welding engineering and geodetic science, and the state's only program in medical communications. Although immensely popular, students report that the English program needs improvement.

The university's fundamental commitment to liberal arts learning means all undergrads must satisfy rigorous general education requirements that include at least one course in math, two each in writing and a foreign language, three in social science, four in natural science, and five in arts and humanities. To top it all off, students must complete a capstone requirement that includes a course on Issues of the Contemporary World. A quarterly selective admissions program has replaced OSU's old open-door policy, but a conditional/unconditional admissions policy allows some poorly prepared students to play catch-up in designated areas. Some 10,500 students receive merit-based scholarships while 560 athletes receive scholarships in 17 sports.

> **"One part of the campus maintains a nostalgic air while another is relatively modern."**

Freshmen, who are grouped together in the University College before entering one of the degree-granting programs, find most introductory lectures huge. Teaching assistants, not professors, hold smaller recitation sections and deal on a personal level with students. "Ohio State is becoming more and more competitive," says an early child development major, "but it is far from overwhelming if you attend class and keep up with the coursework." Students find that class sizes are whittled down as they continue in their fields of study. OSU's honors program allows 2,500 students to take classes that are taught by top professors and limited to 25 students each. Internships are required in some programs and optional in others, and possibilities for study abroad include Japan and the People's Republic of China. A personalized study program enables students to create their own majors.

Inside OSU's ivy-covered halls and modern additions are some of the best up-to-date equipment and facilities, including a "phenomenal" library system with two dozen branches and nearly four million volumes—all coordinated by computer. Professors "are well-informed about their subjects," according to students. "Teachers are passionate about working with students," says a senior. Complaints about long registration lines have been answered by BRUTUS, Ohio State's Touch-Tone telephone registration system, which saves on time but does little to ease class overcrowding.

Eighty-five percent of Ohio State's students come from Ohio, and the balance come largely from adjacent states. Every type of background is represented, most in huge numbers. Paradoxically, this school with its nationally recognized African American studies program has a student body that is 8 percent African American; Hispanics and Asian Americans make up another 7 percent. Several programs are aimed specifically at "enhancing" efforts to attract and retain minority students, including a statewide Young Scholars Program that yearly guarantees admission and financial aid to seventh graders once they complete high school.

"Student involvement is overwhelming."

The residence halls that house 24 percent of the Ohio State masses are located in three areas: North, South, and Olentangy (that is, those closest to the Olentangy River). Freshmen—required to live either at home or in the dorms—are scattered among each of OSU's 27 residence halls. "The dorms are very comfortable," says a student. "Plus, you get a lot of living options." Upperclassmen, when they don't head for off-campus life in Columbus, find the South campus section among the most desirable (it's more sociable, louder, and full of single rooms). The Towers in the Olentangy section have gained more popularity since their conversion to eight-person suites. All in all, students have a choice of single-sex, co-ed (by floor or by room), or married-couples apartments if they want to live in campus housing. Computer labs are located in each residence area. A system of variable room rates based on frills (air-conditioning, private bath, number of roommates), as well as a choice of four meal-plan options, give students flexibility in determining their housing costs. Dormitory students have a choice of five dining halls, but others cook for themselves or eat in fraternity houses.

Such a large student market has, of course, produced a strip of bars, fast-food joints, convenience stores, bookstores, vegetarian restaurants, and you-name-it along the edge of the campus on High Street, and downtown Columbus is just a few minutes away. The fine public transportation system carries students not only throughout this capital city but also around the sprawling campus. In addition to the usual shopping centers, restaurants, golf courses, and movie theaters, Columbus boasts a symphony orchestra and ballet, and its central location in the state makes it easily accessible to Cleveland and Cincinnati. Outdoor enthusiasts can ski in nearby Mansfield, canoe and sail on the Olentangy and Scioto rivers, hike around adjacent quarries, or camp in the nearby woods.

Ohio State is a bustling place on weekends. "Student involvement is overwhelming," says one student. Various social events are planned by on-campus housing

Ohio State operates the mother of all college sports programs—an $85 million operation once led by the only athletic director in the country with his own Bobblehead doll for sale.

Inside OSU's ivy-covered halls and modern additions are some of the best up-to-date equipment and facilities, including a "phenomenal" library system with two dozen branches and nearly four million volumes—all coordinated by computer.

groups—floors, dorms, or sections of the campus. The Michigan–Ohio State football game inspires the best partying of the year, and other annual events include a Renaissance Festival and River Rat Day. Two student unions run eateries as well as movies on Friday and Saturday nights, and High Street's zillion bars, saloons, restaurants, and discos come to life. Campus policies prohibit underage drinking in dorms, but one partier discloses, "I can get served in almost any bar on campus." Just 5 percent of men and 6 percent of women on this vast campus belong to one of the 61 fraternities and sororities. By one account, these students make the Greek system "a way of life and isolate themselves from the rest of the student population."

Ohio State operates the mother of all college sports programs—an $85 million operation once led by the only athletic director in the country with his own Bobblehead doll for sale. The Buckeyes field teams in 36 sports, from women's rifle to men's football. Nonrecruited students should not expect to make any varsity team as walk-ons. Rivalries abound and one student asserts (without a hint of irony), "We party harder, we play harder, and we're more humble [than our rivals]." Many take advantage of an ambitious intramural program that boasts a dozen basketball courts and 26 courts for handball, squash, and racquetball. "It rained one day and 200 softball games were rained out," one student reports. For diehard basketball fans, the first official day of practice, Midnight Basketball, is a favored ritual.

OSU's sheer size is sometimes overwhelming to be sure, but students say they "thrive on the challenge and excitement of a big university." They enjoy "the freedom to pick and choose courses, programs, activities, and friends to fit their needs." For those who really want to be a Buckeye, jump in with both feet and heed the old campus saying: "Welcome to the Nut House."

If You Apply To ➤ | **OSU:** Rolling admissions. Meets demonstrated need of 12 percent. Campus interviews: recommended, informational. No alumni interviews. SATs or ACTs: required. SAT IIs: optional. Accepts the Common Application and electronic applications. Essay question.

Ohio University

Chubb Hall 120, Athens, OH 45701-2979

OU is half the size of Ohio State and plays up its homey feel compared to the cast of thousands in Columbus. The Honors Tutorial College is a sure bet for top students who want close contact with faculty. Communications and journalism top the list of prominent programs.

Website: www.ohiou.edu
Location: Rural
Total Enrollment: 20,143
Undergraduates: 16,950
Male/Female: 47/53
SAT Ranges: V 490–600
    M 490–600
ACT Range: 21–26

With top-notch programs in journalism and business, Ohio University has become a competitive public institution without shedding its small-town roots. It has become known as an important research institution, with studies including dinosaur anatomy and rural diabetes rates. Students here love to hit the town for fun but are quick to hit the books, too. They take pride in their university and Athens, the quintessential college town that surrounds OU. While Athens might seem a bit too quaint for big-city folks, OU students call it home.

Established in 1804 as the first institution of higher learning in the old Northwest Territory, Ohio University is located in Athens, about 75 miles from Columbus, the state capital. Encircled by winding hills, the campus features neo-Georgian architecture, tree-lined redbrick walkways, and white-columned buildings all clustered on "greens," which are like small neighborhoods. Long walks are especially nice during the fall foliage season. The university's newest state-of-the-art classroom facility, Margaret M. Walter Hall, is equipped with the latest in educational technology. Other improvements include a $20 million renovation and expansion of Bentley Hall, the social sciences facility, and the Innovation Center, which provides incubation services to biotechnology and IT companies. A brand-spanking new student center is slated to open in 2007.

One of the focal points of an Ohio University education and something that sets the school apart from run-of-the-mill state institutions is the Honors Tutorial College. Founded in 1972, it's the nation's first multi-disciplinary, degree-granting honors program modeled on the tutorial method used in British universities, notably Oxford and Cambridge. It is ranked as one of the best programs on campus, and the most selective: Students must have at least a 1300 on their SAT or a 30 on their ACT, and only about 60 freshmen get in every year. Students take an individualized curriculum in a major field and spend most of their time in one-on-one weekly tutorials with profs. Other top areas are the College of Communication and its three offspring: the schools of telecommunications, visual communication, and journalism, which feature the latest graphics and computer equipment. The Global Learning Community Certificate is an innovative program that prepares students for leadership opportunities in a rapidly changing world. First-year GLC students work in bi-national teams with students from universities in Hungary, Ecuador, Thailand, and elsewhere. Students can take a new online journalism course, which teaches skills like computer-assisted reporting and Web design. Also new to the curriculum is a certificate program in geographic information science and a bachelor's degree in applied and technical studies.

> "I've never had a problem getting help or getting my questions answered."

General education requirements involve a minimum of one course in math or quantitative skills, two courses in English composition, one senior-level interdisciplinary course, plus 30 quarter hours in applied sciences and technology, social sciences, natural sciences, humanities, and cross-cultural perspectives. To lighten the load, you can take electives such as The Language of Rock Music (so you can communicate better with Mom and Dad?). Study abroad offers worldwide destinations for anywhere from two weeks to one year. Co-op programs are available for engineering students, and nearly anyone can earn credit for an internship.

> "Everyone has a strong sense of pride in our university and our town."

Students say most of their professors are top-notch. "I have had excellent professors," says one junior. "They're very knowledgeable and approachable. I've never had a problem getting help or getting my questions answered." Freshmen often are taught by full professors with TAs handling study sessions. Classes of 100-plus students do exist, but the average class size for freshmen is about 25. Getting into classes can be difficult. "As budgets decrease, the professor staff decreases as well, causing access to classes to be very difficult," one student says. The academic climate at OU is debatable, depending on the classes and major you choose.

You'll find many classmates from the Buckeye State; 92 percent are Ohioans. But students have pride in their school and take every chance to poke fun at their rival, Miami University of Ohio. "Everyone has a strong sense of pride in our university and our town," says a senior. "Our rival seems more uptight and snobbish." Almost everyone at OU attended public high school and 17 percent graduated in

(Continued)

Financial Aid: 49%
Expense: Pub $ $ $ $
Phi Beta Kappa: Yes
Applicants: 12,417
Accepted: 63%
Enrolled: 35%
Grad in 6 Years: 70%
Returning Freshmen: 82%
Academics: ✍ ✍ ✍
Social: ☎ ☎ ☎ ☎
Q of L: ★ ★ ★
Admissions: (740) 593-4100
Email Address:
  admissions@ohiou.edu

Strongest Programs:
Journalism
Business
Engineering
Communications
Film

One of the focal points of an Ohio University education and something that sets the school apart from run-of-the-mill state institutions is the Honors Tutorial College.

Freshmen often are taught by full professors with TAs handling study sessions. Classes of 100-plus students do exist, but the average class size for freshmen is about 25. Getting into classes can be difficult.

You'll find many classmates from the Buckeye State; 92 percent are Ohioans. But students have pride in their school and take every chance to poke fun at their rival, Miami University of Ohio.

the top tenth of their class. The student body is overwhelmingly white, although administrators are trying to attract more minority students and has established an Office of Multicultural Programs. Three percent are African American; Hispanics and Asian Americans combine for 2 percent. The new Gateway Award Program provides financial aid for outstanding students who show academic excellence, financial need, and/or a combination of both.

Campus housing is plentiful (41 dorms) and well liked. Almost everyone lives on campus for two years then moves into neighboring dwellings. Campus housing comes with a variety of options: co-ed, single-sex, quiet study, academic interest, and even an international dorm. At the "mods," six men and six women occupy separate wings but share a living room and study room. Upperclassmen usually move to fraternity or sorority houses, nearby apartments, or rental houses. Five different meal plans are available at four cafeterias and include fast-food counters next to regular dorm-food fare. One student says everything looks good, "but looks can be deceiving." "Some of the things they serve are a little odd—like fish nuggets," another student says.

The social scene is largely off-campus. "Athens is such a unique town," says a senior. "There is so much to do." Uptown is dotted with bars and clubs, campus and community activities such as plays, and guest speakers and performers. Some students also choose to participate in Greek life. Twelve percent of men and 13 percent of women join their ranks. The administration and some students have tried to

"Athens is such a unique town." downplay OU's party-school image by strictly enforcing the alcohol policy. Freshmen are required to pass an online alcohol education course; if they don't, they might not be able to register for OU classes. But despite their efforts, students say that drinking continues. Athens's fabled Halloween celebration is a huge block party with people from all over the Midwest and wouldn't be missed by many students. Students also look forward to homecoming, International Festival, and block parties like Palmerfest and Millfest. "Athens is its own place," says a senior. "You feel at home. It's beautiful and friendly and like no other." Volunteer opportunities, such as Habitat for Humanity and a local homeless shelter, are available through the Center for Community Service. Students also love to hike and camp at the nearby state parks or trek to Columbus for shopping.

Sports are a big draw at Ohio. The men's basketball team were Mid-American Conference champions in 2005, and the men's ice hockey team defeated Penn State to win the 2004 national championship. Intramural sports are popular and include teams for broomball and wallyball (think volleyball using walls.)

Students say OU has a lot to offer, from a vibrant social life to quality professors and challenging academics. "I love this school and the city's community," says one student. "I think most students would not regret their decision to come here."

Overlaps

Ohio State, Miami University (OH), Bowling Green, Kent State, University of Cincinnati

If You Apply To ➤

OU: Rolling admissions. Regular admissions: Feb. 1. Financial aid: March 15. Does not guarantee to meet demonstrated need. Campus and alumni interviews: optional, informational. SATs or ACTs: required. ACT preferred. SAT IIs: optional. Essay question: optional personal essay.

Ohio Wesleyan University

South Sandusky Street, Delaware, OH 43015

OWU serves up the liberal arts with a popular side dish of business-related programs. In a region of beautiful campuses, Ohio Wesleyan's is nondescript. Like Denison, OWU is working hard to make its fraternities behave. Attracts middle-of-the-road to conservative students with preprofessional aspirations.

Ohio Wesleyan University is a small school with a big commitment to providing its students with a well-rounded education. Hallmarks at OWU are strong preparation for graduate and professional school, a solid grounding in the liberal arts, and an emphasis on having fun outside the classroom. Once known for its raucous students, this small university has overcome its hard-partying past and now offers its students a rewarding college experience.

Situated smack in the center of the state, OWU's spacious 200-acre campus is peaceful and quaint, albeit with a highway that runs down the middle. Several buildings are on the National Register of Historic Places. The architecture ranges from Greek Revival to Colonial to modern, with ivy-covered brick academic buildings on one side of a

> **"Courses are rigorous, but the climate is cooperative and challenging."**

busy thoroughfare and dormitories and fraternities on the other side of the highway. Stately Stuyvesant Hall, with its majestic bell tower, is the main campus landmark. The Conrades-Wetherell science center with state-of-the-art laboratories, classrooms, and science library, was recently completed.

Preprofessional education has always been OWU's forte. Between 85 and 90 percent of students in the premed program get accepted to medical schools. The curriculum includes majors in neuroscience and East Asian studies, and the highly popular zoology and microbiology departments are interesting alternatives to the traditional premed route. The Woltemade Center for Economics, Business, and Entrepreneurship caters to budding entrepreneurs, and the music and fine arts programs offer both professional and liberal arts degrees.

A member of the Great Lakes College Association* consortium, Ohio Wesleyan offers numerous innovative curricular programs. The most prominent is the National Colloquium, a yearlong series of lectures on a timely issue. Speakers have included David Wetherell, president and CEO of CMGI, and novelist Gloria Naylor. The honors program offers qualified students one-on-one tutorials and a chance to conduct research with faculty members in areas of mutual interest. The Special Languages program offers the opportunity for self-directed study and tutoring by native speakers in languages such as Arabic, Chinese, Japanese, and Modern Greek. Students can travel to Mexico for a community service experience during spring break, while fine arts, theater, and music majors can spend a semester in New York City to study with professionals there. A major in Latin American studies has been added.

"Courses are rigorous, but the climate is cooperative and challenging," says a freshman economics major. To graduate, OWU students must take a year of foreign language; three courses in each of the social sciences, natural sciences, and humanities; one course in the arts; and one course in cultural diversity. Students must also pass three mandatory writing classes to sharpen their written communication skills, but these aren't burdensome. Students universally laud OWU's faculty for ability and accessibility. "The professors here are all experts in their area. They encourage discussion and questions and are open to one-on-one interaction outside of class," remarks a history major. "The quality of teaching is excellent," a junior adds.

Website: www.owu.edu
Location: Small town
Total Enrollment: 1,909
Undergraduates: 1,909
Male/Female: 47/53
SAT Ranges: V 550–660
    M 560–660
ACT Range: 24–28
Financial Aid: 57%
Expense: Pr $ $
Phi Beta Kappa: Yes
Applicants: 2,803
Accepted: 74%
Enrolled: 27%
Grad in 6 Years: 66%
Returning Freshmen: 78%
Academics: ✍ ✍ ✍ ½
Social: 🐨 🐨 🐨 🐨 🐨
Q of L: ★ ★ ★
Admissions: (740) 368-3020
Email Address:
    owuadmit@owu.edu

Strongest Programs:
Psychology
Zoology
Economics and Management
Sociology/Anthropology
English
History
Politics and Government
Biology

"Freshmen and upper classmen are all taught by the same professors, most of whom have doctoral degrees."

A senior says OWU students are mature, self-defined, passionate leaders. Forty-nine percent of students come from Ohio; another big contingent consists of students from mid-Atlantic and New England states, while recruits from Chicago and California are increasing. Students agree that diversity is valued on campus, but African Americans make up only 4 percent of the student body, Hispanics 2 percent, and Asian Americans 2 percent. Merit scholarships worth an average of $12,296 are available to qualified students; there are no athletic scholarships.

Eighty-four percent of OWU students live in university-sponsored housing. All but one of the dorms are co-ed, and rooms are mostly apartment-style, four-person suites or doubles. Fraternities, unlike sororities, offer a residential option. Special-interest houses, such as Creative Arts House, House of Black Culture, House of Spirituality, and Women's House, are available, as is Welch Hall, which is for students with GPAs over 3.2. "Almost all students live on campus," says one student. "The dorms are very nice and foster a close-knit community of students." Seniors are now permitted to live off campus, a policy change that has received praise. Each meal eaten on the college plan subtracts a certain number of points (far too many in the opinion of most students) from students' accounts, but there are numerous culinary choices, from all-you-can-eat in the three dining halls to pizza and snacks from the college grocery store.

Does the buttoned-down seriousness of recent years mean that OWU has forsaken its heritage of raucous partying? Administrators certainly hope so. Trying to stamp out drunken binges, OWU slaps fines of up to $150 on all underage students caught drinking and puts them on probation after the fourth offense. One student says, "The campus works to educate students on alcohol and to guide students' decision-making."

"The campus works to educate students on alcohol and to guide students' decision-making."

A sophomore adds, "We have substance-free dorms and halls and clubs that provide an alternative to entertainment by booze. They are pretty popular." Part of OWU's commitment to mend its partying ways includes dry rush for all fraternities and an armband policy at parties. Greek membership, however, still attracts 40 percent of men and 28 percent of women. Among OWU's best-loved traditions are Fallfest and Monnett Weekend in the spring—campuswide bashes for students, parents, and alumni that include bonfires, a Fun Run, and open houses for the Greeks. Romantics will enjoy the President's Ball the weekend before finals in the winter, and the famous Little Brown Jug harness race provides offbeat fun.

Delaware, a town of 25,000, is "a classic college town," reports one junior. "Residents are friendly." Another student notes, "Over 80 percent of OWU students are involved with community service efforts in the community." Approximately 85 percent of the students volunteer in the community for Habitat for Humanity and other charitable organizations. Ohio's capital and largest city, Columbus, is only 30 minutes away by car and offers many job and internship opportunities. Lakes, farms, and even ski slopes are within a few hours' drive.

OWU sports rank in the top 10 in the nation, according to the Sears Director's Cup Standings, which rates top all-around programs. Recent NCAC champions include women's soccer and men's soccer and golf. Sports fever carries over into single-sex and co-ed intramurals, and a massive annual game of Capture the Flag begins at 11 one night and lasts until the wee hours.

Ohio Wesleyan University offers a solid liberal arts education devoid of bells and whistles. "Ohio Wesleyan is a place where the education goes well beyond the classroom," explains one student. "The family atmosphere and the opportunities that the college provides you in a diverse environment enrich the entire college experience."

Overlaps

Denison, College of Wooster, DePauw, Kenyon, Miami University (OH), Ohio State

University of Oklahoma

1000 Asp Avenue, Room 127, Norman, OK 73019

Football aside, OU has historically been outclassed by neighbors like the University of Texas at Austin and the University of Kansas. But the signs of the improvement are there. Check out the Honors College, which boasts a living/learning option. OU is strong in engineering and geology-related fields.

The University of Oklahoma has more to brag about than football. Indeed, President David Boren—a former U.S. Senator and Oklahoma governor—has made it a priority to improve both academics and the physical appearance of the state's flagship campus. "There are new buildings everywhere, because President Boren has found the resources to upgrade our university in every way," says a satisfied senior. Couple that with a rigorous honors program and a genuine friendliness among the student body, and it's easy to understand this favorite saying: "Sooner born and Sooner bred, when I die, I'll be Sooner dead!"

Located about 18 miles south of Oklahoma City, OU's 2,000-acre Norman campus features tree-lined streets and predominantly redbrick buildings. Many are historic in nature, and built in the Cherokee or Prairie Gothic style. The Norman campus houses 13 colleges; seven medical and health-related colleges are located on the OU Health Sciences Center campus in Oklahoma City, and programs from colleges on both campuses are also offered at OU's Schusterman Center in Tulsa. The National Weather Research Center under construction on OU's Norman campus will be the largest weather research center of its kind in the nation, while a Center for Genomic and Biogenetic Research is on the drawing board.

All Oklahoma freshmen start out in University College before choosing among OU's degree-granting institutions, including colleges of Architecture, Education, and Fine Arts. The College of Engineering offers aerospace, civil, mechanical and environmental engineering. In January 2006, the new College of Earth and Energy was chartered, consolidating resources related to petroleum and geological engineering, meteorology, geology and geophysics, and geography. OU's petroleum program ranks among the best in the nation, and in the College of Arts and Sciences, the natural sciences, notably chemistry, are strong. The Michael F. Price College of Business, named for the superstar investment manager, Class of '73, now offers a major in entrepreneurship and venture management.

> "You still feel like you have personal relationships with all your professors."

Other well-recognized programs at OU include majors in Native American studies and energy management; the OU Native American studies program teaches more Native American languages for college credit than any other institution in the world. The College of Education's rigorous, nationally accredited five-year teacher-certification program, Teacher Education Plus (TE-PLUS), incorporates field experience, mentoring, and instruction from 30 full-time professors. New majors

Website: www.ou.edu
Location: Suburban
Total Enrollment: 23,399
Undergraduates: 18,401
Male/Female: 49/51
ACT Range: 23–28
Financial Aid: 16%
Expense: Pub $
Phi Beta Kappa: Yes
Applicants: 8,475
Accepted: 79%
Enrolled: 54%
Grad in 6 Years: 56%
Returning Freshmen: 85%
Academics: ✍ ✍ ✍
Social: ☎ ☎ ☎
Q of L: ★★★
Admissions: (405) 325-2252
Email Address:
    admrec@ou.edu

Strongest Programs:
Meteorology
Finance and Accounting
History of Science
Chemistry and Biochemistry
Petroleum and Geological
    Engineering
Music
English
History

include architectural engineering, Chinese, East Asian studies, and Latin American studies; there are also new minors in aviation, enterprise studies, Hebrew, naval science and non-profit organizational studies.

OU's general education requirements consist of three to five courses in symbolic and oral communication, including English composition; two courses in natural science; two courses in social science; four humanities courses; an upper-division general education course outside the major; and a Senior Capstone Experience. The Honors College offers small classes with outstanding faculty members, and independent study, along with its own dorm. Top students may also apply for the Scholarship-Leadership Enrichment Program, under which well-known lecturers given seminars at the university for academic credit.

Although OU is one of the smaller Big 12 schools, it can still overwhelm. Classes are large, and 37 percent of those taken by undergraduates are taught by graduate students, rather than full-fledged faculty. Even so, a political science major says, "you still feel like you have personal relationships with all your professors." In addition, in the past decade, increased private support has helped OU nearly quadruple its endowed faculty positions, helping the school to attract and retain talented professors. Finally, OU brings more than 50 retired faculty members back to campus each year to teach their introductory courses, and even President Boren teaches an introductory course in political science each semester.

OU's student body is primarily homegrown; 72 percent hail from within the Sooner state. African Americans and Asian Americans each make up just over 5 percent of the student body, while Hispanic students comprise 4 percent, and Native Americans add 8 percent. Nine percent of OU students receive scholarships based on academic merit, with awards averaging $1,122. There are also 367 athletic scholarships in 11 sports, and the Presidential Travel and Study Abroad Scholarships, which offer $75,000 for students and faculty to study and conduct research around the globe.

Twenty-six percent of students live in the university's residence halls, most of which are co-ed by floor. The dorms are "well-maintained, but showing their age," says a freshman. Fortunately, says a senior, many have been updated with air-conditioning and color TVs in the lounges; the three tower dorms, the most popular choice for freshmen, are currently undergoing renovations, and many students already benefit from new carpet and tile in the bathrooms, and modular furniture that can be arranged in a variety of ways. Upperclassmen may also choose the new OU Traditions Square apartment community, opened in January 2005. Furnished units in the complex include in-unit washers and dryers, and full kitchens, plus high-speed wired and wireless Internet access, and access to fitness area, pool, sand volleyball courts, and putting green. Sixteen percent of men and 25 percent of women go Greek, but only 9 percent of students live in Greek housing. The dorms and Greek houses went dry in January 2005.

Fraternity parties are the highlight of weekends at OU, but there are plenty of other options, too, including mixers and movies in the student union, and trips across the street to Campus Corner for shopping, dining and entertainment. The town of Norman, pop. 100,000, is Oklahoma's third-largest city, and Oklahoma City is just 20 minutes away. Other popular diversions include the annual road trip to Dallas for the OU–Texas game, the first-of-the-football-season Big Red Rally, the Medieval Festival, and the University Sing, a talent show. The Big Event also brings thousands of students into the community for a day of service each year.

OU sports big-time athletic teams. Sooner football was undefeated in 2000–01 and brought home a national championship under second-year coach Bob Stoops. In 2003–04 and 2004–05, the team again played for the national title. "OU-Texas is insane," says a letters major. "I can't accurately describe it in words. Every football